**FOURTH EDITION**

# Research Methods in Psychology

## EVALUATING A WORLD OF INFORMATION

FOURTH EDITION

# Research Methods in Psychology

## EVALUATING A WORLD OF INFORMATION

## Beth Morling

UNIVERSITY OF DELAWARE

W. W. NORTON & COMPANY
Independent Publishers Since 1923

Editor: Sheri L. Snavely
Senior Developmental Editor: Beth Ammerman
Project Editor: Taylere Peterson
Assistant Editor: Chloe Weiss
Managing Editor, College: Marian Johnson
Production Manager: Jane Searle
Media Editor: Kaitlin Coats
Associate Media Editor: Christina Fuery
Media Project Editor: Danielle Belfiore
Assistant Media Editor: Allison Nicole Smith
Managing Editor, College Digital Media: Kim Yi
Ebook Production Manager: Kate Barnes
Marketing Managers: Ken Barton and Ashley Sherwood
Design Director and Text Design: Rubina Yeh
Director of College Permissions: Megan Schindel
Permissions Specialist: Joshua Garvin
Photo Editor: Mike Cullen
Photo Researcher: Julie Tesser
Composition and Illustration: S4Carlisle Publishing Services
Informational Graphics: OPEN
Manufacturing: LSC-Kendallville

Permission to use copyrighted material is included in the Credits on page 625.

Library of Congress Cataloging-in-Publication Data

Names: Morling, Beth, author.
Title: Research methods in psychology : evaluating a world of information / Beth Morling, University of Delaware.
Description: Fourth Edition. | New York : W. W. Norton & Company, 2020. | Revised edition of the author's Research methods in psychology, [2018] | Includes bibliographical references and index.
Identifiers: LCCN 2020021774 | ISBN 9780393536225 (paperback) | ISBN 9780393536300 (epub)
Subjects: LCSH: Psychology—Research—Methodology—Textbooks. | Psychology, Experimental—Textbooks.
Classification: LCC BF76.5 .M667 2020 | DDC 150.72/1—dc23
LC record available at https://lccn.loc.gov/2020021774

W. W. Norton & Company, Inc., 500 Fifth Avenue, New York, NY 10110
wwnorton.com
W. W. Norton & Company Ltd., 15 Carlisle Street, London W1D 3BS

1 2 3 4 5 6 7 8 9 0

This edition is dedicated to teaching-focused faculty working in universities, whose titles may not reflect their training and experience, whose untenurable status may not acknowledge their equal claim to academic freedom, and whose salaries may not reflect the true value of their work. Thank you for your dedication to students.

# Brief Contents

# About the Author

**BETH MORLING** is Professor of Psychology at the University of Delaware. She attended Carleton College in Northfield, Minnesota, and received her PhD from the University of Massachusetts at Amherst. Before coming to the University of Delaware, she held positions at Union College (New York) and Muhlenberg College (Pennsylvania). In addition to regularly teaching research methods at Delaware, she also teaches undergraduate cultural psychology, a seminar on the self-concept, and a graduate course in the teaching of psychology. Her research in the area of cultural psychology explores how cultural practices shape people's motivations. Dr. Morling has been a Fulbright scholar in Kyoto, Japan, and was the Delaware State Professor of the Year (2014), an award from the Council for Advancement and Support of Education (CASE) and the Carnegie Foundation for the Advancement of Teaching.

# Preface

Students in the psychology major plan to pursue a tremendous variety of careers—not just becoming psychology researchers. So they sometimes ask: Why do we need to study research methods when we want to be therapists, social workers, teachers, lawyers, or physicians? Indeed, many students anticipate that research methods will be "dry," "boring," and irrelevant to their future goals. This book was written with these very students in mind—students who are taking their first course in research methods (usually sophomores) and who plan to pursue a wide variety of careers. Most of the students who take the course will never become researchers themselves, but they can learn to systematically navigate the research information they will encounter in empirical journal articles as well as in online magazines, print sources, blogs, and tweets.

I used to tell students that by conducting their own research, they would be able to read and apply research later, in their chosen careers. But the literature on learning transfer leads me to believe that the skills involved in designing one's own studies will not simply transfer to understanding and critically assessing studies done by others. If we want students to assess how well a study supports its claims, we have to teach them to assess research. That is the approach this book takes.

## Students Can Develop Research Consumer Skills

To be a systematic consumer of research, students need to know what to prioritize when assessing a study. Sometimes random samples matter, and sometimes they do not. Sometimes we ask about random assignment and confounds, and sometimes we do not. Students benefit from having a set of systematic steps to help them prioritize their questioning when they evaluate quantitative information. To provide that, this book presents a framework of **three claims and four validities**, introduced in Chapter 3. One axis of the framework is the three kinds of claims researchers (as well as journalists, bloggers, and commentators) might make: frequency claims (some percentage of people do X), association claims (X is associated with Y), and causal claims (X changes Y). The second axis of the framework is the four validities that are generally agreed upon by methodologists: internal, external, construct, and statistical.

The three claims, four validities framework provides a scaffold that is reinforced throughout. The book shows how almost every term, technique, and piece of information fits into the basic framework.

The framework also helps students set priorities when evaluating a study. Good quantitative reasoners prioritize different validity questions depending on the claim. For example, for a frequency claim, we must ask about measurement (construct validity) and sampling techniques (external validity), but we don't ask about random assignment or confounds, because the claim is not a causal one. For a causal claim, we look closely at internal validity and construct validity, but external validity is usually a lower priority.

Through engagement with a consumer-focused research methods course, students become systematic interrogators. They start to ask more appropriate and refined questions about a study. By the end of the course, students can clearly explain why a causal claim needs an experiment to support it. They know how to evaluate whether a variable has been measured well. They know when it's appropriate to call for more participants in a study. And they can explain when a study must have a representative sample and when such a sample is not needed.

## What About Future Researchers?

This book can also be used to teach the flip side of the question: How can producers of research design better studies? The producer angle is presented so that students will be prepared to design studies, collect data, and write papers in courses that prioritize these skills.

Future researchers will find sophisticated content, presented in an accessible, consistent manner. They learn the difference between mediation (Chapter 9) and moderation (Chapters 8 and 9), an important skill in theory building and theory testing. They learn how to design and interpret factorial designs, even up to three-way interactions (Chapter 12). And in the common event that your students conduct a study that shows a null effect, they can explore the possible reasons (Chapter 11). This book provides the statistical background, ethics coverage, and APA style guidelines (updated to reflect the latest edition of the *APA Manual*) for guiding students through study design, execution, and writing.

To support producers of research, the Fourth Edition has added two optional data-collection exercises in sections titled Replicate the Study. One walks students through a bivariate correlational design (Chapter 8) and the other, a basic experiment (Chapter 10). Students prepare simple materials, organize their data, and analyze the results. Students then complete an APA-style template as a report. In my view, students can conduct one of these studies as an early project, and build upon the scaffold for a later, more independent investigation. Before assigning these educational exercises, instructors should consult their local IRB to find out if approval is needed.

# Organization

Most chapters will be familiar to veteran instructors, including chapters on measurement, experimentation, and factorial designs. However, unlike some methods books, this one devotes two full chapters to correlational research (one on bivariate and one on multivariate studies), which help students learn how to interpret, apply, and interrogate different types of association claims, one of the common types of claims they will encounter.

There are three supplementary chapters on descriptive statistics, inferential statistics, and scientific writing (APA-style reports and posters). These chapters provide a review for students who have already had statistics and provide the tools they need to create research reports and conference posters.

The appendices provide statistical tables for students who are conducting their own research.

# Support for Students and Instructors

The book's pedagogical features employ learning science to emphasize skill building. Each chapter begins with high-level learning objectives—major skills students should expect to remember even "a year from now." Important terms in a chapter are introduced in boldface. The Check Your Understanding questions at the end of each major section provide retrieval practice for key concepts. Each chapter ends with multiple-choice Review Questions and a set of Learning Actively exercises that allow students to apply what they learned. (Answers are provided at the end of the book.) Working It Through sections appear in several chapters (Chapters 3, 4, 5, 8, and 11); each works though a single study in depth so students can observe how the chapter's central concepts are integrated and applied. In addition, selected figures are annotated to help students learn how to interpret graphs and tables. A master table of the three claims and four validities appears inside the book's front cover to remind students of the content scaffold for the course.

I believe the book works pedagogically because it spirals through the three claims, four validities framework, building in repetition and depth. Although each chapter addresses the usual core content of research methods, students are always reminded of how a particular topic helps them interrogate the key validities. The interleaving of content should help students remember and apply this questioning strategy in the future.

To support instructors, I have worked with W. W. Norton to design the media resources for instructors, especially the online Interactive Instructor's Guide. This resource offers in-class activities, a sample syllabus, homework and final assignments, and chapter-by-chapter teaching notes, all based on my own materials and experience. The book has a substantial set of teaching resources to assist both new and experienced research methods instructors, including a robust test bank with over 1,000 questions, the InQuizitive online assessment tool, updated lecture and active learning slides, and more. For a complete list, see p. xix.

## Teachable Examples on the Everyday Research Methods Blog

Students and instructors can find hundreds of examples of psychological science in the news on my blog, Everyday Research Methods (www.everydayresearch methods.com; no password or registration required). I use these examples during class as well as for homework and exams. Students can use the entries as extra practice in reading about research studies in psychology in the popular media. Follow me on Twitter to get the latest blog updates (@bmorling); I usually post twice a month.

## Changes in the Fourth Edition

Instructors who have used earlier editions will be happy to learn that the organization remains the same. I have replaced some chapter examples (see the table), meaning that instructors who assign the Fourth Edition might still use their favorite illustrations from past editions as extra examples while teaching.

The in-text citations, References list, and sample paper now conform to the guidelines in the latest edition of the *Publication Manual of the American Psychological Association* (7th edition, 2020).

The Fourth Edition continues to reflect the new methodological standards developed after psychology's replication crisis. For example, preregistration and replication are now introduced in Chapter 1. Transparent science practices are integrated in Chapters 1, 2, 11, and 14 and the supplemental chapters. I've revised discussions of sample size in light of our field's new emphasis on larger samples. I've also added error bars to the figures in the book, as is becoming standard.

A major change is the statistical validity coverage. Instead of foregrounding the *p*-values and statistical significance of null hypothesis significance testing (NHST), I now use the new statistics, which emphasizes effect size estimation, precision (confidence intervals), and meta-analysis. Psychological statisticians have argued for years in favor of this shift (e.g., Cumming, 2014) and many instructors know they *should* start to teach it—but there are few undergraduate models out there. With this edition, I strove to empower instructors by modeling how to teach the new statistics to students. Trust me: You can do it! In fact, students are more likely to grasp estimation and precision than they are to correctly define statistical significance. Instructors new to the approach should start by reading Chapter S2, including Table S2.3. And rest assured: The book still explains statistical significance. But instead of leading with it, I foreground effect size and 95% confidence intervals, and then simply explain that a statistically significant result is obtained when the confidence interval doesn't contain zero. I am grateful to Dr. Robert Calin-Jageman for helping me learn this approach and for carefully reviewing these sections for accuracy.

As college faculty, we play an essential role in helping our students become information literate. And the last four years have witnessed an alarming increase in the viral spread of disinformation ("fake news") online. Therefore, new content in Chapter 2 addresses disinformation and predatory journals. I'm grateful to my librarian colleagues at UD, Meg Grotti and Alison Wessel, for helping me develop this section.

Here is a detailed list of the changes made to each chapter.

| Chapter | Major Changes in the Fourth Edition |
|---|---|
| 1. Psychology Is a Way of Thinking | I have incorporated preregistration and replication here and added a short section on pseudoscience. There's a new section on Merton's norms of science (see "Scientists Work in a Community"), which provides an excellent model of why science is self-correcting. I also developed the section on why we don't use the term *prove* in science. |
| 2. Sources of Information: Why Research Is Best and How to Find It | In the section "Experience Has No Comparison Group," I replaced the bloodletting example with a new one on radical mastectomy. I've also replaced the contingency tables with bar graphs because the contingency tables confused my students and they are never revisited.<br><br>I added new sections on predatory versus legitimate and open-access versus paywalled journals. There's also a new infographic with guidelines on avoiding disinformation (Figure 2.17: Be Information Literate, Not Gullible or Cynical). To make room for this new material, I omitted the sections on trade books and wikis. |
| 3. Three Claims, Four Validities: Interrogation Tools for Consumers of Research | The three claims, four validities framework is the same, keeping the best teachable examples from the previous edition and adding new examples from recent media. Here's where you'll see the first introduction of the new statistics for statistical validity and a new infographic (Figure 3.5: Navigating Causal Claims: Do Family Meals Really Curb Eating Disorders?).<br><br>I replaced the study on music lessons and IQ with a study on self-regulation in children. The Working It Through section at the end of this chapter was revised around a new example (on head tilt). |
| 4. Ethical Guidelines for Psychology Research | This chapter is similar to the previous edition, but I have added a new discussion of self-plagiarism. |
| 5. Identifying Good Measurement | This chapter retains the same teaching examples as the previous edition. In response to reviewer comments, I improved the section on internal reliability by adding a correlation matrix that depicts correlations among items and introduced the term *average inter-item correlation*. I have refined some of the validity coverage to reflect recent measurement papers by Flake et al. (2017) and Clark and Watson (2019). Although my coverage in this chapter is not as sophisticated as these authors might like, my goal has been to be student friendly as well as accurate. |

*(Continued)*

| Chapter | Major Changes in the Fourth Edition |
|---|---|
| 6. Surveys and Observations: Describing What People Do | In response to a reviewer suggestion, I have integrated research on the prevalence of ACEs, or adverse childhood experiences, a topic of interest to many students. The ACEs data also led me to temper the section on self-reports. I became concerned that the section on flashbulb memories might lead students to mistrust people's reports of *anything* they say happened to them. Therefore, I added content explaining that people generally can report accurately on their own histories of neglect, abuse, or poverty. Also look for a new example of observational research here. |
| 7. Sampling: Estimating the Frequency of Behaviors and Beliefs | Polling strategies are always changing. I've replaced comparisons of cell-phone-only to landline-only samples with a new section on Internet panels, a technique that seems poised to replace telephone polling. |
| 8. Bivariate Correlational Research | There's a new example on brain thickness and time spent sitting (Siddharth et al., 2018), replacing the one on multitasking. The data are open, so your students could even re-create the statistics. However, it's a small sample (only 35 adults) and the estimate has not been replicated. (So don't go out and buy a standing desk just because of this finding!)

The new statistics approach is in full force, including a revised section on effect size. I now downplay Cohen's effect size conventions (both here and in Chapter 10), for two reasons. First, Cohen himself warned people not to rely on them, and by including them in tables I was perpetuating them. Second, the conventions aren't consistent with each other. That is, $r$s of .1, .3, and .5 do not mathematically correspond to $d$s of .2, .5, and .8. Chapter 8 now provides a more nuanced discussion of effect size and importance inspired by Funder and Ozer (2019).

At the end of Chapter 8, you'll find the first Replicate the Study section (Do people who have moved frequently prefer shopping at chain stores?). |
| 9. Multivariate Correlational Research | The core examples have stayed the same. Here you'll notice new language explaining that when a beta is statistically significant, it means that its confidence interval doesn't include zero.

In the mediation section, I removed the section on Kenny's five steps. These steps were too advanced for my own students; furthermore, most researchers today use other techniques to test mediation, such as bootstrapping and SEM. |
| 10. Introduction to Simple Experiments | I replaced the pasta bowl study with a new study on baby persistence because Wansink's research has been widely discredited for its statistical inconsistencies and questionable practices. The new statistics are featured in this chapter again, including new content on replication, effect size, and whether to use $d$ versus original units. Note that I recomputed the effect size of Mueller and Oppenheimer's (2014) study using their open data (it's $d = 0.37$, not 0.77). Be sure to look for some recent studies that failed to replicate Mueller and Oppenheimer in Chapter 14.

At the end of Chapter 10, you'll find the second new Replicate the Study section (Do we remember words better if we process them deeply?). |

| Chapter | Major Changes in the Fourth Edition |
|---|---|
| 11. More on Experiments: Confounding and Obscuring Variables | The first half of this chapter is much the same as past editions. In the second half (on null effects), I have revised the content in light of the new statistics. There is new coverage of sample size, including a table explaining how sample size affects the precision of an estimate (the 95% CI). I have removed the figure on power (the flashlight and candle image) because power is mostly relevant to Type II errors and NHST. |
| 12. Experiments with More Than One Independent Variable | The only major change here (as in all chapters) is the addition of accurate error bars to all figures. The discussion of main effects and interactions is framed more in the NHST format (students learn to ask, Is there a main effect or not?) and less in terms of the new statistics format (which would take the form of "How strong is the main effect?"). I believe this approach will be easier for students to comprehend. |
| 13. Quasi-Experiments and Small-N Designs | There are three excellent new examples of quasi-experiments here: on organ donation, on the opioid crisis in the U.S., and on the Netflix show *13 Reasons Why*. This last one replaces the Danziger study on food breaks and parole decision making, which has been criticized as flawed.<br><br>The four quasi-experimental designs used to be grouped as two between-groups and two within-groups designs, but I removed this distinction. Now they're simply presented as four designs. I have also introduced a new key term, *quasi-independent variable*. |
| 14. Replication, Transparency, and Real-World Importance | This chapter has a new title and has been updated to reflect the current state of the field. There's much more here on replication, including replication projects (such as Many Labs) and two new forest plots. The new Table 14.3 on questionable versus transparent research practices replaces Table 14.1 from the previous edition. To make room for new content, I reluctantly omitted Masuda and Nisbett's (2001) cross-cultural study on memory (the fish figures). |
| Supplementary Chapters | Chapter S1, on descriptive statistics, has not changed much except to add dot plots and box plots. Chapter S2, on inferential statistics, is almost completely new. I hope this chapter is helpful to instructors teaching the new statistics for the first time as well as to students. In Chapter S3, you'll find a new student paper and poster. This paper models the seventh edition of the APA style manual and illustrates how students can integrate open science practices and write about the new statistics. |

# Acknowledgments

Working on this textbook continues to be rewarding and enriching, thanks to the many people who have smoothed the way. To start, I feel fortunate to have collaborated with an author-focused company and an all-around great editor, Sheri Snavely. Through all four editions, she has been both optimistic and realistic, as well as savvy and smart. She also made sure I got the most thoughtful reviews possible and that I was supported by an excellent team at Norton: Kaitlin Coats, Ashley Sherwood, Ken Barton, Chloe Weiss, Christina Fuery, Allison Smith, Taylere Peterson, Jane Searle, Rubina Yeh, Mike Cullen, and Joshua Garvin. I was delighted to work again with the brilliant Beth Ammerman, who has inspected or improved every chapter, sentence, and figure.

I am also thankful for the support and continued enthusiasm I have received from the Norton sales and marketing teams: Michael Wright, Erik Fahlgren, Dennis Fernandes, Annie Stewart, Erin Brown, Amber Watkins, Mary Dudley, Lydia Warren, Jordan Mendez, Deirdre Hall, Jonathan Mason, Dan Horton, and Andrea Knab. I also wish to thank the science and media specialists for their creativity and drive to ensure my book reaches a wide audience, and that all the media work for instructors and students.

I deeply appreciate the support of many colleagues. A former student, Jeong Min Lee, updated and greatly expanded InQuizitive for the Fourth Edition (originally authored by another former student, Patrick Ewell, in the previous edition). My friend Carrie Smith authored the Test Bank for two editions and has made it an authentic measure of quantitative reasoning (as well as sending me things to blog about). Jeong Min Lee, Emily Prince, and Pamela Schuetze carefully checked and revised the Test Bank for this edition. My student Sephora Ferjuste updated all the references to reflect the new guidelines in the latest edition of the APA style manual. My other student Nicolette Del Priore provided page numbers for all of the cross references. Thanks to Max Pochan for updating the lecture slides.

The book's content was reviewed by a cadre of talented research methods professors, and I am grateful to each of them. I'm especially grateful to Dr. Bob Calin-Jageman for his review of the new statistics content and to Dr. Simine Vazire for always moving our science forward on research credibility. Many of the faculty below were asked to review the text or media; others cared enough to send me comments or examples by e-mail. Their students are lucky to have them in the classroom, and my readers will benefit from the time they spent in improving this book:

Eileen Josiah Achorn, *University of Texas, San Antonio*

Sarah Ainsworth, *University of North Florida*

Kristen Weede Alexander, *California State University, Sacramento*

Leola Alfonso-Reese, *San Diego State University*

Cheryl Armstrong, *Fitchburg State University*

Jennifer Asmuth, *Susquehanna University*

Kristin August, *Rutgers University, Camden*

Erika Bagley, *Muhlenberg College*

Jessica L. Barnack-Tavlaris, *The College of New Jersey*

Tyson S. Barrett, *Utah State University*

Gordon Bear, *Ramapo College*

Kathryn Becker Blease, *Oregon State University*

Margaret Elizabeth Beier, *Rice University*

Jeffrey Berman, *University of Memphis*

Brett Beston, *McMaster University*

Alisa Beyer, *Northern Arizona University*

Jui Bhagwat, *Santa Clara University*

Julie Boland, *University of Michigan*

Marina A. Bornovalova, *University of South Florida*

Caitlin Brez, *Indiana State University*

Shira Brill, *California State University, Northridge*

J. Corey Butler, *Southwest Minnesota State University*

Robert Calin-Jageman, *Dominican University*

Emily M. Carstens Namie, *University of North Dakota*

Ricardo R. Castillo, *Santa Ana College*

Amy Corbett, *State University of New York, Cobleskill*

Alexandra F. Corning, *University of Notre Dame*

Kelly A. Cotter, *California State University, Stanislaus*

Lisa Cravens-Brown, *The Ohio State University*

Victoria Cross, *University of California, Davis*

Kelly L. Curtis, *High Point University*

Matthew Deegan, *University of Delaware*

Kenneth DeMarree, *University at Buffalo*

Jessica Dennis, *California State University, Los Angeles*

Nicole DeRosa, *SUNY Upstate Golisano Children's Hospital*

Rachel Dinero, *Cazenovia College*

Dana S. Dunn, *Moravian College*

C. Emily Durbin, *Michigan State University*

Russell K. Espinoza, *California State University, Fullerton*

Patrick Ewell, *Kenyon College*

Iris Firstenberg, *University of California, Los Angeles*

Christina Frederick, *Sierra Nevada College*

Alyson Froehlich, *University of Utah*

Christopher J. Gade, *University of California, Berkeley*

Isabel Gauthier, *Vanderbilt University*

Timothy E. Goldsmith, *University of New Mexico*

Jennifer Gosselin, *Sacred Heart University*

Meg Grotti, *University of Delaware*

John G. Grundy, *Iowa State University*

AnaMarie Connolly Guichard, *California State University, Stanislaus*

Andreana Haley, *University of Texas, Austin*

Edward Hansen, *Florida State University*

Cheryl Harasymchuk, *Carleton University*

Kristina Howansky, *St. Mary's College of Maryland*

Mark J. Huff, *The University of Southern Mississippi*

Richard A. Hullinger, *Indiana State University*

Deborah L. Hume, *University of Missouri*

Kurt R. Illig, *University of St. Thomas*

Jonathan W. Ivy, *Pennsylvania State University, Harrisburg*

W. Jake Jacobs, *University of Arizona*

Matthew D. Johnson, *Binghamton University*

Christian Jordan, *Wilfrid Laurier University*

Linda Juang, *San Francisco State University*

Victoria A. Kazmerski, *Penn State Erie, The Behrend College*

Heejung Kim, *University of California, Santa Barbara*

Greg M. Kim-Ju, *California State University, Sacramento*

Tabitha Kirkland, *University of Washington*

Ari Kirshenbaum, PhD, *St. Michael's College*

Kerry S. Kleyman, *Metropolitan State University*

Timothy S. Klitz, *Washington & Jefferson College*

Penny L. Koontz, *Marshall University*

Christina M. Leclerc, PhD, *State University of New York at Oswego*

Jeong Min Lee, *Georgia State University*

Ellen W. Leen-Feldner, *University of Arkansas*

Carl Lejuez, *University of Maryland*

Marianne Lloyd, *Seton Hall University*

Stella G. Lopez, *University of Texas, San Antonio*

Greg Edward Loviscky, *Pennsylvania State University*

Amber K. Lupo, *Texas State University*

Sara J. Margolin, PhD, *The College at Brockport, State University of New York*

Scott D. Martin, *Brigham Young University – Idaho*

Joshua W. Maxwell, *The University of New Mexico*

Azucena Mayberry, *Texas State University*

Christopher Mazurek, *Columbia College*

Peter Mende-Siedlecki, *University of Delaware*

Molly A. Metz, *Miami University*

Michele M. Miller, PhD, *University of Illinois Springfield*

Daniel C. Molden, *Northwestern University*

J. Toby Mordkoff, *University of Iowa*

Elizabeth Morgan, *Springfield College*

Katie Mosack, *University of Wisconsin, Milwaukee*

Erin Quinlivan Murdoch, *George Mason University*

Stephanie C. Payne, *Texas A&M University*

Anita Pedersen, *California State University, Stanislaus*

Elizabeth D. Peloso, *University of Pennsylvania*

Celeste Pilegard, *University of California, San Diego*

Brad Pinter, *Penn State Altoona*

M. Christine Porter, *College of William and Mary*

Kacy Pula, *University of Idaho*

Joshua Rabinowitz, *University of Michigan*

Elizabeth Riina, *Queens College, City University of New York*

Catherine Riordan, *Western Washington University*

James R. Roney, *University of California, Santa Barbara*

Richard S. Rosenberg, PhD, *California State University, Long Beach*

Carin Rubenstein, *Pima Community College*

Silvia J. Santos, *California State University, Dominguez Hills*

Pamela Schuetze, PhD, *The College at Buffalo, State University of New York*

John N. Schwoebel, PhD, *Utica College*

Mark J. Sciutto, *Muhlenberg College*

Elizabeth A. Sheehan, *Georgia State University*

Victoria A. Shivy, *Virginia Commonwealth University*

Leo Standing, *Bishop's University*

Harold W. K. Stanislaw, *California State University, Stanislaus*

Kenneth M. Steele, *Appalachian State University*

Mark A. Stellmack, *University of Minnesota, Twin Cities*

Eva Szeli, *Arizona State University*

Lauren A. Taglialatela, *Kennesaw State University*

Alison Thomas-Cottingham, *Rider University*

Chantal Poister Tusher, *Georgia State University*

Allison A. Vaughn, *San Diego State University*

Simine Vazire, *University of California, Davis*

Jan Visser, *University of Groningen*

John L. Wallace, PhD, *Ball State University*

Shawn L. Ward, *Le Moyne College*

Christopher Warren, *California State University, Long Beach*

Erika Wells, *Boston University*

Alison Wessel, *University of Delaware*

Shannon N. Whitten, *University of Central Florida*

Jelte M. Wicherts, *Tilburg University*

Antoinette R. Wilson, *University of California, Santa Cruz*

James Worthley, *University of Massachusetts, Lowell*

Charles E. (Ted) Wright, *University of California, Irvine*

Guangying Wu, *The George Washington University*

Paula Yust, *Duke University*

David Zehr, *Plymouth State University*

Peggy Mycek Zoccola, *Ohio University*

I have tried to make the best possible improvements from all of these capable reviewers.

My life as a teaching professor has been enriched by the friendship and support of my students and colleagues at the University of Delaware, colleagues I see each year at the SPSP conference, and all the faculty I see regularly at the National Institute for the Teaching of Psychology, affectionately known as NITOP.

Three teenage boys keep a person both entertained and humbled; thanks to Max (Figure 4.6), Alek (Figure 5.7), and Hugo (Figure 3.1) for providing their services. I remain grateful to my mother-in-law, Janet Pochan, for cheerfully helping on the home front. Finally, I want to thank my husband, Darrin, for encouraging me and for always having the right wine to celebrate (even if it's only Tuesday).

*Beth Morling*

# Media Resources for Instructors and Students

Developed by book author and award-winning teacher Beth Morling, the *Research Methods in Psychology* teaching resources give you all the tools you need to increase student retention, understanding, and engagement.

## InQuizitive

InQuizitive adaptive assessment for *Research Methods in Psychology* is now organized by chapter and expanded by about 35 percent. Developed by a cognitive psychologist, InQuizitive includes a variety of interactive question types, guiding answer-specific feedback, and personalized question sets to help students grasp course concepts faster. Motivating game-like elements engage students and drive them back into the text when they need to review.

## TEST BANK

The test bank for *Research Methods in Psychology* features 1,050 questions (60 multiple-choice and 15 short-answer questions per chapter), including 140 **new** multiple-choice questions. **New** Norton Testmaker makes the test bank easy to customize for your course. You can search and filter test bank questions by chapter, question type, difficulty level, Bloom's taxonomy level, and APA learning outcome. You can also edit questions. Then you can easily export your assessments to Microsoft Word or your LMS.

## INTERACTIVE INSTRUCTOR'S GUIDE

The Interactive Instructor's Guide (IIG) is a searchable, sortable database of author-created resources for engaging students in active and applied learning in the classroom, including the following:

- **New Interactive Lecture PowerPoints**, created by author Beth Morling, support active learning by providing slides with activities, linked videos, discussion questions, and classroom response questions—all integrated with lecture outline slides.

- **Student Exercises** provide detailed plans for skill-based assignments, including learning goals, advice for preparation, step-by-step assignments, and student handouts.

- **Learning Actively Exercises** engage students in critical thinking and applying their knowledge in an active way. The repository of Learning Actively Exercises in the IIG expands on the exercises available in the textbook.

## EVERYDAY RESEARCH METHODS BLOG: *www.everydayresearchmethods.com*

The *Everyday Research Methods* blog, regularly updated by author Beth Morling, includes over 200 teachable articles from blogs, newspapers, research studies, online videos, and more. Key blog posts for each chapter are collected and summarized in the Interactive Instructor's Guide and the Interactive Lecture PowerPoints.

## INTERACTIVES

**New** interactive figures allow students to experience the most challenging and essential concepts from the course firsthand. Created by Beth Morling, these activities engage students in exploring data sets, evaluating scientific evidence, participating in mini-studies, quizzing themselves on key concepts, and more. They can also be used as active learning exercises in lecture or online classes.

## RESOURCES FOR YOUR LMS

Easily add high-quality, integrated Norton digital resources to your online, hybrid, or lecture courses. All activities can be accessed right within your existing learning management system.

# Contents

# PART III  Tools for Evaluating Frequency Claims

# PART V  Tools for Evaluating Causal Claims

## PART VI Balancing Research Priorities

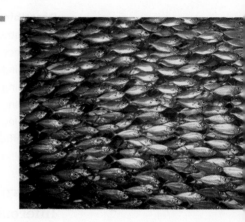

# PART I

# Introduction to Scientific Reasoning

## Scared Straight Programs Are Counterproductive

**PRISON LEGAL NEWS, 2016**

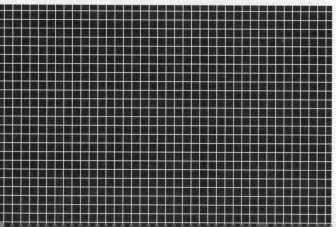

## Mindfulness May Improve Test Scores

**SCIENTIFIC AMERICAN, 2013**

# 1

# Psychology Is a Way of Thinking

THINKING BACK TO YOUR introductory psychology course, what do you remember learning? You might remember that dogs can be trained to salivate at the sound of a bell or that people in a group fail to call for help when the room fills up with smoke. Or perhaps you recall studies in which people administered increasingly stronger electric shocks to an innocent man although he seemed to be in distress. You may have learned what your brain does while you sleep or that you can't always trust your memories. But how come you *did not* learn that "we use only 10% of our brain" or that "hitting a punching bag can make your anger go away"?

You learned some principles and not others because psychological science is based on research done by psychologists. Like other scientists, psychologists are empiricists. Being an empiricist means basing one's conclusions on systematic observations. Psychologists do not simply think intuitively about behavior, cognition, and emotion; they know what they know because they have conducted studies on people and animals acting in their natural environments or in specially designed situations. Research is what tells us that most people will administer electric shock to an innocent man in certain situations, and it also tells us that our brains are usually fully engaged—we use much more than 10%. To think like a psychologist, you must think like a researcher, and taking a course in research methods is crucial to your understanding of psychology.

This book explains the types of studies psychologists conduct as well as the potential strengths and limitations of each type of study. You will learn not only how to plan your own studies but also how to find research, read about it, and ask questions about it. While

**LEARNING OBJECTIVES**

**A year from now, you should still be able to:**

**1.**
Explain what it means to reason empirically.

**2.**
Appreciate how psychological research methods help you become a better producer of information as well as a better consumer of information.

**3.**
Describe five habits that define the work of scientists.

gaining a greater appreciation for the rigorous standards psychologists maintain in their research, you'll find out how to be a systematic and critical consumer of psychological science.

# RESEARCH PRODUCERS, RESEARCH CONSUMERS

Some psychology students are fascinated by the research process and intend to become *producers* of research. Perhaps they hope to get a job studying brain anatomy, documenting the behavior of dolphins or monkeys, administering personality questionnaires, observing children in a school setting, or analyzing data. They expect to write up their results and present them at research meetings. These students dream about working as research scientists or professors. Other psychology students may not want to work in a lab, but they do enjoy reading about the structure of the brain, the behavior of dolphins or monkeys, the personalities of their fellow students, or the behavior of children in a school setting. They are interested in being *consumers* of research information—reading about research so they can later apply it to their work, hobbies, relationships, or personal growth.

In practice, psychologists engage in both roles. When they are planning their research and creating new knowledge, they study the work of others who have gone before them. Research producers and consumers also share a commitment to empiricism—answering psychological questions with direct, formal observations— and to communicating with others about what they have learned.

## Why the Producer Role Is Important

For your future coursework in psychology, it is important to know how to be a producer of research. Of course, students who go to graduate school for psychology will need to know all about research methods. But even if you do not plan to pursue an advanced degree in psychology, you will probably have to write a paper following the style guidelines of the American Psychological Association (APA) before you graduate, and you may be required to do research as part of a course lab section. To succeed, you will need to know why scientists randomly assign people to groups, how to measure attitudes accurately, or how to interpret results from a graph. You will also develop job-related skills such as how to organize and analyze data or how to measure behavior accurately.

Many psychology professors are active researchers, and if you are offered the opportunity to work in their laboratories, take it! Your faculty supervisor may ask you to code behaviors, assign participants to different groups, enter data, or write a report (**Figure 1.1**). This first taste of being a research producer will help you deepen your understanding of psychological inquiry. Although you will be supervised closely, you will be expected to know some basics of conducting research. This book will help you understand why you have to protect the anonymity of your participants, use a coding book, or flip a coin to decide who goes in which group.

## Why the Consumer Role Is Important

Even though they may produce some research during their undergraduate years, most psychology majors do not eventually become full-time researchers. Regardless of the career you choose, however, becoming a savvy consumer of information is essential. You will need to develop the ability to read about research with curiosity and a critical eye.

**FIGURE 1.1**
**Producers of research.**
As undergraduates, some psychology majors work alongside faculty members as producers of information.

Think about how often you encounter news stories or look up information on the Internet. Much of the time, the stories you read and the websites you visit will present information based on data. For example, during an election year, Americans may come across polling information in the media almost every day. Many online sources have science sections that include stories on the latest research. Entire websites are dedicated to psychology-related topics, such as treatments for autism, subliminal learning tapes, or advice for married couples. While some of the research is accurate and useful, some of it is dubious, and some is actually fake. How can you tell high-quality research information when you see it? A course in research methods enables you to ask the appropriate questions so you can evaluate information correctly.

Finally, being a smart consumer of research could be crucial to your future career. Whether your goal is to be a social worker, a teacher, a sales representative, a human resources professional, an entrepreneur, or a parent, you will need to know how to interpret research data with a critical eye. Clinical psychologists, social workers, and family therapists read research to know which therapies are the most effective. In fact, obtaining a license in these helping professions requires knowing the research behind **evidence-based treatments**—that is, therapies that are supported by research. Teachers also use data to find out which methods work best. And the business world depends on quantitative information: Research is used to predict what sales will be like in the future or what consumers will buy.

In this book, you will often see the phrase "interrogating information." Like a detective, a consumer of research needs to know how to ask the right questions and evaluate a study on the basis of the answers. This book will teach you systematic rules for interrogating research information—a skill most employers are looking for.

## The Benefits of Being a Good Consumer

What do you gain by being a critical consumer of information? Imagine, for example, that you are a correctional officer at a juvenile detention center, and you hear of a crime-prevention program called Scared Straight. The program targets teenagers who are at risk for becoming involved in the criminal justice system. They visit prisons, where selected inmates describe the stark, violent realities of prison life (**Figure 1.2**). The idea is that when teens hear about how tough it is in prison, they will be scared into the "straight," law-abiding life. The program makes intuitive sense, and your employer is considering a partnership between the residents of your detention center and the state prison system.

Before starting the partnership, you help your employer find research on the program. You quickly learn that despite the intuitive appeal of the Scared Straight approach, the program doesn't work—in fact, it might even cause criminal activity to get worse! Several published articles have reported the results of randomized, controlled studies in which young adults were assigned to either a Scared Straight program or a control program. The researchers then collected criminal records for 6–12 months. None of the studies showed that Scared Straight attendees committed fewer crimes, and most studies found an *increase* in crime among participants in the Scared Straight programs, compared with the controls (Petrosino et al., 2000). In one case, Scared Straight attendees had committed 20% *more* crimes than the control group. The well-intentioned program that seems to make sense might actually be doing harm. This example illustrates why you should always

**FIGURE 1.2**
**Scared straight.**

Although it makes intuitive sense that young people would be scared into good behavior by hearing from current prisoners, such intervention programs have actually been shown to cause an increase in criminal offenses.

seek empirical evidence to test the efficacy of our interventions. In fact, if you investigate further, you'll find that the U.S. Department of Justice officially warns that such programs are ineffective and can harm youth, and the Juvenile Justice and Delinquency Prevention Act of 1974 was amended to prohibit youth in the criminal justice system from interactions with adult inmates in jails and prisons.

Of course, being a skilled consumer of information can also inform you about programs that *do* work. For example, in your quest to become a better student, suppose you see this headline: "Mindfulness may improve test scores." The practice of mindfulness involves attending to the present moment, on purpose, with a nonjudgmental frame of mind (Kabat-Zinn, 2013). In a mindful state, people simply observe and let go of thoughts rather than elaborating on them. You read a study conducted by Michael Mrazek and his colleagues, who assigned people to take either a 2-week mindfulness training course or a 2-week nutrition course (Mrazek et al., 2013). At the end of the training, only the people who had practiced mindfulness showed less mind wandering and got better GRE scores than they did before the course.

After reading this and several other studies that found similar results, you conclude that the research evidence supports the use of mindfulness for improving test scores, and you decide to try a mindfulness training course. Or if you were a teacher or tutor, you might consider advising your students to practice some of the focusing techniques. (Chapter 10 returns to this example and explains why the Mrazek study stands up to interrogation.) Being a critical consumer of data can help you and your future employers decide to invest time in some programs (such as mindfulness for study skills) but not others (such as Scared Straight for criminal behavior).

---

✔

## CHECK YOUR UNDERSTANDING

1. Explain what the producer of research and consumer of research roles have in common, and describe how they differ.

2. What kinds of jobs would require producer-of-research skills? What kinds of jobs would require consumer-of-research skills?

1. See pp. 6–7. 2. See pp. 7–8.

---

# HOW SCIENTISTS WORK

Psychological scientists are identified not by advanced degrees or white lab coats but by what they do, what they value, and how they think. The rest of this chapter will explain the fundamental ways psychologists approach their work. First, they act as empiricists in their investigations. Second, they test theories through research and, in turn, revise their theories based on the resulting data. Third, they follow norms in the scientific community that prioritize objectivity and fairness. Fourth, they take an empirical approach to both applied research and basic research. Fifth, psychologists make their work public: They submit their results to journals for review and respond to the work of other scientists. Another aspect of making work public involves sharing findings of psychological research with the popular media, who may or may not get the story right.

## Scientists Are Empiricists

» For more on the contrast between empiricism and intuition, experience, and authority, see Chapter 2, pp. 24–38.

Empiricists do not base conclusions on intuition, on casual observations of their own experience, or on what other people—even people with Ph.D.s—say. **Empiricism**, also referred to as the *empirical method* or *empirical research*, involves using evidence from the senses (sight, hearing, touch) or from instruments that assist the senses (such as thermometers, timers, photographs, weight scales, and questionnaires) as the basis for conclusions. Empiricists aim to be systematic and rigorous and to make their work independently verifiable by other observers. In Chapter 2, you will learn more about why empiricism is considered the most reliable basis for conclusions compared with other forms of reasoning, such as experience or intuition. For now, we'll focus on some of the practices in which empiricists engage.

## Scientists Test Theories: The Theory-Data Cycle

In the theory-data cycle, scientists collect data to test, change, or update their theories. Even if you haven't yet conducted formal research, you have probably tested ideas and hunches of your own by asking specific questions that are grounded in theory, making predictions, and reflecting on data.

For example, say you go to check the weather app on your phone but it opens to a blank screen (**Figure 1.3**). What could be wrong? Maybe it's only that one app that isn't working. Does something else, such as Instagram, work? If not, you might ask your roommates, sitting nearby, "Are you having wifi problems?" If their wifi is working fine, you might try resetting your own wireless connection.

Notice the series of steps you took. First, you asked a particular set of questions (Is it only one app? Is it our apartment's wifi?) that reflected your theory that the weather app requires a wireless connection. Because you were operating under this theory, you chose not to ask other kinds of questions (Has a warlock cursed my phone? Does my device have a bacterial infection?). Your theory set you up to ask certain questions and not others. Next, you made specific predictions, which you tested by collecting data. You tested your first idea (It's only the weather app) by making a specific prediction (If I test another app, it will work). You tested your prediction (Does Instagram work?). The data (It doesn't work) told you your initial prediction was wrong. You used that outcome to change your idea about the problem (It's the wireless). And so on. Your process was similar to what scientists do in the theory-data cycle.

## THE CUPBOARD THEORY VERSUS THE CONTACT COMFORT THEORY

A classic example from the psychological study of attachment can illustrate the way researchers use data to test their theories. You've probably observed that animals form strong attachments—emotional bonds—to their caregivers. If you have a dog, you know it's extremely happy to see you when you come home, wagging its tail and jumping all over you. Human babies, once they are able to crawl, may follow their parents or caregivers around, keeping close to them. Baby monkeys exhibit similar behavior, spending hours clinging tightly to the mother's fur. Why do animals form such strong attachments?

**FIGURE 1.3**
**Troubleshooting a phone.**
Troubleshooting an electronic device is a form of engaging in the theory-data cycle.

One theory, referred to as the cupboard theory of mother-infant attachment, is that a mother is valuable to a baby mammal because she is a source of food. The baby animal gets hungry, gets food from the mother by nursing, and experiences a pleasant feeling (reduced hunger). Over time, the sight of the mother acquires positive value because she is the "cupboard" from which food comes. If you've ever assumed your dog loves you only because you feed it, your beliefs are consistent with the cupboard theory.

An alternative theory, proposed by psychologist Harry Harlow (1958), is that babies are attached to their mothers because of the comfort of their warm, fuzzy fur. This is the contact comfort theory. (In addition, it provides a less cynical view of why your dog is happy to see you!) Which theory is right?

In the natural world, a mother provides both food and contact comfort at once, so when the baby clings to her, it is impossible to tell why. To test the alternative theories, Harlow had to separate the two influences—food and contact comfort. The only way he could do so was to create "mothers" of his own. He built two monkey foster "mothers"—the only mothers his lab-reared baby monkeys ever had. One of the mothers was made of bare wire mesh with a bottle of milk built in. This wire mother offered food, but not comfort. The other was covered with fuzzy terrycloth and was warmed by a lightbulb suspended inside, but she had no milk. This cloth mother offered comfort, but not food.

This experiment sets up three possible outcomes. The contact comfort theory would be supported if the babies spent most of their time clinging to the cloth mother. The cupboard theory would be supported if the babies spent most of their

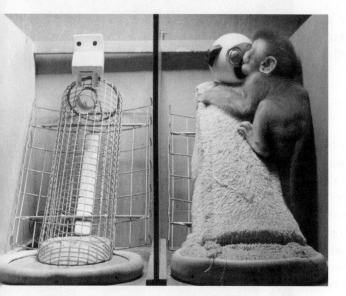

**FIGURE 1.4**

**The contact comfort theory.**

As the theory led Harlow to hypothesize, the baby monkeys spent most of their time on the warm, cozy cloth mother, even though she did not provide any food.

time clinging to the wire mother. Neither theory would be supported if monkeys divided their time equally between the two mothers. In setting up this experiment, Harlow purposely created a situation that might prove his theory wrong.

When Harlow put the baby monkeys in cages with the two mothers, the evidence in favor of the contact comfort theory was overwhelming. Harlow's data showed that the little monkeys would cling to the cloth mother for 12–18 hours a day (**Figure 1.4**). When they were hungry, they would climb down, nurse from the wire mother, and then go right back to the warm, cozy cloth mother. In short, Harlow used the two theories to make specific predictions about how the monkeys would interact with each mother. The data he recorded (how much time the monkeys spent on each mother) supported only one of the theories. The theory-data cycle in action!

### THEORY, HYPOTHESES, AND DATA

A **theory** is a set of statements—as simple as possible—that describes general principles about how variables relate to one another. For example, Harlow's theory was that contact comfort, not food, was the primary basis for a baby's attachment to its mother. This theory led Harlow to investigate particular kinds of questions—he chose to pit contact comfort against food in his research. The theory meant that Harlow also chose *not* to study unrelated questions, such as the babies' food preferences or sleeping habits.

The theory not only led to the questions but also to specific hypotheses about the answers. A **hypothesis**, or *prediction*, is stated in terms of the study design. It's the specific outcome the researcher will observe in a study if the theory is accurate. Harlow's hypothesis stated that the babies would spend more time on the cozy mother than on the wire mother. Notably, one theory can lead to a large number of hypotheses because a single study is not sufficient to test the entire theory—it is intended to test only part of it. Most researchers test theories with a series of empirical studies, each designed to test an individual hypothesis.

**Data** are a set of observations. (Harlow's data were the amount of time the baby monkeys stayed on each mother.) Depending on whether the data are consistent with hypotheses based on a theory, the data may either support or challenge the theory. Data that match the theory's hypotheses strengthen the researcher's confidence in the theory. When the data do not match the theory's hypotheses, however, those results indicate that the theory needs to be revised or the research design needs to be improved.

Ideally, hypotheses are **preregistered**. That is, after the study is designed but before collecting any data, the researcher states publicly what the study's outcome

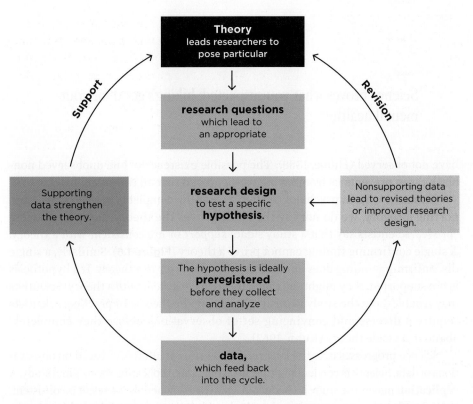

**Support**

**Revision**

**Theory**
leads researchers to
pose particular

**research questions**
which lead to
an appropriate

Supporting
data strengthen
the theory.

**research design**
to test a specific
**hypothesis**.

Nonsupporting data
lead to revised theories
or improved research
design.

The hypothesis is ideally
**preregistered**
before they collect
and analyze

**data,**
which feed back
into the cycle.

**FIGURE 1.5**
**The theory-data cycle.**

is expected to be (perhaps using a time-stamped Internet tool). It's unconvincing if a researcher collects the data first and then claims, "I knew that would happen all along." Instead, the theory-data cycle is like a gamble: Researchers place a public bet in advance that the study will come out in favor of the theory. They are willing to risk being wrong every time they collect data. **Figure 1.5** shows how these steps work as a cycle.

## STUDIES DON'T PROVE THEORIES

The word *prove* is not used in science. Researchers never say they have proved their theories. Why not? As empiricists, scientists avoid inferences they cannot support with direct observation. Consider this set of observations:

> *This raven is black.*
> *That raven is black.*
> *Every raven I have ever seen is black.*

Are we therefore justified in concluding that *All ravens are black*?

Not if we are empiricists. We have not observed all possible ravens, so it is possible that a nonblack raven exists. If scientists take their role as empiricists seriously, they are not justified in making generalizations about phenomena they

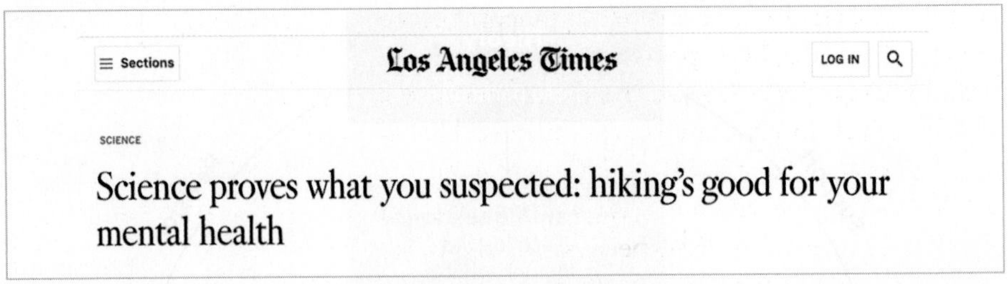

**FIGURE 1.6**
**Scientists don't say "prove."**

When you see the word *prove* in a headline, be skeptical. No single study can prove a theory once and for all. A more scientifically accurate headline would be: "Study Supports the Hypothesis That Hiking Improves Mental Health." (Source: Netburn, LATimes.com, 2015.)

≡ Sections        **Los Angeles Times**        LOG IN   🔍

SCIENCE

Science proves what you suspected: hiking's good for your mental health

have not observed (Hume, 1888). The possible existence of one unobserved non-black raven prevents us from saying we've proved that all ravens are black.

Similarly, when a psychologist such as Harlow completes a single study supporting a theory, we do not say the study proves the theory. Instead of saying "prove," scientists say that a study's data *support* or *are consistent with* a theory. A single confirming finding cannot prove a theory (**Figure 1.6**). Similarly, a single disconfirming finding does not lead researchers to scrap a theory. If a hypothesis is not supported, they might say that data *are inconsistent with* a theory. Scientists may troubleshoot the study instead of rejecting the theory. In practice, scientists require a diverse and convincing set of observations before they completely abandon a viable theory (Kuhn, 1962).

Science progresses over the long run, via a series of inferences based on observations of data. Scientists conduct multiple investigations, replicating the original study. A **replication** means the study is conducted again to test whether the result is consistent. Scientists therefore evaluate their theories based on the **weight of the evidence**—the collection of studies, including replications, of the same theory. Therefore, Harlow's theory of attachment was not "proved" by one single study involving wire and cloth mothers. However, his theory was strongly supported by dozens of individual studies that ruled out alternative explanations and tested the theory's limits.

» For more on replication, see Chapter 14, pp. 437–444.

## GOOD THEORIES ARE FALSIFIABLE

Strong scientific theories set up gambles. A theory should lead to hypotheses that, when tested, could fail to support the theory—in other words, **falsifiability** is a characteristic of good theories (Popper, 1963). Harlow gambled with his study: If the monkeys had spent more time on the *wire* mother than the cloth mother, the study would not have supported the contact comfort theory. Similarly, Mrazek's mindfulness study could have falsified the researchers' theory: If students in the mindfulness training group had shown *lower* GRE scores than those in the nutrition group, the theory of mindfulness and attention would not have been supported.

In contrast, some pseudoscientific techniques have been based on theories that are not falsifiable. Here's an example. Some therapists practice facilitated communication (FC), believing they can help people with developmental disorders communicate by gently guiding their clients' hands over a special keyboard. In simple but rigorous empirical tests, the facilitated messages have been shown to come from the therapist, not the client (Twachtman-Cullen, 1997). All such studies have falsified the theory behind FC. However, FC's supporters don't accept these results. The skepticism inherent in the empirical method, FC supporters say, breaks down trust between the therapist and client and shows a lack of faith in people with disabilities. Therefore, these supporters hold a belief about FC that is not falsifiable. According to its supporters, we can never test the efficacy of FC because it only works as long as it's not scrutinized. To be truly scientific, researchers must take risks, including being prepared to accept data that do not support their theory. Practitioners must be open to such risk as well so they can use techniques that actually work. For another example of an unfalsifiable claim, see **Figure 1.7**.

## Scientists Work in a Community

Scientists are members of a community, and as such, they follow a set of norms—shared expectations about how they should act. Sociologist Robert Merton (1942) identified four norms that scientists attempt to follow, summarized in **Table 1.1**. Following

**FIGURE 1.7**

**An example of a theory that is not falsifiable.**

Certain people might wear a tinfoil hat, operating under the idea that the hat wards off government mental surveillance. But like most conspiracy theories, this notion of remote government mindreading is not falsifiable. If the government has been shown to read people's minds, the theory is supported. But if there is no physical evidence, that also supports the theory because if the government does engage in such surveillance, it wouldn't leave a detectable trace of its secret operations.

**TABLE 1.1**

### Merton's Scientific Norms

| NAME | DEFINITION | INTERPRETATION AND APPLICATION |
|---|---|---|
| **Universalism** | Scientific claims are evaluated according to their merit, independent of the researcher's credentials or reputation. The same preestablished criteria apply to all scientists and all research. | Even a student can do science—you don't need an advanced degree or research position. |
| **Communality** | Scientific knowledge is created by a community and its findings belong to the community. | Scientists should transparently and freely share the results of their work with other scientists and the public. |
| **Disinterestedness** | Scientists strive to discover the truth, whatever it is; they are not swayed by conviction, idealism, politics, or profit. | Scientists should not be personally invested in whether their hypotheses are supported by the data. Scientists do not spin the story; instead, they accept what the data tell them. In addition, a scientist's own beliefs, income, or prestige should not bias their interpretation or reporting of results. |
| **Organized skepticism** | Scientists question everything, including their own theories, widely accepted ideas, and "ancient wisdom." | Scientists accept almost nothing at face value. Nothing is sacred—they always ask to see the evidence. |

the theory-data cycle and the norms and practices of the scientific community means science can progress. By being open to falsification and skeptically testing every assumption, science can become **self-correcting**; that is, it discovers its own mistaken theories and corrects them.

## Scientists Tackle Applied and Basic Problems

The empirical method can be used for both applied and basic research questions. **Applied research** is done with a practical problem in mind and the researchers conduct their work in a local, real-world context. An applied research study might ask, for example, if a school district's new method of teaching language arts is working better than the former one. It might test the efficacy of a treatment for depression in a sample of trauma survivors. Applied researchers might be looking for better ways to identify those who are likely to do well at a particular job, and so on.

The goal of **basic research**, in contrast, is to enhance the general body of knowledge rather than to address a specific, practical problem. Basic researchers might want to understand the structure of the visual system, the capacity of human memory, the motivations of a depressed person, or the limitations of the infant attachment system. However, the knowledge basic researchers generate may be applied to real-world issues later on.

**Translational research** is the use of lessons from basic research to develop and test applications to health care, psychotherapy, or other forms of treatment and intervention. Translational research represents a dynamic bridge from basic to applied research. For example, basic research on the biochemistry of cell membranes might be translated into a new drug for schizophrenia. Or basic research on how mindfulness changes people's patterns of attention might be translated into a study skills intervention. **Figure 1.8** shows the interrelationship of the three types of research.

**Basic Research** → **Translational Research** → **Applied Research**

What parts of the brain are active when experienced meditators are meditating?

In a laboratory study, can meditation lessons improve college students' GRE scores?

Has our school's new meditation program helped students focus longer on their math lessons?

**FIGURE 1.8**
**Basic, applied, and translational research.**
Basic researchers may not have an applied context in mind, and applied researchers may be less familiar with basic theories and principles. Translational researchers attempt to translate the findings of basic research into applied areas.

## Scientists Make Their Work Public

When scientists want to tell the scientific world about the results of their research, they write a paper and submit it to a scientific **journal**. In so doing, they practice the communality norm. Scientific journals usually come out every month and contain articles written by various researchers. Unlike popular newsstand magazines, the articles in a scientific journal are *peer-reviewed*. The journal editor sends the paper to three or four experts on the subject. The experts tell the editor about the work's virtues and flaws and the editor, considering these reviews, decides whether the paper deserves to be published in the journal.

The peer-review process in the field of psychology is intended to be rigorous. Peer reviewers are kept anonymous, so even if they know the author of the article professionally or personally, they can feel free to give an honest assessment of the research. They comment on how important the work is, how it fits with the existing body of knowledge, how competently the research was done, and how convincing the results are. Ultimately, peer reviewers are supposed to ensure that the articles published in scientific journals contain important, well-done studies. When the peer-review process works, research with major flaws does not get published. (Some journals reject more than 90% of submissions after peer review.) The process continues even after a study is published. Other scientists can cite an article and do further work on the same subject. Moreover, scientists who find flaws in the research (perhaps overlooked by the peer reviewers) can publish letters, commentaries, or competing studies. Publication thus helps make science self-correcting.

## Scientists Talk to the World: From Journal to Journalism

One goal of this textbook is to teach you how to interrogate information about psychological science that you find not only in scientific journals but also in more mainstream sources. Psychology's scientific journals are read primarily by other scientists and by psychology students, but rarely by the general public. **Journalism**, in contrast, is a secondhand report about the research, written by journalists or laypeople. A journalist might become interested in a psychology study through a press release written by the scientist's university or by hearing scientists talk about their work at a conference. The journalist turns the research into a news story by summarizing it for a popular audience, giving it an interesting headline and using nontechnical terms.

Science journalism fulfills the communality norm of science by allowing scientists to share potentially valuable work with the general public. Science journalism is easy to access, and understanding it does not require specialized education.

**FIGURE 1.9**

**Getting it right.**

Cartoonist Jorge Cham parodies what can happen when journalists report on scientific research. Here, an original study reported a relationship between two variables. Although the University Public Relations Office relates the story accurately, the strength of the relationship and its implications become distorted with subsequent retellings, much like a game of "telephone."

However, in their effort to tell an engaging, clickable story, journalists might overstate the research or get the details wrong (**Figure 1.9**).

Media coverage of a phenomenon called the "Mozart effect" provides an example of how journalists might misrepresent science when they write for a popular audience (Spiegel, 2010). In 1993, researcher Frances Rauscher found that when students heard Mozart music played for 10 minutes, they performed better on a subsequent spatial intelligence test when compared with students who had listened to silence or to a monotone speaking voice (Rauscher et al., 1993). Rauscher said in a radio interview, "What we found was that the students who had listened to the Mozart sonata scored significantly higher on the spatial temporal task." However, Rauscher added, "It's very important to note that we did not find effects for general intelligence . . . just for this one aspect of intelligence. It's a small gain and it doesn't last very long" (Spiegel, 2010). But despite the careful way the scientists described their results, the media that reported on the story exaggerated its importance:

> The headlines in the papers were less subtle than her findings: "Mozart makes you smart" was the general idea. . . . But worse, says Rauscher, was that her very modest finding started to be wildly distorted. "Generalizing these results to children is one of the first things that went wrong. Somehow or another the myth started exploding that children that listen to classical music from a young age will do better on the SAT, they'll score better on intelligence tests in general, and so forth." (Spiegel, 2010)

**FIGURE 1.10**
**The Mozart effect.**
Journalists sometimes misrepresent research findings. Exaggerated reports of the Mozart effect even inspired a line of consumer products for children.

Perhaps because the media distorted the effects of that first study, a small industry sprang up, recording child-friendly sonatas for parents and teachers (**Figure 1.10**). However, according to research conducted since the first study was published, the effect of listening to Mozart on people's intelligence test scores is not very strong, and it applies to most music, not just Mozart (Pietschnig et al., 2010).

How can you prevent being misled by a journalist's coverage of science? One way is to find the original source, which you'll learn to do in Chapter 2. Reading the original scientific journal article is the best way to get the full story. Another approach is to maintain a skeptical mindset when it comes to popular sources. Chapter 3 explains how to ask the right questions before you allow yourself to accept a writer's claim.

## CHECK YOUR UNDERSTANDING

1. What happens to a theory when the data do not support the theory's hypotheses? What happens to a theory when the data do support the theory's hypotheses?

2. What are the four norms that people in the scientific community strive to follow?

3. Explain the difference between basic research and applied research, and describe how the two interact.

4. Why can't theories be proved in science?

5. When scientists publish their data, what are the benefits?

6. Describe two ways journalists might distort the science they attempt to publicize.

1. See the discussion of Harlow's monkey experiment on pp. 12-13. 2. See p. 15. 3. See p. 16. 4. See p. 17. 5. See pp. 17-19. 6. By overstating results of studies or by getting the details wrong.

# CHAPTER REVIEW

It's time to complete your study experience! Go to INQUIZITIVE to practice actively with this chapter's concepts and get personalized feedback along the way.

## Summary

**Thinking like a psychologist means thinking like a scientist, and thinking like a scientist involves thinking about the empirical basis for what we believe.**

### RESEARCH PRODUCERS, RESEARCH CONSUMERS

- Some students need skills as producers of research; they develop the ability to work in research laboratories and make new discoveries.

- Some students need skills as consumers of research; they need to be able to find, read, and evaluate the research behind important policies, therapies, and workplace decisions.

- Having good consumer-of-research skills means being able to evaluate the evidence behind the claims of a salesperson, journalist, or researcher, and making better, more informed decisions by asking the right questions.

### HOW SCIENTISTS WORK

- As scientists, psychologists are empiricists; they base their conclusions on systematic, unbiased observations of the world.

- Using the theory-data cycle, researchers propose theories, make hypotheses (predictions), and collect data. A good scientific theory is supported by data and is falsifiable. A researcher might say that a theory is well supported or well established, rather than proved, meaning that most of the data have confirmed the theory and very little data have disconfirmed it.

- Applied researchers address real-world problems, and basic researchers work for general understanding. Translational researchers attempt to translate the findings of basic research into applied areas.

- As members of a community, scientists strive to follow four norms: universalism, communality, disinterestedness, and organized skepticism.

- The publication process is part of worldwide scientific communication. Scientists publish their research in journals, following a peer-review process that leads to sharper thinking and improved communication. Even after publication, published work can be approved or criticized by the scientific community.

- Journalists are writers for the popular media who are skilled at transforming scientific studies for the general public, but they don't always get it right. Think critically about what you read online, and when in doubt, go directly to the original source: peer-reviewed research.

## Key Terms

evidence-based treatment, p. 7
empiricism, p. 10
theory, p. 12
hypothesis, p. 12
data, p. 12
preregistered, p. 12
replication, p. 14

weight of the evidence, p. 14
falsifiability, p. 14
universalism, p. 15
communality, p. 15
disinterestedness, p. 15
organized skepticism, p. 15
self-correcting, p. 16

applied research, p. 16
basic research, p. 16
translational research, p. 16
journal, p. 17
journalism, p. 17

To see samples of chapter concepts in the popular media, visit www.everydayresearchmethods.com and click the box for Chapter 1.

## Review Questions

1. Which of the following jobs most likely involves producer-of-research skills rather than consumer-of-research skills?

   a. Police officer

   b. University professor

   c. Physician

   d. Journalist

2. As a true empiricist, one should:

   a. Base one's conclusions on direct observations.

   b. Strive to prove all theories with research.

   c. Be sure that one's research can be applied in a real-world setting.

   d. Discuss one's ideas in a public setting, such as on social media.

3. A statement, or set of statements, that describes general principles about how variables relate to one another is a(n)

   a. prediction

   b. hypothesis

   c. empirical observation

   d. theory

4. Why is publication an important part of the research process?

   a. Because publication enables practitioners to use the research in applied settings.

   b. Because when a study is published, other scientists can verify or challenge it, making science self-correcting.

   c. Because journalists can make the knowledge available to the general public.

   d. Because publication is the first step of the theory-data cycle.

5. Which of the following research questions best illustrates an example of basic research?

   a. Has our company's new marketing campaign led to an increase in sales?

   b. How satisfied are our patients with the sensitivity of the nursing staff?

   c. Does wearing kinesio-tape reduce joint pain in figure skaters?

   d. Can 2-month-old human infants tell the difference between four objects and six objects?

## Learning Actively

1. To learn more about the theory-data cycle, look in the textbooks from your other psychology courses for examples of theories. In your introductory psychology book, you might look up the James Lange theory or the Cannon-Bard theory of emotion. You could look up Piaget's theory of cognitive development, the Young-Helmholtz theory of color vision, or the stage theory of memory. How do the data presented in your textbook show support for the theory? Does the textbook present any data that do not support the theory?

2. Go to an online news website and find a headline that is reporting the results of a recent study. Read the story, and ask: Has the research in the story been published yet? Does the journalist mention the name of a journal in which the results appeared? Or has the study only been presented at a research conference? Then, use the Internet to find examples of how other journalists have covered the same story. What variation do you notice in their stories?

3. A few years ago, psychologist Stanley Coren wrote a *Psychology Today* blog post titled "The Data Says 'Don't Hug the Dog!'" This blog post was later covered by multiple press outlets, including National Public Radio. Why do you think this story proved so popular? Read Coren's blog post and find out (Coren, 2016). Was the original study he reports on peer-reviewed? What do you think of the data he describes? Do any of the media outlets that picked up this story use the word *prove* in their headlines?

# Six Great Ways to Vent Your Frustrations

LIFEHACK.ORG, N.D.

FURY

## Rage Room Helps Cure Your Anger and Frustration Issues

NJ.COM, 2018

# 2

# Sources of Information: Why Research Is Best and How to Find It

HAVE YOU EVER LOOKED online for a stress-relief technique? You might have found aggressive games such as *Kick the Buddy* or downloaded an app such as *Smash Boss*. Maybe you've considered paying for a "rage room" that lets you destroy plates, computers, or teddy bears. Perhaps a friend has suggested posting your complaints publicly in an anonymous chat room. But does venting anger really make people feel better? Does expressing aggression make aggression go away?

Many sources of information promote the idea that venting your frustrations works. You might try a "venting" app yourself and feel good while you're using it. Or you may hear from guidance counselors, friends, or online sources that venting negative feelings is a healthy way to manage anger. But is it accurate to base your conclusions on what well-meaning authorities say? Should you believe what everyone else believes? Does it make sense to base your convictions on your own personal experience?

This chapter discusses three sources of evidence for people's beliefs—experience, intuition, and authority—and compares them to a superior source of evidence: *empirical research*. We will evaluate one particular approach to handling anger: the idea of cathartically releasing bottled-up tension by hitting a punching bag, screaming,

**FIGURE 2.1**
**Anger management.**
Some people believe that venting physically or emotionally is the best way to work through anger. But what does the research suggest?

or expressing your emotions (**Figure 2.1**). Is catharsis a healthy way to deal with feelings of anger and frustration? How could you find credible research on this subject if you wanted to read about it? And why should you trust the conclusions of researchers instead of those based on your own experience or intuition?

## THE RESEARCH VERSUS YOUR EXPERIENCE

When we need to decide what to believe, our own experiences are powerful sources of information. "My Himalayan salt lamp cleans the air and enhances my well-being." "I feel so much better after I vent my anger online." Often, too, we base our opinions on the experiences of friends and family. For instance, suppose you're considering buying a new car. You want the most reliable one, so after consulting *Consumer Reports*, you decide on a Honda Fit, a top-rated car based on its objective road testing and a survey of 1,000 Fit owners. But then you hear about your cousin's Honda Fit, which is always in the shop. Why not trust your own experience—or that of someone you know and trust—as a source of information?

### Experience Has No Comparison Group

There are many reasons not to base beliefs solely on personal experience, but perhaps the most important is that when we do so, we don't have a comparison group. Research, by contrast, asks the critical question: Compared to what? A **comparison group** enables us to compare what would happen both with and without the thing we are interested in—both with and without salt lamps or online games (**Figure 2.2**).

**FIGURE 2.2**
**Your own experience.**
You may think you experienced greater well-being after you installed a Himalayan salt lamp. But does this device really release ions into the air? And does it reduce depression or anxiety?

Here's a medical example of why a comparison group is crucial. In the 1890s, surgeons, led in the United States by William Halsted, believed that the cure for breast cancer was a radical mastectomy—a complete removal of the breast, lymph nodes, chest muscles, and even collarbone. Knowing that cancer spreads, surgeons believed they should remove all parts of the body to which it might potentially metastasize. Radical mastectomy was the accepted treatment for breast cancer for almost a century, to the exclusion of any other approach. In retrospect, the procedure makes little sense: In its early stages, breast cancer is localized, so the surgery goes too far: It's drastic, risky, and disfiguring. In its later stages, breast cancer has already spread throughout the body, and even the most radical mastectomy is not enough.

Nevertheless, surgeons continued to have faith in the procedure for decades. They became emotional in its defense, belittling anyone who dared question the approach (Mukherjee, 2010). It wasn't until 1971 that the U.S. National Cancer

Institute began the first large randomized clinical trial. After 10 years and 1,700 patients, the study found that radical mastectomy was no more effective at curing breast cancer than simple mastectomy, which spares the lymph nodes and chest wall (Fisher et al., 1985, 2002). Today, doctors hardly ever perform radical mastectomies.

Why would surgeons believe for so long that radical mastectomy was working? To test it, surgeons at the time would have had to systematically record the outcomes of women who had the radical surgery and compare them to women who had some other procedure. But surgeons were so convinced of its effectiveness that they never even tried another treatment (Bland, 1981; Mukherjee, 2010). They never had a comparison group to test. "The more fervently surgeons believed in the inherent good of their operations, the more untenable it became to put these to a formal scientific trial" (Mukherjee, 2010, p. 71). They became personally invested in believing that their treatment was working and refused to consider any alternatives.

**Figure 2.3** illustrates the problem. Because they assumed that radical mastectomy was superior to any other treatment, surgeons didn't collect data on a comparison group until the 1960s. **Figure 2.4** illustrates how a comparison group could have revealed one of three possible outcomes. If tested, other treatments might have had (a) a lower long-term survival rate than radical mastectomy, (b) an equivalent long-term survival rate, or (c) a *better* one. By not testing any comparison groups, the surgeons failed to follow Merton's norm of organized skepticism: They

« For all four of Merton's norms of science, see Chapter 1, p. 15.

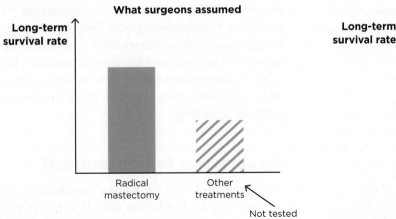

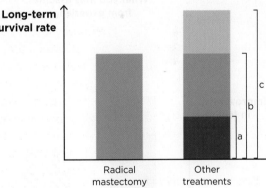

**FIGURE 2.3**
**You need a comparison group.**

From 1890 to the 1970s, most surgeons simply assumed that radical mastectomy was a better treatment for breast cancer. But they only had data on their own procedure; they never collected any data on comparison treatments.

**FIGURE 2.4**
**The power of a comparison group.**

If surgeons had collected data on both radical mastectomies and other treatments, they could have learned whether other treatments were (a) worse than, (b) about the same as, or (c) better than the surgery.

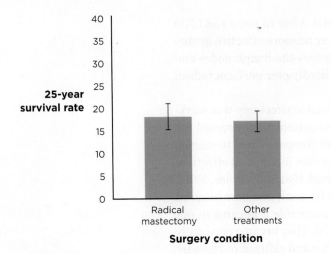

**FIGURE 2.5**

**The study's results.**

Researchers at the National Cancer Institute conducted a randomized clinical trial of nearly 1,700 women, comparing a group with radical mastectomy with other treatments (these included simple mastectomy and simple mastectomy plus radiation). They found that the radical procedure did not lead to better outcomes. Today, radical mastectomy is almost never used. (Figure shows percent of women who were still alive with no further cancer 25 years after treatment; error bars represent standard error of the estimate. Data from Fisher et al., 2002, Table 1.)

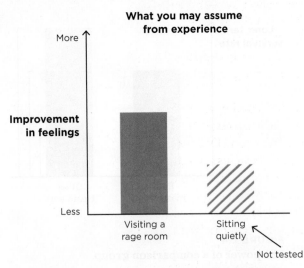

**FIGURE 2.6**

**Experience doesn't have a comparison group.**

You might believe that your visit to a "rage room" made you feel better (compared with sitting quietly), but you do not have comparison data when you only live through one experience.

assumed that their treatment was working instead of looking for the evidence. **Figure 2.5** illustrates the result from the large randomized trial that finally collected data on the comparison group.

Just as the surgeons never compared radical mastectomy with other procedures, when you rely on personal experience to decide what is true, you usually don't have a systematic comparison group because you're observing only one "patient": yourself. Perhaps you try a brain-training course and get higher grades that term. But what grades would you have gotten if you hadn't taken the course? That salt lamp you've been using may seem to be working, but what would have happened *without* it? Maybe you would have felt fine anyway. You might think visiting a rage room makes you calm down when you're angry, but would you have felt even better if you had gone to the gym? What if you had done nothing and just let a little time pass (**Figure 2.6**)?

Basing conclusions on personal experience is problematic because daily life usually doesn't include comparison experiences. In contrast, basing conclusions on systematic data collection has the simple but tremendous advantage of providing a comparison group. Only a systematic comparison can show you whether your well-being improves when you use a salt lamp (compared with when you do not) or whether your anger goes away when you play a violent online game (compared with doing nothing).

## Experience Is Confounded

Another problem with basing conclusions on personal experience is that even if a change has occurred, we often can't be sure what caused it. In everyday life, too much is going on at once. When patients treated with radical mastectomy survived, they might have had earlier-stage cancer to begin with or may have been undergoing chemotherapy or radiation at the same time. Which one caused the improvement? When you noticed a difference in your well-being after buying a salt lamp, maybe you were also getting regular massages or practicing yoga. Which one caused your positive mood? *Smash Boss* provides violent content, but when you play it you might also be distracting yourself or increasing your heart rate. Is it these factors or the game's violence that causes you to feel better after playing it?

In real-world situations, there are several possible explanations for an outcome. In research, these alternative explanations are called **confounds**. Confounded can also mean confused. Essentially, a confound occurs when you think one thing caused an outcome but in fact other things changed, too, so you are confused about what the cause really was. You might think online brain-training exercises are making your grades improve, but because you are also taking different classes and have gained experience as a student, you can't determine which of these factors (or combination of factors) caused the improvement.

What can we do about confounds like these? For a personal experience, it is hard to isolate variables. Think about the last time you had an upset stomach. Which of the many things you ate that day made you sick? Or your allergies—which of the blossoming spring plants are you allergic to? In a research setting, though, scientists can use careful controls to be sure they are changing only one factor at a time.

« For more on confounds and how to avoid them in research designs, see Chapter 10, pp. 286–291.

## Research Is Better Than Experience

What happens when scientists set up a systematic comparison that controls for potential confounds? For example, by using controlled, systematic comparisons, several groups of researchers have tested the hypothesis that venting anger is beneficial (e.g., Berkowitz, 1973; Bushman et al., 2001; Feshbach, 1956; Lohr et al., 2007). One such study was conducted by researcher Brad Bushman (2002). To examine the effect of venting, or catharsis, Bushman systematically compared the responses of angry people who were allowed to vent their anger with the responses of those who did not vent their anger.

First, Bushman needed to make people angry. He invited 600 undergraduates to arrive to a laboratory setting, where each student wrote a political essay. Next, each essay was shown to another person, called Steve, who was actually a **confederate**, an actor playing a specific role for the experimenter. Steve insulted the writer by criticizing the essay, calling it "the worst essay I've ever read," among other unflattering comments. (Bushman knew this technique made students angry because he had used it in previous studies, in which students whose essays were criticized reported feeling angrier than those whose essays were not criticized.)

Bushman then randomly divided the angry students into three groups to systematically compare the effects of venting and not venting anger. Group 1 was instructed to sit quietly in the room for 2 minutes. Group 2 was instructed to punch a punching bag for 2 minutes, having been told it was a form of exercise. Group 3 was instructed to punch a punching bag for 2 minutes while imagining Steve's face on it. (This was the important catharsis group.) Finally, all three groups of students

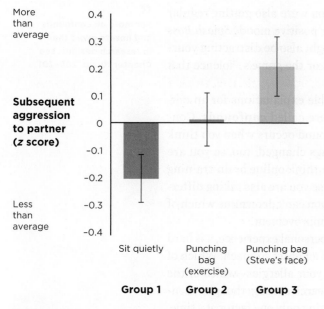

**FIGURE 2.7**

**Results from controlled research on the catharsis hypothesis.**

In this study, after Steve (the confederate) insulted all the students in three groups by criticizing their essays, those in Group 1 sat quietly for 2 minutes, Group 2 hit a punching bag while thinking about exercise, and Group 3 hit a punching bag while imagining Steve's face on it. Later, students in all three groups had the chance to blast Steve with loud noise. (The error bars represent standard error of the estimate. Source: Adapted from Bushman, 2002, Table 1.)

were given a chance to get back at Steve. In the course of playing a quiz game with him, students could blast Steve's ears with a loud noise. (Because Steve was a confederate, he didn't actually hear the noises, but the students thought he did.)

Which group gave Steve the loudest, longest blasts of noise? The catharsis hypothesis predicts that Group 3 should have calmed down the most, and as a result, this group should not have blasted Steve with very much noise. This group, however, gave Steve the loudest noise blasts of all! Compared with the other two groups, those who vented their anger at Steve through the punching bag continued to punish him when they had the chance. In contrast, Group 2, those who hit the punching bag for exercise, subjected him to less noise (not as loud or as long). Those who sat quietly for 2 minutes punished Steve the least of all. So much for the catharsis hypothesis. When the researchers set up the comparison groups, they found the opposite result: People's anger subsided more quickly when they sat in a room quietly than when they tried to vent it. **Figure 2.7** shows the study results in graph form.

Notice the power of systematic comparison here. In a controlled study, researchers can set up the conditions to include at least one comparison group. Contrast the researcher's larger view with the more subjective view, in which each person consults only their own experience. For example, if you had asked some of the students in the catharsis group whether using the punching bag helped their anger subside, they could only consider their own, idiosyncratic experiences. When Bushman looked at the pattern overall—taking into account all three groups—the results indicated that the catharsis group still felt the angriest. The researcher thus has a privileged view—the view from the outside, including all possible comparison groups. In contrast, when you are the one acting in the situation, yours is a view from the inside, and you only see one possible condition.

Researchers can also control for potential confounds. In Bushman's study, all three groups felt equally angry at first. Bushman even separated the effects of aggression only (using the punching bag for exercise) from the effects of aggression toward the person who made the participant mad (using the punching bag as a stand-in for Steve). In real life, these two effects—exercise and the venting of anger—would usually occur at the same time.

Bushman's study is, of course, only one study on catharsis, and scientists always dig deeper. In many other studies, researchers have made people angry, presented them with an opportunity to vent their anger (or not), and then watched their behavior. Research results have repeatedly indicated that people who physically express their anger at a target actually become *more* angry than when they started. Researchers have proposed that venting aggression seems to give people practice at being aggressive (Berkowitz, 1973; Bushman et al., 2001; Feshbach, 1956; Geen & Quanty, 1977; Lohr et al., 2007; Tavris, 1989).

« For more on the value of conducting multiple studies, see Chapter 14, pp. 437–440.

The important point is that the results of a single study, such as Bushman's, are certainly better evidence than experience. In addition, consistent results from several similar studies mean that scientists can be more confident in the findings. As we conduct additional studies, the data can support *theories* about how people can effectively regulate their anger. Psychologist Todd Kashdan referred to this body of catharsis research when he was interviewed for a story about the "rage room" concept, in which people pay to smash objects. He advised the journalist that "it just increases your arousal and thus makes you even more angry. What you really need is to reduce or learn to better manage that arousal" (Dart, 2016).

## Research Results Are Probabilistic

Although research is usually more accurate than individual experience, sometimes our personal stories contradict the research results. Personal experience is powerful, and we often let a single experience distract us from the lessons of more rigorous research. Should you continue to play online games when you're angry because you believe they work for you? Should you disregard *Consumer Reports* because your cousin had a terrible experience with her Honda Fit?

When your experience (or your cousin's) is an exception to what the research finds, you may be tempted to conclude: The research must be wrong. However, the results of behavioral research are **probabilistic**, which means that its findings do not explain all cases all of the time. Instead, the conclusions of research are meant to explain a certain proportion (preferably a high proportion) of the possible cases. In practice, this means scientific conclusions are based on patterns that emerge only when researchers set up comparison groups and test many people. Your own experience is only one point in that overall pattern. Thus, for instance, even though radical mastectomy does not cure cancer, some women did become cancer-free after the surgery. Those patients who recovered do not change the conclusion derived from all of the data. And even though your cousin's Honda needed a lot of repairs, her case is only one out of 1,001 Fit owners, so it doesn't invalidate the general trend. Similarly, just because there is a strong general trend (that Honda Fits are reliable), it doesn't mean *your* Honda will be reliable too. The research may suggest a *strong probability* that your Honda will be reliable, but the prediction is not perfect.

## CHECK YOUR UNDERSTANDING

1. What are two general problems with basing beliefs on experience? How does empirical research work to correct these problems?

2. What does it mean to say that research results are probabilistic?

1. See pp. 24–29. 2. See p. 29.

# THE RESEARCH VERSUS YOUR INTUITION

Personal experience is one way we might reach a conclusion. Another is intuition—using our hunches about what seems "natural," or attempting to think about things "logically." While we may believe our intuition is a good source of information, it can lead us to make less effective decisions.

## Ways That Intuition Can Be Biased

Humans are not natural scientific thinkers. We might be aware of our potential to be biased, but we may be too busy, or not motivated enough, to correct and control for these biases. What's worse, most of us think we aren't biased at all! Fortunately, the formal processes of scientific research help prevent these biases from affecting our decisions. Here are five examples of biased reasoning.

### BEING SWAYED BY A GOOD STORY

One example of a bias in our thinking is accepting a conclusion just because it makes sense or feels natural. We tend to believe good stories—even ones that are false. For example, to many people, bottling up negative emotions seems unhealthy. As with a pimple or a boiling kettle of water, it might seem better to release the pressure by expressing our anger. Sigmund Freud was an early proponent of catharsis, and his biographers speculate that he was influenced by the industrial technology of his day (Gay, 1989). Back then, engines used the power of steam to create vast amounts of energy. If the steam was too compressed, it could have devastating effects on a machine. Freud seems to have reasoned that the human psyche functions the same way. Catharsis makes a good story because it draws on a metaphor (pressure) that is familiar to most people.

Last century's cancer surgeons may have been swayed by a good story, too. Cancer multiplies aggressively and fatally. To surgeons (and even to the women themselves), radical mastectomy may have felt like the right dose of treatment for a terrifying disease. One surgeon wrote in 1956, "the disease, even in its early stage, is such a formidable enemy that it is my duty to carry out as radical an operation as the . . . anatomy permits" (Haagensen, cited in Mukherjee, 2010, p. 194).

The Scared Straight program is another commonsense story that turned out to be wrong. As you read in Chapter 1, such programs propose that when teenagers susceptible to criminal activity hear about the difficulties of prison from actual inmates, they will be scared away from committing crimes in the future. It certainly makes sense that impressionable young people would be frightened and deterred by such stories. However, research has consistently found that Scared Straight programs are ineffective; in fact, they sometimes even cause *more* crime. The intuitive appeal of such programs is strong (which explains why some communities still invest in them), but the research warns against them. One psychologist estimated that the widespread use of the program in New Jersey might have "caused 6,500 kids to commit crimes they otherwise would not have committed" (Wilson, 2011, p. 138). Faulty intuition can even be harmful.

Sometimes a good story will turn out to be accurate, of course, but it's important to be aware of the limitations of intuition. When empirical evidence contradicts what your common sense tells you, be ready to adjust your beliefs on the basis of the research. Automatically believing a story that seems to make sense can lead you astray.

## BEING PERSUADED BY WHAT COMES EASILY TO MIND

Another bias in thinking is the **availability heuristic**, which states that things that pop up easily in our mind tend to guide our thinking (Tversky & Kahneman, 1974). When events or memories are vivid, recent, or memorable, they come to mind more easily, leading us to overestimate how often things happen.

**Figure 2.8** provides an example. Americans are about as likely to die from heart disease as they are from cancer. But Americans are 18 times more likely to use Google to search for information on cancer than information on heart disease. Why? Perhaps because the media report on cancer news more often. If media reports make cancer more cognitively available to us, we may become more concerned and search for it. The figure shows a similar trend for terrorism and homicide: Americans search relatively often for these terms, perhaps reflecting their emotional impact and availability in the media. But very few Americans die from these causes.

The availability heuristic might lead us to wrongly estimate the number of something or how often something happens. For example, if you visited my campus, you might see some women wearing a headcovering (hijab) and conclude there are many Muslim women here. The availability heuristic could lead you to overestimate, simply because hijabi Muslim women stand out visually. People who practice many other religions do not stand out, so you may underestimate their frequency.

Our attention can be inordinately drawn to certain instances, leading to overestimation. A professor may complain that "everybody" uses a cell phone during their class, when in fact only one or two students do so; it's just that their annoying behavior stands out. You might overestimate how often your kid sister leaves

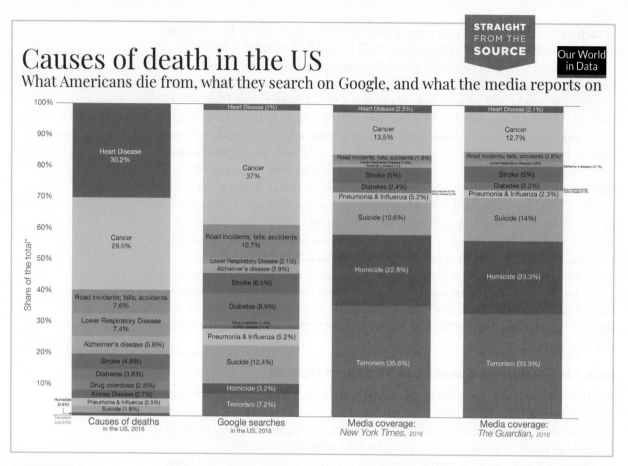

# Causes of death in the US

## What Americans die from, what they search on Google, and what the media reports on

**Causes of deaths** in the US, 2016

- Heart Disease 30.2%
- Cancer 29.5%
- Road incidents; falls; accidents 7.6%
- Lower Respiratory Disease 7.4%
- Alzheimer's disease (5.6%)
- Stroke (4.9%)
- Diabetes (3.8%)
- Drug overdose (2.8%)
- Kidney Disease (2.7%)
- Pneumonia & Influenza (2.5%)
- Suicide (1.8%)
- Homicide (0.9%)
- Terrorism (<0.01%)

**Google searches** in the US, 2016

- Heart Disease (2%)
- Cancer 37%
- Road incidents; falls; accidents 10.7%
- Lower Respiratory Disease (2.1%)
- Alzheimer's disease (2.9%)
- Stroke (6.5%)
- Diabetes (8.9%)
- Drug overdose (1.3%)
- Kidney Disease (1.1%)
- Pneumonia & Influenza (5.2%)
- Suicide (12.4%)
- Homicide (3.2%)
- Terrorism (7.2%)

**Media coverage:** *New York Times*, 2016

- Heart Disease (2.5%)
- Cancer 13.5%
- Road incidents; falls; accidents (1.9%)
- Lower Respiratory Disease (1.2%)
- Alzheimer's disease (1%)
- Stroke (5%)
- Diabetes (2.4%)
- Drug overdose (0.4%)
- Kidney Disease (0.2%)
- Pneumonia & Influenza (5.2%)
- Suicide (10.6%)
- Homicide (22.8%)
- Terrorism (35.6%)

**Media coverage:** *The Guardian*, 2016

- Heart Disease (2.1%)
- Cancer 12.7%
- Road incidents; falls; accidents (2.8%)
- Lower Respiratory Disease (1.6%)
- Alzheimer's disease (<0.1%)
- Stroke (5%)
- Diabetes (2.3%)
- Drug overdose (0.9%)
- Kidney Disease (0.1%)
- Pneumonia & Influenza (2.3%)
- Suicide (14%)
- Homicide (23.3%)
- Terrorism (33.3%)

*Share of the total*

**FIGURE 2.8**

**The availability heuristic.**

Americans' Google search histories suggest that we are overly concerned about certain causes of death—perhaps because they are vivid or because media coverage makes these topics available in our minds. (Source: www.ourworldindata.org)

her bike out in the rain, only because it's harder to notice the times she put it away. When driving, you may complain that you always hit the red lights, only because you spend more time at them; you don't notice the green lights you breeze through. What comes to mind easily can bias our conclusions about how often things happen.

## FAILING TO THINK ABOUT WHAT WE CANNOT SEE

The availability heuristic leads us to overestimate events, such as how frequently people encounter red lights or die from violence. A related problem prevents us from seeing the relationship between an event and its outcome. When deciding if there's a pattern, for example, between a radical mastectomy and full recovery, or between using a salt lamp and feeling calm, people forget to seek out the information that *isn't* there.

In the story "Silver Blaze," the fictional detective Sherlock Holmes investigates the theft of a prize racehorse. The horse was stolen at night while two stable hands and their dog slept, undisturbed, nearby. Holmes reflects on the dog's "curious" behavior that night. When the other inspectors protest that "the dog did nothing in the night-time," Holmes replies, "That was the curious incident." Because the dog did *not* bark, Holmes deduces that the horse was stolen by someone familiar to the dog at the stable (Doyle, 1892/2002, p. 149; see Gilbert, 2005). Holmes solves the crime because he notices the *absence* of something.

When testing relationships, we often fail to look for absences; in contrast, it is easy to notice what is present. This tendency, referred to as the **present/present bias**, reflects our failure to consider appropriate comparison groups (discussed earlier). Surgeons may have fallen prey to the present/present bias when they were observing the effects of radical mastectomies on patients. They focused on patients who received the surgery (treatment was "present") and recovered (recovery was "present") but did not fully account for those who did *not* recover (treatment was "present" but recovery was "absent") or consider other treatments (treatment was "absent").

Did you ever find yourself thinking about an old friend and then get a text message from them? "I must be psychic!" you think. No, it's just the present/present bias in action. You noticed the times when your thoughts coincided with a text message and concluded there was a psychic relationship. But you forgot to consider all the times you thought about people who didn't subsequently text you or the times when people texted you when you weren't thinking about them.

In the context of managing anger, the present/present bias means we will easily notice the times we *did* express frustration at the gym, at the dog, or in an email and subsequently felt better. In other words, we notice the times when both the treatment (venting) and the desired outcome (feeling better) are present but are less likely to notice the times when we didn't express our anger and just felt better anyway. In other words, the treatment was absent but the outcome was still present (**Table 2.1**). When thinking intuitively, we tend to focus only on experiences that fall in the present/present cell: the instances in which catharsis seemed to work. But if we think harder and look at the whole picture, we might conclude expressing frustration doesn't work well at all.

**TABLE 2.1**

### The Present/Present Bias

| | EXPRESSED FRUSTRATION (TREATMENT PRESENT) | DID NOTHING (TREATMENT ABSENT) |
|---|---|---|
| **Felt better (outcome present)** | 5 Present/present | 10 Absent/present |
| **Felt worse (outcome absent)** | 10 Present/absent | 5 Absent/absent |

*Note:* The number in each cell represents the number of times the two events coincided. We are more likely to focus on the times when two factors were both present or two events occurred at the same time (the red present/present cell), rather than on the full pattern of our experiences.

The availability heuristic plays a role in the present/present bias because instances in the "present/present" cell of a comparison stand out. But the present/present bias adds the tendency to ignore "absent" cells, which are essential for testing relationships. To avoid the present/present bias, scientists train themselves always to ask: Compared to what?

## FOCUSING ON THE EVIDENCE WE LIKE BEST

During an election season, you might check opinion polls for your favorite candidate. What if your candidate lags behind in the first opinion poll you see? If you're like most people, you will keep looking until you find a poll in which your candidate has the edge (Wolfers, 2014).

The tendency to look only at information that agrees with what we want to believe is called the **confirmation bias**. We "cherry-pick" the information we take in—seeking and accepting only the evidence that supports what we already think. A lyric by the songwriter Paul Simon captures this well: "Still a man hears what he wants to hear and disregards the rest."

» For more on Merton's norms, see Chapter 1, p. 15.

One study specifically showed how people select only their preferred evidence. The participants took an IQ test and then were told their IQ was either high or low. Shortly afterward, they all had a chance to look at some magazine articles about IQ tests. Those who were told their IQ was low spent more time looking at articles that *criticized* the validity of IQ tests, whereas those who were told their IQ was high spent more time looking at articles that *supported* IQ tests as valid measures of intelligence (Frey & Stahlberg, 1986). They were motivated to think they were smart, so they analyzed the available information in biased ways by selecting only the kinds of evidence they wanted to see.

Without scientific training, we are not very rigorous in gathering evidence to test our ideas. Psychological research has repeatedly found that when people are asked to test a hypothesis, they tend to seek only the evidence that supports their expectations and forget to ask questions that would disconfirm their initial view (Copeland & Snyder, 1995; Klayman & Ha, 1987; Snyder & Campbell, 1980; Snyder & Swann, 1978; Snyder & White, 1981). As a result, people tend to gather only a certain kind of information, and then they conclude that their beliefs are supported. This bias is one reason clinical psychologists and other therapists are required to get a research methods education (**Figure 2.9**). Merton's norm of organized

**FIGURE 2.9**
**Confirmation bias.**

This therapist suspects her client has an anxiety disorder. What kinds of questions should she be asking that would both potentially confirm and potentially disconfirm her hypothesis?

skepticism means that scientists should make a habit of questioning everything and seek evidence both for and against their ideas.

### BIASED ABOUT BEING BIASED

Even when we read about the biased ways people think (such as in a research methods textbook like this one), we nevertheless conclude that those biases do not apply to *us*. We have what's called a **bias blind spot**, the belief that we are unlikely to fall prey to the other biases previously described (Pronin et al., 2004; Pronin et al., 2002). Most of us think we are less biased than others, so when we notice that our own view of a situation is different from that of somebody else, we conclude that "I'm the objective one here" and "you are the biased one."

In one study, researchers interviewed U.S. airport travelers, most of whom said the average American is much more biased than themselves (Pronin et al., 2002). For example, the travelers said that while most others would take personal credit for successes, the travelers themselves would not. Respondents believed other Americans would say a person is smart and competent, just because they are nice; however, they did not believe they themselves had this bias. People believed other Americans would tend to "blame the victims" of random violence for putting themselves in harm's way, even though they would do no such thing themselves (**Figure 2.10**).

**FIGURE 2.10**
**The bias blind spot.**

A physician who receives a free gift from a pharmaceutical salesperson might believe she won't be biased by it, but she may also believe *other* physicians will be persuaded by such gifts to prescribe the drug company's medicines.

The bias blind spot might be the sneakiest of all the biases in human thinking. It makes us trust our faulty reasoning even more. In addition, it can make it difficult for us to initiate the scientific theory-data cycle. We might say, "I don't need to test this conclusion; I already know it is correct." Part of learning to be a scientist is learning not to use feelings of confidence as evidence for the truth of our beliefs. Rather than thinking what they want to, scientists use data.

## The Intuitive Thinker Versus the Scientific Reasoner

When we think intuitively rather than scientifically, we make mistakes. Because of our biases, we tend to notice and actively seek information that confirms our ideas. To counteract biases, adopt the empirical mindset of a researcher. Recall from Chapter 1 that empiricism involves basing beliefs on systematic information from the senses. Now we have an additional nuance for what it means to reason empirically: To be an empiricist, you must also guard against common biases when you look at the data.

Researchers ask: Compared to what? Rather than base their beliefs on their personal conviction, researchers collect data on a comparison group. Knowing they should not simply go along with the story everyone believes, they train themselves to test their intuition with systematic, empirical observations. They strive to collect potentially disconfirming evidence, not just evidence that confirms their hypotheses. Keenly aware that they have biases, scientific reasoners allow the data to speak more loudly than their own confidently held—but possibly faulty—ideas. In short, while researchers are not perfect reasoners themselves, they strive to guard against the many pitfalls of relying on intuition—and they draw more accurate conclusions as a result.

---

**✔**

**CHECK YOUR UNDERSTANDING**

**1.** This section described several ways in which intuition is biased. Can you name all five?

**2.** Why might the bias blind spot be the sneakiest of all the intuitive reasoning biases?

**3.** Do you think you can improve your own reasoning by simply learning about these biases? How?

1. See pp. 30–36. 2. See pp. 35–36. 3. Answers will vary.

---

## TRUSTING AUTHORITIES ON THE SUBJECT

You might have heard statements like these: "We only use 10% of our brains" and "You're either a visual learner, an auditory learner, or a kinesthetic learner." People often state such ideas as if they are facts. However, you should be cautious about basing your beliefs on what everybody says—even when the statement is made by someone who is (or claims to be) an authority. In that spirit, how reliable is the advice of confident surgeons, guidance counselors, talk show hosts, or psychology professors? All these people have some authority. But should you trust them? Recall the surgeons who, for decades, insisted that radical mastectomy was the correct approach to breast cancer; they even blacklisted critics of the procedure. Their authority as high-status, confident surgeons made people less likely to ask for evidence.

Let's consider this example of anger management advice from a person with a master's degree in psychology, several published books on anger management, a thriving workshop business, and his own website. He's certainly an authority on the subject, right? Here is his advice:

> Punch a pillow or a punching bag. Yell and curse and moan and holler. . . . If you are angry at a particular person, imagine his or her face on the pillow or punching bag, and vent your rage. . . . You are not hitting a person, you are hitting the ghost of that person . . . a ghost alive in you that must be exorcised in a concrete, physical way. (Lee, 1993, p. 96)

After reading this chapter, you probably do not trust John Lee's advice. In fact, this is a clear example of how a self-proclaimed "expert" might be wrong.

Before taking the advice of authorities, ask yourself about the source of their ideas. Did the authority systematically and objectively compare different conditions, as a researcher would do? Or maybe they have read the research and are interpreting it for you; they might be practitioners who are basing their conclusions on empirical evidence. In this respect, an authority with a scientific degree may be better able to accurately understand and interpret scientific evidence (**Figure 2.11**). If you know this is the case—in other words, if an authority refers to research evidence in their own area of expertise—their advice might be worthy of attention. However, authorities can also base their advice on their own experience or intuition, just like the rest of us. And they, too, might present only the studies that support their own side.

Also keep in mind that not all research is equally reliable. The research experts use to support their arguments might have been conducted poorly. In the rest of this book, you will learn how to interrogate others' research and form conclusions about its quality. Also, the research someone cites to support an argument may not accurately and appropriately support that particular argument. In Chapter 3, you'll learn more about what kinds of research support different

**FIGURE 2.11**

**Are celebrities authorities to be trusted?**

When celebrities make claims about the health benefits of crystals, herbal supplements, or particular diets, should you believe them? Should you buy their products based only on these celebrities' endorsements?

**FIGURE 2.12**

**A concept map showing sources of information.**

People's beliefs can come from several sources. You should base your beliefs about psychological phenomena on research, rather than experience, intuition, or authority. Research can be found in a variety of sources, some more dependable than others. Ways of knowing that appear in outlined boxes are more trustworthy.

kinds of claims. **Figure 2.12** shows a concept map illustrating the sources of information reviewed in this chapter. Conclusions based on research, outlined in black on the concept map, are the most likely to be correct.

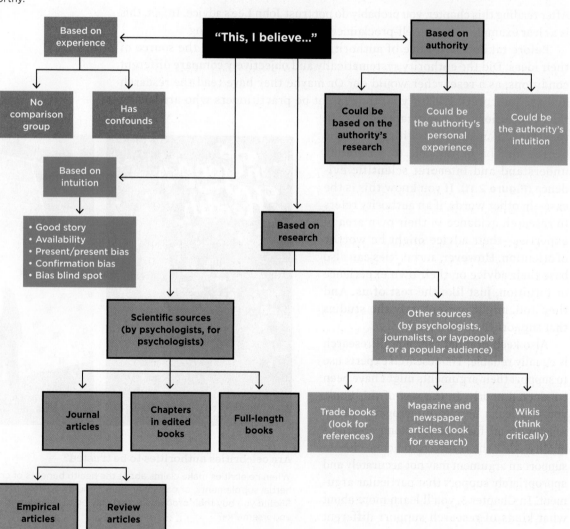

### CHECK YOUR UNDERSTANDING

**1.** When would it be sensible to accept the conclusions of authority figures? When might it not?

1. See p. 37. When authorities base their conclusions on well-conducted research (rather than experience or intuition), it may be reasonable to accept them.

# FINDING AND READING THE RESEARCH

In order to base your beliefs on empirical evidence rather than on experience, intuition, or authority, you will, of course, need to read about that research. But where do you find it and how will you know if the sources you found are high quality?

## Consulting Scientific Sources

Psychological scientists usually publish their research in three kinds of sources. Most often, research results are published as articles in scholarly journals. In addition, psychologists may describe their research in single chapters within edited books, and some researchers also write full-length scholarly books.

### JOURNAL ARTICLES: PSYCHOLOGY'S MOST IMPORTANT SOURCE

Scientific journals come out monthly or quarterly, as magazines do. Unlike popular magazines, however, scientific journals do not have glossy, colorful covers or advertisements. For example, the study by Bushman (2002) described earlier was published in the scientific journal *Personality and Social Psychology Bulletin*.

Journal articles are written for an audience of other psychological scientists and psychology students. They can be either empirical articles or review articles. **Empirical journal articles** report, for the first time, the results of an (empirical) research study. Empirical articles contain details about the study's method, the statistical tests used, and the results of the study. **Figure 2.13** is an example of an empirical journal article.

**Review journal articles** summarize and integrate all the published studies that have been done in one research area. A review article by Alina Nazareth and her colleagues (2019), for example, summarized 266 studies on human sex differences in navigation skills (such as estimating distance or pointing to the right direction). Sometimes a review article uses a quantitative technique called **meta-analysis**, which combines the results of many studies and gives a number that summarizes the magnitude, or the **effect size**, of a relationship. In the Nazareth review (2019), the authors computed the average effect size across all 266 studies. Meta-analysis is valued by psychologists because it weighs each study proportionately and does not allow cherry-picking particular studies.

**《** For a full discussion of meta-analysis, see Chapter 14, pp. 444–447.

Before being published in a journal, both empirical articles and review articles must be peer-reviewed (see Chapter 1). Both types are considered the most prestigious forms of publication, in part because of this peer review process.

### BOOKS AND EDITED BOOKS

One way to get an overview of a body of research is to read a scholarly book or an edited book. Compared with scholars in other disciplines, such as art history or English, psychologists do not write many full-length scientific books

# Does Venting Anger Feed or Extinguish the Flame? Catharsis, Rumination, Distraction, Anger, and Aggressive Responding

STRAIGHT FROM THE SOURCE

**Brad J. Bushman**
*Iowa State University*

*Does distraction or rumination work better to diffuse anger? Catharsis theory predicts that rumination works best, but empirical evidence is lacking. In this study, angered participants hit a punching bag and thought about the person who had angered them (rumination group) or thought about becoming physically fit (distraction group). After hitting the punching bag, they reported how angry they felt. Next, they were given the chance to administer loud blasts of noise to the person who had angered them. There also was a no punching bag control group. People in the rumination group felt angrier than did people in the distraction or control groups. People in the rumination group were also most aggressive, followed respectively by people in the distraction and control groups. Rumination increased rather than decreased anger and aggression. Doing nothing at all was more effective than venting anger. These results directly contradict catharsis theory.*

The belief in the value of venting anger has become widespread in our culture. In movies, magazine articles, and even on billboards, people are encouraged to vent their anger and "blow off steam." For example, in the movie *Analyze This*, a psychiatrist (played by Billy Crystal) tells his New York gangster client (played by Robert De Niro), "You know what I do when I'm angry? I hit a pillow. Try that." The client promptly pulls out his gun, points it at the couch, and fires several bullets into the pillow. "Feel better?" asks the psychiatrist. "Yeah, I do," says the gunman. In a *Vogue* magazine article, female model Shalom concludes that boxing helps her release pent-up anger. She said,

> I found myself looking forward to the chance to pound out the frustrations of the week against Carlos's (her trainer) mitts. Let's face it: A personal boxing trainer has advantages over a husband or lover. He won't look at you accusingly and say, "I don't know where this irritation is

724

coming from." . . . Your boxing trainer knows it's in there. And he wants you to give it to him. ("Fighting Fit," 1993, p. 179)

In a *New York Times Magazine* article about hate crimes, Andrew Sullivan writes, "Some expression of prejudice serves a useful purpose. It lets off steam; it allows natural tensions to express themselves incrementally; it can siphon off conflict through words, rather than actions" (Sullivan, 1999, p. 113). A large billboard in Missouri states, "Hit a Pillow, Hit a Wall, But Don't Hit Your Kids!"

### Catharsis Theory

The theory of catharsis is one popular and authoritative statement that venting one's anger will produce a positive improvement in one's psychological state. The word *catharsis* comes from the Greek word *katharsis*, which literally translated means a cleansing or purging. According to catharsis theory, acting aggressively or even viewing aggression is an effective way to purge angry and aggressive feelings.

Sigmund Freud believed that repressed negative emotions could build up inside an individual and cause psychological symptoms, such as hysteria (nervous outbursts). Breuer and Freud (1893-1895/1955) proposed that the treatment of hysteria required the discharge of the emotional state previously associated with trauma. They claimed that for interpersonal traumas, such as

**Author's Note:** I would like to thank Remy Reinier for her help scanning photo IDs of students and photographs from health magazines. I also would like to thank Angelica Bonacci for her helpful comments on an early ... should ... Iowa St... iastate.e... 

*PSPB*, V...
© 2002 ...

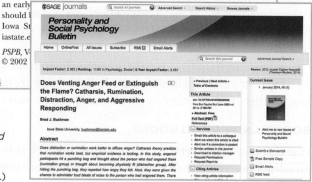

---

**FIGURE 2.13**

### Bushman's empirical article on catharsis.

The first page is shown here, as it appeared in *Personality and Social Psychology Bulletin.* The inset shows how the article appears in an online search in that journal. Clicking "Full Text pdf" takes you to the article shown. (Source: Bushman, 2002.)

for an audience of other psychologists. It is more common to contribute a chapter to an edited book. An edited book is a collection of chapters on a common topic, each chapter of which is written by a different contributor. For example, the edited book *The Handbook of Emotion Regulation* (2014) contains more than 30 chapters, all written by different researchers. Edited book chapters are a good place to find a summary of a set of research a particular psychologist has done. Chapters are not peer-reviewed as rigorously as empirical journal articles or review articles. However, the editor of the book is careful to invite only experts—researchers who are intimately familiar with the empirical evidence on a topic—to write the chapters. The audience is usually other psychologists and psychology students (**Figure 2.14**).

**FIGURE 2.14**
**The variety of scientific sources.**
You can read about research in empirical journal articles, review journal articles, edited books, and full-length books.

## Finding Legitimate Scientific Sources

Your university library's reference staff can be extremely helpful in teaching you how to find appropriate scientific sources. Working on your own, you can also use tools such as PsycINFO and Google Scholar to conduct searches.

### PsycINFO

PsycINFO is a comprehensive tool for sorting through the vast amount of psychological research. Doing a search in PsycINFO is like using Google, but PsycINFO searches only sources in psychology.

PsycINFO has many advantages. It can show you all the articles written by a single author (e.g., "Brad Bushman") or under a single keyword (e.g., "autism"). It tells you whether each source was peer-reviewed. The tool "Cited by" links to other articles that have cited each target article, and the tool "References" links to the other articles each target article used. That means if you've found a great article for your project in PsycINFO, the "Cited by" and "References" lists can be helpful for finding more papers just like it. One disadvantage to PsycINFO is that your college or university library must subscribe; the general public cannot use it.

To use PsycINFO, simply try it yourself or ask a reference librarian to show you the basic steps. One challenge for students is translating curiosity into the correct search terms. Don't get discouraged if your initial search terms are not working. It takes a few rounds to learn the terms that researchers use to study

## TABLE 2.2

## Tips for Turning Your Question into a Successful Database Search

1. **Figure out the best search terms for your question.** Textbooks, topical encyclopedias, and topical dictionaries (available through your college library) can help you find the right terms and give you an overview of the field. An initial Google search on your question can also help.

   **Example:** *Do eating disorders happen more frequently in families that eat dinner together?*

   Instead of "eating disorders," you may need to be more specific. You might need "anorexia nervosa" or "bulimia nervosa."

   Instead of "eating dinner together," you may need to be broader. Terms include "family meal" or "home environment."

   **Example question:** *What motivates people to study?*

   Search terms suggested: "study skills," "academic achievement motivation," "academic self-concept," "study habits," "homework," "learning strategies."

   **Example question:** *Can exposure to negative ions cure depression?*

   Search terms suggested: "seasonal affective disorder" or "light therapy." (And to be unbiased, consider searching the other side: Does exposure to ions NOT affect depression?)

2. **Research is an iterative process. Once you find one suitable article in PsycINFO, do another search.**

   - Look at the PsycINFO "Subject Terms" associated with it and search them in the next attempt.
   - Check whether PsycINFO suggests "Related Items."
   - Use that article's <u>References</u> to find similar work.
   - In PsycINFO, click on <u>Cited by</u> to find other researchers who have used this article.

3. **Adjust your search using "or" and "and."**

   Broaden with OR: Example: "anorexia" or "bulimia" or "eating disorder."

   Narrow with AND: Example: "anorexia" and "adolescence"

your question. **Table 2.2** presents some strategies for turning your questions into successful searches.

## GOOGLE SCHOLAR

The free tool Google Scholar works like the regular Google search engine, except the search results will all be in the form of empirical journal articles and scholarly books. In addition, by visiting the user profile for a particular scientist, you can see all of that research team's publications.

One disadvantage of Google Scholar is that it doesn't let you limit your search terms to specific fields (such as the abstract or title). In addition, it doesn't categorize the articles it finds—for example, as peer-reviewed or not—whereas PsycINFO does. And because Google Scholar contains articles from all scholarly disciplines, it may take more time for you to sort through the results.

## QUALITY MATTERS

Just because you find a scientific journal article through an online search doesn't mean you should use it. Most journals are legitimate: Their research was conducted appropriately, their editors facilitate true peer review, and scientists in the community recognize and trust them (Bergstrom & West, 2017).

Other journals are called "predatory." Their names sound legitimate (e.g., *The Journal of Science* or *Psychiatry and Mental Disorders*), but they publish almost any submission they receive, even fatally flawed studies (Bohannon, 2013). They exist to make money by charging fees to scientists who want to publish their work.

How can you judge journal quality? Your professors and librarians can tell you the names of legitimate journals in psychology—so ask them! You can use an online tool such as Cabell's blacklist of predatory journals. Another rough guide is whether the journal is listed in Journal Citation Reports, which calculates "impact factor." This metric tells you how often, on average, papers in that journal have been cited. The impact factor of the highly respected *Psychological Science* is

6.1, which means that on average its papers are cited 6 times. Impact factor isn't perfect (Chambers, 2017); it cannot tell you whether an article's science is actually sound. But if a journal has an impact factor of at least 1.0, it is more likely to be legitimate (Bergstrom & West, 2017).

## OPEN VERSUS PAYWALLED SOURCES

While you are enrolled in college, you have access to almost any scientific article, through either your own library or interlibrary loan. Once you leave the university, you will learn that some articles are **paywalled**, or subscription only. Other articles are **open access**, or available for free to the general public. Open-access publication of science supports Merton's norm of communality—science should be available for everyone, including the taxpaying public. If you're blocked by a paywall, try the scientist's personal website or the repositories PsyArXiv or PubMed Central (keeping in mind that some manuscripts on PsyArXiv have not yet passed through peer review).

# Reading the Research

Once you have found an empirical journal article or chapter, then what? You might wonder how to go about reading the material. Some journal articles contain an array of statistical symbols and unfamiliar terminology. Even the titles of journal articles and chapters can be intimidating. How is a student supposed to read empirical articles? It helps to know what you will find in an article and to read with a purpose.

## COMPONENTS OF AN EMPIRICAL JOURNAL ARTICLE

Most empirical journal articles (those that report the results of a study for the first time) are written in a standard format, as recommended by the *Publication Manual of the American Psychological Association* (APA, 2020). They usually include certain sections in the same order: abstract, introduction, Method, Results, Discussion, and References. Each section contains a specific kind of information. (For more on empirical journal articles, see Presenting Results: APA-Style Reports at the end of this book.)

**Abstract.** The abstract is a concise summary of the article. It briefly describes the study's hypotheses, method, and major results. When you are collecting articles for a project, the abstracts can help you quickly decide whether each article describes the kind of research you are looking for, or whether you should move on to the next article.

**Introduction.** The introduction is the first section of regular text, and the first paragraphs typically explain the topic of the study. The middle paragraphs lay out the background for the research. What theory is being tested? What have past studies found? Why is the present study important? Pay special attention to the final paragraph, which states the specific research questions, goals, or hypotheses for the current study.

**Method.** The Method section explains in detail how the researchers conducted their study. It usually contains subsections such as Participants, Materials, Procedure, and Apparatus. An ideal Method section gives enough detail that if you wanted to repeat the study, you could do so without having to ask the authors any questions.

**Results.** The Results section describes the quantitative and, as relevant, qualitative results of the study, including the statistical tests the authors used to analyze the data. It usually provides tables and figures that summarize key results. Although you may not understand all the statistics used in the article, you might still be able to understand the basic findings by looking at the tables and figures.

**Discussion.** The opening paragraph of the Discussion section generally summarizes the study's research question and methods and indicates how well the results of the study supported the hypotheses. Next, the authors usually discuss the study's importance: Perhaps their hypothesis was new, or the method they used was a creative and unusual way to test a familiar hypothesis, or the participants were unlike others who had been studied before. In addition, the authors may discuss alternative explanations for their data and pose interesting questions raised by the research.

**References.** The References section contains a full bibliographic listing of all the sources the authors cited in writing their article, enabling interested readers to locate these studies. When you are conducting a literature search, reference lists are excellent places to look for additional articles on a given topic. Once you find one relevant article, the reference list for that article will contain a treasure trove of related work.

### READING WITH A PURPOSE: EMPIRICAL JOURNAL ARTICLES

Here's some surprising advice: Don't read every word of every article, from beginning to end. Instead, *read with a purpose*. In most cases, this means asking two questions as you read: (1) What is the argument? (2) What is the evidence to support the argument? The obvious first step toward answering these questions is to read the abstract, which provides an overview of the study. What should you read next?

Empirical articles are stories from the trenches of the theory-data cycle (see Figure 1.5 in Chapter 1). Therefore, an empirical article reports on data that are generated to test a hypothesis, and the hypothesis is framed as a test of a particular theory. After reading the abstract, try skipping to the end of the introduction, where you'll find the primary goals and hypotheses of the study. After reading the goals and hypotheses, you can read the rest of the introduction to learn more about the theory that the hypotheses are testing. Another place to find the argument of the paper is the first paragraph of the Discussion section, where most authors summarize the key results and state how well the results supported their hypotheses.

Once you have a sense of what the argument is, look for the evidence. In an empirical article, the evidence is contained in the Method and Results sections.

What did the researchers do, and what results did they find? How well do these results support their argument (i.e., their hypotheses)?

## READING WITH A PURPOSE: CHAPTERS AND REVIEW ARTICLES

While empirical journal articles use predetermined headings such as Method, Results, and Discussion, authors of chapters and review articles create their own headings for the topic. You can use these headings to get an overview before you start reading in detail.

As you read these sources, again ask: What is the argument? What is the evidence? The argument will be the purpose of the chapter or review article—the author's stance on the issue. In a review article or chapter, the argument often presents an entire theory (whereas an empirical journal article usually tests only one part of a theory). Here are some examples of arguments you might find:

- Using cell phones impairs driving, even when phones are hands-free (Horrey & Wickens, 2006).
- While speed reading is possible, it comes at the cost of comprehension of the text (Rayner et al., 2016).
- "Prolonged exposure therapy" is effective for treating most people who suffer from posttraumatic stress disorder, though many therapists do not yet use this therapy with their clients (Foa et al., 2013).

The evidence is the research that the author reviews. What research has been done? How strong are the results? What do we still need to know? With practice, you will learn to categorize what you read as argument or evidence, and you will be able to evaluate how well the evidence supports the argument.

# Legitimate Journalism Versus Disinformation

Reading about research in its original form is the best way to get a thorough, accurate, and peer-reviewed report of scientific evidence. But you'll encounter descriptions of psychology research in less scholarly places, too. Journalists can provide good overviews of psychological research, but you should choose and read your sources carefully and be vigilant for disinformation (**Figure 2.15**).

**FIGURE 2.15**

**What you see online may not accurately represent reality.**

## SCIENCE IN THE POPULAR MEDIA

Journalists play an important role in telling the public about findings in psychological science. Psychological research may be covered in specialized outlets such as *Psychology Today* and the *Hidden Brain* podcast, which are devoted exclusively to covering social science research for a popular audience. Research also makes its way to wider news feeds and online newspapers. **Table 2.3** contrasts scientific journals and journalism coverage.

Most science journalists do an excellent job. They read the original research, interview multiple experts, and fact-check. As you read about science in popular sources, it's worth thinking critically about two issues. First, journalists may select a more sensational, clickable story while overlooking its flaws. Second, even when studies are conducted well, journalists may not describe them accurately.

**How Good Is the Study Behind the Story?** When journalists report on a study, have they chosen research that has been conducted rigorously, that tests an important question, and that has been peer-reviewed? Or have they chosen a study simply because it is sensational or moralistic?

For example, one summer the headlines read, "Horns are growing on young people's skulls. Phone use is to blame, research suggests" (**Figure 2.16**). This headline shocked readers and listeners and was covered by multiple news outlets. The "horns" in question referred to bone growths of 10mm or more that were visible via X-ray at the back of people's skulls. The researchers reported that 41% of participants ages 18 to 30 had one of these enlargements on their skulls. The journal publication behind this journalism had been peer-reviewed, usually a sign of the study's quality.

As the "horn" headlines went viral, other journalists began writing stories about the study's flaws. These critical reviews revealed that the study did not

---

**TABLE 2.3**

## Scholarly and Popular Articles About Research Serve Different Goals and Audiences

| | SCHOLARLY ARTICLES (JOURNALS) | POPULAR ARTICLES (JOURNALISM) |
|---|---|---|
| **Example Sources** | *Psychological Science, Child Development, Journal of Experimental Psychology* | *New York Times, Vox, CNN, Time, Scientific American, Wall Street Journal* |
| **Purpose** | Report the results of research after it has been peer-reviewed<br>Discuss ongoing research in detail | Summarize research that may be of interest to the general public |
| **Authors** | Scholars, always named, and often identified by the institution at which they work | Journalists, who are often unnamed |
| **Audience** | Scholars and researchers within a specific field of study | The general public |
| **Language** | Highly specialized and/or technical, and often includes professional jargon not easily understood by the general public | Can be understood by most people |
| **Sources** | Always include sources and full Reference list | Typically do not include footnotes or a list of sources, though they may mention the original researchers and include links to their published journal articles |

Source: Adapted from Butler University Libraries and Center for Academic Technology (https://libguides.butler.edu/c.php?g=117303&p=1940118).

actually measure phone use. Therefore, it could not establish a link between phone use and bone growth. In addition, the X-rays that the study analyzed were exclusively from people who had visited a chiropractor for neck pain. Therefore, it was impossible to know if the reported rates of bone growth would apply to the general population. Finally, the researchers failed to disclose a conflict of interest—at least one author was a chiropractor who sells a pillow designed to improve people's posture.

Two days after the first headline about the horns, the headlines began to change for the better. One read, "Smartphones aren't making millennials sprout horns. Here's how to spot a bad study." Fortunately, in this particular case, you could have obtained a full picture by reading laterally—that is, finding other stories on the same topic written from different perspectives. As you progress in this book, you will learn to read journalism more critically and even spot flawed research yourself.

**FIGURE 2.16**

**Journalists may not cover the best research.**

This sensational news report was based on a single research study that was later widely criticized by other researchers and journalists. Although the news report prominently displays some of the numerical values from the study, the study's method was not adequate to determine that cell phone use was "changing our bodies."

**Is the Story Accurate?**  Even when journalists report on reliable, well-conducted research, they don't always get the story right. Sometimes a journalist does not have the scientific training, motivation, or time before deadline to understand the original science very well. Maybe the journalist sands down the details to make it more accessible to a general audience. And sometimes a journalist wraps up the details of a study with a more dramatic headline than the research can support. For example, in the bone growth study, the original researchers did not use the term "horns." That term was added by a journalist, perhaps to make the story more clickable.

When you read popular media coverage of psychology research, use your skills as a consumer of information to read the content critically—especially if the news is something you wanted to hear. Use PsycINFO or Google Scholar to locate the original empirical article to see how well the journalist summarized the work.

## AVOIDING DISINFORMATION

The specific skill of critically reading science journalism can be generalized to other online content. Did an eagle swoop down and fly off with a human baby? Did a bird poop on Vladimir Putin during a press conference? Was someone paid $3,500 to protest Donald Trump at a rally? Is the @RogueNASA Twitter account really written by a NASA employee? While it's humorous to learn that the eagle and Putin videos are fake, other disinformation may have a more sobering impact on civic engagement.

Disinformation ("fake news") is not simply mainstream journalism that you don't believe or agree with. Instead, **disinformation** is "the deliberate creation and sharing of information known to be false" (Wardle, 2017). It takes many forms. Those who spread disinformation include hate groups who have cloaked false, racist stories in websites disguised to look real (Daniels, 2009). They include false foreign social media accounts aimed at suppressing African American votes in the United States (DiResta et al., 2018; Shane & Frenkel, 2018). People cannot always tell when news is fake; in fact, one poll found that the majority of Americans from both political parties believed fake news headlines they had seen (Silverman & Singer-Vine, 2016). Disinformation matters. It has made some people disengage from voting. It has made others act drastically: In 2016, after reading unfounded conspiracy stories, a man fired a rifle into a pizza restaurant he read was a sex-trafficking site.

**Motives of Disinformation.** People spread deliberately false information for several reasons (Wardle, 2017). *Propaganda, passion,* and *politics* motivate some of it: Disinformation can drive votes and enhance political support. *Provocation* motivates people who want to "punk" others into emotional reactions. *Profit* is a motive too: False scientific claims about salt lamps, herbal supplements, or crystals may accompany a shopping website. There's also the chance that it's *parody*—sites like *The Onion* create false stories only to make us laugh.

**Types of Disinformation.** Some disinformation is completely false. Other disinformation is more subtle: It might attribute false quotes to real people or use a real quote in a false context. Photos and videos can be especially provocative and convincing. Disinformation might involve manipulating photos or videos (as in the eagle and Putin stories) or pasting real images into false contexts.

**Read Critically but Not Cynically.** We need to gather information to fulfill our obligations as citizens. How can we avoid falling for disinformation without giving up and disengaging? It helps to slow down and cross-check. If a social media share makes you feel fearful, angry, or vindicated, track down the source. What's the real context? Is the source neutral or biased? Is it a hoax? **Infographic Figure 2.17** presents ways to verify stories you might be tempted to believe.

---

✔

**CHECK YOUR UNDERSTANDING**

1. How are empirical journal articles different from review journal articles? How is each type of article different from a chapter in an edited book?

2. What two guiding questions can help you read any academic research source?

3. Describe the advantages and disadvantages of using PsycINFO and Google Scholar.

4. What are three steps you can take to guard against disinformation?

1. See pp. 39–41. 2. See p. 44. 3. See pp. 41–42. 4. See pp. 46–48.

---

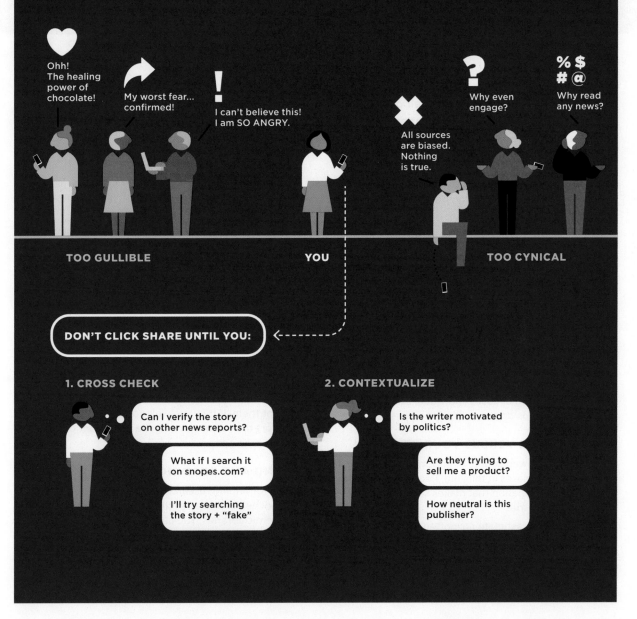

**FIGURE 2.17**

# Be Information Literate, Not Gullible or Cynical

If a social media share makes you feel fearful, angry, or vindicated, track down the source. What's the real context? Is the source neutral or biased? Is it a hoax?

Ohh! The healing power of chocolate!

My worst fear... confirmed!

I can't believe this! I am SO ANGRY.

All sources are biased. Nothing is true.

Why even engage?

Why read any news?

**TOO GULLIBLE**     **YOU**     **TOO CYNICAL**

**DON'T CLICK SHARE UNTIL YOU:**

**1. CROSS CHECK**

Can I verify the story on other news reports?

What if I search it on snopes.com?

I'll try searching the story + "fake"

**2. CONTEXTUALIZE**

Is the writer motivated by politics?

Are they trying to sell me a product?

How neutral is this publisher?

# CHAPTER REVIEW

 It's time to complete your study experience! Go to INQUIZITIVE to practice actively with this chapter's concepts and get personalized feedback along the way.

## Summary

People's beliefs can be based on their own experience, on their intuition, on authorities, or on controlled research. Of these, research information is the most accurate source of knowledge.

### THE RESEARCH VERSUS YOUR EXPERIENCE

- Beliefs based on personal experience may not be accurate. One reason is that personal experience usually does not involve a comparison group. In contrast, research explicitly asks: Compared to what?

- In addition, personal experience is often confounded. In daily life, many things are going on at once, and it is impossible to know which factor is responsible for a particular outcome. In contrast, researchers can closely control for confounding factors.

- Research has an advantage over experience because researchers design studies that include appropriate comparison groups.

- Conclusions based on research are probabilistic. Research findings cannot predict or explain all cases all the time; instead, they aim to predict or explain a high proportion of cases. Individual exceptions to research findings do not nullify the results.

### THE RESEARCH VERSUS YOUR INTUITION

- Intuition is a flawed source of information because it is affected by biases in thinking. People are likely to accept an explanation that makes sense intuitively, even if it is not true.

- People can overestimate how often something happens if they consider only readily available thoughts, those that come to mind most easily.

- People find it easier to notice what is present than what is absent. When people forget to look at the

information that would falsify their belief, they may see relationships that aren't there.

- Intuition is also subject to confirmation bias. We seek out evidence that confirms our initial ideas and fail to seek out evidence that can disconfirm them.

- We all seem to have a bias blind spot and believe we are less biased than everyone else.

- Scientific researchers are aware of their potential for biased reasoning, so they create special situations in which they can systematically observe behavior. They create comparison groups, consider all the data, and allow the data to change their beliefs.

### TRUSTING AUTHORITIES ON THE SUBJECT

- Authorities may attempt to convince us to accept their claims. If their claims are based on their own experience or intuition, we should probably not accept them. If they use well-conducted studies to support their claims, we can be more confident about taking their advice.

### FINDING AND READING THE RESEARCH

- Tools for finding research in psychology include the online database PsycINFO, available through academic libraries. You can also use Google Scholar or the websites of researchers.

- Journal articles, chapters in edited books, and full-length books should be read with a purpose by asking: What is the theoretical argument? What is the evidence? What do the data say?

- Popular media articles and books can be good sources of information about psychology research, as long as you think critically. Journalists might not always cover psychology research accurately. You can compare a popular media story to the original empirical article to be sure.

- Disinformation is news that is deliberately created to mislead or provoke. Many people believe news that is demonstrably false. Think critically and verify popular Internet sources.

## Key Terms

comparison group, p. 24
confound, p. 27
confederate, p. 27
probabilistic, p. 29
availability heuristic, p. 31

present/present bias, p. 33
confirmation bias, p. 34
bias blind spot, p. 35
empirical journal article, p. 39
review journal article, p. 39

meta-analysis, p. 39
effect size, p. 39
paywalled, p. 43
open access, p. 43
disinformation, p. 47

**To see samples of chapter concepts in the popular media, visit www.everydayresearchmethods.com and click the box for Chapter 2.**

## Review Questions

1. Destiny concluded that her new white noise machine helped her fall asleep last night. She based this conclusion on personal experience, which might have confounds. In this context, a confound means:

   a. Another thing might have also occurred last night to help Destiny fall asleep.

   b. Destiny's experience has left her puzzled or confused.

   c. Destiny has not compared last night with times she didn't use the white noise machine.

2. What does it mean to say that research results are probabilistic?

   a. Researchers refer to the probability that their theories are correct.

   b. Research predicts all possible results.

   c. Research conclusions explain a certain proportion of possible cases but may not explain all.

   d. If there are exceptions to a research result, it means the theory is probably incorrect.

3. After two students from his school commit suicide, Marcelino concludes that the most likely cause of death in teenagers is suicide. In fact, suicide is not the most likely cause of death in teens. What happened?

   a. Marcelino was probably a victim of the bias blind spot.

   b. Marcelino was probably influenced by the availability heuristic; he was too influenced by cases that came easily to mind.

   c. Marcelino thought about too many examples of teens who died from other causes besides suicide.

   d. Marcelino did not consider possible confounds.

4. When is it a good idea to base conclusions on the advice of authorities?

   a. When authorities have an advanced degree, such as a Ph.D. or a master's degree.

   b. When authorities base their advice on research that systematically and objectively compares different conditions.

   c. When the authority's website has an official-looking logo or domain name.

   d. When authorities state they have many years of experience in their area.

5. Which of the following is the most reliable source for reading the details of a psychological study?

   a. Scientific journals

   b. Online podcasts

   c. Newspaper science pages

   d. Full-length books

6. In reading an empirical journal article, what two questions should you be asking as you read?

   a. What is the argument? What is the evidence to support the argument?

   b. Why was this research done? Were there any significant findings?

   c. How reputable is (are) the author(s)? Did the findings include support for the hypotheses?

   d. How does this research relate to other research? What are ways to extend this research further?

## Learning Actively

1. Each of the examples below is a statement, based on experience, that does not take a comparison group into account:

   a. My dog doesn't get as upset by fireworks when she wears the "thunder blanket."

   b. My meditation practice has made me feel more peaceful.

   c. The GRE course I took really improved my scores!

   For each statement: (a) Ask: Compared to what? Write a comparison group question that would help you evaluate the conclusion. (b) Get all the information. Draw a simple bar graph, with different possible outcomes that it might show (see Figure 2.4 for a model). (c) Address confounds. Assuming there is a relationship (for example, between meditation and feeling calmer), write down possible confounds for the proposed relationship.

   **Example**: "Since I cut sugar from their diets, I've noticed the campers in my cabin are much more cooperative!"

   a. Compared to what? Would the campers have improved anyway, without the change in diet?

   b. A systematic comparison should be set up as follows:

   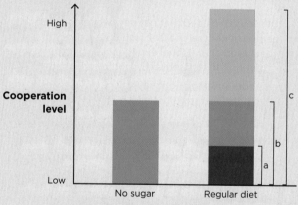

   c. Possible confounds: What other factor might have changed at the same time as the low-sugar diet and also caused more cooperativeness? Possible confounds include the campers simply getting used to camp and settling down. Or maybe a new swimming program started at the same time as the low-sugar diet, and it tired the campers out.

2. Using what you have learned in this chapter, write a sentence or two explaining why the reasoning reflected in each of the following statements is sound or unsound. (a) What are you being asked to believe in each case? (b) What further information might you need to determine the accuracy of the speaker's conclusions? (c) On what is the speaker basing her claim—experience, intuition, or authority?

   a. "I'm positive my cousin has an eating disorder! She's always eating diet bars."

   b. "I read something cool in the paper this morning: They said violent video games basically don't cause aggression. They were talking about some research somebody did."

   c. "It's so clear that our candidate won that debate! Did you hear all the zingers he delivered?"

   d. "Doing these brain games every day helps you get smarter. It's been proved by neuropsychology."

   e. "Binge drinking is totally normal on my campus. Everybody does it almost every weekend."

   f. "Decluttering your closets makes a huge difference. I did it last week, and I feel so much happier when I am in my room."

   g. "When I ride my road bike, I don't get buzzed by cars as much when I wear my local brewery jersey. I think the cars see me as a friend when I wear it."

3. Finding empirical journal articles means figuring out the right search terms. Following the suggestions in Table 2.2, identify initial search terms for these questions. Remember that finding search terms can take several rounds of searching.

   a. Are adults with autism more violent than typical adults?

   b. Does having PTSD put you at risk for alcoholism?

   c. How do we measure narcissism?

4. Choose one of the search terms you found in Question 3. Try finding one empirical article in Google Scholar or PsycINFO. Is the article open source or paywalled? Try to find another article that is related to it, either because it's cited in the References section or because it has cited this article.

5. Visit snopes.com to find an example of disinformation (check the "Hot 50" list). What might be the motive behind it? Provocation, passion, propaganda, punking, profit, or parody?

6. Browse the blog everydayresearchmethods.com to find a popular press story about psychological science. Then find the original empirical journal article behind the popular story. Compare the two. What details did the journalist leave out? What details did the journalist summarize accurately?

## Countries with More Butter Have Happier Citizens

**BIG THINK, 2019**

## Most Students Don't Know When News Is Fake

*WALL STREET JOURNAL*, 2016

## Pretending to Be Batman Helps Kids Stay on Task

**RESEARCH DIGEST, 2017**

# 3

# Three Claims, Four Validities: Interrogation Tools for Consumers of Research

ARTICLES ABOUT PSYCHOLOGY RESEARCH written for a general audience regularly appear in the popular media. Headlines about psychology attract readers because people are interested in such topics as happiness, parenting, and school achievement—among many others. As a psychology student, you're probably interested in these subjects as well. But to what extent should you believe the information you read online? Journalists who report on psychological science should accurately report what the researchers did and why the study was important, but sometimes they misrepresent or overstate the research findings. Even researchers writing an empirical journal article might overstate a study's findings. How do you know if a study really supports what people say about it (**Figure 3.1**)?

Your research methods course will help you determine when the popular press coverage of a research article is accurate. You will learn how to raise the appropriate questions for interrogating the study that is being used to support a writer's claims about human behavior. By extension, the skills you use to evaluate the information behind the research will also help you plan your own studies as a producer of information.

**LEARNING OBJECTIVES**

**A year from now, you should still be able to:**

**1.**
Differentiate the three types of claims: frequency, association, and causal.

**2.**
Ask appropriate questions to help you interrogate each of the four big validities: construct validity, statistical validity, external validity, and internal validity.

**3.**
Explain which validities are most relevant for each of the three types of claims.

**4.**
State which kind of research study is required to support a causal claim.

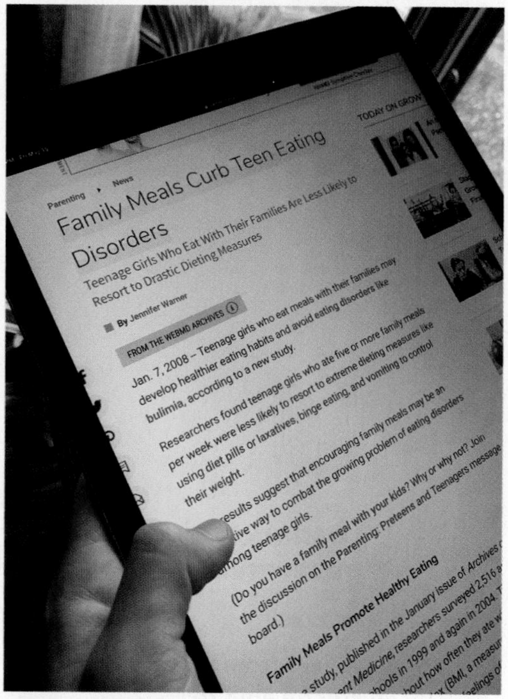

**FIGURE 3.1**
**From journal to journalism.**
The journalist's headline makes a dramatic claim. Is it supported by the scientific study being summarized?

Think of this chapter as a scaffold. All the research information in later chapters will have a place in the framework of the three claims and four validities presented here. The three types of claims—frequency claims, association claims, and causal claims—make statements about variables or about relationships between variables. Variables are the core unit of psychological research.

## VARIABLES

A **variable**, as the word implies, is something that varies, so it must have at least two **levels**, or *values*. Take this headline: "Most students don't know when news is fake." Here, "knowing when news is fake" is the variable, and its levels are knowing when news is fake, and not knowing when news is fake. Similarly, the study that inspired the statement "Countries with more butter have happier citizens" contains two variables: per capita butter consumption (whose levels might go from 0 kilograms per year up to 2 kilograms per year) and the level of happiness (with levels ranging from 1, least happy, to 10, most happy). In contrast, if a study concluded that "15% of Americans smoke," nationality is not a variable because everyone in the study is American. In this example, nationality would be a constant, not a variable. A **constant** is something that could potentially vary but that has only one level in the study in question. (In this example, "smoking" would be a variable, and its levels would be smoker and nonsmoker.)

## Measured and Manipulated Variables

The researchers in any study either measure or manipulate each variable. The distinction is important because some claims are tested with measured variables, while other claims must be tested with both measured and manipulated variables. A **measured variable** is one whose levels are simply observed and recorded. Some variables, such as height and IQ, are measured using familiar tools (a ruler, a test). Other variables, such as gender and hair color, are also said to be "measured." To measure variables such as depression and stress, researchers devise a special set of questions to represent the various levels. In each case, measuring a variable is a matter of recording an observation, a statement, or a value as it occurs naturally.

In contrast, a **manipulated variable** is a variable a researcher controls, usually by assigning study participants to the different levels of that variable. For example, a researcher might give some participants 10 milligrams of a medication, others 20 mg, and still others 30 mg. Or a researcher might assign some people to take a test in a room with many other people and assign others to take the test alone. In both examples, the participants could end up at any of the levels because the researchers do the manipulating, assigning participants to be at one level of the variable or another.

Some variables cannot be manipulated—they can only be measured. Age can't be manipulated because researchers can't assign people to be older or younger; they can only measure what age people already are. IQ is another variable that can't be manipulated. Researchers cannot assign some people to have a high IQ and others to have a low IQ; they can only measure each person's IQ. Even if the researchers choose the 10% of people with the highest IQ and the 10% with the lowest IQ, it is still a measured variable because people cannot be assigned to the highest or lowest 10%.

Other variables cannot be manipulated because it would be unethical to do so. For example, in a study on the long-term effects of childhood trauma, researchers could not ethically assign children to "trauma experience" and "no trauma experience" conditions.

« For a complete discussion of ethical guidelines in research, see Chapter 4.

Some variables, however, can be either manipulated or measured, depending on the goals of a study. If childhood music lessons were your variable of interest, you could *measure* whether children already take music lessons, or you could *manipulate* this variable if you assigned some children to take music lessons and others to take something else (such as drama lessons). If you wanted to study butter consumption, you could *measure* this trait by recording how much butter different nations consume annually (perhaps in kilograms). You could also *manipulate* this variable in the short term if you assigned some willing volunteers to consume a large (versus small) quantity of foods rich in butter.

## From Conceptual Variable to Operational Definition

Each variable in a study can be referred to in two ways. When researchers are discussing their theories and when journalists write about their research, they use more abstract names, called **constructs** or **conceptual variables**. When testing hypotheses with empirical research, they create **operational definitions** of variables, also known as **operational variables**, or *operationalizations*. To **operationalize** a concept of interest means to turn it into a measured or manipulated variable.

For example, a researcher's interest in the construct "coffee consumption" could be operationalized as a structured question in which people tell an interviewer how often they drink coffee. Alternatively, the same construct might be operationalized by having people use an app in which they record everything

TABLE 3.1

## How Do Researchers Describe Variables?

| WAY OF DESCRIBING A VARIABLE | DEFINITION | EXAMPLE 1 | EXAMPLE 2 |
|---|---|---|---|
| **Construct, conceptual variable** | The name of the concept being studied | "Satisfaction with life" | "Perseverance" (in young children) |
| **Conceptual definition** | A careful, theoretical definition of the construct | "A person's cognitive evaluation of his or her life" (Diener et al., 1985) | "The ability to push through when confronted with . . . obstacles" (White et al., 2017) |
| **Operational definition, operationalization** | How the construct is measured or manipulated in an actual study | Five questionnaire items on the Satisfaction with Life scale, answered on a scale of 1 (*strongly disagree*) to 5 (*strongly agree*). An example item is "All in all, I am satisfied with my life" | How long a child will choose to engage in a slow-paced, boring activity that involves pressing a button when they see a picture of cheese on a screen and not pressing it when they see a cat on the screen |

they eat or drink for a period of time. **Table 3.1** explains the ways variables can be defined.

Sometimes this operationalization step is simple and obvious. For example, a researcher interested in a conceptual variable such as "weight gain" in laboratory rats would probably just weigh them. A researcher who is interested in the conceptual variable "income" might operationalize this variable by asking each person about their total income last year. In these two cases, the researcher can operationalize the conceptual variable of interest straightforwardly.

Other times, the concepts researchers wish to study are harder to operationalize because they are difficult to see, touch, or feel. Examples are personality traits, states such as "argumentativeness," and behavior judgments such as "attempted suicide." The abstract nature of these conceptual variables does not stop psychologists from operationalizing them; it just makes studying them a little harder. In such cases, researchers might develop creative or elegant operational definitions to capture the variable of interest. See **Table 3.2** for some examples.

In journal articles, variables are usually referred to at the conceptual level. So to discover how the variable "school achievement" was operationalized, you need to ask: How did the researchers measure "school achievement" in this study? To determine how a variable such as "childhood trauma" was operationalized, ask: How did researchers measure "childhood trauma" in this research? **Figure 3.2** shows how the first variable might be operationalized.

**TABLE 3.2**

## Describing Variables: Examples

| VARIABLE NAME (CONCEPTUAL VARIABLE) | OPERATIONAL DEFINITION (ONE POSSIBILITY) | LEVELS OF THIS VARIABLE | IS THE VARIABLE MEASURED OR MANIPULATED? |
|---|---|---|---|
| Car ownership | Researchers asked people to circle "I own a car" or "I do not own a car" on their questionnaire. | 2 levels: own a car or not | Measured |
| Expressing gratitude to romantic partner | Researchers asked people in relationships the extent to which they agree with items such as "I tell my partner often that s/he is the best." | 7 levels, from 1 (*strongly disagree*) to 7 (*strongly agree*) | Measured |
| Exposure to disinformation | Researchers assigned participants to hear false information either one time or two times. | 2 levels: hearing the false information once or twice. | Manipulated |
| What time children eat dinner | Using a daily food diary, researchers had children write down what time they ate dinner each evening. | Researchers divided children into two groups: those who ate dinner between 2 P.M. and 8 P.M., and those who ate after 8 P.M. | Measured |

**What grades do you get?**
- ◉ All As
- ◉ Mostly As and Bs
- ◉ Mostly Bs
- ◉ Mostly Bs and Cs

Self-report questionnaire          Checking records          Teachers' observations

**FIGURE 3.2**

## Operationalizing "school achievement."

A single conceptual variable can be operationalized in a number of ways.

**CHECK YOUR UNDERSTANDING**

**1.** What is the difference between a variable and its levels? What might be the levels of the variable "favorite color"?

**2.** Explain why some variables can only be measured, not manipulated. Can "history of trauma" be a manipulated variable? Can "level of eye contact" be a manipulated variable?

**3.** What is the difference between a conceptual variable and the operational definition of a variable? How might the conceptual variables "level of eye contact," "intelligence," and "stress" be operationalized by a researcher?

1. See p. 56. 2. See p. 57. "History of trauma" is probably not a manipulated variable, but "level of eye contact" might be manipulated if researchers assigned some people to make regular eye contact with a conversation partner and other people to look away from a conversation partner. 3. See pp. 57–59.

## THREE CLAIMS

A **claim** is an argument someone is trying to make. Internet bloggers might make claims based on personal experience or observation ("The media coverage of congressional candidates has been sexist"). Politicians might make claims based on rhetoric ("I am the candidate of change!"). Literature scholars make claims based on textual evidence ("Based on my reading of the text, I argue that the novel *Frankenstein* reflects a fear of technology"). In this textbook, we focus on claims made by researchers and journalists. Researchers make claims about theories based on data. Journalists make claims when they report on studies they read in empirical journals. Recall from Chapters 1 and 2 that psychologists use systematic observations, or data, to test and refine theories and claims. A psychologist might claim, based on data they have collected, that a certain percentage of teens attempted suicide last year, or that people who exercise earn more money, or that pretending to be a superhero helps kids stay on task.

Notice the different wording in the headlines in **Table 3.3**. In particular, the first statement merely gives a percentage of teens who texted while driving; this and the others in the first row are *frequency claims*. The claims in the middle are *association claims*: For example, one of them suggests that two variables, speech delays and mobile devices, go together, but it does not claim that speech delays cause screen time or that screen time causes speech delays. The claims in the last section of the table, however, are *causal claims*. For example, the verb *help* indicates that pretending to be Batman actually causes children to be more persistent. The kind of claim a psychological scientist makes must be backed up by the right kind of study. How can you identify the types of claims researchers make, and how can you evaluate whether their studies can support each type of claim? If you conduct research yourself, how will you know what kind of study will support the type of claim you wish to make?

# Frequency Claims

Just 15% of Americans Smoke

Seventy-four Percent of the World Smiled Yesterday

Forty-one Percent of Children Worldwide Experience Moderate Food Insecurity

Most Students Don't Know When News Is Fake

**Frequency claims** describe a particular rate or degree of a single variable. In the last example above, "most" refers to a proportion of students (presumably higher than 50%) who could not identify fake news. In the first example, "15%" is the proportion of American adults who smoke. These headlines claim how frequent or common something is. Claims that mention the percentage of a variable, the number of people who engage in some activity, or a certain group's level on a variable can all be called frequency claims.

Frequency claims are easily identified because they focus on only one variable—such as level of food insecurity, rate of smiling, or amount of texting. In addition, in studies that support frequency claims, the variables are always measured, not manipulated. For example, the researchers measured children's food insecurity by using a questionnaire or an interview and reported the results.

Some reports give a list of single-variable results, all of which count as frequency claims. Take, for example, the recent report from Gallup stating that 74% of the world smiled yesterday (Gallup.com, 2019). The same report also found that 49% of people said they learned something interesting yesterday. These are two separate frequency claims—they each measured a single variable one at a time. The researchers were not trying to show an association between these single variables, and the report did not claim that the people who learned something interesting were more likely to smile. It simply stated that a certain percentage of the world's people smiled and a certain percentage learned something interesting.

## TABLE 3.3

### Examples of Each Type of Claim

| CLAIM TYPE | SAMPLE HEADLINES |
|---|---|
| **Frequency claims** | Thirty-nine Percent of Teens Admit to Texting While Driving |
| | In the U.S., 71% Support Transgender People Serving in the Military |
| | Screen Time for Kids Under 2 More Than Doubles, Study Finds |
| | Most Students Don't Know When News Is Fake |
| **Association claims** | Speech Delays Could Be Linked to Mobile Devices |
| | Girls More Likely to Be Compulsive Texters |
| | Suffering a Concussion Could Triple the Risk of Suicide |
| | Countries with More Butter Have Happier Citizens |
| **Causal claims** | Mothers' Friendships Are Good for Babies' Brains |
| | Family Meals Curb Eating Disorders |
| | To Appear More Intimidating, Just Tilt Your Head Down |
| | Pretending to Be Batman Helps Kids Stay on Task |

## Association Claims

Study Links Coffee Consumption to Lower Depression in Women

New Study Links Exercise to Higher Pay

Another Study Points to Connection Between *13 Reasons Why* and Increased Youth Suicide

A Late Dinner Is Not Linked to Childhood Obesity, Study Shows

These headlines are all examples of association claims. An **association claim** argues that one level of a variable is likely to be associated with a particular level of another variable. Variables that are associated are sometimes said to **correlate**, or *covary*, meaning that when one variable changes, the other variable tends to change, too. More simply, they may be said to be *related*.

Notice that there are two variables in each example above. In the first, the variables are amount of coffee consumption and level of depression: Higher coffee consumption is associated with lower levels of depression (and therefore lower coffee consumption goes with higher levels of depression). In the second example, the variables are the amount of exercise and the income level: More frequent exercise goes with higher levels of income.

An association claim states a relationship between at least two variables. To support an association claim, the researcher usually measures the two variables and determines whether they're associated. This type of study, in which the variables are measured and the relationship between them is tested, is called a **correlational study**. Therefore, when you read an association claim, you will usually find a correlational study supporting it.

» For more on correlation patterns, see Chapter 8.

### POSITIVE ASSOCIATION

The headline "New study links exercise to higher pay" is an association in which high goes with high and low goes with low; it's called a **positive association**, or *positive correlation*. Stated another way, high rates of exercise go with higher levels of pay, and low rates of exercise go with lower levels of pay.

One way to represent an association is to use a **scatterplot**, a graph in which one variable is plotted on the y-axis and the other variable is plotted on the x-axis. Each dot represents one participant in the study, measured on the two variables. **Figure 3.3** shows what scatterplots of the associations in three of the example headlines would look like. (Data are fabricated for illustration purposes, and numbers are arbitrary units.) Notice that the dots in **Figure 3.3A** form a cloud of points, as opposed to a straight line. If you drew a straight line through the center of the cloud of points, however, the line would incline upward; in other words, the mathematical slope of the line would be positive.

### NEGATIVE ASSOCIATION

The study behind the claim "Coffee drinking linked to less depression in women" obtained a negative association. In a **negative association** (or *negative correlation*), high goes with low and low goes with high. In other words, high rates of coffee go with less depression, and low rates of coffee go with more depression.

A scatterplot representing this association would look something like the one in **Figure 3.3B**. Each dot represents a person who has been measured on two variables. However, in this example, a line drawn through the cloud of points would slope downward; it would have a negative slope.

In this example, the reverse of the association—that people who drink less coffee are the most depressed—is another way to phrase this negative association.

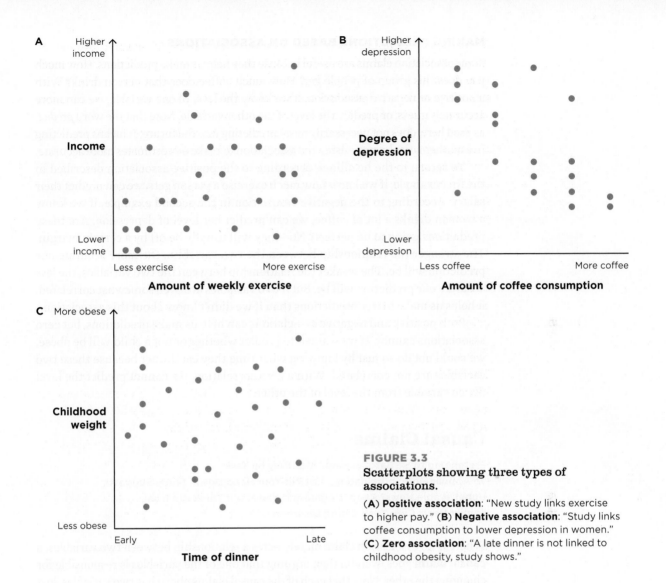

**FIGURE 3.3**
**Scatterplots showing three types of associations.**

(**A**) **Positive association**: "New study links exercise to higher pay." (**B**) **Negative association**: "Study links coffee consumption to lower depression in women." (**C**) **Zero association**: "A late dinner is not linked to childhood obesity, study shows."

Keep in mind that the word *negative* refers only to the slope; it does not mean the association is somehow bad. To avoid this kind of confusion, some people prefer the term *inverse association*.

## ZERO ASSOCIATION

The study behind the headline "A late dinner is not linked to childhood obesity, study shows" is an example of a **zero association**, or no association between the variables (*zero correlation*). In a scatterplot, both early and late levels of dinnertime are associated with all levels of obesity (**Figure 3.3C**). This cloud of points has no slope—or more specifically, a line drawn through it would be nearly horizontal, and a horizontal line has a slope of zero.

## MAKING PREDICTIONS BASED ON ASSOCIATIONS

Some association claims are useful because they help us make predictions. How much pay does this group of people get? How much coffee does that person drink? With a positive or negative association, if we know the level of one variable, we can more accurately guess, or predict, the level of the other variable. Note that the word *predict*, as used here, does not necessarily mean predicting into the future. It means predicting in a mathematical sense—using the association to make our estimates more accurate.

To return to the headlines, according to the positive association described in the first example, if we know how much exercise a person gets, we can predict their salary. According to the negative association in the second example, if we know a woman drinks a lot of coffee, we can predict her level of depression. Are these predictions going to be perfect? No—they will usually be off by a certain margin. The stronger the relationship between the two variables, the more accurate our prediction will be. The weaker the relationship between the two variables, the less accurate our prediction will be. But if two variables are even somewhat correlated, it helps us make better predictions than if we didn't know about this association.

Both positive and negative associations can help us make predictions, but zero associations cannot. If we wanted to predict whether or not a child will be obese, we could not do so just by knowing what time they eat dinner because these two variables are not correlated. With a zero correlation, we cannot predict the level of one variable from the level of the other.

## Causal Claims

Pretending to Be Batman Helps Kids Stay on Task

To Appear More Intimidating, Just Tilt Your Head Down, Study Suggests

Unbelievable News? Read It Again and You Might Think It's True

Family Meals Curb Teen Eating Disorders

Whereas an association claim merely notes a relationship between two variables, a **causal claim** goes even further, arguing that one of the variables is responsible for changing the other. Note that each of the causal claims above has two variables, just like association claims: pretending to be Batman and staying on task, intimidating (versus nonthreatening) appearance and head tilt, family meals and eating disorders.

In addition, like association claims, the causal claims above suggest that the two variables in question covary: Reading a story more than once goes with being more likely to believe that story. Eating family meals goes with lower rates of eating disorders. Kids who pretend to be Batman persist longer (than children who don't), and tilting your head down goes with appearing intimidating. You might also see a causal claim based on a zero association that reports a lack of cause. For example, you might read that vaccines do not cause autism or that being in daycare does not cause behavior problems.

Causal claims, however, go beyond a simple association between the two variables. They use language suggesting that one variable causes the other—verbs such as *cause*, *enhance*, *affect*, *decrease*, and *change*. In contrast, association claims use verbs such as *link*, *associate*, *correlate*, *predict*, *tie to*, and *be at risk for*. In **Table 3.4**, notice the difference between these types of verbs and verb phrases. Causal verbs tend to be more exciting. They are active and forceful, suggesting that one variable comes first in time and acts on the other variable. It's not surprising, then, that journalists may be tempted to describe family dinners as *curbing* eating disorders, for example, because it makes a better story than family meals just *being associated with* eating disorders.

Here's another important point: A causal claim may contain tentative language—*could*, *may*, *seem*, *suggest*, *sometimes*, *potentially*. If a headline read "Music lessons *may* enhance IQ," it would be more tentative, but would still be still considered a causal claim. The verb *enhance* makes it a causal claim, regardless of any softening or qualifying language.

*Advice* is also a causal claim; it implies that if you do X, then Y will happen. For example: "Best way to deal with jerks? Give them the cold shoulder." "Boost your salary by hitting the gym."

Causal claims are a step above association claims. Because they make a stronger statement, we need to hold them to higher standards. To move from the simple language of association to the language of causality, a study has to satisfy three criteria. First, it must establish that the two variables (the causal variable and the outcome variable) are correlated; the relationship cannot be zero. Second, it must show that the causal variable came first and the outcome variable came later. Third, it must establish that no other explanations exist for the relationship. Therefore, when we encounter a causal claim, we must be sure the study can support it. Later in this chapter, you will learn that only one type of study, an experiment, enables researchers to support a causal claim because it meets all three criteria.

**TABLE 3.4**

## Verb Phrases That Distinguish Association and Causal Claims

| ASSOCIATION CLAIM VERBS | CAUSAL CLAIM VERBS | |
| --- | --- | --- |
| is linked to | causes | promotes |
| is at higher risk for | affects | reduces |
| is associated with | may curb | prevents |
| is correlated with | exacerbates | distracts |
| prefers | changes | fights |
| is more/less likely to | may lead to | worsens |
| may predict | makes | increases |
| is tied to | sometimes makes | trims |
| goes with | hurts | adds |

# Not All Claims Are Based on Research

Besides the types of claims mentioned above, you may also encounter stories in the popular media that are not based on research, even if they are related to psychology. For instance:

The Forgotten Mothers and Babies of Zika
A Woman Living with Chronic Pain Describes How It Makes Her Seem "Uninterested"
Guys Reveal How They Found Their Therapists

These kinds of headlines, while interesting, are not frequency, association, or causal claims, in which a writer summarizes the results of a poll, survey, or other research study. Anecdotes and interviews are about people's personal experiences. Such headlines describe a person's experience with a health problem, raise awareness of rare diseases, or share mental health resources. But they don't say anything about the frequency of a problem or how it might be solved using research-based evidence.

✔

**CHECK YOUR UNDERSTANDING**

1. How many variables are there in a frequency claim? An association claim? A causal claim?

2. Which part of speech in a claim can help you differentiate between association and causal claims?

3. How are causal claims special, compared with the other two claim types?

4. What three criteria must causal claims satisfy?

1. See pp. 61–62 and 65–66. 2. The verbs matter; see pp. 65–66 and Table 3.4. 3. See pp. 65–66. 4. See p. 65.

## INTERROGATING THE THREE CLAIMS USING THE FOUR BIG VALIDITIES

You now have the tools to differentiate the three major claims you'll encounter in research journals and the popular media—but your job is just beginning. Once you identify the kind of claim a writer is making, you need to ask targeted questions as a critically minded consumer of information. The rest of this chapter will sharpen your ability to evaluate the claims you come across, using what we'll call the four big validities: construct validity, external validity, statistical validity, and internal validity (Cook & Campbell, 1979; Shadish et al., 2002). **Validity** refers to the appropriateness of a conclusion or decision, and in general, a *valid* claim is reasonable, accurate, and justifiable. In psychological research, however, we do not say a claim is simply "valid." Instead, psychologists specify which of the validities they are applying. As a psychology student, you will learn to pause before you declare a study to be "valid" or "not valid" and to specify which of the four big validities the study has achieved.

Although the focus for now is on how to evaluate other people's claims in terms of the four big validities, you'll also be using this same framework if you plan to conduct your own research. Whether you decide to test a frequency claim, an association claim, or a causal claim, it is essential to plan your research carefully, emphasizing the validities that are most important for your goals.

# Interrogating Frequency Claims

To evaluate how well a study supports a frequency claim, you will focus on two of the big validities: construct validity and external validity. You may decide to ask about statistical validity, too.

## CONSTRUCT VALIDITY OF FREQUENCY CLAIMS

**Construct validity** refers to how well a conceptual variable is operationalized. When you ask how well a study measured or manipulated a variable, you are interrogating the construct validity—be it smiling, smoking, texting, gender identity, food insecurity, or knowing when news is fake. For example, when evaluating the construct validity of a frequency claim, the question is how well the researchers measured their variable of interest. Consider this claim: "39% of teens text while driving." There are several ways to measure this variable, though some are better than others. You could ask teenagers to tell you on an online survey how often they engage in text messaging while they're behind the wheel. You could stand near an intersection and record the behaviors of teenage drivers. You could even use cell phone records to see if a text was sent at the same time a person was known to be driving. You would expect the study behind this claim to use an accurate measure of texting among teenagers, and observing behavior is probably a better way than casually asking, "Have you ever texted while driving?"

To ensure construct validity, researchers must establish that each variable has been measured reliably (meaning the measure yields similar scores on repeated testings) and that different levels of a variable accurately correspond to true differences in, say, texting or happiness. (For more detail on construct validity, see Chapter 5.)

## EXTERNAL VALIDITY OF FREQUENCY CLAIMS

The next important questions to ask about frequency claims concern **generalizability**: How did the researchers choose the study's participants, and how well do those participants represent the intended population? Consider the example "74% of the world smiled yesterday." Did Gallup researchers survey every one of the world's 8 billion people to come up with this number? Of course not. They surveyed a smaller sample of people. Next you ask: Which people did they survey, and how did they choose their participants? Did they include only people in major urban areas? Did they ask only college students from each country? Or did they attempt to randomly select people from every region of the world?

Such questions address the study's **external validity**—how well the results of a study generalize to, or represent, people or contexts besides those in the original study. If Gallup researchers had simply asked people who clicked on the Gallup website whether they smiled yesterday, and 74% of them said they did, the researcher cannot claim that 74% of the entire world did. The researcher cannot even argue that 74% of Gallup website visitors smiled or laughed because the people who choose to answer such questions may not be an accurate representation. Indeed, to claim the 74% number, the researchers would have needed to ensure that the participants in the sample adequately represented all people in the world—a daunting task! Gallup's Global Emotions Report states that their sample includes adults in each of 140 countries who were interviewed by phone or in person (Gallup.com, 2019). The researchers attempted to obtain representative samples in each country (excluding very remote or politically unstable areas of certain countries).

» For more on the procedures that researchers use to ensure external validity, see Chapter 7, pp. 186–191.

### STATISTICAL VALIDITY OF FREQUENCY CLAIMS

Researchers use statistics to analyze their data. **Statistical validity**, also called *statistical conclusion validity*, is the extent to which a study's statistical conclusions are precise, reasonable and replicable. How well do the numbers support the claim?

To understand statistical validity, it helps to know that the value we get from a single study is not an objective truth. Instead, it's an *estimate* of that value in some population. For example, for the report claiming that "39% of teenagers text while driving," researchers interviewed a sample of about 9,000 teen drivers to estimate the behavior of the population of all U.S. teenage drivers. To evaluate statistical validity, we start with the **point estimate**. In a frequency claim, the point estimate is usually a percentage.

Next we ask about the *precision* of that estimate. For a frequency claim, precision is captured by the **confidence interval**, or **margin of error of the estimate**. The confidence interval is a range designed to include the true population value a high proportion of the time. In the report about how many teenagers text while driving, the 39.2% point estimate was accompanied by the confidence interval, 37.0–41.4. This means that the true number of teens who text while driving may be as low as 37% or as high as 41.4%, though our interval might miss the true value (CDC, n.d.). An analogy for the confidence interval is a contractor who estimates your home repair will cost "between $1,000 and $1,500." The repair will probably cost something in that range (but might cost less or cost more).

Finally, statistical validity improves with multiple estimates. Researchers ideally conduct studies more than once and then consider the results of all investigations of the same topic. Combining many estimates is better than using a single one. We should consider each study in the context of multiple results on the same question, collected over the long run.

## Interrogating Association Claims

Correlational studies, which support association claims, measure two variables instead of one. Such studies describe how these variables are related to each other. To interrogate an association claim, you ask how well the correlational study behind the claim supports construct, external, and statistical validities.

## CONSTRUCT VALIDITY OF ASSOCIATION CLAIMS

To support an association claim, a researcher measures two variables, so you have to assess the construct validity of *each* variable. For the headline "Study links coffee consumption to lower depression in women," you should ask how well the researchers measured coffee consumption and how well they measured depression. The first variable, coffee consumption, could be measured by asking people to document their food and drink intake every day for some period of time. The second variable, depression, could be measured using a series of questions developed by clinical psychologists that ask about depression symptoms.

In any study, measuring variables is a fundamental strength or weakness—and construct validity questions assess how well such measurements were conducted. If you conclude that one of the variables was measured poorly, you would not be able to trust the study's conclusions. However, if you conclude that the construct validity of both variables was excellent, you can have more confidence in the association claim being reported.

## EXTERNAL VALIDITY OF ASSOCIATION CLAIMS

You might also interrogate the external validity of an association claim by asking whether it can generalize to other populations, as well as to other contexts, times, or places. For example, the association between coffee consumption and depression came from a study of women. Will the association generalize to men? You can also evaluate generalizability to other contexts by asking, for example, whether the link between coffee consumption and depression might be generalizable to other forms of caffeine (such as tea or cola). Similarly, if a study found a link between exercise and income, you can ask whether the study, conducted on Americans, can generalize to people in Canada, Mexico, or Japan. **Table 3.5** summarizes the four big validities used in this text.

---

**TABLE 3.5**

### The Four Big Validities

| TYPE OF VALIDITY | DESCRIPTION |
| --- | --- |
| Construct validity | How well the variables in a study are measured or manipulated. The extent to which the operational variables in a study are a good approximation of the conceptual variables. |
| External validity | The extent to which the results of a study generalize to some larger population (e.g., whether the results from this sample of teenagers apply to all U.S. teens), as well as to other times or situations (e.g., whether the results based on coffee apply to other types of caffeine). |
| Statistical validity | How well the numbers support the claim—that is, how strong the effect is and the precision of the estimate (the confidence interval). Also takes into account whether the study has been replicated. |
| Internal validity | In a relationship between one variable (A) and another (B), the extent to which A, rather than some other variable (C), is responsible for changes in B. |

## STATISTICAL VALIDITY OF ASSOCIATION CLAIMS

When applied to an association claim, statistical validity considers how strong the estimated association is and how precise that estimate is, and it considers other estimates of the same association.

The first aspect of the statistical validity of an association is strength: How strong is the estimated association? Some associations—such as the association between education and income—are quite strong. People with bachelor's degrees usually earn much more money than those with high school degrees—about 66% more income over a 40-year career (The College Board, n.d., based on data from the U.S. Census Bureau). Other associations—such as the association between exercise and income—are weaker. The study on exercise and income found that frequent exercisers earn about 9% more money than others (Kosteas, 2012).

We can also ask about the *precision* of the estimated association. The estimate of an association (e.g., 9% higher income for frequent exercisers) can be accompanied by a confidence interval, just as it can for frequency claims. We might read for example, that frequent exercisers earn "between 6% and 12%" more income than others. The confidence interval is designed to capture the true relationship between exercising and income in a high proportion of cases. Studies with smaller samples (fewer people) have wider, less precise intervals that reflect uncertainty (e.g., 1% to 25%). Studies with larger samples have narrower, more precise intervals (e.g., 8% to 10%). Finally, we ask whether the study has been conducted more than once, because multiple estimates of the association are better than one.

》
For more about association strength and statistical significance, see Chapter 8, pp. 205–206 and pp. 213–214.

As you might imagine, evaluating statistical validity can be complicated. Full training in how to interrogate statistical validity requires a separate, semester-long statistics class. This book introduces you to the basics and focuses on the strength of the estimated effect, the precision of that estimate (its confidence interval), and replication over the long run.

In sum, when you come across an association claim, you should ask about three validities: construct, external, and statistical. You can ask how well the two variables were measured (construct validity). You can ask whether you can generalize the result to a population (external validity). And you can estimate the strength of the association and the precision of this estimate (statistical validity).

**Table 3.6** gives an overview of the three claims, four validities framework. Before reading about how to interrogate causal claims, use the table to review what we've covered so far.

## Interrogating Causal Claims

An association claim says that two variables are related. A causal claim goes further, saying that one variable causes the other. Instead of using such verb phrases as *is associated with*, *is related to*, and *is linked to*, causal claims use directional

**TABLE 3.6**

## Interrogating the Three Types of Claims Using the Four Big Validities

| TYPE OF VALIDITY | FREQUENCY CLAIMS ("4 IN 10 TEENS ADMIT TO TEXTING WHILE DRIVING") | ASSOCIATION CLAIMS ("STUDY LINKS EXERCISE TO HIGHER PAY") | CAUSAL CLAIMS ("PRETENDING TO BE BATMAN HELPS KIDS STAY ON TASK") |
|---|---|---|---|
| | Usually based on a survey or poll, but can come from other types of studies | Usually supported by a correlational study | Must be supported by an experimental study |
| **Construct validity** | How well has the researcher measured the variable in question? | How well has the researcher measured each of the two variables in the association? | How well has the researcher measured or manipulated the variables in the study? |
| **Statistical validity** | What is the confidence interval (margin of error) of the estimate? Are there other estimates of the same percentage? | What is the estimated effect size: How strong is the association? How precise is the estimate: What is the confidence interval? What do estimates from other studies say? | What is the estimated effect size: How large is the difference between groups? How precise is the estimate: What is the confidence interval? What do estimates from other studies say? |
| **Internal validity** | Frequency claims do not usually assert causality, so internal validity is not relevant. | People who make association claims are not asserting causality, so internal validity is not relevant. A writer should avoid making a causal claim from a simple association, however (see Chapter 8). | Was the study an experiment? Does the study achieve temporal precedence? Does the study control for alternative explanations by randomly assigning participants to groups? Does the study avoid internal validity threats (see Chapters 10 and 11)? |
| **External validity** | To what populations, settings, and times can we generalize this estimate? How representative is the sample? Was it a random sample? | To what populations, settings, and times can we generalize this association claim? How representative is the sample? To what other situations might the association be generalized? | To what populations, settings, and times can we generalize this causal claim? How representative is the sample? How representative are the manipulations and measures? |

verbs such as *affects*, *leads to*, and *reduces*. When you interrogate such a claim, your first step will be to make sure it is backed up by research that fulfills the three criteria for causation: covariance, temporal precedence, and internal validity.

## THREE CRITERIA FOR CAUSATION

Of course, one variable usually cannot be said to cause another variable unless the two are related. **Covariance**, the extent to which two variables are observed to go together, is established by the results of a study. It is the first criterion a study must satisfy in order to establish a causal claim. But showing that two variables are associated is not enough to justify using a causal verb. The research method must

TABLE 3.7

**Three Criteria for Establishing Causation Between Variable A and Variable B**

| CRITERION | DEFINITION |
|---|---|
| Covariance | The study's results show that as A changes, B changes; e.g., high levels of A go with high levels of B, and low levels of A go with low levels of B. |
| Temporal precedence | The study's method ensures that A comes first in time, before B. |
| Internal validity | The study's method ensures that there are no plausible alternative explanations for the change in B; A is the only thing that changed. |

also satisfy two additional criteria: temporal precedence and internal validity (**Table 3.7**).

To say that a study establishes **temporal precedence** means that the method was designed so that the causal variable clearly comes first in time, before the effect variable. To make the claim "Pretending to be Batman helps kids stay on task," a study must show that "pretending to be Batman" came first and staying on task came later. Although this statement might seem obvious, it is not always so. Consider the claim "Pressure to be available 24/7 on social media causes teen anxiety." It might be the case that social media behavior came first, causing anxiety, but it is also possible that teens start out anxious, and that anxiety spreads to their social media behavior. Therefore, to support the causal claim, a study needs to establish that social media behavior came first and the anxiety came later.

Another criterion, called **internal validity**, or the *third-variable criterion*, refers to a study's ability to eliminate alternative explanations for the association. For example, to say "Pretending to be Batman helps kids stay on task" is to claim that pretending to be a hardworking hero like Batman *causes* increased persistence. But an alternative explanation could be that older kids are more likely to pretend to be hardworking heroes and are better able to stay on task. In other words, there could be an internal validity problem. The maturity of the child, not pretending to be Batman, leads children to persist longer.

### EXPERIMENTS CAN SUPPORT CAUSAL CLAIMS

Usually, to support a causal claim, researchers must conduct a well-designed **experiment**, in which one variable is manipulated and the other is measured. Experiments are considered the gold standard of psychological research because of their potential to support causal claims. In daily life, people tend to use the word *experiment* casually, referring to any trial of something to see what happens ("Let's experiment and try making the popcorn with olive oil instead"). In science, including psychology, an experiment is more than just "a study." When psychologists conduct an experiment, they *manipulate* the variable they think is the cause and *measure* the variable they think is the effect (or outcome). In the context of an experiment, the manipulated variable is called the **independent variable** and the measured variable is called the **dependent variable**. To support the claim about Batman, the researchers in that study would have had to manipulate the variable "pretending to be Batman" and measure the persistence variable.

» For examples of independent and dependent variables, see Chapter 10, pp. 281–283.

Remember: To *manipulate* a variable means to assign participants to be at one level or the other. In the study that tested the persistence claim, researcher Rachel White and five research colleagues (2017) recruited 90 typically developing 6-year-old children. They asked all 90 kids to do a slow-paced, boring computer task. The kids were told to work as hard as they could on the boring task, but they could take breaks to play an enticing game on an iPad. (This was how the researchers operationalized "staying on task" in their study.)

The study was meant to test whether kids would stay on the computer task longer if they took a self-distanced perspective. Self-distancing means taking an outsider's view of your own behavior, like being a fly on the wall. White and colleagues manipulated the self-distancing variable by putting kids in one of three groups. Children in one group were encouraged to self-distance by pretending to be a hardworking hero—such as Batman, Bob the Builder, or Dora the Explorer—and were given a costume to wear. The researchers told these children to ask themselves as they worked on the boring task, "Is [Batman/Bob/Dora] working hard?"

A second group of children was told to think of themselves from a third-person perspective, asking "Is [child's name] working hard?" A third group of children was called self-immersed—the condition lowest in self-distancing. They were told to ask the first-person question, "Am I working hard?"

At the conclusion of the study, White and colleagues found that the 6-year-olds who were in the hardworking hero condition spent almost 60% of their time on the boring task (and only 40% on the iPad). Children in the third-person condition spent 45% of their time on the boring task. Children in the self-immersed condition spent only 35% of their time on the boring task (**Figure 3.4**). The results of White et al.'s study showed covariance: Being in the Batman condition covaried with persisting longer on the boring task.

**A Study's Method Can Establish Temporal Precedence and Internal Validity.** Why does the method of manipulating one variable and measuring the other help scientists make causal claims? For one thing, manipulating the independent variable—the causal variable—ensures that it comes first. By manipulating the children's perspective first and then measuring persistence, White and colleagues ensured temporal precedence in their study.

In addition, when researchers manipulate a variable, they have the potential to control for alternative explanations; that is, they can ensure internal validity. When the White team were investigating children's persistence, they

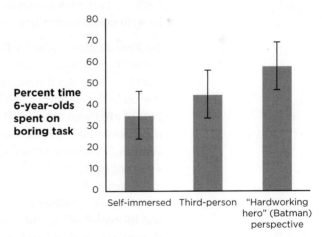

**FIGURE 3.4**

**Interrogating a causal claim.**

What features of White et al.'s study made it possible to support the causal claim that pretending to be Batman causes kids to persist longer at a boring task? (The error bars represent the standard error of the estimate. Source: White et al., 2017.)

ensured that the children in all three conditions were about the same age, because otherwise age would have been an alternative explanation for the results. They also didn't want the children in the Batman condition to be more intelligent, more introverted, or have different kinds of parents than children in the other two conditions, because these could also be alternative explanations.

Therefore, White and her colleagues used a technique called **random assignment** to ensure that the children in all the groups were as similar as possible. They used a method, such as rolling a die, to decide whether each child in the study would follow the hardworking hero, third-person, or self-immersed instructions. By randomly assigning children to one of the groups these researchers could ensure that the children in the Batman condition were as similar as possible, in every other way, to those in the third-person or self-immersed conditions. Random assignment increased internal validity by allowing the researchers to control for potential alternative explanations. They also designed the experiment so the children were all the same age, were all tested in the same laboratory room, worked on the same boring game, and had the same attractive iPad distractor. These methodology choices secured the study's internal validity.

» For more on how random assignment helps ensure that experimental groups are similar, see Chapter 10, pp. 290–291.

The White team's experiment met all three criteria for causation. The results showed covariance, and the method established temporal precedence and internal validity. Therefore, the researchers were justified in making a causal claim from their data. Their study really can be used to support the claim that "pretending to be Batman helps kids stay on task."

### WHEN CAUSAL CLAIMS ARE A MISTAKE

Let's use two other examples to illustrate how to interrogate causal claims made by writers and journalists.

**Do Family Meals Really Curb Eating Disorders?**  To interrogate the causal claim "Family meals curb teen eating disorders" (**Infographic Figure 3.5**), we start by asking about covariance in the study behind this claim. Is there an association between family meals and eating disorders? Yes: The news report says 26% of girls who ate with their families fewer than five times a week had eating-disordered behavior (e.g., the use of laxatives or diuretics, or self-induced vomiting), and only 17% of girls who ate with their families five or more times a week engaged in eating-disordered behaviors (Warner, 2008). The two variables are associated.

What about temporal precedence? Did the researchers make sure family meals had increased before the eating disorders decreased? No: In fact both variables were measured at the same time, so the temporal precedence is not clear from this association. In fact, one of the symptoms of an eating disorder is embarrassment about eating in front of others, so perhaps the eating disorder came first and the decreased family meals came second. Daughters with eating disorders may simply find excuses to avoid eating with their families.

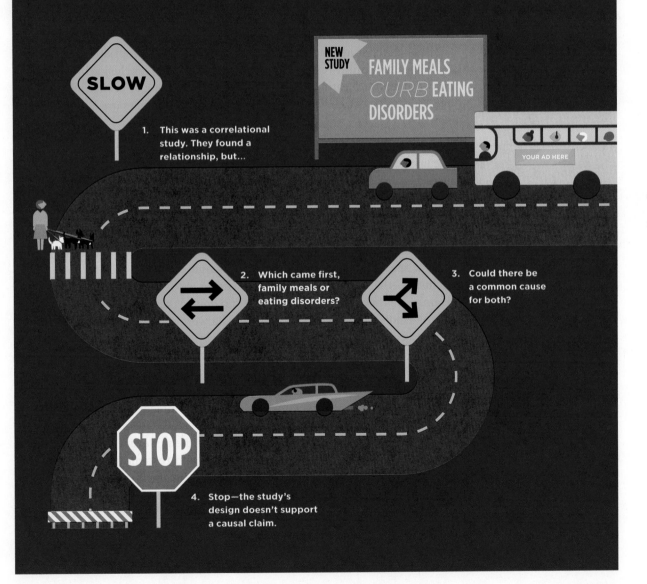

**FIGURE 3.5**

# Navigating Causal Claims: Do Family Meals Really Curb Eating Disorders?

Journalists might make a causal claim from a correlational study. But correlational studies don't establish temporal precedence or internal validity.

**SLOW**

1. This was a correlational study. They found a relationship, but...

**NEW STUDY**

**FAMILY MEALS CURB EATING DISORDERS**

YOUR AD HERE

2. Which came first, family meals or eating disorders?

3. Could there be a common cause for both?

**STOP**

4. Stop—the study's design doesn't support a causal claim.

Internal validity is a problem here, too. Without an experiment, we cannot rule out many alternative, third-variable explanations. Perhaps girls from dual-earner families are less likely to eat with their families and are more vulnerable to eating disorders, whereas girls who have only one working parent are less vulnerable. Maybe academically high-achieving girls are too busy to eat with their families and are also more susceptible to eating-disordered behavior. These are just two possible alternative explanations. Only a well-run experiment could have controlled for these internal validity problems (the alternative explanations), using random assignment to ensure that the girls who had frequent family dinners and those who had less frequent family dinners were comparable in all other ways: dual- versus single-income households, high versus low scholastic achievement, and so on. However, it would be impractical and probably unethical to conduct such an experiment.

Although the study's authors reported the findings appropriately, the journalist wrapped the study's results in an eye-catching causal conclusion by saying that family dinners *curb* eating disorders. The journalist should probably have headlined the study with the association claim, "Family dinners *are linked to* eating disorders."

**Does Social Media Pressure Cause Teen Anxiety?**  Another example of a dubious causal claim is this headline: "Pressure to be available 24/7 on social media causes teen anxiety." In the story, the journalist reported on a study that measured two variables in a set of teenagers. One variable was social media use (especially the degree of pressure to respond to texts and posts), and the other was level of anxiety (ScienceDaily, 2015). The researchers found that those who felt pressure to respond immediately also had higher levels of anxiety.

Let's see if this study's design is adequate to support the journalist's conclusion—that social media pressure *causes* anxiety in teenagers. The study certainly does have covariance: The results showed that teens who felt more pressure to respond immediately to social media were also more anxious. However, this was a correlational study, in which both variables were measured at the same time, so temporal precedence was not established. We cannot know if the pressure to respond to social media increased first, thereby leading to increased anxiety, or if teens who were already anxious expressed their anxiety through social media use, by putting pressure on themselves to respond immediately.

In addition, this study did not rule out possible alternative explanations (internal validity) because it was not an experiment. Several outside variables could potentially correlate with both anxiety and responding immediately to social media. One might be that teens who are involved in athletics are more relaxed (because exercise can reduce anxiety) and less engaged in social media (because busy schedules limit their time). Another might be that certain teenagers are vulnerable to emotional disorders in general. They are already more anxious *and* feel more pressure about the image they're presenting on social media (**Figure 3.6**).

An experiment could potentially rule out such alternative explanations. In this example, though, conducting an experiment would be hard. A researcher cannot randomly assign teens to be concerned about social media or to be anxious. Because the research was not enough to support a causal claim, the journalist should have packaged the description of the study under an association claim headline: "Social media pressure and teen anxiety are linked."

## OTHER VALIDITIES TO INTERROGATE IN CAUSAL CLAIMS

A study can support a causal claim only if the results demonstrate covariance, and only if it used the experimental method, thereby establishing temporal precedence and internal validity. Therefore, internal validity is often the most important validity to evaluate for causal claims. Besides internal validity, the other three validities discussed in this chapter—construct validity, statistical validity, and external validity—should be interrogated, too.

**FIGURE 3.6**
**Support for a causal claim?**
Without conducting an experiment, researchers cannot support the claim that social media pressure causes teen anxiety.

**Construct Validity of Causal Claims.** Take the headline "Pretending to be Batman helps kids stay on task." First, we could ask about the construct validity of the measured variable in this study. How well was "staying on task" measured? Is persistence at the slow, boring computer task an acceptable measure of this variable? Then we would need to interrogate the construct validity of the manipulated variable. In operationalizing manipulated variables, researchers must create a specific task or situation that will represent each level of the variable. In the current example, was the costume and the question "Is Batman working hard?" the best manipulation of the construct, "pretending to be a hardworking hero"?

《
For more on how researchers use data to check the construct validity of their manipulations, see Chapter 10, pp. 303–305.

**External Validity of Causal Claims.** We could ask, in addition, about external validity. The study tested 6-year-old children from Minneapolis, Minnesota. Can this sample generalize to children from other states or other countries? Would it generalize to younger kids? What about generalization to other situations— could the results generalize to other targets, such as pretending to be an admired teacher? (In Chapters 10 and 14, you'll learn more about how to evaluate the external validity of experiments and other studies.)

**Statistical Validity of Causal Claims.** We can also interrogate statistical validity. To start, we would ask: How large was the difference between the groups? In this example, participants in the Batman condition persisted about 60% of the time, compared with 35% of the time for those in the self-immersed condition— nearly twice as long. That seems like a fairly large effect. Next, we can ask about the precision of this estimate. The error bars in Figure 3.4 show the precision of

»

For more on determining the
strength of a relationship
between variables,
see Statistics Review:
Descriptive Statistics,
pp. 468–472.

each percentage estimate (the confidence intervals)—these intervals are somewhat wide, reflecting the relatively small sample size. We can also ask whether this study has been repeated—whether we can consider estimates from multiple studies over time. (In Chapter 10, you'll learn more about interrogating the statistical validity of causal claims.)

## Prioritizing Validities

Which of the four validities is the most important? It depends. When researchers plan studies, they usually find it impossible to conduct a study that satisfies all four validities at once. Depending on their goals, sometimes researchers place a lower priority on certain validities. They decide where their emphasis lies—and so will you, when you participate in producing your own research.

External validity, for instance, is not always possible to achieve—and sometimes it may not be the researcher's priority. As you'll learn in Chapter 7, to be able to generalize results from a sample to a wide population requires a representative sample from that population. Consider the study on children's persistence at a task. Because the researchers were planning to test a causal claim, they wanted to emphasize internal validity so they focused on making the children in the three groups—self-immersed, third-person, and hardworking hero—absolutely equivalent. They were not prioritizing external validity and did not try to sample children from all over the country. However, the study is still important and interesting because it used an internally valid experimental method, even though it did not achieve external validity. Furthermore, although they used a sample of children from Minneapolis, there may be no theoretical reason to assume that the hardworking hero instructions would not improve the persistence of rural children, too. Future research could confirm that the intervention works for other groups of children just as well, but there is no obvious reason to expect otherwise.

In contrast, if some researchers were conducting a telephone survey and did want to generalize its results to, say, the entire Canadian population—to maximize external validity—they would have to randomly select Canadians from all ten provinces. One approach would be to use a random-digit telephone dialing system to call people in their homes, but this technology is expensive. When researchers do use formal, randomly sampled polls, they often have to pay a polling company a fee to administer each question. Therefore, a researcher who wants to evaluate, say, depression levels in a large population may be economically forced to use a short questionnaire or survey. A 2-item measure might not be as good as a 15-item measure, but the longer one would cost more. In this example, the researcher might sacrifice some construct validity in order to achieve external validity.

You'll learn more about these priorities in Chapter 14. The point, for now, is simply that in the course of planning and conducting a study, researchers weigh the pros and cons of methodology choices and decide which validities are most important. When you read about a study, you should not necessarily conclude it is faulty just because it did not meet one of the validities.

**CHECK YOUR UNDERSTANDING**

1. What question(s) would you use to interrogate a study's construct validity?

2. In your own words, describe the three things that statistical validity addresses.

3. Define external validity, using the term *generalize* in your definition.

4. Why can't a correlational study support a causal claim?

5. Why don't researchers usually aim to achieve all four of the big validities at once?

1. See pp. 67, 69, and 77. 2. See pp. 70–71. 3. See pp. 68 and 77–78. 4. See pp. 72–73 and table 3.7. 5. See pp. 78–79.

# REVIEW: FOUR VALIDITIES, FOUR ASPECTS OF QUALITY

As a review, let's apply the four validities discussed in this chapter to another headline from a popular news source: "To appear more intimidating, just tilt your head down, study suggests." The journalist's story was reported in an online magazine (Walton, 2019), and the original research was published in the journal *Psychological Science* (Witkower & Tracy, 2019). Should we consider this a well-designed study? How well does it hold up on each of the four validities? At this stage in the course, you should focus on asking the right questions for each validity. In later chapters, you will also learn how to evaluate the answers to those questions. You can see how we might interrogate this study by reading the Working It Through section.

# To Appear More Intimidating, Just Tilt Your Head Down, Study Suggests

Two researchers conducted a study in which participants were shown photos of different neutral faces—some directly forward, others tilted 10 degrees down, and others tilted 10 degrees back (Witkower & Tracy, 2019). We will work through this example to demonstrate how to apply the concepts from Chapter 3.

| QUESTIONS TO ASK | CLAIMS, QUOTES, OR DATA | INTERPRETATION AND EVALUATION |
|---|---|---|
| What kind of claim is made in the headline?<br><br>What are the variables in the headline?<br><br>Which validities should we interrogate for this claim? | A *Forbes* journalist wrote an article headlined "To appear more intimidating, just tilt your head down, study suggests" (Walton, 2019). | This is a causal claim because it gives advice. The advice suggests that tilting your head down will cause you to appear intimidating.<br><br>One variable is tilting your head down (or not). The other variable is how intimidating, or dominant, you appear.<br><br>We should interrogate a causal claim on all four validities, especially internal validity. |

**The empirical study behind the journalist's story appeared in the journal *Psychological Science*. This article reported three separate studies. We'll be working with the first study here.**

| **Construct validity** | | |
|---|---|---|
| How well did the researchers manipulate "Tilting your head down"? | In the Method section of their article, researchers Witkower and Tracy (2019) report that "Avatars were generated to ensure precise manipulations of targets' head angle while preventing any | By using avatars (computer-generated faces), the researchers could very precisely manipulate the exact head |

| QUESTIONS TO ASK | CLAIMS, QUOTES, OR DATA | INTERPRETATION AND EVALUATION |
|---|---|---|
| **Construct Validity** (*continued*) How well did the researchers manipulate "Tilting your head down"? | incidental facial or body movements; all targets displayed neutral facial expressions. . . . Each target was portrayed with the head tilted upward 10°, the head at a neutral angle (i.e., 0°), or the head tilted downward 10°." | tilts and expressions of the faces that participants would see. The manipulation seems well done. |
| How well did they measure "how intimidating—dominant—you appear"? | The researchers report that participants used "a validated measure of dominance, defined as the use of intimidation or threat to influence other people. . . . These items were as follows: 'This person would enjoy having control over others,' 'This person would be willing to use aggressive tactics to get their way,' 'This person would often try to get his way regardless of what people may want,' and 'This person would try to control others rather than permit them to control him.' For each target, participants rated their agreement with each statement on a scale ranging from 1 (*not at all*) to 7 (*very much*)." | In this passage, the authors give their conceptual definition of dominance ("the use of intimidation or threat to influence other people"). They also describe the operationalization of dominance. The four items they used are a straightforward way of measuring how dominant a target looks. The authors mention that the items were previously shown to accurately measure dominance impressions. Therefore the construct validity of this measure seems excellent. |
| **Statistical validity** How large was the difference in perceived dominance between different head tilt groups? How precise are the estimates? Was the effect replicated? | The researchers report that downward-tilting faces were rated about 5.4 and neutral faces were rated as 4.4 on the 1–7 dominance rating scale. In addition, the authors report the results of two other studies, both of which estimated the effect to be about the same strength. | Tilting the target's head down led to a 1-point increase in dominance on a 7-point scale. That's about a 14% increase. The study was replicated at least two times, and multiple estimates found similar effect sizes. |
| **Internal validity** Was this study an experiment? Are there alternative explanations, other than the head tilt, that could have caused the dominance ratings to increase? | The researchers manipulated the head tilt of the targets; therefore, this was an experiment. Also, because researchers used avatars in the first study, they could make sure that the target faces held the exact same eye expression, mouth movements, hair arrangement, skin tone, and so on. | The only difference between the three conditions was the head tilt, not eye or mouth expression. Therefore, we can be sure that head tilt, not other factors, caused dominance ratings to increase. Internal validity was excellent. |
| **External validity** Can we generalize from the people in this study's sample to some larger population? Can we generalize from avatar targets to the faces of real humans? | The researchers used a sample of North American participants who do studies online for money through a service called MTurk. One of the additional studies used photos of real human targets, not avatars, and found the same pattern of results. | The study's ability to generalize is unknown. However, when researchers conduct experiments to support causal claims, their priority is usually internal validity, not external validity. The effect does appear to generalize from avatars to real human faces. |

# CHAPTER REVIEW

 It's time to complete your study experience! Go to INQUIZITIVE to practice actively with this chapter's concepts and get personalized feedback along the way.

## Summary

The three claims, four validities framework enables you to systematically evaluate any study you read, whether in a journal article or a popular media story. It can also guide you in making choices about research you might conduct yourself.

### VARIABLES

- Variables, concepts of interest that vary, form the core of psychological research. A variable has at least two levels.
- Variables can be measured or manipulated.
- Variables in a study can be described in two ways: as conceptual variables (elements of a theory) and as operational definitions (specific measures or manipulations in order to study them).

### THREE CLAIMS

- As a consumer of information, you will identify three types of claims that researchers, journalists, and other writers make about research: frequency, association, and causal claims.
- Frequency claims make arguments about the level of a single, measured variable in a group of people.
- Association claims argue that two variables are related to each other. An association can be positive, negative, or zero. Association claims are usually supported by correlational studies, in which all variables are measured. When you know how two variables are associated, you can use one to predict the other.
- Causal claims state that one variable is responsible for changes in the other variable. To support a causal claim, a study must meet three criteria—covariance, temporal precedence, and internal validity—which is accomplished only by an experimental study.

### INTERROGATING THE THREE CLAIMS USING THE FOUR BIG VALIDITIES

- To interrogate a frequency claim, ask questions about the study's construct validity (quality of the measurements), external validity (generalizability to a larger population), and statistical validity (the percentage estimate, its confidence interval, and other estimates of the percentage).
- To interrogate an association claim, ask about its construct, external, and statistical validity. Statistical validity addresses the strength of a relationship, the precision with which it is estimated, and whether it has been replicated in other studies.
- To interrogate a causal claim, ask whether the study conducted was an experiment, which is the only way to establish internal validity and temporal precedence. If it was an experiment, further assess internal validity by asking whether the study was designed with any confounds and whether the researchers randomly assigned participants to groups. You can also ask about the study's construct, external, and statistical validity.
- Researchers usually cannot achieve all four validities at once in an experiment, so they prioritize them. Their interest in making a causal statement means they may sacrifice external validity to ensure internal validity.

# Key Terms

variable, p. 56
level, p. 56
constant, p. 56
measured variable, p. 56
manipulated variable, p. 56
construct, p. 57
conceptual variable, p. 57
operational definition, p. 57
operational variable, p. 57
operationalize, p. 57
claim, p. 60
frequency claim, p. 61

association claim, p. 62
correlate, p. 62
correlational study, p. 62
positive association, p. 62
scatterplot, p. 62
negative association, p. 62
zero association, p. 63
causal claim, p. 64
validity, p. 66
construct validity, p. 67
generalizability, p. 67
external validity, p. 67

statistical validity, p. 68
point estimate, p. 68
confidence interval, p. 68
margin of error of the
    estimate, p. 68
covariance, p. 71
temporal precedence, p. 72
internal validity, p. 72
experiment, p. 72
independent variable, p. 72
dependent variable, p. 72
random assignment, p. 74

 **To see samples of chapter concepts in the popular media, visit www.everydayresearchmethods.com and click the box for Chapter 3.**

# Review Questions

1. Which of the following variables are manipulated, rather than measured? (Could be more than one.)

   a. Number of shoes owned, in pairs.

   b. A person's height, in cm.

   c. Amount of aspirin a researcher gives a person to take, either 325 mg or 500 mg.

   d. Degree of happiness, rated on a scale from 1 to 10.

   e. Type of praise a researcher uses in groups of dogs: verbal praise or a clicking sound paired with treats.

2. Which of the following headlines is an association claim?

   a. Chewing Gum Can Improve Your Mood and Focus

   b. Handling Money Decreases Helpful Behavior in Young Children

   c. Workaholism Is Tied to Psychiatric Disorders

   d. Eating Kiwis May Help You Fall Asleep

3. Which of the following headlines is a frequency claim?

   a. Obese Kids Are Less Sensitive to Tastes

   b. Eighty Percent of Women Feel Dissatisfied with How Their Bodies Look

   c. Feeling Fat? Maybe Facebook Is to Blame

   d. Daycare and Behavior Problems Are Not Linked

4. Which of the following headlines is a causal claim?

   a. Taking a Deep Breath Helps Minimize High Blood Pressure, Anxiety, and Depression

   b. Younger People Can't Read Emotions on Wrinkled Faces

   c. Strange But True: Babies Born in the Autumn Are More Likely to Live to 100

   d. Check the Baby! Many New Moms Show Signs of OCD

5. Which validity would you be interrogating by asking: How well did the researchers measure sensitivity to tastes in this study?

   a. Construct validity

   b. Statistical validity

   c. External validity

   d. Internal validity

6. Which validity would you be interrogating by asking: How did the researchers get their sample of people for this survey?

   a. Construct validity

   b. Statistical validity

   c. External validity

   d. Internal validity

7. In most experiments, trade-offs are made between validities because it is not possible to achieve all four at once. What is the most common trade-off?

   a. Internal and external validity.

   b. Construct and statistical validity.

   c. Statistical and internal validity.

   d. External and statistical validity.

## Learning Actively

1. For each boldfaced variable below, indicate how you might describe the variable conceptually and operationally, the variable's levels, and whether the variable is measured or manipulated.

| VARIABLE IN CONTEXT | CONCEPTUAL VARIABLE NAME | OPERATIONALIZATION OF THIS VARIABLE | LEVELS OF THIS VARIABLE | MEASURED OR MANIPULATED |
|---|---|---|---|---|
| A questionnaire study asks for various demographic information, including participants' **level of education.** | Level of education | Asking participants to circle their highest level of education from this list:<br><br>High school diploma<br>Some college<br>College degree<br>Graduate degree | High school diploma<br>Some college<br>College degree<br>Graduate degree | Measured |
| A questionnaire study asks about **anxiety**, measured on a 20-item Spielberger Trait Anxiety Inventory. | | | | |
| A study of readability has people read a passage of text printed in one of two **fonts: sans-serif or serif.** | | | | |
| A study of **school achievement** asks participants to report their SAT scores, as a measure of college readiness. | | | | |
| A researcher studying self-control and **blood sugar levels** gives participants one of two glasses of sweet-tasting lemonade: one has sugar, the other is sugar-free. | | | | |

2. Imagine you encounter each of the following headlines. What questions would you ask if you wanted to understand more about the quality of the study behind the headline? For each question, indicate which of the four validities it is addressing. Follow the model in the Working It Through section.

   a. Chewing Gum Can Improve Your Mood and Focus

   b. Workaholism Is Tied to Psychiatric Disorders

   c. Eighty Percent of Women Feel Dissatisfied with How Their Bodies Look

3. Suppose you want to test the causal claim about chewing gum improving your mood and focus. How could you design an experiment to test this claim? What would the variables be? Would each be manipulated or measured? What results would you expect? Sketch a graph of the outcomes you would predict. Would your experiment satisfy the three criteria for supporting a causal statement?

**PART II**

# Research Foundations for Any Claim

Beneficence

Respect for Persons

Justice

# 4

# Ethical Guidelines for Psychology Research

NO MATTER WHAT TYPE of claim researchers are investigating, they are obligated—by law, by morality, and by today's social norms—to treat the participants in their research with kindness, respect, and fairness. In the 21st century, researchers are expected to follow basic ethical principles in the treatment of humans and other animals. Researchers are also expected to produce research that is meaningful, helpful, and accessible to the public. This chapter introduces the criteria for evaluating whether a set of research was conducted appropriately and ethically.

## HISTORICAL EXAMPLES

In the past, some researchers held different ideas about the ethical treatment of study participants. Two examples of research, one from medicine and one from psychology, follow. The first one clearly illustrates several ethics violations. The second demonstrates the difficult balance of priorities researchers might face when evaluating a study's ethics.

### The Tuskegee Syphilis Study Illustrates Three Major Ethics Violations

In the late 1920s and early 1930s, about 35% of poor Black men living in the southern United States were infected with syphilis. Because the disease was largely untreatable at the time, it interfered with their

**LEARNING OBJECTIVES**

**A year from now, you should still be able to:**

**1.**
Define the three ethical principles of the Belmont Report and describe how each one is applied. Recognize the similarities between the Belmont Report's principles and the five APA Ethical Principles.

**2.**
Describe the procedures that are in place to protect human participants and animal subjects in research.

**3.**
Articulate some of the ways that ethical decision making requires balancing priorities, such as research risks versus benefits, rights of individual participants versus societal gains, free participation versus coercion.

ability to work, contribute to society, and climb out of poverty. In 1932, the U.S. Public Health Service (PHS), cooperating with the Tuskegee (Alabama) Institute, began a study of 600 Black men. About 400 were already infected with syphilis, and about 200 were not. The researchers wanted to study the effects of untreated syphilis on the men's health over the long term. At the time, administering no treatment was a reasonable choice because of the risky and ineffective methods available in 1932 (Jones, 1993). These treatments involved infusions of toxic metals, but when they worked at all they had serious—even fatal—side effects (CDC, 2016). The men were recruited in their community churches and schools, and many of them were enthusiastic about participating in a project that would give them access to medical care for the first time in their lives (Reverby, 2009). However, there is little evidence that the men were told the study was actually about syphilis.

Early in the project, the researchers decided to follow the men infected with syphilis until each one died, to obtain valuable data on how the disease progresses when untreated. The study lasted 40 years, during which the researchers made a long series of unethical choices. Infected men were told they had "bad blood" instead of syphilis. All of them were required to come to the Tuskegee clinic for evaluation and testing, but they were never given any beneficial treatment (**Figure 4.1**). At one point, in fact, the researchers conducted a painful, potentially dangerous spinal tap procedure on every participant in order to follow the progression of the disease. To ensure that the men would come in for the procedure, the researchers lied, telling them it was a "special free treatment" for their illness (Jones, 1993).

As the project continued, 250 of the men registered to join the U.S. Armed Forces, which were then engaged in World War II. As part of the draft process, the men were diagnosed (again) with syphilis and told to reenlist after they had been treated. Instead of following these instructions, however, the researchers interfered and kept the men from being treated. As a result, they could not serve in the armed forces or receive subsequent G.I. benefits (U.S. Public Health Service, 1973).

In 1943, the PHS approved the use of penicillin for treating syphilis, yet the Tuskegee Institute did not provide information about this new cure to the participants in their study. In 1968, PHS employee Peter Buxtun raised concerns with officials at the CDC. However, the researchers decided to proceed as before. The study continued until 1972, when Buxtun told the story to the Associated Press (Gray,

**FIGURE 4.1**
**The Tuskegee Syphilis Study.**
A doctor takes a blood sample from a participant. What unethical decisions were made by the researchers who conducted this study?

1998; Heller, 1972) and the study was widely condemned. Over the years, many of the men in the study got sicker, and dozens died. Several men inadvertently infected their partners, in some cases causing congenital syphilis in their children (Jones, 1993; Reverby, 2009).

In 1974, the families of the participants reached a settlement in a lawsuit against the U.S. government. In 1997, President Bill Clinton formally apologized to the survivors on behalf of the nation (**Figure 4.2**). Nonetheless, the Tuskegee Syphilis Study has contributed to an unfortunate legacy. As a result of this study, some African Americans are suspicious of government health services and research participation (McCallum et al., 2006).

**FIGURE 4.2**
**An official apology in 1997.**

The U.S. government issued an apology to survivors of the Tuskegee Syphilis Study.

## UNETHICAL CHOICES

The researchers conducting this infamous study made a number of choices that are unethical from today's perspective. Later writers have identified these choices as falling into three distinct categories (Childress et al., 2005; Gray, 1998). First, the men were *not treated respectfully*. The researchers lied to them about the nature of their participation and withheld information (such as penicillin as a cure for the disease). In so doing, they did not give the men a chance to make a fully informed decision about participating in the study. If they had known in advance the true nature of the study, some might still have agreed to participate but others might not. After the men died, the doctors offered a generous burial fee to the families, mainly so they could be sure of doing autopsy studies. These low-income families may have felt coerced into agreeing to an autopsy only because of the large payment.

Second, the men in the study were *harmed*. They and their families were not told about a treatment for a disease that, in the later years of the study, could be easily cured. (Many of the men were illiterate and thus unable to learn about the penicillin cure on their own.) They were also subjected to painful and dangerous tests. Third, the researchers *targeted a disadvantaged social group* in this study. Syphilis affects people from all social backgrounds and ethnicities, yet all the men in this study were poor and African American (Gray, 1998; Jones, 1993).

# The Milgram Obedience Studies Illustrate a Difficult Ethical Balance

The Tuskegee Syphilis Study provides several examples of ethics violations, but ethical matters may be more nuanced. Social psychologist Stanley Milgram's series of studies on obedience to authority, conducted in the early 1960s, illustrates some of the difficulties of ethical decision making.

Imagine yourself as a participant in one of Milgram's studies. You are told there will be two participants: you, the "teacher," and another participant, the "learner." As teacher, your job is to punish the learner when he makes mistakes in a learning task. The learner slips into a cubicle where you can't see him, and the session begins (Milgram, 1963, 1974).

As the study goes on, you are told to punish the learner for errors by administering electric shocks at increasingly higher intensities, as indicated on an imposing piece of equipment in front of you: the "shock generator." At first, while receiving the low-voltage shocks, the learner does not complain. But he keeps making mistakes on the learning task, and you are required by the rules of the study to deliver shocks that are 15 volts higher after each mistake (**Figure 4.3**). As the voltage is increased, the learner begins to grunt with pain. At about 120 volts, the learner shouts that the shocks are very painful and says he wants to quit the experiment. At 300 volts, the learner screams that he will no longer respond to the learning task. The experimenter, sitting behind you in a white lab coat, tells you to keep delivering shocks—15 volts more each time, until the machine indicates you're delivering 450-volt shocks. Whereas before the learner screamed in pain with each new shock, after 300 volts you now hear nothing from him. You can't tell whether he is even conscious in his cubicle.

If you protest (and you probably would), the experimenter behind you says calmly, "Continue." If you protest again, the experimenter says, again calmly, "The experiment requires that you continue," or even, "You have no choice, you must go on." What would you do now?

You may believe you would have refused to obey the demands of this inhumane experimenter. However, in the original study, fully 65% of the participants obeyed, following the experimenter's instructions and delivering the 450-volt shock to the learner. Only two or three participants (out of hundreds) refused to give even the first, 15-volt shock. Virtually all participants subjected another person to electric shocks—or at least they thought they did. Fortunately, the learner was a confederate of the experimenter: He was a paid actor playing a role, and he did not actually receive any shocks. But the participants did not know this; they thought the learner was an innocent, friendly man.

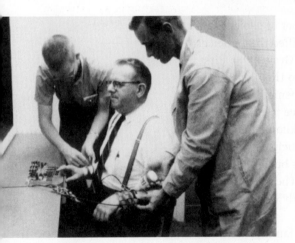

**FIGURE 4.3**

**The Milgram obedience studies.**

In one version, the experimenter (right) and the true participant, or "teacher" (left), help connect the "learner" to the electrodes that would supposedly shock him. Was it ethical for the researchers to invent this elaborate situation, which ultimately caused participants so much stress?

Milgram conducted 18 or more variations of this study. Each time, 40 new participants were asked to deliver painful shocks to the learner (**Figure 4.4**).

## BALANCING RISK TO PARTICIPANTS WITH BENEFIT TO SOCIETY

Was Milgram acting ethically in conducting this research? One psychologist at the time criticized the study because it was extremely stressful to the teacher-participants (Baumrind, 1964). Milgram relayed this observation from one of his research assistants:

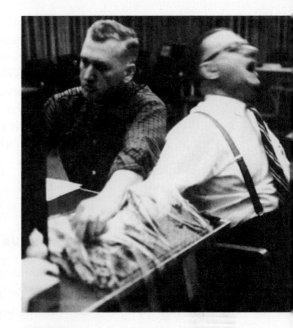

**FIGURE 4.4**
**Balancing ethical concerns.**

In one variation of the Milgram obedience studies, participants were required to force the learner's arm onto a (fake) electric plate. How do you balance potential harm to participants with the benefit to society in this research?

> I observed a mature and initially poised businessman enter the laboratory smiling and confident. Within 20 minutes he was reduced to a twitching, nervous wreck, who was rapidly approaching a point of nervous collapse. He constantly pulled on his earlobe, and twisted his hands. At one point he pushed his fist into his forehead and muttered, "Oh, God, let's stop it." And yet he continued to respond to every word of the experimenter, and obeyed to the very end. (Milgram, 1963, p. 377)

To what extent was it ethical to put unsuspecting volunteers through such a stressful experience?

Some writers have questioned how Milgram's participants coped with their involvement later on. In an interview right after the study, the participants were **debriefed**; that is, they were carefully informed about the study's hypotheses. They shook hands with the learner, who reassured them he was unharmed. However, in order to avoid influencing potential future participants, the debriefing never mentioned that the learner did not receive shocks (Perry, 2013). In interviews years later, some participants reported worrying for weeks about the learner's welfare (Perry, 2013).

Milgram claimed that his results—65% obedience—surprised him (Milgram, 1974; but see Perry, 2013). Experts at the time predicted that only 1–2% of people would obey the experimenter up to 450 volts. After the first iteration of the study, however, Milgram knew what kind of behavior to expect. Once he knew that many of the people in the study would experience anxiety and stress, Milgram might have taken steps to stop, or modify, the procedure, and yet he did not.

An ethical debate about the Milgram studies must also weigh the lessons learned, and Milgram himself emphasized their social impact. Some argue the studies contributed crucial lessons about obedience to authority and the "power of the situation"—lessons we would not have learned without his research (Blass, 2002). The research may have benefited individual participants: Milgram had an associate call some of the participants at home, months later, to ask about their current state of well-being. Some of them felt they had learned something important. For example, one participant reported: "What appalled me was that I could possess this capacity for obedience and compliance. . . . I hope I can deal more effectively with future conflicts of values I encounter" (Milgram, 1974, p. 54). Thus, there is a fundamental conundrum in deciding whether this research is ethical—trying to balance the potential *risks to participants* and *the value of the knowledge* gained. In cases like the Milgram studies, it is not an easy decision.

---

**CHECK YOUR UNDERSTANDING**

1. What three categories of ethics violations are illustrated by the Tuskegee Syphilis Study?

2. What ethical concerns have been raised regarding the Milgram obedience studies?

1. See pp. 89–91. 2. See pp. 92–94.

## CORE ETHICAL PRINCIPLES

Organizations around the world have developed formal statements of ethics. Following World War II, the Nuremberg Trials revealed the horror of medical experiments conducted on concentration camp victims in Nazi-occupied Europe and resulted in the Nuremberg Code. Although it is not a formal law in any nation, the ten-point Nuremberg Code influences the ethical research laws of many countries (Shuster, 1997). In addition, many national leaders have signed the Declaration of Helsinki, which guides ethics in medical research and practice. Within the United States, ethical systems are also based on the Belmont Report, which defines the ethical guidelines researchers should follow. All of these ethical statements are grounded in the same core principles.

### The Belmont Report: Principles and Applications

In 1976, a commission of physicians, ethicists, philosophers, scientists, and other citizens gathered at the Belmont Conference Center in Eldridge, Maryland, at the request of the U.S. Congress. They intensively discussed basic ethical principles researchers should follow. The commission was created partly in response to the serious ethics violations of the Tuskegee Syphilis Study (Jonsen, 2005).

The contributors produced a short document called the Belmont Report, which outlines three main principles for guiding ethical decision making: respect for persons, beneficence, and justice. Each principle has standard applications. The guidelines are intended for use in many disciplines, including medicine, sociology, anthropology, and basic biological research, as well as psychology.

## THE PRINCIPLE OF RESPECT FOR PERSONS

In the Belmont Report, the **principle of respect for persons** includes two provisions. First, individuals potentially involved in research should be treated as autonomous agents: They should be free to make up their own minds about whether they wish to participate in a research study. Applying this principle means that every participant is entitled to the precaution of **informed consent**: Each person learns about the research project, considers its risks and benefits, and decides whether to participate.

In obtaining informed consent, researchers are not allowed to mislead people about the study's risks and benefits. Nor may they coerce or unduly influence a person into participating, because doing so would violate the principle of respect for persons. Coercion is an implicit or explicit suggestion that those who do not participate will suffer a negative consequence; for example, a professor implying that students' grades will be lower if they don't participate in a particular study. Undue influence is offering an incentive too attractive to refuse, such as an irresistible amount of money in exchange for participating. The report notes that financially poor individuals may be more easily swayed into participating if a research study provides a large payment.

The second application of respect for persons states that some people have less autonomy, so they are entitled to special protection when it comes to informed consent. For example, children, people with intellectual or developmental disabilities, and prisoners should be protected, according to the Belmont Report. Children and certain other individuals might be unable to give informed consent because of not understanding the procedures involved well enough to make a responsible decision (**Figure 4.5**). Prisoners are especially susceptible to coercion, according to the Belmont Report, because they may perceive requests to participate in research as demands, rather than as invitations. All these populations should be treated with special consideration.

## THE PRINCIPLE OF BENEFICENCE

To comply with the **principle of beneficence**, researchers must take precautions to protect participants from harm and to ensure their well-being. To apply this principle, researchers carefully assess the risks and benefits of the study they

**FIGURE 4.5**
**Vulnerable populations in research.**
Why might children be considered a vulnerable population that requires special ethical consideration?

plan to conduct. In addition, they must consider how the community might benefit or be harmed. Will a community gain something of value from the knowledge this research is producing? Will there be costs to a community if this research is not conducted?

The Tuskegee Syphilis Study failed to treat the participants in accordance with the principle of beneficence. The researchers harmed participants through risky and invasive medical tests, and they harmed the participants' families by exposing them to untreated syphilis. The researchers also withheld benefits from the men in the study. Today, researchers may not withhold treatments that are known to be helpful to study participants. For example, if preliminary results indicate, halfway through a study, that a treatment is advantageous for an experimental group, the researcher must give the participants in the control group the opportunity to receive that treatment, too.

Another potential risk is having people's personal information (their behavior, mental health information, or private reactions) revealed to others. To prevent harm, researchers usually make participant information either anonymous or confidential. In an **anonymous study,** researchers do not collect any potentially identifying information, including names, birthdays, photos, and so on. Anonymous online surveys will even strip away the identifiers of the computer used. In a **confidential study**, researchers collect some identifying information (for contacting people at a later date if needed) but prevent it from being disclosed. They may save data in encrypted form or store people's names separately from their other data.

Risks and benefits are generally easy to assess when it comes to physical health, the type measured in medical research. Is a person's health getting worse or better? Is the community going to be healthier because of this research, or not? In contrast, some psychological studies can expose participants to emotional or psychological harm, such as anxiety, stress, depression, or mental strain, and these may be harder to evaluate.

Consider the participants in the Milgram studies, who were clearly experiencing stress. How might you assess the harm done in this situation? Because it's hard to evaluate emotional or psychological harm, it is difficult to evaluate how damaging a study like Milgram's might be. However, the principle of beneficence demands that researchers consider such risks (and benefits) before beginning each study. As a point of reference, some institutions ask researchers to estimate how stressful a study's situation would be compared with the normal stresses of everyday life.

The other side of the balance—the benefits of psychological research to the community—may not be easy to assess either. One could argue that Milgram's results are valuable, but their value is impossible to quantify in terms of lives or dollars saved. Nevertheless, to apply the principle of beneficence, researchers must attempt to predict the risks and benefits of their research—to both participants and the larger community.

## THE PRINCIPLE OF JUSTICE

The **principle of justice** calls for a fair balance between the kinds of people who participate in research and the kinds of people who benefit from it. For example, if a research study discovers that a procedure is risky or harmful, the participants, unfortunately, "bear the burden" of that risk, while other people—those not in the study—may benefit from the research results (Kimmel, 2007). The Tuskegee Syphilis Study illustrates a violation of this principle of justice: Anybody, regardless of race or income, can contract syphilis and benefit from research on it, but the participants in the study—who bore the burden of untreated syphilis—were all poor African American men. Therefore, these participants bore an undue burden of risk.

When the principle of justice is applied, it means that researchers consider the extent to which the participants involved in a study are representative of the kinds of people who would also benefit from its results. If researchers decide to study a sample from only one ethnic group or only a sample of institutionalized individuals, they must demonstrate that the problem they are studying is especially prevalent in that ethnic group or in that type of institution. For example, it would violate the justice principle if researchers studied a group of prisoners mainly because they were convenient. However, it might be perfectly acceptable to study only institutionalized people for a study on tuberculosis because tuberculosis is particularly prevalent in institutions where people live together in a confined area.

## ETHICAL PRINCIPLES IN PRACTICE

Just as panels of judges interpret a country's laws, panels of people interpret the guidelines in the Belmont Report (Jonsen, 2005). Most universities and research hospitals have committees that decide whether research and practice are complying with ethical guidelines. In the United States, federally funded agencies must follow the Common Rule, which describes detailed ways the Belmont Report should be applied in research (U.S. Department of Health and Human Services, 2009). For example, it explains informed consent procedures and ways to approve research before it is conducted.

At many colleges and universities, policies require anyone involved in research with human participants (professors, graduate students, undergraduates, or research staff) to be trained in ethically responsible research. Your institution might require you to complete online training, such as the course Responsible Conduct of Research, administered by the CITI program. By learning the material in this chapter, you will be better prepared for CITI courses if you're required to take them (**Figure 4.6**).

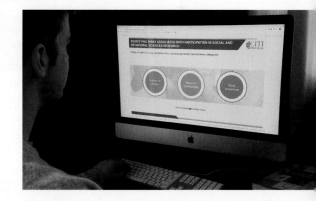

**FIGURE 4.6**
**Student researchers must train in the ethical conduct of research.**

Many colleges and universities use the CITI training program to prepare researchers.

# GUIDELINES FOR PSYCHOLOGISTS: THE APA ETHICAL PRINCIPLES

In addition to the Belmont Report, institutional policies, and federal laws, American psychologists can consult the Ethical Principles of Psychologists and Code of Conduct, written by the American Psychological Association (2002) (**Figure 4.7**). This broad set of guidelines governs three common roles of psychologists: as research scientists, as educators, and as practitioners (usually as therapists). Psychological associations in other countries have similar codes of ethics, and other professions have codes of ethics as well (Kimmel, 2007).

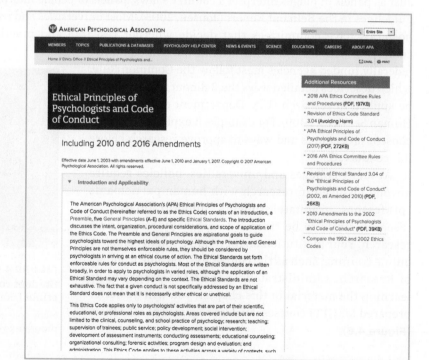

**FIGURE 4.7**

**The APA website.**

The full text of the APA's ethical principles can be found on the website. If you are considering becoming a therapist or counselor someday, you may find it interesting to read the other APA ethical standards that were written specifically for practitioners.

# Belmont Plus Two: APA's Five General Principles

The APA outlines five general principles for guiding individual aspects of ethical behavior. These principles are intended to protect not only research participants but also students in psychology classes and clients of professional therapists. As you can see in **Table 4.1**, three of the APA principles (A, D, and E in the table) are identical to the three main principles of the Belmont Report (beneficence, justice, and respect for persons). Another principle is *fidelity and responsibility* (e.g., a clinical psychologist teaching in a university may not serve as a therapist to one of his or her classroom students, and psychologists must avoid sexual relationships with their students or clients). The last APA principle is *integrity* (e.g., professors are obligated to teach accurately, and therapists are required to stay current on the empirical evidence for therapeutic techniques).

# Ethical Standards for Research

In addition to the five general principles, the APA lists ten specific ethical standards. These standards are similar to enforceable rules or laws. Psychologist members of the APA who violate any of these standards can lose their professional license or may be disciplined in some other way by the association.

TABLE 4.1

## The Belmont Report's Basic Principles and the APA's Five General Principles Compared

| BELMONT REPORT (1979) | APA ETHICAL PRINCIPLES (2002) | DEFINITION |
|---|---|---|
| **Beneficence** | **A. Beneficence and nonmaleficence** | Treat people in ways that benefit them. Do not cause suffering. Conduct research that will benefit society. |
| | B. Fidelity and responsibility | Establish relationships of trust; accept responsibility for professional behavior (in research, teaching, and clinical practice). |
| | C. Integrity | Strive to be accurate, truthful, and honest in one's role as researcher, teacher, or practitioner. |
| **Justice** | **D. Justice** | Strive to treat all groups of people fairly. Sample research participants from the same populations that will benefit from the research. Be aware of biases. |
| **Respect for persons** | **E. Respect for people's rights and dignity** | Recognize that people are autonomous agents. Protect people's rights, including the right to privacy, the right to give consent for treatment or research, and the right to have participation treated confidentially. Understand that some populations may be less able to give autonomous consent, and take precautions against coercing such people. |

Note: The principles in boldface are shared by both documents and specifically involve the treatment of human participants in research. The APA guidelines are broader; they apply not only to how psychologists conduct research but also to how they teach and conduct clinical practice.

Of its ten ethical standards, Ethical Standard 8 is written specifically for psychologists in their role as researchers. (The other standards are more relevant to their roles as therapists, consultants, and teachers.) The next sections outline some of the details of the APA's Ethical Standard 8.

## INSTITUTIONAL REVIEW BOARDS (STANDARD 8.01)

An **institutional review board** (**IRB**) is a committee responsible for interpreting ethical principles and ensuring that research using human participants is conducted ethically. Most colleges and universities, as well as research hospitals, have an IRB. If a U.S. institution uses federal money (such as government grants) to carry out research projects, a designated IRB is required. However, in the United States, research conducted by private businesses does not have to use an IRB or follow any particular ethical guidelines (though businesses may write their own ethics policies).

An IRB panel in the U.S. includes five or more people, some of whom must come from specified backgrounds. At least one member must be a scientist, one must have academic interests outside the sciences, and one (or more) must be a community member who has no ties to the institution (such as a local pastor, a community leader, or an interested citizen). In addition, when the IRB discusses a proposal to use prison participants, one member must be recruited as a designated prisoner advocate. The IRB must consider particular questions for any research involving children. In most other countries, IRBs follow similar mandates for their composition.

Before conducting a study, researchers must fill out a detailed application describing their study, its risks and benefits (to both participants and society), its procedures for informed consent, and its provisions for protecting people's privacy. The IRB then reviews each application.

Different IRBs have different procedures. At most universities, when a study is judged to be of little or no risk (such as a completely anonymous questionnaire), the IRB does not meet to discuss it in person. In most institutions, though, a study that poses risks to humans or that involves vulnerable populations must be reviewed by an in-person IRB meeting. Ideally, IRB oversight provides a neutral, multiperspective judgment on any study's ethicality. An effective IRB should not permit research that violates people's rights, research that poses unreasonable risk, or research that lacks a sound rationale. However, an effective IRB should not obstruct research, either. It should not prevent controversial—but still ethical—research questions from being investigated. Ideally, the IRB attempts to balance the welfare of research participants and the researchers' goal of contributing important knowledge to the field.

## INFORMED CONSENT (STANDARD 8.02)

As mentioned earlier, informed consent is the researcher's obligation to explain the study to potential participants in everyday language and give them a chance to decide whether to participate. In most studies, informed consent is obtained by providing a written document that outlines the procedures, risks, and benefits of the research, including a statement about any treatments that are experimental.

In certain circumstances, the APA standards (and other federal laws that govern research) indicate that informed consent procedures are not necessary. If the study is not likely to cause harm, involves a completely anonymous questionnaire, or takes place in an educational setting, written informed consent might not be required. Similarly, when the study involves naturalistic observation of participants in low-risk public settings, such as a museum, classroom, or mall, people can reasonably expect to be observed by others anyway. The individual institution's regulations determine these exceptions to informed consent, and those studies still must be approved by an IRB. In addition, researchers are always ethically obliged to respect participants' rights.

Obtaining informed consent also involves informing people whether the data they provide in a research study will be treated as private and confidential. In the course of research, people might report on their health status, political attitudes, test scores, or study habits—information they might not want others to know. Therefore, informed consent procedures ordinarily outline which parts of the data are confidential and which, if any, are not. If data are to be treated as confidential, researchers agree to remove names and other identifiers. Such things as handwriting, birthdays, and photographs might reveal personal data, and researchers must be careful to protect that information if they have promised to do so. At many institutions, confidentiality procedures are not optional. Many institutions require researchers to store any identifiable data in a locked area or on secure computers.

## DECEPTION (STANDARD 8.07)

You may have read about psychological research in which the researchers lied to participants. In the Milgram obedience studies described earlier, the participants did not know the learner was not really being shocked. In another study, an experimental confederate posed as a thief, stealing money from a person's bag while an unsuspecting bystander sat reading at a table (**Figure 4.8**). In some versions of this study, the "thief," the "victim," and a third person who sat calmly nearby pretending to read, were all experimental confederates. That makes three confederates and a fake crime—all in one study (Shaffer et al., 1975).

Even in the most straightforward study, participants are not told about all the comparison conditions. For example, in the study described in Chapter 3, the children were aware they were performing a boring task dressed as Batman, but they didn't know others were performing the task as themselves (White et al., 2019). All these studies contained an element of **deception**. In some cases, researchers withheld some details of the study from participants—deception through *omission*. In other cases, researchers actively lied to participants—deception through *commission*.

Consider how these studies might have turned out if there had been no such deception. Suppose the researchers had said, "We're going to see whether you're willing to help prevent a theft. Wait here. In a few moments, we will stage a theft and see what you do." Or "We want to know if you'll work harder at this boring task if you're dressed as Batman. Ready?" Obviously, the data would be useless.

**FIGURE 4.8**
**Deception in research.**

A study on bystander action staged a theft at a library table.

Deceiving research participants by lying to them or by withholding information is, in many cases, necessary in order to obtain meaningful results.

Is deception ethical? In a deception study, researchers must still uphold the principle of respect for persons by informing participants of the study's activities, risks, and benefits. The principle of beneficence also applies: What are the ethical costs and benefits of doing the study with deception, compared with the ethical costs of not doing it this way? It's important to find out what kinds of situational factors influence someone's willingness to report a theft and to test hypotheses about what motivates students in school. Because most people consider these issues to be important, some researchers argue that the gain in knowledge seems worth the cost of lying (temporarily) to the participants (Kimmel, 1998). Even then, the APA principles and federal guidelines require researchers to avoid using deceptive research designs except as a last resort and to debrief participants after the study.

Despite such arguments, some psychologists believe that deception undermines people's trust in the research process and should never be used in a study design (Ortmann & Hertwig, 1997). Still others suggest deception is acceptable in certain circumstances (Bröder, 1998; Kimmel, 2012; Pittenger, 2008). Researchers have investigated how undergraduates respond to participating in a study that uses deception. Results indicate that students usually tolerate minor deception and even some discomfort or stress, considering them necessary parts of research. When students do find deception to be stressful, these negative effects are diminished when the researchers fully explain the deception in a debriefing session (Bröder, 1998; Sharpe et al., 1992; Smith & Richardson, 1983).

### DEBRIEFING (STANDARD 8.08)

When researchers have used deception, they must spend time after the study talking with each participant in a structured conversation. In a debriefing session, the researchers describe the nature of the deception and explain why it was necessary. Emphasizing the importance of their research, they attempt to restore an honest relationship with the participant. As part of the debriefing process, the researcher describes the design of the study, thereby giving the participant some insight about the nature of psychological science (**Figure 4.9**).

Nondeceptive studies may include a debriefing session, too. At many universities, student participants in research receive a written description of the study's goals and hypotheses, along with references for further reading. The intention is to make participation in research a worthwhile educational experience, so students can learn more about the research process in general, understand how their participation fits into the larger context of theory testing, and learn how their participation might benefit others. In debriefing sessions,

**FIGURE 4.9**
**Debriefing.**

After any study, the researcher talks with participants and educates them about the research process.

researchers might also offer to share results with the participants. Even months after their participation, people can request a summary of the study's results.

## RESEARCH MISCONDUCT

Most discussions of ethical research focus on protection and respect for participants, and rightly so. However, the publication process also involves ethical decision making. As an example, it is considered ethical to publish one's results. After participants have spent their time in a study, it is only fair to make the results known publicly for the benefit of society. Psychologists must also treat their data and their sources accurately.

**Data Fabrication (Standard 8.10) and Data Falsification.** Two forms of research misconduct involve manipulating results. **Data fabrication** occurs when, instead of recording what really happened in a study (or sometimes instead of running a study at all), researchers invent data that fit their hypotheses. **Data falsification** occurs when researchers influence a study's results, perhaps by selectively deleting observations from a data set or by influencing their research subjects to act in the hypothesized way.

One case exemplifies both of these breaches. In 2012, social psychologist Diederik Stapel was fired from his job as a professor at Tilburg University in the Netherlands because he fabricated data in dozens of his studies (Stapel Investigation, 2012). Three graduate students became suspicious of his actions and bravely informed their department head. Soon thereafter, committees at the three universities where he had worked began documenting years of fraudulent data collection by Stapel. In written statements, he admitted that at first he changed occasional data points (data falsification), but later he found himself typing in entire datasets to fit his and his students' hypotheses (data fabrication). The scientific journals that published his fraudulent data have retracted more than 58 articles to date, according to the website Retraction Watch, which tracks cases of research fraud across the sciences.

Creating fabricated or falsified data is clearly unethical and has far-reaching consequences. When people fabricate data, they mislead others about the actual support for a theory. Fabricated data might inspire other researchers to spend time (and often grant money) following a false lead or to be more confident in theories than they should be. In the case of Stapel, the fraud cast a shadow over the careers of the graduate students and coauthors he worked with. Even though the collaborators did not know about or participate in the fabrication, Stapel's collaborators subsequently found many of their own published papers on the retraction list. Psychologists are concerned that Stapel's fraud could potentially harm psychology's reputation, even though psychology as a field is not uniquely vulnerable to fraud (Stroebe et al., 2012).

The costs were especially high for a fraudulent study that suggested a link between the measles, mumps, rubella (MMR) vaccine and autism (Wakefield et al., 1998). The study was discussed worldwide among frightened parents. Some parents still refuse to vaccinate their children, even though the paper has

« For more on the theory-data cycle, see Chapter 1, pp. 10–13.

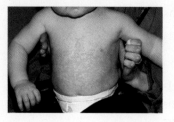

## FIGURE 4.10

**Fabricated and falsified data have consequences.**

This paper on vaccines was retracted from *The Lancet* after the authors admitted to fabricating results, selectively reporting data (falsification), and failing to report their financial interest. The cost of this fraud can be measured in loss of life from reduced vaccination rates and increased rates of diseases like measles. (Source: Wakefield et al., 1998. Originally published in *The Lancet*.)

been retracted from the journal *The Lancet* because the authors admitted fraud (**Figure 4.10**). Even now, there are measles outbreaks in the United Kingdom and the United States attributable to inadequate vaccination rates.

Why might a researcher fabricate or falsify data? In many universities, the reputations, income, and promotions of professors are based on their publications and their influence in the field. In high-pressure circumstances, the temptation might be great to delete contradictory data or create supporting data (Stroebe et al., 2012). In addition, countering Merton's norm of disinterestedness, some researchers become personally invested in their own hypotheses and believe that any data that do not support their predictions must be inaccurate. Writing about his first instance of falsification, Stapel wrote, "I changed an unexpected 2 into a 4 . . . I looked at the [office] door. It was closed. When I saw the new results, the world had returned to being logical" (quoted in Borsboom & Wagenmakers, 2013). Unethical scientists may manipulate their data to coincide with their intuition rather than with formal observations, as a true empiricist would.

Most recent cases of research fraud have been detected not by the peer-review process but by people who work with the perpetrator (Stroebe et al., 2012). If colleagues or students of a researcher in the United States suspect such misconduct, they may report it to the scientist's institution. If the research project is federally

**»**

To review the quality of different sources of information, see Chapter 2, pp. 39–49 and Figure 2.12.

funded, suspected misconduct can be reported to the Office of Research Integrity, a branch of the Department of Health and Human Services, which then has the obligation to investigate.

## OPENNESS AND TRANSPARENCY

Research misconduct violates two current goals of psychological science: openness and transparency. As part of the publication process, researchers increasingly share their raw data via websites such as the Open Science Framework. (Before making their data open, they remove all identifying information about the participants.) Open data upholds Merton's norm of communality, which states that science belongs to everyone. Open data supports scientific progress because other scientists can replicate published work and test their own novel hypotheses.

As part of reporting a study, transparency also matters. Researchers might measure multiple variables in a study and test dozens of hypotheses. This practice is acceptable when researchers report their process transparently—describing all measured variables and statistical analyses in the Method section (Simmons et al., 2012). However, it is ethically and scientifically questionable to test multiple hypotheses and then report only the variables or results that worked, because this misleads readers about the full picture of evidence.

« For more on Merton's four norms of science see Chapter 1, p. 15.

## PLAGIARISM (STANDARD 8.11)

Another form of research misconduct is **plagiarism**, usually defined as representing the ideas or words of others as one's own. A formal definition, provided by the U.S. Office of Science and Technology Policy, states that plagiarism is "the appropriation of another person's ideas, processes, results, or words without giving appropriate credit" (Federal Register, 2000). Academics and researchers consider plagiarism a violation of ethics because it is unfair for a researcher to take credit for another person's intellectual property: It is a form of stealing.

To avoid plagiarism, you must cite the sources of all ideas that are not your own, to give appropriate credit to the original authors. Psychologists follow the style guidelines for citations in the *Publication Manual of the American Psychological Association* (APA, 2019). When using another person's exact words, put quotation marks around the quoted text and add the page number where the quotation appeared in the original source. When you describe or paraphrase another person's ideas, you cite the original author's last name and the year of publication, but be careful not to paraphrase the original text too closely. (**Figure 4.11** presents examples of paraphrasing, quoting, and plagiarizing.)

Researchers also should not recycle their own text, or **self-plagiarize**. When researchers publish multiple articles in a line of research, they may end up recycling portions of the Method section from previous work. But they should not repeat sentences verbatim in the introduction or Discussion section. In a Results section, recycling sentences is unacceptable because it means the article is presenting previously published data as if it were new (BioMed Central & COPE, n.d.).

Plagiarism is a serious offense—not only in published work by professional researchers but also in papers students submit for college courses. Every university

*Research Article*

ASSOCIATION FOR
PSYCHOLOGICAL SCIENCE

Psychological Science
2019, Vol. 30(6) 893–906
© The Author(s) 2019
Article reuse guidelines:
sagepub.com/journals-permissions
DOI: 10.1177/0956797619838762
www.psychologicalscience.org/PS

$SAGE

# A Facial-Action Imposter: How Head Tilt Influences Perceptions of Dominance From a Neutral Face

**Zachary Witkower and Jessica L. Tracy**
Department of Psychology, The University of British Columbia

**Abstract**
Research on face perception tends to focus on facial morphology and the activation of [...] any impact of head position. We raise questions about this approach by demonstratin[...] dramatically shift the appearance of the face to shape social judgments without engagin[...] studies (total *N* = 1,517), we found that when eye gaze was directed forward, tilting one's [...] with a neutral angle) increased perceptions of dominance, and this effect was due to [...] lowered and V-shaped eyebrows caused by a downward head tilt. Tilting one's head d[...] as an *action-unit imposter*, creating the artificial appearance of a facial action unit that [...] perception. Social judgments about faces are therefore driven not only by facial shape [...] movements in the face's physical foundation: the head.

**Keywords**
face perception, nonverbal behavior, social perception, dominance, head tilt, open data,

Received 6/14/18; Revision accepted 1/24/19

The current research provides the first evidence that tilting one's head downward causes the eyebrows to lower and take on a V shape, creating the illusion of corrugator activity, or Action Unit 4, and this illusory movement in turn increases perceptions of dominance when eye gaze is directed forward. Across five studies, we found that tilting one's head downward functions as an action-unit imposter, generating the appearance of facial-muscle activity that has a strong impact on social perceptions when no such activity exists. This finding emerged from studies showing that (a) the effect of a downward head tilt on dominance perceptions cannot be attributed to alternative mechanisms

---

**OK**

*Correct presentation of a direct quotation from the article (quotation marks, author and year, and page number are employed).*

---

The authors explained that when people tilt their heads down, they are "creating the illusion of corrugator activity" and that "this illusory movement in turn increases perceptions of dominance when eye gaze is directed forward" (Witkower & Tracy, 2019, p. 902).

---

**OK**

*Correct presentation of a paraphrase.*

---

The authors explained that when people tilt their heads down, it creates a smaller gap between the eyebrows and the eyes. It's only an illusion, but this smaller gap makes people think the face is more intimidating (Witkower & Tracy, 2019).

---

**Plagiarism**

*Paraphrasing too close to the original (the highlighted areas are not set off in quotes, so it implies that this passage is the writer's own words. Therefore this passage is plagiarized even though it is cited).*

---

The authors explained that when people tilt their heads down, they create an illusion of eyebrow activity, which in turn increases perceptions of being intimidating when people's gaze is directed forward (Witkower & Tracy, 2019).

---

## FIGURE 4.11

### Avoiding plagiarism.

Writers must cite direct quotations using quotation marks, author name, year of publication, and page number. Paraphrasing must be cited with the author name and year. Paraphrasing that is too close to the original is plagiarism, even when it is cited.

and college has plagiarism policies that prohibit students from copying the words or ideas of others without proper credit. Students who plagiarize in their academic work are subject to disciplinary action—including expulsion, in some cases.

## ANIMAL RESEARCH (STANDARD 8.09)

In some branches of psychology, research is conducted almost entirely on animal subjects: rats, mice, cockroaches, sea snails, dogs, rabbits, cats, chimpanzees, and others. The ethical debates surrounding animal research can be just as complex as those for human participants. Most people have a profound respect for animals and compassion for their well-being. Psychologists and nonpsychologists alike want to protect animals from undue suffering.

« For further discussion of plagiarism in writing and the APA guidelines, see Presenting Results at the end of this book.

**Legal Protection for Laboratory Animals.** In Standard 8.09, the APA lists ethical guidelines for the care of animals in research laboratories. Psychologists who use animals in research must care for them humanely, must use as few animals as possible, and must be sure the research is valuable enough to justify using animal subjects.

In addition to these APA standards, psychologists follow federal and local laws for animal care and protection. In the United States, the Animal Welfare Act (AWA) outlines standards and guidelines for the treatment of animals (Animal Welfare Act, 1966). The AWA applies to many species of animals in research laboratories and other contexts, including zoos and pet stores.

The AWA mandates that relevant research institutions have a local board called the Institutional Animal Care and Use Committee (IACUC, pronounced "EYE-a-kuk"). Similar to an IRB, the IACUC must approve any animal research project before it can begin (Animal Welfare Act, 1966). It must contain a veterinarian, a practicing scientist who is familiar with the goals and procedures of animal research, and a member of the local community who is unconnected with the institution. The IACUC requires researchers to submit an extensive protocol specifying how animals will be treated and protected. The IACUC application also includes the scientific justification for the research: Applicants must demonstrate that the proposed study has not already been done and explain why the research is important. The AWA does not cover mice, rats, and birds, but such species are included in the oversight of IACUC boards.

After approving a research project, the IACUC monitors the treatment of animals throughout the research process. It inspects the labs every 6 months. If a laboratory violates a procedure outlined in the proposal, the IACUC or a government agency can stop the experiment, shut the lab down, or discontinue government funding. In European countries and Canada, similar laws apply.

**Animal Care Guidelines and the Three Rs.** Animal researchers in the United States use the resources of the *Guide for the Care and Use of Laboratory Animals*, which focuses on what's known as the Three Rs: replacement, refinement, and reduction (National Research Council, 2011).

- *Replacement* means researchers should find alternatives to animals in research when possible. For example, some studies can use computer simulations instead of animal subjects.

- *Refinement* means researchers must modify experimental procedures and other aspects of animal care to minimize or eliminate animal distress.
- *Reduction* means researchers should adopt experimental designs and procedures that require the fewest animal subjects possible.

In addition, the manual provides guidelines for housing facilities, diet, and other aspects of animal care in research. The guide indicates which species must be housed in social groups and specifies cage sizes, temperature and humidity ranges, air quality, lighting and noise conditions, sanitation procedures, and enrichments such as toys and bedding.

**Attitudes of Scientists and Students Toward Animal Research.** In surveys, the majority of psychology students and faculty support the use of animals in research (Plous, 1996a). Nationally, about 47% of Americans favor the use of animals in research, and the more science knowledge people have, the more likely they are to back it (Strauss, 2018). In fact, when people read about the requirements stated in the AWA, they become more supportive of animal research (Metzger, 2015). In other words, people seem to favor animal research more if they know it protects the welfare of animal subjects.

**Attitudes of Animal Rights Groups.** Since the mid-1970s in the United States, some groups have assumed a more extreme position—arguing for animal rights, rather than animal welfare (**Figure 4.12**). Animal rights groups generally base their activities on one of two arguments (Kimmel, 2007). First, they may believe animals are just as likely as humans to experience suffering. They feel humans should not be elevated above other animals. Because all kinds of animals can suffer, all of them should be protected from painful research procedures. According to this view, certain types of research with animals could be allowed, but only if they might also be permitted with human participants.

Second, some groups also believe animals have inherent rights, equal to those of humans. These activists draw on the principle of justice, as outlined in the Belmont Report and the APA Ethical Principles. Animal rights activists do not believe animals should unduly bear the burden of research that benefits a different species (humans). Animal rights groups conclude that many research practices using animals are morally wrong (Kimmel, 2007).

The members of these groups may be politically active, vocal, and sincerely devoted to the protection of animals. In a survey, Herzog (1993) concluded they are "intelligent, articulate, and sincere . . . [and] eager to discuss their views about the treatment of animals" with a scientist (quoted in Kimmel, 2007, p. 118). Consistent

**FIGURE 4.12**
A protest opposing animal research.

with this view, Plous (1998) polled animal rights activists and found most to be open to compromise via a respectful dialogue with animal researchers.

**Ethically Balancing Animal Welfare, Animal Rights, and Animal Research.** Given the laws governing animal welfare and given the visibility of animal rights arguments, you can be sure that today's research with animals in psychological science is not conducted lightly or irresponsibly. On the contrary, though research with animals is widespread, animal researchers are generally thoughtful and respectful of animal welfare.

Animal researchers defend their use of animal subjects with three primary arguments. The first is that animal research has resulted in numerous benefits to humans and animals alike (**Figure 4.13**). Animal research has contributed countless valuable discoveries about basic processes of vision, the organization of the brain, the course of infection, disease prevention, and therapeutic drugs. Therefore, as outlined in the Belmont Report and APA Ethical Principles, ethical thinking means that research scientists and the public must evaluate the costs and benefits of research projects—in terms of both the subjects used and the potential outcomes.

**FIGURE 4.13**

**A protest supporting animal research.**
How do researchers achieve an ethical balance between concern for animal welfare and the benefits to society from research using animals?

Second, supporters argue that animal researchers are sensitive to animal welfare. They think about the pain and suffering of animals in their studies and take steps to avoid or reduce it. The IACUC oversight process and the *Guide for the Care and Use of Laboratory Animals* help ensure that animals are treated with care. Third, researchers have successfully reduced the number of animals they need to use because of new procedures that do not require animal testing (Kimmel, 2007). Some animal researchers even believe animal rights groups have exaggerated (or fabricated, in some cases) the cruelty of animal research (Coile & Miller, 1984) and that some activists have largely ignored the valuable scientific and medical discoveries that have resulted from animal research.

---

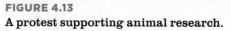

**CHECK YOUR UNDERSTANDING**

1. What are the five ethical principles outlined by the APA? Which two are not included in the three principles of the Belmont Report?

2. Name several ways the Animal Welfare Act, IACUC boards, and the *Guide for the Care and Use of Laboratory Animals* shape animal research.

1. See p. 98–99 and Table 4.1. 2. See pp. 107–109.

# ETHICAL DECISION MAKING: A THOUGHTFUL BALANCE

Ethical decision making, as you have learned, does not involve simple yes-or-no decisions; it requires a balance of priorities. When faced with a study that could possibly harm human participants or animals, researchers (and their IRBs) consider the potential benefits of the research: Will it contribute something important to society? Many people believe that research with some degree of risk is justified if the benefit gained from the results is great. In contrast, if the risk to participants becomes too high, the new knowledge may not be valuable enough to justify the harm.

Another example of this careful balance comes from the way researchers implement the informed consent process. On the one hand, researchers may want to demonstrate their gratitude and respect for participants by compensating them with money or some other form of reward. Paying participants might help ensure that the samples represent a variety of populations, as the principle of justice requires, because some people might not participate in a study without a financial incentive. On the other hand, offering participants rewards that are too great could tip the balance. If monetary rewards become too attractive, potential participants may no longer be able to freely consent.

Although in some cases it is easy to conduct important research that has a low degree of risk to participants, other ethical decisions are extremely difficult. Researchers try to balance respect for animal subjects and human participants, protections from harm, benefits to society, and awareness of justice. As this chapter has emphasized, they do not weigh the factors in this balance alone. Influenced by IRBs, IACUCs, peers, and sociocultural norms, they strive to conduct ethical research that is valuable to society.

Ethical research practice is not performed according to a set of permanent rules. It is an evolving and dynamic process that takes place in historical and cultural contexts. Researchers refine their ethical decision making in response to good and bad experiences, changing social norms (even public opinion), and scientific discoveries. By following ethical principles, researchers make it more likely that their work will benefit, and be appreciated by, the general public.

The Working It Through section shows how ethical principles can be applied to a controversial research example.

✔

## CHECK YOUR UNDERSTANDING

**1.** Give some examples from the preceding discussion of how the ethical practice of research balances priorities.

1. Answers will vary.

## WORKING IT THROUGH

# Did a Study Conducted on Facebook Violate Ethical Principles?

A few years ago, researchers from Facebook and Cornell University collaborated to test the effect of emotional contagion through online social networks (Kramer et al., 2014). Emotional contagion is the tendency for emotions to spread in face-to-face interactions. When people express happiness, people around them become happier, too. Researchers randomly selected more than 600,000 Facebook users and withheld certain posts from their newsfeeds. From one group, they withheld posts with positive emotion words (such as *happy* and *love*). From a second group, they withheld posts at random (not altering their emotional content). And from the third group, they withheld negative posts. The researchers measured how many positive and negative emotion words people subsequently used on their own Facebook timelines. The results showed that the group who had seen fewer positive posts tended to use fewer positive and more negative emotion words on their own pages. The effect size was extremely small, but the researchers concluded that emotional contagion can happen even through online text. After the media publicized the study's results, commentators raised an alarm: Facebook manipulated people's newsfeeds? Is that ethical? We can organize the critiques of this study around the topics in Chapter 4.

| QUESTIONS TO ASK | DETAILS FROM THE STUDY | INTERPRETATION AND EVALUATION |
|---|---|---|
| **Institutional review board**<br>Was the study reviewed by an IRB? | The study's lead scientist was employed by Facebook, and as a private company, Facebook is not required to follow federal ethical guidelines such as the Common Rule.<br><br>The other two scientists had the study reviewed by Cornell University's IRB, as required. The Cornell IRB decided the study did not fall under its program because the data had been collected by Facebook. | This example highlights that private businesses sometimes conduct research on people who use their products and such research might not be reviewed for ethics. |

*(Continued)*

| QUESTIONS TO ASK | DETAILS FROM THE STUDY | INTERPRETATION AND EVALUATION |
|---|---|---|
| **Informed consent**<br><br>Were Facebook users able to decide whether they wanted to participate? | The study's authors reported that when people create a Facebook account, they agree to a data use policy, and this constituted informed consent. | Not all critics agreed. The journal in which the study was published attached an editorial statement of concern stating that, though it had agreed to publish the paper, it was concerned that the study did not allow participants to opt out (Flick, 2016). |
| **Deception and debriefing**<br><br>Were participants deceived about the study? If so, were they debriefed? | Participants were not told their newsfeeds might have been manipulated for research purposes. | Participants were deceived through omission of information.<br><br>In addition, people were not debriefed afterward. Even now, people cannot find out whether they participated in this study or not. |
| If an IRB had considered this study in advance, they would have evaluated it, first, in terms of **respect for persons**. | Respect for persons requires informed consent. Participants did not consent to this particular study. | Although people did not provide informed consent for this particular study, informed consent might not be deemed necessary when a study takes place in a public place where people can reasonably expect to be observed. Do you think the Facebook study falls into that category? |
| An IRB would also ask about **beneficence**: Did the research harm anyone, and did it benefit society? | The study itself demonstrated that people felt worse when positive emotion posts were removed.<br><br>The researchers argued that the study benefited society. Social media plays a role in many people's daily lives, and emotions are linked to well-being. | People may have suffered a bit, but was their distress any greater than it might have been in daily life? (Perhaps not, because the effect size was so small.)<br><br>In addition, Facebook already manipulates newsfeeds, selecting stories and posts according to a computerized algorithm.<br><br>The results did show that social media is a source of emotional contagion that could potentially affect public well-being. Do you find this study to be beneficial to society? |
| An IRB would consider whether the principle of **justice** was met. Were the people who participated in the study representative of the people who can benefit from its findings? | The study randomly selected hundreds of thousands of people who read Facebook in English. | Because the sample was selected at random, it appears that the people who "bore the burden" of research participation were the same types who could benefit from its findings. The principle of justice has probably been met. |

# CHAPTER REVIEW

 It's time to complete your study experience! Go to INQUIZITIVE to practice actively with this chapter's concepts and get personalized feedback along the way.

## Summary

Whether psychologists are testing a frequency, association, or causal claim, they strive to conduct their research ethically. Psychologists are guided by standard ethical principles as they plan and conduct their research.

### HISTORICAL EXAMPLES

- The Tuskegee Syphilis Study, which took place in the United States during the 1930s through the 1970s, illustrates the ethics violations of harming people, not asking for consent, and targeting a particular group in research.

- The Milgram obedience studies illustrate the gray areas in ethical research, including how researchers define harm to participants and how they balance the importance of a study with the harm it might do.

### CORE ETHICAL PRINCIPLES

- Achieving an ethical balance in research is guided by standards and laws. Many countries' ethical policies are governed by the Nuremberg Code and the Declaration of Helsinki. In the United States, federal ethical policies are based on the Common Rule, which is grounded in the Belmont Report.

- The Belmont Report outlines three main principles for research: respect for persons, beneficence, and justice. Each principle has specific applications in the research setting.

- Respect for persons involves the process of informed consent and the protection of special groups in research, such as children and prisoners.

- Beneficence involves the evaluation of risks and benefits to participants in the study and to society as a whole.

- Justice involves the way participants are selected for the research. One group of people should not bear an undue burden for research participation, and participants should be representative of the groups that will also benefit from the research.

### GUIDELINES FOR PSYCHOLOGISTS: THE APA ETHICAL PRINCIPLES

- The APA guides psychologists by providing a set of principles and standards for research, teaching, and other professional roles.

- The APA's five general principles include the three Belmont Report principles, plus two more: the principle of fidelity and responsibility and the principle of integrity.

- The APA's Ethical Standard 8 provides enforceable guidelines for researchers to follow. It includes specific information for informed consent, institutional review boards, deception, debriefing, research misconduct, and animal research.

### ETHICAL DECISION MAKING: A THOUGHTFUL BALANCE

- For any type of claim psychologists are investigating, ethical decision making requires balancing a variety of priorities.

- Psychologists must balance benefits to society with risks to research participants and balance compensation for participants with undue coercion for their involvement.

## Key Terms

debriefed, p. 93

principle of respect for persons, p. 95

informed consent, p. 95

principle of beneficence, p. 95

anonymous study, p. 96

confidential study, p. 96

principle of justice, p. 97

institutional review board (IRB), p. 100

deception, p. 101

data fabrication, p. 103

data falsification, p. 103

plagiarism, p. 105

self-plagiarism, p. 105

 **To see samples of chapter concepts in the popular media, visit www.everydayresearchmethods.com and click the box for Chapter 4.**

## Review Questions

1. Which of the following is not one of the three principles of the Belmont Report?

   a. Respect for persons

   b. Justice

   c. Beneficence

   d. Fidelity and responsibility

2. In a study of a new drug for asthma, a researcher finds that the group receiving the drug is doing much better than the control group, whose members are receiving a placebo. Which principle of the Belmont Report requires the researcher to also give the control group the opportunity to receive the new drug?

   a. Informed consent

   b. Justice

   c. Beneficence

   d. Respect for persons

3. To study a sample of participants from only one ethnic group, researchers must first demonstrate that the problem being studied is especially prevalent in that ethnic group. This is an application of which principle from the Belmont Report?

   a. Respect for persons

   b. Beneficence

   c. Special protection

   d. Justice

4. Following a study using deception, how does the researcher attempt to restore an honest relationship with the participant?

   a. By apologizing to the participant and offering monetary compensation for any discomfort or stress.

   b. By debriefing each participant in a structured conversation.

   c. By reassuring the participant that all names and identifiers will be removed from the data.

   d. By giving each participant a written description of the study's goals and hypotheses, along with references for further reading.

5. What type of research misconduct involves representing the ideas or words of others as one's own?

   a. Plagiarism

   b. Obfuscation

   c. Suppression

   d. Data falsification

6. Which of the following is not one of the Three R's provided by the *Guide for the Care and Use of Laboratory Animals*?

   a. Reduction

   b. Replacement

   c. Restoration

   d. Refinement

# Learning Actively

1. A developmental psychologist applies to an institutional review board (IRB), proposing to observe children ages 2–10 playing in the local McDonald's play area. Because the area is public, the researcher does not plan to ask for informed consent from the children's parents. What ethical concerns exist for this study? What questions might an IRB ask?

2. A social psychologist plans to hand out surveys in her 300-level undergraduate class. The survey asks about students' study habits. The psychologist does not ask the students to put their names on the survey; instead, students will put completed surveys into a large box at the back of the room. Because of the low risk involved in participation and the anonymous nature of the survey, the researcher requests to be exempted from formal informed consent procedures. What ethical concerns exist for this study? What questions might an IRB ask?

3. Consider the use of deception in psychological research. Does participation in a study involving deception (such as the Milgram obedience studies) necessarily cause harm? Recall that when evaluat-ing the risks and benefits of a study, the researcher considers both the participants in the study and society as a whole—anyone who might be affected by the research. What might be some of the costs and benefits to participants who are deceived? What might be some of the costs and benefits to society of studies involving deception?

4. Use the Internet to look up your college's definition of plagiarism. Does it match the one given in APA Ethical Standard 8.11? If not, what does it exclude or add? What are the consequences for plagiarism at your college?

5. Use the Internet to find out the procedures of the IRB at your college. According to your college's policies, do undergraduates like you need special ethics training before they can conduct research? Does research conducted in a research methods class need formal IRB approval? Does your college categorize studies that are "exempt" from IRB review versus "Expedited" versus "Full Board" review? If so, what kinds of studies are considered exempt?

## What's the Happiest Country in the World?

GALLUP, 2019

## Can Money Buy You Happiness?

*WALL STREET JOURNAL*, 2014

## Gratitude Is for Lovers

GREATER GOOD, 2013

# 5

# Identifying Good Measurement

WHETHER STUDYING THE NUMBER of polar bears left in the Arctic Circle, the infection rate of the COVID-19 virus, the number of steps people take each day, or the level of human happiness, every scientist faces the challenge of measurement. When researchers test theories, they have to systematically measure phenomena by collecting data. These measurements must be good ones—or else they are useless.

Measurement in psychological research can be particularly challenging. Many of the phenomena psychologists are interested in—motivation, emotion, thinking, reasoning—are difficult to measure directly. Happiness, the topic of much research, is a good example of a construct that could be hard to assess. Is it really possible to quantify how happy people are? Are the measurements accurate? Before testing, for example, which country is the happiest, we might ask whether we can really measure happiness. Maybe people misrepresent their level of well-being, or maybe people aren't aware of how happy they are. How do we evaluate who is truly happy and who isn't? This chapter explains how to ask questions about the quality of a study's measures—the construct validity of quantifications of things like happiness, gratitude, or wealth. Construct validity, remember, refers to how well a study's variables are measured or manipulated.

Construct validity is a crucial piece of any psychological research study—for frequency, association, or causal claims. This chapter focuses on the construct validity of *measured variables*. You will learn, first, about different ways researchers operationalize

**LEARNING OBJECTIVES**

**A year from now, you should still be able to:**

**1.**
Interrogate the construct validity of a study's measured variables.

**2.**
Describe the kinds of evidence that support the construct validity of a measured variable.

» For a review of measured and manipulated variables, see Chapter 3, pp. 56–57.

measured variables. Then you'll learn how you can evaluate the reliability and validity of those measurements. The construct validity of *manipulated variables* is covered in Chapter 10.

# WAYS TO MEASURE VARIABLES

The process of measuring variables involves some key decisions. As researchers decide how they should operationalize each variable in a study, they choose among three common types of measures: self-report, observational, and physiological. They also decide on the most appropriate scale of measurement for each variable they plan to investigate.

## More About Conceptual and Operational Variables

In Chapter 3, you learned about operationalization, the process of turning a construct of interest into a measured or manipulated variable. Much psychological research requires two definitions of each variable. The **conceptual definition**, or construct, is the researcher's definition of the variable in question at a theoretical level. The operational definition represents a researcher's specific decision about how to measure or manipulate the conceptual variable.

### OPERATIONALIZING "HAPPINESS"

Let's take the variable "happiness," for example. One research team, led by noted psychologist  Ed Diener, began their study of happiness by developing a precise conceptual definition. Specifically, Diener's team reasoned that the word *happiness* might have a variety of meanings, so they explicitly limited their interest to "subjective well-being" (or well-being from a person's own perspective).

After defining happiness at the conceptual level, Diener and his colleagues developed an operational definition. Because they were interested in people's perspectives on their own well-being, they chose to operationalize subjective well-being, in part, by asking people to report on their own happiness in a questionnaire format. The researchers decided people should use their own criteria to describe what constitutes a "good life" (Pavot & Diener, 1993). They worded their questions so people could think about the interpretation of life satisfaction that was appropriate for them. These researchers operationally defined, or measured, subjective well-being by asking people to respond to five items about their satisfaction with life using a 7-point scale; 1 corresponded to "strongly disagree" and 7 corresponded to "strongly agree":

_____ 1.  In most ways my life is close to my ideal.

_____ 2.  The conditions of my life are excellent.

_____ 3.  I am satisfied with my life.

_____ 4.  So far, I have gotten the important things I want in life.

_____ 5.  If I could live my life over, I would change almost nothing.

The unhappiest people would get a total score of 5 on this self-report scale because they would answer "strongly disagree," or 1, to all five items (1 + 1 + 1 + 1 + 1 = 5). The happiest people would get a total score of 35 on this scale because they would answer "strongly agree," or 7, to all five items (7 + 7 + 7 + 7 + 7 = 35). Those at the neutral point would score 20—right in between satisfied and dissatisfied (4 + 4 + 4 + 4 + 4 = 20). Diener and Diener (1996) reported some data based on this scale, concluding that most people are happy, scoring above 20. For example, 63% of high school and college students scored above 20 in one study, and 72% of disabled adults scored above 20 in another study.

In choosing this operational definition of subjective well-being, the research team started with only one possible measure, even though there are many other ways to study this concept. Another way to measure happiness is to use a single question called the Ladder of Life (Cantril, 1965). The question goes like this:

Imagine a ladder with steps numbered from 0 at the bottom to 10 at the top. The top of the ladder represents the best possible life for you and the bottom of the ladder represents the worst possible life for you. On which step of the ladder would you say you personally stand at this time?

On this measure, participants respond by giving a value between 0 and 10. The Gallup polling organization uses the Ladder of Life scale in its daily Gallup-Healthways Well-Being Index.

Which one of these operational definitions do you think is a better measure of happiness? Diener's research team and Gallup have collected data on their measures of happiness and determined that they both do a good job of measuring the construct, as we'll see later in this chapter.

## OPERATIONALIZING OTHER CONCEPTUAL VARIABLES

To study conceptual variables other than happiness, researchers follow a similar process: They start by stating a definition of their construct (the conceptual variable) and then create an operational definition. For example, to measure the association between wealth and happiness, researchers need to measure both happiness and wealth. They might operationally define wealth by asking about salary in dollars, by asking for bank account balances, or even by observing the kind of car people drive.

Consider another variable that has been studied in research on relationships: gratitude toward one's partner. Researchers who measure gratitude toward a relationship partner might operationalize it by asking people how often they thank their partner for something they did. Or they might ask people how appreciative they usually feel. Even a simple variable such as gender must be operationalized.

**TABLE 5.1**

## Variables and Operational Definitions

| VARIABLE | ONE POSSIBLE OPERATIONAL DEFINITION (OPERATIONALIZATION) | ANOTHER POSSIBLE OPERATIONAL DEFINITION |
|---|---|---|
| Gratitude toward one's relationship partner | Asking people if they agree with the statement, "I appreciate my partner." | Watching couples interact and counting how many times they thank each other. |
| Gender identity | Asking people to report on a survey whether they identify as male, female, or nonbinary. | In phone interviews, a researcher guesses gender through the sound of the person's voice. |
| Wealth | Asking people to report their income within various ranges (less than $20,000, between $20,000 and 50,000, and more than $50,000). | Coding the value of a car from 1 (older, lower-status vehicle) to 5 (new, high-status vehicle in good condition). |
| Intelligence | An IQ test that includes problem-solving items, memory and vocabulary questions, and puzzles. | Recording brain activity while people solve difficult problems. |
| Well-being (happiness) | 10-point Ladder of Life scale. | Diener's 5-item subjective well-being scale. |

As **Table 5.1** shows, any conceptual variable can be operationalized in a number of ways. In fact, operationalizations are one place where creativity comes into the research process, as researchers work to develop new and better measures of their constructs.

## Three Common Types of Measures

The types of measures psychological scientists typically use to operationalize variables generally fall into three categories: self-report, observational, and physiological.

### SELF-REPORT MEASURES

A **self-report measure** operationalizes a variable by recording people's answers to questions about themselves in a questionnaire or interview. Diener's five-item scale and the Ladder of Life question are both examples of self-report measures about life satisfaction. Similarly, asking people how much they appreciate their partner and asking about gender identity are both self-report measures. If stress is the variable being studied, researchers might ask people to self-report on the frequency of specific events they've experienced in the past year, such as marriage, divorce, or moving (e.g., Holmes & Rahe, 1967).

In research on children, self-reports may be replaced with parent reports or teacher reports. These measures ask parents or teachers to respond to a series of questions, such as describing the child's recent life events, the words the child knows, or the child's typical classroom behaviors. (Chapter 6 discusses situations when self-report measures are likely to be accurate and when they might be biased.)

## OBSERVATIONAL MEASURES

An **observational measure**, sometimes called a behavioral measure, operationalizes a variable by recording observable behaviors or physical traces of behaviors. For example, a researcher could operationalize happiness by observing how many times a person smiles. Intelligence tests can be considered observational measures, because the people who administer such tests in person are observing people's intelligent behaviors (such as being able to correctly solve a puzzle or quickly detect a pattern). Coding how much a person's car cost would be an observational measure of wealth (Piff et al., 2012).

Observational measures may record physical traces of behavior. Stress behaviors could be measured by counting the number of tooth marks left on a person's pencil, or a researcher could measure stressful events by consulting public legal records to document whether people have recently married, divorced, or moved. (Chapter 6 addresses how an observer's ratings of behavior might be accurate and how they might be biased.)

## PHYSIOLOGICAL MEASURES

A **physiological measure** operationalizes a variable by recording biological data, such as brain activity, hormone levels, or heart rate. Physiological measures usually require the use of equipment to amplify, record, and analyze biological data. For example, moment-to-moment happiness has been measured using facial electromyography (EMG)—a way of electronically recording tiny movements in the muscles in the face. Facial EMG can be used to detect a happy facial expression because people who are smiling show particular patterns of muscle movement around the eyes and cheeks.

Other constructs might be measured using a brain scanning technique called functional magnetic resonance imaging, or fMRI. In a typical fMRI study, people engage in a carefully structured series of psychological tasks (such as looking at three types of photos or playing a series of rock-paper-scissors games) while lying in an MRI machine. The MRI equipment records and codes the relative changes in blood flow in particular regions of the brain, as shown in **Figure 5.1**. When more

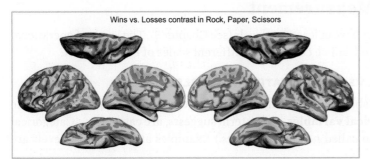

Wins vs. Losses contrast in Rock, Paper, Scissors

**FIGURE 5.1**

**Images from fMRI scans showing brain activity.**

In this study of how people respond to rewards and losses, the researchers tracked blood flow patterns in the brain when people had either won, lost, or tied a rock-paper-scissors game played with a computer. They found that many regions of the brain respond more to wins than to losses, as indicated by the highlighted regions. (Source: Vickery, Chun, & Lee, 2011.)

blood flows to a brain region while people perform a certain task, researchers conclude that brain area is activated because of the patterns on the scanned images.

Some research indicates a way fMRI might be used to measure intelligence in the future. Specifically, the brains of people with higher intelligence may be more efficient at solving complex problems, and their fMRI scans show relatively less brain activity for complex problems (Deary et al., 2010). Therefore, future researchers may be able to use the efficiency of brain activity as a physiological measure of intelligence. In contrast, head circumference, a physiological measure from a century ago, turned out to be flawed, because smarter brains are not necessarily stored inside larger skulls (Gould, 1996).

A physiological way to operationalize stress might be to measure the amount of the hormone cortisol released in saliva because people under stress show higher levels of cortisol (Carlson, 2009). Skin conductance, an electronic recording of the activity in the sweat glands of the hands or feet, is another way to measure stress physiologically. People under more stress have more activity in these glands. Another physiological measure detects electrical patterns in different brain regions near the scalp, using electroencephalography (EEG).

### WHICH OPERATIONALIZATION IS BEST?

A single construct can be operationalized in several ways, from self-report to behavioral observation to physiological measures. Some people erroneously believe physiological measures are the most accurate. But even physiological results have to be validated by using other measures. For instance, as mentioned above, researchers used fMRI to learn that the brain works more efficiently relative to level of intelligence. But how was participant intelligence established in the first place? Before doing the fMRI scans, the researchers gave the participants an IQ test—an observational measure (Deary et al., 2010). Similarly, researchers might trust an fMRI pattern to indicate when a person is genuinely happy. However, the only way a researcher could know that some pattern of brain activity was associated with happiness would be by asking each person how happy they felt (a self-report measure) at the same time the brain scan was being done. As you'll learn later in this chapter, researchers normally expect self-report, observational, and physiological measures to show similar patterns of results.

## Scales of Measurement

All variables must have at least two levels (see Chapter 3). The levels of operational variables, however, can be coded using different scales of measurement.

### CATEGORICAL VS. QUANTITATIVE VARIABLES

Operational variables are primarily classified as categorical or quantitative. The levels of **categorical variables**, as the term suggests, are categories. (Categorical variables are also called *nominal variables*.) Examples are sex, whose levels are male and female, and species, whose levels in a study might be rhesus macaque, chimpanzee, and bonobo. A researcher might decide to assign numbers to the levels of a categorical variable (e.g., using "1" to represent rhesus macaques, "2" for chimps, and "3" for bonobos) during the data-entry process. However, the numbers do not have numerical meaning—a bonobo is different from a chimpanzee, but being a bonobo ("3") is not quantitatively "higher" than being a chimpanzee ("2").

In contrast, the levels of **quantitative variables** (also called continuous variables) are coded with *meaningful* numbers. Height and weight are quantitative because they are measured in numbers, such as 170 centimeters or 65 kilograms. Diener's scale of subjective well-being is quantitative too, because a score of 35 represents more happiness than a score of 7. IQ score, level of brain activity, and amount of salivary cortisol are also quantitative variables.

## THREE TYPES OF QUANTITATIVE VARIABLES

For certain kinds of statistical tests, researchers need to further classify a quantitative variable in terms of ordinal, interval, or ratio scale.

An **ordinal scale** of measurement applies when the numerals of a quantitative variable represent a ranked order. For example, a bookstore's website might display the top 10 best-selling books. We know that the #1 book sold more than the #2 book, and that #2 sold more than #3, but we don't know whether the number of books that separates #1 and #2 is equal to the number of books that separates #2 and #3. In other words, the intervals may be unequal. Maybe the first two rankings are only 10 books apart, and the second two rankings are 150,000 books apart. Similarly, a professor might use the order in which exams were turned in to operationalize how fast students worked. This represents ordinal data because the fastest exams are on the bottom of the pile—ranked 1. However, this variable has not quantified *how much* faster each exam was turned in, compared with the others.

An **interval scale** of measurement applies to the numerals of a quantitative variable that meet two conditions: First, the numerals represent equal intervals (distances) between levels, and second, there is no "true zero" (a person can get a score of 0, but the 0 does not literally mean "nothing"). An IQ test is an interval scale—the distance between IQ scores of 100 and 105 represents the same as the distance between IQ scores of 105 and 110. However, a score of 0 on an IQ test does not mean a person has "no intelligence." Body temperature in degrees Celsius is another example of an interval scale—the intervals between levels are equal; however, a temperature of 0 degrees does not mean a person has "no temperature." Most researchers assume questionnaire scales like Diener's (scored from 1 = *strongly disagree* to 7 = *strongly agree*) are interval scales. They do not have a true zero, but we assume the distances between numerals, from 1 to 7, are equivalent. Because they do not have a true zero, interval scales cannot allow a researcher to say things like "twice as hot" or "three times happier."

Finally, a **ratio scale** of measurement applies when the numerals of a quantitative variable have equal intervals and when the value of 0 truly means "none"

**TABLE 5.2**

## Measurement Scales for Operational Variables

| TYPE OF VARIABLE | CHARACTERISTICS | EXAMPLES |
|---|---|---|
| **Categorical** | Levels are categories. | Nationality. Type of music. Kind of phone people use. |
| **Quantitative** | Levels are coded with meaningful numbers. | |
| Ordinal | A quantitative variable in which numerals represent a rank order. Distance between subsequent numerals may not be equal. | Order of finishers in a swimming race. Ranking of 10 shows from most to least favorite. |
| Interval | A quantitative variable in which subsequent numerals represent equal distances, but there is no true zero. | IQ score. Shoe size. Degree of agreement on a 1-7 scale. |
| Ratio | A quantitative variable in which numerals represent equal distances and zero represents "none" of the variable being measured. | Number of exam questions answered correctly. How many episodes of a show watched. Height in cm. |

of the variable being measured. On a knowledge test, a researcher might measure how many items people answer correctly. On this scale, 0 truly represents "nothing correct" (0 answers correct). Even if nobody scores a 0, this value would still be meaningful. If a researcher measures how frequently people blink their eyes in a stressful situation, the number of eyeblinks is a ratio scale because 0 would represent zero eyeblinks. Because ratio scales do have a meaningful zero, a researcher can say something like "Alek answered twice as many problems as Hugo." **Table 5.2** summarizes all the above variations.

### ✔ CHECK YOUR UNDERSTANDING

1. Explain why a variable usually has only one conceptual definition but can have multiple operational definitions.

2. Name the three common ways in which researchers operationalize their variables.

3. In your own words, describe the difference between categorical and quantitative variables. Come up with new examples of variables that would fit the definition of ordinal, interval, and ratio scales.

1. See pp. 118-120. 2. See pp. 120-122. 3. See pp. 122-124.

# RELIABILITY OF MEASUREMENT: ARE THE SCORES CONSISTENT?

Once the variables in a study have been operationalized, we can ask the important construct validity question: How do we know that the operationalizations are appropriate? The construct validity of a measure has two aspects. **Reliability** refers to how consistent the results of a measure are, and **validity** refers to whether the operationalization is measuring what it is supposed to measure.

## Introducing Three Types of Reliability

Researchers use data to decide which measures to use in a study, because establishing reliability is an empirical question. A measure's reliability is just what the word suggests: whether or not researchers can rely on a particular score. If an operationalization is reliable, it will yield a consistent pattern of scores every time.

Reliability can be assessed in three ways, depending on how a variable was operationalized, and all three involve consistency in measurement. When a measure has **test-retest reliability**, a study participant will get pretty much the same score each time they are measured with it. With **interrater reliability**, consistent scores are obtained no matter who measures the variable. With **internal reliability** (also called *internal consistency*), a study participant gives a consistent pattern of answers, no matter how the researchers phrase the question.

### TEST-RETEST RELIABILITY

To illustrate test-retest reliability, let's suppose a sample of people took an IQ test today. When they take it again 1 month later, the pattern of scores should be consistent: People who scored the highest at Time 1 should also score the highest at Time 2. Even if all the scores from Time 2 have increased since Time 1 (due to practice or schooling), the pattern should be consistent: The highest-scoring Time 1 people should still be the highest scoring people at Time 2. Test-retest reliability can apply whether the operationalization is self-report, observational, or physiological, but it's most relevant when researchers are measuring constructs (such as intelligence, personality, or gratitude) that are theoretically stable. Happy mood, for example, may reasonably fluctuate from month to month or year to year for a particular person, so less consistency would be expected in this variable.

### INTERRATER RELIABILITY

With interrater reliability, two or more independent observers will come up with consistent (or very similar) findings. Interrater reliability is most relevant for observational measures. Suppose you are assigned to observe the number of times each child smiles in 1 hour at a childcare playground. Your lab partner is assigned to sit on the other side of the playground and make their own count of the same children's smiles. If, for one child, you record 12 smiles during the first hour and your lab partner also records 12 smiles in that hour for the same child, there is interrater reliability. Any two observers watching the same children at the same time should agree about which child has smiled the most and which child has smiled the least.

## INTERNAL RELIABILITY

The third kind of reliability, internal reliability, applies to measures that combine multiple items. Suppose a sample of people take Diener's five-item subjective well-being scale. The questions on his scale are worded differently, but each item is intended to measure the same construct. Therefore, people who agree with the first item on the scale should also agree with the second item (as well as with Items 3, 4, and 5). Similarly, people who disagree with the first item should also disagree with Items 2, 3, 4, and 5. If the pattern is consistent across items in this way, the scale has internal reliability.

## Using a Scatterplot to Quantify Reliability

Before using a particular measure in a study they are planning, researchers may collect data to see if it is reliable. They may also rely on data collected on the measure by other researchers. Two statistical devices researchers can use for data analysis are scatterplots (see Chapter 3) and the correlation coefficient $r$ (discussed below). In fact, evidence for reliability is a special example of an association claim—the association between an earlier time and a later time, between one coder and another, or between one version of the measure and another.

Here's an example of how correlations are used to document reliability. Years ago, when some people thought smarter people had larger heads, they used head circumference as an operationalization of intelligence. Would this measure be reliable? Probably. Suppose you record the head circumference, in centimeters, for everyone in a classroom, using an ordinary tape measure. To see whether the measurements were reliable, you could measure all the heads twice (test-retest reliability) or you could measure them first, and then have someone else measure the same set (interrater reliability).

**Figure 5.2** shows how the results of such a measurement might look, in the form of a data table and a scatterplot. In the scatterplot, the first measurements of head circumference for four students are plotted on the y-axis. The circumferences as measured the second time—whether by you again (test-retest) or by a second observer (interrater)—are plotted on the x-axis. In this scatterplot, each dot represents a person measured twice.

We would expect the two measurements of head circumference to be about the same for each person. They are, so the dots on the scatterplot all fall almost exactly on the sloping line that would indicate perfect agreement. The two measures won't always be exactly the same because there is likely to be some measurement error

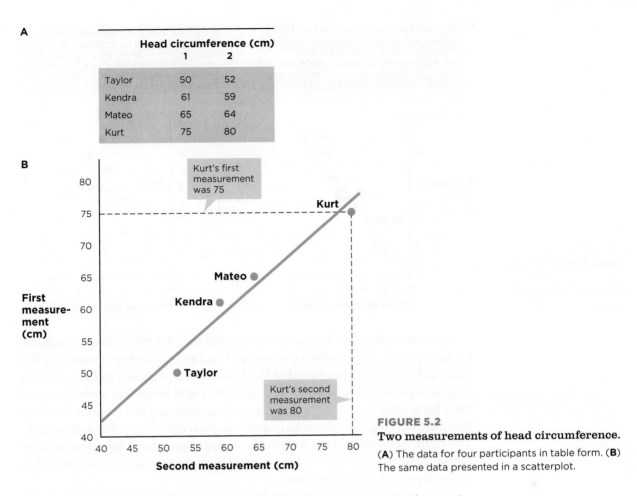

**FIGURE 5.2**
**Two measurements of head circumference.**
(**A**) The data for four participants in table form. (**B**) The same data presented in a scatterplot.

that will lead to slightly different scores even for the same person (such as variations in the tape measure placement for each person).

## SCATTERPLOTS CAN SHOW INTERRATER AGREEMENT OR DISAGREEMENT

In a different scenario, suppose ten young children are being observed at a playground. Two independent observers, Mark and Matt, rate how happy each child appears to be, on a scale of 1 to 10. They later compare notes to see how well their ratings agree. From these notes, they create a scatterplot, plotting Observer Mark's ratings on the *x*-axis and Observer Matt's ratings on the *y*-axis.

If the data looked like those in **Figure 5.3A**, the ratings would have high interrater reliability. Both Mark and Matt rate Jay's happiness as 9—one of the happiest kids on the playground. Observer Mark rates Jackie a 2—one of the least happy kids. Observer Matt agreed because he rates her 3, and so on. The two observers do not show perfect agreement, but there are no great disagreements about the happiest and least happy kids. Again, the points are a bit scattered, but they cluster close to the sloping line that would indicate perfect agreement.

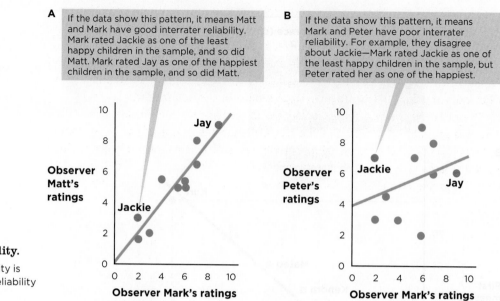

**A** If the data show this pattern, it means Matt and Mark have good interrater reliability. Mark rated Jackie as one of the least happy children in the sample, and so did Matt. Mark rated Jay as one of the happiest children in the sample, and so did Matt.

**B** If the data show this pattern, it means Mark and Peter have poor interrater reliability. For example, they disagree about Jackie—Mark rated Jackie as one of the least happy children in the sample, but Peter rated her as one of the happiest.

**FIGURE 5.3**
**Interrater reliability.**
(**A**) Interrater reliability is high. (**B**) Interrater reliability is low.

In contrast, suppose the data looked like **Figure 5.3B**, which shows much less agreement. Here, the two observers are Mark and Peter, and they are watching the same children at the same time, but Mark gives Jay a rating of 9 and Peter thinks he rates only a 6. Mark considers Jackie's behavior to be shy and withdrawn and rates her a 2, but Peter thinks she seems calm and content and rates her a 7. Here the interrater reliability would be considered unacceptably low. One reason could be that the observers did not have a clear enough operational definition of "happiness" to work with. Another reason could be that one or both of the coders has not been trained well enough yet.

A scatterplot can thus be a helpful tool for visualizing the agreement between two administrations of the same measurement (test-retest reliability) or between two coders (interrater reliability). Using a scatterplot, you can see whether the two ratings agree (if the dots are close to a straight line drawn through them) or whether they disagree (if the dots scatter widely from a straight line drawn through them).

## Using the Correlation Coefficient *r* to Quantify Reliability

Scatterplots can provide a picture of a measure's reliability. However, a more common and efficient way to see if a measure is reliable is to use the correlation coefficient. Researchers can use a single number, called a **correlation coefficient**, or *r*, to indicate how close the dots, or points, on a scatterplot are to a line drawn through them.

Notice that the scatterplots in **Figure 5.4** differ in two important ways. One difference is that the scattered clouds of points slope in different directions. In Figure 5.4A and Figure 5.4B the points slope upward from left to right, in Figure 5.4C they slope downward, and in Figure 5.4D they do not slope up or down at all. This

» For more on the slope of a scatterplot, see Chapter 3, pp. 62–63.

slope is referred to as the direction of the relationship, and the **slope direction** can be positive, negative, or zero—that is, sloping up, sloping down, or not sloping at all.

The other way the scatterplots differ is that in some, the dots are close to a straight, sloping line; in others, the dots are more spread out. This spread corresponds to the **strength** of the relationship. In general, the relationship is strong when dots are close to the line; it is weak when dots are spread out.

The numbers below the scatterplots are the correlation coefficients, or $r$. The $r$ indicates the same two things as the scatterplot: the direction of the relationship and the strength of the relationship, both of which psychologists use in evaluating reliability evidence. Notice that when the slope is positive, $r$ is positive; when the slope is negative, $r$ is negative. The value of $r$ can fall only between 1.0 and –1.0. When

«
For more on how to compute $r$, see Statistics Review: Descriptive Statistics, pp. 480–484.

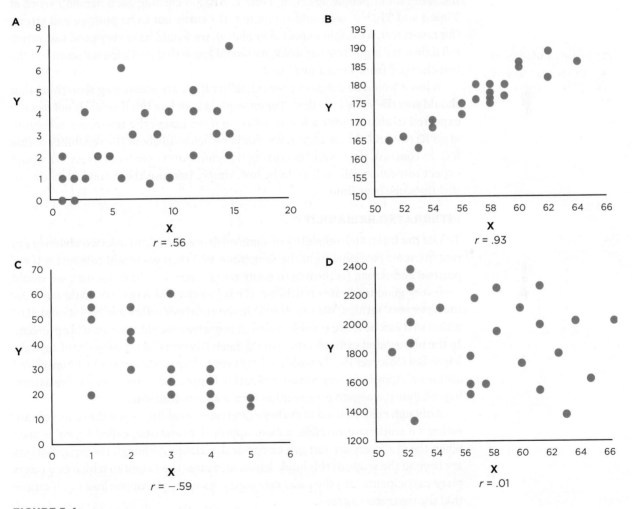

**FIGURE 5.4**

**Correlation coefficients.**

Notice the differences in the correlation coefficients ($r$) in these scatterplots. The correlation coefficient describes both the direction and the strength of the association between the two variables, regardless of the scale on which the variables are measured.

the relationship is strong, $r$ is close to either 1 or –1; when the relationship is weak, $r$ is closer to zero. An $r$ of 1.0 represents the strongest possible positive relationship, and an $r$ of –1.0 represents the strongest possible negative relationship. If there is no relationship between two variables, $r$ will be .00 or close to .00 (i.e., .02 or –.04).

Those are the basics. How do psychologists use the strength and direction of $r$ to evaluate reliability evidence?

## TEST-RETEST RELIABILITY

To assess the test-retest reliability of some measure, we would assess the same set of participants on that measure at least twice. First, we'd give the set of participants the measure at Time 1. Then we'd wait a while (say, 2 months) and contact the same set of people again, at Time 2. After recording each person's score at Time 1 and Time 2, we could compute $r$. If $r$ turns out to be positive and strong (for test-retest, we might expect .5 or above), we would have very good test-retest reliability. If $r$ is positive but weak, we would know that participants' scores on the test changed from Time 1 to Time 2.

A low $r$ would be a sign of poor reliability if we are measuring something that should stay the same over time. For example, a trait like intelligence is not usually expected to change over a few months, so if we assess the test-retest reliability of an IQ test and obtain a low $r$, we would be doubtful about the reliability of this test. In contrast, if we were measuring flu symptoms or seasonal stress, we would expect test-retest reliabilities to be low, simply because these constructs do not stay the same over time.

## INTERRATER RELIABILITY

To test the interrater reliability of some measure, we might ask two observers to rate the same participants at the same time, and then we would compute $r$. If $r$ is positive and strong (according to many researchers, $r = .70$ or higher), we would have very good interrater reliability. If $r$ is positive but weak, we could not trust the observers' ratings. We would retrain the coders or refine our operational definition so it can be more reliably coded. A negative $r$ would indicate a big problem. In the playground example, that would mean Observer Mark considered Jay very happy but Observer Peter considered Jay very unhappy, Observer Mark considered Jackie unhappy but Peter considered Jackie happy, and so on. When we're assessing reliability, a negative correlation is rare and undesirable.

Although $r$ can be used to evaluate interrater reliability when the observers are rating a quantitative variable, a more appropriate statistic, called *kappa*, is used when the observers are rating a categorical variable. Although the computations are beyond the scope of this book, kappa measures the extent to which two raters place participants into the same categories. As with $r$, a kappa close to 1.0 means that the two raters agreed.

## INTERNAL RELIABILITY

Internal reliability is relevant for measures that use multiple items or observations to get at the same construct. On self-report scales such as Diener's five-item subjective well-being scale, people answer the same question worded in multiple ways. Researchers usually plan to sum all the items to create a single composite score. Before combining the items, researchers assess the scale's internal reliability to evaluate whether people responded consistently to each item, despite the different wordings.

Let's consider the following adaptation of Diener's well-being scale. Would a group of people give consistent responses to all five items? Would people who agree with Item 1 also agree with Items 2, 3, 4, and 5?

_____ 1. In most ways my life is close to my ideal.
_____ 2. The conditions of my life are excellent.
_____ 3. I am satisfied with my life.
_____ 4. I am fond of polka dots.
_____ 5. If I could live my life over, I would change almost nothing.

You can see that only some of these items go together. Items 1 and 2 are probably correlated, since they are similar to each other, but Items 1 and 4 are probably not correlated, since people can like polka dots whether or not they are living their ideal lives. How do we quantify these intuitions?

First, researchers ask a large sample of participants to answer all of the items. Then they compute the correlations between every item and every other item (see **Table 5.3**). Next, they compute the **average inter-item correlation (AIC)**,

**TABLE 5.3**

### Internal Reliability

| | ITEM 1 | ITEM 2 | ITEM 3 | ITEM 4 | ITEM 5 |
|---|---|---|---|---|---|
| Item 1. "In most ways my life is close to my ideal." | | | | | |
| Item 2. "The conditions of my life are excellent." | .21 | | | | |
| Item 3. "I am satisfied with my life." | .22 | .25 | | | |
| Item 4. "I am fond of polka dots." | .01 | −.05 | .02 | | |
| Item 5. "If I could live my life over, I would change almost nothing." | .32 | .40 | .23 | −.01 | |

*Note:* This matrix shows the correlations among the five items listed on page 131. To assess internal reliability, we start by computing the correlation of each item with every other item. To find the correlation (*r*) between two items, locate where one item's column and another item's row intersect (for example, the correlation between Item 1 and Item 3 is *r* = .22). You can see that Items 1, 2, 3, and 5 correlate with one another, but Item 4 (the one about polka dots) does not correlate with any of the other items. The pattern suggests that Item 4 is problematic and this set of items is not internally reliable. (Data are fabricated for illustration purposes.)

which is the average of all these correlations (for example, all 10 correlations in Table 5.3). An AIC between .15 and .50 means that the items go reasonably well together (Clark & Watson, 2019). After that, researchers might compute **Cronbach's alpha** (or *coefficient alpha*), which mathematically combines the AIC and the number of items in the scale. The closer Cronbach's alpha is to 1.0, the better the scale's reliability. For self-report measures, researchers are looking for Cronbach's alpha of .80 or higher (Clark & Watson, 2019). If the AIC or Cronbach's alpha is acceptable, the researchers determine that there is good internal reliability and they can sum all the items together. If the AIC or Cronbach's alpha is unacceptable, the researchers look carefully at the items, perhaps revising or omitting some.

## Reading About Reliability in Journal Articles

Authors of empirical journal articles usually present reliability information for the measures they are using. One example of such evidence is shown in **Figure 5.5**, which comes from an actual journal article. According to the table, the subjective well-being scale called Satisfaction with Life (SWL) had been used in six studies. The table shows the internal reliability (labeled as coefficient alpha) from each of these studies as well as test-retest reliability for each one. The table did not present interrater reliability because the scale is a self-report measure, and interrater reliability is relevant only when two or more observers are rating something. Based on the evidence in this table, we can conclude that the subjective well-being scale has acceptable internal reliability and acceptable test-retest reliability. You'll see another example of how reliability is discussed in a journal article in the Working It Through section at the end of this chapter.

**STRAIGHT**
FROM THE
**SOURCE**

Table 2
*Estimates of Internal Consistency and Temporal Reliability for the Satisfaction with Life Scale*

| Sample | Coefficient alpha | Test–retest | Temporal interval |
|---|---|---|---|
| Alfonso & Allison (1992a) | .89 | .83 | 2 weeks |
| Pavot et al. (1991) | .85 | .84 | 1 month |
| Blais et al. (1989) | .79–.84 | .64 | 2 months |
| Diener et al. (1985) | .87 | .82 | 2 months |
| Yardley & Rice (1991) | .80, .86 | .50 | 10 weeks |
| Magnus, Diener, Fujita, & Pavot (1992) | .87 | .54 | 4 years |

**FIGURE 5.5**
**Reliability of the well-being scale.**

The researchers created this table to show how six studies supported the internal reliability and test-retest reliability of their SWL scale.
(Source: Pavot & Diener, 1993, Table 2.)

Authors of study using SWL scale.

Coefficient (Cronbach's) alpha above .80 means SWL scale has good internal reliability.

High correlation of $r = .83$ for retesting 2 weeks apart means scale has good test-retest reliability.

## CHECK YOUR UNDERSTANDING

1. Reliability is about consistency. Define the three kinds of reliability, using the word *consistent* in each of your definitions.

2. For each of the three common types of operationalizations—self-report, observational, and physiological—indicate which type(s) of reliability would be relevant.

3. Which of the following correlations is the strongest: $r = .25$, $r = -.65$, $r = -.01$, or $r = .43$?

# VALIDITY OF MEASUREMENT: DOES IT MEASURE WHAT IT'S INTENDED TO MEASURE?

As they prepare to use some measure, researchers not only check to be sure it is reliable; they also want to be sure it measures the conceptual variables it was intended for. That's construct validity. You might ask how well the five-item well-being scale reflects Diener's theoretical definition of subjective well-being. Or you might ask whether a self-report measure of gratitude really reflects how thankful people are. You might ask whether recording the value of the car a person drives reflects that person's wealth.

Measurement reliability and measurement validity are separate steps in establishing construct validity. To demonstrate the difference between them, consider the example of head circumference as an operationalization of intelligence. Head size measurements are usually reliable because circumference is easy to measure. However, head circumference is not related to intelligence (Gould, 1996). Therefore, like a bathroom scale that always reads too light (**Figure 5.6**), the head circumference test may be reliable, but it is not valid as an intelligence test: It does not adequately capture the construct of intelligence.

## Measurement Validity of Abstract Constructs

Does anyone you know use an activity monitor? Your friends may feel proud when they reach a daily steps goal or boast about how many miles they've covered

**FIGURE 5.6**

**Reliability is not the same as validity.**

This person's bathroom scale may report that he weighs 50 pounds (22.7 kg) every time he steps on it. The scale is certainly reliable, but it is not valid.

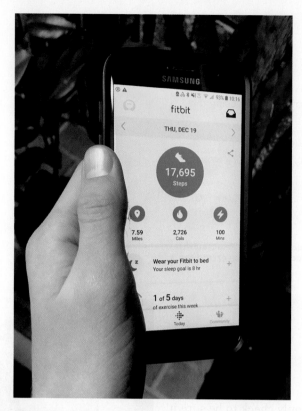

**FIGURE 5.7**
**Are activity monitors valid?**

A friend wore a pedometer during a hike and recorded these values. What data could you collect to know whether or not it accurately counted his steps?

that day (**Figure 5.7**). How can you know for sure that these pedometers are accurate? Of course, it's straightforward to evaluate the validity of a pedometer: You'd simply walk around, counting your steps while wearing one, and then compare your own count to that of your device. If you're sure you walked 200 steps and your pedometer says you walked 200, then your device is probably valid. Similarly, if your pedometer recorded the correct distance after you've walked around a track or some other path with a known mileage, it's probably a valid monitor.

In the case of an activity monitor, we are lucky to have concrete, straightforward standards for accurate measurement. But psychological scientists often want to measure abstract constructs such as happiness, intelligence, stress, or self-esteem, which we can't simply count (Clark & Watson, 2019; Cronbach & Meehl, 1955; Smith, 2005a, 2005b). Construct validity is therefore especially important when a construct is not directly observable. Take happiness: We have no means of directly measuring how happy a person is. We could estimate it in a number of ways, such as scores on a well-being inventory, daily smile rate, blood pressure, stress hormone levels, or even the activity levels of certain brain regions. Yet each of these measures of happiness is indirect. And that is the challenge: How can we know if operationalizations are measuring our intended construct, happiness, and not something else?

We know by collecting a variety of data and evaluating it in light of our theory about the construct (Cronbach & Meehl, 1955). The evidence for construct validity is a matter of degree. Psychologists do not say a particular measure is or is not valid. Instead, they ask: What is the weight of evidence in favor of this measure's validity? Several kinds of evidence can convince a researcher, and we'll discuss them below. First, take a look at **Figure 5.8**, an overview of the reliability and validity concepts covered in this chapter.

## Face Validity and Content Validity: Does It Look Like a Good Measure?

A measure has **face validity** if it is subjectively considered to be a plausible operationalization of the conceptual variable in question. Face-valid measures align well with the conceptual definition of a construct. Head circumference has high face validity as a measurement of hat size, but it has low face validity

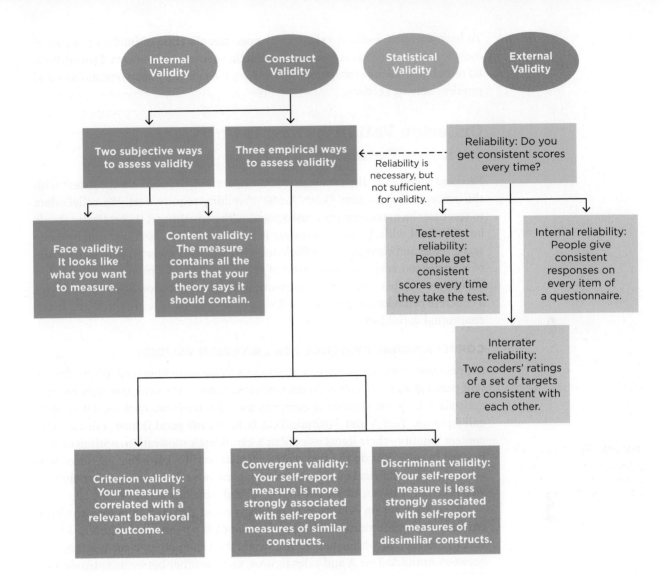

**FIGURE 5.8**
**A concept map of measurement reliability and validity.**

Construct validity is one of the four big validities, and it is supported by a variety of evidence.

as an operationalization of intelligence. In contrast, speed of problem solving, vocabulary size, and curiosity have higher face validity as operationalizations of intelligence. Researchers might check face validity by consulting experts. For example, we might assess the face validity of Diener's well-being scale by consulting people who are experts in the theoretical construct of well-being: Do they think the items are consistent with the construct?

**Content validity** also requires knowledge of the conceptual definition: A measure must capture all parts of a defined construct. For example, consider this conceptual definition of intelligence, which contains distinct elements, including the ability to "reason, plan, solve problems, think abstractly, comprehend complex ideas, learn quickly, and learn from experience" (Gottfredson, 1997, p. 13).

To have adequate content validity, any operationalization of intelligence should include questions or items to assess each of these seven components. Indeed, most IQ tests have multiple categories of items, such as memory span, vocabulary, and problem-solving sections.

## Criterion Validity: Does It Correlate with Key Behaviors?

Face and content validity establish that the operationalizations are consistent with the conceptual definition. Other forms of validity require data. We collect data to test that the measurement is associated with something it theoretically *should* be associated with. In some cases, such relationships can be illustrated by using scatterplots and correlation coefficients. They can be illustrated with other kinds of evidence too, such as comparisons of groups with known properties. **Criterion validity** evaluates whether the measure under consideration is associated with a concrete behavioral outcome that it should be associated with, according to the conceptual definition.

### CORRELATIONAL EVIDENCE FOR CRITERION VALIDITY

Suppose you work for a company that wants to measure how well job applicants will perform as salespeople. Of the several commercially available tests of sales aptitude, which one should the company use? You have two choices, which we'll call Aptitude Test A and Aptitude Test B. Both look good in terms of face and content validity—their items ask about a candidate's motivation, optimism, and interest in sales. But do the test scores correlate with a key behavior: success in selling? It's an empirical question. Your company can collect data to tell them how well each of the two aptitude tests is correlated with success in selling.

To assess criterion validity, your company could give both sales tests to all the current sales representatives and then find out each person's sales figures—a measure of their selling performance. You would then compute two correlations: one between Aptitude Test A and sales figures, and the other between Aptitude Test B and sales figures. **Figure 5.9A** shows scatterplot results for Test A. The score on Aptitude Test A is plotted on the *x*-axis, and actual sales figures are plotted on the *y*-axis. (Alex scored 39 on the test and brought in $38,000 in sales, whereas Irina scored 98 and brought in $100,000.) **Figure 5.9B**, in contrast, shows the association of sales performance with Aptitude Test B.

Looking at these two scatterplots, we can see that the correlation in the first one is much stronger than in the second one. In other words, future sales performance is correlated more strongly with scores on Aptitude Test A than with scores on Aptitude Test B. If the data looked like this, the company would conclude that Aptitude Test A has better criterion validity as a measure of selling ability, so it seems better for hiring salespeople. In contrast, the other data show that scores on Aptitude Test B do not predict future sales performance; it has poor criterion validity as a measure of sales aptitude.

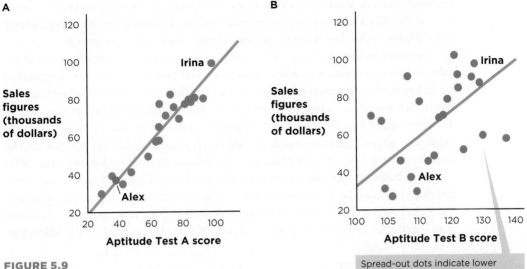

**A**

**B**

Spread-out dots indicate lower correlation between Test B scores and sales figures, so this test has lower criterion validity as a measure of sales performance.

**FIGURE 5.9**

**Correlational evidence for criterion validity.**

(**A**) Aptitude Test A predicts sales performance, so criterion validity is high. (**B**) Aptitude Test B does not predict sales as well, so criterion validity is lower. A company would probably want to use Test A for identifying potential selling ability when selecting future salespeople.

Criterion validity is especially important for self-report measures because the correlation can indicate how well people's self-reports predict their actual behavior. Criterion validity provides some of the strongest evidence for a measure's construct validity. For example, Gallup presents criterion validity evidence for the 10-point Ladder of Life scale they use to measure happiness. They report that Ladder of Life scores correlate with key behavioral outcomes, such as becoming ill and missing work (Gallup, n.d.).

If an IQ test has criterion validity, it should be correlated with behaviors consistent with the construct of intelligence, such as how fast people can learn a complex set of symbols (an outcome that represents the conceptual definition of intelligence). Of course, the ability to learn quickly is only one component of that definition. Further criterion validity evidence could show that IQ scores are correlated with other behavioral outcomes that are theoretically related to intelligence, such as the ability to solve problems and indicators of life success (e.g., graduating from college, being employed in a high-level job, being curious and thoughtful).

**KNOWN-GROUPS EVIDENCE FOR CRITERION VALIDITY**

Another way to gather evidence for criterion validity is to use a **known-groups paradigm**, in which researchers see whether scores on the measure can discriminate among two or more groups whose behavior is already confirmed. For example, to validate the use of salivary cortisol as a measure of stress, a researcher could compare the salivary cortisol levels in two groups of people: those who are about to give a speech in front of a classroom and those who are in the audience. Public speaking is recognized as being a stressful situation for almost everyone. Therefore, if salivary cortisol is a valid measure of stress, people in the speech group should have higher levels of cortisol than those in the audience group.

Lie detectors are another good example. These instruments record a set of physiological measures (such as skin conductance and heart rate) that are supposed to be different when a person is lying versus telling the truth. If skin conductance and heart rate are valid measures of lying, we could conduct a known-groups test in which we know in advance which of a person's statements are true and which are false. The physiological measures should be elevated only for the lies, not for the true statements. (For a review of the mixed evidence on lie detection, see Saxe, 1991.)

The known-groups method can also be used to validate self-report measures. Psychiatrist Aaron Beck and his colleagues developed the Beck Depression Inventory (BDI), a 21-item self-report scale with items that ask about major symptoms of depression (Beck et al., 1961). Participants circle one of four choices, such as the following:

0   I do not feel sad.
1   I feel sad.
2   I am sad all the time and I can't snap out of it.
3   I am so sad or unhappy that I can't stand it.

0   I have not lost interest in other people.
1   I am less interested in other people than I used to be.
2   I have lost most of my interest in other people.
3   I have lost all of my interest in other people.

A clinical scientist adds up the scores on each of the 21 items for a total BDI score, which can range from a low of 0 (not at all depressed) to a high of 63.

To test the criterion validity of the BDI, Beck and his colleagues gave this self-report scale to two known groups of people. They knew one group was suffering from clinical depression and the other group was not because they had asked psychiatrists to conduct clinical interviews and diagnose each person. The researchers computed the mean BDI scores of the two groups and created a bar graph, shown in **Figure 5.10**. The evidence supports the criterion validity of the BDI. The graph shows the expected result: The average BDI score of the known group of depressed people was higher than the average score of the known group who were not depressed. Because its criterion validity was established in this way, the BDI is still widely used today when researchers need a quick and valid way to identify people who are vulnerable to depression.

Beck also used the known-groups paradigm to calibrate low, medium, and high scores on the BDI. When the psychiatrists

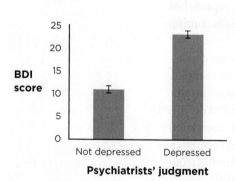

**FIGURE 5.10**

**BDI scores of two known groups.**

This pattern of results provides evidence for the criterion validity of the BDI using the known-groups method. Clients judged to be more depressed by psychiatrists also scored higher. Error bars indicate standard error of each mean. (Source: Adapted from Beck et al., 1961.)

interviewed the people in the sample, they evaluated not only whether they were depressed but also the level of depression in each person: none, mild, moderate, or severe. As expected, the BDI scores of the groups rose as their level of depression (assessed by psychiatrists) was more severe (**Figure 5.11**). This result was even clearer evidence that the BDI was a valid measure of depression. With the BDI, clinicians and researchers can confidently use specific ranges of BDI scores to categorize how severe a person's depression might be.

Diener's subjective well-being scale is another example of using the known-groups paradigm for criterion validity. In one review article, he and his colleague presented the subjective well-being scale averages from several studies. Each study had given the scale to different groups of people who could be expected to vary in happiness level (Pavot & Diener, 1993). For example, male prison inmates, a group that would be expected to report low subjective well-being, showed a lower mean score on the scale than Canadian college students, who averaged much higher—indicated by the *M* column in **Table 5.4**. Such known-groups patterns provide strong evidence for the criterion validity of the subjective well-being scale. Researchers can therefore have more confidence in the scale's validity.

What about the Ladder of Life scale, the measure of happiness used in the Gallup-Healthways Well-Being Index? This measure also has some known-groups evidence to support its criterion validity. National scores on this measure dropped, as you might expect, during the first months of the coronavirus pandemic (Witters & Harter, 2020). Scores also generally drop during economic recessions and rise during the summer months. These results fit what we would expect if the Ladder of Life is a valid measure of well-being.

## Convergent Validity and Discriminant Validity: Does the Pattern Make Sense?

Criterion validity examines whether a measure correlates with key behavioral outcomes. Another form of validity evidence is whether

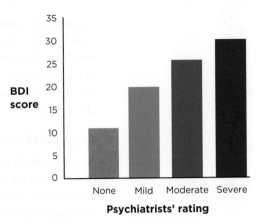

**FIGURE 5.11**

**BDI scores of four known groups.**

This pattern of results means it is valid to use BDI cutoff scores to decide if a person has mild, moderate, or severe depression. (Source: Adapted from Beck et al., 1961.)

**TABLE 5.4**

**Subjective Well-Being Scores for Known Groups from Several Studies**

| SAMPLE CHARACTERISTICS | N | M | SD | STUDY REFERENCE |
|---|---|---|---|---|
| American college students | 244 | 23.7 | 6.4 | Pavot & Diener (1993) |
| French Canadian college students (male) | 355 | 23.8 | 6.1 | Blais et al. (1989) |
| Korean university students | 413 | 19.8 | 5.8 | Suh (1993) |
| Printing trade workers | 304 | 24.2 | 6.0 | George (1991) |
| Veterans Affairs hospital inpatients | 52 | 11.8 | 5.6 | Frisch (1991) |
| Abused women | 70 | 20.7 | 7.4 | Fisher (1991) |
| Male prison inmates | 75 | 12.3 | 7.0 | Joy (1990) |

*Note: N* = Number of people in group. *M* = Group mean on subjective well-being. *SD* = Group standard deviation.
Source: Adapted from Pavot & Diener, 1993, Table 1.

there is a meaningful pattern of similarities and differences among related measures. A self-report measure should correlate more strongly with measures of similar constructs than it does with those of dissimilar constructs. The patterns of correlations with measures of theoretically similar and dissimilar constructs are called **convergent validity** and **discriminant validity** (or *divergent validity*), respectively.

### CONVERGENT VALIDITY

As an example of convergent validity, let's consider Beck's depression scale, the BDI, again. One team of researchers wanted to test the convergent and discriminant validity of the BDI (Segal et al., 2008). If the BDI really quantifies depression, the researchers reasoned, it should be correlated with (should converge with) other self-report measures of depression. Their sample of 376 adults completed the BDI and a number of other questionnaires, including a self-report instrument called the Center for Epidemiologic Studies Depression scale (CES-D).

As expected, BDI scores were positively, strongly correlated with CES-D scores ($r = .68$). People who scored as depressed on the BDI also scored as depressed on the CES-D; likewise, those who scored as not depressed on the BDI also scored as not depressed on the CES-D. **Figure 5.12** shows a scatterplot of the results. (Notice that most of the dots fall in the lower left portion of the scatterplot because most people in the sample are not depressed; they score low on both the BDI and the CES-D.) This correlation between similar self-report measures of the same construct (depression) provided evidence for the convergent validity of the BDI.

This example of convergent validity is somewhat obvious: A measure of depression should correlate with a different measure of the same construct—depression.

»

For more on the strength of correlations, see Chapter 8, Table 8.4, and Statistics Review: Descriptive Statistics, pp. 480–488.

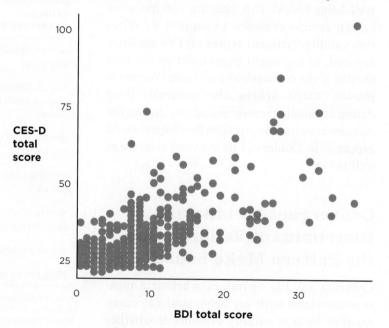

**FIGURE 5.12**
**Evidence supporting the convergent validity of the BDI.**

The BDI is strongly correlated with another measure of depression, the CES-D ($r = .68$), providing evidence for convergent validity. (Source: Segal et al., 2008.)

But convergent validity evidence also includes *similar* constructs, not just the same one. The researchers showed, for instance, that the BDI scores were strongly correlated with a score quantifying psychological well-being ($r = -.65$). The strong negative correlation they observed made sense as a form of convergent validity because people who are depressed are also expected to have lower levels of well-being (Segal et al., 2008).

## DISCRIMINANT VALIDITY

The BDI should *not* correlate strongly with measures of constructs that are very different from depression—it should show discriminant validity with them. For example, depression is not the same as a person's perception of their overall physical health. Although mental health problems, including depression, do overlap somewhat with physical health problems, we would not expect the BDI to be strongly correlated with a measure of perceived physical health problems. More important, we would expect the BDI to be more strongly correlated with the CES-D than it is with physical health problems. Sure enough, Segal and his colleagues found a correlation of only $r = .16$ between the BDI and a measure of perceived physical health problems. This weak correlation shows that the BDI is different from people's perceptions of their physical health, so we can say that the BDI has discriminant validity with physical health problems.

**Figure 5.13** shows a scatterplot of the results. Notice that most of the dots fall in the lower left portion of the scatterplot because most people in the sample reported few health problems and were not depressed: They scored low on both the BDI and on the perceived physical health problems scale.

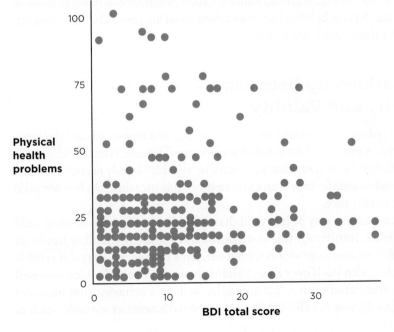

**FIGURE 5.13**

**Evidence supporting the discriminant validity of the BDI.**

As expected, the BDI is only weakly correlated with perceived health problems ($r = .16$), providing evidence for discriminant validity. (Source: Segal et al., 2008.)

As another example of discriminant validity, consider that many developmental disorders have similar symptoms, but diagnoses can vary. It might be important to specify, for instance, whether a child has autism or only a language delay. Therefore, a screening instrument for identifying autism should have discriminant validity; it should not accidentally diagnose that same child as having a language delay. Similarly, a scale that is supposed to diagnose learning disabilities should not be correlated with IQ because learning disabilities are not related to general intelligence.

It is usually not necessary to establish discriminant validity between a measure and something that is completely unrelated. Because depression is not likely to be associated with how many movies you watch or the number of siblings you have, we would not need to examine its discriminant validity with these variables. Instead, researchers focus on discriminant validity for "near neighbors": similar but different constructs. Does the BDI measure depression or perceived health problems? Does Diener's subjective well-being scale measure enduring happiness or just temporary mood? Does a screening technique identify autism or language delay?

Convergent validity and discriminant validity are usually evaluated together, as a pattern of correlations among self-report measures. A measurement should have higher correlations (higher $r$ values) with similar traits (convergent validity) than it does with dissimilar traits (discriminant validity). There are no strict rules for what the correlations should be. Instead, the overall pattern of convergent and discriminant validity helps researchers decide whether their operationalization really measures the construct they want it to measure.

Finally, recall that construct validity requires evaluating the *weight* of the evidence; no single definitive outcome will establish validity of a measure (Smith, 2005a). A set of convergent and discriminant validity correlations (such as those in Figures 5.12 and 5.13) is helpful, but researchers must also consider face, content, and criterion validity evidence as well.

## The Relationship Between Reliability and Validity

One essential point is worth reiterating: The validity of a measure is not the same as its reliability. A person might boast that some operationalization of behavior is "a very reliable test." But to say that a measure is "reliable" is only part of the story. Recall that head circumference is an extremely reliable measure, but it is not valid for assessing intelligence.

Although a measure may be less valid than it is reliable, it cannot be more valid than it is reliable. Intuitively, this statement makes sense. Reliability has to do with how well a measure correlates with itself. For example, an IQ test is reliable if it is correlated with itself over time. Validity, however, has to do with how well a measure is associated with something else, such as a behavior that indicates intelligence. An IQ test is valid if it is associated with another variable, such as school grades or life success. If a measure does not even correlate with itself, then how can it be more strongly associated with some other variable?

As another example, suppose you used your pedometer to count how many steps you take in your daily walk from your parking spot to your building. If the pedometer reading is very different from day to day, then the measure is unreliable—and of course, it also cannot be valid because the true distance of your walk has not changed. Therefore, reliability is necessary (but not sufficient) for validity.

---

✔

**CHECK YOUR UNDERSTANDING**

1. What do face validity and content validity have in common?

2. Many researchers believe criterion validity is more important than convergent and discriminant validity. Can you see why?

3. Which requires stronger correlations for its evidence: convergent validity or discriminant validity? Which requires weaker correlations?

4. Can a measure be reliable but not valid? Can it be valid but unreliable?

1. They both require an expert's judgment; see pp. 134–136. 2. Because only criterion validity establishes how well a measure correlates with a behavioral outcome, not simply with other self-report measures; see pp. 136–142. 3. Convergent validity; discriminant validity. 4. It can be reliable but not valid, but a measure cannot be valid if it is unreliable; see pp. 142–143.

---

# REVIEW: INTERPRETING CONSTRUCT VALIDITY EVIDENCE

Before using a stopwatch in a track meet, a coach wants to be sure the stopwatch is working well. Before taking a patient's blood pressure, a nurse wants to be sure the cuff she's using is reliable and accurate. Similarly, before conducting a study, researchers want to be sure all the measures they plan to use are reliable and valid ones. When you read empirical articles, look for the validity evidence for the measures the researchers used. You'll usually find reliability and validity information in the Method section, where the authors describe their measures. You should ask: Did the researchers present evidence that the measures they used have construct validity?

It turns out that many researchers report only internal reliability (Cronbach's alpha); they do not provide any other convergent, discriminant, or criterion validity evidence. That's a problem (Flake et al., 2017). However, some researchers get it right. The Working It Through section presents a good example of how validity information was described in a study by Gordon and colleagues (2012).

**Item**

1. I tell my partner often that s/he is the best.
2. I often tell my partner how much I appreciate her/him.
3. At times I take my partner for granted. (reverse scored item)
4. I appreciate my partner.
5. Sometimes I don't really acknowledge or treat my partner like s/he is someone special. (reverse scored item)
6. I make sure my partner feels appreciated.
7. My partner sometimes says that I fail to notice the nice things that s/he does for me. (reverse scored item)
8. I acknowledge the things that my partner does for me, even the really small things.
9. I am sometimes struck with a sense of awe and wonder when I think about my partner being in my life.

**FIGURE 5.14**

**Items in the Appreciation in Relationships (AIR) Scale.**

These items were used by the researchers to measure how much people appreciate their relationship partner. Do you think these items have face validity as a measure of appreciation? (Source: Gordon et al., 2012.)

The evidence reported by Gordon et al. (2012) supports the Appreciation in Relationships (AIR) scale as a reliable and valid scale (**Figure 5.14**). It has internal and test-retest reliability, and there is evidence of its convergent, discriminant, and criterion validity. The researchers were confident they could use AIR when they later tested their hypothesis that more appreciative couples would have healthier relationships. Many of their hypotheses about gratitude (operationalized by the AIR scale) were supported. One of the more dramatic results was from a study that followed couples over time. The authors reported: "We found that people who were more appreciative of their partners were significantly more likely to still be in their relationships at the 9-month follow-up" (Gordon et al., 2012, p. 268).

This empirical journal article illustrates how researchers use data to establish the construct validity of the measure they plan to use. Their research was picked up by the popular press and given the headline "Gratitude is for lovers."

# How Well Can We Measure the Amount of Gratitude Couples Express to Each Other?

What do partners bring to a healthy romantic relationship? One research team proposed that gratitude toward one's partner would be important (Gordon et al., 2012). They predicted that when people are appreciative of their partners, close relationships are happier and last longer. In an empirical journal article, the researchers reported how they tested this hypothesis. But before they could study how the concept of gratitude contributes to relationship health, they needed to be able to measure the variable "gratitude" in a reliable and valid way. They created and tested the Appreciation in Relationships, or AIR, scale. We will work through the ways this example illustrates concepts from Chapter 5.

| QUESTIONS TO ASK | CLAIMS, QUOTES, OR DATA | INTERPRETATION AND EVALUATION |
| --- | --- | --- |
| **Conceptual and Operational Definitions**<br><br>How did they operationalize the conceptual variable "gratitude"? | "In the first step, we created an initial pool of items based on lay knowledge, theory, and previous measures of appreciation and gratitude. . . . These items were designed to capture a broad conceptualization of appreciation by including items that assess the extent to which people recognize and value their partner as a person as well as the extent to which they are grateful for a partner's kind deeds" (p. 260). | This quoted passage describes how Gordon and her colleagues developed and selected the AIR items. Notice how they wrote items to capture their conceptual definition of gratitude (see Figure 5.14). |

*(Continued)*

| QUESTIONS TO ASK | CLAIMS, QUOTES, OR DATA | INTERPRETATION AND EVALUATION |
|---|---|---|

**Was the AIR scale reliable? Did the scale give consistent scores?**

### Internal Reliability

When a self-report scale has multiple items, it should have good internal reliability. Did the AIR scale have good internal reliability?

"In the initial online survey, participants completed a questionnaire with basic demographic information. Participants completed the AIR scale . . . α = .87" (p. 266).

In this passage, the authors report the internal reliability of the AIR scale. The value α = .87 indicates that people in the Gordon study answered all the AIR items consistently. A Cronbach's alpha above .80 is considered good internal reliability.

### Test-Retest Reliability

We might expect the AIR scale to have test-retest reliability because gratitude should be stable over time. Were the AIR scores stable over time?

"The AIR scale had strong test-retest reliability from baseline to the 9-month follow-up (. . . r = .61, p = .001)" (p. 267).

This passage reports the test-retest correlation, which was r = .61. Those who were the most appreciative at Time 1 were also the most appreciative at Time 2; similarly, those who were least appreciative at Time 1 were also least appreciative at Time 2.

### Interrater Reliability

Because the AIR scale is a self-report measure, the researchers do not need to report interrater reliability evidence.

**The evidence indicates the AIR scale has adequate internal and test-retest reliability. What evidence is there for its validity? Does the scale really measure the concept of gratitude?**

### Convergent and Discriminant Validity

Do AIR scores correlate more strongly with measures similar to gratitude and less strongly with measures dissimilar to gratitude?

In a section on convergent and discriminant validity, the authors write: "As expected, . . . [the AIR scale was] positively correlated with the extent to which people had a grateful disposition [r = .25], as well as with people's gratitude in response to their partners' kind acts [r = .60]. In contrast, [the AIR scale was not] associated with people's feelings of indebtedness to their partners [r = .19]" (p. 262).

In this passage, the authors give convergent and discriminant validity evidence. The AIR scale has convergent validity with other measures of gratitude and discriminant validity with a measure of indebtedness. In other words, there was a pattern of higher correlations with gratitude than with indebtedness.

### Criterion Validity

Does the AIR scale predict relevant behavioral outcomes?

The "final study allowed us to provide additional evidence for the validity of the AIR scale by examining cross-partner associations. . . . [P]eople who reported feeling more appreciative of their partners had partners who felt more appreciated by them, β = .50, t(66) = 5.87, p < .001, . . . suggesting that the AIR scale is capturing the interpersonal transmission of appreciation from one partner to the other" (p. 269).

In this passage, the authors present criterion validity evidence. If the AIR scale is a valid measure, you'd expect partners with higher AIR scores to also have partners who notice this appreciation. Because the results showed that AIR scores were associated with this relevant outcome, there is evidence for the AIR scale's criterion validity.

# CHAPTER REVIEW

It's time to complete your study experience! Go to INQUIZITIVE to practice actively with this chapter's concepts and get personalized feedback along the way.

## Summary

The construct validity of a study's measured variables is something you will interrogate for any type of claim.

### WAYS TO MEASURE VARIABLES

- Psychological scientists measure variables in every study they conduct. Three common types of measures are self-report, in which people report on their own behaviors, beliefs, or attitudes; observational measures, in which raters record the visible behaviors of people or animals; and physiological measures, in which researchers measure biological data, such as heart rate, brain activity, and hormone levels.

- Depending on how they are operationalized, variables may be categorical or quantitative. The levels of categorical variables are categories. The levels of quantitative variables are meaningful numbers, in which higher numbers represent more of some variable.

- Quantitative variables can be further classified in terms of ordinal, interval, or ratio scales.

### RELIABILITY OF MEASUREMENT: ARE THE SCORES CONSISTENT?

- Both measurement reliability and measurement validity are important for establishing a measure's construct validity.

- Researchers use scatterplots and correlation coefficients (among other methods) to evaluate evidence for a measure's reliability and validity.

- To establish a measure's reliability, researchers collect data to see whether the measure works consistently. There are three types of measurement reliability.

- Test-retest reliability establishes whether a sample gives a consistent pattern of scores at more than one testing.

- Interrater reliability establishes whether two observers give consistent ratings to a sample of targets.

- Internal reliability is established when people answer similarly worded items in a consistent way.

- Measurement reliability is necessary but not sufficient for establishing measurement validity.

### VALIDITY OF MEASUREMENT: DOES IT MEASURE WHAT IT'S INTENDED TO MEASURE?

- Measurement validity can be established with subjective judgments (face validity and content validity) or with empirical data.

- Criterion validity requires collecting data that show a measure is correlated with expected behavioral outcomes.

- Convergent and discriminant validity require collecting data that show a measure is correlated more strongly with measures of similar constructs than with measures of dissimilar constructs.

### REVIEW: INTERPRETING CONSTRUCT VALIDITY EVIDENCE

- Measurement reliability and validity evidence are reported in the Method section of empirical journal articles. Details may be provided in the text, as a table of results, or through cross-reference to a longer article that presents full reliability and validity evidence.

# Key Terms

conceptual definition, p. 118
self-report measure, p. 120
observational measure, p. 121
physiological measure, p. 121
categorical variable, p. 122
quantitative variable, p. 123
ordinal scale, p. 123
interval scale, p. 123
ratio scale, p. 123
reliability, p. 125

validity, p. 125
test-retest reliability, p. 125
interrater reliability, p. 125
internal reliability, p. 125
correlation coefficient r, p. 128
slope direction, p. 129
strength, p. 129
average inter-item correlation, (AIC) p. 131
Cronbach's alpha, p. 132

face validity, p. 134
content validity, p. 135
criterion validity, p. 136
known-groups paradigm, p. 137
convergent validity, p. 140
discriminant validity, p. 140

 **To see samples of chapter concepts in the popular media, visit www.everydayresearchmethods.com and click the box for Chapter 5.**

# Review Questions

1. Classify each operational variable below as categorical or quantitative. If the variable is quantitative, further classify it as ordinal, interval, or ratio.

   a. Degree of pupil dilation in a person's eyes in a study of romantic couples (measured in millimeters).

   b. Number of books a person owns.

   c. A book's sales rank on Amazon.com.

   d. The language a person speaks at home.

   e. Nationality of the participants in a cross-cultural study of Canadian, Ghanaian, and French students.

   f. A student's grade in school.

2. Which of the following correlation coefficients best describes the pictured scatterplot?

   a. $r = .78$

   b. $r = -.95$

   c. $r = .03$

   d. $r = -.45$

3. Classify each of the following results as an example of internal reliability, interrater reliability, or test-retest reliability.

   a. A researcher finds that people's scores on a measure of extroversion stay stable over 2 months.

   b. An infancy researcher wants to measure how long a 3-month-old baby looks at a stimulus on the right and left sides of a screen. Two undergraduates watch a tape of the eye movements of ten infants and time how long each baby looks to the right and to the left. The two sets of timings are correlated $r = .95$.

   c. A researcher asks a sample of 40 people a set of five items that all capture how extroverted they are. The Cronbach's alpha for the five items is found to be .85.

4. Classify each result below as an example of face validity, content validity, convergent and discriminant validity, or criterion validity.

   a. A professor gives a class of 40 people his five-item measure of conscientiousness (e.g., "I get chores done right away," "I follow a schedule," "I do not make a mess of things"). Average scores are correlated ($r = -.20$) with how many times each student has been late to class during the semester.

b. A professor gives a class of 40 people his five-item measure of conscientiousness (e.g., "I get chores done right away," "I follow a schedule," "I do not make a mess of things"). Average scores are more highly correlated with a self-report measure of tidiness ($r = .50$) than with a measure of general knowledge ($r = .09$).

c. The researcher e-mails his five-item measure of conscientiousness (e.g., "I get chores done right away," "I follow a schedule," "I do not make a mess of things") to 20 experts in personality psychology and asks them if they think his items are a good measure of conscientiousness.

d. The researcher e-mails his five-item measure of conscientiousness (e.g., "I get chores done right away." "I follow a schedule," "I do not make a mess of things") to 20 experts in personality psychology and asks them if they think he has included all the important aspects of conscientiousness.

## Learning Actively

1. For each measure below, indicate which kinds of reliability would need to be evaluated. Then draw a scatterplot indicating that the measure has good reliability and another one indicating the measure has poor reliability. (Pay special attention to how you label the axes of your scatterplots.)

   a. Researchers place unobtrusive video recording devices in the hallway of a local high school. Later, coders view tapes and code how many students are using cell phones in the 4-minute period between classes.

   b. Clinical psychologists have developed a seven-item self-report measure to quickly identify people who are at risk for panic disorder.

   c. Psychologists measure how long it takes a mouse to learn an eyeblink response. For 60 trials, they present a mouse with a distinctive blue light followed immediately by a puff of air. The 5th, 10th, and 15th trials are test trials, in which they present the blue light alone (without the air puff). The mouse is said to have learned the eyeblink response if observers record that it blinked its eyes in response to a test trial. The earlier in the 60 trials the mouse shows the eyeblink response, the faster it has learned the response.

   d. Educational psychologists use teacher ratings of classroom shyness (on a 9-point scale, where 1 = *not at all shy in class* and 9 = *very shy in class*) to measure children's temperament.

2. Consider how you might validate the 9-point classroom shyness rating example in Question 1d. First, what behaviors might be relevant for establishing this rating's criterion validity? Draw a scatterplot showing the results of a study in which the classroom shyness rating has good criterion validity (be careful how you label the axes). Second, come up with ways to evaluate the convergent and discriminant validity of this rating system. What traits should correlate strongly with shyness? What traits should correlate only weakly or not at all? Explain why you chose those traits. Draw a scatterplot showing the results of a study in which the shyness rating has good convergent or discriminant validity (be careful how you label the axes).

3. This chapter included the example of a sales ability test. Search online for "sales ability assessment" and see what commercially available tests you can find. Do the websites present reliability or validity evidence for the measures? If so, what form does the evidence take? If not, what kind of evidence would you like to see? You might frame your predictions in this form: "If this sales ability test has convergent validity, I would expect it to be correlated with . . . ."; "If this sales ability test has discriminant validity, I would expect it *not* to be correlated with . . . ."; "If this sales ability test has criterion validity, I would expect it to be correlated with . . . ."

# PART III

# Tools for Evaluating Frequency Claims

> "Should we eat at this restaurant? It got 4 stars on Yelp."

REAL CLEAR POLITICS

RCP POLL AVERAGE
2020 Democratic Presidential Nomination

| 27.8 Biden +6.5 | 21.3 Warren | 17.5 Sanders | 5.3 Buttigieg |
| 4.7 Harris | 3.3 Yang | 2.5 O'Rourke | Castro |
| 1.5 Booker | 1.3 Klobuchar | 1.0 Gabbard | 0.8 Bennet |
| 0.7 Steyer | 0.5 Delaney | 0.5 Ryan | 0.4 Bullock |
| Sestak | 0.3 Williamson | Messam | |

## Chabot Polling at 50%

**REALCLEARPOLITICS, 2016**

## Two-Thirds of Adults Have Had an Adverse Childhood Experience

**ACESTOOHIGH, 2017**

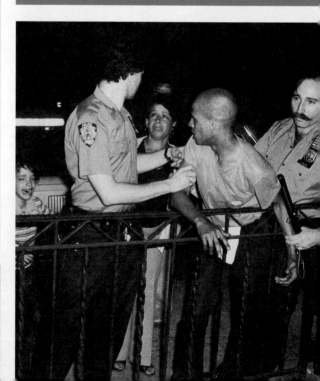

# 6

# Surveys and Observations: Describing What People Do

YOU SHOULD BE ABLE to identify the three statements that open this chapter as single-variable frequency claims. Each claim is based on data from one self-reported variable: the rated quality of a restaurant, support for a congressional candidate, or people's history of adverse childhood experiences (such as abuse or neglect). Where do the data for such claims come from? This chapter focuses on the construct validity of surveys and polls, in which research-ers ask people questions, as well as observational studies, in which researchers watch the behavior of people or animals, often without asking them questions at all. Researchers use surveys, polls, and observations to measure variables for any type of claim. However, in this chapter and the next, many of the examples focus on how surveys and observations are used to measure one variable at a time for frequency claims.

## CONSTRUCT VALIDITY OF SURVEYS AND POLLS

Researchers use surveys and polls to ask people questions over the Internet, in door-to-door interviews, or on the phone. You may have been asked to take surveys in various situations. Perhaps after you

A year from now, you should still be able to:

**1.**
Explain how carefully prepared questions improve the construct validity of a poll or survey.

**2.**
Describe how researchers can make observations with good construct validity.

purchased an item from an Internet retailer, you got an e-mail asking you to post a review. While you were reading news online, maybe a survey popped up. A polling organization such as Gallup may have called your cell phone.

The word *survey* is often used when people are asked about a consumer product, whereas the word *poll* is used when people are asked about their social or political opinions. However, in this book, **survey** and **poll** both mean the same thing: a method of posing questions to people online, in personal interviews, or in written questionnaires.

How much can you learn about a phenomenon just by asking people questions? It depends on how well you ask. As you will learn, researchers who develop their questions carefully can support frequency, association, or causal claims that have excellent construct validity.

## Choosing Question Formats

Survey questions can follow several formats. Researchers may ask **open-ended questions** that allow respondents to answer any way they like. They might ask people to name the public figure they admire the most. Departing overnight guests might be asked to comment on their experience at a hotel. People's various responses to these open-ended questions provide researchers with spontaneous, rich information. The drawback is that the responses must be coded and categorized, a process that is difficult and time-consuming. In the interest of efficiency, researchers in psychology often restrict the answers people can give.

One specific way to ask survey questions uses **forced-choice questions**, in which people give their opinion by picking the best of two or more options. Forced-choice questions are often used in political polls, such as asking: If the Ohio congressional election were held today, would you vote for the Republican Steve Chabot? Or the Democrat Aftab Pureval?

Forced-choice questions are also used to measure personality. An example comes from the Narcissistic Personality Inventory (NPI; Raskin & Terry, 1988). This instrument asks people to choose one statement from each of 40 pairs of items, such as the following:

1. _____ I really like to be the center of attention.
   _____ It makes me uncomfortable to be the center of attention.
2. _____ I am going to be a great person.
   _____ I hope I am going to be successful.

To score a survey like this, the researcher adds up the number of times people choose the "narcissistic" response over the "non-narcissistic" one (in the pairs above, the narcissistic response is the first option).

Simple yes/no questions are also considered a forced-choice format. The Adverse Childhood Experiences (ACE) study asks about early history of violence, abuse, and neglect with simple yes/no questions like those depicted in **Figure 6.1** (Merrick et al., 2018).

Before your 18th birthday, did a parent or other adult in the household often or very often . . .

swear at you, insult you, put you down, or humiliate you?

*or*

act in a way that made you afraid that you might be physically hurt?

Before your 18th birthday, did a parent or other adult in the household often or very often . . .

push, grab, slap, or throw something at you?

*or*

hit you so hard that you had marks or were injured?

**FIGURE 6.1**
**ACE Questions.**

Questions from an online version of the Adverse Childhood Experiences (ACE) survey, which asks about early experiences with violence, abuse, and neglect.

In another question format, people are presented with a statement and are asked to use a rating scale to indicate their degree of agreement. When such a scale contains more than one item and each response value is labeled with the specific terms *strongly agree, agree, neither agree nor disagree, disagree,* and *strongly disagree,* it is often called a **Likert scale** (Likert, 1932). If it does not follow this format exactly (e.g., if it has only one item, or if its response labels differ from the original Likert labels), it may be called a *Likert-type scale.* Here is one of the ten items from a commonly used measure called the Rosenberg Self-Esteem Scale (Rosenberg, 1965), which uses a Likert scale:

*I am able to do things as well as most other people.*

| 1 | 2 | 3 | 4 | 5 |
|---|---|---|---|---|
| Strongly disagree | | | | Strongly agree |

Instead of degree of agreement, respondents might be asked to rate a target object using a numeric scale that is anchored with adjectives; this is called a **semantic differential format**. For example, on the Internet site RateMyProfessors.com, students assign ratings to a professor using the following adjective phrases:

*Overall Quality:*

Profs get F's too    1    2    3    4    5    A real gem

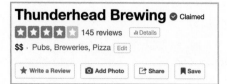

**FIGURE 6.2**
**A five-star restaurant rating on the Internet.**

Online ratings of products and services are examples of frequency claims. Is a five-star rating a valid indicator of a restaurant's quality?

*Level of Difficulty:*

| Show up and pass | 1 | 2 | 3 | 4 | 5 | Hardest thing I've ever done |

The five-star rating format that Internet rating sites (like Yelp) use is another example of this technique (**Figure 6.2**). Generally one star means "poor" or (on Yelp) "Eek! Methinks not," and five stars means "outstanding" or even "Woohoo! As good as it gets!"

There are other question types, of course, and researchers might combine formats on a single survey. The point is that the format of a question (open-ended, forced-choice, or Likert scale) does not make or break its construct validity. The way the questions are worded and the order in which they appear are much more important.

## Writing Well-Worded Questions

When you interrogate a survey result, your first question is about construct validity: How well was that variable measured? The way a question is worded and presented in a survey can make a tremendous difference in how people answer. It is crucial that each question be clear and straightforward. Poll and survey creators work to ensure that the wording and order of the questions do not influence respondents' answers.

### QUESTION WORDING MATTERS

An example of the way question wording can affect responses comes from survey research on a random sample of Delaware voters (Wilson & Brewer, 2016). The poll asked about people's support for voter identification laws, which require voters to show a photo ID before casting a ballot. Participants heard one of several different versions of the question. **Table 6.1** presents the results.

As you can see, different versions of the question led to different results. The second and third wordings might be called **leading questions**, because their wording leads people to a particular response. The results show that the wording matters. When people answer questions that suggest a particular viewpoint, at least some people change their answers.

In general, if the intention of a survey is to capture respondents' true opinions, the survey writers might attempt to word every question neutrally, avoiding potentially emotional terms. When researchers want to measure how much the wording matters for their topic, they word each question more than one way. If the results are the same regardless of the wording, they can conclude that question wording does not affect people's responses to that particular topic. If

TABLE 6.1

## Question wording matters

A random sample of Delaware voters were randomly assigned to one of three versions of a voter ID question.

| WHEN THE QUESTION WAS WORDED LIKE THIS: | DELAWARE VOTERS' SUPPORT FOR VOTER ID LAWS WAS: |
|---|---|
| What is your opinion? Do you strongly favor, mostly favor, mostly oppose, or strongly oppose voter ID laws? | 79% |
| Opponents of voter ID laws argue that they will prevent people who are eligible to vote from voting. What is your opinion? Do you strongly favor, mostly favor, mostly oppose, or strongly oppose voter ID laws? | 69% |
| Opponents of voter ID laws argue that they will prevent people who are eligible to vote from voting, and that the laws will affect African American voters especially hard. What is your opinion? Do you strongly favor, mostly favor, mostly oppose, or strongly oppose voter ID laws? | 61% |

the results differ, then they may need to report the results separately for each version of the question.

### DOUBLE-BARRELED QUESTIONS

The wording of a question is sometimes so complicated that respondents have trouble answering in a way that accurately reflects their opinions. In a survey, it is always best to ask a simple question. When people understand the question, they can give a clear, direct, and meaningful answer, but sometimes survey writers forget this basic guideline. For example, an online survey from the National Rifle Association asked this question:

> Do you agree that the Second Amendment to our United States Constitution guarantees your individual right to own a gun and that the Second Amendment is just as important as your other Constitutional rights?
>
> _____ Support
> _____ Oppose
> _____ No opinion

This is called a **double-barreled question**; it asks two questions in one. Double-barreled questions have poor construct validity because people might be responding to the first half of the question, the second half, or both. Therefore, the item could be measuring the first construct, the second construct, or both. Careful researchers would have asked each question separately:

**Do you agree that the Second Amendment guarantees your individual right to own a gun?**

_____ Support
_____ Oppose
_____ No opinion

**Do you agree that the Second Amendment is just as important as your other Constitutional rights?**

_____ Support
_____ Oppose
_____ No opinion

## NEGATIVE WORDING

**Negatively worded questions** are another way survey items can be unnecessarily complicated. Whenever a question contains negative phrasing, it can cause confusion, thereby reducing the construct validity of a survey or poll (Schwarz & Oyserman, 2001).

A classic example comes from a survey on Holocaust denial, which found that 20% of Americans denied that the Nazi Holocaust ever happened. In the months that followed the publication of this survey's results, writers and journalists criticized and analyzed the "intensely disturbing" news (Kagay, 1994).

Upon further investigation, the Roper polling organization reported that the people in the original telephone poll had been asked, "Does it seem possible or does it seem impossible to you that the Nazi extermination of the Jews never happened?" Think for a minute about how you would answer that question. If you wanted to convey the opinion that the Holocaust did happen, you would have to say, "It's impossible that it never happened." In order to give your opinion about the Holocaust accurately, you must also be able to unpack the double negative of *"impossible"* and *"never."* So instead of measuring people's beliefs, the question may be measuring people's working memory or their motivation to pay attention.

We know that this negatively worded question may have affected people's responses because the same polling organization repeated the survey less than a year later, asking the question more clearly: "Does it seem possible to you that the Nazi extermination of the Jews never happened, or do you feel certain that it happened?" This time, only 1% responded that the Holocaust might not have happened, 8% did not know, and 91% said they were certain it happened (Kagay, 1994). This later result, as well as other polls reflecting similarly low levels of Holocaust denial, indicates that the question as it was originally worded had poor construct validity: It probably did not measure people's true beliefs.

Sometimes even one negative word can make a question difficult to answer. For example, consider the following question:

*Abortion should never be restricted.*

| 1 | 2 | 3 | 4 | 5 |
|---|---|---|---|---|
| Disagree | | | | Agree |

To answer this question, those who oppose abortion must think in the double negative ("I *disagree* that abortion should *never* be restricted"), while those who support abortion rights would be able to answer more easily ("I agree—abortion should never be restricted").

When possible, negative wording should be avoided, but researchers sometimes ask questions both ways, like this:

*Abortion should never be restricted.*

| 1 | 2 | 3 | 4 | 5 |
|---|---|---|---|---|
| Disagree | | | | Agree |

*I favor strong restrictions on abortion.*

| 1 | 2 | 3 | 4 | 5 |
|---|---|---|---|---|
| Disagree | | | | Agree |

After asking the question both ways, the researchers can study the items' internal consistency (using Cronbach's alpha) to see whether people respond similarly to both questions. (In this case, agreement with the first item should correlate with disagreement with the second item.) Like double-barreled questions, negatively worded ones can reduce construct validity because they might capture people's ability to figure out the question rather than their true opinions.

« For more on Cronbach's alpha, see Chapter 5, pp. 131–132.

## QUESTION ORDER

The order in which questions are asked can also affect the responses to a survey. We might safely assume that respondents' answers to the first question on a survey is unaffected by any other questions, but the earlier questions sometimes change the way respondents understand and answer the later questions. For example, a question on a parenting survey such as "How often do your children play?" would have different meanings if the previous questions had been about sports versus music versus daily activities.

Consider this example: Political opinion researcher David Wilson and his colleagues asked people whether they supported affirmative action for different groups (Wilson et al., 2008). Half the participants were asked two forced-choice questions in this order:

1. Do you generally favor or oppose affirmative action programs for women?
2. Do you generally favor or oppose affirmative action for racial minorities?

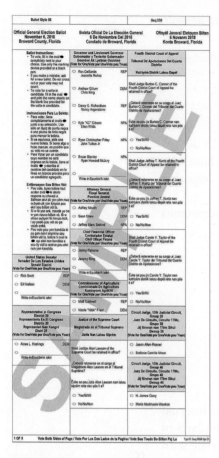

**FIGURE 6.3**

**Question order matters.**

People are up to 5% more likely to vote for the first person they see on a ballot (Miller & Krosnick, 1998). Because of this research, a Florida court ruled in 2019 that the party in power does not have the right to list its own candidates first.

The other half were asked the same two questions, but in the opposite order:

1. Do you generally favor or oppose affirmative action for racial minorities?
2. Do you generally favor or oppose affirmative action programs for women?

Wilson found that Whites reported more support for affirmative action for minorities when they had first been asked about affirmative action for women. Presumably, most Whites support affirmative action for women more than they do for minorities. To appear consistent, they might feel obligated to express support for affirmative action for racial minorities if they have just indicated their support for affirmative action for women (**Figure 6.3**).

The most direct way to control for the effect of question order is to prepare different versions of a survey, with the questions in different sequences. If the results for the first order differ from the results for the second order, researchers can report each set of results separately.

## Encouraging Accurate Responses

Careful researchers pay attention to how they word and order their survey questions. But what about the people who answer them? Overall, people can give meaningful responses to many kinds of questions (Paulhus & Vazire, 2007; Schwarz & Oyserman, 2001). In certain situations, people might give inaccurate answers because they don't make an effort to think about each question, because they want to look good, or because they are simply unable to report accurately about their own motivations and memories.

### PEOPLE CAN GIVE MEANINGFUL RESPONSES

Many students start out skeptical that people's self-reports can be trusted. But in fact self-reports can be ideal. People are able to report their own gender identity, happiness, income, ethnicity, and so on; there is no need to use expensive or difficult measures to collect such information. People can accurately report on things they did or that happened to them. More important, self-reports often provide the only meaningful information you can get. Diener and his colleagues were specifically interested in subjective well-being (see Chapter 5), so it made sense to ask participants to self-report on aspects of their life satisfaction (Diener et al., 1985). Who else but you knows how happy you feel?

In some cases, self-reports might be the only option. For example, researchers who study dreaming can monitor brain activity to identify *when* someone is dreaming, but they need to use self-reports to find out the *content* of the person's dreams. Other traits are not very observable, such as how anxious somebody is feeling or whether someone has been a victim of violence. Therefore, it is meaningful and effective to ask people to self-report on their own experiences (Becker-Blease & Freyd, 2006; Vazire & Carlson, 2011).

## SOMETIMES PEOPLE USE SHORTCUTS

At times, however, self-reports are imperfect. **Response sets**, also known as *non-differentiation*, are a type of shortcut people can take when answering survey questions. Although response sets do not cause many problems for answering a single, stand-alone item, people might adopt a consistent way of answering all the questions—especially toward the end of a long questionnaire (Lelkes et al., 2012). Rather than thinking carefully about each question, people might answer all of them positively, negatively, or neutrally. Response sets weaken construct validity because these survey respondents are not saying what they really think.

One potential response set is **acquiescence**, or *yea-saying*. This occurs when people say "yes" or "strongly agree" to every item instead of thinking carefully about each one. For example, a respondent might answer "5" to every item on Diener's scale of subjective well-being—not because the respondent is happy, but because that person is using a yea-saying shortcut (**Figure 6.4**). People apparently have a bias to agree with (say "yes" to) any item—no matter what it states (Krosnick, 1999). Acquiescence can threaten construct validity because instead of measuring the construct of true feelings of well-being, the survey could be measuring the tendency to agree or the lack of motivation to think carefully.

How can researchers tell the difference between a respondent who is yea-saying and one who really does agree with all the items? The most common way is by including reverse-worded items. Diener might have changed the wording of some items to mean their opposite; for instance, "If I had my life to live over, I'd change almost *everything*." One benefit is that reverse-worded items might slow people down so they answer more carefully. (Before computing a scale average for each person, the researchers rescore only the reverse-worded items such that, for example, "strongly disagree" becomes a 5 and "strongly agree" becomes a 1.) The scale with reverse-worded items would have more construct validity because high or low averages would be measuring true happiness or unhappiness, instead of acquiescence.

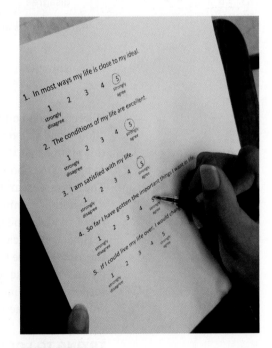

**FIGURE 6.4**
**Response sets.**

When people use an acquiescent response set, they agree with almost every question or statement. It can be hard to know whether they really mean it or whether they're just using a shortcut to respond to the questions.

A drawback of reverse-wording is that sometimes it results in negatively worded items, which are more difficult to answer.

Another specific response set is **fence sitting**—playing it safe by answering in the middle of the scale, especially when survey items are controversial. People might also answer in the middle (or say "I don't know") when a question is confusing or unclear. Fence sitters can weaken a survey's construct validity when middle-of-the-road scores suggest that some responders don't have an opinion, though they actually do. Of course, some people honestly may have no opinion on the questions; in that case, they choose the middle option for a valid reason. It can be difficult to distinguish those who are unwilling to take a side from those who are truly ambivalent.

Researchers may try to jostle people out of this tendency. One approach is to take away the neutral option. Compare these two formats:

*Race relations are going well in this country.*

    ◯      ◯      ◯      ◯      ◯

Strongly                             Strongly
disagree                             agree

*Race relations are going well in this country.*

    ◯      ◯      ◯      ◯

Strongly                     Strongly
disagree                   agree

When a scale contains an even number of response options, the person has to choose one side or the other because there is no neutral choice. The drawback of this approach is that sometimes people really do not have an opinion or an answer, so having to choose a side is an invalid representation of their truly neutral stance. Therefore, researchers must carefully consider which format is best.

Another common way to get people off the fence is to use forced-choice questions, in which people must pick one of two answers. Although this reduces fence sitting, again it can frustrate people who feel their own opinion is somewhere in the middle of the two options. In some telephone surveys, interviewers will write down a response of "I don't know" or "No opinion" if a person volunteers that response. Thus, more people get off the fence, but truly ambivalent people can also validly report their neutral opinions.

**TRYING TO LOOK GOOD**

Most of us want to look good in the eyes of others, but when survey respondents give answers that make them look better than they really are, these responses decrease the survey's construct validity. This phenomenon is known as **socially desirable responding**, or **faking good**. The idea is that because respondents are embarrassed, shy, or worried about giving an unpopular opinion, they will not tell the truth on a survey or other self-report measure. A similar, but less common, phenomenon is called **faking bad**.

To avoid socially desirable responding, a researcher might ensure that the participants know their responses are anonymous—perhaps by conducting the survey online, or in the case of an in-person interview, reminding people of their anonymity right before asking sensitive questions (Schwarz & Oyserman, 2001). However, anonymity may not be a perfect solution. Anonymous respondents may treat surveys less seriously. In one study, anonymous respondents were more likely to start using response sets in long surveys. In addition, anonymous people were less likely to accurately report a simple behavior, such as how many candies they had just eaten, which suggests they were paying less attention to details (Lelkes et al., 2012).

One way to minimize this problem is to include special survey items that identify socially desirable responders with target items like these (Crowne & Marlowe, 1960):

> My table manners at home are as good as when I eat out in a restaurant.
> I don't find it particularly difficult to get along with loud-mouthed, obnoxious people.

If people agree with many such items, researchers may discard that individual's data from the final set, under suspicion that they are exaggerating on the other survey items or not paying close attention in general.

Researchers can also ask people's friends to rate them. When it comes to domains where we want to look good (e.g., on how rude or how smart we are), others know us better than we know ourselves (Vazire & Carlson, 2011). Thus, researchers might be better off asking people's friends to rate them on traits that are observable but desirable.

Finally, researchers may use computerized measures to evaluate people's implicit opinions about sensitive topics. One widely used test, the Implicit Association Test, asks people to respond quickly to positive and negative words on the right and left of a computer screen (Greenwald et al., 2003). Intermixed with the positive and negative words are instances of different social groups, such as males and females, Blacks and Whites, or Middle Eastern females and White females. People respond to all possible pairs. For example, they respond to positive words with Black faces, negative words with White faces, negative words with Black faces, and positive words with White faces. When people respond more efficiently to the White-positive/Black-negative combination than to the White-negative/Black-positive combination, researchers infer that the person may hold negative attitudes on an implicit, or unconscious, level (Jost, 2019).

## SELF-REPORTING "MORE THAN THEY CAN KNOW"

In general, people are *capable* of reporting accurately on their own feelings, thoughts, and actions. Everyone knows their opinions better than anyone else does. Only *I* know my level of support for a political candidate. Only *the patrons* know how much they liked that restaurant. In certain cases, however, self-reports can be inaccurate, especially when people are asked to describe *why* they are thinking, behaving, or feeling the way they do. When asked, most people willingly provide an explanation or an opinion to a researcher, but sometimes they unintentionally give inaccurate responses.

Psychologists Richard Nisbett and Timothy Wilson (1977) conducted a set of studies to demonstrate this phenomenon. In one study, they put six pairs of nylon stockings on a table and asked female shoppers in a store to tell them which of the stockings they preferred. As it turned out, almost everyone selected the last pair on the right. The reason for this preference was something of a mystery—especially since all the stockings were exactly the same! (Researchers have speculated people are biased toward the last item they evaluate.) Next, the researchers asked each woman why she selected the pair she did. Every participant reported that she selected the pair on the right for its excellent quality. Even when the researchers suggested they might have chosen the pair because it was on the far right side of the table, the women insisted they made their choices based on the quality of the stockings. In other words, the women easily formulated answers for the researchers, but their answers had nothing to do with the real reason they selected the one pair of stockings (**Figure 6.5**). Moreover, the women did not seem to be aware they were inventing a justification for their preference. They gave a sincere, reasonable response—one that just happened to be wrong. Therefore, researchers cannot assume the reasons people give for their own behavior are their actual reasons. People may not be able to accurately explain *why* they acted as they did.

### SELF-REPORTING MEMORIES OF EVENTS

What about people's memories for events in their own lifetimes? People can usually report accurately on what happened a few days ago, but what about more distant memories?

Memories for significant life experiences can be quite accurate. For example, studies have tested ways to validate adult reports of adverse childhood experiences (ACEs). One way is to locate cases of childhood abuse that were officially documented by courts or hospitals. When researchers have given ACE-related questions to court-documented victims of abuse (without revealing why they were asking), most of them did report a history of abuse, as we would expect. Other studies have shown that people accurately recalled their own abuse, even if they were not accurate about details of specific incidents (see Hardt & Rutter, 2004, for a review). The conclusion

**FIGURE 6.5**
**The accuracy of self-reports.**

If you ask this shopper why he chooses one of these items, he will probably give you a reasonable answer. But does his answer represent the true reason for making his choice?

here is that people's accounts of adverse events—and many other events—should be trusted (Becker-Blease & Freyd, 2006).

In some cases, people's certainty about their memories might not match their accuracy. For example, some people failed to recall abuse that had been documented (so-called false negatives; Hardt & Rutter, 2004; Williams, 1994). They were certain they had never been victimized, despite records from their childhood that confirmed abuse.

Another example comes from people's vivid memories of exactly where they were when they heard the news that two planes had crashed into New York's World Trade Center on September 11, 2001. Cognitive psychologists have checked the accuracy of such "flashbulb memories." To conduct such a study, researchers administer a short questionnaire to people on the day after a dramatic event, asking them to recall where they were, with whom, and so forth. A few weeks or years later, the same people answer the same questions as before and also rate how vivid their memories are and how confident they are in them. People's flashbulb memories remain vivid over time (Talarico & Rubin, 2003), even as they decline in accuracy. For example, years later, about 73% of people recalling their memories of the 9/11 attacks remembered seeing the first plane hit the World Trade Center on TV, when in fact no such footage was available at that time (Pezdek, 2003).

The important finding from these studies is that vividness and confidence are unrelated to how accurate the memories actually are. Years later, people who are extremely confident in their memories are about as likely to be wrong as people who report their memories with little or no confidence (Neisser & Harsch, 1992). People's feelings of confidence in their memories do not, by themselves, inform us about their accuracy.

## RATING CONSUMER PRODUCTS

What about the special case of online product ratings? Online ratings are examples of frequency claims. Are consumers able to make good judgments about products they have purchased and used? One study found little correspondence between five-star ratings on Amazon.com and the ratings of the same products by Consumer Reports, an independent product rating firm (De Langhe et al., 2016). The researchers found that consumers' ratings were, instead, correlated with the cost of the product and the prestige of its brand. Studies like these suggest that people may not always be able to accurately report on the quality of products they buy (**Figure 6.6**).

**FIGURE 6.6**

**Do consumer ratings match expert ratings?**

This camera's online reviews were positive, but Consumer Reports (an independent rating firm) ranked it second to last. While consumers may be able to report their subjective experience with a product, their ratings might not accurately predict product quality.

**CHECK YOUR UNDERSTANDING**

1. What are three potential problems related to the wording of survey questions? Can they be avoided?

2. Name at least two ways to ensure that survey questions are answered accurately.

3. For which topics, and in what situations, are people most likely to answer survey questions accurately ?

1. See pp. 156–159. 2. See pp. 160–163. 3. See pp. 159–160.

# CONSTRUCT VALIDITY OF BEHAVIORAL OBSERVATIONS

Survey and poll results are among the most common types of data used to support a frequency claim—the kind you read most often in newspapers or on websites. Researchers also study people simply by watching them in action. When a researcher watches people or animals and systematically records how they behave or what they are doing, it is called **observational research**. Because people cannot always report on their behavior or past events accurately, some scientists believe observing behavior is better than collecting self-reports through surveys. Given the potential effects of question order, response sets, socially desirable responding, and other problems, many psychologists trust behavioral data more than survey data, at least for some variables.

Observational research can be the basis for frequency claims. Researchers might record how much people eat in fast-food restaurants or observe whether drivers stop for a pedestrian in a crosswalk. They might test the balance of athletes who have been hit on the head during practice or watch families as they eat dinner. Observational research is not just for frequency claims: Observations can also be used to operationalize variables in association claims and causal claims. Regardless of the type of claim, it is important that observational measures have good construct validity.

## Some Claims Based on Observational Data

Self-report questions can be excellent measures of what people *think* they are doing and of what they *think* is influencing their behavior. But if you want to know what people are *really* doing or what *really* influences their behavior, you should probably watch them. Here are three examples of how observational methods have been used to answer research questions in psychology.

## OBSERVING HOW MUCH PEOPLE TALK

Matthias Mehl and his colleagues kept track of what people say in everyday contexts (Mehl et al., 2007). The researchers recruited several samples of students and asked them to wear an electronically activated recorder (EAR) for 2–10 days (depending on the sample). This device contains a small, clip-on microphone and a digital sound recorder similar to an iPod (**Figure 6.7A**). At 12.5-minute intervals throughout the day, the EAR records 30 seconds of ambient sound. Later, research assistants transcribe everything the person says during the recorded time periods. The published data demonstrate that, on average, women spoke 16,215 words per day, while men spoke 15,669 (**Figure 6.7B**). This difference is tiny (about 3% more), so despite stereotypes of women being the chattier gender, women and men showed the same level of speaking, at least in this sample.

## OBSERVING WHERE BABIES AND CAREGIVERS LOOK

A team of researchers investigated babies and their parents during play to determine how much time they spent looking at each other's faces versus looking at the toys. Individual parents and their 12-month-old babies participated in pairs. Each was fitted with a special device that recorded their eye movements while

**A**

**B**

STRAIGHT FROM THE SOURCE

**Table 1.** Estimated number of words spoken per day for female and male study participants across six samples. *N* = 396. Year refers to the year when the data collection started; duration refers to the approximate number of days participants wore the EAR; the weighted average weighs the respective sample group mean by the sample size of the group.

| Sample | Year | Location | Duration | Age range (years) | Sample size (*N*) | | Estimated average number (SD) of words spoken per day | |
|---|---|---|---|---|---|---|---|---|
| | | | | | Women | Men | Women | Men |
| 1 | 2004 | USA | 7 days | 18–29 | 56 | 56 | 18,443 (7460) | 16,576 (7871) |
| 2 | 2003 | USA | 4 days | 17–23 | 42 | 37 | 14,297 (6441) | 14,060 (9065) |
| 3 | 2003 | Mexico | 4 days | 17–25 | 31 | 20 | 14,704 (6215) | 15,022 (7864) |
| 4 | 2001 | USA | 2 days | 17–22 | 47 | 49 | 16,177 (7520) | 16,569 (9108) |
| 5 | 2001 | USA | 10 days | 18–26 | 7 | 4 | 15,761 (8985) | 24,051 (10,211) |
| 6 | 1998 | USA | 4 days | 17–23 | 27 | 20 | 16,496 (7914) | 12,867 (8343) |
| | | | | | Weighted average | | 16,215 (7301) | 15,669 (8633) |

**FIGURE 6.7**

**Observational research on daily spoken words.**

(**A**) Study participants wore a small recording device to measure how many words they spoke per day. (**B**) This table shows the study's results as they were reported in the original empirical journal article. (Source: Mehl et al., 2007, Table 1.)

Infant's view   Caregiver's view

Third-person view

walking wings

**FIGURE 6.8**

**Using eye trackers in observational research.**

**Bottom panel:** A baby and her mother wear special cameras that detect exactly where their eyes are directed. **Upper left:** This camera shows the infant's viewpoint. The crosshairs indicate the baby is looking at the toy apple. **Upper right:** This camera shows the parent's viewpoint. The crosshairs indicate the parent is looking at her baby's face. (Source: Franchak et al., 2016.)

they played freely in a laboratory playroom (Franchak et al., 2016; **Figure 6.8**). Later, the researchers looked frame-by-frame at the resulting video and recorded where each person was looking. One key result was that babies spent much more time looking at toys than at their parent, but that caregivers looked equally at the toys and their baby.

### OBSERVING FAMILIES IN THE EVENING

A third example comes from a study of families in which both parents work (Campos et al., 2013). The researchers had camera crews follow both parents from a sample of 30 dual-earner families from the time they got home from work until 8:00 PM. Later, teams of assistants coded a variety of behaviors from the resulting videotapes. The researchers studied two aspects of family life: the emotional tone of the parents and the topics of conversation during dinner.

To code emotional tone, they watched the videos, rating each parent on a 7-point scale. The rating scale went from 1 (cold/hostile) to 4 (neutral) to 7 (warm/happy). The results showed that emotional tone in the families was very slightly positive in the evening hours (around 4.2 on the 7-point scale). In addition, they found that kids and parents differed in what they discussed at dinnertime. The kids were more likely to express distaste at the food, while the parents talked about how healthy it was (**Figure 6.9**). In addition to these frequency estimates, the researchers also studied associations. For example, they found that mothers' (but not fathers') emotional tone was more negative when children complained about the food at dinner.

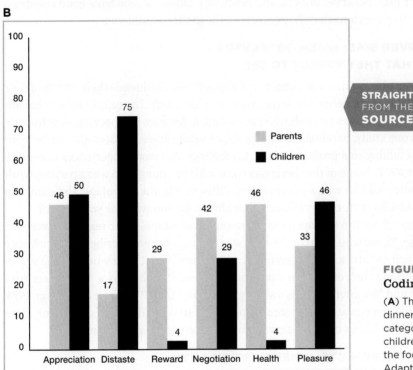

**A**

**Dinnertime talk.** Coders documented whether each family member present engaged in each of the following six types of food-related talk: (a) expressions of appreciation, (b) expressions of distaste, (c) reference to health, (d) reference to pleasure, (e) reference to food as a reward, and (f) negotiation over the terms of food rewards or penalties.

**B**

STRAIGHT
FROM THE
SOURCE

**FIGURE 6.9**
**Coding dinnertime topics.**

(**A**) The coders assigned each piece of dinnertime conversation to one of six categories. (**B**) The results showed that children were most likely to express distaste at the food their parents had prepared. (Source: Adapted from Campos et al., 2013.)

## OBSERVATIONS CAN BE BETTER THAN SELF-REPORTS

The previous examples illustrate a variety of ways researchers have conducted observational studies. Let's reflect on the benefits of behavioral observation in these cases. What might have happened if the researchers had asked the participants to self-report? The college students certainly would not have been able to estimate how many words they spoke each day. Parents might report that they look more at their adorable babies than at toys, but the babies could not have reported at all! And while parents could report on how they were feeling in the evening and at dinner, they might not have been able to describe how emotionally warm their expressions appeared to others—the part that matters to their partners and children. Observations can sometimes tell a more accurate story than self-reporting (Vazire & Carlson, 2011).

# Making Reliable and Valid Observations

Observational research is a way to operationalize a conceptual variable, so when interrogating a study we need to ask about the construct validity of any observational measure. We ask: What is the variable of interest, and did the observations accurately measure that variable? Although observational research may seem straightforward, researchers must work diligently to be sure their observations are reliable and valid.

The construct validity of observations can be threatened by three problems: observer bias, observer effects, and reactivity. Observations have good construct validity to the extent that they can avoid these three problems.

## OBSERVER BIAS: WHEN OBSERVERS SEE WHAT THEY EXPECT TO SEE

**Observer bias** occurs when observers' expectations influence their interpretation of the participants' behaviors or the outcome of the study. Instead of rating behaviors objectively, observers rate behaviors according to their own expectations or hypotheses. In one study, psychoanalytic therapists were shown a videotape of a 26-year-old man talking to a professor about his feelings and work experiences (Langer & Abelson, 1974). Some of the therapists were told the young man was a patient, while others were told he was a job applicant. After seeing the videotape, the clinicians were asked for their observations. What kind of person was this young man?

Although all the therapists saw the same videotape, their reactions were not the same. Those who thought the man was a job applicant described him with such terms such as "attractive," "candid," and "innovative." Those who saw the videotape thinking the young man was a patient described him as a "tight, defensive person" and "frightened of his own aggressive impulses" (Langer & Abelson, 1974, p. 8). Since everyone saw the same tape, these striking differences can only have reflected the biases of the observers in interpreting what they saw.

## OBSERVER EFFECTS: WHEN PARTICIPANTS CONFIRM OBSERVER EXPECTATIONS

It is problematic when observer biases affect researchers' own interpretations of what they see. It is even worse when the observers inadvertently change the behavior of those they are observing, such that participant behavior changes to match observer expectations. Known as **observer effects**, or *expectancy effects*, this phenomenon can occur even in seemingly objective observations.

**Bright and Dull Rats.** In a classic study of observer effects, researchers Rosenthal and Fode (1963) gave each student in an advanced psychology course five rats to test as part of a final lab experience in the course. Each student timed how long it took for their rats to learn a simple maze, every day for several days. Although each student received a randomly selected group of rats, the researchers told half of them that their rats were bred to be "maze-bright" and the other half that their rats were bred to be "maze-dull."

Even though all the rats were genetically similar, those that were believed to be maze-bright completed the maze a little faster each day and with fewer mistakes. In contrast, the rats believed to be maze-dull did not improve their performance over the testing days. Each group of rats behaved in ways that matched their observers' expectations. This study showed that observers not only see what they expect to see; sometimes they even cause the behavior of those they are observing to conform to their expectations.

**Clever Hans.** A horse nicknamed Clever Hans provides another classic example of how observers' subtle behavior changed a subject's behavior—and how scientifically minded observers corrected the problem (Heinzen et al., 2015). More than 100 years ago, a retired schoolteacher named William von Osten tutored his horse, Hans, in mathematics. If he asked Hans to add 3 and 2, for example, the horse would tap his hoof five times and then stop. After 4 years of daily training, Clever Hans could perform math at least as well as an average fifth-grader, identify colors, and read German words (**Figure 6.10**). Von Osten allowed many scientists to test his horse's abilities, and all were satisfied that von Osten was not giving Hans cues on the sly because the horse apparently could do arithmetic even when his owner was not present.

**FIGURE 6.10**
**William von Osten and Clever Hans.**

The horse Clever Hans could detect nonverbal gestures from anybody—not just his owner—so his behavior even convinced a special commission of experts in 1904.

Just when other scientists had concluded Clever Hans was truly capable of doing math, an experimental psychologist, Oskar Pfungst, came up with a more rigorous set of checks (Pfungst, 1911). Suspecting the animal was sensing subtle nonverbal cues from his human questioners, Pfungst showed the horse a series of cards printed with numbers. He alternated situations in which the questioner could or could not see each card. As Pfungst suspected, Hans was correct only when his questioner saw the card.

As it turned out, the horse *was* extremely clever—but not at math. He was smart at detecting the subtle head movements of the questioner. Pfungst noticed that a questioner would lean over to watch Hans tap his foot, raising his head a bit at the last correct tap. Clever Hans had learned this slight move was the cue to stop tapping (Heinzen et al., 2015).

## PREVENTING OBSERVER BIAS AND OBSERVER EFFECTS

Researchers must ensure the construct validity of observational measures by taking steps to avoid observer bias and observer effects. First and foremost, careful researchers train their observers well. They develop clear rating instructions, often called *codebooks*, so the observers can make reliable judgments with minimal bias. Codebooks are precise statements of how the variables are operationalized, and the more precise and clear the codebook statements are, the more valid the

*Emotional tone.* To measure emotional tone, coders rated the extent to which the behavior of each parent was marked by verbal and nonverbal markers of coldness/hostility or warmth/happiness on a Likert scale (1 = *cold/hostile*; 4 = *neutral*; 7 = *warm/happy*). Cold/hostile emotional tone was defined as short communication, flat or angry affect, and no evidence of positive affect. Neutral tone was defined as a task oriented, practical tone that was neither cold/hostile nor warm/happy. Warm/happy emotional tone was defined as warm voice tones, smiles, laughter, and head nods with no evidence of negative affect. Coders independently rated a parent's emotional tone when they appeared in the video (a) alone, (b) with their partner (if present), or (c) with their 7- to 12-year-old child (if present). The latter rating was restricted to the 7- to 12-year-old child that all families were required to have to standardize interaction that might otherwise vary with stage of child development. Thus, up to three emotional tone variables could be rated for each parent in each 30-s video slice. Interrater reliabilities for emotional tone alone (ICC = .92), with partner (ICC = .91), and with child (ICC = .95) were high.

> Interrater reliability of this observation.

**FIGURE 6.11**

**Coding emotional tone.**

Here is how the researchers reported the way they coded emotional tone in the Method section of their article. (Source: Adapted from Campos et al., 2013.)

operationalizations will be. **Figure 6.11** shows how emotional tone was coded in the family observation study.

Researchers can assess the construct validity of a coded measure by using multiple observers. Doing so allows the researchers to assess the interrater reliability of their measures. The excerpt shown in Figure 6.11 shows how researchers discuss the interrater reliability of the emotional tone ratings. The abbreviation ICC is a correlation that quantifies degree of agreement. The closer the correlation is to 1.0, the more the observers agreed with one another. The coders in this case showed acceptable interrater reliability.

»
For more on interrater reliability, see Chapter 5, pp. 125–132.

Using multiple observers does not eliminate anyone's biases, of course, but if two observers of the same event agree on what happened, the researchers can be more confident. If there is disagreement, the researchers may need to train their observers better, develop a clearer coding system for rating the behaviors, or both.

Even when an operationalization has good interrater reliability, it still might not be valid. When two observers agree with each other, they might share the same biases, so their common observations are not necessarily valid. Think about the therapists in the Langer and Abelson (1974) study. Those who were told the man in the videotape was a patient might have showed interrater reliability in their descriptions of how defensive or frightened he appeared. But because they shared similar biases, their reliable ratings were not valid descriptions of the man's behavior. Therefore, interrater reliability is only half the story; researchers should employ methods that minimize observer bias and observer effects.

**Masked Research Design.** The Rosenthal and Fode (1963) study and the Clever Hans effect both demonstrate that observers can give unintentional cues that influence the behavior of their subjects. A common way to prevent observer bias and observer effects is to use a **masked design**, or *blind design*, in which the observers are unaware of the purpose of the study and the conditions to which participants have been assigned.

If Rosenthal and Fode's students had not known which rats were expected to be bright and dull, the students would not have evoked different behavior in their charges. Similarly, when Clever Hans' observers did not know the right answer to the questions they were asking, the horse acted differently and seemed much less intelligent. These examples make it clear that coders and observers should not be aware of a study's hypotheses, or steps should be taken to mask the conditions they are observing.

## REACTIVITY: WHEN PARTICIPANTS REACT TO BEING WATCHED

Sometimes the mere presence of an outsider is enough to change the behavior of those being observed. Suppose you're visiting a first-grade classroom to observe the children. You walk quietly to the back of the room and sit down to watch what the children do. What will you see? A roomful of little heads swiveled around looking at you! Do first graders usually spend most of their time staring at the back of the room? Of course not. What you are witnessing is an example of reactivity.

**Reactivity** is a change in behavior when study participants know another person is watching. They might react by being on their best behavior—or in some cases, their worst—rather than displaying their typical behavior. Reactivity occurs not only with human participants but also with animal subjects. If people and animals can change their behavior just because they are being watched, what should a careful researcher do?

**Solution 1: Blend In.** One way to avoid observer effects is to make **unobtrusive observations**—that is, make yourself less noticeable. A developmental psychologist doing research might sit behind a one-way mirror, like the one shown in **Figure 6.12**, in order to observe how children interact in a classroom without letting them know. In a public setting, a researcher might act like a casual onlooker—another face in the crowd—to watch how other people behave.

**Solution 2: Wait It Out.** Another solution is to wait out the situation. A researcher who plans to observe at a school might let the children get used to his or her presence until they forget they're being watched. The anthropologist Jane Goodall, in her studies of chimpanzees in the wild, used a similar tactic. When she began introducing herself to the chimps in the

**FIGURE 6.12**
**Unobtrusive observations.**

This one-way mirror lets researchers unobtrusively record the behaviors of children in a preschool classroom.

Gombe National Park in Africa, they fled or stopped whatever else they were doing to focus on her. After several months, the chimps got used to having her around and were no longer afraid to go about their usual activities in her presence. Similarly, participants in the Mehl EAR study reported that after a couple of days of wearing the device, they did not find it to be invasive (Mehl & Pennebaker, 2003).

**Solution 3: Measure the Behavior's Results.** Another way to avoid reactivity is to use unobtrusive data. Instead of observing behavior directly, researchers measure the traces a particular behavior leaves behind. For example, in a museum, wear-and-tear on the flooring can signal which areas of the museum are the most popular, and the height of smudges on the windows can indicate the age of visitors. The number of empty liquor bottles in residential garbage cans indicates how much alcohol is being consumed in a community (Webb et al., 1966). Using these indirect methods, researchers can measure behavior without doing any direct participant observation.

## OBSERVING PEOPLE ETHICALLY

Is it ethical for researchers to observe the behaviors of others? It depends. Most psychologists believe it is ethical to watch people in museums and classrooms, at sports events, or even at the sinks of public bathrooms because in those settings people can reasonably expect their activities to be public, not private. Of course, when psychologists report the results of such observational studies, they do not specifically identify any of the people who were observed.

More secretive methods, such as one-way mirrors and covert video recording, are also considered ethical in some conditions. In most cases, psychologists doing research must obtain permission in advance to watch or to record people's private behavior. If hidden video recording is used, the researcher must explain the procedure at the conclusion of the study. If people object to having been recorded, the researcher must erase the file without watching it.

Certain ethical decisions may be influenced by the policies of a university where a study is conducted. As discussed in Chapter 4, institutional review boards (IRBs) assess each study to decide whether it can be conducted ethically.

---

✔

### CHECK YOUR UNDERSTANDING

1. Sketch a concept map of observer bias, observer effects, and reactivity, and indicate the approaches researchers can take to minimize each problem.

2. Explain why each of these three problems can threaten construct validity, using this sentence structure for each issue:

   If an observational study suffers from _____, then the researcher might be measuring _____ instead of _____.

1. See pp. 170–174. 2. See pp. 170 and 172.

# CHAPTER REVIEW

 It's time to complete your study experience! Go to INQUIZITIVE to practice actively with this chapter's concepts and get personalized feedback along the way.

## Summary

Surveys, polls, and observational methods are used to support frequency claims, but they also measure variables for association and causal claims. When interrogating a claim based on data from a survey or an observational study, we ask about the construct validity of the measurement.

### CONSTRUCT VALIDITY OF SURVEYS AND POLLS

- Survey question formats include open-ended, forced-choice, Likert scale, and semantic differential.

- Sometimes the way a survey question is worded can lead people to be more likely or less likely to agree with it.

- Double-barreled and negatively worded questions are difficult to answer in a valid way.

- People sometimes answer survey questions with an acquiescent or fence-sitting response tendency or in a way that makes them look good. To avoid some of these problems, researchers can add items to a survey or change the way questions are written.

- Surveys are efficient and accurate ways to assess people's subjective feelings and opinions; they may be less appropriate for assessing people's actual behavior, motivations, or certain memories.

### CONSTRUCT VALIDITY OF BEHAVIORAL OBSERVATIONS

- Observational studies record people's true behavior, rather than what people say about their behavior.

- Well-trained coders and clear codebooks help ensure that observations will be reliable and not influenced by observer expectations.

- Some observational studies are susceptible to reactivity. Masked designs and unobtrusive observations make it more likely that observers will not make biased ratings, and that participants will not change their behavior in reaction to being observed.

- Local IRB guidelines may vary, but in general, it is considered ethical to conduct observational research in public settings where people expect to be seen by others.

## Key Terms

To see samples of chapter concepts in the popular media, visit www.everydayresearchmethods.com and click the box for Chapter 6.

# Review Questions

1. The following item appears on a survey: "Was your cell phone purchased within the last two years and have you downloaded the most recent updates?" What is the biggest problem with this wording?

   a. It is a leading question.

   b. It involves negative wording.

   c. It is a double-barreled question.

   d. It is not on a Likert scale.

2. When people are using an acquiescent response set they are:

   a. Trying to give the responses they think the researcher wants to hear.

   b. Misrepresenting their views to appear more socially acceptable.

   c. Giving the same, neutral answer to each question.

   d. Tending to agree with every item, no matter what it says.

3. In which of the following situations do people most accurately answer survey questions?

   a. When they are describing the reasons for their own behavior.

   b. When they are describing what happened to them, especially after important events.

   c. When they are describing their subjective experience; how they personally feel about something.

   d. People almost never answer survey questions accurately.

4. Which of the following makes it more likely that behavioral observations will have good interrater reliability?

   a. A masked study design

   b. A clear codebook

   c. Using naive, untrained coders

   d. Open-ended responses

5. Which one of the following is a means of controlling for observer bias?

   a. Using unobtrusive observations.

   b. Waiting for the participants to become used to the observer.

   c. Making sure the observer does not know the study's hypotheses.

   d. Measuring physical traces of behavior rather than observing behavior directly.

6. Which of the following is a way of preventing reactivity?

   a. Waiting for the participants to become used to the observer.

   b. Making sure the observers do not know the study's hypotheses.

   c. Making sure the observer uses a clear codebook.

   d. Ensuring the observers have good interrater reliability.

# Learning Actively

1. Consider the various survey question formats: open-ended, forced-choice, Likert scale, and semantic differential. For each of the following research topics, write a question in each format, keeping in mind some of the pitfalls in question writing. Which of the questions you wrote would have the best construct validity, and why?

   a. A study that measures attitudes about women serving in combat roles in the military.

   b. A customer service survey asking people about their satisfaction with their most recent shopping experience.

   c. A poll that asks people which political party they have supported in the past.

2. As part of their Well-Being Index, the Gallup organization asks a daily sample of Americans, "In the last seven days, on how many days did you exercise

for 30 or more minutes?" If people say they have exercised three or more days, Gallup classifies them as "frequent exercisers." Gallup finds that between about 47% (in the winter months) and 55% (in the summer) report being frequent exercisers (Gallup, n.d.). What kind of question is this: forced-choice, Likert scale, semantic differential, or some other format? Does the item appear to be leading, negatively worded, or double-barreled? Do you think it leads to accurate responses?

3. Plan an observational study to see which kind of drivers are more likely to stop for a pedestrian in a crosswalk: male or female drivers. Think about how to maximize your construct validity. Will observers be biased about what they record? How might they influence the people they're watching, if at all? Where should they stand to observe driver behavior? How will you evaluate the interrater reliability of your observers? Write a two- to three-sentence operational definition of what it means to "stop for a pedestrian in a crosswalk." The definition should be clear enough that if you asked two friends to use it to code "stopping for pedestrian" behavior, it would have good reliability and validity.

4. To study the kinds of faces babies usually see, researchers asked parents to place tiny video cameras on their 1-month-old and 3-month-old infants during their waking hours (Sugden et al., 2013). Coders viewed the resulting video footage frame by frame, categorizing the gender, race, and age of the faces each baby saw. The results revealed that babies are exposed to faces 25% of their waking hours. In addition, the babies in the sample were exposed to female faces 70% of the time, and 96% of the time they were exposed to faces that were the same race as themselves. What questions might you ask to decide whether the observational measures in this study were susceptible to observer bias, observer effects, or reactivity?

**8 Out of 10 Drivers Say They Experience Road Rage**

CBS LOCAL, 2016

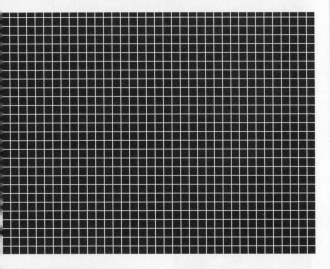

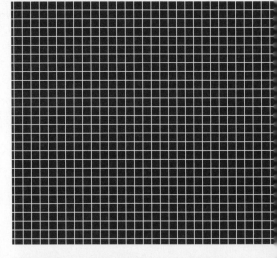

**Nearly 9 in 10 Afghans Are Suffering**

GALLUP, 2019

**61% Said This Shoe "Felt True to Size"**

ZAPPOS.COM

 *Fit Survey:* **61%** Felt true to size

# 7

# Sampling: Estimating the Frequency of Behaviors and Beliefs

THE CLAIMS THAT OPEN this chapter address a variety of topics: driving behavior, well-being, and the fit of a pair of shoes. The target population in each case is different. One example is about American drivers, one applies to people in Afghanistan, and the last represents online shoppers. In all three claims, we are being asked to believe something about a larger group of people (e.g., all U.S. drivers or all 35 million people of Afghanistan), based on data from a smaller sample that was actually studied. In this chapter, you'll learn when we can use a sample to generalize to a population, and when we cannot. In addition, you'll learn when we really care about being able to generalize to a population, and when it's less important.

## GENERALIZABILITY: DOES THE SAMPLE REPRESENT THE POPULATION?

When interrogating external validity, we ask whether the results of a particular study can be generalized to some larger population of interest. External validity is often extremely important for frequency claims. To interrogate the external validity of frequency claims such as those discussed in Chapter 6 and also presented here, we might ask the following types of questions:

"Does the sample of drivers who were asked about road rage adequately represent American drivers?"

"Can feelings of the Afghan people in the sample generalize to all the people in Afghanistan?"

"Do the people who reviewed the fit of these shoes represent the population of people who wear them?"

as well as (from Chapter 6) . . .

"Do the people who responded to this survey about adverse childhood experiences represent the larger population of our country?"

"Can we predict the results of the election if the polling sample consisted of 1,500 people?"

Recall that external validity concerns both *samples* and *settings*. A researcher may intend the results of a study to generalize to the other members of a certain population, as in the questions above. Or a researcher may intend the results to generalize to other settings, such as other shoes from the same manufacturer, other products, or other classes taught by the same professor. This chapter focuses on the external validity of samples.

## Populations and Samples

Have you ever been offered a free sample in a grocery store? Say you tried a sample of spinach mini-quiche and you loved it. You probably assumed that all 50 in the box would taste just the same. Maybe you liked one baked pita chip and assumed all the chips in the bag would be good, too. The single bite you tried is the sample. The box or bag it came from is the population. A **population** is the entire set of people or products in which you are interested. The **sample** is a smaller set, taken from that population. You don't need to eat the whole bag (the whole population) to know whether you like the chips; you only need to test a small sample. If you did taste every chip in the population, you would be conducting a **census**.

Researchers usually don't need to study every member of the population either—that is, they do not need to conduct a census. Instead, they study a sample of people, assuming that if the sample behaves a certain way, the population will do the same. The external validity of a study concerns whether the sample used in the study is adequate to represent the unstudied population. If the sample can generalize to the population, there is good external validity. When a sample has good external validity, we can also say the sample "is representative of" a population of

**TABLE 7.1**

### Synonymous Sampling Terms Used in This Chapter

| EXTERNALLY VALID | UNKNOWN EXTERNAL VALIDITY |
|---|---|
| Unbiased sample | Biased sample |
| Probability sample | Nonprobability sample |
| Random sample | Nonrandom sample |
| Representative sample | Unrepresentative sample |

interest. If the sample is biased in some way, then external validity is unknown. **Table 7.1** lists synonymous terms you will learn in this chapter.

### WHAT IS THE POPULATION OF INTEREST?

The world's population is around 7.5 billion people, but researchers rarely have that entire population in mind when they conduct a study. Before researchers can decide whether a sample is biased or unbiased, they have to specify a population to which they want to generalize: the *population of interest*. Instead of "the population" as a whole, a research study's intended population is more limited. A population of interest might be laboratory mice. It might be undergraduate women. It might be men with dementia. At the grocery store, the population of interest might be the 50 mini-quiches in the box or the 200 pita chips in the bag.

If a sample of people rated a style of shoes on how well they fit, we might be interested in generalizing to the population of people who have worn those shoes. If we are considering the results of a national election poll, we might care primarily about the population of people who will vote in the next election in the country. To say that a sample generalizes to a population, we must first decide which population we are interested in.

### COMING FROM A POPULATION VERSUS GENERALIZING TO THAT POPULATION

Just because a sample *comes from* a population does not mean it *generalizes to* that population. Just because a sample consists of American drivers does not mean it represents all American drivers. Just because a sample contains Afghan people doesn't mean the sample can generalize to the population of Afghanistan.

Samples are either biased or representative. In a **biased sample**, also called an *unrepresentative sample*, some members of the population of interest have a much higher probability than other members of being included in the sample. In an **unbiased sample**, also called a *representative sample*, all members of the population have an equal chance of being included in the sample. Only unbiased samples

TABLE 7.2

**Biased and Unbiased Samples of Different Populations of Interest**

| POPULATION OF INTEREST | BIASED SAMPLING TECHNIQUE | UNBIASED SAMPLING TECHNIQUE |
|---|---|---|
| Democrats in Texas | Recruiting people sitting in the front row at the Texas State Democratic Convention. | Obtaining a list of all registered Texas Democrats from public records and calling a sample of them through randomized digit dialing. |
| Drivers | Asking drivers to complete a survey when they stop to add money to a parking meter. | Obtaining a list of licensed drivers in each state, and selecting a sample using a random number generator. |
| Students who have taken a class with Professor A | Including only students who have written comments about Professor A on a website. | Obtaining a list of all of Professor A's current and former students, and selecting every fifteenth student for study. |

allow us to make inferences about the population of interest. **Table 7.2** lists a few examples of biased and unbiased samples.

## When Is a Sample Biased?

Let's return to the food examples to explore biased and unbiased samples further. If you reached all the way to the bottom of the bag to select your sample pita chip, that sample would be *biased,* or *unrepresentative*. Broken chips at the bottom of the bag are not representative of the population, and choosing a broken chip might cause you to draw the wrong conclusions about the quality of that bag of chips. Similarly, suppose the box of 50 quiches was a variety pack, containing various flavors of quiche. In that case, a sample spinach quiche would be unrepresentative, too. If the other types of quiche are not as tasty as the spinach, you would draw incorrect conclusions about the varied population.

In a consumer survey or an online opinion poll, a biased sample could be like getting a handful from the bottom of the bag, where the broken pita chips are more likely to be. In other words, a researcher's sample might contain too many of the most *unusual* people. For instance, the students who rate a professor on a website might tend to be the ones who are angry or disgruntled, and they might not represent the rest of the professor's students very well. A biased study sample could also be like an unrepresentative spinach quiche. A researcher's sample might include only one kind of people, when the population of interest is more like a variety pack. Imagine a study that sampled only men when the population of interest contains both men and women. Or imagine a poll that sampled only Democrats when the population of interest contains Republicans, Democrats, and people with other political views (**Figure 7.1**).

Of course, the population of interest is what the researcher says it is, so if the population of interest is U.S. Democrats, it is appropriate to use only people who are registered Democrats in the sample. Even then, the researcher would want

**FIGURE 7.1**
**Biased, or unrepresentative, samples.**
If the population of interest includes members of all political parties, a sample from a single party's political convention would not provide a representative sample.

to be sure the Democrats in the sample are representative of the population of Democrats.

## WAYS A SAMPLE MAY BE BIASED

A sample could be biased in at least two ways: Researchers might study only those they can contact conveniently or only those who volunteer to respond. These two biases can threaten the external validity of a study because people who are convenient or more willing might have different opinions from those who are less handy and less willing.

**Sampling Only Those Who Are Easy to Contact.** Many studies incorporate **convenience sampling**, using a sample of people who are easy to contact and readily available to participate. Psychology studies are often conducted by psychology professors, and they find it handy to use college students as participants. The Mehl study on how much people talk is an example (see Chapter 6). However, those easy-to-reach college students may not be representative of other populations that are less educated, older, or younger (e.g., Connor et al., 2005).

Another form of convenience sampling is used in online studies. Psychologists may conduct research through websites such as Prolific Academic or Amazon's Mechanical Turk (**Figure 7.2**). People who want to earn money for participating in research can do so online. Even though these samples are convenient, those who complete studies on websites sometimes differ slightly from other adult samples in terms of personality traits and political beliefs (Clifford et al., 2015; Goodman et al., 2013).

Here's another example. Imagine you are conducting an exit poll during a presidential election and you've hired interviewers to ask people who they voted for as they're leaving the polling place. (Exit polls are widely used in the United States to

**FIGURE 7.2**
**Online studies normally use convenience samples.**

People who participate in online research for payment, such as at the Prolific Academic website, are considered a convenience sample. How might they differ from college student samples, or from representative samples of people from the same country?

help the media predict the results of an election before the votes are completely counted.) The sample for your exit poll might be biased in a couple of ways. For one, maybe you had only enough money to send interviewers to polling places that were nearby and easy to reach. The resulting sample might be biased because the neighboring precincts might be different from the district as a whole. Therefore, it would be better to send interviewers to a sample of precincts that represent the entire population of precincts. In addition, at a particular precinct, the interviewers might approach the population of exiting voters in a biased way. Untrained exit poll workers may feel most comfortable approaching voters who look friendly, look similar to themselves, or look as if they are not in a hurry. For instance, younger workers might find it easiest to approach younger voters. Yet because younger voters tend to be more liberal, that sample's result might lead you to conclude the voters at that location voted for a Democratic candidate more often than they really did. In this case, sampling only the people who are convenient would lead to a biased sample. Effective pollsters train their staff to interview exiting voters according to a predetermined, randomized schedule.

Researchers might also end up with a convenience sample if they are *unable* to contact an important subset of people. They might not be able to study those who live far away or who don't show up to a study appointment. Such circumstances may result in a biased sample when the people the researchers *can* contact are different from the population to which they want to generalize.

At one time, companies conducting surveys selected their samples from landline telephone numbers. This approach made sense when almost all Americans had telephones in their homes. Today, many people only have wireless phones. Wireless-only people are generally younger and have lower incomes than people who have landlines. Therefore, today's surveys and polls call both wireless and landline numbers for greater accuracy.

Even when a polling organization calls both types of numbers (landline and wireless), people may not answer the phone. This problem is getting worse: In 2018, a polling organization found that fewer than 6% answer such calls (Kennedy & Hartig, 2019; **Figure 7.3**). Polls with low response rates may still be accurate, depending on the polling topic. Nevertheless, Pew Research and other polling organizations have started conducting more polls via Internet panels. First, they mail paper invitations to a random sample of home addresses and invite the person with the next birthday to participate. Panel members respond using their computers or mobile devices. If an invited panelist does not have Internet access, the organizations offer free tablets and wireless Internet access to them, to be sure these people are included. An advantage to such online panels is that organizations can follow up with the same randomly selected people repeatedly. That means they can track how people change their opinions over time (Keeter, 2019).

**Sampling Only Those Who Volunteer.** Another way a sample might be biased is through **self-selection**, a term used when a sample is known to contain only people who volunteer to participate. Self-selection can cause serious problems for external validity.

When Internet users choose to rate something—a product on Amazon.com, an online quiz on Twitter or BuzzFeed.com, a professor on RateMyProfessors.com—they are self-selecting when doing so (**Figure 7.4**). The people who rate the items are not necessarily representative of the population of all people who bought that product, follow that Twitter account, visited that website, or took that class. Researchers do not always know how online "raters" differ from "nonraters," but they speculate that the people who take the time to rate things might have stronger opinions or might be more willing to share ideas with others.

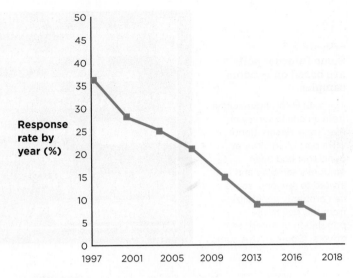

**FIGURE 7.3**

**Declining rates of answering polling phone calls.**

Since 1997, fewer and fewer people pick up the phone when a pollster calls. For this reason, polling organizations are developing and using Internet-based polling methods. (Source: Pew Research, 2019.)

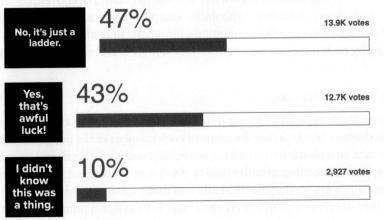

### 3. You've avoided walking under a ladder before.

| No, it's just a ladder. | 47% | 13.9K votes |
| Yes, that's awful luck! | 43% | 12.7K votes |
| I didn't know this was a thing. | 10% | 2,927 votes |

**FIGURE 7.4**

**Some Internet polls are based on self-selected samples.**

This poll was posted on BuzzFeed.com. Why can't we generalize from this sample of over 20,000 to the population of young adults who read BuzzFeed?

**FIGURE 7.5**

**Some Internet polls are based on random samples.**

The data in this figure came from an online survey on road rage. Respondents were part of an Internet panel that had been randomly sampled and invited to respond, so we can probably generalize from this poll to the population of American drivers. (Source: AAA.com.)

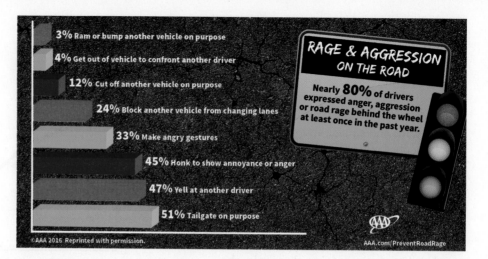

Remember, though, not all Internet-based surveys are subject to self-selection bias. When members of an Internet survey panel are invited via random selection, then self-selection bias can be ruled out. The road rage survey conducted by the American Automobile Association (**Figure 7.5**) is an example of an externally valid Internet survey.

## Obtaining a Representative Sample: Probability Sampling Techniques

When external validity is vital and researchers need an unbiased, representative sample from a population, probability sampling is the best option. There are several techniques for probability sampling, but they all involve an element of random selection. In **probability sampling**, also called *random sampling*, every member of the population of interest has an equal and known chance of being selected for the sample, regardless of whether they are convenient or motivated to volunteer. Therefore, probability samples have excellent external validity and can generalize to the population of interest. In contrast, **nonprobability sampling** techniques involve nonrandom sampling and result in a biased sample.

### SIMPLE RANDOM SAMPLING

The most basic form of probability sampling is **simple random sampling**. To visualize this process, imagine that the name of each member of the population of interest is written on a plastic ball. The balls are rolled around in a bowl, and then a mechanism spits out a number of balls equal to the size of the desired sample. The people whose names are on the selected balls will make up the sample.

Another way to create a simple random sample is to assign a number to each individual in a population and then select certain ones using a table of random

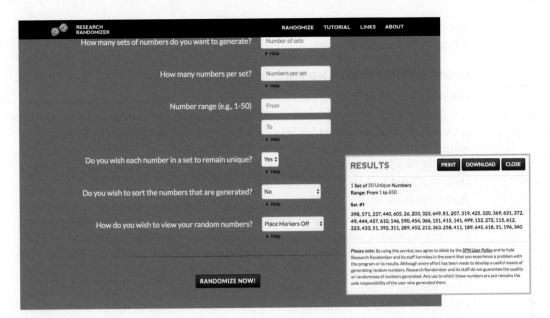

**FIGURE 7.6**
**Computerized randomizers.**

This website generates lists of random numbers. In this example, the user requested a list of 50 random members of a population of 650. Each individual in the original population must first be assigned a number from 1 to 650. The randomizer tool determines which of the 50 individuals should be in the random sample. (Source: randomizer.org.)

numbers. Researchers use software to generate random numbers (**Figure 7.6**). When pollsters need a random sample, they program computers to randomly select telephone numbers or home addresses from a database of eligible people.

**《**
For a sample table of random numbers, see Appendix A, pp. 567–569.

### SYSTEMATIC SAMPLING

In **systematic sampling**, using a computer or a random number table, the researcher starts by selecting two random numbers—say, 4 and 7. If the population of interest is a roomful of students, the researcher would start with the fourth person in the room and then count off, choosing every seventh person until the sample is the desired size. Mehl and his colleagues (2007) used the EAR device to sample conversations every 12.5 minutes (see Chapter 6). Although they did not choose this value (12.5 min) at random, the effect is essentially the same as being a random sample of participants' conversations. (Recall that although external validity often involves generalizing to populations of *people*, researchers may also generalize to settings—in this case, to a population of conversations.)

Although simple random sampling and systematic sampling work well in theory, they can be surprisingly difficult and time consuming. It can be nearly impossible to find and enumerate every member of the population of interest, so researchers usually use variants of the basic technique. The variants below are

**《**
For more on random numbers and how to use them, see Appendix A, pp. 565–569.

just as externally valid as simple random sampling because they all contain an element of random selection.

## CLUSTER SAMPLING AND MULTISTAGE SAMPLING

**Cluster sampling** is an option when people are already divided into arbitrary groups. Clusters of participants within a population of interest are randomly selected, and then all individuals in each selected cluster are used. If a researcher wanted to randomly sample high school students in the state of Pennsylvania, for example, he could start with a list of the 952 public high schools (clusters) in that state, randomly select 100 of those high schools (clusters), and then include every student from each of those 100 schools in the sample.

In the related technique of **multistage sampling**, two random samples are selected: a random sample of clusters and then a random sample of people within those clusters. In the high school example, the researcher would start with a list of high schools (clusters) in the state and select a random 100 of those schools. Then, instead of including all students at each school, the researcher would select a random sample of students from each of the selected schools. Both cluster sampling and multistage sampling are easier than sampling from all Pennsylvania high schools, and both should still produce a representative sample because they involve random selection.

## STRATIFIED RANDOM SAMPLING

Another multistage technique is **stratified random sampling**, in which the researcher purposefully selects particular demographic categories, or strata, and then randomly selects individuals within each of the categories, proportionate to their assumed membership in the population. For example, a group of researchers might want to be sure their sample of 1,000 Canadians includes people of South Asian descent in the same proportion as in the Canadian population (which is 4%). Thus, they might have two categories (strata) in their population: South Asian Canadians and other Canadians. In a sample of 1,000, they would make sure to include at least 40 members of the category of interest (South Asian Canadians). Importantly, however, all 1,000 members of both categories are selected at random.

Stratified random sampling differs from cluster sampling in two ways. First, strata are meaningful categories (such as ethnic or religious groups), whereas clusters are more arbitrary (any random set of high schools would do). Second, the final sample sizes of the strata reflect their proportion in the population, whereas clusters are not selected with such proportions in mind. **Figure 7.7** illustrates the similarities and differences between simple random, cluster, and stratified random sampling.

## OVERSAMPLING

A variation of stratified random sampling is called **oversampling**, in which the researcher intentionally overrepresents one or more groups. Perhaps researchers

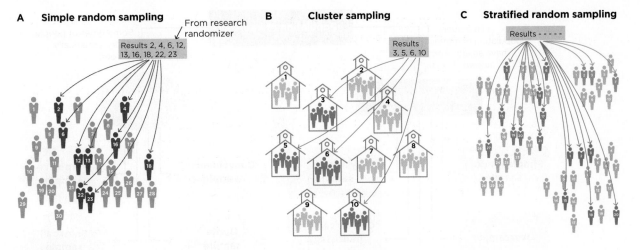

**FIGURE 7.7**

**Three common forms of probability sampling.**

(**A**) To obtain a simple random sample of 10 of these 30 individuals, we requested 10 random numbers from Research Randomizer. (**B**) To obtain a cluster sample, we selected 4 of these 10 schools at random (using Research Randomizer). We will study all the students within each selected school. (**C**) To obtain a stratified sample of hospital employees, we first divided this population into three meaningful strata: 10 social workers, 20 doctors, and 30 nurses. We randomly selected 3 social workers, 6 doctors, and 9 nurses. Therefore, our sample's proportions of social workers, doctors, and nurses are proportional to those in the full population. (In practice, the samples studied will much larger than those depicted here.)

want to sample 1,000 people, making sure to include South Asians in the sample. Maybe the researchers' population of interest has a low percentage of South Asians (say, 4%). Because 40 individuals may not be enough to make precise statistical estimates, the researchers decide that of the 1,000 people they sample, a full 100 will be sampled at random from the Canadian South Asian community. In this example, the ethnicities of the participants are still the categories, but the researchers are oversampling the South Asian population: The South Asian group will constitute 10% of the sample, even though it represents only 4% of the population. A survey that includes an oversample adjusts the final results so members in the oversampled group are weighted to their actual proportion in the population. However, this is still a probability sample because the 100 South Asians in the final sample were sampled randomly from the population of South Asians.

## COMBINING TECHNIQUES

When reading about studies in the news or in empirical journal articles, you'll probably come across methods of sampling that combine the techniques described here. Researchers might use a combination of multistage sampling and oversampling, for example. As long as clusters and individuals are selected at random, the sample will represent the population of interest and will have good external validity.

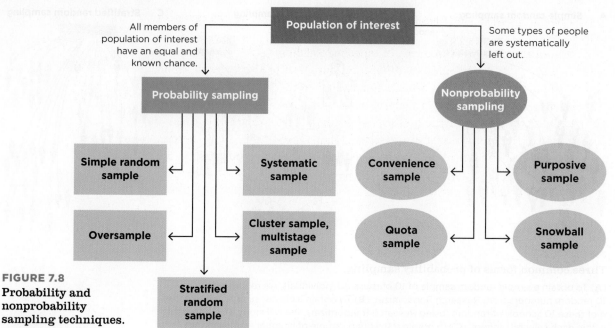

**FIGURE 7.8**
**Probability and nonprobability sampling techniques.**

Probability sampling techniques all involve an element of random selection and result in samples that resemble the population. Nonprobability sampling techniques are biased because they exclude systematic subsets of individuals; they cannot be generalized to the population.

In addition, to control for bias, researchers might supplement random selection with a statistical technique called *weighting*. If they determine that the final sample contains fewer members of a subgroup than it should (such as fewer young adults or fewer low-income people), they adjust the data so responses from members of underrepresented categories count more and overrepresented members count less.

In sum, there are many acceptable ways to obtain a representative sample. Because all these probability sampling techniques involve a component of randomness, they all ensure that each individual, cluster, or systematic interval has an equal and known chance of being selected. In other words, people are not excluded from the sample for any of the reasons that might lead to bias. **Figure 7.8** provides a visual overview of the probability and nonprobability sampling techniques.

### RANDOM SAMPLING AND RANDOM ASSIGNMENT

In conversation you might hear, "I have a random question . . .," meaning an unexpected one. But in research, *random* has a more precise meaning: occurring without any order or pattern. Each coin flip in a series is random because you cannot predict (beyond 50% certainty) whether it will come up heads or tails; there's no predictable order.

In the context of research methods, it's important not to confuse random sampling and random assignment. With random sampling (probability sampling), researchers create a sample using some random method, such as drawing names from a hat or using a random-digit phone dialer, so that each member of the population has an equal chance of being in the sample. Random sampling enhances *external validity*.

**Random assignment** is used only in experimental designs. When researchers want to place participants into two different groups (such as a treatment group and a comparison group), they usually assign them at random. Random assignment enhances *internal validity* by helping ensure that the comparison group and the treatment group have the same kinds of people in them, thereby controlling for alternative explanations. For example, in an experiment testing how exercise affects well-being, random assignment would make it likely that the people in the treatment and comparison groups are about equally happy at the start. (For more detail on random assignment, see Chapters 3 and 10.)

## Settling for an Unrepresentative Sample: Nonprobability Sampling Techniques

Samples obtained through random selection achieve excellent external validity, but such samples can be difficult to obtain. For example, the Gallup organization really does survey people in 160 countries—including Afghanistan—by either calling random samples of people in each country or traveling in person to randomly selected remote villages. You can appreciate the expense and effort required to obtain the estimate that "nearly 9 in 10 Afghans are suffering."

In cases where external validity is *not* vital to a study's goals, researchers might be content with a nonprobability sampling technique. Depending on the type of study, they can choose among a number of techniques for gathering such a sample.

### CONVENIENCE SAMPLING

Convenience sampling (introduced earlier) is the most common sampling technique, but researchers have other options available.

### PURPOSIVE SAMPLING

If researchers want to study only certain kinds of people, they recruit only those particular participants. When this is done in a nonrandom way, it is called **purposive sampling**. Researchers wishing to study, for example, the effectiveness of a specific intervention to quit smoking would seek only smokers for their sample. Notice that limiting a sample to only one type of participant does not make a sample purposive. If researchers recruit smokers by contacting community members at random, that sample would not be considered purposive because it is a random sample. However, if researchers recruit the sample of smokers by posting flyers at a local tobacco store, that action makes it a purposive sample, because only smokers will participate and because the smokers are not randomly selected. Researchers studying a weight management program might study only people in a diabetes clinic. Such a sample would not be, and might not need to be, representative of the population of obese people in some area.

## SNOWBALL SAMPLING

One variation on purposive sampling that can help researchers find rare individuals is **snowball sampling**, in which participants are asked to recommend a few acquaintances for the study. For a study on coping behaviors in people who have Crohn's disease, for example, a researcher might start with one or two people who have the condition, and then ask them to recruit people from their support groups. Each of them might, in turn, recruit one or two more acquaintances until the sample is large enough. Snowball sampling is unrepresentative because people are recruited via social networks, which are not random. You might be familiar with this approach from online surveys that urge you to forward the survey link to a few more people in your social network.

## QUOTA SAMPLING

In **quota sampling**, which is similar to stratified random sampling, the researcher identifies subsets of the population of interest and then sets a target number for each category in the sample (e.g., 80 Asian Americans, 80 African Americans, and 80 Latinx). Next, the researcher samples from the population of interest nonrandomly until the quotas are filled. As you can see, both quota sampling and stratified random sampling specify subcategories and attempt to fill targeted percentages or numbers for each subcategory. However, in quota sampling the participants are selected nonrandomly (perhaps through convenience or purposive sampling), and in stratified random sampling they are selected using a random selection technique.

---

✔

### CHECK YOUR UNDERSTANDING

1. What are five techniques for selecting a probability sample of a population of interest? Where does random selection enter into each of these five selection processes?

2. In your own words, define the word *random* in the research methods context. Then describe the difference between random sampling and random assignment.

3. What are four ways of selecting a nonprobability sample? What types of people might be more likely to be selected in each case?

4. Why are convenience, purposive, snowball, and quota sampling *not* examples of representative sampling?

1. See pp. 186–191. 2. See pp. 190–191. 3. See pp. 191–192. 4. Because none of them involve selecting participants at random.

---

# INTERROGATING EXTERNAL VALIDITY: WHAT MATTERS MOST?

A sample is either externally valid for a population of interest or it has unknown external validity. Although external validity is crucial for many frequency claims, it might not always matter. When researchers study association claims or causal claims, they are often comfortable with unknown external validity.

## In a Frequency Claim, External Validity Is a Priority

Frequency claims, as you know, are claims about how often something happens in a population. When you read headlines like these—"8 out of 10 drivers say they experience road rage," "Almost 9 out of 10 Afghans are suffering," or "Two-thirds of adults have had an adverse childhood experience"—it might be obvious to you that external validity is important. If the driving study used sampling techniques that contained mostly urban residents, the road rage estimate might be too high because urban driving may be more stressful. If the Gallup poll included too many people from impoverished regions in Afghanistan, the 9-out-of-10 estimate might be too high. In such claims, external validity, which relies on probability sampling techniques, is crucial.

In certain cases, the external validity of surveys based on random samples can actually be confirmed. In political races, the accuracy of pre-election opinion polling can be compared with the final voting results. In most cases, however, researchers are not able to check the accuracy of their samples' estimates because they hardly ever complete a full census of a population on the variable of interest. For example, we could never evaluate the well-being of all the people in Afghanistan to find out the true percentage of those who are struggling or suffering. Similarly, a researcher can't locate all the owners of a particular style of shoe to ask them whether their shoes "fit true to size." Because you usually cannot directly check accuracy when interrogating a frequency claim, the best you can do is examine the method the researchers used. As long as it was a probability sampling technique, you can be more confident in the external validity of the result.

## When External Validity Is a Lower Priority

Even though you need a probability sample to support a frequency claim, many associations and causes can still be accurately detected even in a nonprobability sample. Researchers might not have the funds to obtain random samples for their studies, and their priorities lie elsewhere. For example, as you will learn, random assignment is prioritized over random sampling when conducting an experiment.

What about a frequency claim that is *not* based on a probability sample? It might matter a lot, or it might not. You will need to carefully consider whether the reason for the sample's bias is relevant to the claim.

## NONPROBABILITY SAMPLES IN THE REAL WORLD

» For more on when external validity may not be a priority, see Chapter 8, pp. 224–225; Chapter 10, pp. 306–308; and Chapter 14.

Consider whether self-selection affects the results of an online shopping rating, as in the Zappos.com headline "61% said this shoe felt true to size." You can be pretty sure the people who rated the fit of these shoes are self-selected and therefore don't represent all the people who own that model. The raters obviously have Internet access, whereas some of the shoe owners might not. The raters probably cared enough to rate the shoes online. Another reason people respond might be that they are conscientious. They like to keep others informed, so they tend to rate everything they buy. In this case, the shopping rating sample is self-selected to include people who are more helpful than average.

The question is: Do the opinions of these nonrandom shoppers apply to other shoppers and to how the shoes will fit *you*? Are the feet of opinionated or conscientious raters likely to be very different from those of the general population? Probably not, so their opinions about the fit of the shoes might generalize. The raters' fashion sense might even be the same as yours. (After all, they were attracted to the same image online.) If you believe the characteristics of this self-selected sample are roughly the same as those of others who bought the shoes, their ratings might be accurate for you after all.

Here's another example. Let's say a driver uses a navigation app to report a slowdown on a specific highway (**Figure 7.9**). This driver is not a randomly selected sample of drivers on that stretch of road; in fact, this driver is more conscientious and thus more likely to report problems. However, these traits are not that relevant. Traffic is the same for everybody, conscientious or not, so even though this driver is a nonrandom sample, the traffic report can probably generalize to the other drivers on that road. The feature that has biased the sample (being conscientious) is not relevant to the variable being measured (being in traffic).

In short, when you know a sample is not representative, you should think carefully about how much it matters. Are the characteristics that make the sample biased relevant to what you are measuring? In certain cases, it's reasonable to trust the reports of unrepresentative samples.

**FIGURE 7.9**

**Nonrandom samples might not matter.**

A driver who reports traffic is probably not representative of all the drivers on that stretch of road. Nevertheless, the report from this nonrandom sample might be accurate.

## NONPROBABILITY SAMPLES IN RESEARCH STUDIES

Let's use this reasoning to work through a couple of other examples. Recall from Chapter 6 the 30 dual-earner families who allowed the researchers to videotape their evening activities (Campos et al., 2013). Only certain kinds of families will let researchers walk around the house and record everyone's behavior. Would this self-selection affect the conclusions of the study? It seems possible that a family that volunteers for such intrusion has a warmer emotional tone than the full population of dual-earning families. Without more data on families who do not readily agree to be videotaped, we cannot know for sure. The researchers may have to live with some uncertainty about the generalizability of their data.

What about the study in which two-thirds of the sample had experienced at least one adverse childhood experience (ACE)? The sample of participants was not drawn randomly from a population of Americans. Instead, the insurance company Kaiser Permanente gave the ACE questionnaire (see Chapter 6) to more than 17,000 people in the San Diego area. The study did not attempt to select people at random (Felitti et al., 1998). Therefore, we have to live with some uncertainty about whether the "two-thirds" estimate from this study can generalize. However, our uncertainty does not mean that the results are wrong or even uninteresting. It is sobering to read that two-thirds of people in this sample have experienced an adverse childhood event. In addition, other studies have found similar rates (with around 60% of adults reporting at least one ACE) using random samples from the United States (CDC, 2010).

## Larger Samples Are Not More Representative

For external validity, is a bigger sample always a better sample? The answer may surprise you: not really. The idea that larger samples are more externally valid than smaller samples is perhaps one of the most persistent misconceptions in a research methods course.

When a phenomenon is rare, we do need a large random sample in order to locate enough instances of that phenomenon for valid statistical analysis. For example, in a study of religion in American life, the Pew Research Center contacted a random sample of 35,071 adults. The large size enabled them to obtain and analyze sufficiently large samples of small religious groups, such as Jehovah's Witnesses, who make up less than 1% of Americans (Pew Research Center, 2015). But for most variables, when researchers are striving to generalize from a sample to a population, the size of the sample is in fact much less important than how that sample was selected. When it comes to the external validity of the sample, it's *how*, not *how many*.

Suppose you want to predict the outcome of the U.S. presidential election by polling 4,000 people at the Republican National Convention. You would have a grand old sample, but it would not tell you anything about the opinions of the entire country's voting population because everyone you sampled would be a member of one political party. Many Internet polls are so popular that thousands of people choose to vote in them. Look back at the BuzzFeed poll about superstitions (see Figure 7.4). More than 29,000 people chose to respond, yet we have no idea to whom the results generalize and we might guess that this sample probably contains a high proportion of young people. Similarly, the San Diego ACE study had a large sample (more than 17,000), but people were not randomly selected. Therefore, we are not sure to whom this sample can generalize.

When researchers do use random sampling, it turns out that 1,000–2,000 people are all they usually need—even for populations as large as the U.S. population of 330 million. For reasons of statistical accuracy, many polls shoot for, at most, a sample of 2,000. A researcher chooses a sample size for the poll in order to optimize the margin of error of the estimate. Introduced in Chapter 3, the margin of error is a statistic that sets up the confidence interval for a study's estimate. For instance, you might read that 35% of Canadians in some poll support the Liberal Party, plus or minus 3%. Margins of error ("plus or minus 3%"), such as the range 32% to 38%, are created so they are likely to contain the true percentage of Canadians who support the Liberal Party. As **Figure 7.10** illustrates, as a polling

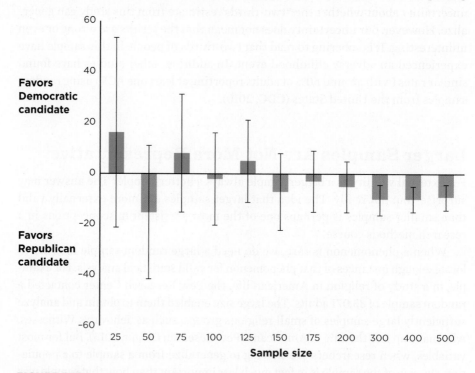

**FIGURE 7.10**

**Smaller samples give unstable estimates with large margins of error.**

During an election cycle, media outlets may call a random sample of voters and ask each respondent whether they plan to vote for one candidate or the other. In this example, the polling estimate was plotted repeatedly as the sample got larger and larger. At lower sample sizes, the estimate is volatile, but as the sample size increases, the estimate changes less and the margin of error (confidence interval) becomes narrower. (Data are fabricated for illustration purposes, based on real polling data.)

sample gets larger, its margin of error becomes more precise. However, the *external validity* of the poll comes from its sampling method, not the sample size.

**Table 7.3** shows the margin of error for random samples of different sizes. First, you can see that the larger the sample size, the smaller the margin of error—that is, the more accurately the sample's results estimate the views of the population. Second, after a random sample size of 1,000, it takes many more people to gain just a little more accuracy in the margin of error. That's why many researchers consider 1,000 to be an optimal balance between statistical accuracy and polling effort. A sample of 1,000 people, *as long as it is random*, allows them to generalize to the population (even a population of 330 million) quite accurately. In effect, sample size is not an external validity issue; it is a statistical validity issue.

**TABLE 7.3**

## Margins of Error Associated with Different Random Sample Sizes

| IF THE PERCENTAGE IS ESTIMATED ON A RANDOM SAMPLE OF SIZE | MARGIN OF ERROR ON THE PERCENTAGE IS |
|---|---|
| 2,000 | Plus or minus 2% |
| 1,500 | Plus or minus 3% |
| 1,000 | Plus or minus 3% |
| 500 | Plus or minus 4% |
| 200 | Plus or minus 7% |
| 100 | Plus or minus 10% |
| 50 | Plus or minus 10% |

*Note:* Margin of error varies as a function of sample size and the percentage result of the poll. In this table, estimates were based on a 50% polling result (e.g., if 50% of people supported a candidate).

## CHECK YOUR UNDERSTANDING

1. When might researchers decide to use a nonprobability sample, even though a probability sample would ensure external validity?

2. For what type of claim is it most important for a researcher to use a representative sample?

3. Which of these samples is more likely to be representative of a population of 100,000?
   a. A convenience sample of 50,000 people
   b. A cluster sample of 500 people

4. Explain why a larger sample is not necessarily more externally valid than a smaller one.

1. See pp. 194-195. 2. A frequency claim; see p. 193. 3. b. 4. See pp. 195-197.

# CHAPTER REVIEW

It's time to complete your study experience! Go to INQUIZITIVE to practice actively with this chapter's concepts and get personalized feedback along the way.

## Summary

When a claim makes a statement about a population of interest, you can ask how well the sample that was studied (such as a sample of online shoppers) represents the population in the claim (all online shoppers).

### GENERALIZABILITY: DOES THE SAMPLE REPRESENT THE POPULATION?

- The quality of a frequency claim usually depends on the ability to generalize from the sample to the population of interest. Researchers use samples to estimate the characteristics of a population.

- When a sample is externally valid, we can also say it is unbiased, generalizable, or representative.

- When generalization is the goal, random sampling techniques—rather than sample size—are vital because they lead to unbiased estimates of a population.

- Nonrandom and self-selected samples do not represent the population. Such biased samples may be obtained when researchers sample only those who are easy to reach or only those who are more willing to participate.

- Probability sampling techniques can result in a representative sample; they include simple random sampling, cluster sampling, multistage sampling, stratified random sampling, oversampling, systematic sampling, and combinations of these. All of them select people or clusters at random, so all members

of the population of interest are equally likely to be included in the sample.

- Nonprobability sampling techniques include convenience sampling, purposive sampling, snowball sampling, and quota sampling. Such sampling methods do not allow generalizing from the sample to a population.

### INTERROGATING EXTERNAL VALIDITY: WHAT MATTERS MOST?

- When researchers intend to generalize from the sample to the population, probability sampling (random sampling) is essential.

- Random samples are crucial when researchers are estimating the frequency of a particular opinion, condition, or behavior in a population. Nonprobability (nonrandom) samples can occasionally be appropriate when the cause of the bias is not relevant to the survey topic.

- For external validity, the size of a sample is not as important as whether the sample was selected randomly.

## Key Terms

population, p. 180
sample, p. 180
census, p. 180

biased sample, p. 181
unbiased sample, p. 181
convenience sampling, p. 183

self-selection, p. 185
probability sampling, p. 186
nonprobability sampling, p. 186

**To see samples of chapter concepts in the popular media, visit www.everydayresearchmethods.com and click the box for Chapter 7.**

# Review Questions

1. Which of the following four terms is not synonymous with the others?

   a. Generalizable sample

   b. Externally valid sample

   c. Representative sample

   d. Biased sample

2. A researcher's population of interest is New York City dog owners. Which of the following samples is most likely to generalize to this population of interest?

   a. A sample of 25 dog owners visiting dog-friendly New York City parks.

   b. A sample of 25 dog owners who have appointments for their dogs at veterinarians in the New York City area.

   c. A sample of 25 dog owners selected at random from New York City pet registration records.

   d. A sample of 25 dog owners who visit New York City's ASPCA website.

3. Which of the following samples is most likely to generalize to its population of interest?

   a. A convenience sample of 12,000

   b. A quota sample of 120

   c. A stratified random sample of 120

   d. A self-selected sample of 120,000

4. Externally valid samples are more important for some research questions than for others. For which of the following research questions will it be most important to use an externally valid sampling technique?

   a. Estimating the proportion of U.S. teens who are depressed.

   b. Testing the association between depression and illegal drug use in U.S. teens.

   c. Testing the effectiveness of support groups for teens with depression.

# Learning Actively

1. During a U.S. election, the news media interviewed a group of women in Florida. Although opinion polls supported the liberal candidate, these conservative women were still optimistic that their own side would win. One woman said, "I don't think those polls are very good—after all, they've never called *me*. Have they called any of you ladies?" Is this woman's critique of polling techniques appropriate? Why or why not?

2. Imagine you're planning to estimate the price of the average book at your college bookstore. The bookstore carries 13,000 titles, but you plan to sample only 200 books. You will select a sample of 200 books, record the price of each book, and use the average of the 200 books in the sample to estimate the average price of the 13,000 titles in the bookstore. Assume the bookstore can give you access to a database that lists all 13,000 titles it carries. Based on this information, answer the following questions:

   a. What is the sample in this study, and what is the population of interest?

   b. How might you collect a simple random sample of books?

   c. How might you collect a stratified random sample? (What would your strata be?)

   d. How might you collect a convenience sample?

   e. How might you collect a systematic random sample?

   f. How might you collect a cluster sample?

   g. How might you collect a quota sample?

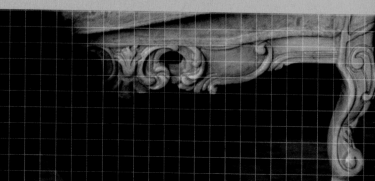

# PART IV

# Tools for Evaluating Association Claims

## Meaningful Conversations Linked to Happier People

*SCIENTIFIC AMERICAN, 2010*

## Couples Who Meet Online Have Better Marriages

*FREAKONOMICS, 2013*

# 8

# Bivariate Correlational Research

THE TWO STATEMENTS ON the opposite page are examples of association claims that are supported by correlational studies. Each one is an association claim because it describes a relationship between variables: meaningful conversations and happiness, where people met their spouse and marriage quality.

The verbs used in each case are association verbs. In the first claim, the verb is *linked*, and the second claim's verb is *have*. Neither statement argues that X *causes* Y, or X *makes* Y *happen*, or X *increases rates of* Y. (If they did, they would be causal claims, not association claims.)

What about the studies behind these statements? Even without reading the full details of each study, we might guess that the variables were all measured. Researchers can measure where people met their spouses, but they can't reasonably assign people to meet their spouse either online or in person. Researchers can measure marital satisfaction, but they can't assign people to be satisfied or not. They can evaluate people's meaningful conversations and their levels of happiness, but it might be difficult to assign people to have deep conversations or assign people to have certain levels of happiness. Because it's a plausible assumption that the two variables in each claim were measured (rather than manipulated), we suspect the studies behind the claims were correlational.

This chapter describes the kinds of studies that can support association claims, explains what kinds of graphs and statistics are used to describe the associations, and shows how you can systematically

**LEARNING OBJECTIVES**

A year from now, you should still be able to:

**1.**
Explain that measured variables, not any particular statistic, make a study correlational.

**2.**
Interrogate the construct validity and statistical validity (and, of lower priority, external validity) of an association claim.

**3.**
Explain why a correlational study can support an association claim but not a causal claim.

interrogate an association claim using the four big validities framework. What kinds of questions should you ask when you encounter an association claim? What should you keep in mind if you plan to conduct a study to test such a claim?

# INTRODUCING BIVARIATE CORRELATIONS

An association claim describes the relationship found between two measured variables. A **bivariate correlation**, or *bivariate association*, is an association that involves exactly two variables. Chapter 3 introduced the three types of associations: positive, negative, and zero. To investigate associations, researchers need to measure the first variable and the second variable in the same group of people. Then they use graphs and simple statistics to describe the type of relationship the variables have with each other.

To test the relationship between meeting one's spouse online and marital satisfaction, researcher John Cacioppo and his colleagues emailed surveys to thousands of people who participate in uSamp, an online market research project (Cacioppo et al., 2013). More than 19,000 respondents answered questions about where they met their spouse—online or not. Then, to evaluate marital satisfaction, the researchers used a 4-item measure called the Couples Satisfaction Index (CSI), which asks questions such as "Indicate the degree of happiness, all things considered, of your marriage," with a 7-point rating scale from 1 (*extremely unhappy*) to 7 (*perfect*). Sample data for this study appear in **Table 8.1**. People who met online scored a little higher on the CSI.

Another correlational study investigated the association between sitting during the workweek and the thickness of certain brain regions. Prabha Siddarth and her colleagues tested a sample of 35 adults, aged 45 and older. They asked each person how many hours they typically spend sitting on weekdays, and then, by imaging each person's brain in an MRI scanner, measured the thickness of their medial-temporal lobes (MTL; Siddarth et al., 2018). They focused on the MTL because these parts of the brain are smaller in people who have Alzheimer's disease or declines in memory. Sample data for this study appear in **Table 8.2**.

## TABLE 8.1

### Sample Data from the Cacioppo Study on Marital Satisfaction

| RESPONDENT | WHERE DID YOU MEET SPOUSE? | MARITAL SATISFACTION RATING |
| --- | --- | --- |
| a | Online | 6.2 |
| b | Offline | 5.5 |
| c | Online | 7.0 |
| d | Offline | 4.2 |
| ... | ... | ... |
| yy | Online | 7.0 |

*Note:* Data are fabricated for illustration purposes.
Source: Adapted from Cacioppo et al., 2013.

## TABLE 8.2

### Sample Data from the Siddarth Study on Sitting and MTL Thickness

| ADULT | TIME SPENT SITTING (HOURS) | MTL TOTAL THICKNESS |
| --- | --- | --- |
| A | 10 | 2.67 |
| B | 11 | 2.56 |
| C | 5 | 2.70 |
| D | 7 | 2.34 |
| ... | | ... |
| JJ | 3 | 2.51 |

Source: Adapted from Siddarth et al., 2018. MTL = medial-temporal lobe.

To investigate the association between meaningful, substantive conversations and happiness, Matthias Mehl and his colleagues (2010) measured people's happiness by combining Pavot and Diener's (1993) subjective well-being scale (see Chapter 5) with a measure of overall happiness. Then they measured people's level of "deep talk" by having them wear an electronically activated recorder (EAR) for 4 days. (The EAR, introduced in Chapter 6, is an observational measurement device, an unobtrusive microphone worn by a participant that records 30 seconds of ambient sound every 12.5 minutes.) After 79 people's daily conversations were recorded and transcribed, researchers coded the extent to which the recorded snippets represented "deep talk" or "substantive conversation." Each participant was assigned a value representing the percentage of time spent in substantive conversation. Sample data for this study appear in **Table 8.3**. Those with deeper conversations had higher well-being scores.

In the sample data tables, notice that each row shows one person's scores on two measured variables. Even though each study measured more than two variables, an analysis of bivariate correlations looks at only two variables at a time. Therefore, a correlational study might have measured multiple variables, but the authors present the bivariate correlations between different pairs of variables separately.

**TABLE 8.3**

**Sample Data from the Mehl Study on Well-Being and Deep Talk**

| PERSON | SCORE ON WELL-BEING SCALE | PERCENTAGE OF CONVERSATIONS RATED AS DEEP TALK |
|---|---|---|
| A | 1.2 | 80 |
| B | 0.3 | 52 |
| C | −0.4 | 35 |
| D | 1.4 | 42 |
| ... | ... | ... |
| ZZ | −1.6 | 16 |

*Note:* Data are fabricated for illustration purposes.
Source: Adapted from Mehl et al., 2010.

## Review: Describing Associations Between Two Quantitative Variables

After recording the data, the next step in testing an association claim is to describe the relationship between the two measured variables using scatterplots and the correlation coefficient *r*. We could create a scatterplot for the relationship between deep talk and well-being, for example, by placing scores on the well-being scale on the *x*-axis and percentage of conversations that include deep talk on the *y*-axis, placing a dot on the graph to represent each person (**Figure 8.1**).

In addition to creating the scatterplot, Mehl and his team computed the correlation coefficient

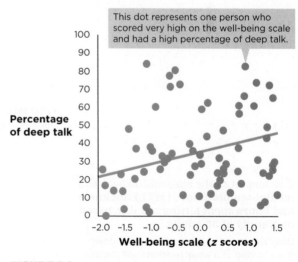

**FIGURE 8.1**

**Scatterplot of the association between deep talk and well-being.**

(Source: Adapted from Mehl et al., 2010.)

for their data and came up with an *r* of .26. As discussed in Chapter 5, a positive *r* means that the relationship is positive: High scores on one variable go with high scores on the other. In other words, high percentages of substantive conversation go with high levels of well-being, and low percentages of substantive conversation go with low levels of well-being. The magnitude of *r* was estimated to be .26.

Recall that *r* has two qualities: direction and strength. Direction refers to whether the association is positive, negative, or zero. The strength refers to "how much": how closely related the two variables are. The more closely related two variables are, the closer the *r* will be to 1.0 or –1.0. Across many areas of psychology, correlations are typically around *r* = .20, but some areas of psychology might average as high as *r* = .40 (Gignac & Szodorai, 2016; Rubio-Aparicio et al., 2018; Schäfer & Schwarz, 2019). Later in this chapter we'll talk about how to evaluate the strength of an *r* of .26.

**Figure 8.2** shows a scatterplot for the study correlating the time spent sitting with total MTL thickness. When Siddarth's team computed the correlation coefficient between those two variables, they found an *r* of –.37. The negative *r* means that more time spent sitting is associated with a thinner MTL, and less time spent sitting is associated with a thicker MTL.

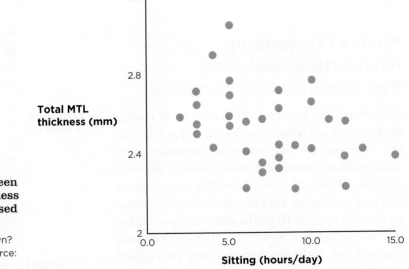

**FIGURE 8.2**

**Scatterplot of the association between medial-temporal lobe (MTL) thickness and hours spent sitting per day, based on a study of 35 adults.**

Does this cloud of points slope up or down? Is it a strong or a weak relationship? (Source: Adapted from Siddarth et al., 2018.)

# Describing Associations with Categorical Data

In the examples we have discussed so far, the nature of the association can be described with scatterplots and the correlation coefficient $r$. For the association between marital satisfaction and online dating, however, the dating variable is *categorical*; its values fall in either one category or another. A person meets their spouse either online or offline. The other variable in this association, marital satisfaction, is *quantitative*; 7 means more marital satisfaction than 6, 6 means more than 5, and so on.

For more on categorical and quantitative variables, see Chapter 5, pp. 122–123.

## GRAPHING ASSOCIATIONS WHEN ONE VARIABLE IS CATEGORICAL

When both variables in an association are measured on quantitative scales (as were the number of substantive conversations and happiness), a scatterplot is usually the best way to represent the data. But is a scatterplot the best representation of an association in which one of the variables is measured categorically? **Figure 8.3** shows how a scatterplot for the association between meeting location and marital satisfaction might look.

As in all scatterplots, one variable is plotted on the *x*-axis and the other on the *y*-axis, and one dot represents one person (in a study with a very large sample, one dot could represent several people who had the same scores). You can even look for an association in this graph: Do the scattered points slope up from right to left, do

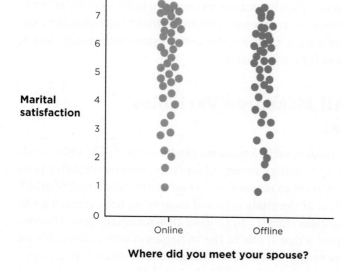

**Where did you meet your spouse?**

**FIGURE 8.3**

**Scatterplot of meeting location and marital satisfaction.**

Do you see an association here between meeting location and marital satisfaction? (The dots in this graph are "jittered," which means that they are spread out horizontally so you can see more dots at once. Data are fabricated for illustration purposes.)
(Source: Adapted from Cacioppo et al., 2013.)

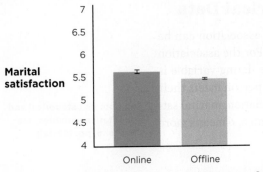

**FIGURE 8.4**
**Bar graph of meeting location and marital satisfaction.**

This is the same outcome as in Figure 8.3, graphed differently. Do you see an association here between meeting location and marital satisfaction? The error bars in this graph represent the 95% CI for each mean. These CIs are very narrow, reflecting the large sample size in the study. (Source: Adapted from Cacioppo et al., 2013.)

they slope down, or is the slope flat? If you answered that you see a very slight downward slope, you would be right. You'd conclude there's an association between where people meet their spouse and marital satisfaction, and that those who met online have slightly happier marriages, just as the researchers found when they conducted their study (Cacioppo et al., 2013). If you computed the correlation between these two variables, you would get $r = -.06$.

Although you can make a scatterplot of such data, researchers may also plot the results of an association with a categorical variable as a bar graph, as in **Figure 8.4**. Each person is not represented by one data point; instead, the graph shows the **mean** marital satisfaction rating (the arithmetic average) for all the people who met their spouses online and the mean marital satisfaction rating for those who met their spouses in person.

When you use a bar graph, you usually examine the *difference* between the group averages to see whether there is an association. In the graph of meeting location and marital satisfaction in Figure 8.4, you can see that the average satisfaction score is slightly higher in the online than the offline group. The difference in means indicates an association between where people met their spouse and marital satisfaction.

### ANALYZING ASSOCIATIONS WHEN ONE VARIABLE IS CATEGORICAL

When at least one of the variables in an association claim is categorical, as in the online dating example, researchers may use different statistics to analyze the data. Although they occasionally use *r*, it is more common to estimate the magnitude of difference between means (group averages).

## A Study with All Measured Variables Is Correlational

It might seem confusing that association claims can be supported by either scatterplots or bar graphs, and by using a variety of statistics, such as *r* or differences between means. It's important to remember that no matter what kind of graph you see, when the method of the study involved measuring both variables, the study is correlational, and therefore it can support an association claim. (In contrast, recall from Chapter 3 that if one of the variables is *manipulated*, it's an experiment, which is more appropriate for testing a causal claim.) An association claim is not supported by a particular kind of statistic or a particular kind of graph; it is supported by a study design—correlational research—in which all the variables are measured.

**CHECK YOUR UNDERSTANDING**

1. At minimum, how many variables are there in an association claim?

2. What characteristic of a study makes it correlational?

3. Sketch three scatterplots: one showing a positive correlation, one showing a negative correlation, and one showing a zero correlation.

4. Sketch two bar graphs: one that shows a correlation between two variables, and one that shows no correlation.

5. When do researchers typically use a bar graph, as opposed to a scatterplot, to display correlational data?

1. Two. 2. All variables are measured; see p. 204. 3. Answers may vary; see Figures 8.1, 8.2, and 8.3 for models. 4. A bar graph that shows a correlation should have bars at different heights; a bar graph with a zero correlation would show two bars of the same height. 5. See pp. 208–209.

# INTERROGATING ASSOCIATION CLAIMS

With an association claim, the two most important validities to interrogate are construct validity and statistical validity. You might also ask about the external validity of the association. Although internal validity is relevant for causal claims, not association claims, you need to be able to explain why correlational studies do not establish internal validity. We'll now discuss the questions you'll use to interrogate each of the four big validities specifically in the context of association claims.

## Construct Validity: How Well Was Each Variable Measured?

An association claim describes the relationship between two measured variables, so it is relevant to ask about the construct validity of *each* variable. How well was each of the two variables measured?

To interrogate the Mehl study, for example, you would ask questions about the researchers' operationalizations of deep talk and well-being. Recall that deep talk in this study was observed via the EAR recordings and coded later by research assistants, while well-being was measured using the subjective well-being scale. Once you know what kind of measure was used for each variable, you can ask questions to assess each one's construct validity: Does the measure have good reliability? Is it measuring what it's intended to measure? What is the evidence for its face validity, its concurrent validity, its discriminant and convergent validity? For example, you could ask whether the 4-item measure of marital satisfaction used in the Caccioppo study had good internal reliability and whether it had convergent validity. Does it correlate with other measures of marital happiness?

## Statistical Validity: How Well Do the Data Support the Conclusion?

When you ask about the statistical validity of an association claim, you are asking about factors that might have affected the scatterplot, correlation coefficient *r*, bar graph, or difference score that led to your association claim. You need to consider the strength and precision of your estimate, if it has been replicated, any outliers that might have affected the overall findings, restriction of range, and whether a seemingly zero association might actually be curvilinear.

» For more on the correlation coefficient *r*, see Statistics Review: Inferential Statistics, pp. 480–488.

### STATISTICAL VALIDITY QUESTION 1: HOW STRONG IS THE RELATIONSHIP?

All associations are not equal; some are stronger than others. The term **effect size** describes the strength of a relationship between two or more variables. As an example, **Figure 8.5** depicts two associations: Both are positive, but the one in part B is stronger (its *r* is closer to 1). In other words, part B depicts a stronger relationship.

Psychologists sometimes use the terms *weak*, *moderate*, and *strong* to describe *r*s of .1, .3, and .5, respectively (Cohen, 1992). It's better, however, to think about effect sizes in nuanced ways. Effect size indicates the importance of a relationship, but our judgments also depend on the context.

**All Else Being Equal, Larger Effect Sizes Are More Important.** The first thing to understand is that effect sizes can indicate the importance of a result. When all else is equal, a larger effect size is often considered more important than

**FIGURE 8.5**

**Two scatterplots depicting different association strengths.**

Both of these are positive associations. Which scatterplot shows the stronger relationship, part A or part B?

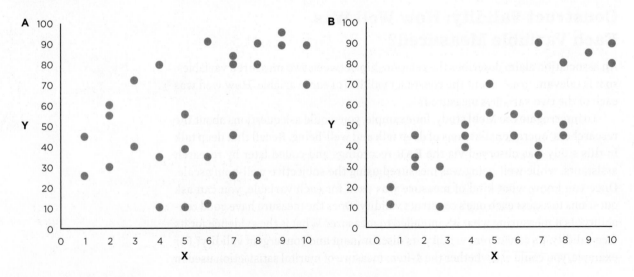

a small one. By this criterion, the association between deep talk and happiness ($r$ = .26) may be more important than the weaker one between meeting online and having a happier marriage ($r$ = .06).

However, depending on the context, even a tiny effect size can be important. At the Olympic level, a tiny adjustment to an athlete's form or performance might mean the difference between earning a medal and not reaching the podium at all. On the earth, a very small change in average global temperature can lead to major sea-level rise.

**"Small" Effect Sizes Can Compound Over Many Observations.** Second, when a seemingly tiny effect size is aggregated (combined) over many people or situations, it can have an important impact. In baseball, when star batters are compared with average batters, the star batters are better at getting on base during any one batting turn, but only by a tiny amount: $r$ = .05 (Abelson, 1985). This difference seems small, but over the course of a full season of baseball (more than 550 turns batting), the star batters score many more runs.

Another example of aggregation comes from the personality trait agreeableness, which refers to how warm, kind, and cooperative people are. More agreeable people have more enjoyable social interactions, with an effect size of about $r$ = .07 (Ozer & Benet-Martìnez, 2006). This might appear to be a small effect, but imagine a first-year college student who is high in agreeableness and who has a couple hundred social interactions during the first weeks in the dorm. That tiny effect of agreeableness could add up, meaning the student can accrue much more popularity, compared with a less-agreeable roommate (Funder & Ozer, 2019; **Figure 8.6**).

Tiny effect sizes can become important when aggregated over many situations, and they can also become important when aggregated over many *people*. An example comes from a study that tested high school students from across the United States. A large sample of teens completed a one-hour online lesson that taught the growth mindset about intelligence (Yeager et al., 2019). People who have a growth mindset believe they can become smarter by using effort and good learning strategies. To find out how well the growth mindset lesson worked, the researchers tracked high school grades. Teens who had been randomly assigned to the growth mindset group (compared with a control group) had better grades, with an effect size of $r$ = .05. The researchers estimated that an effect this size was enough to prevent 79,000 U.S. teens from scoring in the "D" or "F" grade range.

When the outcome is not as extreme as success or failure, a very small effect size might indeed be negligible. For instance, at $r$ = .06, the effect size of the association

**FIGURE 8.6**
**Tiny effects can add up.**

The correlation between the personality trait of agreeableness and the success of a single social interaction may be "only" .07, but when this effect is aggregated over the course of a couple hundred social interactions, an agreeable person will actually be more popular than a less agreeable person (Funder & Ozer, 2019).

between meeting online and marital satisfaction corresponds to a difference on the 7-point satisfaction scale of only .16 (5.64 versus 5.48). It's hard to picture what sixteen one-hundredths of a point difference means in practical terms, but it doesn't seem like a large effect. Similarly, the Cacioppo team also collected the divorce rates in the two groups. They found that the divorce rate for couples who met online was 5.87%, compared with 7.73% for couples who met offline, which corresponds to an effect size of $r = .02$. That is also a very small effect size, representing about two extra divorces per 100 couples. In your opinion, is it important? What's more, does the effect size correspond to the headlines used by journalists who covered the study in the press?

**Benchmarks: Compared to What?** A third way to think about effect size is to compare it to well-understood benchmarks. Recall that the average effect size in psychology studies is around $r = .20$ and may only rarely be as high as $r = .40$. If we use the descriptions in **Table 8.4**, we might conclude that the $r = .26$ association between deep talk and well-being in the Mehl study was fairly typical for a personality or social psychology study. In the Siddarth study, the association between time spent sitting and MTL thickness was $r = -.37$, which is fairly large by psychology standards. According to Funder & Ozer (2019), we might even be suspicious of an association this large—is it too good to be true? The next section explains that when effect sizes come from relatively small samples (in this case, only 35 adults), the estimates are not very precise.

TABLE 8.4

## Guidelines for Interpreting the Magnitude of an Effect Size $r$

| ASSUMING IT WAS BASED ON A LARGE SAMPLE (1,500 OR MORE), AN $r$ OF | MIGHT INITIALLY BE DESCRIBED AS | A NONPSYCHOLOGICAL EXAMPLE OF THIS EFFECT SIZE |
|---|---|---|
| .05 (or -.05) | Very small or very weak | The correlation between a baseball player's overall batting average and success at any one batting turn |
| .10 (or -.10) | Small or weak | Correlation between taking antihistamine medication and runny nose symptoms ($r = -.11$) |
| .20 (or -.20) | Moderate | Difference between men and women in average body weight (males higher, $r = .26$) |
| .30 (or -.30) | Fairly powerful effect | Correlation between a town's elevation above sea level and its annual temperature ($r = -.34$) |
| .40 (or -.40) | Unusually large in psychology—either very powerful or possibly too good to be true (based on a small sample) | Correlation between height and weight in adults ($r = .44$) |

Sources: Funder & Ozer, 2019; also Abelson, 1985; Kraft, 2020; Meyer et al., 2001; Ozer & Benet-Martinez, 2006.

## STATISTICAL VALIDITY QUESTION 2: HOW PRECISE IS THE ESTIMATE?

A study's correlation coefficient is the point estimate of the true correlation in the population. But how precise is that estimate? That is, How wrong could it be? To communicate the precision of their estimate of $r$, researchers report a 95% confidence interval (95% CI), introduced in Chapter 3. The CI calculations ensure that 95% of CIs will contain the true population correlation.. Recall the analogy—your contractor might estimate the true cost of your home repair to be between $1,000 and $1,500.

Consider the correlation between time spent sitting and MTL thickness. The relationship was estimated to be $r = -.37$, and its 95% CI is [−.07, −.64]. (The 95% CI is usually reported in square brackets.) We cannot know the true population relationship between sitting and MTL thickness, but we do know that CIs are designed to capture the true relationship in 95% of studies like this. Therefore we can't rule out that the true $r$ is around −.07 or even as high as around −.64.

**Sample Size and Precision.** You might observe that the interval of [−.07, −.64] seems wide, meaning the estimate is imprecise. That's because this estimate of $r = -.37$ is based on a relatively small sample of only 35 adults. When an estimate is based on a small sample, it is less stable. If the researchers add a few more adults to the existing sample, the additional participants could potentially alter the estimate substantially. Reflecting this instability, small samples have wider (less precise) confidence intervals. The CI has to be wide to capture the degree of uncertainty we have when the sample is small. Indeed, if other researchers conducted a replication of this study, we would not be too surprised if they found a correlation very close to .00 or an $r$ stronger than −.37.

In contrast, large samples result in estimates with much narrower, more precise confidence intervals. Recall the association between where people meet their spouse and their marital satisfaction, $r = .06$. This study surveyed more than 19,000 people, so the estimate is fairly stable. Even if the study added a few more adults, their results would be unlikely to budge this estimate of $r = .06$. Indeed, the 95% CI was quite narrow: [.05, .07] (**Figure 8.7**). Both endpoints depict weak relationships, but the precise estimate gives us a strong guide to what to expect for a future study. Assuming all else is equal, we can predict that future estimates will mostly be in this narrow range.

**CIs That Do Not Contain Zero.** It is notable that the 95% CI for the association between sitting and MTL thickness [−.07, −.64] does not include zero. The CI for

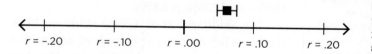

**FIGURE 8.7**

**95% CI for the association between meeting one's spouse online and marital satisfaction.**

This CI is very narrow, reflecting the very large sample in this study.

meeting one's spouse online [.05, .07] doesn't include zero either. In both of these cases, we can infer that the true relationship is unlikely to be zero. When the 95% CI does not include zero, it is common to say that the association is **statistically significant**. The definition of a statistically significant correlation is one that is unlikely to have come from a population in which the association is zero.

**CIs That Do Contain Zero.** In contrast, if a 95% CI does include zero, we can't rule out that the true association is zero. For example, in the MTL study, the researchers had also computed the correlation between amount of exercise people got and their MTL thickness. This correlation was estimated at $r = .02$, with a 95% CI of [−.32, .34]. The interpretation is that the true association between exercise and MTL thickness could be negative or positive, and we can't rule out zero. When the 95% CI contains zero, it is common to say that the association is "not statistically significant."

» For a full introduction to statistical significance, see Statistics Review: Inferential Statistics, pp. 516–518.

### STATISTICAL VALIDITY QUESTION 3: HAS IT BEEN REPLICATED?

The effect size and 95% CI provide important information about how strong the relationship might be. Another step in estimating the population association is to conduct the study again (a process called **replication**) and find multiple estimates.

For example, the correlation between deep talk and well-being was originally estimated at $r = .26$, 95% CI [.04, .45]. A few years later, a research team analyzed four additional samples in which people's conversations were recorded using the EAR device (Milek et al., 2018), obtaining four additional estimates of this association. One sample contained 184 adults, another 122, and two other samples included about 50 people each. The research team computed the $r$ and its 95% CI for each additional sample. **Figure 8.8** shows the five results. Each correlation is plotted as a black square, and the wings on each side of the square indicate the width of the 95% CI for that estimate. The vertical line on the graph marks a zero association. As you can see, the 95% CI for three of the five correlations did not include zero, and all but one of the estimated correlations are positive. The authors concluded that they "found solid evidence that engaging in substantive conversations was moderately associated with life satisfaction" (Milek et al., 2018, p. 1,459).

The Siddharth et al. (2018) study on MTL thickness has not been replicated yet, and neither has the study on marriage satisfaction. Based on what you know so far, which of these two studies

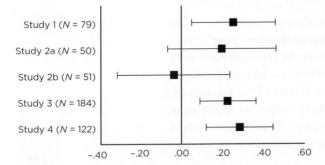

**FIGURE 8.8**

**Multiple estimates of the association between substantive conversations and well-being.**

Milek et al. (2018) computed five estimates. Each correlation (*r*) is plotted as a black square. Most estimates are to the right of the solid vertical line representing zero, which means that the estimate is a positive relationship. The wings on each side of the square indicate the width of the 95% CI. The vertical line on the graph marks a zero association. As you can see, the 95% CI for three of the five correlations did not include zero. (Source: Computed from open data provided by Milek et al., 2018.)

do you think will be most important to try to replicate—the one with the smaller sample or the one with the larger sample?

«
For a full discussion of replication, including meta-analysis, see Chapter 14, pp. 437–447.

## STATISTICAL VALIDITY QUESTION 4: COULD OUTLIERS BE AFFECTING THE ASSOCIATION?

An **outlier** is an extreme score—a single case (or a few cases) that stands out from the pack. Depending on where it sits in relation to the rest of the sample, a single outlier can have an effect on the correlation coefficient $r$. The two scatterplots in **Figure 8.9** show the potential effect of an outlier, a single person who happened to score high on both $x$ and $y$. Why would a single outlier be a problem? As it turns out, adding that one data point changes the correlation from $r = .26$ to $r = .37$. Depending on where the outlier is, it can make a medium-sized correlation appear stronger, or a strong one appear weaker, than it really is.

Outliers can be problematic because even though they are only one or two data points, they may exert disproportionate influence. Think of an association as a seesaw. If you sit close to the center of the seesaw, you don't have much power to make it move, but if you sit way out on one end, you have a much larger influence on whether it moves. Outliers are like people on the far ends of a seesaw: They can have a large impact on the direction or strength of the correlation.

In a bivariate correlation, outliers are mainly problematic when they involve extreme scores on *both* variables. In evaluating the positive correlation between height and weight, for example, a person who is both extremely tall and extremely heavy would make the $r$ appear stronger; a person who is extremely short and extremely heavy would make the $r$ appear weaker. When interrogating an association claim, it is therefore important to ask whether a sample has any outliers. The best way to find them is to look at the scatterplots and see if one or a few data points stand out.

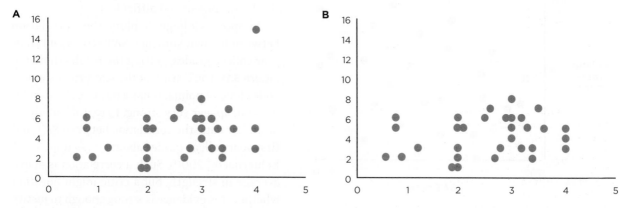

**FIGURE 8.9**
**The effects of an outlier.**
These two scatterplots are identical, except for the outlier in the top-right corner of part A. **(A)** $r = .37$. **(B)** $r = .26$.

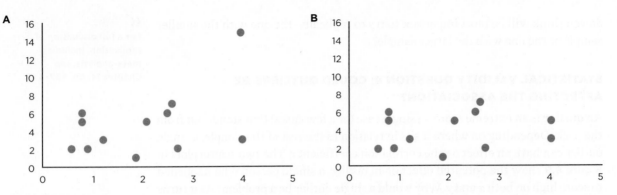

**A**

**B**

## FIGURE 8.10
**Outliers matter most when the sample is small.**

Again, these two scatterplots are identical except for the outlier. But in this case, removing the outlier changed the correlation from $r = .49$ to $r = .15$; this is a much bigger jump than in Figure 8.9, which has more data points.

Just as a small sample has a wider confidence interval, outliers matter the most when a sample is small (**Figure 8.10**). If there are 500 points in a scatterplot (a whole bunch of people sitting in the middle of the seesaw), one outlier is not going to have as much impact. But if there are only 12 points in a scatterplot (only a few people in the middle of the seesaw), an outlier has much more influence on the pattern.

### STATISTICAL VALIDITY QUESTION 5: IS THERE RESTRICTION OF RANGE?

In a correlational study, if there is not a full range of scores on one of the variables in the association, it can make the correlation appear smaller than it really is. This situation is known as **restriction of range**.

To understand the problem, imagine a selective college (College S) that admits only students with high SAT scores. To support this admissions practice, the college might claim that SAT scores are associated with academic success. To support their claim with data, they would use the correlation between SAT scores and first-year college grades. (Those grades are an appropriate measure for such a study because for many students, first-year college courses are similar in content and difficulty.)

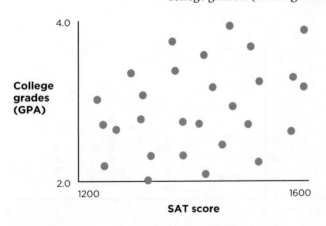

**College grades (GPA)**

**SAT score**

## FIGURE 8.11
**Correlation between SAT scores and first-year college grades.**

College S might observe a scatterplot like this for its enrolled students. (Data are fabricated for illustration purposes.)

Suppose College S plots the correlation between its own students' SAT scores and first-year college grades, getting the results shown in **Figure 8.11**. You'll see that the scatterplot shows a wide cloud of points. It has a positive slope, but it does not appear very strong. In real-life analyses of similar data, the correlation between SAT and first-year college grades about $r = .33$ (Camara & Echternacht, 2000). Such a correlation is above average in strength, but a critic might question whether this evidence is strong enough to justify using the SAT for admissions.

Here's where restriction of range comes in. As you may know, student scores on the SAT currently range from 400 to 1,600. But selective

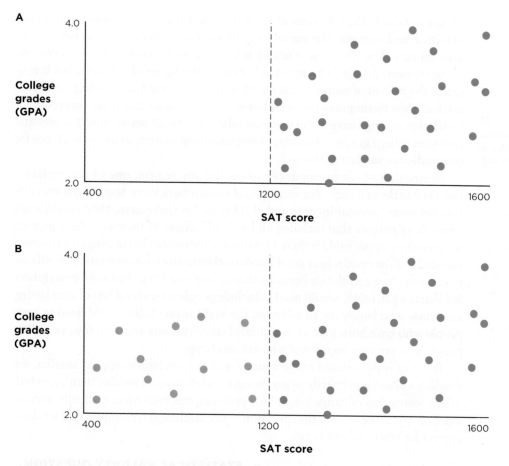

## FIGURE 8.12
**Restriction of range underestimates the true correlation.**

(**A**) College S admits only those students whose SAT scores are above 1200, so its observed correlation between SAT and GPA is about *r* = .33. (**B**) If we could include estimates of the scores for students who were not admitted, the correlation between SAT and GPA would be stronger, about *r* = .57. (Data are fabricated for illustration purposes.)

College S admits only students who score 1,200 or higher on their SATs, as shown in **Figure 8.12A**. Therefore, the true range of SAT scores is *restricted* in College S from 1,200 to 1,600 out of a possible 400 to 1,600.

If we assume the pattern in Figure 8.12A continues in a linear fashion, we can see what the scatterplot would look like if the range on SAT scores were not restricted, as shown in **Figure 8.12B**. The admitted students' scatterplot points are in exactly the same pattern as they were before, but now we have scatterplot points for the unadmitted students. Compared with the range-restricted correlation in part A, the full sample's correlation in part B is stronger. In other words, the restriction of range situation means College S originally *underestimated* the true correlation between SAT scores and grades.

What do researchers do when they suspect restriction of range? A study could obtain the true correlation between SAT scores and college grades by admitting all students to College S (regardless of their SAT scores), see what grades they obtained, and compute the correlation. Of course, College S would not be very keen on that idea. The second option is to use a statistical technique, *correction for restriction of range*. The formula is beyond the scope of this text, but it estimates the full set of scores based on what we know about an existing, restricted set, and then recomputes the correlation. Actual studies that have corrected for restriction of range have estimated a correlation of $r = .57$ between SAT scores and first-year college grades—a stronger association and more convincing evidence for the predictive validity of the SAT.

» Restriction of range is similar to ceiling and floor effects; see Chapter 11, pp. 345–346.

Restriction of range can apply when, for any reason, one of the variables has very little variance. For example, if researchers were testing the correlation between parental income and child school achievement, they would want a sample of parents that included all levels of income. If their sample of parents were entirely upper middle class, there would be restriction of range on parental income, and the researchers would underestimate any true correlation. Similarly, to get at the true correlation between sitting time and MTL thickness, researchers Siddharth et al. (2018) would need to include people who spend lots of time sitting and those who barely do. In addition, the Mehl team (2010) would need to have people who have both a lot of meaningful conversations and very few, as well as people who are very happy and who are less happy.

Because restriction of range usually makes correlations appear smaller, we would ask about it primarily when the correlation appears weaker than expected. When restriction of range might be a problem, researchers can, ideally, recruit more people at the ends of the spectrum or use statistical techniques that let them correct for restriction of range.

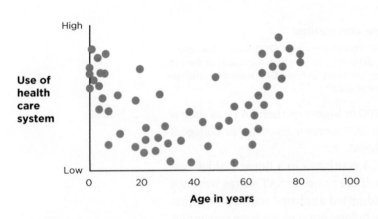

**FIGURE 8.13**

**A curvilinear association.**

With increasing age, people's use of the health care system decreases and then increases again. A curvilinear association is not captured adequately by the simple bivariate correlation coefficient *r*. In these data, $r = .01$, a value that does not accurately describe the relationship. (Data are fabricated for illustration purposes.)

## STATISTICAL VALIDITY QUESTION 6: IS THE ASSOCIATION CURVILINEAR?

When a study reports that there is no relationship between two variables, the relationship might truly be zero. In rare cases, however, there might be a **curvilinear association**, in which the relationship between two variables is not a straight line; it might be positive up to a point and then become negative.

A curvilinear association exists, for example, between age and the use of health care services, as shown in **Figure 8.13**. As people get older, their use of the health care system decreases up to a point. Then, as they approach age 60 and beyond, health care use increases again. When we compute a simple bivariate correlation coefficient $r$ on these data, we get only $r = -.01$ because $r$ is designed to describe the slope of the best-fitting *straight line* through the scatterplot. When the slope of the scatterplot goes up and then down (or down and then up), $r$ does not describe the pattern very well. The straight line that fits best through this set of points is flat and horizontal, with a slope of zero. Therefore, if we looked only at the $r$ and not at the scatterplot, we might conclude there is no relationship between age and use of health care. When researchers suspect a curvilinear association, they might compute the correlation between one variable and the square of the other.

## Internal Validity: Can We Make a Causal Inference from an Association?

Even though it's not necessary to formally interrogate internal validity for an association claim, we must guard against the powerful temptation to make a causal inference from any association claim we read. We hear that couples who meet online have happier marriages, so we advise our single friends to sign up for Match.com (thinking online dating will *make* their future marriages more happy). In fact, a press release erroneously wrapped the dating study in the causal head-line, "Meeting online *leads to* happier, more enduring marriages" (Harms, 2013; emphasis added). Journalists' reports on the Siddharth et al. (2018) finding were headlined, "Standing at your desk could make you smarter." Oops—the strong verb *made* turned the claim into a causal one (Friedman, 2018). What's more, the study didn't measure how "smart" people were—only their MTL thickness. When we read a correlational result, the temptation to make a causal claim can be almost irresistible.

### APPLYING THE THREE CAUSAL CRITERIA

Because the causal temptation is so strong, we have to remind ourselves repeat-edly that correlation is not causation. Why is a simple association insufficient to establish causality? As discussed in Chapter 3, to establish causation, a study must satisfy three criteria:

1. *Covariance of cause and effect.* The results must show a correlation, or associa-tion, between the cause variable and the effect variable.
2. *Temporal precedence.* The method must ensure that the cause variable preceded the effect variable; it must come first in time.
3. *Internal validity.* There must be no plausible alternative explanations for the relationship between the two variables.

The temporal precedence criterion is sometimes called the **directionality problem** because we don't know which variable came first. The internal validity criterion is often called the **third-variable problem**: When we can come up with

**1.** *Covariance:* Do the results show that the variables are correlated?

**2.** *Temporal precedence* (directionality problem): Does the method establish which variable came first in time?

(If we cannot tell which came first, we cannot infer causation.)

**3.** *Internal validity* (third-variable problem): Is there a C variable that is associated with both A and B, independently?

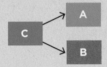

(If there is a plausible third variable, we cannot infer causation.)

**FIGURE 8.14**
**The three criteria for establishing causation.**
When variable A is correlated with variable B, does that mean A causes B? To decide, apply the three criteria.

an alternative explanation for the association between two variables, that alternative is some lurking third variable. **Figure 8.14** provides a shorthand description of these three criteria.

Let's apply these criteria to the deep talk and well-being association, to see whether we can conclude that meaningful conversations *cause* an increase in well-being:

1. *Covariance of cause and effect.* Based on the results of five studies, we already know deep talk is associated positively with well-being. As the percentage of deep talk goes up, well-being goes up, thus showing covariance of the proposed cause and the proposed effect.

2. *Temporal precedence.* In the studies' methods, deep talk and well-being were measured during the same short time period, so we cannot be sure whether people engaged in deep talk first, followed by an increase in well-being, or whether people were happy first and later engaged in more meaningful conversations.

3. *Internal validity.* The association between deep talk and well-being could be attributable to some third variable connected to both deep talk and well-being. For instance, a busy, stressful life might lead people to report lower well-being and have less time for substantive talks. Or perhaps in this college sample, having a strong college-preparatory background is associated with both deep conversations and having higher levels of well-being in college (because those students are better prepared). But be careful—not any third variable will do. The potential third variable, to be plausible, must correlate logically with *both* of the measured variables in the original association. For example, we might propose that income is an alternative explanation, arguing that people with higher incomes will have greater well-being. For income to work as a plausible third variable, though, we would have to explain how higher income is related to more deep talk, too.

As you can see, the bivariate correlation between well-being and deep talk doesn't let us make the causal claim that high levels of substantive conversation cause high levels of well-being. We also cannot make a causal claim in the other direction—that high levels of well-being cause people to engage in more deep conversations. Although the two variables are associated, the study has met only one of the three causal criteria: covariance. Further research using a different kind of study would be needed to establish temporal precedence and internal validity before we would accept this relationship as causal.

What about the press release stating that meeting one's spouse online is associated with a happier marriage? Consider whether this finding justifies the headline "Meeting online leads to happier, more enduring marriages" (Harms, 2013). Let's see how this study stands up to the three causal criteria:

1. *Covariance of cause and effect.* The study reported an association between meeting online and greater marital satisfaction. As discussed earlier, the association in the original study was very weak, but its 95% CI did not contain zero. There seems to be a relationship there.
2. *Temporal precedence.* We can be sure that the meeting location variable came first and marital satisfaction came later. People usually do have to meet somebody (either online or offline) before getting married!
3. *Internal validity.* This criterion is not met by the study. It is possible that certain types of people are more likely to both meet people online and be happier in their marriages. For example, people who are especially motivated to be in a relationship may be more likely to sign up for, and meet their spouses on, online dating sites. And these same relationship-motivated people may be especially prepared to feel happy in their marriages.

In this case, the two variables are associated, so the study has established covariance, and the temporal precedence criterion has also been satisfied. However, the study does not establish internal validity, so we cannot make a causal inference.

## MORE ON INTERNAL VALIDITY: WHEN IS THAT POTENTIAL THIRD VARIABLE A PROBLEM?

When we think of a reasonable third variable explanation for an association claim, how do we know if it's an internal validity problem? In the Mehl study (2010) about deep talk and well-being, we thought level of stress might be a third variable that explains this association. As mentioned earlier, it could be that people under stress are both less happy *and* have less time for meaningful conversations, and that's why deep talk is correlated with well-being. Stress level makes a reasonable third variable here, but is it really responsible for the relationship the Mehl team found? We have to dig deeper.

Sometimes a potential third variable really is a problem. Imagine you measure a large sample of people on both their height and their hair length. You'd probably find a negative correlation: Taller people have shorter hair. But the potential

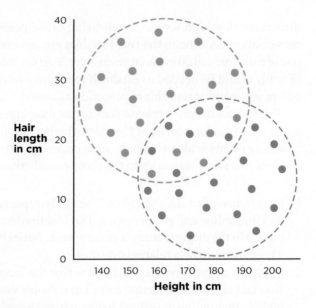

**Hair length in cm**

40

30

20

10

0

140  150  160  170  180  190  200

**Height in cm**

**FIGURE 8.15**

**A third variable, gender: an internal validity problem.**

Women (green dots) are both higher in hair length and lower in height, compared with men (blue dots). Within each gender group, there is no relationship between these two variables. This outcome means that gender is really the reason hair length and height are negatively correlated. (Data are fabricated for illustration purposes.)

third variable here is gender. Although there are lots of exceptions, men tend to be taller than women and tend to have shorter hair. Looking at **Figure 8.15** overall, you would see a negative correlation. However, in this figure, the green dots represent women, who are generally higher on hair length and lower on height. The blue dots represent men, who are generally lower on hair length and higher on height. What's more, if you look at just the green dots by themselves (that is, if you consider the women only), you won't find any relationship between height and hair length. This pattern means that the relationship we see in the overall sample is attributable to the third variable: gender. In such situations, the original relationship between height and hair length is referred to as a **spurious association**. The bivariate correlation is there, but only because of some third variable (gender).

Other times we propose a potential third variable, but it turns out *not* to be a problem. Imagine you measure a large sample of people on their height and weight. You'd probably find a positive correlation overall—in general, taller people weigh more than shorter people. A potential third variable here is gender again: Men tend to be taller than women and to weigh more than women. Could gender be a third variable this time? Look at **Figure 8.16**. You'll notice the overall, positive correlation, and you'll also see that the overall pattern is still there when you consider only the green dots (women) or the blue dots (men) separately. Even though gender is a potential third variable, when we dig deeper, we see that height and weight are still correlated *within* the two gender groups. These data don't support the notion that gender is a third variable in this relationship.

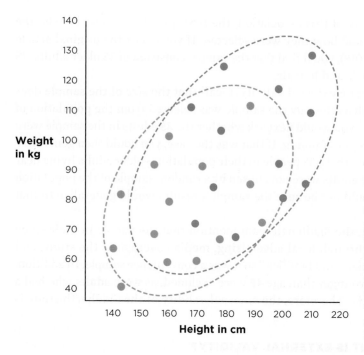

**FIGURE 8.16**

**A third variable, gender: not an internal validity problem.**

Women (green dots) are lower in both height and weight than men (blue dots). However, within each gender group there is still a positive relationship between height and weight. This outcome means that gender does not actually pose an internal validity problem in this relationship; height and weight are still correlated even within the two gender subgroups. (Data are fabricated for illustration purposes.)

When we propose a third variable that could explain a bivariate correlation, it's not necessarily going to present an internal validity problem. We can ask the researchers if their bivariate correlation is still present within potential subgroups. In the Mehl study, if there's still a correlation between deep talk and well-being even within a group of highly stressed people (and within a group of less-stressed people), then stress is unlikely to be a third-variable problem. In Chapter 9, you'll learn more about how to dig deeper to explore whether or not potential third variables are really a problem.

In sum, when we're interrogating a simple association claim, it is not necessary to focus on internal validity as long as it's just that: an association claim. However, we must keep reminding ourselves that covariance satisfies only the first of the three criteria for causation. Before assuming that an association supports a causal claim, we have to apply what we know about temporal precedence and internal validity.

## External Validity: To Whom Can the Association Be Generalized?

When interrogating the external validity of an association claim, you ask whether the association can generalize to other people, places, and times. For example, consider again the association between sitting and MTL thickness. To interrogate

>>
For more on sampling techniques, see Chapter 7, pp. 186–192.

the external validity of this association, the first questions would be who the participants were and how they were selected. If you check the original article (Siddharth et al., 2018), you'll find that the sample consisted of 35 older adults, 25 of whom were female and 10 male.

As you interrogate external validity, recall that the *size* of the sample does not matter as much as the *way* the sample was selected from the population of interest. Therefore, you would next ask whether the 35 adults in the sample were selected using random sampling. If that was the case, you could then generalize the association from these 35 people to their population—older adults living near Los Angeles. If the adults were not chosen by a random sample of the population of interest, you could not be sure the sample's results would generalize to that population.

As it turns out, the Siddharth team mention that the people in their study were "recruited through local advertising, media coverage of the study, and referrals by physicians and families," so it was a convenience sample. In addition, people who were younger than age 45 were excluded, as were adults who had a history of dementia. Therefore, the external validity of the Siddharth study is unknown.

## HOW IMPORTANT IS EXTERNAL VALIDITY?

What should you conclude when a study does not use a random sample? Is it fair to disregard the entire study? In the case of the Siddharth study, we might decide that the construct validity is sound if the measures of sitting time and MTL thickness were acceptable. The researchers did not make any causal claims that would render internal validity relevant. The study had a relatively small sample, so the 95% CI was relatively wide (the estimate is imprecise). But what about its external validity?

This correlational study may not have used a random sample, but you should not automatically reject the association for that reason. Instead, you can accept the study's results and leave the question of generalization to the next study, which might test the association between these two variables in some other population.

Furthermore, many associations do generalize—even to samples that are very different from the original one. Imagine a study of college students in the United States that found men to be taller than women. Would this finding generalize to people in the Netherlands, who are, overall, taller than Americans? Most likely it would: We'd still find the same *association* between sex and height because Dutch men are taller than Dutch women.

Similarly, you might predict that the MTL result would not generalize to younger people, ages 20 to 45, because you might assume the MTL regions of young people's brains have not yet aged and younger people are more likely to move around at work (rather than sit). You might be correct about these mean (average) differences between the samples. However, *within* a sample of people

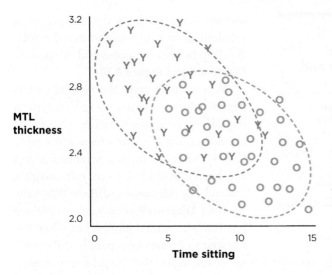

**FIGURE 8.17**

**An association in two different samples.**

Older adults (represented by O) might spend more time sitting than younger adults (Y), and they might have thinner MTL measurements. But the association between the two variables *within* each sample of people may exist. (Data are fabricated for illustration purposes.)

in the 20 to 45 age range, those who spend more time sitting may still be the ones with thinner MTL. The younger sample of people might score lower, on average, on both variables in the association claim, but even so, the association might still hold true within the younger sample. In a scatterplot that includes both these samples, the association would hold true within each subgroup (**Figure 8.17**).

## MODERATING VARIABLES

When the relationship between two variables changes depending on the level of another variable, that other variable is called a **moderator**. Let's consider a study on the correlation between professional sports games attendance and the success of the team. You might expect to see a positive correlation: The more a team wins, the more people will attend the games. However, research by Shige Oishi and his colleagues shows that this association is moderated by the franchise city's level of residential mobility (Oishi et al., 2007). In cities with high residential mobility (such as Phoenix, Arizona), people move in and out of the city frequently. Because frequent movers don't develop ties to their community, the researchers theorized, they would be "fair weather" fans whose interest in the local team depends on whether the team wins. In contrast, in cities with low residential mobility (such as Pittsburgh, Pennsylvania), people live in the city for a long time. They develop strong community ties and are loyal to their sports team even when it loses.

Using data gathered from major league baseball games, Oishi and his team determined that in cities with high residential mobility, there is a positive correlation between success and attendance, indicating a fair-weather fan base. In cities with low residential mobility, there is not a strong correlation between success

TABLE 8.5

### A City's Residential Mobility Moderates the Relationship Between Sports Team Success and Game Attendance

| CITY | ASSOCIATION (*r*) BETWEEN TEAM SUCCESS AND GAME ATTENDANCE |
|---|---|
| Phoenix, AZ (high residential mobility) | .29; 95% CI [.06, .49] |
| Pittsburgh, PA (low residential mobility) | –.16; 95% CI [–.39, .09] |

Source: Adapted from Oishi et al., 2007.

and attendance. We say that the degree of residential mobility moderates the relationship between success and attendance (**Table 8.5** and **Figure 8.18**).

When we identify the type of city as a moderator, we do not mean that type of city affects only one variable. That is, we are not saying Arizona's team wins more than Pittsburgh's or that Arizona's games are better attended than Pittsburgh's. Instead, the *relationship* differs: When the Arizona Diamondbacks lose, people are less likely to attend games, but when the Pittsburgh Pirates lose, people still attend.

For another example, consider a study of teenagers that found a relationship between compulsive texting and school grades. Compulsive texting was defined as being preoccupied with texting, as well as texting that interferes with important life activities. The study found a relationship among girls but not among boys. Therefore, gender moderated the relationship between compulsive texting and grades, such that the relationship was negative for girls but zero for boys (Lister-Landman et al., 2015).

Finally, Mehl et al. (2010) looked for moderators in the relationship they found between deep talk and well-being. They wondered if the relationship would differ depending on whether substantive conversations took place on a weekend or a

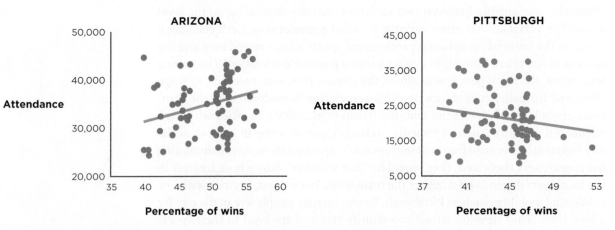

**FIGURE 8.18**

**A moderating variable.**

A city's degree of residential mobility moderates the relationship between local sports team success and attendance at games. Each dot represents one major league baseball season. The Arizona Diamondbacks are based in Phoenix, a high residential mobility city; that pattern shows people are more likely to attend games there when the team is having a winning season. Pittsburgh is a low residential mobility city; that pattern shows Pittsburgh Pirates fans attend games regardless of how winning the season is. (Source: Adapted from Oishi et al., 2007.)

weekday. However, the results suggested that weekend/weekday status did not moderate the relationship between deep talk and well-being: The relationship was positive and of equal strength in both time periods (**Table 8.6**).

In correlational research, moderators can inform external validity. When an association is moderated by residential mobility, type of relationship, day of the week, or some other variable, we know it does not generalize from one of these situations to the others. For example, in asking whether the association between multitasking frequency and ability would generalize to people in their 70s and 80s, you would be asking whether that association would be moderated by age. Similarly, the Mehl team found that the association between deep talk and well-being does generalize from the weekends to weekdays: The strength of the association is almost the same in the two contexts.

Review what you've learned in this chapter by studying the Working It Through section.

« In Chapter 12, you will learn that another way of understanding moderators is to describe them as interactions; see p. 370.

**TABLE 8.6**

**Weekend/Weekday Status Does Not Moderate the Relationship Between Deep Talk and Well-Being**

| DAY OF WEEK | ASSOCIATION (*r*) BETWEEN PERCENTAGE OF SUBSTANTIVE CONVERSATIONS AND WELL-BEING |
|---|---|
| Weekday | .28; 95% CI [.07, .47] |
| Weekend | .27; 95% CI [.06, .46] |

*Note:* Substantive conversations are associated with happiness on both weekdays and weekends.
Source: Adapted from Mehl et al., 2006.

---

✔

**CHECK YOUR UNDERSTANDING**

1. In one or two brief sentences, explain how you would interrogate the construct validity of a bivariate correlation.

2. What are six questions you can ask about the statistical validity of a bivariate correlation? Do all the statistical validity questions apply the same way when bivariate correlations are represented as bar graphs?

3. Which of the three rules of causation is almost always met by a bivariate correlation? Which two rules might not be met by a correlational study?

4. Give examples of some questions you can ask to evaluate the external validity of a correlational study.

5. If we found that gender moderates the relationship between deep talk and well-being, what might that mean?

1. See pp. 209–210. 2. See pp. 210–219; questions about outliers and curvilinear associations may not be relevant for correlations represented as bar graphs. 3. See pp. 219–220. 4. See pp. 224–225. 5. It would mean the relationship between deep talk and well-being is different for men than for women. For example, the relationship might be stronger for women than it is for men.

# Are Parents Happier Than People with No Children?

Some researchers have found that people with children are less happy than people who don't have kids. In contrast, a popular media story reports on a study in which parents are, in fact, happier. We will work through this example of a bivariate correlational study to illustrate the concepts from Chapter 8.

| QUESTIONS TO ASK | CLAIMS, QUOTES, OR DATA | INTERPRETATION AND EVALUATION |
|---|---|---|
| What kind of claim is being made in the journalist's headline?<br><br>What are the two variables in the headline?<br><br>Association claims can be supported by correlational studies. Why can we assume the study was correlational? | "Parents are happier than non-parents" (Welsh, 2012).<br><br>The journalist reported: "Parents may not be the overtired, overworked and all-around miserable individuals they are sometimes made out to be, suggests new research finding. Mom and Dad (particularly fathers) experience greater levels of happiness and meaning from life than nonparents" (Welsh, 2012). | The simple verb *are* made this an association claim. Parenting goes with being happier.<br><br>The two variables are "being a parent or not" and "level of happiness."<br><br>We can assume this is a correlational study because parenting and level of happiness are probably measured variables (it's not realistically possible to manipulate them). In a correlational study, all variables are measured. |

**The journal article reports on three studies of parenting and happiness, and we'll focus on Study 2 (Nelson et al., 2013).**

| | | |
|---|---|---|
| Are the variables categorical or quantitative? | The Method section describes how the researchers distributed pagers to 329 adults, about half of whom were parents. The adults reported on their happiness (on a 7-point scale) at different times of the day. | One variable is categorical: People were either parents or not.<br><br>The other variable, happiness, was quantitative because people could range from low to high. |

| QUESTIONS TO ASK | CLAIMS, QUOTES, OR DATA | INTERPRETATION AND EVALUATION |
|---|---|---|
| What were the results? | 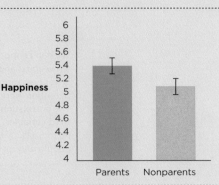 | Because one variable was categorical and the other was quantitative, the researchers presented the results as a bar graph. Parents had a higher average well-being than nonparents. |

## Construct Validity

| | | |
|---|---|---|
| How well was each variable measured? | To measure parenting status, the researchers simply asked people if they were parents. | It seems unlikely that people would lie about their parental status, so we can assume a self-report was a valid measure of parenting. |
| | To measure happiness, participants wore devices that paged them five times daily. At each page, the participant rated 8 positive emotions (such as pride, joy) and 11 negative emotions (such as anger, guilt). The researchers subtracted the ratings of negative emotions from positive ones at each time point and averaged across each person's 35 reports for a week. | It seems reasonable that people who have positive emotions throughout the day are happier, so this operationalization of happiness has face validity. Notably, happiness was based on an "in-the-moment" response, not a global judgment, so it may be more accurate. However, the researchers don't present any criterion validity or convergent validity evidence for the measure. |

## Statistical Validity

| | | |
|---|---|---|
| What is the effect size? How precise is it? Has it been replicated? | The researchers reported: "As in Study 1, we first examined the relationship between parenthood and happiness with $t$ tests. Parents reported higher levels of global well-being, including more happiness, $t(325) = 2.68$, $p = .008$, $r = .15 . . .$" (Nelson et al., 2013, p. 7). | The authors report an effect size of $r = .15$, and $p = .008$. This effect size is somewhat smaller than the average correlation in psychology studies. The 95% CI is [.04, .25], which is rather uncertain: The true relationship could be very small or even moderate. The article reports three studies, all of which replicated the effect that parents are happier than nonparents. |
| Are there outliers? | | The researchers don't mention outliers, but in a sample this large, outliers are unlikely to have an impact on the overall pattern. |
| Is the association curvilinear? | | Parenting is a two-category variable. Without some middle category we can't have a curvilinear association. |
| Could there be restriction of range? | | We look for restriction of range when the results are smaller than expected. Perhaps because these researchers found an effect, they did not test for restriction of range. |

*(Continued)*

| QUESTIONS TO ASK | CLAIMS, QUOTES, OR DATA | INTERPRETATION AND EVALUATION |
|---|---|---|
| **Internal Validity**<br><br>Can the study support the claim that parenthood *causes* people to be happy? | | We can't support a causal claim. The results show covariance, but temporal precedence is not present because happiness and parenting were measured at the same time. The correlational method could not rule out third variables. For example, parents may be more likely to be married, and married people may also be happier. |
| **External Validity**<br><br>To whom can we generalize this association? | The article reports that the sample of 329 adults came from "a study on emotional experience in adulthood" (p. 4). | The authors did not state that the sample was selected at random, so we do not know to whom this association can generalize. |

# CHAPTER REVIEW

 It's time to complete your study experience! Go to INQUIZITIVE to practice actively with this chapter's concepts and get personalized feedback along the way.

## Summary

Association claims state that two variables are linked, but they do not state that one causes the other. Association claims are supported by correlational research, in which both variables are measured in a set of participants. (If either of the variables is manipulated, the study is an experiment, which could potentially support a causal claim.)

### INTRODUCING BIVARIATE CORRELATIONS

- The variables in a bivariate correlational study can be either quantitative or categorical. If both variables are quantitative, the data are usually depicted in a scatterplot; if one variable is categorical, the data are usually depicted in a bar graph.

- For a scatterplot, the correlation coefficient $r$ can be used to describe the relationship. For a bar graph, the difference between the two group means is used to describe the relationship.

- Regardless of whether an association is analyzed with scatterplots or bar graphs, if both variables are measured, the study is correlational.

### INTERROGATING ASSOCIATION CLAIMS

- Because a correlational study involves two measured variables, the construct validity of each measure must be interrogated in a bivariate correlation study.

- Interrogating the statistical validity of an association claim involves six areas of inquiry: effect size (strength of $r$), precision (confidence interval of $r$), replication of the study, the presence of outliers, possible restriction of range, and whether the association is curvilinear.

- Internal validity addresses the degree to which a study supports a causal claim. Although it is not necessary to interrogate internal validity for an association claim because it does not make a causal statement, it can be tempting to assume causality from a correlational study.

- Correlational studies do not satisfy all three criteria for a causal claim: They may show covariance but do not usually satisfy temporal precedence, and they cannot establish internal validity.

- Interrogating the external validity of an association claim involves asking whether the sample is representative of some population. If a correlational study does not use a random sample of people or contexts, the results cannot necessarily generalize to the population from which the sample was taken.

- A lack of external validity should not disqualify an entire study. If the study fulfills the other three validities and its results are sound, the question of generalizability can be left for future investigation.

- A bivariate correlation is sometimes moderated, which means the relationship changes depending on the levels of another variable, such as gender, age, or location.

# Key Terms

bivariate correlation, p. 204
mean, p. 208
effect size, p. 210
statistical significance, p. 214

replication, p. 214
outlier, p. 215
restriction of range, p. 216
curvilinear association, p. 218

directionality problem, p. 219
third-variable problem, p. 219
spurious association, p. 222
moderator, p. 225

**To see samples of chapter concepts in the popular media, visit www.everydayresearchmethods.com and click the box for Chapter 8.**

# Review Questions

1. Suppose you hear that conscientious people are more likely to get regular health checkups. Which of the following correlations between conscientiousness and getting checkups would probably support this claim?

   a. $r = .03$

   b. $r = .45$

   c. $r = -.35$

   d. $r = -1.0$

2. Which of these associations will probably be plotted as a bar graph rather than a scatterplot?

   a. The more conscientious people are, the greater the likelihood they'll get regular health checkups.

   b. Level of depression is linked to the amount of exercise people get.

   c. Students at private colleges get higher GPAs than those at public colleges.

   d. Level of chronic stomach pain in kids is linked to later anxiety as adults.

3. A study found that people who like spicy foods are generally risk takers. Which of the following questions interrogates the construct validity of this correlation?

   a. How strong is the effect?

   b. Did the study use a random sample of people?

   c. Were there any outliers in the relationship?

   d. How well did they measure each variable: risk taking and liking spicy foods?

4. Darrin reads a story reporting that students at private colleges get higher GPAs than those at public colleges. He wonders if this means going to a private college causes you to have a higher GPA. If so, he'll go to a private college! Applying the three causal criteria, Darrin knows there is covariance here. He also knows there is temporal precedence because you choose a college first, and then you get your GPA. Which of the following questions would help Darrin ask about the third criterion, internal validity?

   a. Could there be restriction of range?

   b. Is the link between private college and high grades the same for both men and women?

   c. How did they decide what qualifies a college as private or public?

   d. Is there some other reason these two are related? Maybe better students are more likely to go to private colleges, and they are also likely to get better grades?

5. Which of the following sentences describes a moderator for the relationship between risk taking and liking spicy foods?

   a. There is a positive relationship between liking spicy foods and risk taking for men, but no relationship for women.

   b. Older adults tend to like spicy foods less than younger adults.

   c. The relationship between liking spicy foods and risk taking is the same for people in cities and in rural areas.

# Learning Actively

1. For each of the following examples, sketch a graph of the result (either a bar graph or a scatterplot). Then interrogate the construct validity, the statistical validity, and the external validity of each association claim. What questions would you ask? What answers would you expect?

   a. "Chronic stomach pain in kids is linked to adult anxiety disorders in later life." In this study, the researchers "followed 332 children between the ages of 8 and 17 who were diagnosed with functional abdominal pain and 147 with no pain for an average of eight years. . . . On follow-up, the researchers interviewed the volunteers—who were on average age 20 at that point—either in person or by phone. . . . Of adults who had abdominal pain as children, 51 percent had experienced an anxiety disorder during their lives, compared to 20 percent of those who didn't experience tummy aches as children" (Carroll, 2013).

   b. "Kids with ADHD may be more likely to bully." In this study, the researchers "followed 577 children—the entire population of fourth graders from a municipality near Stockholm—for a year. The researchers interviewed parents, teachers and children to determine which kids were likely to have ADHD. Children showing signs of the disorder were then seen by a child neurologist for diagnosis. The researchers also asked the kids about bullying. [The study found that] children with attention deficit hyperactivity disorder are almost four times as likely as others to be bullies" (Carroll, 2008).

2. A researcher conducted a study of 34 scientists (Grim, 2008). He reported a correlation between the amount of beer each scientist drank per year and the likelihood of that scientist publishing a scientific paper. The correlation was reported as $r = -.55$, 95% CI [-.74, -.27].

   a. What does a negative correlation mean in this example? Is this relationship strong or weak?

   b. What does 95% CI [-.74, -.27] mean in this result?

   c. Draw a scatterplot of this association. What might happen to this correlation if you added one person in the sample who drank much more beer than other scientists and also published far fewer papers than other scientists?

   d. A popular media report about this article was headlined "Suds seem to skew scientific success" (*San Diego Union-Tribune*, 2008). Is such a causal claim justified?

   e. Perhaps academic discipline is a moderator of this relationship. Create a moderator table, using Table 8.5 as a model, showing that the association between beer drinking and publications is stronger for science faculty than it is for humanities faculty.

# Do people who have moved frequently prefer shopping at chain stores?

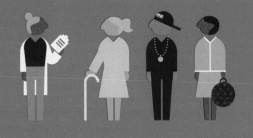

You and a lab partner can work together to try to replicate a study that tested the relationship between residential mobility and preference for familiarity. The theory behind this study states residential mobility (that is, moving to a new area) can be stressful and disruptive. In response, people who have moved a lot should prefer familiar objects over unfamiliar ones. For a person who is distressed by frequent moves, spending time with familiar objects can be comforting. A research team led by Shige Oishi conducted a series of studies to test this theory (Oishi et al., 2012). They chose to use retail stores as a way of evaluating preference for "familiar objects." The team asked people to imagine that they needed to make a variety of purchases (for example, a digital camera or a cup of coffee). For each product they were supposed to buy, participants indicated whether they would prefer to shop at a U.S. national chain store or a local store. Then, participants reported how often they had moved to a different house during their school years. The authors found that the more people had moved in their lifetimes, the more they preferred chain stores such as Best Buy or Starbucks (Oishi et al., 2012). The original study reported two correlations, based on two similar studies: $r$ (128) = .20, 95% CI [.03, .36] (Study 2a) and $r$ (102) = .33, 95% CI [.15, .49] (Study 2b).

In this exercise, you'll replicate the study that tested this hypothesis.

## STEP 1 ▸ Prepare your materials.

Working with your partner, you will prepare a survey containing questions about people's moving history and their preference for chain stores versus local stores. You can use a tool such as Google Forms, Qualtrics, or Survey Monkey to create the survey, or you can just print it on paper.

Here are the items used in the original study. First, to measure moving history, the researchers used this measure:

> How many times did you move to a new city or town during elementary school?
>
> How many times did you move to a new city or town during middle school?
>
> How many times did you move to a new city or town during high school?

Second, to measure preference for chain stores over local stores, they used these instructions:

> Imagine you are out on a shopping trip in California and have to buy a number of items. For each item, you have a choice of one of two stores. The two stores are approximately equal in their variety of goods and the quality of the goods. They are also equal in price. Some of the stores are local California stores, whereas others are national chain stores. Please indicate which of the two stores you would like to visit to purchase the item listed.

To compute preference for chain stories, they assigned people one point for each time they selected the national chain over the local one. Then they summed up all the points (for a maximum score of 14).

To compute residential mobility, they added up the number of moves in each time period (elementary, middle, and high school).

**Coffee:**
- ⚪ Malibou
- ⚪ Starbucks*

**Dinner:**
- ⚪ Red Lobster*
- ⚪ Seafood Grill

**Digital camera:**
- ⚪ Camera World
- ⚪ Best Buy*

**Pizza:**
- ⚪ Firenche
- ⚪ Domino's*

**Books:**
- ⚪ Barnes & Noble*
- ⚪ Morgen's Book Store

**Ice cream:**
- ⚪ Baskin-Robbins*
- ⚪ Olivier

**Stationery:**
- ⚪ Paper & Pencil
- ⚪ Staples*

**Gifts:**
- ⚪ Rene's House
- ⚪ Hallmark*

**Bakery:**
- ⚪ Monte
- ⚪ Panera Bread*

**Chocolate:**
- ⚪ Godiva*
- ⚪ La Chocola

**Hardware:**
- ⚪ Lowe's*
- ⚪ Orchard Supply

**Furniture:**
- ⚪ Richard's Furnishing
- ⚪ Ethan Allen*

**Grocery:**
- ⚪ Whole Foods*
- ⚪ Fresh Mart

**Pharmacy:**
- ⚪ Raymond's
- ⚪ CVS*

*Note:* * Indicates the national chain option for each item. When you show these options to participants, you should omit the *.

## STEP 2  Collect data.

Find some classmates or friends who are willing to participate. As you invite people to participate, ask each person for permission. You can follow this script:

"Hi! I'm wondering if you have a few minutes to help me out for my psychology class. I'm practicing research and I am looking for volunteers to be in a short study where you answer questions about yourself and about where you might shop. There are no risks or benefits in this study, and your participation would be voluntary. I'm also not going to collect your name. Would you be willing to participate?"

If your friends agree, you can hand them the paper survey, or send them the link to the online survey.

## STEP 3  Enter your data.

**TIP:** If you use Google Forms to administer your survey, the data will already be collected in a Google Sheet.

When we enter the data into a data matrix, each person gets a row and each variable gets a column. You'll need a column for each variable ("elementary school moves," "middle school moves," "high school moves") as well as a column for each of the shopping choices (coffee, camera, etc.).

When you enter the data, if a person chooses a national chain, they get a "1" for that category. For example, if they choose Starbucks for coffee, they get a "1" in that cell. If they chose Malibou, they'd get a "0."

Your data matrix will look something like this:

Have your partner(s) check your data entry to make sure you've done it correctly.

## STEP 4  Compute the summary scores.

After your data are entered, add these new columns:

Sum of number of moves

Sum of preferences for national chain stores

Optional column: In the original article, the researchers found that the total number of moves was positively skewed; therefore, they created a new variable that was the **square root of the total number of moves**.

Using the function tool, compute three scores for each person.

**Sum of number of moves** is the sum of the three time periods (elementary, middle, and high school moves)

**Sum of preferences for national chains** is the sum of the 14 shopping choices, which are scored as "1" or "0" (Coffee, camera, etc).

**Optional: Square root of the total number of moves** is the square root of the sum of number of moves.

(Please see the formulas used in the sample data set for help; your instructor can provide the link.)

---

**STEP 5** **Use the statistics program JASP to calculate descriptive statistics, correlation, and CI.**

A. Save your data as .csv.
B. Open JASP on your computer. (Obtain this free program at jasp-stats.org.)
C. In JASP, select File/Open/Computer to find the .csv data file you just downloaded.

D. Once the file is open, select the Common tab to get to the data view. Change variable types if needed (next to each variable name).
E. First, look at the summary statistics. Select **Descriptives**. Move your two primary variables—the **total number of moves** and the **total preference for chain stores**—over into the empty box.

Take note of the N ("Valid"), the minimum, maximum, mean, and standard deviation. You'll be including these values in your report. As you see below, the sample data has 19 participants, the mean preference for national chains is 6.16, and the mean preference for number of moves is 1.68.

## Descriptives

**Descriptive Statistics**

|  | Sum national chains | Total number of moves |
|---|---|---|
| Valid | 19 | 19 |
| Missing | 0 | 0 |
| Mean | 6.158 | 1.684 |
| Std. Deviation | 2.609 | 2.162 |
| Minimum | 2.000 | 0.000 |
| Maximum | 11.00 | 7.000 |

**F.** Next, compute the correlation between the two variables. Select Regression/Correlation Matrix:

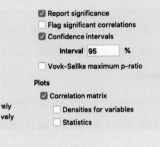

**Correlation Matrix** ▼

Pearson Correlations ▼

| | | Total number of moves | Sum national chains |
|---|---|---|---|
| **Total number of moves** | Pearson's r | — | |
| | p-value | — | |
| | Upper 95% CI | — | |
| | Lower 95% CI | — | |
| **Sum national chains** | Pearson's r | 0.265 | — |
| | p-value | 0.272 | — |
| | Upper 95% CI | 0.642 | — |
| | Lower 95% CI | −0.215 | — |

You can also create a scatterplot of the association by selecting "Correlation matrix" under Plots:

Move two variables over to the window: **Total number of moves** and the **sum of the national chains**. Check the box for "confidence intervals."

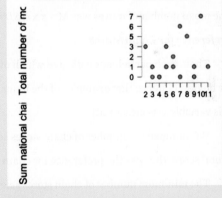

The results below come from a different set of data; your own results will vary. However, use the table to find your own data's *r* (called Pearson's *r*) and your own data's 95% CI.

In the sample data, the *r* is .272, and the 95% CI is [-.215, .642].

**STEP 6 Report your results.**

Write up a mini version of your study (Method, Results, and Discussion sections only) using this APA-style template. You should fill in all the blanks and provide any content noted with [square brackets]. Take the brackets out after you add the content, with the exception of 95% CIs, which are normally shown in square brackets.

## APA paper template:

### Method

This was a bivariate correlational study in which two variables were measured: _____ and _____. Our hypothesis was that _____.

### Participants

Participants were [number] volunteers who were students at _____. They participated voluntarily in [location].

### Procedure

The participants participated individually [describe how they answered the questions—on paper? online? How were they recruited?].

#### *Number of Moves*

Participants indicated how many times they had moved during their childhood by answering the questions [describe the items you used]. We computed the total number of moves by [describe].

The minimum number of moves was x.xx and the maximum was x.xx. The mean number of moves was $M$ = x.xx, $SD$ = x.xx.

#### *Preference for Chain Stores*

Then, each participant indicated which of two stores they would shop at for buying 14 items: [list examples of the items here, and say more about how this variable was measured].

We summed the number of chain stores selected across the 14 items to get a total score; this was the preference for chain scores variable.

The minimum number of chain stores selected was x.xx and the maximum was x.xx. The mean number of chain stores selected was $M$ = x.xx, $SD$ = x.xx.

Data were analyzed using [JASP/SPSS/Excel].

## Results

The correlation between number of moves and preference for chain stores was ($r$ = .xx, 95% CI [.xx, .xx]). This is a [positive/negative/zero] correlation. This CI means that [explain].

This 95% CI [does/does not] contain zero, so we can conclude that the relationship between the two variables [is not/is] statistically significant.

## Discussion

The results of this correlational study can be compared to two original correlations of $r$ = .20, 95% CI [.03, .36] (Study 2a) and $r$ = .33, 95% CI [.15, .49] (Study 2b) between number of moves and preference for chain stores, reported by Oishi et al., 2012. The correlation we obtained is [stronger/weaker/about the same] as these. Therefore, our results [replicate/do not replicate] the correlations obtained in the original study.

[Here you can make a comment about your study's internal, external, and construct validities.]

---

**COMPREHENSION QUESTIONS**

1. What makes this a correlational study?
2. The original study tested this correlation two times, in Study 2a and Study 2b. The original correlations were $r$ = .20, 95% CI [.03, .36] and $r$ = .33, 95% CI [.15, .49]. Given these two previously published confidence intervals, are you surprised by the results you got? Why do you think your results are the same, or different from, the Oishi et al., 2012, study?
3. What might be a third variable that could be associated with both number of residential moves and preference for chain stores?
4. Can your study support the causal claim that "moving a lot as a child causes you to prefer familiar national chain stores"? Why or why not? (Apply the three causal criteria.)

**The Origins of Narcissism: Children More Likely to Be Self-Centered if They Are Praised Too Much**

*INDEPENDENT, 2015*

**Study Links Teen Pregnancy to Sex on TV Shows**

**NEWSMAX.COM, 2008**

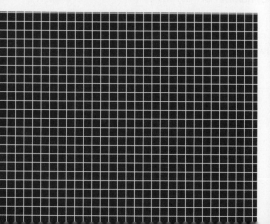

# 9

# Multivariate Correlational Research

CORRELATIONAL STUDIES CAN PROVIDE interesting new information in their own right. The opening headlines provide examples. It might interest us to read that children who are praised too much are also self-centered or narcissistic. We might be surprised to learn that watching sex on TV shows is linked to teen pregnancy. Often, however, a correlational result is an early step in establishing a causal relationship between two variables. Psychological scientists (among many others) want to know about causes and effects, not just correlations, because they may suggest treatments. If praise is linked to narcissism, we might wonder whether or not the praise *makes* kids narcissistic. If it does, parents might change how they express approval. When reading that sexual content on TV is linked to teenage pregnancy, we may wonder whether watching sexual material *causes* behavior that leads to pregnancy. If it does, then pediatricians, teachers, or advocacy groups could argue for restricting teens' exposure to certain kinds of TV shows. However, if the relationships are not causal, such interventions would not work.

Because correlation is not causation, what are the options? Researchers have developed some techniques that enable them to test for cause. The best of these is experimentation: Instead of measuring both variables, researchers manipulate one variable and measure the other. (Experimental designs are covered in Chapters 10–12.) Even without setting up an experiment, however, researchers can use some advanced correlational techniques to get a bit closer to

**LEARNING OBJECTIVES**

**A year from now, you should still be able to:**

**1.**
State why simple bivariate correlations are not sufficient for establishing causation.

**2.**
Explain how longitudinal correlational designs can establish temporal precedence.

**3.**
Explain how multiple-regression analyses can rule out some (but not all) third variables.

**4.**
Describe the value of pattern and parsimony, in which a variety of research results support a single, parsimonious causal theory.

**5.**
Explain the function of a mediating variable.

making a causal claim. This chapter outlines three such techniques: longitudinal designs, which allow researchers to establish temporal precedence in their data; multiple-regression analyses, which help researchers rule out certain third-variable explanations; and the "pattern and parsimony" approach, in which the results of a variety of correlational studies all support a single, causal theory. In the three techniques, as in all correlational studies, the variables are measured—that is, none are manipulated.

## REVIEWING THE THREE CAUSAL CRITERIA

The bivariate examples in Chapter 8 involved only two measured variables. In contrast, longitudinal designs, multiple-regression designs, and the pattern and parsimony approach are **multivariate designs**, which involve more than two measured variables. While these techniques are not perfect solutions to the causality conundrum, they are extremely useful and widely used tools, especially when experiments are impossible to run.

Remember that the three criteria for establishing causation are covariance, temporal precedence, and internal validity. We might apply these criteria to correlational research on the association between parental praise and narcissism.

In the research you'll read about in this chapter, narcissism is studied as a personality trait in which people feel superior to others, believe they deserve special treatment, and respond strongly when others put them down. Parental overpraise, the other variable discussed in this example, occurs when parents tell kids they are exceptional or more special than other children. It's important to note that childhood narcissism is different from high self-esteem (a trait that is considered healthy). Similarly, overpraising is different from parents expressing warmth and love for their children.

Let's examine the three criteria:

1. *Is there covariance?* At least one study did find covariance (Otway & Vignoles, 2006). Adults who were narcissistic remembered their parents praising them for almost everything they did. The correlation was around $r = .20$.
2. *Is there temporal precedence?* A correlational study like Otway and Vignoles's does not establish temporal precedence because both variables were measured at the same time. In a single session, adults rated their narcissism and also reflected on their parents' past behavior. Therefore, their current self-views could have colored their recall of the past. It's not clear which variable came first in time.
3. *Is there internal validity?* The association between parental praise and child narcissism might be explained by a third variable. Perhaps parents praise boys more than girls, and boys are also more likely to have narcissistic traits. Or perhaps parents who are themselves narcissistic simply overpraise their children and, independently, their narcissism is mimicked by their kids.

**CHECK YOUR UNDERSTANDING**

1. Why can't a simple bivariate correlational study meet all three criteria for establishing causation?

1. See p. 242.

# ESTABLISHING TEMPORAL PRECEDENCE WITH LONGITUDINAL DESIGNS

A **longitudinal design** can provide evidence for temporal precedence by measuring the same variables in the same people at several points in time. Longitudinal research is used in developmental psychology to study changes in a trait or an ability as a person grows older. In addition, this type of design can be adapted to test causal claims.

Researchers conducted such a study on a sample of 565 children and their mothers and fathers living in the Netherlands (Brummelman et al., 2015). The parents and children were contacted four times, every 6 months. Each time, the children completed questionnaires in school, responding to items about narcissism (e.g., "Kids like me deserve something extra"). Parents also completed questionnaires about overpraising their children, which was referred to in the study as overvaluation (e.g., "My child is more special than other children").

This study was longitudinal because the researchers measured the *same* variables in the *same* group of people across time—every 6 months. It is also a multivariate correlational study because eight variables were considered: child narcissism at Times 1, 2, 3, and 4, and parental overvaluation at Times 1, 2, 3, and 4.

## Interpreting Results from Longitudinal Designs

Because there are more than two variables involved, a multivariate design gives several individual correlations, referred to as cross-sectional correlations, autocorrelations, and cross-lag correlations. The Brummelman researchers conducted their analyses on mothers' and fathers' overvaluation separately, in order to investigate the causal paths for each parent separately. We present the results for mothers here, but the results were similar for fathers.

### CROSS-SECTIONAL CORRELATIONS

The first set of correlations are **cross-sectional correlations**; they test to see whether two variables, measured at the same point in time, are correlated. For example, the study reports that the correlation between mothers' overvaluation

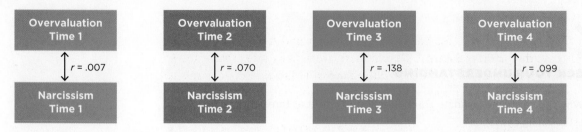

**FIGURE 9.1**
**Cross-sectional correlations.**

Look at the correlations of the variables when measured at the same time. Within each time period, the mothers' overvaluation is weakly associated with child narcissism. Notice that the arrows point in both directions because in these cross-sectional correlations, the two variables were measured at the same time, so we don't know which came first. The figure shows zero-order (bivariate) correlations. (Source: Adapted from Brummelman et al., 2015.)

at Time 4 and children's narcissism at Time 4 was $r = .099$. This correlation is consistent with the hypothesis. However, because both variables in a cross-sectional correlation were measured at the same time, this result alone cannot establish temporal precedence. Either one of these variables might have led to changes in the other. **Figure 9.1** depicts how this study was designed and shows all of the cross-sectional correlations.

## AUTOCORRELATIONS

The next step was to evaluate the correlation of each variable with itself across time. For example, the Brummelman team asked whether mothers' overvaluation at Time 1 was associated with mothers' overvaluation at Times 2, 3, and 4; they also asked whether children's narcissism at Time 1 was associated with their scores at Times 2, 3, and 4. Such correlations are sometimes called **autocorrelations** because they determine the correlation of one variable with itself, measured on two different occasions. The results in **Figure 9.2** suggest that both overvaluation and narcissism are fairly consistent over time.

» Autocorrelations are the same as test-retest reliability correlations (see Chapter 5).

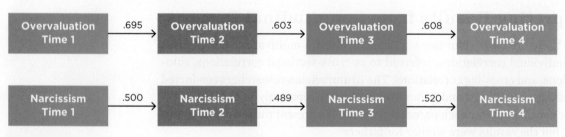

**FIGURE 9.2**
**Autocorrelation.**

In a longitudinal study, researchers also investigate the autocorrelations. These results indicate that both variables seem to be relatively stable over time. Notice that the arrows point in only one direction, because we are sure that the Time 1 measurements came before the Time 2 measurements. (Source: Adapted from Brummelman et al., 2015.)

## CROSS-LAG CORRELATIONS

So far, so good. However, cross-sectional correlations and autocorrelations are generally not the primary interest. Researchers are usually most interested in **cross-lag correlations**, which show whether the earlier measure of one variable is associated with the later measure of the other variable. Cross-lag correlations thus address the directionality problem and help establish temporal precedence.

In the Brummelman study, the cross-lag correlations show how strongly mothers' overvaluation at Time 1 is correlated with child narcissism later on, compared with how strongly child narcissism at Time 1 is correlated with mothers' overvaluation later on. By inspecting the cross-lag correlations in a longitudinal design, we can investigate how one variable correlates with another one (that's the "cross" part of its name) over time (that's the "lag" part). Cross-lag correlations establish temporal precedence. In Brummelman's results, only one set of the cross-lag correlations was greater than zero; the other set was not (**Figure 9.3**).

**Statistically significant correlations.** Notice that Brummelman's team reported the point estimates for the correlations but did not report the 95% CIs for each. Instead, they used the shorthand of statistical significance, which is related to the 95% CI. Perhaps the correlation of $r = .071$ in Figure 9.3 (the association between Time 1 overvaluation and Time 2 narcissism) had a 95% CI of [.01, .15], which does not include zero. As you learned in Chapter 8, when a 95% CI for a correlation does not include zero, researchers can also say that the correlation is "statistically significant." In contrast, perhaps the correlation from Time 1 narcissism to Time 2 overvaluation had a 95% CI of [–.09, .07]. Because this CI does include zero, we can also say that the correlation is "not significant," abbreviated "n.s." Brummelman's team used this shorthand instead of reporting the 95% CIs for each correlation.

Taken together, the cross-lag correlations mean that mothers who overvalued their children at one time had children who were higher in narcissism 6 months later. In contrast, children who were higher in narcissism at a particular time did

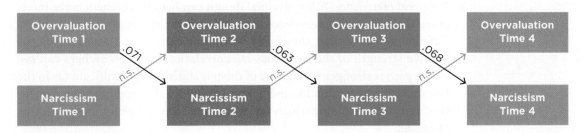

**FIGURE 9.3**
**Results of a cross-lag study.**
The cross-lag correlations in this study are consistent with the conclusion that parental overpraise comes before narcissism because overpraise in early time periods significantly predicts later narcissism, but narcissism in earlier time periods was not significantly (n.s.) related to later overpraise. The arrows point in only one direction because in each case the method makes clear which variable came first in time; Time 1 always comes before Time 2, and so on. Values shown are associated with mothers' overpraise. (Source: Adapted from Brummelman et al., 2015.)

not have mothers who overvalued them 6 months later. Because the "overvaluation-to-narcissism" correlations are significant and the "narcissism-to-overvaluation" correlations are not, the results suggest the overvaluation, not the narcissism, came first.

**Three Possible Patterns from a Cross-Lag Study.** The results of the cross-lag correlations in the Brummelman study could have followed one of three patterns. The study did show that parental overpraise (overvaluation) at earlier times was correlated with child narcissism at the later times. Such a pattern was consistent with the argument that overpraise leads to increases in narcissism over time. However, the study could have shown the opposite result—that narcissism at earlier times was correlated with overpraise later. Such a pattern would have indicated that the childhood narcissistic tendency came first, leading parents to change their type of praise later.

Finally, the study could have shown that *both* correlations were different from zero—that overpraise at Time 1 predicted narcissism at Time 2 *and* that narcissism at Time 1 predicted overpraise at Time 2. If that had been the result, it would mean excessive praise and narcissistic tendencies are mutually reinforcing. In other words, there is a cycle in which overpraise leads to narcissism, which leads parents to overpraise, and so on.

## Longitudinal Studies and the Three Criteria for Causation

Longitudinal designs can provide some evidence for a causal relationship by means of the three criteria for causation:

1. *Covariance.* Statistical relationships in longitudinal designs help establish covariance. When two variables are correlated and their 95% CIs do not contain zero (as in the cross-lag correlations in Figure 9.3), there is covariance.
2. *Temporal precedence.* A longitudinal design can help researchers make inferences about temporal precedence. Because each variable is measured at clearly different points in time, they know which one came first. By comparing the relative strength of the two cross-lag correlations, the researchers can see which path is stronger. If only one of them is statistically significant (as in the Brummelman overvaluation and narcissism study), the researchers move a little closer to determining which variable comes first and closer to establishing causation.
3. *Internal validity.* When conducted simply—by measuring only the two key variables—longitudinal studies may not help rule out third variables. For example, the Brummelman results presented in Figure 9.3 cannot clearly rule out the possible third variable of socioeconomic status. It's possible that parents in higher income brackets overpraise their children, and that children in upper-income families are also more likely to think they're better than other kids.

However, researchers can sometimes design their studies or conduct subsequent analyses in ways that address some third variables. For example, in the Brummelman study, one possible third variable is gender. What if boys show higher levels of narcissism than girls, and what if parents of boys are also more likely to overpraise them? Gender might be associated with both variables. Participant gender does not threaten internal validity here, however, because Brummelman and his colleagues report that the pattern was the same when boys and girls were examined separately. Thus, gender is a potential third variable, but by studying the longitudinal patterns of boys and girls separately, the Brummelman team was able to rule it out.

## Why Not Just Do an Experiment?

Why would Brummelman and his team go to the trouble of tracking children every 6 months for 2 years? Why didn't they just do an experiment? After all, conducting experiments is the only certain way to confirm or disconfirm causal claims. The problem is that in some cases people cannot be randomly assigned to a causal variable of interest. For example, we cannot manipulate personality traits, such as narcissism in children. Similarly, while parents might be able to learn new ways to praise their children, they can't easily be assigned to daily parenting styles, so it's hard to manipulate this variable.

In addition, it could be unethical to assign some people, especially children, to a condition in which they receive a certain type of praise, especially over a long time period, particularly if we suspect that one type of praise might make children narcissistic. Similarly, if researchers suspect that smoking causes lung cancer or sexual content on TV causes pregnancy, it would be unethical (and difficult) to ask study participants to smoke cigarettes or watch certain TV shows for several years. When an experiment is not practical or ethical, a longitudinal correlational design is a good option.

Nevertheless, researchers who investigate how children react to different types of praise have not relied solely on correlational data. They have developed ethical experiments to study such reactions, at least over a short time period (Brummelman et al., 2016; Mueller & Dweck, 1998). By randomly assigning children to receive praise for who they are (e.g., "You are so smart") versus praise for how hard they worked (e.g., "You must have worked hard at these problems"), researchers have produced some solid evidence that children really do change their behavior and attitudes in response to adult praise (**Figure 9.4**). Because it is ethically questionable to expose children to potentially harmful feedback, such studies had to pass strict ethical review and approval before they were conducted (see Chapter 4). In addition, the exposure time was short (only one instance of praise per study, and no instances of criticism). It would be much more challenging to do an ethical experimental study of the effects of long-term

**FIGURE 9.4**
**Praising children.**

Correlational and experimental studies suggest that when adults praise children's learning strategies and efforts (compared with praising the type of person they are), kids respond favorably and continue to work hard.

exposure to potentially maladaptive praise at home. That makes longitudinal correlational designs an attractive alternative.

✔

**CHECK YOUR UNDERSTANDING**

**1.** Why is a longitudinal design considered a multivariate design?

**2.** What are the three kinds of correlations obtained from a longitudinal design? What does each correlation represent?

**3.** Describe which patterns of temporal precedence are indicated by different cross-lag correlational results.

1. See p. 243. 2. See pp. 243–246. 3. See pp. 245–246.

# RULING OUT THIRD VARIABLES WITH MULTIPLE-REGRESSION ANALYSES

Groundbreaking research suggests that pregnancy rates are much higher among teens who watch a lot of TV with sexual dialogue and behavior than among those who have tamer viewing tastes. (CBSNews, 2008)

This news item, referring to a study on TV content and teenage pregnancy, reports a simple association between the amount of sexual content teens watch on TV and their likelihood of becoming pregnant (Chandra et al., 2008). But is there a causal link? Does sexual TV content *cause* pregnancy? Apparently there is covariance: According to the published study, teens who watched more sexual material on TV were more likely to get pregnant. What about temporal precedence? Did the TV watching come before the pregnancy? According to the report, this study did establish temporal precedence because the researchers first asked teens to report the types of TV shows they like to watch and followed up 3 years later with the same teens to find out if they had experienced a pregnancy.

What about internal validity? Third variables could explain the association. Perhaps one is age: Older teenagers might watch more mature TV programs, and they're also more likely to be sexually active. Or perhaps parenting is a third variable: Stricter parents might monitor their teens' TV use and also put tighter limits on their behavior.

How do we know whether one of these variables—or some other one—is the true explanation for the association? This study used a statistical technique called **multiple regression** (or *multivariate regression*), which can help rule out some third variables, thereby addressing some internal validity concerns.

# Measuring More Than Two Variables

In the sexual TV content and pregnancy study, the researchers investigated a sample of 1,461 teenagers on the two key variables (Chandra et al., 2008). To measure the amount of sexual TV content viewed, they had participants report how often they watched 23 programs popular with teens. Then coders watched 14 episodes of each show, counting how many scenes involved sex, including passionate kissing, sexually explicit talk, or intercourse. To assess pregnancy rates 3 years later, they asked girls, "Have you ever been pregnant?" and asked boys, "Have you ever gotten a girl pregnant?" The two variables were positively correlated: Watching higher amounts of sex on TV was associated with a higher risk of pregnancy (**Figure 9.5**).

If the researchers had stopped there and measured only these two variables, they would have conducted a bivariate correlational study. However, they also measured several other variables, including the total amount of time teenage participants spent watching any kind of TV, their age, their academic grades, and whether they lived with both parents. By measuring all these variables instead of just two (with the goal of testing the interrelationships among them all), they conducted a multivariate correlational study.

## USING STATISTICS TO CONTROL FOR THIRD VARIABLES

By using a multivariate design, researchers can evaluate whether a relationship between two key variables still holds when they **control for** another variable. To introduce what "controlling for" means, let's focus on one potential third variable: age. Perhaps sexual content and pregnancy are correlated only because older teens are both more likely to watch more mature shows and more likely to be sexually active. If this is the case, all three variables are correlated with one another: Viewing sex on TV and getting pregnant are correlated, as we already determined, but

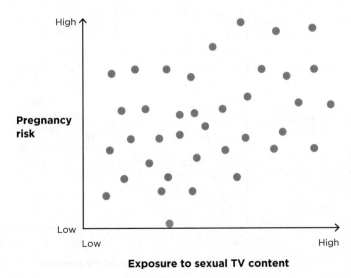

**FIGURE 9.5**

**Correlating sexual TV content with pregnancy risk.**

Higher rates of sexual content on TV go with higher risk of pregnancy, and lower rates of sexual content go with lower risk of pregnancy. (Data are fabricated for illustration purposes.)

sex on TV and age are also correlated with each other, and age and pregnancy are correlated, too. The researchers want to know whether age, as a third variable correlated with both the original variables, can account for the relationship between sexual TV content and pregnancy rates. To answer the question, they see what happens when they control for age.

You'll learn more about multiple-regression computations in a full-semester statistics course. This book will focus on a conceptual understanding of what these analyses mean. The most statistically accurate way to describe the phrase "control for age" is to talk about proportions of variability. Researchers are asking whether, after they take the relationship between age and pregnancy into account, there is still a portion of variability in pregnancy that is attributable to watching sexy TV. But this is extremely abstract language. As an analogy, you might compare this variability to the overall movement (the variance) of your wiggling, happy dog when you return home. You can ask, "What portion of the variability in my dog's overall movement is attributable to his tail moving? To his shoulders moving? To his back legs moving?" You can ask, "Will the dog still be moving when he greets me, even if I were to hold his tail constant—hold it still?"

Another way to understand "controlling for" is to recognize that testing a third variable with multiple regression means identifying subgroups. We can think of it like this: We start by looking only at the oldest age group (say, 20-year-olds) and see whether viewing sexual TV content and pregnancy are still correlated. Then we move to next oldest group (age 18), then the youngest group (age 16). We ask whether the bivariate relationship still holds at all ages.

There are a couple of possible outcomes from such a subgroup analysis, and one is shown in the scatterplot in **Figure 9.6**. Here, the overall association is positive—the more sexual TV programs teens watch, the higher the chance of getting pregnant. In addition, the oldest teens (the 20 symbols) are, overall, higher on sexual

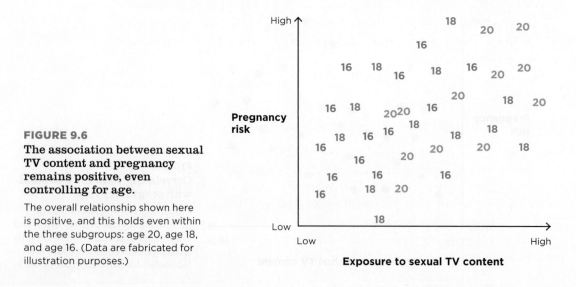

**FIGURE 9.6**
**The association between sexual TV content and pregnancy remains positive, even controlling for age.**

The overall relationship shown here is positive, and this holds even within the three subgroups: age 20, age 18, and age 16. (Data are fabricated for illustration purposes.)

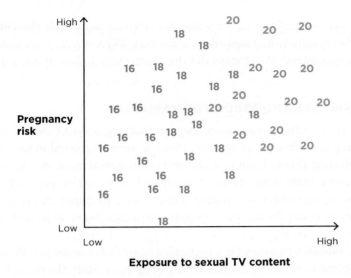

**FIGURE 9.7**

**The association between sexual TV content and pregnancy goes away, controlling for age.**

The overall association shown here is positive, but if we separately consider the subgroups of age 20, age 18, or age 16, there is no relationship between the two variables. (Data are fabricated for illustration purposes.)

TV content and higher in chance of pregnancy. The youngest teens (16 symbols) are, overall, lower on sexual TV content and lower in chance of pregnancy. If we look *only* at the 20-year-olds, or *only* at the 16-year-olds, however, the scatterplots still show the key relationship between sexy TV and pregnancy: It remains positive even within these age subgroups. Therefore, the relationship is still there, even when we hold age constant.

In contrast, the second possible outcome is shown in **Figure 9.7**. Here, the overall relationship is still positive, just as before—the more sexual content teens watch on TV, the higher the chance of pregnancy. In addition, just as before, the 20-year-olds watch more sexy TV and are more likely to become pregnant. However, this time, when we look *only* at the age 20 subgroup or *only* the age 16 subgroup, the key relationship between sexy TV and pregnancy is absent. The scatterplots *within* the age subgroups do not show the relationship anymore. Therefore, the association between watching sexual TV content and getting pregnant goes away when we control for age. In this case, age was, indeed, the third variable that was responsible for the relationship.

## Regression Results Indicate Whether a Third Variable Affects the Relationship

Which one of the two scatterplots, Figure 9.6 or Figure 9.7, best describes the relationship between sexual content on TV and pregnancy? The statistical technique of multiple regression can tell us. When researchers use regression, they are testing whether some key relationship holds true even when a suspected third variable is statistically controlled for.

As a consumer of information, you'll probably work with the end result of this process, when you encounter regression results in tables in empirical journal articles. Suppose you're reading an article and you come across a table showing what the regression results would look like for the sexy TV/pregnancy example. What do the numbers mean? What steps did the researchers follow to come up with them?

## CRITERION VARIABLES AND PREDICTOR VARIABLES

When researchers use multiple regression, they are studying three or more variables. The first step is to choose the variable they are most interested in understanding or predicting; this is known as the **criterion variable**, or *dependent variable*. The Chandra team were primarily interested in predicting pregnancy, so they chose that as their criterion variable. The criterion (dependent) variable is usually specified in either the top row or the title of a regression table, such as **Table 9.1**.

The rest of the variables measured in a regression analysis are called **predictor variables**, or *independent variables*. In the sexy TV/pregnancy study, the predictor variables are the amount of sexual content teenagers reported viewing on TV and the age of each teen. In Table 9.1, the two predictor variables are listed below the criterion variable.

## USING BETA TO TEST FOR THIRD VARIABLES

The point of the multiple-regression results in Table 9.1 is to see whether the relationship between exposure to sex on TV and pregnancy might be explained by a third variable—age. Does the association remain, even within each age group (as in Figure 9.6)? Or does the relationship between sexy TV and pregnancy go away within each age group (as in Figure 9.7)? The betas in Table 9.1 help answer this central question.

**Beta Basics.** In a regression table like Table 9.1, there is often a column labeled beta (or β, or even standardized beta). There will be one beta value for each predictor variable. Beta is similar to *r*, but it reveals more than *r* does. A positive beta, like a positive *r*, indicates a positive relationship between that predictor variable and the criterion variable, when the other predictor variables are statistically controlled for. A negative beta, like a negative *r*, indicates a negative relationship between two variables (when the other predictors are controlled for). A beta that is zero, or nearly zero, represents no relationship (when the other predictors are controlled for). Therefore, betas are similar to correlations in that they denote the direction and strength of a

**TABLE 9.1**

### Multiple-Regression Results from a Study Predicting Pregnancy from Sexual Content on TV and Age

| CRITERION (DEPENDENT) VARIABLE: PREGNANCY RISK | BETA | 95% CI FOR BETA | STATISTICAL SIGNIFICANCE |
|---|---|---|---|
| Predictor (independent) variables: | | | |
| Exposure to sex on TV | 0.25 | [.14, .36] | * |
| Age | 0.33 | [.20, .46] | * |

*Note:* Data are fabricated, based on imagined results if the researchers had used only two predictor variables.
*p < .05, meaning the result is statistically significant and the 95% CI does not include zero.

relationship. The higher beta is, the stronger the relationship is between that predictor variable and the criterion variable. The smaller beta is, the weaker the relationship.

« For more on confidence intervals of beta, see Statistics Review: Inferential Statistics, p. 513.

Within a single regression table, we can usually compare predictor variables that show larger betas to predictor variables with smaller betas—the larger the beta, the stronger the relationship. For example, in Table 9.1 we can say that the beta for the age predictor appears a bit stronger than the beta for the exposure to sex on TV predictor. Keep in mind, however, that it is not appropriate to compare the strengths of betas from one regression table to the strengths of betas from another one. The reason is that betas change, depending on what other predictor variables are being used—being controlled for—in the regression (Rohrer, 2018; Westfall & Yarkoni, 2016).

Sometimes a regression table will include the symbol $b$ instead of beta. The coefficient $b$ represents an unstandardized coefficient. A $b$ is similar to beta in that the sign of $b$—positive or negative—denotes a positive or negative association (when the other predictors are controlled for). But unlike two betas, we cannot compare two $b$ values within the same table to each other. The reason is that $b$ values are computed from the original measurements of the predictor variables (such as dollars, centimeters, or inches), whereas betas are computed from predictor variables that have been changed to standardized units. A predictor variable that shows a large $b$ may not actually denote a stronger relationship to the criterion variable than a predictor variable with a smaller $b$.

**Interpreting Beta.** In Table 9.1, notice that the predictor variable "exposure to sex on TV" has a beta of 0.25. This positive beta, like a positive $r$, means higher levels of sex on TV go with higher pregnancy risk (and lower levels of sex on TV go with lower pregnancy risk), *even when we statistically control for the other predictor on this table—age.* In other words, even when we hold age constant statistically, the relationship between exposure to TV sex and pregnancy is still there. This result is consistent with the relationship depicted in Figure 9.6, not the one in Figure 9.7.

The other beta in Table 9.1, the one associated with the age predictor variable, is also positive. This beta means that older age is associated with higher pregnancy rates, *when exposure to sex on TV is controlled for.* In other words, when we hold exposure to sex on TV constant, age predicts pregnancy, too. In sum, the beta that is associated with a predictor variable represents the relationship between that predictor variable and the criterion variable, when the other predictor variables in the table are controlled for.

**95% CIs and Statistical Significance of Beta.** The regression tables in empirical journal articles, especially those published in recent years, have a column labeled 95% CI, which presents the confidence interval for each beta. Regression tables published longer ago may only have a column labeled sig or $p$, or may have an asterisked footnote giving a $p$ value for each beta. Recall that a $p$ value of .05 complements the .95 from a 95% CI. Specifically, when the $p$ value is less

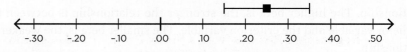
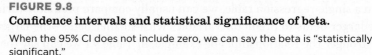

**FIGURE 9.8**
**Confidence intervals and statistical significance of beta.**

When the 95% CI does not include zero, we can say the beta is "statistically significant."

than .05, you can infer that the 95% CI for that beta does not contain zero and is therefore considered statistically significant. When *p* is greater than .05, the beta is considered not significant (n.s.), and you can infer that its 95% CI *does* contain zero (**Figure 9.8**).

Table 9.1 contains both pieces of information (even though they mean the same thing). Each of the betas reported there has a 95% CI that does not include zero, and both are noted as *p* < .05, or statistically significant. Both columns share similar information, but the 95% CI is more informative because it communicates the precision with which beta is estimated (narrower CIs are more precise). **Table 9.2** gives several appropriate ways to explain what the beta for the TV variable means.

**What If Beta Is Close to Zero?**  To answer this question, we'll use an example from a different line of research: family meals and child academic achievement. When these two variables are studied as a bivariate relationship, researchers find that children in families that eat many meals together (dinners and breakfasts) tend to be more academically successful, compared with kids in families that eat only a few meals together.

Once again, this simple bivariate relationship is not enough to show causation. In many studies, family meal habits and academic success are measured at the same time, so there is a temporal precedence problem: Did family meals come first and reinforce key academic skills, leading to higher achievement? Or did high academic success come first, perhaps making it more pleasant for parents to have

**TABLE 9.2**

**Describing the Beta of 0.25 in Table 9.1**

**EACH OF THESE SENTENCES IS AN APPROPRIATE DESCRIPTION OF THE RELATIONSHIP:**

- The relationship between exposure to sex on TV and pregnancy is positive (high levels of sex on TV are associated with higher levels of pregnancy risk), even when age is controlled for.

- The 95% CI for the relationship between exposure to sex on TV and pregnancy does not contain zero, suggesting that this relationship is positive, controlling for age.

- The relationship between exposure to sex on TV and pregnancy is positive (high levels of sex on TV are associated with higher pregnancy risk) and is not attributable to the third variable of age because it holds even when age is held constant.

TABLE 9.3

## Multiple-Regression Results from a Study Predicting Academic Success from Frequency of Family Meals and Parental Involvement

| CRITERION (DEPENDENT) VARIABLE: ACADEMIC SUCCESS | BETA | 95% CI FOR BETA | STATISTICAL SIGNIFICANCE |
|---|---|---|---|
| **Predictor (independent) variables:** | | | |
| Frequency of family meals | −0.01 | [−0.06, 0.03] | n.s. |
| Parental involvement | 0.09 | [0.06, 0.12] | * |

*Note:* Data are fabricated but reflect actual research. The study controlled for not only parental involvement but also income, family structure, school quality, birth weight, school type, and many other possible third variables. When controlling for all these in a sample of more than 20,000 children, the researchers found that the beta for frequency of family meals was not significant.
*$p < .05$, meaning the result is statistically significant and the 95% CI does not include zero.
Source: Adapted from Miller et al., 2012.

meals with their kids? In addition, there are third variables that present an internal validity concern. For instance, more involved parents might arrange more family meals, and more involved parents might also have higher-achieving children.

A multiple-regression analysis could hold parental involvement constant and see if family meal frequency is still associated with academic success. In one such study, the researchers found that when parental involvement was held constant (along with other variables), family meal frequency was no longer a strong predictor of school success (Miller et al., 2012). This pattern of results means that the only reason family meals were correlated with academic success was because of the third-variable problem of parental involvement (**Table 9.3**).

In other words, although frequency of family meals and academic success are related in their bivariate relationship, that relationship goes away when potential third variables, such as parental involvement, are controlled for. When you hold parental involvement constant, there is no longer a relationship between frequency of family meals and academic success (**Table 9.4**).

TABLE 9.4

### Describing the Beta of −0.01 in Table 9.3

**EACH OF THESE SENTENCES IS AN APPROPRIATE DESCRIPTION OF THE RELATIONSHIP:**

- When controlling for parental involvement, the relationship between family meal frequency and child academic success has a 95% CI that contains zero (is not significant).

- The relationship between family meal frequency and child academic success can likely be explained by the third variable of parental involvement.

- The relationship between family meal frequency and child academic success goes away when parental involvement is controlled for.

# Adding More Predictors to a Regression

Up to now, when considering the relationship between sexual TV content and pregnancy, we've focused on only one potential internal validity problem—age. But remember there are many other possible third variables. What about participation in school activities? What about living with one versus two parents? In fact, the Chandra team measured each of those third variables and even added a few more, such as parental education, ethnicity, and having a history of problem behaviors (Chandra et al., 2008). **Table 9.5** shows every variable tested, as well as the multiple-regression results for all the other variables. Because the Chandra team did not report 95% CIs, only the statistical significance is listed here.

Even when there are many more predictor variables in the table, beta still means the same thing. The beta for the exposure to sex on TV is positive: High levels of sex on TV are associated with higher pregnancy rate, when the researchers controlled for age, total TV exposure, lower grades, parent education, educational aspirations, and so on, down to intention to have children before age 22. Even after controlling for all variables listed in Table 9.5, the researchers found that more exposure to sex on TV predicts a higher chance of pregnancy.

Adding several predictors to a regression analysis can help answer two kinds of questions. First, it helps control for several third variables at once. In the Chandra study, even after all other variables were controlled for, exposure to sex on TV still predicted pregnancy. A result like that gets the researchers a bit closer to making a causal claim because the relationship between the suspected cause (sexy TV) and the suspected effect (pregnancy) does not appear to be attributable to any of the other variables that were measured.

Second, by looking at the betas for all the other predictor variables, we can get a sense of which other factors predict chance of pregnancy. One strong predictor is gender, which, as you can see, has a beta of 1.20, even when the other variables are controlled for. This result means girls are more likely to report becoming pregnant than boys are to report getting a girl pregnant. (Even though it takes two to cause a pregnancy, presumably boys are sometimes unaware of getting a girl pregnant, whereas a girl is more certain.) We also notice that teens with a history of deviant behavior also have a higher risk of pregnancy, controlling for exposure to sex on TV, age, grades, and

**TABLE 9.5**

**Multiple-Regression Results from a Study Predicting Pregnancy from Exposure to Sex on TV and Other Variables**

| CRITERION (DEPENDENT) VARIABLE: PREGNANCY RISK | BETA | SIG |
|---|---|---|
| **Predictor (independent) variables:** | | |
| Exposure to sex on TV | 0.44 | * |
| Total television exposure | −0.42 | * |
| Age | 0.28 | * |
| Lower grades | 0.21 | n.s. |
| Parent education | 0.00 | n.s. |
| Educational aspirations (highest level of school you plan to finish) | −0.14 | n.s. |
| Being Hispanic (vs. other ethnicities) | 0.86 | n.s. |
| Being Black (vs. other ethnicities) | 1.20 | * |
| Being female | 1.20 | * |
| Living in a 2-parent household | −1.50 | * |
| History of deviant or problem behavior (e.g., skipping school, stealing, cheating on a test) | 0.43 | * |
| Intention to have children before age 22 | 0.61 | n.s. |

*$p < .05$, meaning that the 95% CI for this beta does not contain zero.
Source: Adapted from Chandra et al., 2008, Table 2.

the other variables in the table. In fact, the predictive power of history of deviant behavior is about the same magnitude as that of exposure to sex on TV. Even though the authors of this study were most interested in describing the potential risk of viewing sexual content on TV, they were also able to evaluate which other variables are important in predicting pregnancy. (Recall, however, that when a table presents $b$ values, or unstandardized coefficients, it is not appropriate to compare their *relative* strength. We can only do so with beta, and even then, remember that betas change depending on what other predictor variables are used.)

## Regression in Popular Media Articles

When making association claims in the popular media—magazines, newspapers, websites—journalists seldom discuss betas, 95% CIs, or predictor variables. Because they're writing for a general audience, they assume most of their readers will not be familiar with these concepts. However, if you read carefully, you can detect when a multiple regression has been used if a journalist uses one of the phrases in the sections that follow.

### "CONTROLLED FOR"

The phrase "controlled for" is one common sign of a regression analysis. For example, when journalists covered the story about family meals and academic success, they stated the findings like this:

> Researchers . . . determined that there wasn't any relationship between family meals and a child's academic outcomes or behavior. . . . Miller and his team also *controlled for factors* such as parental employment, television-watching, the quality of school facilities, and the years of experience the children's teachers had, among others. (Family Dinner Benefits, Huffingtonpost.com, 2012; emphasis added)

### "ADJUSTING FOR"

Here's another example from an article about how dog ownership is associated with a longer lifespan:

> In another study, [researchers] looked over a 12-year period at dog owners in Sweden who have cardiovascular disease. They adjusted for the kinds of things we know affect cardiovascular health—age, demographics, socioeconomic status, marital status, number of children at home—and even after adjusting for all of that, they found a benefit of dog ownership. (Chen, NPR.org, 2019)

The phrase "even after adjusting for all of that" means the researchers conducted multiple-regression analyses. Even when they controlled for age, demographics,

**FIGURE 9.9**

**Multiple regression in the popular media.**

This journalist wrote that people who ate more chocolate had lower body mass index, and that the researchers adjusted their results for several variables. The phrase "adjusted for" signals a regression analysis, thereby ruling out those variables as internal validity problems. (Source: O'Connor, 2012.)

**The Chocolate Diet?**

"Since so many complicating factors can influence results, it is difficult to pinpoint cause and effect. But the researchers adjusted their results for a number of variables, including age, gender, depression, vegetable consumption, and fat and calorie intake."

socioeconomic status, marital status, and number of children at home, they still found a relationship between dog ownership and lifespan.

And here's a study that found a relationship between eating chocolate and body mass (**Figure 9.9**):

> The people who ate chocolate the most frequently, despite eating more calories and exercising no differently from those who ate the least chocolate, tended to have lower B.M.I.'s. . . . The researchers *adjusted their results for* a number of variables, including age, gender, depression, vegetable consumption, and fat and calorie intake. "It didn't matter which of those you added, the relationship remained very stably significant." (O'Connor, Nytimes.com, 2012; emphasis added)

### "CONSIDERING"

When the sexy TV/pregnancy study was reported online, the journalist mentioned the simple relationship between exposure to sexual TV content and getting pregnant, and then wrote:

> Chandra said TV watching was strongly connected with teen pregnancy even when other factors were considered, including grades, family structure, and parents' education level. (CBSNews, 2008)

The phrase "even when other factors were considered" indicates the researchers used multiple regression.

In sum, journalists can use a variety of phrases to describe a study's use of multiple regression. When you encounter an association claim in a magazine, newspaper, or online, one of your questions should be whether the researchers controlled for possible third variables. If you can't tell from the story what the researchers controlled for, it's reasonable to suspect that certain third variables cannot be ruled out.

# Regression Does Not Establish Causation

Multiple regression might seem to be a foolproof way to rule out all kinds of third variables. If you look at the data in Table 9.5 on exposure to TV sex and pregnancy, for example, you might think you can safely make a causal statement now, since the researchers controlled for so many internal validity problems. They seem to have thought of everything! Not so fast. One problem is that even though multivariate designs analyzed with regression statistics can control for third variables, they cannot always establish temporal precedence. Of course, the Chandra study did measure viewing sexual TV content 3 years before pregnancies occurred. But others, such as the study on family meals and academic achievement, may not.

Even when a study takes place over time (longitudinally), another very important problem is that researchers cannot control for variables they do not measure. Even though multiple regression controls for any third variables the researchers do measure in the study, some other variable they did not consider could account for the association. In the sexy TV/pregnancy study, some unmeasured variable—maybe the teenagers' level of religiosity or the geographic area where they live—might account for the relationship between watching sex on TV and getting pregnant. But since those possible third variables were not measured (or even considered), there is no way of knowing (**Figure 9.10**).

In fact, some psychological scientists have critiqued media studies like this one, arguing that certain types of teenagers are predisposed to watching sexual TV content, and these same teens are also more likely to be sexually active (Steinberg & Monahan, 2011). These critics contend that the relationship between sexual media content and sexual activity is attributable to this predisposition (see Collins et al., 2011).

The "lurking-variable," or third-variable problem is one reason a well-run experimental study is ultimately more convincing in establishing causation than a correlational study. An experimental study on TV, for example, would randomly assign a sample of people to watch either sexy TV shows or programs without sexual content. The power of random assignment would make the two groups likely to be equal on any third variables the researchers did not happen to measure, such as religiosity, social class, or parenting styles. But of course, just like randomly assigning children to get one type of praise or another, it is ethically questionable to conduct an experiment on sexual TV content.

A randomized experiment is the gold standard for determining causation. Multiple regression, in contrast, allows researchers to control for potential third variables, but only for the variables they choose to measure.

**FIGURE 9.10**

**Possible third variables in the association between sexual TV content and pregnancy.**

What additional third variables, not already measured by the researchers, might be associated with both watching sex on TV and getting pregnant?

**CHECK YOUR UNDERSTANDING**

1. Describe what it means to say that some variable "was controlled for" in a multivariate study.

2. How many criterion variables are there in a multiple-regression analysis? How many predictor variables?

3. What is the relationship between the 95% CI for beta and the beta's statistical significance?

4. Give at least two phrases indicating that a study used a multiple-regression analysis.

5. What are two reasons that multiple-regression analyses cannot completely establish causation?

1. See pp. 249–251. 2. One criterion variable, and at least two predictor variables. See p. 252. 3. When the 95% CI does not include zero, we can say that the beta is statistically significant, $p < .05$. See also pp. 253–255. 4. See pp. 257–258. 5. See p. 259.

# GETTING AT CAUSALITY WITH PATTERN AND PARSIMONY

So far this chapter has focused on two multivariate techniques that help researchers investigate causation, even when they're working with correlations among measured variables. Longitudinal correlational designs can satisfy the temporal precedence criterion. Multiple-regression analyses statistically control for some potential internal validity problems (third variables).

In this section, we explore how researchers can investigate causality by using a variety of correlational studies that all point in a single, causal direction. This approach can be called "pattern and parsimony" because there's a pattern of results best explained by a single, parsimonious causal theory. **Parsimony** is the degree to which a scientific theory provides the simplest explanation of some phenomenon. In the context of investigating a causal claim, parsimony means the simplest explanation of a pattern of data—the theory that requires making the fewest exceptions or qualifications.

## The Power of Pattern and Parsimony

A classic example of pattern and parsimony is the case of smoking and lung cancer. This example was first articulated by the psychological scientist Robert Abelson. Decades ago, it started becoming clear that smokers had higher rates of lung cancer than nonsmokers (the correlation has been estimated at

$r$ = .49, 95% CI [.39, .58]; Remen et al., 2018). Did the smoking *cause* the cancer? Cigarette manufacturers certainly did not want people to think so. If someone argued that this correlation was causal, a critic might counter that the cigarettes were not the cause; perhaps people who smoked were more stressed, which predisposed them to lung cancer. Or perhaps smokers also drank a lot of coffee, and it was the coffee, not the cigarettes, that caused cancer. The list of third-variable explanations could go on and on. Even though multiple-regression analyses could control for these alternative explanations, critics could always argue that regression cannot control for every possible third variable.

Another problem, of course, is that even though an experiment could rule out third-variable explanations, a smoking experiment would not be ethical or practical. A researcher could not reasonably assign a sample of volunteers to become lifetime smokers or nonsmokers. The only data researchers had to work with were correlational.

The solution to this problem, Abelson explains, is to specify a mechanism for the causal path. Specifically, in the case of cigarettes, researchers proposed that cigarette smoke contains chemicals that are toxic when they come into contact with human tissue. The more contact a person has with these chemicals, the greater the toxicity exposure. This simple theory leads to a set of predictions, all of which could be explained by the single, parsimonious theory that chemicals in cigarettes cause cancer (Abelson, 1995, p. 184):

1. The longer a person has smoked cigarettes, the greater their chance of getting cancer.
2. People who stop smoking have lower cancer rates than people who keep smoking.
3. Smokers' cancers tend to be in the lungs and of a particular type.
4. Smokers who use filtered cigarettes have a somewhat lower rate of cancer than those who use unfiltered cigarettes.
5. People who live with smokers have higher rates of cancer, too, because of their passive exposure to the same chemicals.

This process exemplifies the theory-data cycle (see Chapter 1). A theory—cigarette toxicity—led to a particular set of research questions. The theory also led researchers to frame hypotheses about what the data should show.

Indeed, converging evidence from several individual studies conducted by medical researchers has supported each of these separate predictions (their evidence became part of the U.S. Surgeon General's warning in 1964), and that's where parsimony comes in. Because all five of these diverse predictions are tied back to one central principle (the toxicity of the chemicals in cigarette smoke), there is a strong case for parsimony (**Figure 9.11**).

Notice, also, that the diversity of these five empirical findings makes it much harder to raise third-variable explanations. Suppose a critic

**FIGURE 9.11**
**Pattern and parsimony.**

Many studies, using a variety of methods, provide converging evidence to support the causal claim that cigarettes contain toxic chemicals that harm humans. Although each of the individual studies has methodological weaknesses, taken together, they all support the same, parsimonious conclusion.

argued that coffee drinking was a third variable. Coffee drinking could certainly explain the first result (the longer one smokes—and presumably drinks coffee, too—the higher the rates of cancer). But it cannot explain the effect of filtered cigarettes or the cancer rates among secondhand smokers. The most parsimonious explanation of this entire pattern of data—and the weight of the evidence—is the toxicity of cigarettes.

» To review the concept of weight of the evidence, see Chapter 1, p. 14.

It is hard to overstate the strength of the pattern and parsimony technique. In psychology, researchers commonly use a variety of methods and many studies to explore the strength and limits of a particular research question. Another example comes from research on TV violence and aggression. Many studies have investigated the relationship between watching violence on TV and violent behavior. Some studies are correlational; some are experimental. Some are on children; others on adults. Some are longitudinal; others are not. But in general, the evidence all points to a single, parsimonious conclusion that watching violence on TV causes people to behave a little more aggressively (Anderson et al., 2003).

Many psychological scientists build their careers by doing study after study devoted to one research question. Scientists use a variety of methods, combining results to develop their causal theories and to support them with converging evidence.

## Pattern, Parsimony, and the Popular Media

When journalists write about science, they do not always fairly represent pattern and parsimony in research. Instead, they may report only the results of the latest study. For example, they might present a news story on the most recent nutrition research, without describing the other studies done in that area. They might report that certain brain regions are thicker in people who spend less time sitting but fail to cover the full pattern of studies on exercise or on brain plasticity. They might report on a single study that showed an association between eating chocolate and body mass, without mentioning the rest of the studies on that same topic and without tying the results to the theory they are supporting.

When journalists report only one study at a time, they selectively present only a part of the scientific process. They might not describe the context of the research, such as what previous studies have revealed or what theory the study was testing. Reporting on the latest study without giving the full context can make it seem as though scientists conduct unconnected studies on a whim. It might even give the impression that one study can reverse decades of previous research. In addition, skeptics who read such science stories might find it easy to criticize the results of a single, correlational study. As you have learned, science accumulates incrementally. Ideally, journalists should report on the entire body of evidence, as well as the theoretical background, for a particular claim.

» For more on replication and the weight of the evidence, see Chapter 1, p. 14 and Chapter 14, pp. 437–444.

# MEDIATION

Once researchers have established a relationship between two variables using the research designs and statistical tools discussed in this chapter, they often want to explore it further by thinking about *why*. For example, they might ask why watching sexual content on TV predicts a higher pregnancy risk, or why people who engage in meaningful conversations are happier. Many times, these explanations suggest a **mediator**, or *mediating variable*, between two of the variables. A study does not have to be correlational to include a mediator; experimental studies can also test them. However, researchers might test mediation analyses using multivariate tools such as multiple regression, so it makes sense to learn about mediators here.

Consider this example. We know conscientious people are more physically healthy than less conscientious people. But why? The mediator of this relationship might be the fact that conscientious people are more likely to follow medical advice and instructions, and that's why they're healthier. Following doctor's orders would be the mediator of the relationship between the trait, conscientiousness, and the outcome, better health (Hill & Roberts, 2011).

Similarly, we know there's an association between having deep conversations and feelings of well-being (see Chapter 8). Researchers might next propose a reason—a mediator of this relationship. One likely mediator could be social ties: Deeper conversations might help build social connections, which in turn can lead to increased well-being. The researchers could draw this mediation hypothesis, as shown in **Figure 9.12**. They would propose an overall

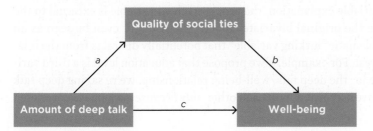

**FIGURE 9.12**
**A proposed mediation model.**

We could propose that deep talk leads to stronger social ties, which leads to increased well-being. Researchers use statistics to estimate how well their data fit this model (see Chapter 8, p. 402).

relationship, $c$, between deep talk and well-being. However, this overall relationship exists only because there are two other relationships: $a$ (between deep talk and social ties) and $b$ (between social ties and well-being). In other words, social ties mediate the relationship between deep talk and well-being. (Of course, there are other possible mediators, such as intellectual growth or taking a break from technology. Those mediators could be tested, too, in another study.)

Researchers use a few statistical techniques to test for mediation. For example, they may compute the relationships between all three variables (for example, deep talk, social ties, and well-being) and use multiple regression to test for mediation (Kenny, 2008). Or they may use structural equation modeling, with or without bootstrapping (Hayes, 2017). These statistical beliefs are beyond the scope of this textbook, but they are all designed to estimate the extent to which the relationships observed in the data fit the mediation hypothesis.

Because mediation hypotheses are causal claims, mediation is definitively established only in conjunction with temporal precedence: when the proposed causal variable is measured or manipulated first in a study, followed some time later by the mediating variable, followed by the proposed outcome variable (Maxwell & Cole, 2007). In other words, to establish mediation in this example, the researchers must conduct a study in which the amount of deep talk is measured (or manipulated) first, followed shortly afterward by a measure of social tie strength. They have to measure well-being last of all, to rule out the possibility that the well-being led to having deeper conversations.

If researchers want to examine whether following doctor's orders is the mediator of the relationship between conscientiousness and good health, the design of the study should ideally measure conscientiousness first, and then later measure medical compliance, and then later measure health. If the design establishes temporal precedence *and* the statistical results support the hypothesis, there is evidence for mediation (Jaremka & Morling, 2019).

## Mediators Versus Third Variables

Mediators are similar to third-variable explanations because both of them can be tested with multiple regression. However, they tell different theoretical stories about a relationship.

In a third-variable explanation, the proposed third variable is external to the two variables in the original bivariate correlation. It might even be seen as an accident—a problematic "lurking variable" that potentially distracts from the relationship of interest. For example, if we propose that education level is a third variable responsible for the deep talk/well-being relationship, we're saying deep talk and well-being are correlated with each other *only because* each one is correlated

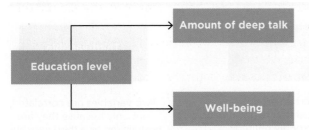

FIGURE 9.13
**A third variable.**

In a third-variable scenario, the third variable is seen as external to the original two variables. Here, deep talk and higher well-being might both be associated with education level.

separately with education, as shown in **Figure 9.13**. In other words, the relationship between deep talk and well-being is there only because both of those variables happen to vary with the outside third variable, education level. The third variable may seem like a nuisance; it might not be of central interest to the researchers. (If they are really interested in deep talk and well-being, they have to control for education level first.)

In contrast, a mediation hypothesis tells a theoretically meaningful, step-by-step story in which "A leads to M leads to B" (for example, deep talk leads to social ties, which lead to well-being). A mediator variable is of direct interest to the researchers rather than a nuisance. In the deep talk example, the researchers believe stronger social ties is the important aspect, or outcome, of deep talk that is responsible for increasing well-being.

## Mediators Versus Moderators

Similar-sounding names can make mediators and moderators confusing at first. (Recall that moderators were introduced in Chapter 8.) However, testing for mediation versus moderation involves asking different questions (Baron & Kenny, 1986). When researchers test for mediating variables, they ask: Why are these two variables linked? When they test for moderating variables, they ask: Are these two variables linked the same way for everyone, or in every situation? Mediators ask: Why? Moderators ask: Who is most vulnerable? For whom is the association strongest?

A mediation hypothesis could propose, for instance, that medical compliance is the reason conscientiousness is related to better health. In contrast, a moderation hypothesis could propose that the link between conscientiousness and good health is strongest among older people (whose health may be more vulnerable to neglecting doctor's orders) and weakest among younger people (who might stay healthy even if they ignore doctor's orders).

As the name implies, the mediating variable comes in the middle of the other two variables. The word *moderate* can mean "to change," and a moderating variable can change the relationship between the other two variables (making it more intense or less intense). **Figure 9.14** diagrams the differences between mediation, moderation, and third variables.

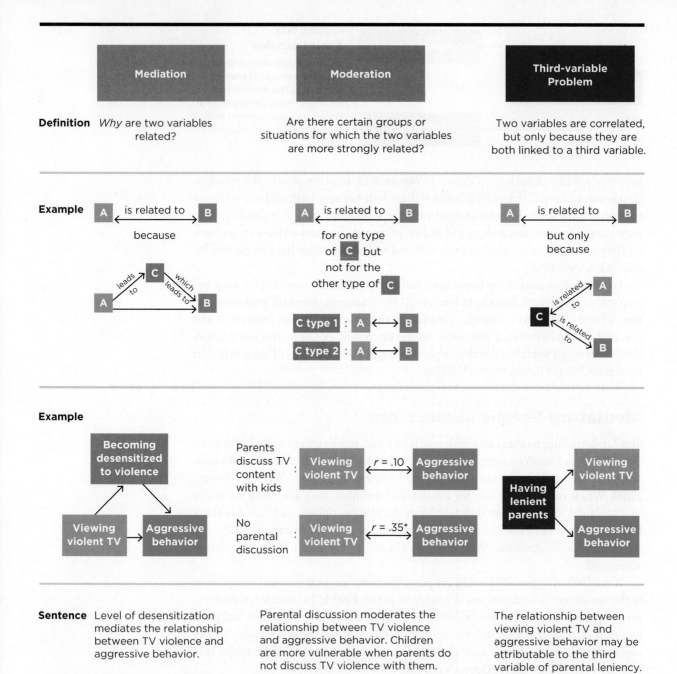

|  | Mediation | Moderation | Third-variable Problem |
|---|---|---|---|
| **Definition** | *Why* are two variables related? | Are there certain groups or situations for which the two variables are more strongly related? | Two variables are correlated, but only because they are both linked to a third variable. |

**Example**

A is related to B because

A leads to C which leads to B

A is related to B for one type of C but not for the other type of C

C type 1 : A ⟷ B
C type 2 : A ⟷ B

A is related to B but only because

C is related to A
C is related to B

**Example**

Becoming desensitized to violence

Viewing violent TV → Aggressive behavior

Parents discuss TV content with kids : Viewing violent TV — $r = .10$ — Aggressive behavior

No parental discussion : Viewing violent TV — $r = .35^*$ — Aggressive behavior

Having lenient parents → Viewing violent TV

Having lenient parents → Aggressive behavior

**Sentence** | Level of desensitization mediates the relationship between TV violence and aggressive behavior. | Parental discussion moderates the relationship between TV violence and aggressive behavior. Children are more vulnerable when parents do not discuss TV violence with them. | The relationship between viewing violent TV and aggressive behavior may be attributable to the third variable of parental leniency.

**FIGURE 9.14**

**Mediation, moderation, and third variables.**

How are they different? ($^*p < .05$)

## MULTIVARIATE DESIGNS AND THE FOUR VALIDITIES

Researchers use multivariate correlational research, such as longitudinal designs and multiple-regression analyses, to get closer to making causal claims. Longitudinal designs help establish temporal precedence, and multiple-regression analysis helps rule out third variables, thus providing some evidence for internal validity. We must remember, however, to interrogate the other three major validities—construct, external, and statistical validity—as well.

For any multivariate design, as for any bivariate design, it is appropriate to interrogate the construct validity of the variables in the study by asking how well each variable was measured. In the Brummelman study (2015) on overpraise and narcissism, is asking parents what they say to their kids a reliable and valid way to measure their actual level of overpraise? Similarly, is self-report a reliable and valid way to measure a child's levels of narcissism? In the Chandra study (2008), what about the measures of exposure to sex on TV and pregnancy? Did the coders who rated TV show content have interrater reliability? Did coders identify sexual content in a valid way?

We can also interrogate the external validity of a multivariate design. In the Brummelman study on narcissism, the researchers invited all children from 17 schools in the Netherlands to participate, and 565 (75%) of them agreed. Volunteers are not a random sample, so we are uncertain whether we can generalize from this sample to the population of children in the 17 schools. We might also ask whether the association generalizes to other kinds of praise, such as praise from teachers or other adults.

To interrogate the external validity of the sexual TV content and pregnancy study, we can ask whether the teenagers were sampled randomly, and from what kind of population. In fact, the Chandra study came from a sample of U.S. teens from all states, and the sample's demographic characteristics were similar to those for the entire country. However, the researchers do not report whether or not their sample was selected randomly (Chandra et al., 2008).

For interrogating a multivariate correlational research study's statistical validity, we can ask about the point estimates and confidence intervals and ask whether the study has been replicated (see Chapter 8). In the case of the sexy TV/pregnancy study, we know the beta was 0.44. However, there are no guidelines for what constitutes a "large" or "small" beta. The authors of the study also presented the pregnancy risk of low-sexual-content viewers, compared with medium and high viewers (**Figure 9.15**). These data show that among 20-year-olds, those who had watched the most sexual TV had a pregnancy risk twice as high as those who had watched the least. Because the risk of pregnancy doubled, it was interpreted as a strong effect size by the authors.

Other statistical validity questions apply to multivariate designs, too. The 95% CIs convey the precision of each estimate. Additional studies can tell us whether

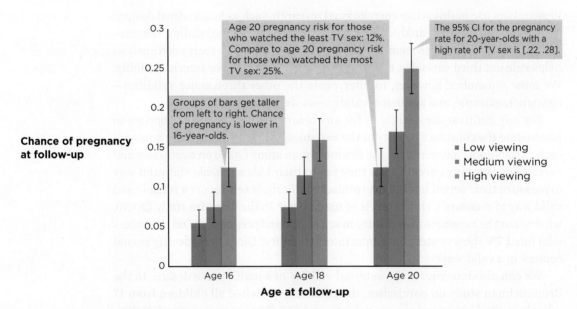

**FIGURE 9.15**
**Effect size and precision in the sexual TV content and pregnancy study.**
The researchers calculated the pregnancy risk among teens who reported watching the lowest levels of sexual content (low viewing), as well as medium and high viewing levels. Different age groups were calculated separately. The graph depicts a large effect size for sexual content because the pregnancy risk for the highest viewers is double that for the lowest viewers. The error bars indicate the 95% CI for each estimate. (Source: Adapted from Chandra et al., 2008.)

the findings have been replicated. And when researchers use multivariate designs, they need to take precautions to look for outliers and curvilinear associations, all of which can be more complicated to detect when there are more than two variables.

**CHECK YOUR UNDERSTANDING**

1. Give an example of a question you would ask to interrogate each of the four validities for a multivariate study.

1. See p. 267.

# CHAPTER REVIEW

It's time to complete your study experience! Go to INQUIZITIVE to practice actively with this chapter's concepts and get personalized feedback along the way.

## Summary

Research often begins with a simple bivariate correlation, which cannot establish causation. Researchers can use multivariate techniques to get closer to making a causal claim.

### REVIEWING THE THREE CAUSAL CRITERIA

- In a multivariate design, researchers measure more than two variables and look for the relationships among them.

- A simple, bivariate correlation indicates that there is covariance but cannot always indicate temporal precedence or internal validity, so it cannot establish causation.

### ESTABLISHING TEMPORAL PRECEDENCE WITH LONGITUDINAL DESIGNS

- Longitudinal designs start with two key variables, on which the same group of people are measured at multiple points in time. Researchers can tell which variable came first in time, thus helping establish temporal precedence.

- Longitudinal designs produce cross-sectional correlations (correlations between the two key variables at any one time period) and autocorrelations (correlations between one variable and itself, over time).

- Longitudinal designs also produce cross-lag correlations. By comparing the relative strengths of the two cross-lag correlations, researchers can infer which of the variables probably came first in time (or if they are mutually reinforcing each other).

### RULING OUT THIRD VARIABLES WITH MULTIPLE-REGRESSION ANALYSES

- In a regression design, researchers start with a bivariate correlation and then measure other potential third variables that might affect it.

- Using multiple-regression analysis, researchers can see whether the basic relationship is still present, even when they statistically control for one or more third variables. If the beta is still significant for the key variable when the researchers control for the third variables, it means the key relationship is not explained by those third variables.

- If the beta approaches zero when the researchers control for a third variable, then the key relationship can be attributed to that third variable.

- Even though regression analyses can rule out third variables, they cannot definitively establish causation because they can only control for possible third variables that the researchers happened to measure. Only an experiment can definitively establish causation.

### GETTING AT CAUSALITY WITH PATTERN AND PARSIMONY

- Researchers can approach causal certainty through pattern and parsimony by specifying a mechanism for the causal relationship and combining the results from a variety of research questions. When a single causal theory explains all of the disparate results, researchers are closer to supporting a causal claim.

### MEDIATION

- In a mediation hypothesis, researchers specify a variable that comes between the two variables of interest as a possible reason the two variables are associated. After collecting data on all three variables (the original two, plus the mediator), they use statistical techniques to evaluate how well the data support the mediation hypothesis.

## MULTIVARIATE DESIGNS AND THE FOUR VALIDITIES

- Interrogating multivariate correlational designs involves investigating not only internal validity and temporal precedence but also construct validity, external validity, and statistical validity. While no single study is perfect, exploring each validity in turn is a good way to systematically assess a study's strengths and weaknesses.

## Key Terms

multivariate design, p. 242
longitudinal design, p. 243
cross-sectional correlation, p. 243
autocorrelation, p. 244

cross-lag correlation, p. 245
multiple regression, p. 248
control for, p. 249
criterion variable, p. 252

predictor variable, p. 252
parsimony, p. 260
mediator, p. 263

 To see samples of chapter concepts in the popular media, visit www.everydayresearchmethods.com and click the box for Chapter 9.

## Review Questions

1. A headline about social media use makes the following (bivariate) association claim: "Social media use is linked to lower grades in college." The two variables in this headline are:

    a. Social media use and quality of grades.

    b. High social media use or low social media use.

    c. Good grades or poor grades.

2. Suppose a researcher uses a longitudinal design to study the relationship between social media use (e.g., Instagram and Snapchat) and grades over time. She measures both of these variables in Year 1 and then measures both variables again in Year 2. Which of the following is an example of an autocorrelation in the results?

    a. The correlation between social media use in Year 1 and social media use in Year 2.

    b. The correlation between social media use in Year 1 and grades in Year 2.

    c. The correlation between grades in Year 1 and social media use in Year 2.

    d. The correlation between grades in Year 1 and social media use in Year 1.

3. In the longitudinal study described in Question 2, which pattern of cross-lag correlations would indicate that social media use leads to lower grades (rather than the reverse)?

    a. Grades at Year 1 shows a strong correlation with social media use at Year 2, but social media use at Year 1 shows a weak correlation with grades at Year 2.

    b. Grades at Year 1 shows a weak correlation with social media use at Year 2, but social media use at Year 1 shows a strong correlation with grades at Year 2.

    c. Grades at Year 1 shows a strong correlation with social media use at Year 2, and social media use at Year 1 shows a strong correlation with grades at Year 2.

4. Consider this statement: "People who use social media got worse grades in college, even when the researchers controlled for the level of college preparation (operationalized by SAT scores) of the students." What does it mean?

    a. Social media use and grades are correlated only because both of these are associated with SAT score.

    b. SAT score is a third variable that seems to explain the association between social media use and grades.

    c. SAT score can be ruled out as a third variable explanation for the correlation between social media use and college grades.

5. Which of the following statements is an example of a mediator of the relationship between social media use and college grades?

   a. Social media use and college grades are more strongly correlated among nonathletes, and less strongly correlated among athletes.

   b. Social media use and college grades are only correlated with each other because they are both related to the difficulty of the major. Students in more difficult majors get worse grades, and those in difficult majors have less time to use social media.

   c. Social media use and college grades are correlated because social media use leads to less time studying, which leads to lower grades.

6. A news outlet reported on a study of people with dementia. The study found that among patients with dementia, bilingual people had been diagnosed 3–4 years later than those who were monolingual. What are the variables in this bivariate association?

   a. Being bilingual or monolingual

   b. Being bilingual or not, and age at dementia diagnosis

   c. Age at dementia diagnosis

7. The journalist reported that the relationship between bilingualism and age at diagnosis did not change, even when the researchers controlled for level of education. What does this suggest?

   a. That the relationship between bilingualism and dementia onset is probably attributable to the third variable: level of education.

   b. That the relationship between bilingualism and dementia onset is not attributable to the potential third variable: level of education.

   c. That being bilingual can prevent dementia.

8. Researchers speculated that the reason bilingualism is associated with later onset of dementia is that bilingual people develop richer connections in the brain through their experiences in managing two languages, and these connections help stave off dementia symptoms. This statement describes:

   a. A mediator

   b. A moderator

   c. A third variable

## Learning Actively

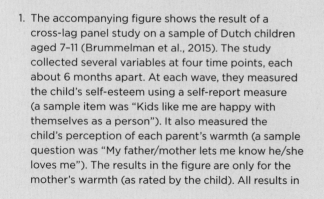

1. The accompanying figure shows the result of a cross-lag panel study on a sample of Dutch children aged 7–11 (Brummelman et al., 2015). The study collected several variables at four time points, each about 6 months apart. At each wave, they measured the child's self-esteem using a self-report measure (a sample item was "Kids like me are happy with themselves as a person"). It also measured the child's perception of each parent's warmth (a sample question was "My father/mother lets me know he/she loves me"). The results in the figure are only for the mother's warmth (as rated by the child). All results in the figure are statistically significant (their 95% CIs do not include zero).

   a. Point to the autocorrelations in the figure.

   b. Are there cross-sectional correlations in the figure?

   c. Overall, what do the cross-lag correlations suggest? Does parental warmth lead to higher self-esteem, or does higher self-esteem lead to parental warmth, or is there a mutually reinforcing relationship?

2. Indicate whether each statement below is describing a mediation hypothesis, a third-variable argument,

or a moderator result. First, identify the key bivariate relationship. Next, decide whether the extra variable comes between the two key variables or is causing the two key variables simultaneously. Then draw a sketch of each explanation, following the examples in Figure 9.14.

a. Having a dog is associated with a longer lifespan because people with fewer health problems are more able to have dogs, and people who have fewer health problems live longer.

b. Having a dog is associated with a longer lifespan, but especially among people living alone; the relationship is weaker among people who live with others.

c. Having a dog is associated with a longer lifespan because people who have dogs get more exercise and exercise makes them healthier (and live longer).

d. Being a victim of sibling aggression is associated with poor mental health in childhood, but the link is especially strong for later-born children and weaker in firstborn children.

e. Sibling aggression is associated with poor childhood mental health because child victims of sibling aggression are more likely to feel lonely at home. Sibling aggression leads to loneliness, which leads to mental health problems.

f. Sibling aggression is associated with poor childhood mental health only because of parental conflict. Sibling aggression is more likely among parents who argue frequently, and arguing also affects kids' mental health.

3. Do victims of sibling aggression suffer worse mental health? A study investigated this question (Tucker et al., 2013). The researchers wondered whether sibling aggression was linked to poor mental health in children, and whether sibling victimization was as bad for kids as peer victimization. In a large sample of children and youths, ages 2–17, they measured several kinds of sibling aggression (e.g., physical assault, taking something away from the child, breaking the child's toys on purpose, calling names). They also measured mental health using a trauma symptom checklist, on which high scores indicate the child has more symptoms of anxiety, depression, and other signs of mental disturbances. The researchers also measured parents' education, child's age, and so on. The regression table in **Table 9.6** comes from their article.

a. What is the criterion (dependent) variable in this study, and where do you find it?

b. How many predictor variables are there in this study?

## TABLE 9.6

## Multiple Regression Predicting Children's and Adolescents' Mental Health

**CRITERION VARIABLE: TRAUMA SYMPTOM CHECKLIST SCORE**

| Predictor variable | BETA |
|---|---|
| Parent education: some college | −0.02 |
| College degree or more | −0.04 |
| Ethnicity | |
| Black | −0.05* |
| Hispanic, any race | −0.01 |
| Other or mixed | −0.00 |
| Language of interview in Spanish | −0.01 |
| Child age 10 plus | −0.13* |
| Child gender male | 0.00 |
| Child maltreatment | 0.15* |
| Sexual victimization | 0.06* |
| School victimization | 0.05* |
| Internet victimization | 0.02 |
| Witness family violence | 0.17* |
| Witness community violence | 0.07* |
| Total types of sibling victimization | 0.15* |
| Total types of peer victimization | 0.25* |
| Total sibling × peer types of victimization | −0.02 |
| $R^2$ | 0.27 |

*$p < .05$
Source: Tucker et al., 2013.

c. Write a sentence that describes what the beta for the "Total types of sibling victimization" predictor means. (Use the sentences in Table 9.2 as a model.)

d. Write a sentence that describes what the beta for the "Total types of peer victimization" predictor variable means.

e. Write a sentence that describes what the beta for the "Child maltreatment" predictor variable means.

f. Write a sentence that describes what the beta for the "Internet victimization" predictor means.

g. Using the magnitude of the betas to decide, which of the predictors is most strongly associated with poor childhood mental health? What about the researchers' initial question: Is sibling victimization just as bad for kids as peer victimization?

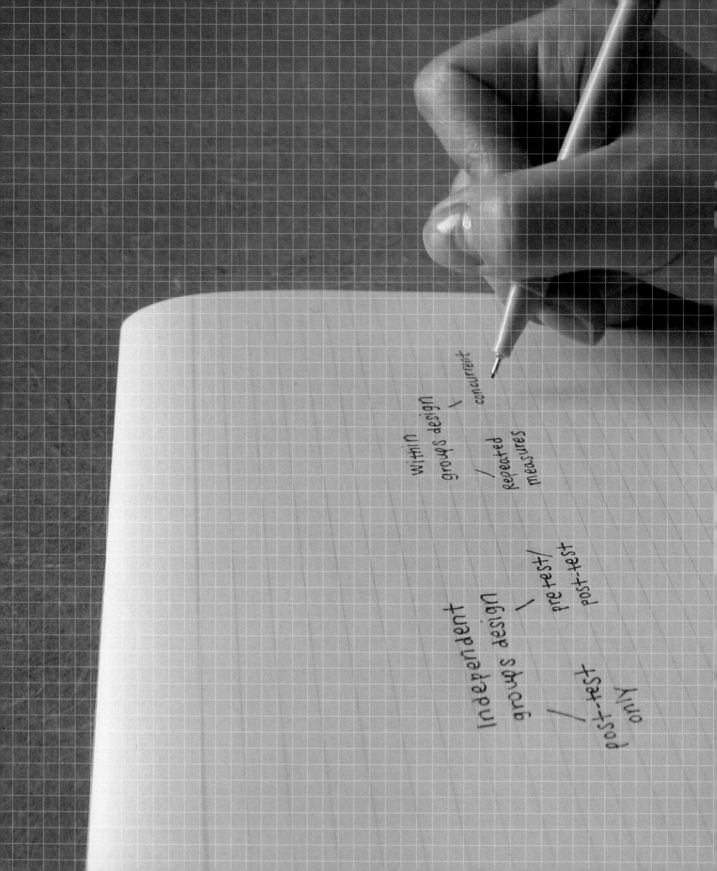

**PART V**

# Tools for Evaluating Causal Claims

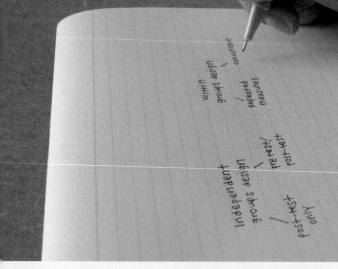

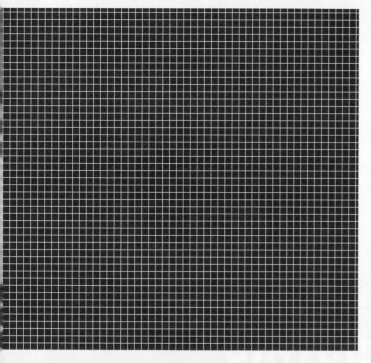

A Learning Secret: Don't Take Notes with a Laptop

*SCIENTIFIC AMERICAN*, 2014

Infants Can Learn the Value of Perseverance by Watching Adults

*THE ATLANTIC*, 2017

# 10

# Introduction to Simple Experiments

A CAUSAL CLAIM IS the boldest kind of claim a scientist can make. A causal claim replaces verb phrases such as *related to, is associated with,* or *linked to* with powerful verbs such as *makes, influences,* or *affects.* Causal claims are special: When researchers make a causal claim, they are also stating something about interventions and treatments. The advice to not take notes with a laptop is based on a causal inference: Taking notes on a laptop causes something negative. Similarly, if babies are influenced by watching adults, those adults should think carefully about what behaviors they model. Interventions are often the ultimate goal of psychological studies, and they must be based on sound experimental research. Experiments are the only way to investigate such causal issues.

## TWO EXAMPLES OF SIMPLE EXPERIMENTS

Let's begin with two examples of experiments that supported valid causal claims. As you read about the two studies, consider how each one differs from the bivariate correlational studies in Chapter 8. What makes each of these studies an experiment? How does the experimental design allow the researchers to support a causal claim rather than an association claim?

## Example 1: Taking Notes

Do you bring a pen to class for taking notes on what your professor is saying? Or do you open your laptop and type? If you're like most students, you use the notetaking habit you think works for you. But should you trust your own experience? Maybe one way of taking notes is actually better than the other (**Figure 10.1**).

Researchers Pam Mueller and Daniel Oppenheimer (2014) decided to conduct an experiment that compared the two practices. When they considered the processes involved, both approaches seemed to have advantages. Typing is faster than longhand, they reasoned, so students can easily transcribe the exact words and phrases a professor is saying, resulting in seemingly more complete notes. However, students might not think about the material when they're typing. When taking handwritten notes, in contrast, students can summarize, paraphrase, or make drawings to connect ideas—even if they record fewer words than they would on a computer. Longhand notes could result in deeper processing of the material and more effective comprehension. Which way would be better?

Sixty-seven college students were recruited to come to a laboratory classroom, usually in pairs. The classroom was prepared in advance: Half the time it contained laptops; the other half, notebooks and pens. Having selected five TED talks on interesting topics, the researchers showed one of the lectures on a video screen. They told the students to take notes on the lectures using their assigned method (Mueller & Oppenheimer, 2014). After the lecture, students spent 30 minutes doing another activity meant to distract them from thinking about the lecture.

**FIGURE 10.1**
**Take note.**
Which form of notetaking would lead to better learning?

Then they were tested on what they had learned from the TED talk. The essay questions asked about straightforward factual information (e.g., "Approximately how many years ago did the Indus civilization exist?") as well as conceptual information (e.g., "How do Japan and Sweden differ in their approaches to equality in their societies?"). Their answers were scored by a research assistant who did not know which form of notetaking each participant had used.

The results Mueller and Oppenheimer obtained are shown in **Figure 10.2**. Students in both the laptop and the longhand groups scored about equally on the factual questions, but the longhand group scored higher on the conceptual questions.

Mueller and Oppenheimer didn't stop at just one study. They wanted to demonstrate that the original result could happen again. Their journal article reports two other studies, each of which compared longhand to laptop notetaking, and each of which showed the same effect: The longhand group performed better on conceptual test questions. (The two other studies, unlike the first, showed that longhand notetakers did better on factual questions, too.) The authors made a causal claim: Taking notes in longhand *causes* students to better understand what they hear. Do you think their study supports the causal claim?

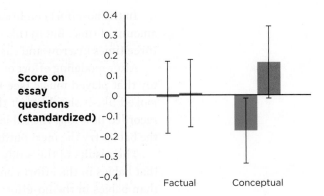

**FIGURE 10.2**

**The effect of laptop and longhand notetaking on test performance.**

In this study, performance on factual questions was the same in the laptop and longhand groups, but performance on conceptual questions was better for those who took handwritten notes. The error bars represent standard error of each mean. (Source: Adapted from Mueller & Oppenheimer, 2014.)

## Example 2: Motivating Babies

In an article with this headline—"Infants can learn the value of perseverance by watching adults"—journalist Ed Yong (2017) summarized a series of studies on how watching adult models can motivate babies to persist at difficult tasks. What were the studies behind this science writer's story?

The studies took place at a play lab at the Boston Children's Museum. The researchers (Leonard et al., 2017) recruited more than 100 babies, aged 13 to 18 months, to participate. Parents sat next to their babies during the study but were asked not to help. Behind the scenes, the researchers had flipped a coin to assign half of the babies to an "effort" condition and half to a "no-effort" condition. In the effort condition, the babies watched a model try to get a toy frog out of a plastic box. The model kept repeating, "How do I get this out?" After trying several ways, she finally opened the box's secret door, saying, "I got it out!" Then the model tried to unhook a toy from a carabiner, saying, "How do I get this off?" After several tries, she finally released the toy and said, "Yay!"

In the no-effort condition, the model worked with the same toys for the same amount of time. But in this condition, she simply took the toy frog out of the box three times in a row and easily took the toy off the carabiner three times.

After modeling effort or no effort, the model handed the baby a cube-shaped toy that played music (see **Figure 10.3**). The toy had a large white button that looked like it should start the music, but it was actually inert. The researchers recorded how long the babies spent playing with the toy. How many times would the babies try the inert button?

The results of the study are depicted in **Figure 10.4**. The researchers found that babies in the effort condition pressed the inert button about 11 times more than babies in the no-effort condition. The researchers wrote, "Seeing just two examples of an adult working hard to achieve her goals can lead infants to work harder at a novel task relative to infants who see an adult succeed effortlessly" (Leonard et al., 2017, p. 357). What do you think: Do the results of this study support the researcher's causal claim?

## EXPERIMENTAL VARIABLES

The word *experiment* is common in everyday use. Colloquially, "to experiment" means to try something out. A cook might say they experimented with a recipe by replacing the eggs with applesauce. A friend might say they experimented

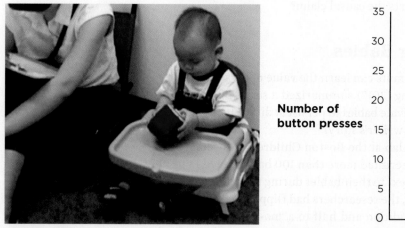

**FIGURE 10.3**

**Measuring persistence.**

A baby tries to get the toy to play music in the persistence study. The researchers measured how many times the baby pressed the large, inert button on the toy.

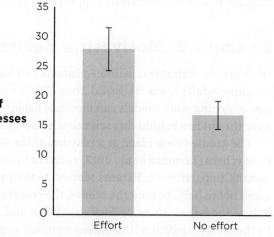

**Number of button presses**

**FIGURE 10.4**

**The results of Leonard et al.'s study on persistence in babies.**

The error bars represent standard error of each mean. (Source: Adapted from Leonard et al., 2017.)

with a different driving route to the beach. In psychological science, however, the term **experiment** specifically means that the researchers manipulated at least one variable and measured another (as you learned in Chapter 3). Experiments can take place in a laboratory, a school, or just about anywhere a researcher can manipulate one variable and measure another.

A **manipulated variable** is a variable that is controlled, such as when the researchers assign participants to a particular level (value) of the variable. For example, Mueller and Oppenheimer (2014) manipulated notetaking by flipping a coin to determine whether a person would take notes with a laptop or in longhand. (In other words, the participants did not get to choose which form they would use.) Notetaking method was a variable because it had more than one level (laptop and longhand), and it was a manipulated variable because the experimenter assigned each participant to a particular level. The Leonard team (2017) similarly manipulated which model the babies watched by flipping a coin ahead of time to decide which session participants were in. (Parents did not choose which type of model their babies would see.)

**Measured variables** take the form of records of behavior or attitudes, such as self-reports, behavioral observations, or physiological measures (see Chapter 5). After an experimental situation is set up, the researchers simply record what happens. In their first study, Mueller and Oppenheimer measured student performance on the essay questions. After manipulating the notetaking method, they watched and recorded—that is, they measured—how well people answered the factual and conceptual questions. The Leonard team manipulated the adult model's effort behavior and then measured how many times each baby pressed the inert button.

## Independent and Dependent Variables

In an experiment, the manipulated (causal) variable is the **independent variable**. The name comes from the fact that the researcher has some "independence" in assigning people to different levels of this variable. A study's independent variable should not be confused with its levels, which are also referred to as **conditions**. The independent variable in the Leonard study was the adult model's effort behavior, which had two conditions: effort and no effort.

The measured variable is the **dependent variable**, or *outcome variable*. How a participant acts on the measured variable *depends* on the level of the independent variable. Researchers have less control over the dependent variable; they manipulate the independent variable and then watch what happens to people's self-reports, behaviors, or physiological responses. A dependent variable is not the same as its levels, either. The dependent variable in the Leonard study was the number of button presses (not "25 presses").

Experiments must have at least one independent variable and one dependent variable, but they often have more than one dependent variable. For example, the notetaking study had two dependent variables: performance on factual questions and performance on conceptual questions. Similarly, the baby persistence study's main dependent variable was the number of button presses, but the researchers also measured how long each baby played with the toy during a 2-minute interval. When the dependent variables are measured on different scales (e.g., button presses and seconds), they are usually presented on separate graphs. (Experiments can also have more than one independent variable; Chapter 12 introduces this type of experiment.)

Here's a way to tell the two kinds of variables apart. When researchers graph their results, the independent variable is almost always on the *x*-axis, and the dependent variable is almost always on the *y*-axis (see Figures 10.2 and 10.4 for examples). A mnemonic for remembering the two types of variables is that the independent variable comes first in time (and the letter I looks like the number 1), and the dependent variable is measured afterward (or second).

## Control Variables

When researchers are manipulating an independent variable, they need to make sure they are varying only one thing at a time—the potential causal force or proposed "active ingredient" (e.g., only the form of notetaking, or only the amount of effort the adult model displays). Therefore, besides the independent variable, researchers also control potential third variables (or nuisance variables) in their studies by holding all other factors constant between the levels of the independent variable. For example, Mueller and Oppenheimer (2014) manipulated the method people used to take notes, but they held constant several other potential variables: People in both groups watched lectures in the same room and had the same experimenter. They watched the same videos and answered the same questions about them, and so on. Any variable that an experimenter holds constant on purpose is called a **control variable**.

In the Leonard et al. study (2017), one control variable was the toys the model was using. In both conditions, she modeled the same frog-in-the-box and carabiner toys. She used the same cheerful, enthusiastic voice. The researchers also kept constant how long the model demonstrated each toy (30 seconds each), the gender of the model (always female), the chair the infant sat in, the cubicle where the experiment took place, and so on.

Control variables are not really variables at all because they do not vary; experimenters keep the levels the same for all participants. Clearly, control variables are essential in experiments. They allow researchers to separate one potential cause from another and thus eliminate alternative explanations for results. Control variables are therefore important for establishing internal validity.

# WHY EXPERIMENTS SUPPORT CAUSAL CLAIMS

In both of the examples above, the researchers manipulated one variable and measured another, so both studies can be considered experiments. But are these researchers really justified in making causal claims on the basis of these experiments? Yes. To understand how experiments support causal claims, you can first apply the three rules for causation to the baby persistence study. The three rules should be familiar to you by now:

1. *Covariance.* Do the results show that the causal variable is related to the outcome variable? Are distinct levels of the independent variable associated with different levels of the dependent variable?
2. *Temporal precedence.* Does the study design ensure that the causal variable comes before the outcome variable in time?
3. *Internal validity.* Does the study design rule out alternative explanations for the results?

## Experiments Establish Covariance

The results of the experiment by Leonard and her colleagues did show covariance between the causal variable (the independent variable: model's behavior) and the outcome variable (the dependent variable: button presses). On average, babies who saw the "effort" model pressed the button 11 times more often than babies who saw the "no-effort" model (see Figure 10.4). In this case, covariance is indicated by a *difference* in the group means: The number of button presses was different in the effort condition than it was in the no-effort condition. The notetaking study's results also showed covariance, at least for conceptual questions: Longhand notetakers had higher scores than laptop notetakers on conceptual questions.

## INDEPENDENT VARIABLES ANSWER "COMPARED TO WHAT?"

The covariance criterion might seem obvious. In our everyday reasoning, though, we tend to ignore its importance because most of our personal experiences do not have the benefit of a **comparison group**, or *comparison condition*. For instance, you might have wondered if your painstaking, handwritten notes are making you learn more, but without comparing longhand with laptop notetaking for the same class session, you cannot know for sure. An experiment, in contrast, provides the comparison group you need. Therefore, an experiment is a better source of information than your own experience because an experiment allows you to ask and answer: Compared to what? (For a review of experience versus empiricism, see Chapter 2.)

If independent variables did not vary, a study could not establish covariance. For example, a few years ago, a psychology blogger described a study he had conducted informally, concluding that dogs don't like being hugged (Coren, 2016). The press widely covered the conclusion, but the study behind it was flawed. Having collected Internet photos of people hugging their dogs, the researcher reported that 82% of the hugged dogs showed signs of stress. However, this study did not have a comparison group: Coren did not collect photos of dogs *not* being hugged. Therefore, we cannot know, based on this study, if signs of stress are actually higher in hugged dogs than not-hugged dogs. In contrast, true experiments manipulate an independent variable. Because every independent variable has at least two levels, true experiments are always set up to look for covariance.

## COVARIANCE: IT'S ALSO ABOUT THE RESULTS

Manipulating the independent (causal) variable is necessary for establishing covariance, but the results matter, too. Suppose the baby researchers had found no difference in how babies behaved in the two conditions. In that case, the study would have found no covariance, and the experimenters would have had to conclude that persistent adult models do not cause babies to persist more. After all, if button presses did not covary with the effort/no-effort conditions, there is no causal impact to explain.

## CONTROL GROUPS, TREATMENT GROUPS, AND COMPARISON GROUPS

There are a couple of ways an independent variable might be designed to show covariance. Your early science classes may have emphasized the importance of a control group in an experiment. A **control group** is a level of an independent variable that is intended to represent "no treatment" or a neutral condition. When a study has a control group, the other level or levels of the independent variable are usually called the **treatment group(s)**. For example, if an experiment is testing the effectiveness of a new medication, the researchers might assign some participants to take the medication (the treatment group) and other participants to take an inert sugar pill (the control group). When the control group is exposed to an inert treatment such as a sugar pill, it is called a **placebo group**, or a *placebo control group*.

Not every experiment has—or needs—a control group, and often, a clear control group does not even exist. The Mueller and Oppenheimer notetaking study (2014) had two comparison groups—laptop and longhand—but neither was a control group, in the sense that neither of them clearly established a "no notetaking" condition.

Also consider the experiment by Harry Harlow (1958), discussed in Chapter 1, in which baby monkeys were put in cages with artificial "mothers" made of either cold wire or warm cloth. There was no control group, just a carefully designed comparison condition. When a study uses comparison groups, the levels of the independent variable differ in some intended and meaningful way. All experiments need a comparison group so the researchers can compare one condition to another, but the comparison group may not need to be a control group.

« For more details on the placebo effect and how researchers control for it, see Chapter 11, pp. 335–337.

## Experiments Establish Temporal Precedence

The experiment by Leonard's team also established temporal precedence. The experimenters manipulated the causal (independent) variable (adult model's effort behavior) to ensure that it came first in time. Then the babies took the musical cube and pressed its button. The causal variable clearly did come before the outcome (dependent) variable. This ability to establish temporal precedence, by controlling which variable comes first, is a strong advantage of experimental designs. By manipulating the independent variable, the experimenter virtually ensures that the cause comes before the effect (or outcome).

The ability to establish temporal precedence is a feature that makes experiments superior to correlational designs. A simple correlational study is a snapshot—all variables are measured at the same time, so when two variables covary (such as time spent sitting and measured cortical thickness, or deep conversations and well-being), it's impossible to tell which variable came first. In contrast, experiments unfold over time, and the experimenter makes sure the independent variable comes first.

## Well-Designed Experiments Establish Internal Validity

Did the Mueller and Oppenheimer study establish internal validity? Are there any alternative explanations for why students in the longhand condition scored better on conceptual tests than students in the laptop condition?

A well-designed experiment establishes internal validity, which is one of the most important validities to interrogate when you encounter causal claims.

To be internally valid, a study must ensure that the causal variable (the active ingredient), and not other factors, is responsible for the change in the outcome variable. You can interrogate internal validity by exploring potential alternative explanations. For example, you might ask whether the students in the laptop notes group were given more difficult test questions than those in the handwritten notes group. If so, the difficulty of the test would be an alternative explanation for why laptop students did worse (**Figure 10.5**). However, the researchers gave the same test to both groups. In fact, the difficulty of the test was a control variable: It was held constant for all participants, for just this reason.

You also might be wondering whether the experimenters in the Leonard et al. study treated the babies in the two groups differently. Maybe the model acted more cheerful with the babies in one condition than she did with those in the other. That would have been another threat to internal validity, so it's important to know whether the models knew the hypothesis of the study.

For any given research question, there can be several possible alternative explanations, which are known as **confounds**, or potential threats to internal validity. The word *confound* can mean "confuse": When a study has a confound, you are confused about what is causing the change in the dependent variable. Is it the intended causal variable (such as the effort shown by the model)? Or is there some alternative explanation (such as the model's cheerful attitude)? Internal validity is subject to a number of distinct threats, three of which—design confounds, selection effects, and order effects—are discussed in this chapter, and the rest in Chapter 11. As experimenters design and interpret studies, they keep these threats to internal validity in mind and try to avoid them.

### DESIGN CONFOUNDS

A **design confound** is an experimenter's mistake in designing the independent variable; it occurs when a second variable happens to vary systematically

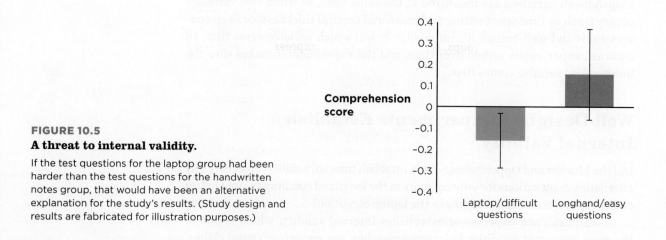

**FIGURE 10.5**
**A threat to internal validity.**
If the test questions for the laptop group had been harder than the test questions for the handwritten notes group, that would have been an alternative explanation for the study's results. (Study design and results are fabricated for illustration purposes.)

along with the intended independent variable. The accidental second variable is therefore an alternative explanation for the results. As such, a design confound is a classic threat to internal validity. If the adult models in the baby study had accidentally exhibited more cheerful attitudes in the effort than the no-effort condition, the study would have a design confound because the second variable (model's cheerfulness) would have systematically varied along with the independent variable (effort versus no effort). If the test for the laptop group was harder than the test for the longhand notes group, then test difficulty would have been a design confound, too.

However, the researchers did not make these errors. The models in the Leonard team's study were carefully trained to express the same emotion in both conditions. And the notetaking researchers gave the same questions to all participants, no matter what condition they were in, so there would be no systematic differences between the groups.

When an experiment has a design confound, it has poor internal validity and cannot support a causal claim. Because the Leonard et al. study did not have any apparent design confounds, its internal validity is sound. The researchers carefully thought about confounds in advance and turned them into control variables instead. Similarly, Mueller and Oppenheimer controlled for a number of potential design confounds, such as question difficulty, experimenter expectations, room conditions, and so on. In both cases, the researchers took steps to help them justify making a causal claim.

**Systematic Variability Is the Problem.** You need to be careful before accusing a study of having a design confound. Not every potentially problematic variable is a confound. Consider the example of the baby persistence study. It might be the case that some of the adult models were cheerful and others were more reserved. The emotional expression of the models is a problem for internal validity *only if* it shows **systematic variability** with the independent variable. Did the cheerful models work only in the effort condition and the reserved ones only in the no-effort condition? Then it would be a design confound. However, if the adult models' demeanor showed **unsystematic variability** (random or haphazard) across both groups, then their emotional expression would not be a confound.

Here's another example. Perhaps some of the participants in the notetaking study were interested in the video lectures and others were not. This variability in interest would not be a design confound unless it varied systematically with the notetaking condition to which they were assigned. If those in the longhand group all happened to be very interested in the lectures and those in the laptop group were all uninterested, level of interest would vary systematically with the notetaking condition and would be a confound. But if some participants in each condition were interested and some were not, that would be unsystematic variability and would not be a confound.

Unsystematic variability can lead to other problems in an experiment. Specifically, it can obscure, or make it difficult to detect differences in, the dependent variable, as discussed fully in Chapter 11. However, unsystematic variability should not be called a design confound (**Figure 10.6**).

Some babies like music more than others, some babies can sit still longer than others, and some babies just had a nap while others are tired. But individual differences don't become a confound unless one type of baby ends up in one group

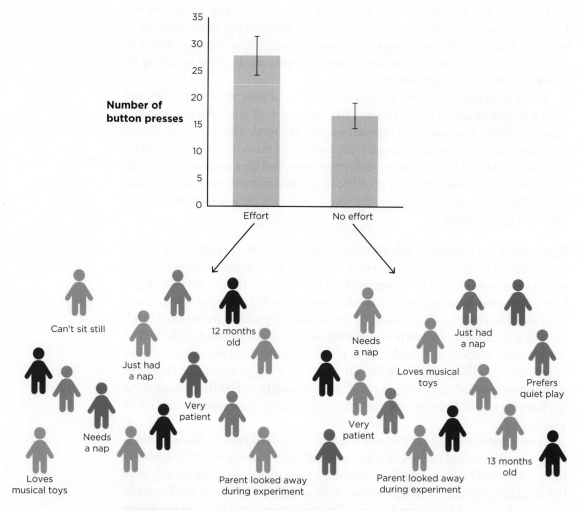

**FIGURE 10.6**

**Unsystematic variability is not the same as a confound.**

Some babies like music more than others, some babies can sit still longer than others, and some babies just had a nap while others are tired. But individual differences don't become a confound unless one type of baby ends up in one group systematically more than another group. If individual differences are distributed evenly in both groups, they are not a confound.

systematically more than another group. If individual differences are distributed evenly in both groups, they are not a confound.

## SELECTION EFFECTS

In an experiment, when the kinds of participants in one level of the independent variable are systematically different from those in the other, **selection effects** can result. They can also happen when the experimenters let participants choose (select) which group they want to be in. A selection effect may result if the experimenters assign one type of person (e.g., all the women, or all who sign up early in the semester) to one condition, and another type of person (e.g., all the men, or all those who wait until later in the semester) to another condition.

Here's a real-world example. A study was designed to test a new intensive therapy for autism, involving one-on-one sessions with a therapist for 40 hours per week (Lovaas, 1987; see Gernsbacher, 2003). To determine whether this therapy would cause a significant improvement in children's autism symptoms, the researchers recruited 38 families that had children with autism and arranged for some children to receive the new intensive treatment while others received their usual treatment. The researchers initially intended to randomly assign families to either the intensive-treatment group or the treatment-as-usual group. However, some of the families lived too far away to receive the new treatment; other parents protested that they preferred to be in the intensive-treatment group. Thus, not all the families were randomly assigned to the two groups.

At the end of the study, the researchers found that the symptoms of the children in the intensive-treatment group had improved more than the symptoms of those who received their usual treatment. However, this study suffered from a clear selection effect: The families in the intensive-treatment group were probably systematically different from the treatment-as-usual group because the groups self-selected. Many parents in the intensive-treatment group were placed there because of their eagerness to try a focused, 40-hour-per-week treatment regimen. Therefore, parents in that group may have been more motivated to help their children, so there was a clear threat to internal validity.

Because of the selection effect, it's impossible to tell the reason for the results (**Figure 10.7**). Did the children in that group improve because of the intensive treatment? Or did they improve because the families who selected the new therapy were simply more engaged in their children's treatment? Of course, in any study that tests a therapy, some participants will be more motivated than others. This variability in

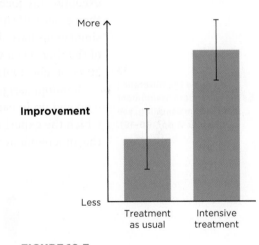

**FIGURE 10.7**
**Selection effects.**

In a study for treating autism, some parents insisted that their children be in the new intensive-treatment group rather than the treatment-as-usual group. Because they had this choice, it's not possible to determine whether the improvement in the intensive group was caused by the treatment itself or by the fact that the more motivated parents chose it. (Data and error bars are fabricated for illustration purposes.)

motivation becomes a confound only when the more motivated folks tend to be in one group—that is, when the variability is systematic.

**Avoiding Selection Effects with Random Assignment.** Well-designed experiments often use **random assignment** to avoid selection effects. In the baby study, an experimenter flipped a coin to determine which participants would be in each group, so each one had an *equal chance* of being in the effort or no-effort condition. What does this mean? Suppose that, of the 100 babies in the study, 20 were exceptionally focused. Probabilistically speaking, the flips of the coin would have placed about 10 of these very focused babies in the effort condition and about 10 in the no-effort condition. Similarly, if 12 of the babies were acting fussy that day, random assignment would place about 6 of them in each group. In other words, since the researchers used random assignment, it's very unlikely, given the random (deliberately unsystematic) way people were assigned to each group, that all the focused or fussy babies would have been clustered in the same group.

Assigning participants at random to different levels of the independent variable—by flipping a coin, rolling a die, or using a random number generator—controls for all sorts of potential selection effects (**Figure 10.8**). Of course, random assignment may not always create numbers that are perfectly even. The 20 exceptionally focused babies may be distributed as 9 and 11, or 12 and 8, rather than exactly 10 and 10. However, random assignment almost always works. In fact, simulations have shown that random assignment creates similar groups up to 98% of the time, even when there are as few as 4 people in each group (Sawilowsky, 2005; Strube, 1991).

**»**
To review the difference between random assignment and random sampling, see Chapter 7, pp. 190–191.

Random assignment is a way of desystematizing the types of participants who end up in each level of the independent variable. It creates a situation in which the experimental groups will become virtually equal, on average, *before* the independent variable is applied. After random assignment (and before

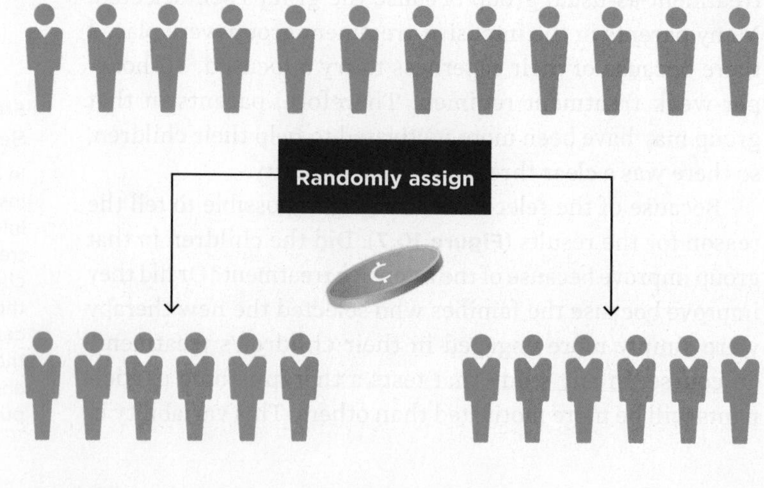

**FIGURE 10.8**
**Random assignment.**

Random assignment ensures that every participant in an experiment has an equal chance to be in each group.

**Randomly assign**

manipulating the independent variable), researchers should be able to test the experimental groups for intelligence, extroversion, motivation, and so on, and averages of each group should be comparable on these traits.

**Avoiding Selection Effects with Matched Groups.** In the simplest type of random assignment, researchers assign participants at random to one condition or another in the experiment. For certain studies, researchers may wish to be absolutely sure the experimental groups are as equal as possible before they administer the independent variable. In these cases, they may choose to use **matched groups**, or *matching*.

To create matched groups from a sample of 30, the researchers would first measure the participants on a particular variable that might matter to the dependent variable. Student achievement, operationalized by GPA, for instance, might matter in the study of notetaking. The researchers would next match up participants in pairs, starting with the two having the highest GPAs, and *within that matched set*, randomly assign one of them to each of the two notetaking conditions. They would then take the pair with the next-highest GPAs and within that set again assign randomly to the two groups. They would continue this process until they reach the participants with the lowest GPAs and assign them at random too (**Figure 10.9**).

Matching has the advantage of randomness. Because each member of the matched pair is randomly assigned, the technique prevents selection effects. This method also ensures that the groups are equal on some important variable, such as GPA, before the manipulation of the independent variable. The disadvantage is that the matching process requires an extra step—in this case, finding out people's GPA before assigning to groups. Matching therefore requires more time and often more resources than random assignment.

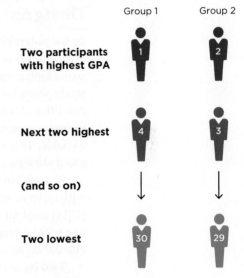

**FIGURE 10.9**

**Matching groups to eliminate selection effects.**

To create matched groups, participants are sorted from lowest to highest on some variable and grouped into sets of two. Individuals within each set are then assigned at random to the two experimental groups.

---

✔

## CHECK YOUR UNDERSTANDING

1. Why do experiments usually satisfy the three causal criteria?

2. How are design confounds and control variables related?

3. How does random assignment prevent selection effects?

4. How does using matched groups prevent selection effects?

1. See pp. 283–286. 2. See pp. 286–287; control variables are used to eliminate potential design confounds. 3. See pp. 290–291. 4. See p. 291.

# INDEPENDENT-GROUPS DESIGNS

Although the minimum requirement for an experiment is that researchers manipulate one variable and measure another, experiments can take many forms. One of the most basic distinctions is between independent-groups designs and within-groups designs.

## Independent-Groups Versus Within-Groups Designs

In the notetaking and baby persistence studies, there were different participants at each level of the independent variable. In the notetaking study, some participants took notes on laptops and others took notes in longhand. In the persistence study, some babies were in the effort condition and others were in the no-effort condition. Both of these studies used an **independent-groups design**, in which separate groups of participants are placed into different levels of the independent variable. This type of design is also called a *between-subjects design* or *between-groups design*.

In a **within-groups design**, or *within-subjects design*, each person is presented with *all* levels of the independent variable. For example, Mueller and Oppenheimer (2014) used an independent-groups design. But they might have run their study as a within-groups design if they had asked each participant to take notes on two videos—using a laptop for one and handwriting their notes for the other.

Two basic forms of independent-groups designs are the posttest-only design and the pretest/posttest design. The two types of designs are used in different situations.

## Posttest-Only Design

The **posttest-only design**, also known as an *equivalent groups, posttest-only design*, is one of the simplest independent-groups experimental designs. In this design, participants are randomly assigned to independent variable groups and are tested on the dependent variable once (**Figure 10.10**). The notetaking study is an

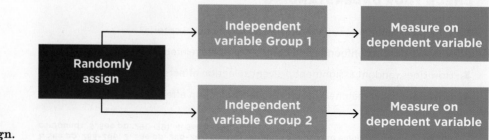

**FIGURE 10.10**
**A posttest-only design.**

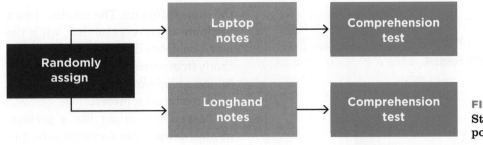

**FIGURE 10.11**
**Studying notetaking: a posttest-only design.**

example of a posttest-only design, with two independent variable levels (Mueller & Oppenheimer, 2014). Participants were randomly assigned to a laptop condition or a longhand condition (**Figure 10.11**), and they were tested only once on the video they watched.

Posttest-only designs satisfy all three criteria for causation. They allow researchers to test for covariance by detecting differences in the dependent variable. (Having at least two groups makes it possible to do so.) They establish temporal precedence because the independent variable comes first in time. And when they are conducted well, they establish internal validity. When researchers use appropriate control variables, there should be no design confounds, and random assignment takes care of selection effects.

## Pretest/Posttest Design

In a **pretest/posttest design**, or *equivalent groups, pretest/posttest design*, participants are randomly assigned to at least two groups and are tested on the key dependent variable twice—once before and once after exposure to the independent variable (**Figure 10.12**).

A study on the effects of mindfulness training, introduced in Chapter 1, is an example of a pretest/posttest design. In this study, 48 students were randomly assigned to participate in either a 2-week mindfulness class or a 2-week nutrition class (Mrazek et al., 2013). One week before starting their respective classes, all students completed a verbal-reasoning section of a GRE test. One week after their classes ended, all students completed another verbal-reasoning GRE test of

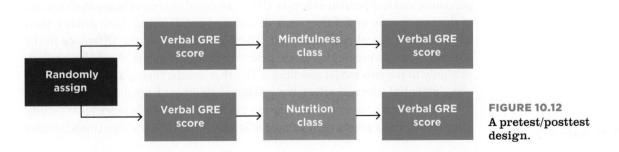

**FIGURE 10.12**
**A pretest/posttest design.**

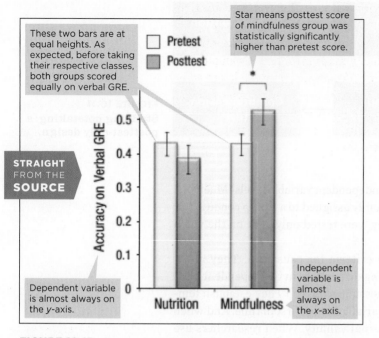

These two bars are at equal heights. As expected, before taking their respective classes, both groups scored equally on verbal GRE.

Star means posttest score of mindfulness group was statistically significantly higher than pretest score.

□ Pretest
■ Posttest

STRAIGHT FROM THE SOURCE

Dependent variable is almost always on the *y*-axis.

Independent variable is almost always on the *x*-axis.

Nutrition    Mindfulness

**FIGURE 10.13**

**Results using a pretest/posttest design.**

In this study, mindfulness training caused students to improve their GRE verbal scores. (Source: Mrazek et al., 2013, Fig. 1A.)

the same difficulty. The results, shown in **Figure 10.13**, revealed that, while the nutrition group did not improve significantly from pretest to posttest, the mindfulness group scored significantly higher at posttest than at pretest.

Researchers might use a pretest/posttest design when they want to be sure random assignment made groups equal. In this case, a pretest/posttest design means researchers can be absolutely sure there is no selection effect in a study. If you examine the white pretest bars in Figure 10.13, you'll see the nutrition and mindfulness groups had almost identical pretest scores, indicating that random assignment worked as expected.

In addition, pretest/posttest designs enable researchers to track people's change in performance over time. Although the two groups started out, as expected, with about the same GRE ability, only the mindfulness group improved their GRE scores.

## Which Design Is Better?

Why might researchers choose to do a posttest-only experiment rather than a pretest/posttest design? Shouldn't they always make sure groups are equal on GRE ability or persistence *before* they experience a manipulation?

Not necessarily. In some situations, it is problematic to use a pretest/posttest design. Imagine that the Leonard team had pretested the babies to see how persistent they were at pressing an inert button. If they had, the babies might have become too frustrated to continue. (Studies with babies need to be short!) Instead, the researchers trusted in random assignment to create equivalent groups. More persistent and less persistent babies all had an equal chance of being in either one of the two groups, and if they were distributed evenly across both groups, their effects would cancel each other out. Therefore, any observed difference in the number of button presses between these two groups of babies should be attributable only to the two model conditions. In other words, "being a persistent baby" was a potential selection effect, but random assignment helped avoid it.

In contrast, a pretest/posttest design made sense for the Mrazek team's study. They could justify giving their sample of students the GRE test two times because they had told participants they were studying ways of "improving cognitive performance."

In short, the posttest-only design may be the most basic type of independent-groups experiment, but its combination of random assignment plus a manipulated variable can lead to powerful causal conclusions. The pretest/posttest design adds a pretesting step to the most basic independent-groups design. Researchers might use a pretest/posttest design if they want to study improvement over time, or to be extra sure that two groups are equivalent at the start—as long as the pretest does not make the participants change their subsequent behavior.

**CHECK YOUR UNDERSTANDING**

1. What is the difference between independent-groups and within-groups designs? Use the term *levels* in your answer.

2. Describe why posttest-only and pretest/posttest designs are both independent-groups designs. Explain how they differ.

1. See p. 292. 2. See pp. 292–294.

## WITHIN-GROUPS DESIGNS

There are two basic types of within-groups designs. When researchers expose participants to all levels of the independent variable, they might do so by repeated exposures, over time, to different levels, or they might do so concurrently.

## Repeated-Measures Design

A **repeated-measures design** is a type of within-groups design in which participants are measured on a dependent variable more than once, after exposure to each level of the independent variable. Here's an example. Humans are social animals, and we know that many of our thoughts and behaviors are influenced by the presence of other people. Happy times may be happier, and sad times sadder, when experienced with others. Researchers Erica Boothby and her colleagues used a repeated-measures design to investigate whether a shared experience would be intensified even when people do not interact with the other person (Boothby et al., 2014). They hypothesized that sharing a good experience with another person makes it even better than it would have been if experienced alone, and that sharing a bad experience would make it even worse.

They recruited 23 college women to come to a laboratory. Each participant was joined by a female confederate (a research assistant pretending to be a participant). The two sat side-by-side, facing forward, and never spoke to each other. The experimenter explained that each person in the pair would do a variety of activities, including tasting some dark chocolates and viewing some paintings. During the experiment, the order of activities was determined by drawing cards, but the drawings were rigged so that the real participant's first two activities were always tasting chocolates. In addition, the real participant tasted one chocolate at the same time the confederate was also tasting it, but she tasted the other chocolate while the confederate was viewing a painting. The participant was told that the two chocolates were different, but in fact they were exactly the same. After tasting each chocolate, participants rated how much they liked it. The results showed that people liked the chocolate more when the confederate was also tasting it (**Figure 10.14**).

In this study, the independent variable had two levels: sharing and not sharing an experience. Participants experienced both levels, making it a within-groups design. The dependent variable was participants' rating of the chocolate. It was a repeated-measures design because each participant rated the chocolate twice (i.e., repeatedly).

## Concurrent-Measures Design

In a **concurrent-measures design**, participants are exposed to all the levels of an independent variable at roughly the same time, and a single attitudinal or behavioral preference is the dependent variable. An example is a study investigating infant cognition, in which infants were shown a male face and a female face

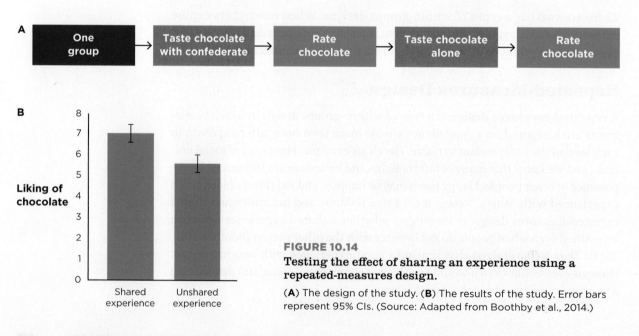

**FIGURE 10.14**

**Testing the effect of sharing an experience using a repeated-measures design.**

(**A**) The design of the study. (**B**) The results of the study. Error bars represent 95% CIs. (Source: Adapted from Boothby et al., 2014.)

at the same time, and an experimenter recorded which face they looked at the longest (Quinn et al., 2002). The independent variable was the gender of the face, and babies experienced both levels (male and female) at the same time. The baby's looking preference was the dependent variable (**Figure 10.15**). This study found that babies show a preference for looking at female faces, unless their primary caretaker is male.

Harlow also used a concurrent-measures design when he presented baby monkeys with both a wire and a cloth "mother" (Harlow, 1958). The monkeys indicated their preference by spending more time with one mother than the other. In Harlow's study, the type of mother was the independent variable (manipulated as within-groups), and each baby monkey's clinging behavior was the dependent variable.

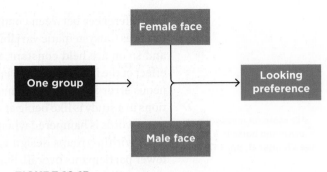

**FIGURE 10.15**

**A concurrent-measures design for an infant cognition study.**

Babies saw two faces simultaneously, and the experimenters recorded which face they looked at more.

## Advantages of Within-Groups Designs

The main advantage of a within-groups design is that it ensures the participants in the two groups will be equivalent. After all, they are the same participants! For example, some people really like dark chocolate and others do not. But in a repeated-measures design, people bring their same liking of chocolate to both conditions, so their individual liking for the chocolate stays the same. The only difference between the two conditions can be attributed to the independent variable (whether people were sharing the experience with the confederate or not). In a within-groups design such as the chocolate study, researchers say that each woman "acted as her own control" because individual or personal variables are kept constant.

Similarly, when the Quinn team (2002) studied whether infants prefer to look at male or female faces as a within-groups design, they did not have to worry (for instance) that all the girl babies would be in one group or the other, or that babies with older siblings or who go to daycare would be in one group or the other. Every baby saw both types of faces, which kept any extraneous personal variables constant across the two facial gender conditions.

The idea of "treating each participant as his or her own control" also means matched-groups designs can be treated as within-groups designs. As discussed earlier, in a matched-groups design, researchers carefully match sets of participants on some key control variable (such as GPA) and assign each member of a set to a different group. The matched participants in the groups are assumed to be more similar to each other than in a more traditional independent-groups design, which uses random assignment.

« To review matched-groups designs, see p. 291.

Besides providing the ability to use each participant as his or her own control, within-groups designs also enable researchers to make more precise estimates of the differences between conditions. Statistically speaking, when extraneous differences (unsystematic variability) in personality, food preferences, gender, ability, and so on are held constant across all conditions, researchers can estimate the effect of the independent variable manipulation more precisely—there is less extraneous error in the measurement. Having extraneous differences between conditions in a study is like being at a noisy party: Your ability to understand somebody's exact words is hampered when many other conversations are going on around you.

» For more on measurement error and noise in a study, see Chapter 11, pp. 347–350.

A within-groups design can also be attractive because it generally requires fewer participants overall. Suppose a team of researchers is running a study with two conditions. If they want 50 participants in each condition, they will need a total of 100 people for an independent-groups design. However, if they run the same study as a within-groups design, they will need only 50 participants because each participant experiences all levels of the independent variable (**Figure 10.16**). In this way, a repeated-measures design can be much more efficient.

## Covariance, Temporal Precedence, and Internal Validity in Within-Groups Designs

Do within-groups designs allow researchers to make causal claims? In other words, do they stand up to the three criteria for causation?

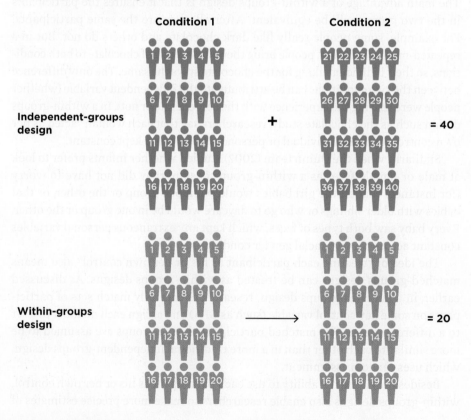

**FIGURE 10.16**

**Within-groups designs require fewer participants.**

If researchers want a certain number of participants in each of two experimental conditions, a within-groups design is more efficient than an independent-groups design. Although only 40 participants are shown here (for reasons of space), psychologists usually need to use larger samples than this in their studies.

Because within-groups designs enable researchers to manipulate an independent variable and incorporate comparison conditions, they provide an opportunity for establishing covariance. The Boothby team (2014) observed, for example, that the chocolate ratings covaried with whether people shared the tasting experience or not.

A repeated-measures design also establishes temporal precedence. The experimenter controls the independent variable and can ensure that it comes first. In the chocolate study, each person tasted chocolate as either a shared or an unshared experience *and then* rated the chocolate. In the infant cognition study, the researchers presented the male and female faces first *and then* measured looking time.

What about internal validity? For a within-groups design, researchers don't have to worry about selection effects because participants are exactly the same in the two conditions. They do need to avoid design confounds, however. For example, Boothby's team made sure both chocolates were exactly the same. If the chocolate that people tasted in the shared condition was of better quality, the experimenters would not know if it was the chocolate quality or the shared experience that was responsible for higher ratings. Similarly, Quinn's team made sure the male and female faces they presented to the babies were equally attractive and of the same ethnicity.

## INTERNAL VALIDITY: CONTROLLING FOR ORDER EFFECTS

Within-groups designs have the potential for a particular threat to internal validity: Sometimes, being exposed to one condition first changes how participants react to the later condition. Such responses are called **order effects**, and they happen when exposure to one level of the independent variable influences responses to the next level. An order effect in a within-groups design is a confound, meaning that behavior at later levels of the independent variable might be caused not by the experimental manipulation but rather by the sequence in which the conditions were experienced.

Order effects can include **practice effects**, also known as *fatigue effects*, in which a long sequence might lead participants to get better at the task or to get tired or bored toward the end. Order effects also include **carryover effects**, in which some form of contamination carries over from one condition to the next. For example, imagine sipping orange juice right after brushing your teeth; the first taste contaminates your experience of the second one.

An order effect in the chocolate-tasting study could have occurred if people rated the first chocolate higher than the second simply because the first bite of chocolate is always the best; subsequent bites are never quite as good. That would be an order effect and a threat to internal validity because the order of tasting chocolate is confounded with the condition (shared versus unshared experiences).

## AVOIDING ORDER EFFECTS BY COUNTERBALANCING

Because order effects are potential internal validity problems in a within-groups design, experimenters want to avoid them. When researchers use **counterbalancing**, they present the levels of the independent variable to participants in different

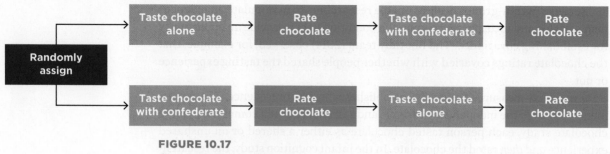

**FIGURE 10.17**
**Counterbalanced design.**
Using counterbalancing in an experiment will cancel out any order effects in a repeated-measures design.

sequences. With counterbalancing, any order effects should cancel each other out when all the data are combined.

Boothby and her colleagues (2014) used counterbalancing in their experiment (**Figure 10.17**). Half the participants tasted their first chocolate in the shared condition followed by a second chocolate in the unshared condition. The other half tasted chocolate in the unshared followed by the shared condition. Therefore, the potential order effect of "first taste of chocolate" was present for half of the people in each condition. When the data were combined from these two sequences, any order effect dropped out of the comparison between the shared and unshared conditions. As a result, the researchers knew that the difference they noticed was attributable only to the shared (versus unshared) experiences, and not to practice, carryover, or some other order effect.

**Procedures Behind Counterbalancing.** When researchers counterbalance conditions (or levels) in a within-groups design, they split their participants into groups, and each group receives one of the condition sequences. How do the experimenters decide which participants receive the first order of presentation and which ones receive the second? Through random assignment, of course! They might recruit, say, 50 participants to a study and randomly assign 25 of them to receive the order A then B, and assign 25 of them to the order B then A.

There are two methods for counterbalancing an experiment: full and partial. When a within-groups experiment has only two or three levels of an independent variable, researchers can use **full counterbalancing**, in which all possible condition orders are represented. For example, a repeated-measures design with two conditions is easy to counterbalance because there are only two orders (A → B and B → A). In a repeated-measures design with three conditions—A, B, and C—each group of participants could be randomly assigned to one of the six following sequences:

$$A \rightarrow B \rightarrow C \qquad B \rightarrow C \rightarrow A$$
$$A \rightarrow C \rightarrow B \qquad C \rightarrow A \rightarrow B$$
$$B \rightarrow A \rightarrow C \qquad C \rightarrow B \rightarrow A$$

As the number of conditions increases, however, the number of possible orders needed for full counterbalancing increases dramatically. For example, a study with four conditions requires 24 possible sequences. If experimenters want to put at least a few participants in each order, the need for participants can quickly increase, counteracting the typical efficiency of a repeated-measures design. Therefore, they might use **partial counterbalancing**, in which only some of the possible condition orders are represented. One way to partially counterbalance is to present the conditions in a randomized order for every subject. (This is easy to do when an experiment is administered by a computer; the computer delivers conditions in a new random order for each participant.)

Another technique for partial counterbalancing is to use a **Latin square**, a formal system to ensure that every condition appears in each position at least once. A Latin square for six conditions (conditions 1 through 6) looks like this:

```
1   2   6   3   5   4
2   3   1   4   6   5
3   4   2   5   1   6
4   5   3   6   2   1
5   6   4   1   3   2
6   1   5   2   4   3
```

The first row is set up according to a formula, and then the conditions simply go in numerical order down each column. Latin squares work differently for odd and even numbers of conditions. If you wish to create your own, you can find formulas for setting up the first rows of a Latin square online.

## Disadvantages of Within-Groups Designs

Within-groups designs are true experiments because they involve a manipulated variable and a measured variable. They potentially establish covariance, they ensure temporal precedence, and when experimenters control for order effects and design confounds, they can establish internal validity, too. So why wouldn't a researcher choose a within-groups design all the time?

Within-groups designs have three main disadvantages. First, as noted earlier, repeated-measures designs have the potential for order effects, which can threaten internal validity. But a researcher can usually control for order effects by using counterbalancing, so they may not be much of a concern.

A second possible disadvantage is that a within-groups design might not be possible or practical. Suppose someone has devised a new way of teaching children how to ride a bike, called Method A. She wants to compare Method A with the older method, Method B. Obviously, she cannot teach a group of children to ride a bike with Method A and then return them to baseline and teach them again with Method B. Once taught, the children are permanently changed. In such a case, a within-groups design, with or without counterbalancing, would make no sense. The study on mindfulness training and GRE scores fits in this category. Once people had participated in mindfulness training, they presumably could apply their new skill indefinitely.

A third problem occurs when people see all levels of the independent variable and then change the way they would normally act. Imagine a study that asks people to rate the attractiveness of two photographed people—one Black and one White. Participants in such a study might think, "I know I'm participating in a study at the moment; seeing both a White and a Black person makes me wonder whether it has something to do with prejudice." As a result, they might change their spontaneous behavior. A cue that can lead participants to guess an experiment's hypothesis is known as a **demand characteristic**, or an *experimental demand*. Demand characteristics create an alternative explanation for a study's results. You would have to ask: Did the manipulation really work, or did the participants simply guess what the researchers expected them to do and change their behavior accordingly?

## Is Pretest/Posttest a Repeated-Measures Design?

You might wonder whether pretest/posttest independent-groups design should be considered a repeated-measures design. After all, in both designs, participants are tested on the dependent variable twice.

In a true repeated-measures design, however, participants are exposed to all levels of a meaningful independent variable, such as a shared or unshared experience, or the gender of the face they're looking at. The levels of such independent variables can also be counterbalanced. In contrast, in a pretest/posttest design, participants see only one level of the independent variable, not all levels (**Figure 10.18**). **Table 10.1** summarizes the four types of experimental designs covered in this chapter.

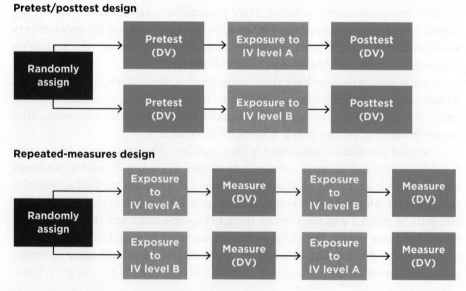

**FIGURE 10.18**
**Pretest/posttest design versus repeated-measures design.**

In a pretest/posttest design, participants see only one level of the independent variable, but in a repeated-measures design, they see all the levels. (DV = dependent variable. IV = independent variable.)

**TABLE 10.1**

## Two Independent-Groups Designs and Two Within-Groups Designs

| INDEPENDENT-GROUPS DESIGNS | | WITHIN-GROUPS DESIGNS | |
|---|---|---|---|
| **Definition: Different participants at each level of independent variable** | | **Definition: Same participants see all levels of independent variable** | |
| Posttest-only design | Pretest/posttest design | Repeated-measures design | Concurrent-measures design |

# INTERROGATING CAUSAL CLAIMS WITH THE FOUR VALIDITIES

To interrogate an experimental design using the four big validities as a framework, what questions should you ask, and what do the answers mean? Let's use Mueller and Oppenheimer's (2014) study on notetaking as an illustration.

## Construct Validity: How Well Were the Variables Measured and Manipulated?

In an experiment, researchers operationalize two constructs: the independent variable and the dependent variable. When you interrogate the construct validity of an experiment, you should ask about the construct validity of each of these variables.

### DEPENDENT VARIABLES: HOW WELL WERE THEY MEASURED?

Chapters 5 and 6 explained in detail how to interrogate the construct validity of a dependent (measured) variable. To interrogate construct validity in the notetaking study, you would start by asking how well the researchers measured their dependent variables: factual knowledge and conceptual knowledge.

One aspect of good measurement is face validity. Mueller and Oppenheimer (2014) provided examples of the factual and conceptual questions they used, so you can examine these and evaluate whether they actually constitute good measures of factual learning (e.g., "What is the purpose of adding calcium propionate to bread?") and conceptual learning (e.g., "If a person's epiglottis was not working properly, what would be likely to happen?"). These two examples do seem to be appropriate types of questions because the first asks for direct recall of a lecture's factual information, and the second requires people to understand the epiglottis and make an inference. The researchers also noted that each of these open-ended questions was graded by two coders. The two sets of scores, they reported, showed good interrater reliability (.89). In this study, the strong interrater reliability indicates that the two coders agreed about which participants got the right answers and which ones did not.

« To review interrater reliability, see Chapter 5, pp. 125–126.

## INDEPENDENT VARIABLES: HOW WELL WERE THEY MANIPULATED?

To interrogate the construct validity of the independent variables, you would ask how well the researchers manipulated (or operationalized) them. In the Mueller and Oppenheimer study, this was straightforward: People were given either a pen or a laptop. This operationalization clearly manipulated the intended independent variable.

**Manipulation Checks and Pilot Studies.**  In other studies, researchers need to use manipulation checks to collect empirical data on the construct validity of their independent variables. A **manipulation check** is an extra dependent variable that researchers can insert into an experiment to convince them that their experimental manipulation worked.

A manipulation check was not necessary in the notetaking study because research assistants could simply observe participants to make sure they were actually using the laptops or pens they had been assigned. Manipulation checks are more likely to be used when the intention is to make participants think or feel certain ways. For example, researchers may want to manipulate feelings of anxiety by telling some students they have to give a public speech. Or they may wish to manipulate people's empathy by showing a poignant film. They may manipulate amusement by telling jokes. In these cases, a manipulation check can help researchers determine whether the operationalization worked as intended.

Here's an example. Researchers were interested in investigating whether humor would improve students' memory of a college lecture (Kaplan & Pascoe, 1977). Students were randomly assigned to listen to a serious lecture or one punctuated by humorous examples, and the key dependent variable was their memory for the material. In addition, to ensure they actually found the humorous lecture funnier than the serious one, students rated the lecture on how "funny" and "light" it was. As expected, the students in the humorous lecture condition rated the speaker as funnier and lighter than students in the serious lecture condition. The researchers concluded that the manipulation worked as expected.

A similar procedure, called a **pilot study**, is a simple study, using a separate group of participants, that is completed before (or sometimes after) the study of primary interest to confirm the effectiveness of the manipulations. Kaplan and Pascoe (1977) might have exposed a separate group of students to either a serious or a humorous lecture and then asked them how amusing they found it.

## CONSTRUCT VALIDITY AND THEORY TESTING

Experiments are designed to test theories. Therefore, interrogating the construct validity of an experiment requires you to evaluate how well the measures and manipulations researchers used in their study capture the conceptual variables in their theory.

Recall that Mueller and Oppenheimer (2014) originally proposed that laptop notetaking would let students more easily take notes verbatim, compared with taking handwritten notes. In fact, their study included measures of "verbatim overlap" so they could test their theory about why laptop notetakers might perform worse. After transcribing each person's notes, they measured how closely the notes overlapped verbatim with the video lecture narration. It turned out that people in the laptop condition had, in fact, written more verbatim notes than people in the longhand condition. In addition, the more people wrote verbatim notes, the worse they did on the essay test. The researchers supported their theory by measuring key constructs that their theory proposed.

Here's another example of how theory guides the variables researchers manipulate and measure in an experiment. Recall that the chocolate-tasting study was designed to test the theory that sharing an experience makes it more intense (Boothby et al., 2014). In addition to showing that good-tasting chocolate tastes better when another person is tasting it, the researchers also needed to demonstrate the same effect in response to a negative experience. Using the same repeated-measures design, in a second study they used squares of 90% dark chocolate, containing almost no sugar, so it was more bitter than the chocolate in the first study. People rated their liking for the bitter chocolate lower when the experience was shared, compared with unshared (**Figure 10.19**).

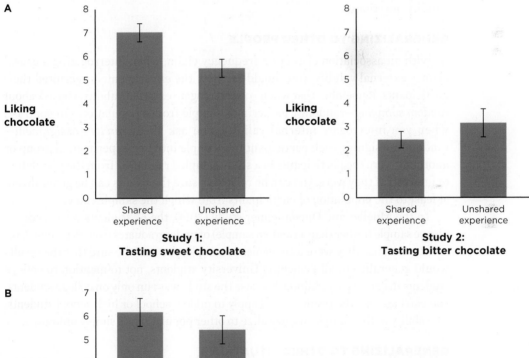

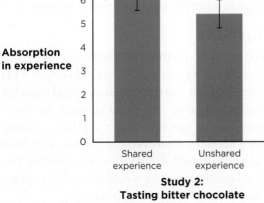

**FIGURE 10.19**

**Construct validity is theory-driven.**

(**A**) When people tasted bitter chocolate in this study, they rated it more negatively when the experience was shared than when it was unshared. They also rated both of the bitter chocolates lower than the sweet chocolates in the first study, providing construct validity evidence that the experience in the second study was negative. (**B**) People were more absorbed in the shared experience, evidence that the shared versus unshared experience was manipulated as intended. Error bars represent 95% CIs. (Source: Adapted from Boothby et al., 2014.)

Two main results of the chocolate studies support their construct validity: (1) People in the first study rated the chocolate higher overall than those in the second study, which is what you'd expect if one was supposed to represent a positive experience and the other a negative experience. (2) People reported being more absorbed in the shared experience than the unshared one. This result supports the theory that shared experiences should be more intense (absorbing) than unshared ones.

## External Validity: To Whom or What Can the Causal Claim Generalize?

Chapters 7 and 8 discussed external validity in the context of frequency claims and association claims. Interrogating external validity in the context of causal claims is similar. You ask whether the causal relationship can generalize to other people, places, and times. (Chapter 14 goes into even more detail about external validity questions.)

### GENERALIZING TO OTHER PEOPLE

As with an association claim or a frequency claim, when interrogating a causal claim's external validity, you should ask how the experimenters recruited their participants. Remember that when you interrogate external validity, you ask about *random sampling*—randomly gathering a sample from a population. (In contrast, when you interrogate internal validity, you ask about *random assignment*—randomly assigning each participant in a sample into one experimental group or another.) Were the participants in a study sampled randomly from the population of interest? If they were, you can be relatively sure the results can be generalized, at least to the population of participants from which the sample came.

In the Mueller and Oppenheimer study (2014), the 67 students were a convenience sample (rather than a random sample) of undergraduates from Princeton University. Because they were a convenience sample, you can't be sure that the results would generalize to all Princeton University students, not to mention to college students in general. In addition, because the study was run only on college students, you can't assume the results would apply to middle school or high school students. The ability of this sample to generalize to other populations is simply unknown.

### GENERALIZING TO OTHER SITUATIONS

External validity also applies to the types of situations to which an experiment might generalize. For example, the notetaking study used five videotaped TED talk lectures. In their published article, Mueller and Oppenheimer (2014) reported two additional experiments, each of which used new video lectures. All three experiments found the same pattern, so you can infer that the effect of laptop notetaking does generalize to other TED talks. However, you can't be sure from this study whether laptop notetaking would generalize to a live lecture class. You also don't know whether the effect of laptop notetaking would generalize to other kinds of college teaching, such as team-based learning or lab courses.

To decide whether an experiment's results can generalize to other situations, we need to conduct more research. One experiment, conducted after Mueller and Oppenheimer's three studies, helped demonstrate that the laptop notetaking effect can generalize to live lecture classes (Carter et al., 2016). College student cadets at West Point were randomly assigned to their real, semester-long economics classes. There were 30 sections of the class, which all followed the same syllabus, used the same textbook, and gave almost the same exams. In 10 of the sections, students were not allowed to use laptops or tablets, and in another 10 sections, they were allowed to use them. In the last 10 sections, students could use tablets as long as they were kept flat on their desk during the class. The results indicated that students in the two computerized sections scored lower on exams than students in the computer-free classrooms. This study helps us generalize from Mueller and Oppenheimer's short-term lecture situation to a real, semester-long college class. Similarly, you might ask if Boothby et al.'s hypothesis about shared experiences might generalize to other experiences besides tasting chocolate (**Figure 10.20**).

## WHAT IF EXTERNAL VALIDITY IS POOR?

Should you be concerned that Mueller and Oppenheimer did not select their participants at random from the population of college students? Should you be concerned that all three of their studies used TED talks instead of other kinds of classroom material?

Remember from Chapter 3 that in an experiment, researchers usually prioritize experimental control—that is, internal validity. To get a clean, confound-free manipulation, they may have to conduct their study in an artificial environment like a university laboratory. Such locations may not represent situations in the real world. Although it's possible to achieve both internal and external validity in a single study, doing so can be difficult. Therefore, many experimenters decide to sacrifice real-world representativeness for internal validity.

«
For more discussion on prioritizing validities, see Chapter 14, pp. 438–452.

**FIGURE 10.20**
**Generalizing to other situations.**

The chocolate-tasting study showed that flavors are perceived as more intense when the experience is shared. A future study might explore whether the shared experiences effect generalizes to other situations, such as watching a happy or sad movie.

Testing their theory and teasing out the causal variable from potential confounds were the steps Mueller and Oppenheimer, like most experimenters, took care of first. In addition, running an experiment on a relatively homogenous sample (such as college students) meant that the unsystematic variability was less likely to obscure the effect of the independent variable (see Chapter 11). Replicating the study using several samples in a variety of contexts is a step saved for later. Although Mueller and Oppenheimer sampled only college students and ran their studies in a laboratory, at least one other study demonstrated that taking notes by computer can cause lower grades even in real, semester-long courses. Future researchers might also be interested in testing the effect of using laptops among younger students or for other subjects (such as psychology or literature courses). Such studies would demonstrate whether longhand notetaking is more effective than laptop notetaking for all subjects and for all types of students.

## Statistical Validity: How Much? How Precise? What Else Is Known?

Interrogating the statistical validity of an experiment involves asking about effect size, precision of the estimate, and replication. In your statistics class, you will learn how to ask other questions, such as whether the researchers conducted the right statistical tests.

### HOW LARGE IS THE EFFECT?

The first question we can ask is, How large is the difference between the laptop and longhand groups? It appears that longhand groups learned more, but how much more? Asking this question helps you evaluate covariance (i.e., the difference between the experimental groups). In general, the larger the difference, the more important, and the stronger, the causal effect.

When we do experiments, we have two ways to express effect size. The first is to use original units. In Mueller and Oppenheimer's studies, the original units for the dependent variable were the number of points people scored correctly. Participants were tested on both factual and conceptual questions, but we'll focus on the conceptual questions here. People in the longhand condition earned an average of 4.29 points on the conceptual questions, compared with 3.77 in the laptop condition. Therefore, the effect size in original units is 0.52 points of improvement. On the 7-question test, that might be the difference between a grade of A or B.

The second way is to use a standardized effect size. In Chapter 8, you learned that the correlation coefficient $r$ helps researchers evaluate the effect size (strength) of an association. When there are two groups in an experiment, we often use an indicator called $d$. This standardized effect size takes into account both the difference between means and the spread of scores within each group (the standard deviation). When $d$ is large, it means the independent variable caused a large change in the dependent variable, relative to how spread out the scores are. When $d$ is small, it means the scores of participants in the two experimental

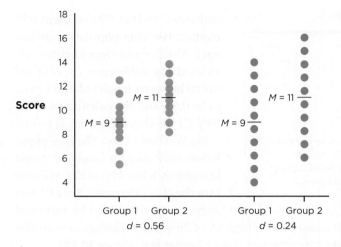

**FIGURE 10.21**

**Effect size and overlap between groups.**

Effect sizes are larger when the scores in the two experimental groups overlap less. Overlap is a function of how far apart the group means are as well as how variable the scores are within each group. On both sides of the graph, the two group means (*M*) are the same distance apart (about 2 units), but the overlap of the scores between groups is greater in the blue scores on the right. Because there is more overlap between groups, the effect size is smaller.

groups overlap more. **Figure 10.21** shows what two *d* values might look like when a study's results are graphed, showing all participants. Even though the difference between means is exactly the same in the two graphs, the effect sizes reflect the different degrees of overlap between the group participants.

In Mueller and Oppenheimer's first study (2014), the effect size for the difference in conceptual test performance between the longhand and laptop groups was *d* = 0.38. This means the laptop group scored 0.38 of a standard deviation higher than the longhand group. Psychologists sometimes start by saying a *d* of 0.2 should be considered small, a *d* of 0.5 is moderate, and a *d* of 0.8 is large (Cohen, 1992; in Chapter 8 you learned that that comparable benchmarks for *r* were .1, .3, and .5, respectively.) According to these guidelines, a *d* of 0.38 would be considered small to moderate. However, you also need context. As you learned in Chapter 8, a "small" effect size (such as a tiny adjustment to an athlete's form) can have a large real-world impact, especially when accumulated over multiple people or situations.

Which one should you use—original units or *d*? It depends on your goal. Original units are useful when you want to estimate the real-world impact of an intervention: How much would taking laptop notes affect a course grade? Standardized effect sizes are useful when you want to compare effect sizes that are based on different units. For example, using *d* you can compare effect sizes for exam points, time spent reading, and words used. Because *d* is standardized, it also enables you to compare the results found in one study to a body of knowledge. For example, in education research, one review found that the average effect size across experimental tests of educational interventions for high school students was *d* = 0.27 (Hill et al., 2008). It might be helpful to know that the pen versus laptop effect is in this same ballpark.

## HOW PRECISE IS THE ESTIMATE?

In addition to estimating the size of the effect, we can also compute its 95% confidence interval (CI). Confidence intervals, introduced in Chapters 3 and 8, are

«

For more detail on standard deviation and effect size, see Statistics Review: Descriptive Statistics, pp. 472–477 and pp. 484–488.

«

For more questions to ask when interrogating statistical validity, see Statistics Review: Inferential Statistics, pp. 491–493.

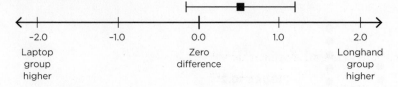

## FIGURE 10.22
### 95% CI for the difference in original units.

In Mueller and Oppenheimer's Study 1, the estimate of the difference in conceptual test score between laptop and longhand conditions was 0.52 points (out of 7 possible); here's one calculation of its 95% CI. (Source: Open data from Mueller & Oppenheimer, 2014; no covariates used.)

computed so that 95% of them will contain the true population difference. Mueller and Oppenheimer calculated the difference (in original units) between longhand and laptop to be 0.52, and one calculation of the 95% CI for this difference is [–0.16, 1.20]. You don't know the true population difference for longhand versus laptop notes, but 95% of CIs will contain the true difference. This CI also suggests we should not be surprised if the true difference turns out to be as large as a 1.20-point advantage or even that the laptop group scored a bit *higher* (–0.16 on a 7-point test; **Figure 10.22**).

The width of the 95% CI reflects precision. When a study has a relatively *small* sample and *more* variability in the data, the CI will be relatively wide (less precise). When a study has a *larger* sample and *less* variability, then the CI will be narrower (more precise). If there were a narrower CI—say, [0.04, 0.72] for the notetaking study—it would suggest that we can probably rule out zero as the true difference between the two conditions; we'd call this result "statistically significant."

Instead of using original units, we can also compute the 95% CI for the *d* of 0.38, which might be presented like this: 95% CI for *d* [–0.16, 1.20]. Just as for original scores, 95% of the CIs for *d* will contain the *d* for the population. The more people in the study and the less variability, the more precise (narrow) the 95% CI will be.

» For details on how the CI is computed, see Statistics Review: Inferential Statistics, pp. 493–495.

## REPLICATION

Each experiment we conduct uses data from a sample (something we know) to make an inference about a true population effect (which we may never know). A single 95% CI provides important information about how large the population effect might be. Another step in estimating the population effect is to conduct the study again and find multiple estimates.

The baby persistence researchers replicated their study exactly and reported both studies' data in their empirical journal article. Science journalist Ed Yong interviewed Leonard and reported, "After Leonard had spent a year studying the value of persistence, her advisor Laura Schulz told her to do the experiment again. 'It was a very meta moment,' she says. She recruited another 120 infants. . . . And to her delight, she got exactly the same results" (Yong, 2017). Mueller and Oppenheimer's study was published alongside two other studies, almost identical to the first, that manipulated pen versus laptop notetaking and measured factual and conceptual knowledge; all three studies found similar effects. Nevertheless, some other researchers have found smaller, and even no, benefits of longhand over laptop notes (Luo et al., 2018; Morehead et al., 2019; Urry et al., 2020). When the studies you encounter have been replicated, you can combine their estimates to get an even better estimate of the true population value.

# Internal Validity: Are There Alternative Explanations for the Results?

When you are interrogating causal claims, keep in mind that internal validity is often the priority. Experimenters isolate and manipulate a key causal variable, while controlling for all other possible variables, precisely so they can achieve internal validity. If the internal validity of an experiment is sound, you know that a causal claim is almost certainly appropriate. But if there is some confound, a causal claim would be inappropriate. It should instead be demoted to an association claim.

Three potential threats to internal validity have already been discussed in this chapter. These fundamental internal validity questions are worth asking of any experiment:

« For a full discussion of replication, including meta-analysis, see Chapter 14, pp. 437–447.

1. Did the experimental design ensure that there were no design confounds, or did some other variable accidentally covary along with the intended independent variable? (Mueller and Oppenheimer made sure people in both groups saw the same video lectures, were in the same room, and so on.)

2. If the experimenters used an independent-groups design, did they control for selection effects by using random assignment or matching? (Random assignment controlled for selection effects in the notetaking study.)

3. If the experimenters used a within-groups design, did they control for order effects by counterbalancing? (Counterbalancing is not relevant in Mueller and Oppenheimer's design because it was an independent-groups design.)

Chapter 11 goes into further detail on these threats to internal validity and covers nine more threats.

---

✔️

## CHECK YOUR UNDERSTANDING

1. How do manipulation checks provide evidence for the construct validity of an experiment's independent variable? Why does theory matter in evaluating construct validity?

2. Besides generalization to other people, what other aspect of generalization does external validity address?

3. What does it mean when an effect size is large (as opposed to small) in an experiment?

4. Summarize the three threats to internal validity discussed in this chapter.

1. See pp. 304–306. 2. Generalization to other situations; see pp. 306–307 3. See pp. 308–309. 4. See p. 311.

# CHAPTER REVIEW

It's time to complete your study experience! Go to INQUIZITIVE to practice actively with this chapter's concepts and get personalized feedback along the way.

## Summary

Causal claims are special because they can lead to advice, treatments, and interventions. The only way to support a causal claim is to conduct a well-designed experiment.

### TWO EXAMPLES OF SIMPLE EXPERIMENTS

- An experiment showed that taking notes on a laptop rather than in longhand caused students to do worse on a conceptual test of lecture material.

- An experiment showed that babies who watch adults being persistent try harder on a subsequent task.

### EXPERIMENTAL VARIABLES

- Experiments study the effect of an independent (manipulated) variable on a dependent (measured) variable.

- Experiments deliberately keep all extraneous variables constant as control variables.

### WHY EXPERIMENTS SUPPORT CAUSAL CLAIMS

- Experiments support causal claims because they potentially allow researchers to establish covariance, temporal precedence, and internal validity.

- The three potential internal validity threats covered in this chapter that researchers work to avoid are design confounds, selection effects, and order effects.

### INDEPENDENT-GROUPS DESIGNS

- In an independent-groups design, different participants are exposed to each level of the independent variable.

- In a posttest-only design, participants are randomly assigned to one of at least two levels of an independent variable and then measured once on the dependent variable.

- In a pretest/posttest design, participants are randomly assigned to one of at least two levels of an independent variable and are then measured on a dependent variable twice—once before and once after they experience the independent variable.

- Random assignment or matched groups can help establish internal validity in independent-groups designs by minimizing selection effects.

### WITHIN-GROUPS DESIGNS

- In a within-groups design, the same participants are exposed to all levels of the independent variable.

- In a repeated-measures design, participants are tested on the dependent variable after each exposure to an independent variable condition.

- In a concurrent-measures design, participants are exposed to at least two levels of an independent variable at the same time and then indicate a preference for one level (the dependent variable).

- Within-groups designs allow researchers to treat each participant as his or her own control and require fewer participants than independent-groups designs. Within-groups designs also present the potential for order effects and demand characteristics.

## INTERROGATING CAUSAL CLAIMS WITH THE FOUR VALIDITIES

- Interrogating construct validity involves evaluating whether the variables were manipulated and measured in ways consistent with the theory behind the experiment.

- Interrogating external validity involves asking whether the experiment's results can be generalized to other people or to other situations and settings.

- Interrogating statistical validity starts by asking about the effect size, precision of the estimate as assessed by the 95% CI, and whether the study has been replicated.

- Interrogating internal validity involves looking for design confounds and seeing whether the researchers used techniques such as random assignment and counterbalancing.

## Key Terms

experiment, p. 281
manipulated variable, p. 281
measured variable, p. 281
independent variable, p. 281
condition, p. 281
dependent variable, p. 281
control variable, p. 282
comparison group, p. 284
control group, p. 284
treatment group, p. 284
placebo group, p. 285
confound, p. 286

design confound, p. 286
systematic variability, p. 287
unsystematic variability, p. 287
selection effect, p. 289
random assignment, p. 290
matched groups, p. 291
independent-groups design, p. 292
within-groups design, p. 292
posttest-only design, p. 292
pretest/posttest design, p. 293
repeated-measures design, p. 295
concurrent-measures design, p. 296

order effect, p. 299
practice effect, p. 299
carryover effect, p. 299
counterbalancing, p. 299
full counterbalancing, p. 300
partial counterbalancing, p. 301
Latin square, p. 301
demand characteristic, p. 302
manipulation check, p. 304
pilot study, p. 304

**To see samples of chapter concepts in the popular media, visit www.everydayresearchmethods.com and click the box for Chapter 10.**

## Review Questions

Max ran an experiment in which he asked people to shake hands with an experimenter (played by a female friend) and rate the experimenter's friendliness using a self-report measure. The experimenter was always the same person and used the same standard greeting for all participants. People were randomly assigned to shake hands with her either after she had cooled her hands under cold water or after she had warmed her hands under warm water. Max's results found that people rated the experimenter as friendlier when her hands were warm than when they were cold.

1. Why does Max's experiment satisfy the causal criterion of temporal precedence?

   a. Because Max found a difference in rated friendliness between the two conditions, cold hands and warm hands.

   b. Because the participants shook the experimenter's hand before rating her friendliness.

   c. Because the experimenter acted the same in all conditions, except having cold or warm hands.

   d. Because Max randomly assigned people to the warm hands or cold hands condition.

2. In Max's experiment, what was a control variable?

   a. The participants' rating of the friendliness of the experimenter.

   b. The temperature of the experimenter's hands (warm or cold).

   c. The gender of the students in the study.

   d. The standard greeting the experimenter used while shaking hands.

3. What type of design is Max's experiment?

   a. Posttest-only design

   b. Pretest/posttest design

   c. Concurrent-measures design

   d. Repeated-measures design

4. Max randomly assigned people to shake hands either with the "warm hands" experimenter or the "cold hands" experimenter. Why did he randomly assign participants?

   a. Because he had a within-groups design.

   b. Because he wanted to avoid selection effects.

   c. Because he wanted to avoid an order effect.

   d. Because he wanted to generalize the results to the population of students at his university.

5. Which of the following questions would you use to interrogate the construct validity of Max's experiment?

   a. How large is the effect size comparing the rated friendliness of the warm hands and cold hands conditions?

   b. How well did Max's "experimenter friendliness" rating capture participants' actual impressions of the experimenter?

   c. Were there any confounds in the experiment?

   d. Can we generalize the results from Max's friend to other experimenters with whom people might shake hands?

## Learning Actively

1. Design a posttest-only experiment that would test each of the following causal claims. For each one, identify the study's independent variable(s), identify its dependent variable(s), and suggest some important control variables. Then sketch a bar graph of the results you would predict (remember to put the dependent variable on the y-axis). Finally, apply the three causal criteria to each study.

   a. Having a friendly (versus a stern) teacher for a brief lesson causes children to score better on a test of material for that lesson.

   b. Practicing the piano for 30 minutes a day (compared with 10 minutes a day) causes new neural connections in the temporal region of the brain.

   c. Drinking sugared lemonade (compared with sugar-free lemonade) makes people perform better on a task that requires self-control.

2. For each of the following independent variables, how would you design a manipulation that uses an independent-groups design? How would you design a manipulation that uses a within-groups design? Explain the advantages and disadvantages of manipulating each independent variable as independent-groups versus within-groups.

   a. Listening to a lesson from a friendly teacher versus a stern teacher.

   b. Practicing the piano for 30 minutes a day versus 10 minutes a day.

   c. Drinking sugared versus sugar-free lemonade.

3. To study people's willingness to help others, social psychologists Latané and Darley (1969) invited people to complete questionnaires in a lab room. After handing out the questionnaires, the female experimenter went next door and staged a loud accident: She pretended to fall off a chair and get hurt (she actually played an audio recording of this accident). Then the experimenters observed whether each participant stopped filling out the questionnaire and went to try to help the "victim."

Behind the scenes, the experimenters had flipped a coin to assign participants randomly to either an "alone" group, in which they were in the questionnaire room by themselves, or a "passive confederate" group, in which they were in the questionnaire room with a confederate (an actor) who sat impassively during the "accident" and did not attempt to help the "victim."

In the end, Latané and Darley found that when participants were alone, 70% reacted, but when participants were with a passive confederate, only 7% reacted. This experiment supported the researchers' theory that during an accident, people take cues from others, looking to them to decide how to interpret the situation.

a. What are the independent, dependent, and control variables in this study?

b. Sketch a graph of the results of this study.

c. Is the independent variable in this study manipulated as independent-groups or as repeated-measures? How do you know?

d. For this study, ask at least one question for each of the four validities.

# Do we remember words better if we process them deeply?

You and a lab partner can work together to replicate a memory effect associated with levels of processing theory. The theory states that when we are learning new information (such as a list of words), we remember it better when we process it deeply; that is, make connections to what we already know (Craik & Lockhart, 1972). In this experiment, you'll replicate a classic study on the levels of processing effect.

**STEP 1** **Prepare your materials.**

Working with your partner, prepare a list of 24 common words, making sure that some are pleasant and some are not, and making sure that some of them contain the letters a or e, and some do not (for example: *sunset*, *snow*, *cupcake*, *war*, *closet*).

**STEP 2** **Prepare two sets of instructions.**

Prepare two sets of instructions. One page should have Instruction 1, followed by the response table, and the other page should have Instruction 2, followed by the same response table. Prepare enough copies for each person in your study.

Your participants will be reading these instructions privately to themselves before they participate.

---

## Instructions 1

After you hear each word, answer this question: Does the word contain an e or a g? Answer yes or no. Please use this table to enter your responses after I read each word.

| Item | Response (Y/N) |
|------|----------------|
| 1. | |
| 2. | |
| 3. | |
| . . . | |
| 24. | |

## Instructions 2

After you hear each word, answer this question: Is the word pleasant? Answer yes or no. Please use this table to enter your responses after I read each word.

| Item | Response (Y/N) |
|------|----------------|
| 1. | |
| 2. | |
| 3. | |
| . . . | |
| 24. | |

## STEP 3 ▸ Run the experimental session.

Your experimental session will take about 10 minutes. Find some classmates or friends willing to participate. It's preferable to run a group of people all at the same time. That way, each person will be following one of two different instructions, but you will be keeping constant several variables, such as the inflection of your voice, the time of day, and so on.

As you invite people to participate, ask each person for permission. You can follow this script:

> "Hi! I'm wondering if you have 10 minutes to help me out for my psychology class. I'm practicing research and I am looking for volunteers to be in a short study where you rate 24 words. There are no risks or benefits in this study, and your participation would be voluntary. I'm also not going to collect your name. Would you be willing to participate?"

As each person says yes, you and your partner will need to randomly assign them to one of the two conditions. Therefore, flip a coin for each person (heads gets Instruction 1 and tails gets Instruction 2). Alternatively, you can fan out a shuffled set of copies of Instruction 1 and Instruction 2, and ask each participant to choose one page.

When everyone has a page of instructions, it's time to read the words on your word list. As you read your list of 24 words out loud, people will answer their assigned question in the blanks provided. After they are done, say:

> "Thanks for rating all the words. Now I'd like you all to do one more thing for me. Please turn your page over and write down all the words that you can remember. I'll give you 2 minutes for this part."

After 2 minutes you may thank your participants and send them on their way.

## STEP 4 ▸ Enter your data.

When we enter data into a data matrix, each person gets a row and each variable gets a column. Therefore, you'll need one column labeled "Condition" and one labeled "Words Recalled." The "words recalled" variable is simply your count, for each person, of how many words they remembered from the study. The data matrix will look something like this:

Have your partner(s) check your data entry to make sure you've done it correctly.

## STEP 5 ▸ Use the statistics program JASP to calculate means and CIs.

A. Save your data as .csv.
B. Open JASP on your computer. (Obtain this free program at www.jaspstats.org.)

**C.** In JASP, select File/Open/Computer to find the .csv data file you have downloaded.

**D.** Once the file is open, select the Common tab to get to the data view. Change each variable type to "Scale" if needed (next to each variable name). Select T-Tests, Independent Samples T-test.

**E.** "Condition" is the Grouping Variable and "Words Recalled" is the Dependent Variable. You should also check the boxes for several Additional Statistics as in the image below.

**F.** The results below come from a different set of data; your own results will vary.

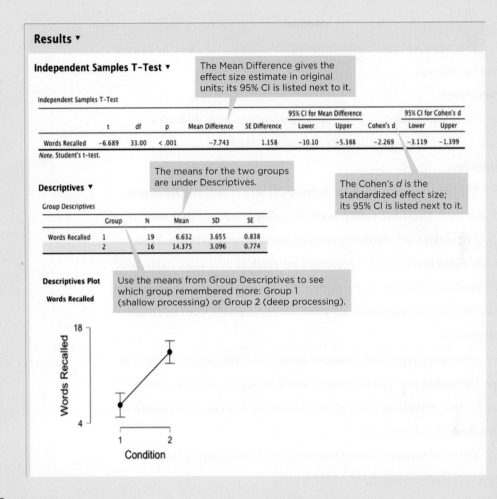

## Results ▾

### Independent Samples T-Test ▾

The Mean Difference gives the effect size estimate in original units; its 95% CI is listed next to it.

Independent Samples T-Test

| | t | df | p | Mean Difference | SE Difference | 95% CI for Mean Difference | | Cohen's d | 95% CI for Cohen's d | |
| --- | --- | --- | --- | --- | --- | --- | --- | --- | --- | --- |
| | | | | | | Lower | Upper | | Lower | Upper |
| Words Recalled | −6.689 | 33.00 | < .001 | −7.743 | 1.158 | −10.10 | −5.388 | −2.269 | −3.119 | −1.399 |

*Note.* Student's t-test.

The Cohen's *d* is the standardized effect size; its 95% CI is listed next to it.

### Descriptives ▾

The means for the two groups are under Descriptives.

Group Descriptives

| | Group | N | Mean | SD | SE |
| --- | --- | --- | --- | --- | --- |
| Words Recalled | 1 | 19 | 6.632 | 3.655 | 0.838 |
| | 2 | 16 | 14.375 | 3.096 | 0.774 |

### Descriptives Plot

Words Recalled

Use the means from Group Descriptives to see which group remembered more: Group 1 (shallow processing) or Group 2 (deep processing).

---

**STEP 6** ▶ **Report your results.**

Write up a mini version of your study (Method, Results, and Discussion section only) using this APA-style template. You should fill in all the blanks and provide any content noted with [square brackets]. Take the brackets out after you add the content, with the exception of 95% CIs, which are normally shown in square brackets.

**APA paper template:**

### Method

This was a posttest-only design in which _____ was the independent variable and _____ was the dependent variable.

#### Participants

Participants were _____ volunteers who were students at _____. They participated voluntarily in [location].

#### Procedure

The participants participated in groups of [size of groups]. One experimenter read a list of 24 common words, including [list 5–6 of your words here].

Participants were randomly assigned to one of two conditions. Those receiving the shallow level of processing instructions were asked to [describe this condition]. Those receiving the deep level of processing instructions were asked to [describe each condition]. Participants rated each word on a paper rating sheet.

After rating each word, the experimenter asked the participants to turn over their rating page and list as many words as they recalled out of the 24 rated words. Participants were given 2 minutes for this task. Participants were then thanked and dismissed.

The experimenters counted how many words each participant recalled. Data were analyzed using [JASP/SPSS/Excel].

### Results

Participants in the deep level of processing condition ($M$ = x.xx, $SD$ = x.xx) remembered [more/less] words than those in the shallow level of processing condition ($M$ = x.xx, $SD$ = x.xx). Therefore, the difference in the number of words recalled was x.xx. The 95% CI on this difference was [x.xx, x.xx]. This CI means that [explain].

The standardized effect size of the difference between deep and shallow processing was $d$ = x.xx, and the 95% CI was [x.xx, x.xx].

These 95% CIs [do/do not] contain zero, so we can conclude that the difference between the two conditions [is not/is] statistically significant.

## Discussion

The results of this experiment suggest that when people engage in deep processing about words (rather than shallow), they remember [a lot more/a few more about the same number/a few less/a lot less] of those words.

[Here you can make a comment about your study's internal, external, and construct validities.]

---

**COMPREHENSION QUESTIONS**

1. This was billed as a posttest-only experiment. Why does it fit that label?

2. What was the independent variable? What were its levels?

3. What was the dependent variable?

4. Using your own words, what does the 95% CI for the difference between the two groups in original units mean?

5. Can we use the results of this study to support the causal claim that "evaluating how pleasant words are leads to better memory for those words, compared with deciding if the word contains a certain letter"? Why or why not? Apply the three causal criteria.

"Was it really the intervention, or something else, that caused things to improve?"

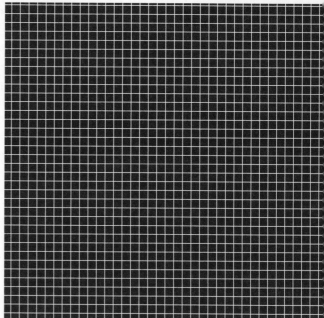

"How should we interpret a null result?"

# 11

# More on Experiments: Confounding and Obscuring Variables

CHAPTER 10 COVERED THE basic structure of an experiment, and this chapter addresses a number of questions about experimental design. Why is it so important to use a comparison group? Why do many experimenters create a standardized, controlled, seemingly artificial environment? Why do researchers use so many participants? Why do they often use special technologies to measure their variables? Why do they insist on double-blind study designs? For the clearest possible results, responsible researchers specifically design their experiments with many factors in mind. They want to correctly estimate real effects, and they want to determine conclusively when their predictions are wrong.

The first section of this chapter describes potential internal validity problems and how researchers usually avoid them. The second section discusses some of the reasons experiments may yield null results.

# THREATS TO INTERNAL VALIDITY: DID THE INDEPENDENT VARIABLE REALLY CAUSE THE DIFFERENCE?

When you interrogate an experiment, internal validity is the priority. As discussed in Chapter 10, three possible threats to internal validity include design confounds, selection effects, and order effects. All three of these threats involve an alternative explanation for the results.

With a design confound, there is an alternative explanation because the experiment was poorly designed; another variable happened to vary systematically along with the intended independent variable. Chapter 10 presented the study on pen versus laptop notetaking and comprehension. If the test questions assigned to the laptop condition were more difficult than the those assigned to the pen condition, that would have been a design confound (see Figure 10.5). It would not be clear whether the notetaking format or the difficulty of the questions caused the handwritten notes group to score better.

With a selection effect, a confound exists because the different independent variable groups have systematically different types of participants. In Chapter 10, the example was a study of an intensive therapy for autism, in which children who received the intensive treatment did improve over time. However, we are not sure if their improvement was caused by the therapy or by greater overall involvement on the part of the parents who elected to be in the intensive-treatment group. Those parents' greater motivation could have been an alternative explanation for the improvement of children in the intensive-treatment group.

With an order effect (in a within-groups design), there is an alternative explanation because the outcome might be caused by the independent variable, but it might also be caused by the order in which the levels of the variable are presented. When there is an order effect, we do not know whether the independent variable is really having an effect, or whether the participants are just getting tired, bored, or well-practiced.

These types of threats are just the beginning. There are other ways—about twelve in total—in which a study might be at risk for a confound. Experimenters think about all of them, and they plan studies to avoid them. Normally, a well-designed experiment can prevent these threats and make strong causal statements (Shadish et al., 2002).

## The Really Bad Experiment (A Cautionary Tale)

Previous chapters have used examples of published studies to illustrate the material. In contrast, this chapter presents three fictional experiments. You will rarely encounter published studies like these because, unlike the designs in Chapter 10, the basic design behind these examples has so many internal validity problems.

Nikhil, a summer camp counselor and psychology major, has noticed that his current cabin of 15 boys is an especially rowdy bunch. He's heard a change in diet might help them calm down, so he eliminates the sugary snacks and desserts from their meals for 2 days. As he expected, the boys are much quieter and calmer by the end of the week, after refined sugar has been eliminated from their diets.

Dr. Yuki has recruited a sample of 40 depressed women, all of whom are interested in receiving psychotherapy to treat their depression. She measures their level of depression using a standard depression inventory at the start of therapy. For 12 weeks, all the women participate in Dr. Yuki's style of cognitive therapy. At the end of the 12-week session, she measures the women again and finds that, on the whole, their levels of depression have significantly decreased.

A dormitory on a university campus has started a Go Green social media campaign, focused on persuading students to turn out the lights in their rooms when they're not needed. Dorm residents receive emails and see posts on social media that encourage energy-saving behaviors. At the start of the campaign, the head resident noted how many kilowatt hours the dorm was using by checking the electric meters on the building. At the end of the 2-month campaign, the head resident checks the meters again and finds that the usage has dropped. He compares the two measures (pretest and posttest) and finds they are significantly different.

Notice that all three of these examples fit the same template, as shown in **Figure 11.1**. If you graphed the data of the first two studies, they would look something like the two graphs in **Figure 11.2**. Consider the three examples: What alternative explanations can you think of for the results of each one?

The formal name for this kind of design is the **one-group, pretest/posttest design**. A researcher recruits one group of participants; measures them on a pretest; exposes them to a treatment, intervention, or change; and then measures them on a posttest. This design differs from the true pretest/posttest design you learned in Chapter 10 because it has only one group, not two. There is no comparison group. Therefore, a better name for this design might be "the really bad experiment." Understanding why this design is problematic can help you learn about threats to internal validity and how to avoid them with better designs.

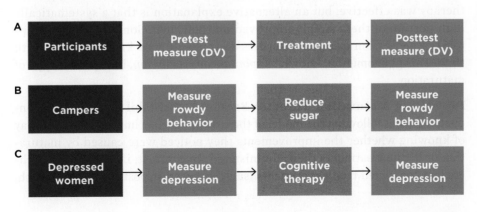

**FIGURE 11.1**
**The really bad experiment.**

(**A**) A general diagram of the really bad experiment, or the one-group, pretest/posttest design. Unlike the pretest/posttest design, it has only one group: no comparison condition. (**B, C**) Possible ways to diagram two of the examples given in the text. Using these as a model, try sketching a diagram of the Go Green example.

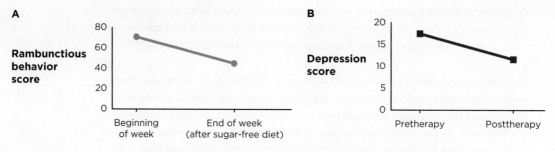

**A**

Rambunctious behavior score

80
60
40
20
0

Beginning of week — End of week (after sugar-free diet)

**B**

Depression score

20
15
10
5
0

Pretherapy — Posttherapy

**FIGURE 11.2**

**Graphing the really bad experiment.**

The first two examples can be graphed this way. Using these as a model, try sketching a graph of the Go Green example.

## Six Potential Internal Validity Threats in One-Group, Pretest/Posttest Designs

By the end of this chapter, you will have learned a total of 12 internal validity threats. Three of them we just reviewed: design confounds, selection effects, and order effects. Several of the internal validity threats apply especially to the really bad experiment, but they can be prevented with a good experimental design. These include maturation threats, history threats, regression threats, attrition threats, testing threats, and instrumentation threats. The final three threats (observer bias, demand characteristics, and placebo effects) potentially apply to any study.

### MATURATION THREATS TO INTERNAL VALIDITY

Why did the boys in Nikhil's cabin start behaving better? Was it truly because they had eaten less sugar? Perhaps. An alternative explanation, however, is that most of them simply settled in, or "matured into," the camp setting after they got used to the place. The boys' behavior improved on its own; the low-sugar diet may have had nothing to do with it. Such an effect is called a **maturation threat**, a change in behavior that emerges more or less spontaneously over time. People adapt to changed environments; children get better at walking and talking; plants grow taller—but not because of any outside intervention. It just happens.

Similarly, the depressed women may have improved because the cognitive therapy was effective, but an alternative explanation is that a systematically high portion of them simply improved on their own. Sometimes the symptoms of depression or other disorders disappear, for no known reason, with time. This phenomenon, known as *spontaneous remission*, is a specific type of maturation.

**Preventing Maturation Threats.** Because both Nikhil and Dr. Yuki conducted studies following the model of the really bad experiment, there is no way of knowing whether the improvements they noticed were caused by maturation or by the treatments they administered. In contrast, if the two researchers had conducted true experiments (such as a pretest/posttest design, which, as you learned in Chapter 10, has at least two groups, not one), they would also have included an appropriate comparison group. Nikhil would have observed a comparison group of equally lively campers who did not switch to a low-sugar diet. Dr. Yuki would have studied a comparison group of women who started out equally depressed but did not receive the cognitive therapy. If the treatment groups improved significantly more than the comparison groups did, these researchers could essentially subtract out the effect of maturation when they interpret their results. **Figure 11.3** illustrates the benefits of a comparison group in preventing a maturation threat for the depression study.

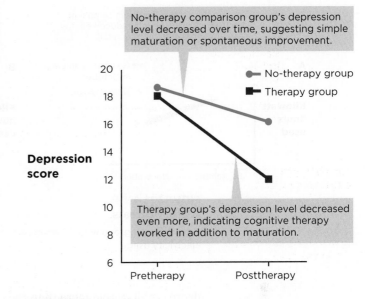

**FIGURE 11.3**
**Maturation threats.**

A pretest/posttest design would help control for the maturation threat in Dr. Yuki's depression study.

## HISTORY THREATS TO INTERNAL VALIDITY

Sometimes a threat to internal validity occurs not just because time has passed, but because something specific has happened between the pretest and posttest. In the third example, why did the dorm residents use less electricity? Was it the Go Green campaign? Perhaps. But a plausible alternative explanation is that the weather got cooler and most residents did not use air conditioning as much. Why did the campers' behavior improve? It could have been the low-sugar diet, but maybe they all started a difficult swimming course in the middle of the week and the exercise tired most of them out.

These alternative explanations are examples of **history threats**, which result from a "historical" or external factor that systematically affects *most members* of the treatment group at the same time as the treatment itself, making it unclear whether the change is caused by the treatment received. To be a history threat, the external factor must affect most people in the group in the same direction (systematically), not just a few people (unsystematically).

**Preventing History Threats.** As with maturation threats, a comparison group can help control for history threats. In the Go Green study, the students would need to measure the kilowatt usage in another, comparable dormitory during the same 2 months, but not give the students in the second dorm the Go Green campaign materials. (This would be a pretest/posttest design rather than a one-group, pretest/posttest design.) If both groups decreased their electricity usage about the same over time (**Figure 11.4A**), the decrease probably resulted from the change of seasons, not from the Go Green campaign. However, if the treatment group

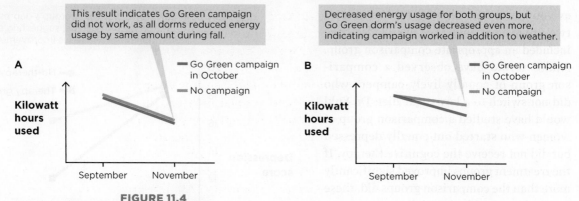

**FIGURE 11.4**
**History threats.**

A comparison group would help control for the history threat of seasonal differences in electricity usage.

»

For more on pretest/posttest design, see Chapter 10, pp. 293–294.

»

For more detail on arithmetic mean, see Statistics Review: Descriptive Statistics, p. 471.

decreased its usage more than the comparison group did (**Figure 11.4B**), you can rule out the history threat. Both the comparison group and the treatment group experienced the same seasonal "historical" changes, so including the comparison group controls for this threat.

## REGRESSION THREATS TO INTERNAL VALIDITY

A **regression threat** refers to a statistical concept called **regression to the mean**. When a group average (mean) is unusually extreme at Time 1, the next time that group is measured (Time 2), it is likely to be less extreme—closer to its typical or average performance.

**Everyday Regression to the Mean.** Real-world situations can help illustrate regression to the mean. For example, during an early round of the 2019 Women's World Cup, the team from Italy outscored the team from Jamaica 5–0. That's a big score; soccer (football) teams hardly ever score 5 points in a game. Without being familiar with either team, people who know about soccer would predict that in their next game, Italy would score fewer than 5 goals. Why? Simply because most people have an intuitive understanding of regression to the mean.

Here's the statistical explanation. The Italian team's score was exceptionally high partly because of the team's talent, and partly because of a unique combination of random factors that happened to come out in their favor. It was an early-round game, and the players felt confident because they were higher seeded. The team's injury level was, just by chance, much lower than usual. The European setting may have favored Italy. Therefore, despite Italy's legitimate talent as a team, they also benefited from randomness—a chance combination of lucky events that would probably never happen in the same combination again, like flipping a coin and getting eight heads in a row. Overall, the team's score in the subsequent game would almost necessarily be worse than in this game—not all eight flips will turn out in their favor again. Indeed, the team did regress: In their next game, they lost to Brazil, 0–1. In other words, Italy finished closer to an average level of performance.

Here's another example. Suppose you're normally cheerful and happy, but on any given day your usual upbeat mood can be affected by random factors, such as the weather, your friends' moods, and even parking problems. Every once in a while, just by chance, several of these random factors will affect you negatively: It will pour rain, your friends will be grumpy, and you won't be able to find a parking space. Your day is terrible! The good news is that tomorrow will almost certainly be better because all three of those random factors are unlikely to occur in that same, unlucky combination again. It might still be raining, but your friends won't be grumpy, and you'll quickly find a good parking space. If even one of these factors is different, your day will go better and you will regress toward your average, happy mean.

Regression works at both extremes. An unusually good performance or outcome is likely to regress downward (toward its mean) the next time. And an unusually bad performance or outcome is likely to regress upward (toward its mean) the next time. Either extreme is explainable by an unusually lucky, or an unusually unlucky, combination of random events.

**Regression and Internal Validity.** Regression threats occur only when a group is measured twice, and only when the group has an extreme score at pretest. If the group has been selected because of its unusually high or low group mean at pretest, you can expect them to regress toward the mean somewhat when it comes time for the posttest.

You might suspect that the 40 depressed women Dr. Yuki studied were, as a group, quite depressed. Their group average at pretest was partly due to their true, baseline level of depression, but it's also true that people seek treatment when they are especially low. In this group, a proportion are feeling especially depressed partly because of random events (e.g., the winter blues, a recent illness, family or relationship problems, job loss, divorce). At the posttest, the same unlucky combination of random effects on the group mean probably would not be the same as they were at pretest (maybe some saw their relationships get better, or the job situation improved for a few), so the posttest depression average would go down. The change would not occur because of the treatment, but simply because of regression to the mean, so in this case there would be an internal validity threat.

**Preventing Regression Threats.** Once again, comparison groups can help researchers prevent regression threats, along with a careful inspection of the pattern of results. If the comparison group and the experimental group are equally extreme at pretest, the researchers can account for any regression effects in their results.

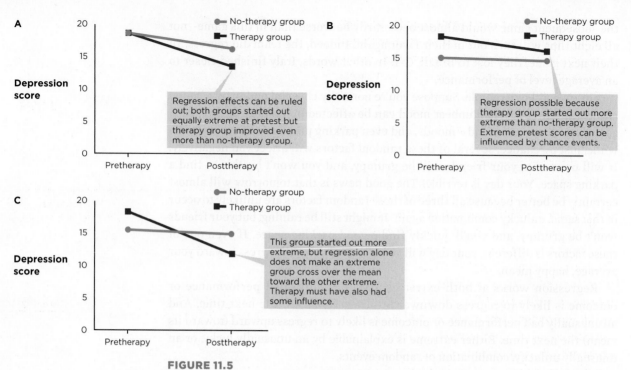

**A**

Depression score

No-therapy group
Therapy group

Regression effects can be ruled out; both groups started out equally extreme at pretest but therapy group improved even more than no-therapy group.

Pretherapy          Posttherapy

**B**

Depression score

No-therapy group
Therapy group

Regression possible because therapy group started out more extreme than no-therapy group. Extreme pretest scores can be influenced by chance events.

Pretherapy          Posttherapy

**C**

Depression score

No-therapy group
Therapy group

This group started out more extreme, but regression alone does not make an extreme group cross over the mean toward the other extreme. Therapy must have also had some influence.

Pretherapy          Posttherapy

**FIGURE 11.5**

**Regression threats to internal validity.**

Regression to the mean can be analyzed by inspecting different patterns of results.

In **Figure 11.5A**, you can rule out regression and conclude that the therapy really does work: If regression played a role, it would have done so for both groups because they were equally at risk for regression at the start. In contrast, if you saw the pattern of results shown in **Figure 11.5B**, you would suspect that regression had occurred. Regression is a particular threat in exactly this situation—when one group has been selected for its extreme mean. In **Figure 11.5C,** in contrast, the therapy group started out more extreme on depression, and therefore probably regressed to the mean. However, regression alone can't make a group cross over the comparison group, so the pattern shows an effect of therapy, in addition to a little help from regression effects.

## ATTRITION THREATS TO INTERNAL VALIDITY

Why did the average level of rambunctious behavior in Nikhil's campers decrease over the course of the week? It could have been because of the low-sugar diet, but maybe it was because the most unruly camper had to leave camp early.

Similarly, the level of depression among Dr. Yuki's patients might have decreased because of the cognitive therapy, but it might have been because three of the most depressed women in the study could not maintain the treatment regimen and dropped out of the study. The posttest average is lower only because these extra-high scores are not included.

In studies that have a pretest and a posttest, attrition (sometimes referred to as *mortality*) is a reduction in participant numbers that occurs when people drop out before the end. Attrition can happen when a pretest and posttest are administered on separate days and some participants are not available on the second day. An **attrition threat** becomes a problem for internal validity when attrition is systematic; that is, when only a certain kind of participant drops out. If any random camper leaves midweek, it might not be a problem for Nikhil's research, but it is a problem when the most rambunctious camper leaves early. His departure creates an alternative explanation for Nikhil's results: Was the posttest average lower because the low-sugar diet worked, or because one extreme score is gone?

Similarly, as shown in **Figure 11.6**, it would not be unusual if two of 40 women in the depression therapy study dropped out over time. However, if the two most depressed women *systematically* drop out, the mean for the posttest is going to be lower only because it does not include these two extreme scores (not because of the therapy). Therefore, if the depression score goes down from pretest to posttest, you wouldn't know whether the decrease occurred because of the therapy or because of the alternative explanation—that the highest-scoring women had dropped out.

**Preventing Attrition Threats.** An attrition threat is fairly easy for researchers to identify and correct. When participants drop out of a study, most researchers will remove those participants' scores from the pretest average too. That way, they look only at the scores of those who completed both parts of the study. Another approach is to check the pretest scores of the dropouts. If they have extreme scores on the pretest, their attrition is more of a threat to internal validity than if their scores are closer to the group average.

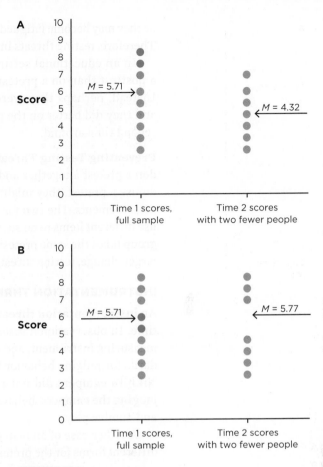

**FIGURE 11.6**
**Attrition threats.**
(**A**) If two people (noted by blue dots) drop out of a study, both of whom scored at the high end of the distribution on the pretest, the group mean changes substantially when their scores are omitted, even if all other scores stay the same. (**B**) If the dropouts' scores on the pretest are close to the group mean, removing their scores does not change the group mean as much.

## TESTING THREATS TO INTERNAL VALIDITY

A **testing threat**, a specific kind of order effect, refers to a change in the participants as a result of taking a test (dependent measure) more than once. People might have become more practiced at taking the test, leading to improved scores, or they may become fatigued or bored, which could lead to worse scores over time. Therefore, testing threats include practice effects (see Chapter 10).

In an educational setting, for example, students might perform better on a posttest than on a pretest, but not because of any educational intervention. Instead, perhaps they were inexperienced the first time they took the test, and they did better on the posttest simply because they had more practice the second time around.

**Preventing Testing Threats.** To avoid testing threats, researchers might abandon a pretest altogether and use a posttest-only design (see Chapter 10). If they do use a pretest, they might opt to use alternative forms of the test for the two measurements. The two forms might both measure depression, for example, but use different items to do so. A comparison group will also help. If the comparison group takes the same pretest and posttest but the treatment group shows an even larger change, testing threats can be ruled out (**Figure 11.7**).

## INSTRUMENTATION THREATS TO INTERNAL VALIDITY

An **instrumentation threat** occurs when a measuring instrument changes over time. In observational research, the people who are coding behaviors are the measuring instrument, and over a period of time, they might change their standards for judging behavior by becoming stricter or more lenient. Thus, maybe Nikhil's campers did not really become less disruptive; instead, the people judging the campers' behavior became more tolerant of loud voices and rough-and-tumble play.

Another case of an instrumentation threat would be when a researcher uses different forms for the pretest and posttest, but the two forms are not sufficiently

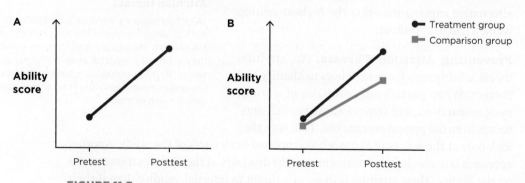

**FIGURE 11.7**

**Testing threats.**

(**A**) If there is no comparison group, it's hard to know whether the improvement from pretest to posttest is caused by the treatment or simply by practice. (**B**) The results from a comparison group can help rule out testing threats. Both groups might improve, but the treatment group improves even more, suggesting that both practice *and* a true effect of the treatment are causing the improvement.

equivalent. Dr. Yuki might have used a measure of depression at pretest on which people tend to score a little higher, and another measure of depression at posttest that tends to yield lower scores. As a result, the pattern she observed was not a sign of how good the cognitive therapy is, but merely reflected the way the alternative forms of the test are calibrated.

**Preventing Instrumentation Threats.** To prevent instrumentation threats, researchers can switch to a posttest-only design, or they can take steps to ensure that the pretest and posttest measures are equivalent. To do so, they might collect data from each instrument to be sure the two are calibrated the same. To avoid shifting standards of behavioral coders, researchers might retrain their coders throughout the experiment, establishing their reliability and validity at both pretest and posttest. Using clear coding manuals would be an important part of this process. Another simple way to prevent an instrumentation threat is to use a posttest-only design (in which behavior is measured only once).

Finally, to control for the problem of different forms, Dr. Yuki could also counterbalance the versions of the test, giving some participants version A at pretest and version B at posttest, and giving other participants version B, and then version A.

**Instrumentation Versus Testing Threats.** These two threats are pretty similar, but here's the difference: An instrumentation threat means the *measuring instrument* has changed from Time 1 to Time 2, whereas a testing threat means the *participants* change over time from having been tested before.

## COMBINED THREATS

You have learned throughout this discussion that true pretest/posttest designs (those with two or more groups) normally take care of many internal validity threats. However, in some cases, a study with a pretest/posttest design might combine selection threats with history or attrition threats. In a **selection-history threat**, an outside event or factor affects only those at one level of the independent variable. For example, perhaps the dorm that was used as a comparison group was undergoing construction, and the construction crew used electric tools that drew on only that dorm's power supply. Therefore, the researcher won't be sure: Was it because the Go Green campaign reduced student energy usage? Or was it only because the comparison group dorm used so many power tools?

Similarly, in a **selection-attrition threat**, only one of the experimental groups experiences attrition. If Dr. Yuki conducted her depression therapy experiment as a pretest/posttest design, it might be the case that the most severely depressed people dropped out—but only from the treatment group, not the control group. The treatment might have been especially arduous for the most depressed people, so they dropped out of the study. Because the control group was not undergoing treatment, they are not susceptible to the same level of attrition. Therefore, selection and attrition can combine to make Dr. Yuki unsure: Did the cognitive therapy really work, compared with the control group? Or is it just that the most severely depressed people dropped out of the treatment group?

## Three Potential Internal Validity Threats in Any Study

Many internal validity threats are likely to occur in the one-group, pretest/posttest design, and these threats can often be examined simply by adding a comparison group. Doing so would result in a pretest/posttest design. The posttest-only design is another option (see Chapter 10). However, three more threats to internal validity—observer bias, demand characteristics, and placebo effects—might apply even for designs with a clear comparison group.

### OBSERVER BIAS

Observer bias can be a threat to internal validity in almost any study in which there is a behavioral dependent variable. **Observer bias** occurs when researchers' expectations influence their interpretation of the results. For example, Dr. Yuki might be a biased observer of her patients' depression: She expects to see her patients improve, whether they do or do not. Nikhil may be a biased observer of his campers: He may expect the low-sugar diet to work, so he views the boys' posttest behavior more positively.

Although comparison groups can prevent many threats to internal validity, they do not necessarily control for observer bias. Even if Dr. Yuki used a no-therapy comparison group, observer bias could still occur: If she knew which participants were in which group, her biases could lead her to see more improvement in the therapy group than in the comparison group.

Observer bias can threaten two kinds of validity in an experiment. It threatens internal validity because an alternative explanation exists for the results. Did the therapy work, or was Dr. Yuki biased? It can also threaten the construct validity of the dependent variable because it means the depression ratings given by Dr. Yuki do not represent the true levels of depression of her participants.

» For more on observer bias, see Chapter 6, p. 170.

### DEMAND CHARACTERISTICS

**Demand characteristics** are a problem when participants guess what the study is supposed to be about and change their behavior in the expected direction. For example, Dr. Yuki's patients know they are getting therapy. If they think Dr. Yuki expects them to get better, they might change their self-reports of symptoms in the expected direction. Nikhil's campers, too, might realize something fishy is going on when they're not given their usual snacks. Their awareness of a menu change could certainly change the way they behave.

» For more on demand characteristics, see Chapter 10, p. 302.

**Controlling for Observer Bias and Demand Characteristics.** To avoid observer bias and demand characteristics, researchers must do more than add a comparison group to their studies. The most appropriate way to avoid such problems is to conduct a **double-blind study**, in which neither the participants nor the researchers who evaluate them know who is in the treatment group and who is in the comparison group.

Suppose Nikhil decides to test his hypothesis as a double-blind study. He could arrange to have two cabins of equally lively campers and replace the sugary snacks with good-tasting low-sugar versions for only one group. The boys would not know which kind of snacks they were eating, and the people observing their behavior would also be blind to which boys were in which group.

When a double-blind study is not possible, a variation might be an acceptable alternative. In some studies, participants know which group they are in, but the observers do not; this is called a **masked design**, or *blind design* (see Chapter 6). The students exposed to the Go Green campaign would certainly be aware that someone was trying to influence their behavior. Ideally, however, the raters who were recording their electrical energy usage should not know which dorm was exposed to the campaign and which was not. Of course, keeping observers unaware is even more important when they are rating behaviors that are more difficult to code, such as symptoms of depression or behavior problems at camp.

Recall the study by Mueller and Oppenheimer (2014) from Chapter 10, in which people took notes in longhand or on laptops. The research assistants in that study were blind to the condition each participant was in when they graded their tests on the lectures. The participants themselves were not blind to their notetaking method. However, since the test-takers participated in only one condition (an independent-groups design), they were not aware that the form of notetaking was an important feature of the experiment. Therefore, they were blind to the *reason* they were taking notes in longhand or on a laptop.

## PLACEBO EFFECTS

The women who received Dr. Yuki's cognitive therapy may have improved because her therapeutic approach really works. An alternative explanation is that there was a placebo effect. A **placebo effect** occurs when people receive a treatment and really improve—but only because the recipients believe they are receiving a valid treatment. In most studies on the effectiveness of medications, for example, one group receives a pill or an injection with the real drug, while another group receives a pill or an injection with no active ingredients—a sugar pill or a saline solution. People can even receive placebo psychotherapy, in which they simply talk to a friendly listener about their problems, but these placebo conversations have no therapeutic structure. The inert pill, injection, or therapy is the placebo. Often people who receive the placebo see their symptoms improve because they believe the treatment they are receiving is supposed to be effective. In fact, the placebo effect can occur whenever any kind of treatment is used to control symptoms, such as an herbal remedy to enhance wellness (**Figure 11.8**).

Placebo effects are not imaginary. Placebos have been shown to reduce real symptoms and side effects, both psychological and physical, including depression (Kirsch & Sapirstein, 1998), postoperative pain or anxiety (Benedetti et al., 2006), terminal cancer pain, and epilepsy (Beecher, 1955). They are not always beneficial or harmless; physical side effects, including skin rashes and headaches, can be caused by placebos, too. People's symptoms appear to respond not just to the active ingredients in medications or to psychotherapy, but also to their belief in what the treatment can do to alter their situation.

A placebo can be strong medicine. Kirsch and Sapirstein (1998) reviewed studies that gave either antidepressant medication, such as Prozac, or a placebo to depressed patients, and concluded that the placebo groups improved almost as much as groups that received real medicine. In fact, up to 75% of the depression improvement in the Prozac groups was also achieved in placebo groups.

**FIGURE 11.8**

**Are herbal remedies placebos?**

It is possible that perceived improvements in mood, joint pain, or wellness promised by herbal supplements are simply due to the belief that they will work, not because of the specific ingredients they contain.

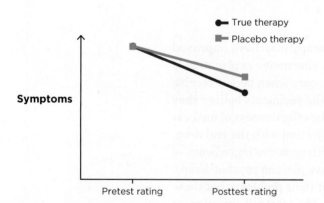

**FIGURE 11.9**

**A double-blind placebo control study.**

Adding a placebo comparison group can help researchers separate a potential placebo effect from the true effect of a particular therapy.

**Designing Studies to Rule Out the Placebo Effect.** To determine whether an effect is caused by a therapeutic treatment or by placebo effects, the standard approach is to include a special kind of comparison group. As usual, one group receives the real drug or real therapy, and the second group receives the placebo drug or placebo therapy. Crucially, however, neither the people treating the patients nor the patients themselves know whether they are in the real group or the placebo group. This experimental design is called a **double-blind placebo control study**.

The results of such a study might look like the graph in **Figure 11.9**. Notice that both groups improved, but the group receiving the real drug improved even more, showing placebo effects *plus* the effects of the real drug. If the results turn out like this, the researchers can conclude that the treatment they are testing does cause improvement above and beyond a placebo effect. Once again, an internal validity threat—a placebo effect—can be avoided with a careful research design.

**Is That Really a Placebo Effect?** If you thought about it carefully, you probably noticed that the results in Figure 11.9 do not definitively show a placebo effect pattern. Both the group receiving the real drug and the group receiving the placebo improved over time. However, some of the improvement in both groups could have been caused by maturation, history, regression, testing, or instrumentation threats (Kienle & Kiene, 1997). If you were interested in showing a placebo effect specifically, you would have to include a no-treatment comparison group—one that receives neither drug nor placebo.

Suppose your results looked something like those in **Figure 11.10**. Because the placebo group improved over time, even more than the no-therapy/no-placebo group, you can attribute the improvement to placebo and not just to maturation, history, regression, testing, or instrumentation.

## With So Many Threats, Are Experiments Still Useful?

After reading about a dozen ways a good experiment can go wrong, you might be tempted to assume that most experiments you read about are faulty. However, responsible researchers consciously avoid internal validity threats when they design and interpret their work. Many of the threats discussed in this chapter are a problem only in one-group, pretest/posttest studies—those with no comparison group. As shown in the Working It Through section (p. 340), a carefully designed comparison group will correct for many of these threats. The section analyzes the study on mindfulness (Mrazek et al., 2013) discussed in Chapter 10 and presented again here in **Figure 11.11**. **Table 11.1** summarizes the internal validity threats in Chapters 10 and 11 and suggests ways to find out whether a particular study is vulnerable.

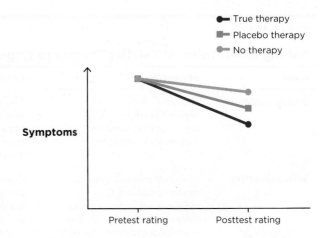

**FIGURE 11.10**

**Identifying a placebo effect.**

Definitively showing a placebo effect requires three groups: one receiving the true therapy, one receiving the placebo, and one receiving no therapy. If there is a placebo effect, the pattern of results will show that the no-therapy group does not improve as much as the placebo group.

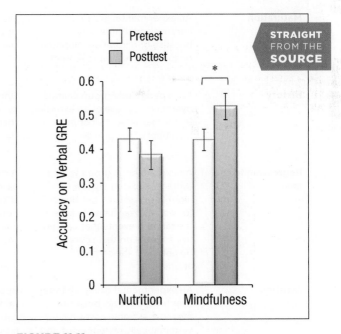

**FIGURE 11.11**

**Mindfulness study results.**

This study showed that mindfulness classes, but not nutrition classes, were associated with an increase in GRE scores. Can the study rule out all twelve internal validity threats and support a causal claim? (Source: Mrazek et al., 2013, Fig. 1A.)

TABLE 11.1

## Asking About Internal Validity Threats in Experiments

| NAME | DEFINITION | EXAMPLE | QUESTIONS TO ASK |
|---|---|---|---|
| **Design confound** | A second variable that unintentionally varies systematically with the independent variable. | *From Chapter 10*: If people who take notes on laptops answer harder questions than those who take notes longhand. | Did the researchers turn potential third variables into control variables—for example, keeping question difficulty constant? |
| **Selection effect** | In an independent-groups design, when the two independent variable groups have systematically different kinds of participants in them. | *From Chapter 10*: In the autism study, some parents insisted they wanted their children to be in the intensive-treatment group rather than the control group. | Did the researchers use random assignment or matched groups to equalize groups? |
| **Order effect** | In a repeated-measures design, when the effect of the independent variable is confounded with carryover from one level to the other, or with practice, fatigue, or boredom. | *From Chapter 10*: People rated the shared chocolate higher only because the first taste of chocolate is always more delicious than the second one. | Did the researchers counterbalance the orders of presentation of the levels of the independent variable? |
| **Maturation** | An experimental group improves over time only because of natural development or spontaneous improvement. | Disruptive boys settle down as they get used to the camp setting. | Did the researchers use a comparison group of boys who had an equal amount of time to mature but who did not receive the treatment? |
| **History** | An experimental group changes over time because of an external factor that affects all or most members of the group. | Dorm residents use less air conditioning in November than September because the weather is cooler. | Did the researchers include a comparison group that had an equal exposure to the external factor but did not receive the treatment? |
| **Regression to the mean** | An experimental group whose average is extremely low (or high) at pretest will get better (or worse) over time because the random events that caused the extreme pretest scores do not recur the same way at posttest. | A group's average is extremely depressed at pretest, in part because some members volunteered for therapy when they were feeling much more depressed than usual. | Did the researchers include a comparison group that was equally extreme at pretest but did not receive the therapy? |
| **Attrition** | An experimental group changes over time, but only because the most extreme cases have systematically dropped out and their scores are not included in the posttest. | Because the most rambunctious boy in the cabin leaves camp early, his unruly behavior affects the pretest mean but not the posttest mean. | Did the researchers compute the pretest and posttest scores with only the final sample included, removing any dropouts' data from the pretest group average? |

| NAME | DEFINITION | EXAMPLE | QUESTIONS TO ASK |
|------|-----------|---------|------------------|
| **Testing** | A type of order effect: An experimental group changes over time because repeated testing has affected the participants. Practice effects (fatigue effects) are one subtype. | GRE verbal scores improve only because students take the same version of the test both times and therefore are more practiced at posttest. | Did the researchers have a comparison group take the same two tests? Did they use a posttest-only design, or did they use alternative forms of the measure for the pretest and posttest? |
| **Instrumentation** | An experimental group changes over time, but only because the measurement instrument has changed. | Coders get more lenient over time, so the same behavior is coded as less disruptive at posttest than at pretest. | Did the researchers train coders to use the same standards when coding? Are pretest and posttest measures demonstrably equivalent? |
| **Observer bias** | An experimental group's ratings differ from a comparison group's, but only because the researcher expects the groups' ratings to differ. | The researcher expects a low-sugar diet to decrease the campers' unruly behavior, so he notices only calm behavior and ignores wild behavior. | Were the observers of the dependent variable unaware of which condition participants were in? |
| **Demand characteristic** | Participants guess what the study's purpose is and change their behavior in the expected direction. | Campers guess that the low-sugar diet is supposed to make them calmer, so they change their behavior accordingly. | Were the participants kept unaware of the purpose of the study? Was it an independent-groups design, which makes participants less able to guess the study's purpose? |
| **Placebo effect** | Participants in an experimental group improve only because they believe in the efficacy of the therapy or drug they receive. | Women receiving cognitive therapy improve simply because they believe the therapy will work for them. | Did a comparison group receive a placebo (inert) drug or a placebo therapy? |

---

![checkmark icon]

## CHECK YOUR UNDERSTANDING

1. How does a one-group, pretest/posttest design differ from a pretest/posttest design, and which threats to internal validity are especially applicable to this design?

2. Using Table 11.1 as a guide, indicate which of the internal validity threats would be relevant even to a (two-group) posttest-only design.

1. See p. 325. 2. See pp. 338–339.

## WORKING IT THROUGH

# Did Mindfulness Training Really Cause GRE Scores to Improve?

In Chapter 10, you read about a pretest/posttest design in which students were randomly assigned to a mindfulness training course or to a nutrition course (Mrazek et al., 2013). Students took GRE verbal tests both before and after their assigned training course. Those assigned to the mindfulness course scored significantly higher on the GRE posttest than pretest. The authors would like to claim that the mindfulness course caused the improvement in GRE scores. Does this study rule out internal validity threats?

| QUESTIONS TO ASK | CLAIMS, QUOTES, OR DATA | INTERPRETATION AND EVALUATION |
|---|---|---|
| **Is the study susceptible to any of these internal validity threats?**<br><br>Design confound | The paper reports that classes met for 45 minutes four times a week for 2 weeks and were taught by professionals with extensive teaching experience in their respective fields. "Both classes were taught by expert instructors, were composed of similar numbers of students, were held in comparable classrooms during the late afternoon, and used a similar class format, including both lectures and group discussions" (p. 778). | These passages indicate that the classes were equal in their time commitment, the quality of the instructors used, and other factors, so these are not design confounds. It appears the two classes did not accidentally vary on anything besides their mindfulness versus nutrition content. |
| Selection effect | The article reports that "students . . . were randomly assigned to either a mindfulness class . . . or a nutrition class" (p. 777). | Random assignment controls for selection effects, so selection is not a threat in the study. |
| Order effect | | Order effects are relevant only for repeated-measures designs, not independent-groups designs like this one. |

| QUESTIONS TO ASK | CLAIMS, QUOTES, OR DATA | INTERPRETATION AND EVALUATION |
|---|---|---|
| Maturation threat | | While it's possible that people could simply get better at the GRE over time, maturation would have happened to the nutrition group as well (but it did not). We can rule out maturation. |
| History threat | | Could some outside event, such as a free GRE prep course on campus, have improved people's GRE scores? We can rule out such a history threat because of the comparison group: It's unlikely a campus GRE program would just happen to be offered only to students in the mindfulness group. |
| Regression threat | | A regression threat is unlikely here. First, the students were randomly assigned to the mindfulness group, not selected on the basis of extremely low GRE scores. Second, the mindfulness group and the nutrition group had the same pretest means. They were equally extreme, so if regression had affected one group, it would also have affected the other. |
| Attrition threat | There's no indication in the paper that any participants dropped out between pretest and posttest. | Because all participants apparently completed the study, attrition is not a threat. |
| Testing threat | | Participants did take the verbal GRE two times, but if their improvement was simply due to practice, we would see a similar increase in the nutrition group, and we do not. |
| Instrumentation threat | The study reports, "We used two versions of the verbal GRE measure that were matched for difficulty and counterbalanced within each condition" (p. 777). | The described procedure controls for any difference in test difficulty from pretest to posttest. |
| Observer bias | "We minimized experimenter expectancy effects by testing participants in mixed-condition groups in which nearly all task instructions were provided by computers" (p. 778). | Experimenter expectancy is another name for observer bias. These procedures seem to be reasonable ways to prevent an experimenter from leading participants in one group to be more motivated to do well on the dependent measure. |
| Demand characteristics or placebo effects | "All participants were recruited under the pretense that the study was a direct comparison of two equally viable programs for improving cognitive performance, which minimized motivation and placebo effects" (p. 778). | This statement argues that all students expected their assigned program to be effective. If true, then placebo effects and demand characteristics were equal in both conditions. |

**This study's design and results have controlled for virtually all the internal validity threats in Table 11.1, so we can conclude its internal validity is strong and the study supports the claim that mindfulness training improved students' GRE verbal scores. (Next you could interrogate this study's construct, statistical, and external validity!)**

# INTERROGATING NULL EFFECTS: WHAT IF THE INDEPENDENT VARIABLE DOES NOT MAKE A DIFFERENCE?

So far, this chapter has discussed cases in which a researcher works to ensure that any covariance found in an experiment was caused by the independent variable, not by a threat to internal validity. What if the independent variable did not make much difference in the dependent variable? What if the 95% CI for the effect includes zero, such as a 95% CI of [−.21, .18]? Such an outcome may be called a *null result,* or **null effect**. Research that finds null effects are surprisingly common—something many students learn when they start to conduct their own studies. If researchers expected to find a large difference but obtained a 95% CI that contained zero instead, they sometimes say their study "didn't work." What might null effects mean?

Here are three hypothetical examples:

Many people believe having more money will make them happy. But will it? A group of researchers designed an experiment in which they randomly assigned people to three groups. They gave one group nothing, gave the second group a little money, and gave the third group a lot of money. The next day, they asked each group to report their happiness on a mood scale. The groups who received cash (either a little or a lot) were not significantly happier, or in a better mood, than the group who received nothing. The 95% CIs for the groups overlapped completely.

Do online reading games make kids better readers? An educational psychologist recruited a sample of 5-year-olds, all of whom did not yet know how to read. She randomly assigned the children to two groups. One group played with a commercially available online reading game for 1 week (about 30 minutes per day), and the other group continued "treatment as usual," attending their normal kindergarten classes. Afterward, the children were tested on their reading ability. The reading game group's scores were a little higher than those of the kindergarten-as-usual group, but the 95% CI for the estimated difference between two groups included zero.

Researchers have hypothesized that feeling anxious can cause people to reason less carefully and logically. To test this hypothesis, a research team randomly assigned people to three groups: low, medium, and high anxiety. After a few minutes of being exposed to the anxiety manipulation, the participants solved problems requiring logic, rather than emotional reasoning. Although the researchers had predicted the anxious people would do worse on the problems, participants in the three groups scored roughly the same.

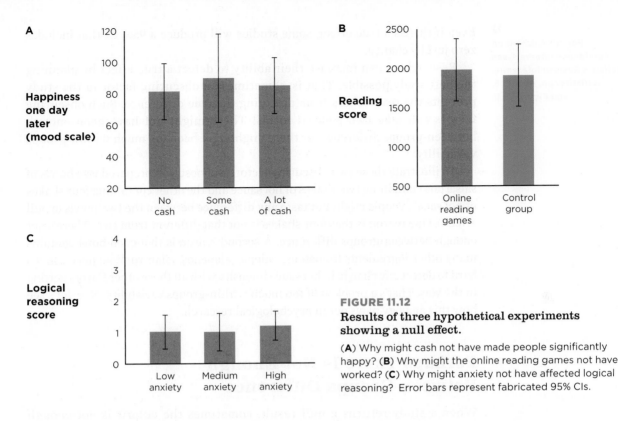

**A** — Happiness one day later (mood scale): No cash, Some cash, A lot of cash

**B** — Reading score: Online reading games, Control group

**C** — Logical reasoning score: Low anxiety, Medium anxiety, High anxiety

**FIGURE 11.12**

**Results of three hypothetical experiments showing a null effect.**

(**A**) Why might cash not have made people significantly happy? (**B**) Why might the online reading games not have worked? (**C**) Why might anxiety not have affected logical reasoning? Error bars represent fabricated 95% CIs.

These three examples of null effects, shown as graphs in **Figure 11.12**, are all posttest-only designs. However, a null effect can happen in a within-groups design or a pretest/posttest design, too (and even in a correlational study). In all three of these cases, the independent variable manipulated by the experimenters did not result in a change in the dependent variable. Why didn't these experiments show covariance between the independent and dependent variables?

Any time an experiment gives a null result, it might be the case that the independent variable has virtually no effect on the dependent variable. In the real world, perhaps money does not make people any happier, online reading games improve kids' reading skill only a tiny amount, and being anxious has virtually no effect on logical reasoning. In other words, the experiment gave an accurate estimate, showing that the manipulation the researchers used caused hardly any change in the dependent variable. Therefore, when we obtain a null result, it can tell us something valid and valuable: The independent variable does not cause much of a difference.

A different possibility is that there is a true effect, but this particular study did not detect it. Research takes place over the long run, and scientists conduct multiple replication studies testing the same theory. Because of chance variations from study to study, we should expect slight variations in the 95% CIs.

»
For more details on confidence intervals, see Statistics Review: Inferential Statistics, pp. 493–495, and Figure S2.9.

Even if there's a true effect, some studies will produce a 95% CI that includes zero just by chance.

Researchers can increase their ability to detect a true effect by planning the best study possible. That is, sometimes an obscuring factor in the study prevents the researchers from detecting the true difference. Such obscuring factors can take two general forms: There might not have been enough between-groups difference, or there might have been too much within-groups variability.

To illustrate these two obscuring factors, suppose you prepared two bowls of salsa: one containing two shakes of hot sauce and the other containing four shakes of hot sauce. People might not taste any difference between the two bowls (a null effect!). One reason is that four shakes is not that different from two: There's not enough between-groups difference. A second reason is that each bowl contains many other ingredients (tomatoes, onions, jalapeños, cilantro, lime juice), so it's hard to detect any change in hot sauce intensity with all those other flavors getting in the way. That's a problem of too much within-groups variability. Now let's see how this analogy plays out in psychological research.

## Perhaps There Is Not Enough Between-Groups Difference

When a study returns a null result, sometimes the culprit is not enough between-groups difference. Weak manipulations, insensitive measures, ceiling and floor effects, and reverse design confounds might prevent study results from revealing a true difference that exists between two or more experimental groups.

### WEAK MANIPULATIONS

Why did the study show that money had little effect on people's moods? You might ask how much money the researchers gave each group. What if the amounts were $0.00, $0.25, and $1.00? In that case, it might be no surprise that the manipulation didn't have a strong effect. A dollar doesn't seem like enough money to affect most people's mood. Like the difference between two shakes and four shakes of hot sauce, it's not enough of an increase to matter. Similarly, perhaps a 1-week exposure to reading games is not sufficient to cause any change in reading scores. Both of these would be examples of weak manipulations, which can obscure a true causal relationship.

When you interrogate a null result, then, it's important to ask how the researchers operationalized the independent variable. In other words, you have to ask about construct validity. The money and mood researchers might have obtained a very different pattern of results if they had given $0.00, $5.00, and

$150.00 to the three groups. The educational psychologist might have found that reading games improve scores if played daily for 3 months rather than just a week.

## INSENSITIVE MEASURES

Sometimes a study finds a null result because the researchers have not used an operationalization of the dependent variable with enough sensitivity. If a medication reduces fever by a tenth of a degree, you wouldn't be able to detect it with a thermometer that was calibrated in one-degree increments—it wouldn't be sensitive enough. Similarly, if online reading games improve reading scores by about 2 points, you wouldn't be able to detect the improvement with a simple pass/fail reading test (either passing or failing, nothing in between). When it comes to dependent measures, it's smart to use ones that have detailed, quantitative increments—not just two or three levels.

« For more on scales of measurement, see Chapter 5, pp. 122–124.

## CEILING AND FLOOR EFFECTS

In a **ceiling effect**, all the scores are squeezed together at the high end. In a **floor effect**, all the scores cluster at the low end. As special cases of weak manipulations and insensitive measures, ceiling and floor effects can cause independent variable groups to score almost the same on the dependent variable.

**Ceilings, Floors, and Independent Variables.**  Ceiling and floor effects can be the result of a problematic independent variable. For example, if the researchers really did manipulate the independent variable by giving people $0.00, $0.25, or $1.00, that would be a floor effect because these three amounts are all low—they're squeezed close to a floor of $0.00.

Consider the example of the anxiety and reasoning study. Suppose the researcher manipulated anxiety by telling the groups they were about to receive an electric shock. The low-anxiety group was told to expect a 10-volt shock, the medium-anxiety group a 50-volt shock, and the high-anxiety group a 100-volt shock. This manipulation would probably result in a ceiling effect because expecting *any* amount of shock would cause anxiety, regardless of the shock's intensity. As a result, the various levels of the independent variable would appear to make no difference.

**Ceilings, Floors, and Dependent Variables.**  Poorly designed dependent variables can also lead to ceiling and floor effects. Imagine if the logical reasoning test in the anxiety study was so difficult that nobody could solve the problems. That would cause a floor effect: The three anxiety groups would score the same, but only because the measure for the dependent variable results in low scores in all groups.

« Ceiling and floor effects are examples of restriction of range; see Chapter 8, pp. 216–218.

Or suppose the reading test used in the online game study asked the children to point to the first letter of their own name. Almost all 5-year-olds can do this, so the measure would result in a ceiling effect. All children would get a perfect score,

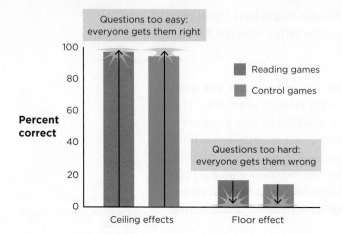

**FIGURE 11.13**
**Ceiling and floor effects.**

A ceiling or floor effect on the dependent variable can obscure a true difference between groups. If all the questions on a test are too easy, everyone will get a perfect score. If the questions are too hard, everyone will score low.

and there would be no room for between-groups variability on this measure. Similarly, if the reading test asked children to analyze a passage of Tolstoy, almost all children would fail, creating a floor effect (**Figure 11.13**).

## MANIPULATION CHECKS HELP DETECT WEAK MANIPULATIONS, CEILINGS, AND FLOORS

When you interrogate a study with a null effect, it is important to ask how the independent and dependent variables were operationalized. Was the independent variable manipulation strong enough to cause a difference between groups? And was the dependent variable measure sensitive enough to detect that difference?

Recall from Chapter 10 that a **manipulation check** is a separate dependent variable that experimenters include in a study, specifically to make sure the manipulation worked. For example, in the anxiety study, after telling people they were going to receive a 10-volt, 50-volt, or 100-volt shock, the researchers might have asked: How anxious are you right now, on a scale of 1 to 10? If the manipulation check showed that participants in all three groups felt nearly the same level of anxiety (**Figure 11.14A**), you'd know the researchers did not effectively manipulate what they intended to manipulate. If the manipulation check showed that the independent variable levels differed in an expected way— participants in the high-anxiety group really felt more anxious than those in the other two groups (**Figure 11.14B**)—then you'd know the researchers did effectively manipulate anxiety. If the manipulation check worked, the researchers could look for another reason for the null effect of anxiety on logical reasoning. Perhaps the dependent measure has a floor effect; that is, the logical reasoning test might be too difficult, so everyone scores low (see Figure 11.13). Or perhaps the effect of anxiety on logical reasoning is truly negligible.

## DESIGN CONFOUNDS ACTING IN REVERSE

Confounds are usually considered to be internal validity threats—alternative explanations for some observed difference in a study. However, they can apply to null effects, too. A study might be designed in such a way that a design confound actually counteracts, or reverses, some true effect of an independent variable.

In the money and happiness study, for example, perhaps the students who received the most money happened to be given the money by a grouchy experimenter, while those who received the least money were exposed to a more

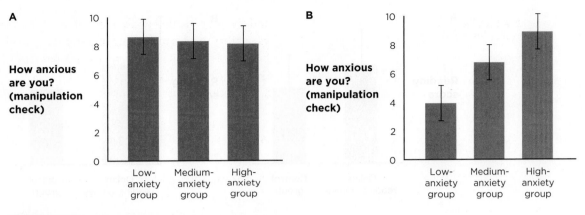

**FIGURE 11.14**

**Possible results of a manipulation check.**

(**A**) These results suggest the anxiety manipulation did not work because people at all three levels of the independent variable reported being equally anxious. (**B**) These results suggest the manipulation did work because the anxiety of people in the three independent variable groups did vary in the expected way. The error bars depict fabricated 95% CIs.

cheerful person. This confound would have worked against any true effect of money on mood.

## Perhaps Within-Groups Variability Obscured the Group Differences

Another reason a study might return a null effect is that there is too much unsystematic variability within each group. This is referred to as **noise** (also known as *error variance* or *unsystematic variance*). In our salsa analogy, noise refers to the great number of the other flavors in the two bowls. Noisy within-groups variability can get in the way of detecting a true difference between groups.

Consider the sets of scores in **Figure 11.15**. The bar graphs and scatterplots depict the same data, but in two graphing formats. In each case, the mean difference *between* the two groups is the same. However, the variability *within* each groups is much larger in part A than part B. You can see that when there is more variability within groups, it obscures the differences between the groups because more overlap exists between the members of the two groups. It's a statistical validity concern: The greater the overlap, the less precisely the two group means are estimated and the smaller the standardized effect size.

When the data show less variability within the groups (see Figure 11.15B), the 95% CI will be narrower and the standardized effect size will be larger. With less within-groups variability, our estimate of the group difference is more precise. If the two bowls of salsa contained nothing but tomatoes, the difference between two and four shakes of hot sauce would be more easily detectable because there would be fewer competing, "noisy" flavors within bowls.

« For more on statistical significance, see Chapter 8, pp. 213–214; and Statistics Review: Inferential Statistics.

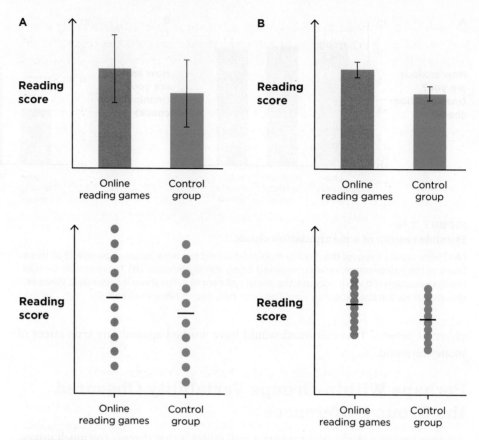

**FIGURE 11.15**

**Within-groups variability can obscure group differences.**

Notice that the group averages are the same in both versions, but the variability within each group is greater in part A than part B. Part B is the situation researchers prefer because it enables them to better detect true differences in the independent variable (error bars represent fabricated standard errors).

In sum, the more unsystematic variability there is within each group, the more the scores in the two groups overlap with each other. The greater the overlap, the less apparent the average difference. As described next, most researchers try to keep within-groups variability to a minimum by attending to measurement error, irrelevant individual differences, and situation noise.

## MEASUREMENT ERROR

One reason for high within-groups variability is **measurement error**, a human or instrument factor that can randomly inflate or deflate a person's true score on the dependent variable. For example, a person who is 160 centimeters tall might be measured at 160.25 cm because of the angle of vision of the person using the meter stick, or they might be recorded as 159.75 cm because they slouched a bit.

All dependent variables involve a certain amount of measurement error, but researchers try to keep those errors as small as possible. For example, the reading test used as a dependent variable in the educational psychologist's study is not perfect. Indeed, a group's score on the reading test represents the group's "true" reading ability—that is, the actual level of the construct in a group—plus or minus some random measurement error. Maybe one child's batch of questions happened to be more difficult than average. Perhaps another student just happened to be exposed to the tested words at home. Maybe one child was especially distracted during the test, and another was especially focused. When these distortions of measurement are random, they cancel each other out across a sample of people and will not affect the group's average, or mean. Nevertheless, an operationalization with a lot of measurement error will result in a set of scores that are more spread out around the group mean (see Figure 11.15A).

A child's score on the reading measure can be represented with the following formula:

child's reading score =
  child's true reading ability +/– random error of measurement

Or, more generally:

dependent variable score =
  participant's true score +/– random error of measurement

The more sources of random error there are in a dependent variable's measurement, the more variability there will be within each group in an experiment (see Figure 11.15A). In contrast, the more precisely and carefully a dependent variable is measured, the less variability there will be within each group (see Figure 11.15B). And lower within-groups variability is better, making it easier to detect a difference (if one exists) between the different independent variable groups.

**Solution 1: Use Reliable, Precise Tools.** When researchers use measurement tools that have excellent reliability (internal, interrater, and test-retest), they can reduce measurement error (see Chapter 5). When such tools also have good construct validity, there will be a lower error rate as well. More precise and accurate measurements have less error.

**Solution 2: Measure More Instances.** A precise, reliable measurement tool is sometimes impossible to find. What then? In this case, the best alternative is to use a larger sample (e.g., more people, more animals) or take multiple measurements on the sample you have. In other words, one solution to measuring badly is to take more measurements. When a tool potentially causes a great deal of random error, the researcher can cancel out many errors simply by including more people in the sample or measuring multiple observations.

Is one person's score 2 points too high because of a random measurement error? If so, it's not a problem, as long as another participant's score is 2 points too low because of a random measurement error. The more participants or items there are, the better the chances of having a full representation of all the possible errors. The random errors cancel each other out, and the result is a better estimate of the "true" average for that group.

## INDIVIDUAL DIFFERENCES

Individual differences can be another source of within-groups variability. They can be a problem in independent-groups designs. In the experiment on money and mood, for example, the normal mood of the participants must have varied. Some people are naturally more cheerful than others, and these individual differences have the effect of spreading out the scores of the students within each group, as **Figure 11.16** shows. In the $1.00 condition is Candace, who is typically unhappy. The $1.00 gift might have made her happier, but her mood would still be relatively low because of her normal level of saltiness. Michael, a cheerful guy, was in the no-money control condition, but he still scored high on the mood measure.

Looking over the data, you'll notice that, on average, the participants in the experimental condition did score a little higher than those in the control condition. But the data are mixed and far from consistent; there's a lot of overlap between the scores in the money group and the control group. Because of this overlap, any effect of a money gift is swamped by these individual differences in mood. The effect of the gift would be small compared to the variability within each group.

**Solution 1: Change the Design.** One way to accommodate individual differences is to use a within-groups design instead of an independent-groups design. In **Figure 11.17**, each pair of points, connected by a line, represents a single person whose mood was measured under both conditions. The top pair of points represents Michael's mood after a money gift and after no gift. Another pair of points represents Candace's mood after a money gift and after no gift. Do you see what happens? The individual data points are exactly where they were in Figure 11.16,

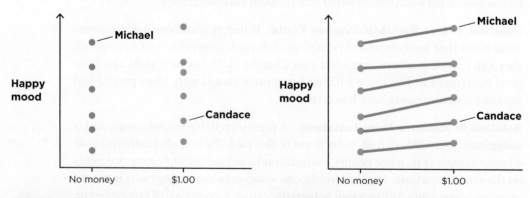

**FIGURE 11.16**
**Individual differences.**

Overall, students who received money were slightly more cheerful than students in the control group, but the scores in the two groups overlapped a great deal.

**FIGURE 11.17**
**Within-groups designs control for individual differences.**

When each person participates in both levels of the independent variable, the individual differences are controlled for, and it is easier to see the effect of the independent variable.

but the pairing process has turned a scrambled set of data into a clear and very consistent finding: Every participant was a little happier after receiving a money gift than after no gift. This included Michael, who is always cheerful, and Candace, who is usually unhappy, as well as others in between.

A within-groups design, in which all participants are compared with themselves, controls for irrelevant individual differences. Finally, notice that the study required only half as many participants as the original independent-groups experiment. You can see again the two strengths of within-groups designs (introduced in Chapter 10): They control for irrelevant individual differences, and they require fewer participants than independent-groups designs.

**Solution 2: Add More Participants.** If within-groups or matched-groups designs are inappropriate (and sometimes they are, because of order effects, demand characteristics, or other practical concerns), another solution to individual difference variability is to measure more people. The principle is the same as it is for measurement error: When a great deal of variability exists because of individual differences, a simple solution is to increase the sample size. The more people you measure, the less impact any single person will have on the group's average. Adding more participants reduces the influence of individual differences *within* groups, thereby enhancing the study's ability to detect differences *between* groups.

Another reason to use a larger sample is that it leads to a more precise estimate. Computing the 95% CI for a set of data requires three elements: a variability component (based on the standard deviation), a sample size component (where sample size goes in the denominator), and a constant. The larger the sample size, the more precise our estimate is and the narrower our CI is (see **Table 11.2**).

« 
For more on computing confidence intervals, see Statistical Review: Inferential Statistics, pp. 493–505.

### SITUATION NOISE

Besides measurement error and irrelevant individual differences, **situation noise**—external distractions—is a third factor that could cause variability within

---

**TABLE 11.2**

### The 95% CI represents the precision of our statistical estimates

This table summarizes the relationship between the 95% CI and measurement error, irrelevant individual differences, and situation noise.

| COMPONENTS OF A 95% CI | ROLE IN THE 95% CI | TO INCREASE THE PRECISION OF THE 95% CI (MAKE IT NARROWER), RESEARCHERS CAN: |
|---|---|---|
| **Variability component** | As error variability decreases, the 95% CI will become narrower (more precise). | Reduce error variability in the study by using precise measurements, reducing situation noise, or studying only one type of person or animal. |
| **Sample size component** | As sample size increases, the 95% CI will become narrower (more precise). | Increase the number of participants studied. |
| **Constant (such as a *z* or *t* value)** | In a 95% CI, the constant is at least 1.96. | We have no real control over the constant when we estimate a 95% CI. |

groups and obscure true group differences. Suppose the money and mood researchers had conducted their study in the middle of the student union on campus. The sheer number of distractions in this setting would make a mess of the data. The smell of the nearby coffee shop might make some participants feel cozy, seeing friends at the next table might make some feel extra happy, and seeing the cute person from sociology class might make some feel nervous or self-conscious. The kind and amount of distractions in the student union would vary from participant to participant and from moment to moment. The result, once again, would be unsystematic variability within each group. Unsystematic variability, like that caused by random measurement error or irrelevant individual differences, will obscure true differences between groups.

Researchers may attempt to minimize situation noise by carefully controlling the surroundings of an experiment. The investigators might choose to distribute money and measure people's moods in a consistently undistracting laboratory room, far from coffee shops and classmates. Similarly, the researcher studying anxiety and logical reasoning might reduce unsystematic situation noise by administering the logical reasoning test on a computer in a standardized classroom environment. The educational psychologist might avoid unsystematic variability in the dependent variable, reading performance, by limiting children's exposure to alternative reading activities. **Table 11.3** summarizes the possible reasons for a null result in an experiment.

## TABLE 11.3

### Reasons for a Null Result

| OBSCURING FACTOR | EXAMPLE | QUESTIONS TO ASK |
|---|---|---|
| **NOT ENOUGH VARIABILITY BETWEEN LEVELS** | | |
| Ineffective manipulation of independent variable | One week of reading games might not improve reading skill (compared with a control group), but 3 months might improve scores. | How did the researchers manipulate the independent variable? Was the manipulation strong? Do manipulation checks suggest the manipulation did what it was intended to do? |
| Insufficiently sensitive measurement of dependent variable | Researchers used a pass/fail measure, when the improvement was detectable only by using a finer-grained measurement scale. | How did the researchers measure the dependent variable? Was the measure sensitive enough to detect group differences? |
| Ceiling or floor effects on independent variable | Researchers manipulated three levels of anxiety by threatening people with 10-volt, 50-volt, or 100-volt shocks (all of which make people very anxious). | Are there meaningful differences between the levels of the independent variable? Do manipulation checks suggest the manipulation did what it was intended to do? |
| Ceiling or floor effects on dependent variable | Researchers measured logical reasoning ability with a very hard test (a floor effect on logical reasoning ability). | How did the researchers measure the dependent variable? Do participants cluster near the top or near the bottom of the distribution? |

| OBSCURING FACTOR | EXAMPLE | QUESTIONS TO ASK |
|---|---|---|
| **TOO MUCH VARIABILITY WITHIN LEVELS** | | |
| Measurement error | Logical reasoning test scores are affected by multiple sources of random error, such as item selection, participant's mood, fatigue, etc. | Is the dependent variable measured precisely and reliably? Does the measure have good construct validity? If measurements are imprecise, did the experiment include enough participants or observations to counteract this obscuring effect? |
| Individual differences | Reading scores are affected by irrelevant individual differences in motivation and ability. | Did the researchers use a within-groups design to better control for individual differences? If an independent-groups design is used, larger sample size can reduce the impact of individual differences. |
| Situation noise | The money and happiness study was run in a distracting location, which introduced several external influences on the participants' mood. | Did the researchers attempt to control any situational influences on the dependent variable? Did they run the study in a standardized setting? |
| **IF THE STUDY WAS SOUND, PLACE IT IN CONTEXT OF THE BODY OF EVIDENCE:** | | |
| The independent variable could, in truth, have almost no effect on the dependent variable. | Did the researchers use a very large sample and take precautions to maximize between-groups variability and minimize within-groups variability? | If so, it's useful evidence that the independent variable has little effect on the dependent variable. Additional studies will strengthen this conclusion: What does the body of evidence (including meta-analyses) say? |
| The independent variable could have a true effect on the dependent variable, but because of random errors of measurement or sampling, this one study didn't detect it. | When several studies are conducted on the same phenomenon, the 95% CIs will differ from each other just by chance. | Again, additional studies help us evaluate this possibility. What does the body of evidence (including meta-analyses) say? If most studies show an effect, this one null result might be a fluke. |

## The Opposite of Obscuring: Power and Precision

When researchers use a within-groups design, employ a strong manipulation, carefully control the experimental situation, or add more participants to a study, they are increasing the precision of their estimates and increasing the study's power. **Power** is an aspect of statistical validity; it is the likelihood that a study will return an accurate result when the independent variable really has an effect. If online reading games cause even a small improvement or if anxiety affects problem solving even by a small amount, will the experiment estimate that effect precisely? Will the 95% CI be reasonably narrow? A within-groups design, a strong manipulation, a larger number of participants, and less situation noise are all things that can improve the precision of our estimates. Of these, the easiest way to increase precision and power is to add more participants.

Studies with large samples have two major advantages. First, as already discussed, large samples make the CI narrow—they lead to a more precise estimate of any statistic, whether it's a mean, a correlation, or a difference between groups. Large samples are more likely to lead to statistically significant results (CIs that do not include zero) when an effect is real.

Second, effects detected from small samples sometimes can't be repeated. Imagine a study on online reading games that tested only 10 children. Even if reading games don't work, it's possible that just by chance, three children show a terrific improvement in reading after using them. Those children would have a disproportionate effect on the results because the sample was so small. And because the result was due primarily to three exceptional children, researchers may not be able to replicate it. Indeed, the CI for such a small sample will be very wide, reflecting how difficult it is to predict what the next study will show. In contrast, in a larger sample (say, 100 children), three exceptional kids would have much less impact on the overall pattern. In short, large samples have a better chance of estimating real effects.

## Null Effects Should Be Reported Transparently

When an experiment results in a null effect (the CI includes zero), what should you conclude? The study might have an obscuring factor, so you might first ask whether it was designed to elicit and detect between-groups differences. Was the manipulation strong? Was the dependent measure sensitive enough? Could either variable be limited to a ceiling or floor effect? Are any design confounds working against the independent variable? You would also ask about the study's ability to minimize within-groups differences. Was the dependent variable measured as precisely as possible, to reduce measurement error? Could individual differences be obscuring the effect of the independent variable? Did the study include enough participants to detect an effect? Was the study conducted with appropriate situational controls? Any of these factors, if problematic, could explain why an experiment showed a null effect.

If you find the experiment was conducted in ways that maximized its power and precision and yielded a narrow CI that includes zero, then you have evidence that the independent variable has little effect on the dependent variable. Maybe online reading games truly do not help children read better. Perhaps anxiety has hardly any effect on logical reasoning. If you read about a study that used a strong manipulation, precise measurement, and a very large sample yet still didn't find anything—that's a sign there's probably no effect (or only a negligible effect) to be found.

Null effects may seem disappointing to a researcher. Indeed, researchers may be tempted to hide null effects and not report them—a reaction that would violate

Merton's norm of disinterestedness. Instead, we should accept what the data tell us. In fact, for the purposes of self-correcting scientific progress, null effects are informative. It's useful to learn which interventions do not work, as well as which ones do. Null effects push us to revise theories.

Like all results, null effects should be considered along with other studies testing the same question. Ideally, scientists conduct and publish replication studies that provide multiple estimates, so we can consider a full body of evidence, often summarized via meta-analysis. Therefore, null effects should be published (rather than hidden away), because they allow us to see all the evidence openly.

There are many examples of true null effects in science. In Chapter 2 you read about a study of 1,700 women that showed no difference in outcome between radical mastectomy and a less drastic procedure (Figure 2.5; Fisher et al., 2002). An analysis of 1.2 million children concluded that vaccinating children does not cause autism (Taylor et al., 2014). Some therapeutic programs apparently do not have the intended effect (such as the Scared Straight program, discussed in Chapter 1). After a certain level of income, money does not appear to be related to happiness (Diener et al., 1985; Lyubomirsky et al., 2005; Lucas & Schimmack, 2009; Myers, 2000). And despite the common belief, sugar does not make children hyperactive (Wolraich et al., 1994).

The Working It Through section provides an example of a series of studies that found no effect of exposure to money on political beliefs.

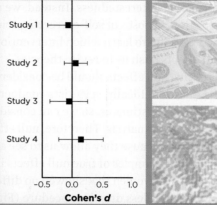

Cohen's *d*

## WORKING IT THROUGH

# Do People's Political Views Change When They See Money?

One theory proposed that subtle exposure to money (for example, being shown photos of dollar bills) leads people to adopt political views in favor of economic inequality (Caruso et al., 2013). A group of researchers conducted four studies to test this hypothesis, and all four studies resulted in null effects (Rohrer et al., 2015). In one of the studies, for example, online participants were randomly assigned to read the instructions against a neutral background or against a background showing dollar bills (see inset). Then participants completed a short questionnaire measuring "system justification." This scale measures how much people think the current social system in the United States is fair and legitimate (a sample item is "Most policies serve the greater good"; Kay & Jost, 2003). Rohrer's results showed that, counter to the theory, participants in the money condition showed slightly lower scores on the system justification measure. The *d* was –0.07 and the 95% CI of the *d* was [–0.41, 0.27].

What should we make of this null effect? We'll work through the questions in Table 11.3 to find out.

| QUESTIONS TO ASK | CLAIMS, QUOTES, OR DATA | INTERPRETATION AND EVALUATION |
|---|---|---|
| **Was there enough variability between levels?** | | |
| Were the neutral background and the money background different enough from each other? | The photos used in the first study are pictured above. One is of money, and the other is a degraded version of the same photo (Caruso et al., 2013). | The money photo is in gray tones, so it might be too subtle to evoke a response. However, the theory specified "subtle" money cues, so it was probably appropriate to use this image even if it's not a strong manipulation. |
| Could there have been a floor effect on the dependent variable? | The system justification items were answered on a 1 to 7 scale, and the means in the two groups were 3.76 and 3.83. | These means are not close to 1.0 or 7.0, suggesting no floor or ceiling effect on the dependent variable. |
| Could there be a confound acting in reverse? | In this study, the only difference between the two conditions were the photos. | There do not appear to be any confounds in this design. |

| QUESTIONS TO ASK | CLAIMS, QUOTES, OR DATA | INTERPRETATION AND EVALUATION |
|---|---|---|
| **Was there too much variability within levels?**<br><br>Was there situation noise or individual differences?<br><br>Was the sample size large enough to counteract situation noise and individual differences? | People completed questionnaires online, so there could be some situation noise. In addition, individuals probably differ in their current political views.<br><br>The sample sizes in the two groups were fairly large (about 67 in each group). | There was likely some within-groups variability due to situation noise and irrelevant individual differences.<br><br>But the sample size was probably large enough to counteract these influences. In addition, the three other studies reported in the paper also had large sample sizes (of 420, 156, and 116). |
| **This study seems sound. What does the body of evidence say?** | The researchers conducted a total of four studies using subtle money cues. All four had null effects, with 95% CIs that included zero. A separate study of more than 6,000 people also found a null effect (Klein et al., 2014).<br><br>Some previously published studies have found effects of money priming on political beliefs (see Vohs, 2015). However, the authors of some of these previous studies admitted that they did not report some null results obtained in the course of their research. | In total, four studies suggest that looking at money does not change political beliefs very much, if at all. Their 95% CIs are plotted above.<br><br>The previous studies on this topic used smaller samples than did Rohrer's team. And any previous null effects should be considered as part of the body of evidence.<br><br>Given this mixed set of results, what do you conclude? |

## CHECK YOUR UNDERSTANDING

1. How can a study maximize variability between independent variable groups? (There are four ways.)

2. How can a study minimize variability within groups? (There are three ways.)

3. In your own words, describe how within-groups designs minimize unsystematic variability.

4. When a study results in a null effect, should it be published? Why or why not?

1. See pp. 344–346 and Table 11.3. 2. See pp. 347–352 and Table 11.3. 3. See pp. 347–348.
4. See pp. 353–355.

# CHAPTER REVIEW

 It's time to complete your study experience!  Go to INQUIZITIVE to practice actively with this chapter's concepts and get personalized feedback along the way.

## Summary

Responsible experimenters may conduct double-blind studies, measure variables precisely, or put people in controlled environments to eliminate internal validity threats and increase a study's power to avoid false null effects.

### THREATS TO INTERNAL VALIDITY: DID THE INDEPENDENT VARIABLE REALLY CAUSE THE DIFFERENCE?

- When an experiment finds that an independent variable affected a dependent variable, you can interrogate the study for twelve possible internal validity threats.

- The first three threats to internal validity to consider are design confounds, selection effects, and order effects (introduced in Chapter 10).

- Six threats to internal validity are especially relevant to the one-group, pretest/posttest design: maturation, history, regression, attrition, testing, and instrumentation threats. All of them can usually be ruled out if an experimenter conducts the study using a comparison group (either a posttest-only design or a pretest/posttest design).

- Three more internal validity threats could potentially apply to any experiment: observer bias, demand characteristics, and placebo effects.

- By interrogating a study's design and results, you can decide whether the study has ruled out all twelve threats. If it passes all your internal validity queries, you can conclude with confidence that the study was a strong one: You can trust the result and make a causal claim.

### INTERROGATING NULL EFFECTS: WHAT IF THE INDEPENDENT VARIABLE DOES NOT MAKE A DIFFERENCE?

- If you encounter a study in which the independent variable had no effect on the dependent variable (a null effect), you can review the possible obscuring factors.

- Obscuring factors can be sorted into two categories of problems. One is the problem of not enough between-groups difference, which results from weak manipulations, insensitive measures, ceiling or floor effects, or a design confound acting in reverse.

- The second problem is too much within-groups variability, caused by measurement error, irrelevant individual differences, or situation noise. These problems can be counteracted by using multiple measurements, more precise measurements, within-groups designs, large samples, and very controlled experimental environments.

- If you can be reasonably sure a study avoided all the obscuring factors, then the study provides valuable evidence. You should consider it, along with other studies on the same topic, to evaluate how strong some effect is in the real world.

# Key Terms

one-group, pretest/posttest design, p. 325

maturation threat, p. 326

history threat, p. 327

regression threat, p. 328

regression to the mean, p. 328

attrition threat, p. 331

testing threat, p. 331

instrumentation threat, p. 332

selection-history threat, p. 333

selection-attrition threat, p. 333

observer bias, p. 334

demand characteristics, p. 334

double-blind study, p. 335

masked design, p. 335

placebo effect, p. 335

double-blind placebo control study, p. 336

null effect, p. 342

ceiling effect, p. 345

floor effect, p. 345

manipulation check, p. 346

noise, p. 347

measurement error, p. 348

situation noise, p. 351

power, p. 353

 To see samples of chapter concepts in the popular media, visit www.everydayresearchmethods.com and click the box for Chapter 11.

# Review Questions

1. Dr. Weber conducted a long-term study in which people were tested on happiness, asked to make two new friends, and then tested on happiness 1 month later. He noticed that six of the most introverted people dropped out by the last session. Therefore, his study might have which of the following internal validity threats?

   a. Attrition

   b. Maturation

   c. Selection

   d. Regression

2. How is a testing threat to internal validity different from an instrumentation threat?

   a. A testing threat can be prevented with random assignment; an instrumentation threat cannot.

   b. A testing threat applies only to within-groups designs; an instrumentation threat applies to any type of study design.

   c. A testing threat can be prevented with a double-blind study; an instrumentation threat can be prevented with a placebo control.

   d. A testing threat refers to a change in the participants over time; an instrumentation threat refers to a change in the measuring instrument over time.

3. A regression threat applies especially:

   a. When there are two groups in the study: an experimental group and a control group.

   b. When the researcher recruits a sample whose average is extremely low or high at pretest.

   c. In a posttest-only design.

   d. When there is a small sample in the study.

4. Dr. Banks tests to see how many training sessions it takes for dogs to learn to "Sit and stay." She randomly assigns 60 dogs to two reward conditions: one is miniature hot dogs, the other is small pieces of steak. Surprisingly, she finds the dogs in each group learn "Sit and stay" in about the same number of sessions. Given the design of her study, what is the *most likely* explanation for this null effect?

   a. The dogs loved both treats (her reward manipulation has a ceiling effect).

   b. She used too many dogs.

   c. She didn't use a manipulation check.

   d. There were too many individual differences among the dogs.

5. Dr. Banks modifies her design and conducts a second study. She uses the same number of dogs and the same design, except now she rewards one group of dogs with miniature hot dogs and another group with pieces of apple. She finds a big difference, with the hot-dogs group learning the command faster. Dr. Banks avoided a null result this time because her design:

a. Increased the between-groups variability.

b. Decreased the within-groups variability.

c. Improved the study's internal validity.

6. When a study has a large number of participants and a small amount of unsystematic variability (low measurement error, low levels of situation noise), then it has a lot of:

a. Internal validity

b. Manipulation checks

c. Dependent variables

d. Power and precision

## Learning Actively

The scenarios described in items 1–3 below contain threats to internal validity. For each scenario:

a. Identify the independent variable (IV) and dependent variable (DV).

b. Identify the design (posttest-only; pretest/posttest; repeated measures; one-group, pretest/posttest).

c. Sketch a graph of the results. (Reminder: Put the dependent variable on the *y*-axis.)

d. Decide whether the study is subject to any of the internal validity threats listed in Table 11.1.

e. Indicate whether you could redesign the study to correct or prevent any of the internal validity threats.

1. For his senior thesis, Jack was interested in whether viewing alcohol advertising would cause college students to drink more alcohol. He recruited 25 seniors for a weeklong study. On Monday and Tuesday, he had them use a secure website and record how many alcoholic beverages they had consumed the day before. On Wednesday, he invited them to the lab, where he showed them a 30-minute TV show interspersed with entertaining ads for alcoholic products. Thursday and Friday were the follow-up measures: Students logged in to the website and recorded their alcoholic beverage consumption again. Jack found that students reported increased drinking after seeing the alcohol advertising, and he concluded the advertising caused them to drink more.

2. In a cognitive psychology class, a group of student presenters wanted to demonstrate the power of retrieval cues. First, the presenters had the class memorize a list of 20 words that were read aloud to them in a random order. One minute later, the class members wrote down as many words as they could remember. On average, the class recalled 6 words. Second, the presenters told the class to try sorting the words into categories as the words were read (color words, vehicle words, and sports words). The presenters read the same words again, in a different random order. On the second test of recall, the class remembered, on average, 14 words. The presenters told the class this experiment demonstrated that categorizing helps people remember words because of the connections they can develop between various words.

3. A group of researchers investigated the effect of mindfulness meditation on mental health workers, 10 weeks after a major hurricane. A sample of 15 mental health workers were pretested on their depression and anxiety symptoms. Then they engaged in meditation training for 8 weeks. After the training was completed, they were tested on their symptoms again, using the same test. The study found that anxiety and depression symptoms were lower at posttest (the 95% CI for the drop in scores excluded zero). The researchers concluded the meditation training helped the participants (based on Waelde et al., 2008).

4. Dr. Dove was interested in the effects of eating chocolate on well-being. She randomly assigned 20 participants to two groups. Both groups ate as they normally would, but one group was instructed to eat a 1-ounce square of dark chocolate after lunch. After 4 weeks on this diet, they completed a questionnaire measuring their level of well-being (happiness, contentment). Dr. Dove was surprised to find the chocolate had no effect: Both groups, on average, scored the same on the well-being measure, and their 95% CIs overlapped. Help Dr. Dove troubleshoot her study. What should she do next time to improve her chances of precisely estimating the effect for the chocolate-enhanced diet, if eating chocolate really does improve well-being?

# The Link Between Alcohol and Aggression

VERYWELLMIND.COM, 2019

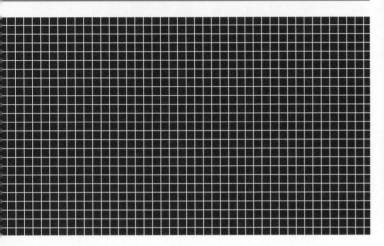

# The Dangers of Distracted Driving

FEDERAL COMMUNICATIONS COMMISSION, N.D.

# 12

# Experiments with More Than One Independent Variable

SO FAR, YOU HAVE read two chapters about evaluating causal claims. Chapters 10 and 11 introduced experiments with one independent variable and one dependent variable. What happens when more independent variables are added to the mix?

## REVIEW: EXPERIMENTS WITH ONE INDEPENDENT VARIABLE

Let's start with the first headline on the opposite page: Is there a connection between alcohol and aggression? According to research, there's almost no doubt that drunk people are more aggressive than sober ones. In several studies, psychologists have brought participants into comfortable laboratory settings, had them drink various amounts of alcohol, and then placed them in different situations to measure their aggressive tendencies. For example, a team of researchers led by Aaron Duke invited community members into their lab (Duke et al., 2011). After screening out volunteers who had problem drinking behaviors, were pregnant, or had other risky health conditions, they randomly assigned the remaining volunteers to drink a glass of orange juice that contained different amounts of alcohol. The "active placebo" group drank orange juice with a very small amount of vodka—enough to smell and to taste, but not enough to make them drunk. Another group was assigned to drink enough vodka to get drunk, by reaching a

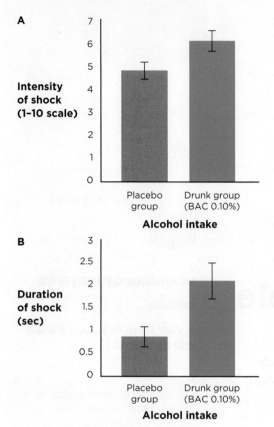

**A**

Intensity
of shock
(1–10 scale)

Alcohol intake

**B**

Duration
of shock
(sec)

Alcohol intake

**FIGURE 12.1**

**Alcohol intake and aggressive tendencies.**

Compared with a placebo group in this study, drunk participants delivered shocks of (**A**) higher intensity and (**B**) longer duration. These results demonstrated that alcohol causes people to behave aggressively. The error bars in these graphs indicate the standard error of each mean. (Source: Adapted from Duke et al., 2011.)

» To review counterbalancing, see Chapter 10, pp. 299–301.

blood alcohol concentration (BAC) of 0.10% (legally impaired is BAC 0.08% or higher).

After confirming the two groups' intoxication levels with a breathalyzer test, the researchers had the volunteers play a computer game with an opponent who was supposedly in another room (the opponent was actually a computer programmed in advance). The players took turns, and when one made a mistake, the opponent was allowed to deliver a shock as punishment. Players chose the intensity of the shock their opponents would receive for each mistake (on a scale of 1 to 10), and they could hold the shock delivery button down for different lengths of time. The researchers measured the intensity and duration of the shocks each participant delivered. The more intense the shocks and the longer their duration, the more aggressive the participants were said to be. Results showed a difference: Drunk participants were more aggressive (**Figure 12.1**).

The second headline reviews research showing that using a cell phone while behind the wheel impairs a person's ability to drive. An early experiment on this question came from the research lab of David Strayer and his colleagues (e.g., Strayer & Drews, 2004), who asked people to talk on hands-free cell phones in a driving simulator that looked almost exactly like a real car. As the participants drove, the researchers recorded several dependent variables, including driving speed, braking time, and following distance. In a repeated-measures (within-groups) design, they had participants drive on several 10-mile segments of highway in the simulator. For two of the segments, the drivers carried on a conversation on a hands-free cell phone. For the other two segments, drivers were not on the phone (of course, the order of the different segments was counterbalanced). The results showed that when drivers were simply talking on cell phones (not even texting or using apps), their reactions to road hazards were 18% slower. Drivers on cell phones also took longer to regain their speed after slowing down and got into more (virtual) accidents (**Figure 12.2**).

The Strayer and Drews study, like the Duke team's study, had one independent variable (cell phone use, manipulated as a within-groups variable) and one dependent variable (driving quality). Their study also showed a *difference* between conditions: People drove more poorly while using cell phones. These two studies were analyzed with a simple difference score: placebo minus drunk conditions, or cell phone minus control.

# EXPERIMENTS WITH TWO INDEPENDENT VARIABLES CAN SHOW INTERACTIONS

The Strayer and Drews study found that hands-free cell phones cause people to drive badly. These researchers also wondered whether that overall difference would apply in all situations and to all people. For example, might younger drivers be less distracted by using cell phones than older drivers? On the one hand, they might, because they grew up using cell phones and are more accustomed to them. On the other hand, older drivers might be less distracted because they have more years of driving experience. By asking these questions, the researchers were thinking about adding another independent variable to the original study: driver age, and the levels could be old and young. Would the effect of driving while using a cell phone depend on age?

Adding an additional independent variable allows researchers to look for an **interaction effect** (or *interaction*)—whether the effect of the original independent variable (cell phone use) *depends on* the level of another independent variable (driver age). Therefore, an interaction of two independent variables allows researchers to establish whether or not "it depends." They can now ask: Does the effect of cell phones depend on age?

The mathematical way to describe an interaction of two independent variables is to say that there is a "difference in differences." In the driving example, the *difference* between the cell phone and control conditions (cell phone minus control) might be *different* for older drivers than younger drivers.

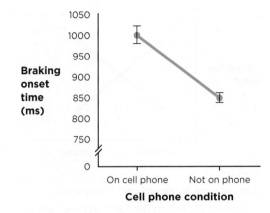

**FIGURE 12.2**
**Cell phone use and driver reaction time.**

In this study, drivers using hands-free cell phones were slower to hit the brakes in response to a road hazard. The error bars in this graph indicate the standard error of each mean. (Source: Adapted from Strayer & Drews, 2004.)

Interaction = a difference in differences = the effect of one independent variable depends on the level of the other independent variable

## Intuitive Interactions

Behaviors, thoughts, motivations, and emotions are rarely simple; they usually involve interactions between two or more influences. Therefore, some of the most important research in psychology explores interactions among multiple independent variables. What's the best way to understand what an interaction means?

Here's one example of an interaction: Do you like hot foods or cold foods? It probably depends on the food. You probably like your ice cream cold, but you like your pancakes hot. In this example, there are two independent variables: the food you are judging (ice cream or pancakes) and the temperature of the food (cold or

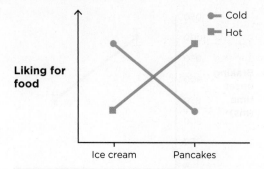

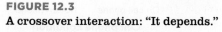

**Liking for food**

Ice cream    Pancakes

**FIGURE 12.3**

**A crossover interaction: "It depends."**

How much you like certain foods depends on the temperature at which they are served. It's equally correct to say that the temperature you prefer depends on which food you're eating.

hot). The dependent variable is how much you like the food. A graph of the interaction is shown in **Figure 12.3**. Notice that the lines cross each other; this kind of interaction is sometimes called a *crossover interaction,* and the results can be described with the phrase "it depends." People's preferred food temperature depends on the type of food.

To describe this interaction, you could say that when people eat ice cream, they like their food cold more than hot; when people eat pancakes, they like their food hot more than cold. You could also apply the mathematical definition by saying that there is a *difference in differences.* You like ice cream cold more than you like it hot (cold minus hot is a positive value), but you like pancakes cold less than you like them hot (cold minus hot is a negative value).

Here's another example. Most people know that either bacon or avocado will make a sandwich taste better. However, if you use both ingredients, the sandwich becomes particularly delicious. **Figure 12.4** shows a graph of this interaction. Notice that the lines are not parallel and they do not cross over each other. This kind of interaction is sometimes called a *spreading interaction,* and the pattern can be described with the phrase "especially": Sandwiches taste better when you add either bacon or avocado alone, but they taste especially good if you add both. In this example, the deliciousness multiplies—it's more than the sum of the two ingredients together.

Here is the mathematical description of this interaction: When there's no bacon on a sandwich, adding avocado leads to a small increase in deliciousness (avocado minus no avocado equals a small value). When there is bacon on a sandwich, adding avocado leads to a large increase in deliciousness (avocado minus no avocado equals a large value). There is a difference in differences.

When psychological scientists think about behavior, they might start with a simple link between an independent and a dependent variable, but often they find they need a second independent variable to tell the full story. For example,

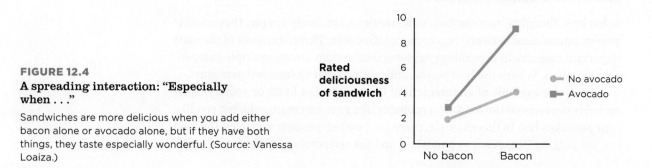

**FIGURE 12.4**

**A spreading interaction: "Especially when . . ."**

Sandwiches are more delicious when you add either bacon alone or avocado alone, but if they have both things, they taste especially wonderful. (Source: Vanessa Loaiza.)

**Rated deliciousness of sandwich**

No bacon    Bacon

No avocado
Avocado

in a romantic relationship, are positive attitudes, such as forgiveness, healthy? (In other words, does the independent variable of positive versus negative attitudes affect the dependent variable, relationship health?) The answer depends on how serious the disagreements are. Research shows that when difficulties are minor, positive attitudes are healthy for the relationship, but when the issues are major (e.g., one partner is abusive to the other or is drug-dependent), positive attitudes seem to prevent a couple from addressing their problems (McNulty, 2010). Thus, the degree of severity of the problems (minor versus major) is the second independent variable.

Does going to daycare hurt children's social and intellectual development? It seems to depend on the quality of care. According to one study, high-quality daycare can benefit the social and intellectual development of kids (compared with children who have only parental care); when the quality of daycare is poor, development might be impaired (Vandell et al., 1988). Reflect for a moment: What would the dependent and independent variables be in this example?

## Factorial Designs Study Two Independent Variables

When researchers want to test for interactions, they do so with factorial designs. A **factorial design** is one in which there are two or more independent variables (also referred to as *factors*). In the most common factorial design, researchers *cross* the two independent variables; that is, they study *each possible combination* of the independent variables. Strayer and Drews (2004) created a factorial design to test whether the effect of driving while talking on a cell phone depended on the driver's age. They used two independent variables (cell phone use and driver age), creating a condition representing each possible combination of the two. As shown in **Figure 12.5**, to cross the two independent variables, they essentially overlaid one independent variable on top of another. This overlay process created four unique conditions, or **cells**: younger drivers using cell phones, younger drivers not using cell phones, older drivers using cell phones, and older drivers not using cell phones.

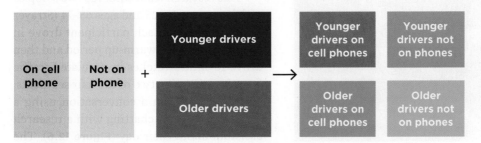

**FIGURE 12.5**
**Factorial designs cross two independent variables.**
A second independent variable was overlaid on top of a first independent variable, creating (in this case) four new experimental conditions, or cells.

Figure 12.5 shows the simplest possible factorial design. There are two independent variables (two factors)—cell phone use and age—and each one has two levels (driving while using a cell phone or not; younger or older driver). This particular design is called a 2 × 2 (two-by-two) factorial design, meaning that two levels of one independent variable are crossed with two levels of another independent variable. Since 2 × 2 = 4, there are four cells in this design.

### USING FACTORIAL DESIGNS TO STUDY MANIPULATED VARIABLES OR PARTICIPANT VARIABLES

You might have noticed that one of the variables, cell phone use, was truly manipulated; the researchers had participants either talk or not talk on cell phones while driving (Strayer & Drews, 2004). The other variable, age, was not manipulated; it was a measured variable. The researchers did not assign people to be older or younger; they simply selected participants who fit those levels. Age is an example of a **participant variable**—a variable whose levels are selected (i.e., measured), not manipulated. Because the levels are not manipulated, variables such as age, gender, and ethnicity are not truly "independent" variables. However, when they are studied in a factorial design, researchers often call them independent variables for the sake of simplicity.

## Factorial Designs Can Test Limits

One reason researchers conduct studies with factorial designs is to test whether an independent variable affects different kinds of people, or people in different situations, in the same way. The study on cell phone use while driving is a good example of this purpose. By crossing age and cell phone use, the researchers were asking whether the effect of using a cell phone was limited to one age group only, or whether it would have the same effect on people of different ages.

This research team observed two samples of drivers: ages 18–25 and ages 65–74 (Strayer & Drews, 2004). Each participant drove in the simulator for a warm-up period and then drove 10-mile stretches in simulated traffic four times. During two of the four segments, drivers carried on a conversation using a hands-free phone, chatting with a research assistant about their day (**Figure 12.6**). The researchers collected data on a variety of dependent variables, including accidents, following distance, and braking onset time

**FIGURE 12.6**

A young driver using a hands-free cell phone while driving in a simulator.

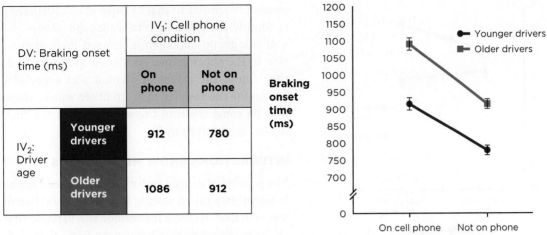

**FIGURE 12.7**
**Factorial design results in table and graph formats.**
The error bars indicate the estimated standard errors of each mean.
(Source: Adapted from Strayer & Drews, 2004.)

(how long it takes, in milliseconds, for a driver to brake for an upcoming road hazard). **Figure 12.7** shows the results for braking onset time. Notice that the same results are presented in two ways: as a table and as a graph.

The results might surprise you. The primary conclusion from this study is that the effect of talking on a cell phone did not depend on age. Older drivers did tend to brake more slowly than younger ones, overall; that finding is consistent with past research on aging drivers. However, Strayer and Drews wanted to know whether the *difference* between the cell phone and control conditions would be *different* for older drivers. The answer was no. The effect of using a cell phone (i.e., the simple difference between the cell phone condition and the control condition) was about the same in both age groups. In other words, cell phone use *did not interact with* (did not *depend on*) age. At least for these two age groups, the harmful effect of cell phone use was similar.

## A FORM OF EXTERNAL VALIDITY

You might have recognized this goal of testing limits as being related to external validity. When researchers test an independent variable in more than one group at once, they are testing whether the effect generalizes. Sometimes, as in the example of age and cell phone use while driving, the independent variable affects the groups in the same way, suggesting that the effect of cell phone use generalizes to drivers of all ages.

In other cases, groups might respond differently to an independent variable. In one study, for instance, researchers tested whether the effect of alcohol intake on aggressive behavior depends on body weight (DeWall et al., 2010). Using a

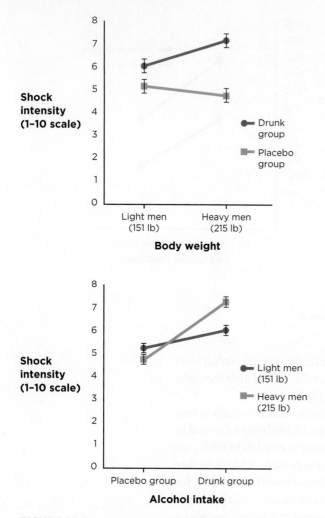

**FIGURE 12.8**

**Testing limits with factorial design.**

According to this study, the effect of alcohol on aggression is stronger in heavier men than lighter men. The same results are graphed two ways, with different independent variables on the *x*-axis. The error bars in this graph indicate the estimated standard errors of each mean. (Source: Adapted from DeWall et al., 2010.)

» To review how moderators work in correlational designs, see Chapter 8, pp. 225–227.

» To review the theory-data cycle, see Chapter 1, pp. 10–15.

procedure similar to that of Duke et al. (2011), they randomly assigned men to a placebo group and a drunk group and then measured their aggression in the shock game. As shown in **Figure 12.8**, they found the effect of alcohol was especially strong for the heavier men. In other words, there may be some truth to the stereotype of the "big, drunk, aggressive guy."

## INTERACTIONS SHOW MODERATORS

The process of using a factorial design to test limits is sometimes called testing for moderators. Recall from Chapter 8 that a moderator is a variable that changes the relationship between two other variables. In factorial design language, a moderator is an independent variable that changes the relationship between another independent variable and a dependent variable. In other words, a moderator results in an interaction; the effect of one independent variable depends on (is moderated by) the level of another independent variable. When Strayer and Drews studied whether driver age would interact with cell phone use, they found that driver age did not moderate the impact of cell phone use on braking onset time. However, DeWall and his colleagues showed that body weight moderates the effect of alcohol on aggression.

# Factorial Designs Can Test Theories

Researchers can use factorial designs not only to test the generalizability of a causal variable but also to test theories. The goal of most experiments in psychological science is to test hypotheses derived from theories. Indeed, many theories make statements about how variables interact with one another. The best way to study how variables interact is to combine them in a factorial design and measure whether the results are consistent with the theory.

## USING A FACTORIAL DESIGN TO TEST A THEORY OF ALCOHOL CUES

Once studies established that alcohol intake can lead to aggressive behavior, researchers wanted to dig deeper. They theorized about *why* drinking alcohol causes aggression. One idea is that alcohol impairs the brain's executive functioning; it interferes with people's ability to consider the consequences of their actions (Giancola, 2000). In addition to pharmacological effects, another theory suggests that through exposure to cultural messages and stereotypes about drinking behavior, people learn to cognitively associate alcohol with aggression. Merely *thinking* about alcohol might prime people to think about aggression. Researchers Bruce Bartholow and Adrienne Heinz (2006) sought to test the theory that alcohol can become cognitively associated with thoughts of aggression. They didn't get anybody drunk in their research; they simply exposed them to pictures of alcohol.

In the lab, participants viewed a series of images and words on a computer screen. Their task was to indicate whether a string of letters was a word or a nonword. For example, the letter string EDVIAN would be classified as a nonword, and the letter string INVADE would be classified as a word. Some of the words were aggression-related (e.g., *hit, combat,* or *fight*) and others were neutral (e.g., *sit, wonder,* or *caught*).

Before seeing each of the word strings, participants viewed a photograph on the computer screen for a brief period (300 ms). Sometimes the photograph was related to alcohol, perhaps a beer bottle or a martini glass. Other times the photograph was not related to alcohol; it was a photo of a plant. The researchers hypothesized that people would be faster to identify aggression-related words after seeing the photos of alcohol. They used the computer to measure how quickly people responded to the words.

As shown in **Figure 12.9**, Bartholow and Heinz were interested in the interaction of two independent variables: photo type (alcohol or plant) and word type (aggressive or neutral). The results told the story they hypothesized: When people had just seen a photo of alcohol, they were quicker to identify an

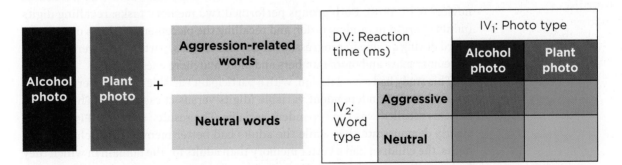

**FIGURE 12.9**
**Theory testing by crossing two independent variables.**

This type of design creates all possible combinations of the independent variables. Here, one independent variable (photo type) is crossed with another independent variable (word type) to create all four possible combinations.

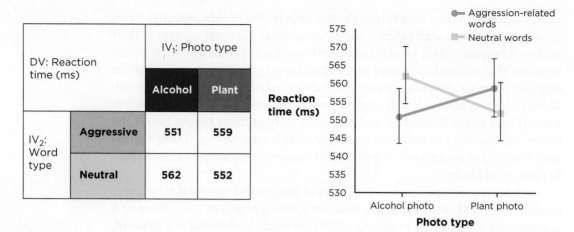

| DV: Reaction time (ms) | | IV₁: Photo type | |
|---|---|---|---|
| | | Alcohol | Plant |
| IV₂: Word type | Aggressive | 551 | 559 |
| | Neutral | 562 | 552 |

**FIGURE 12.10**
**Factorial study results in table and graph formats.**

The error bars in this graph indicate the standard error of each mean. (Source: Adapted from Bartholow & Heinz, 2006.)

aggressive word. When people had just seen a photo of a plant, they were slower to identify an aggressive word (**Figure 12.10**).

This study is a good example of how a researcher can test a theory using a factorial design. The resulting interaction supported one theory of why alcohol intake causes aggressive behavior: People cognitively associate alcohol cues with aggressive concepts.

### USING AN INTERACTION TO TEST A MEMORY THEORY

Another study used a factorial design to test why memory capacity develops as children get older. One theory stated that adults remember more than children do simply because of accumulated knowledge. A richer knowledge structure enables adults to make more mental connections for storing new information. One researcher tested this theory by comparing the memory abilities of two groups: Children who were chess experts (recruited from a chess tournament) and adults who were chess novices (Chi, 1978). Both groups performed two memory tasks: recalling digits (numbers) read in random order, and recalling the placement of pieces on a chessboard during a game in progress. Over a series of trials, participants were asked to remember more and more numbers and more and more chess pieces.

This study had a 2 × 2 design, with a participant variable (child experts or adult novices) and an independent variable (digits versus chess pieces). The number of items recalled was the dependent variable. The results, shown in **Figure 12.11**, clearly demonstrate that while the adults had better memory than children for digits, the children had a better memory than adults for the domain in which they had more knowledge: chess pieces.

In this study, the researchers used a factorial design to test their theory about why memory develops with age. The results showed the interaction predicted by the theory: Children's memory capacity can be better than adults when they have expertise in the topic.

| DV: Items recalled | | IV₁: Participant type | |
|---|---|---|---|
| | | **Child chess experts** | **Adult novices** |
| **IV₂: Type of item** | **Chess pieces** | 9.3 | 5.9 |
| | **Digits** | 6.1 | 7.8 |

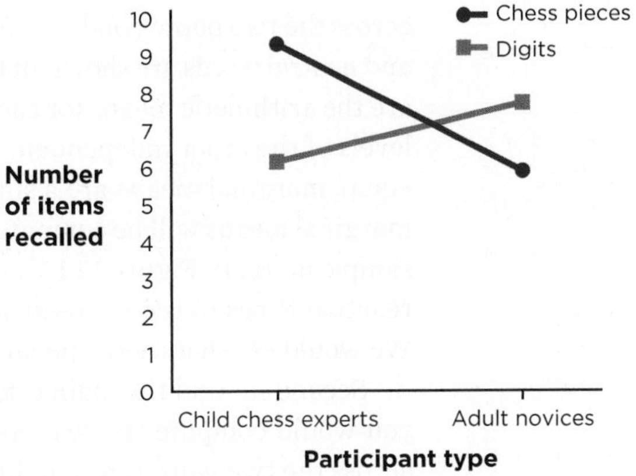

**FIGURE 12.11**
**A factorial study of memory development.**

Do children have less memory capacity than adults? It depends on the type of memory task. (Source: Adapted from Chi, 1978. Error bars are omitted because the relevant information was not available in the original article.)

# Interpreting Factorial Results: Main Effects and Interactions

After running a study with a factorial design with two independent variables, researchers, of course, want to analyze the results. In a design with two independent variables, there will be three results to inspect: two main effects and one interaction effect.

## MAIN EFFECTS: IS THERE AN OVERALL DIFFERENCE?

In a factorial design, researchers test each independent variable to look for a **main effect**—the overall effect of one independent variable on the dependent variable, averaging over the levels of the other independent variable. In other words, a main effect is a simple difference. In a factorial design with two independent variables, there are two main effects.

**Figure 12.12** shows the data from the Bartholow and Heinz (2006) study on word association. One independent variable, word type, is highlighted in blue; the other, photo type, is highlighted in yellow. First, to look for a main effect of word type, you would compute the reaction time to aggressive words (averaging across the two photo conditions) and the reaction time to neutral words (averaging

**FIGURE 12.12**
**Using marginal means to look for main effects.**

Looking for the main effect of an independent variable (IV) involves computing the overall score for each level of that IV, averaging over the levels of the other IV. Neither main effect in this study is statistically significant. (DV = dependent variable.) (Source: Adapted from Bartholow & Heinz, 2006.)

| DV: Reaction time (ms) | | IV₁: Photo type | | |
|---|---|---|---|---|
| | | **Alcohol** | **Plant** | Main effect for IV₂: Word type |
| **IV₂: Word type** | **Aggressive** | 551 | 559 | **555 (average of 551 and 559)** |
| | **Neutral** | 562 | 552 | **557 (average of 562 and 552)** |
| Main effect for IV₁: Photo type | | **556.5 (average of 551 and 562)** | **555.5 (average of 559 and 552)** | |

across the two photo conditions). The resulting two marginal means for aggressive and neutral words are shown in the far-right column of the table. **Marginal means** are the arithmetic means for each level of an independent variable, averaging over levels of the other independent variable. If the sample size in each cell is exactly equal, marginal means are a simple average. If the sample sizes are unequal, the marginal means will be computed using the weighted average, counting the larger sample more. In Figure 12.12, notice there's not much difference overall between reaction times to the aggressive words (555 ms) and the neutral words (557 ms). We would say that there appears to be no main effect of word type.

Second, to find the main effect of photo type, the other independent variable, you would compute the reaction time after seeing the alcohol photos, averaged across the two word type conditions, and the reaction time after seeing the plant photos, also averaged across the two word type conditions. These two marginal means are shown in the bottom row of the table. Here again, there is not much overall difference: On average, people are about as fast to respond after an alcohol photo (556.5 ms) as they are after a plant photo (555.5 ms). There appears to be no main effect of photo type.

»
For more on effect sizes, 95% CIs, and statistical significance, see Chapter 10, pp. 308–310, and Statistics Review: Inferential Statistics, pp. 499–500.

**Estimating How Large Each Main Effect Is.** To inspect the main effects in a factorial design, researchers calculate the difference between the marginal means and, often, compute the 95% confidence interval (CI) of this difference. If the 95% CI does not include zero, then the difference between the marginal means is called a "statistically significant main effect." Bartholow and Heinz estimated the magnitude of the overall difference in reaction times to the two word types. They also estimated the magnitude of the overall difference in reaction times after the two types of photos. In their study, neither of these main effects was statistically significant (their 95% CIs included zero).

Sometimes statistical significance tests indicate that a main effect is, in fact, statistically significant. For example, **Figure 12.13** shows results from the study that measured aggression in drunk and sober men (DeWall et al., 2010). The analysis of the marginal means revealed a main effect for the drinking condition, such that drunk men were more aggressive than sober men. It also revealed a main

**FIGURE 12.13**

**A study with two main effects.**

The marginal means on the right show a statistically significant main effect of alcohol intake (such that drunk men are more aggressive than sober men). The marginal means in the bottom row show a statistically significant main effect of body weight (heavy men are more aggressive than light men). (Source: Adapted from DeWall et al., 2010.)

| DV: Shock intensity (1–10 scale) | | IV₁: Body weight | | |
|---|---|---|---|---|
| | | **Light men (151 lb)** | **Heavy men (215 lb)** | Main effects for IV₂: Drinking condition |
| IV₂: Drinking condition | **Placebo group** | 5.09 | 4.72 | 4.91 (average of 5.09 and 4.72) |
| | **Drunk group** | 6.00 | 7.19 | 6.60 (average of 6.00 and 7.19) |
| Main effect for IV₁: Body weight | | **5.55 (average of 5.09 and 6.00)** | **5.96 (average of 4.72 and 7.19)** | |

effect for body weight, such that heavy men were more aggressive than light men. Both main effects were statistically significant.

**Main Effect = Overall Effect.** The term *main effect* may be misleading because it seems to suggest that it is the most important effect in a study. It is not. In fact, when a study's results show an interaction, the interaction itself is the most important effect. Think of a main effect instead as an *overall effect*—the overall effect of one independent variable at a time.

## INTERACTIONS: IS THERE A DIFFERENCE IN DIFFERENCES?

In a factorial design with two independent variables, the first two results obtained are the main effects for each independent variable. The third result is the interaction effect. Whereas the main effects are simple differences, the interaction effect is the difference in differences.

**Estimating Interactions from a Table.** You can use a table to estimate whether a study's results show an interaction. Because an interaction is a difference in differences, you start by computing two differences. **Figure 12.14** shows the process using the Bartholow and Heinz (2006) study. Begin with one level of the first independent variable: the alcohol photos. The difference in reaction time between the aggressive and neutral words for the alcohol photos is 551 – 562 = –11 ms. Then go to the second level of the first independent variable: the plant photos. The difference in reaction time between the aggressive and neutral words for the plant photos is 559 – 552 = 7 ms. (Be sure to compute the difference in the same direction both times; in this case, always subtracting the results for the neutral words from those for the aggressive words.) There are two differences: –11 ms and 7 ms. These differences are different: One is negative and one is positive (and they are 18 points apart). Indeed, statistical tests told the researchers that the difference of 18 ms is statistically significant. Therefore, you can conclude that there is an interaction in this factorial study.

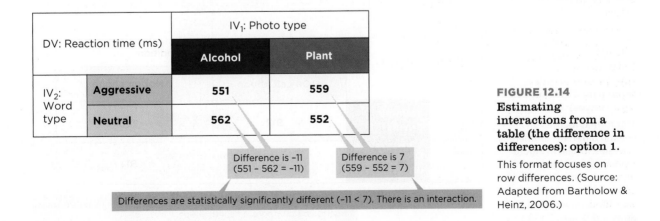

**FIGURE 12.14**

**Estimating interactions from a table (the difference in differences): option 1.**

This format focuses on row differences. (Source: Adapted from Bartholow & Heinz, 2006.)

You could estimate the difference in differences the other way instead, by computing the difference in reaction times to the alcohol and plant photos, first for aggressive words (551 – 559 = –8 ms) and then for neutral words (562 – 552 = 10 ms). Although the values will be slightly different this time, you will reach the same conclusion: There is an interaction. The differences are different—they are 18 points apart (–8 is different from 10).

Similarly, **Figure 12.15** shows how to compute the interaction for the Strayer and Drews (2004) study on using cell phones while driving. Again, if you start with one level of one independent variable, the younger drivers, the difference in braking onset time between drivers using cell phones and drivers who are not using cell phones is 912 – 780 = 132 ms. Next, among the older drivers, the difference in braking onset time between drivers using cell phones and drivers not using cell phones is 1086 – 912 = 174 ms. Are the two differences, 132 and 174, different? They do look different, but this is where statistics are helpful. Just as with main effects, researchers can ask how large the difference in differences is and whether the CI for it includes zero. Strayer and Drews's tests told them that the two differences are *not* significantly different. In this case, there is not a significant difference in differences. In fact, at each age level, there is a 15% drop in braking onset time.

**Detecting Interactions from a Graph.** While it's possible to compute interactions from a table, it is sometimes easier to notice them on a graph. When results from a factorial design are plotted as a line graph and the lines are not parallel, there may be an interaction, something you would confirm with a statistical test. In **Figure 12.16A**, you would suspect an interaction because the lines cross (indeed, the researchers report that the interaction is significant). If the lines are parallel (or "parallel-ish"), as in **Figure 12.16B**, there probably is *no* interaction (these researchers reported that the interaction was not significant). Notice that lines don't have to cross to indicate an interaction; they simply have to be nonparallel. For example, look back at the first graph in Figure 12.8, where the nonparallel lines indicate an interaction between aggression and body weight.

**FIGURE 12.15**
**Estimating interactions from a table (the difference in differences): option 2.**

This format focuses on column differences, whereas the table format in Figure 12.14 focused on row differences. Interactions can be computed either way. (Source: Adapted from Strayer & Drews, 2004.)

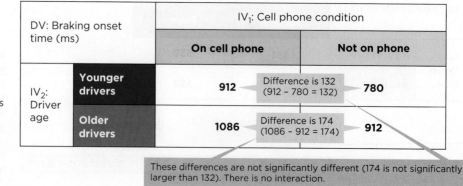

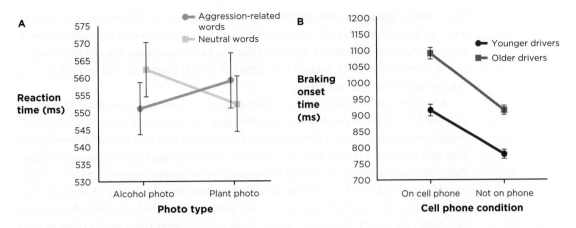

**FIGURE 12.16**
**Detecting interactions from a line graph.**

(**A**) An interaction in the Bartholow and Heinz (2006) study—the lines are not parallel.
(**B**) No interaction in the Strayer and Drews (2004) study—the lines are nearly parallel.
The error bars in these graphs indicate the standard error of each mean.

You can also estimate interactions from a bar graph. As you inspect the bar graphs in **Figure 12.17** (parts A and B), imagine drawing a line to connect the tops of each pair of same-color bars. Would those lines be nearly parallel or not? Or you might notice whether the differences between the bar heights change as you scan across the *x*-axis. Are the differences different, or are they the same? Remember that statistical tests help estimate how large the difference in differences is likely to be.

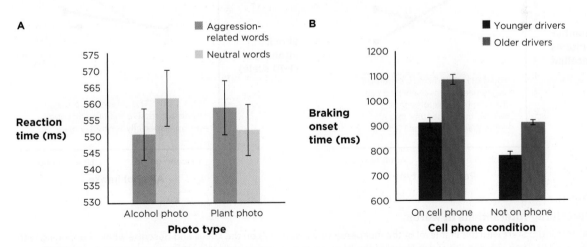

**FIGURE 12.17**
**Detecting interactions from a bar graph.**

(**A**) Results of the Bartholow and Heinz (2006) study. (**B**) Results of the Strayer and Drews (2004) study. Is it easier to detect interactions in this format or in the line graphs in Figure 12.16? The error bars in this graph indicate the standard error of each mean.

**Describing Interactions in Words.** It's one thing to determine that a study has an interaction effect; it's another to describe the pattern of the interaction in words. Since there are many possible patterns for interactions, there's no standard way to describe one: It depends on how the graph looks, as well as on how the researcher frames the results.

A foolproof way to describe an interaction is to start with one level of the first independent variable (that is, the first category on the *x*-axis), explain what's happening with the second independent variable, then move to the next level of the first independent variable (the next category on the *x*-axis) and do the same thing. For example, you might describe the interaction in the Bartholow and Heinz study (see Figures 12.16 and 12.17) like this: "When people saw photos of alcohol, they were quicker to recognize aggression words than neutral words, but when people saw photos of plants, they were slower to recognize aggression words than neutral words." As you move across the *x*-axis, you make it clear that the effect of the other independent variable (word type) is changing.

Another way to describe interactions involves key phrases. Some interactions, like the crossover interaction in **Figure 12.18A**, can be described using the phrase "it depends," as in: "The memory capacity of children depends on their level of expertise." Other interactions, like those in **Figure 12.18B**, can be described using the phrases "only for" or "especially for," as in: "Alcohol leads to aggression, especially for heavy guys."

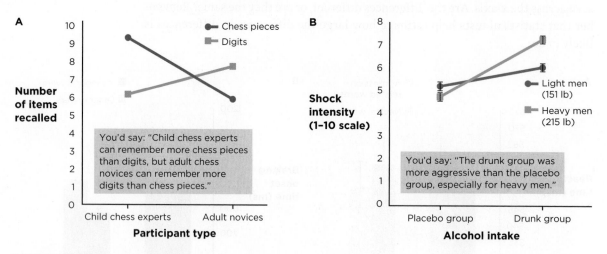

**FIGURE 12.18**

**Describing interactions in words.**

(**A**) Method 1: Start with the first level of the independent variable (IV) on the *x*-axis and describe what's happening with the other IV. Then move to the second level of the IV on the *y*-axis and describe what's happening with the other IV. (**B**) Method 2: Describe the difference in differences, using phrases like "especially for," "only for," and "depends on." Error bars are omitted in Panel A because the relevant information was not available in the original article. In Panel B, the error bars indicate the standard error of each mean.

## INTERACTIONS ARE MORE IMPORTANT THAN MAIN EFFECTS

When researchers analyze the results of a factorial design, they look at main effects for each independent variable and they look for interactions. When a study shows both a main effect and an interaction, *the interaction is almost always more important.*

The study on alcohol, aggression, and body weight provides an example of this principle (DeWall et al., 2010). This factorial design resulted in a main effect for body weight (heavy men were more aggressive than light men), a main effect for alcohol intake (alcohol made people more aggressive than the placebo), and a significant interaction. However, the overall difference (main effect) for body weight actually hides the fact that body weight influences aggressive behavior only when men are drunk. And the overall difference (main effect) for alcohol intake actually hides the fact that alcohol intake makes a difference *especially* for heavy men. So there may be real differences in the marginal means, but the exciting—and most accurate—story in this study is the interaction.

## POSSIBLE MAIN EFFECTS AND INTERACTIONS IN A 2 × 2 FACTORIAL DESIGN

**Figure 12.19** shows a variety of hypothetical outcomes from a single study. In all the examples, the independent variables are the same: a cell phone condition and an age condition. The dependent variable is the average number of accidents. This figure presents a variety of outcomes, all of which were invented in order to show different possible combinations of main effects and interactions in a 2 × 2 factorial design. Note, too, how each main effect and interaction can be described in words.

✔

### CHECK YOUR UNDERSTANDING

1. Describe why Bartholow and Heinz's word association study on alcohol and thoughts of aggression was a factorial design.

2. What are two common reasons to use a factorial design?

3. How can you detect an interaction from a table of means? From a line graph?

4. Why might it be better to call a main effect an "overall effect"?

1. It's factorial because they used all possible combinations of two independent variables; see p. 367.
2. See pp. 368–372. 3. See pp. 375–377. 4. See p. 375.

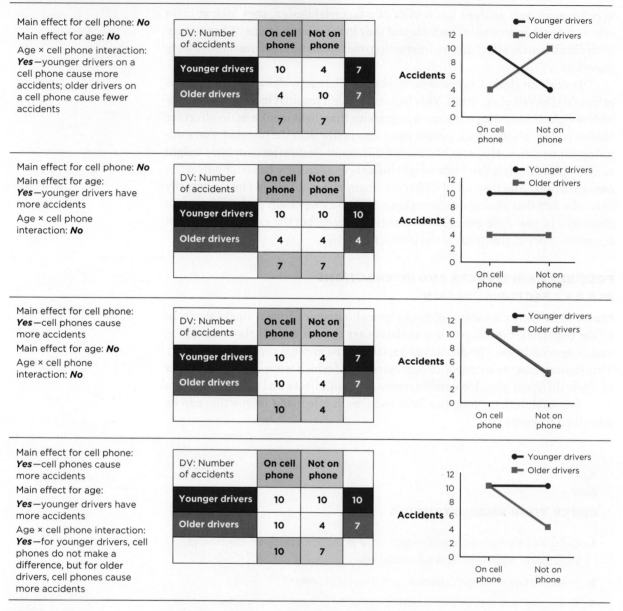

**FIGURE 12.19**

**A range of possible outcomes from a single 2 × 2 factorial design.**

Use this chart to study how various outcomes result in different patterns of main effects and interactions. (All data are fabricated for illustration purposes and error bars are omitted.)

| **Summary of effects** | **Cell means and marginal means** | **Line graph of the results** |
| --- | --- | --- |

Main effect for cell phone: **Yes**—cell phones cause more accidents

Main effect for age: **Yes**—older drivers have more accidents

Age × cell phone interaction: **Yes**—impact of a cell phone is larger for older than for younger drivers

| DV: Number of accidents | On cell phone | Not on phone | |
| --- | --- | --- | --- |
| **Younger drivers** | 8 | 2 | 5 |
| **Older drivers** | 12 | 3 | 7.5 |
| | 10 | 2.5 | |

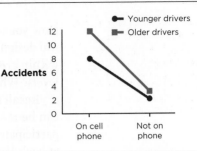

---

Main effect for cell phone: **No**

Main effect for age: **No**

Age × cell phone interaction: **No**

| DV: Number of accidents | On cell phone | Not on phone | |
| --- | --- | --- | --- |
| **Younger drivers** | 5 | 5 | 5 |
| **Older drivers** | 5 | 5 | 5 |
| | 5 | 5 | |

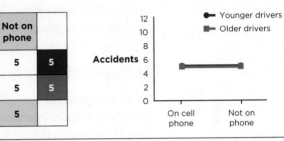

---

Main effect for cell phone: **Yes**—cell phones cause more accidents

Main effect for age: **No**

Age × cell phone interaction: **Yes**—for younger drivers, cell phones make no difference, but for older drivers, cell phones cause more accidents

| DV: Number of accidents | On cell phone | Not on phone | |
| --- | --- | --- | --- |
| **Younger drivers** | 5 | 5 | 5 |
| **Older drivers** | 8 | 2 | 5 |
| | 6.5 | 3.5 | |

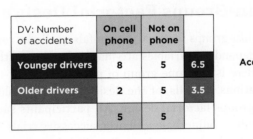
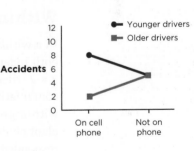

---

Main effect for cell phone: **No**

Main effect for age: **Yes**—younger drivers have more accidents

Age × cell phone interaction: **Yes**—for younger drivers, cell phones cause more accidents, but for older drivers, cell phones cause fewer accidents

| DV: Number of accidents | On cell phone | Not on phone | |
| --- | --- | --- | --- |
| **Younger drivers** | 8 | 5 | 6.5 |
| **Older drivers** | 2 | 5 | 3.5 |
| | 5 | 5 | |

# FACTORIAL VARIATIONS

Now you're ready to explore some advanced variations on the basic 2 × 2 factorial design. What happens when one of the independent variables is manipulated within groups? What happens when an independent variable has more than two levels? What if there's a third independent variable?

Recall from Chapter 10 that in a simple experiment, the independent variable can be manipulated as either an independent-groups variable (different people participate at each level) or a within-groups variable (the same people participate at each level, as in a repeated-measures design). The same is true for factorial designs. Researchers can choose whether to manipulate *each* independent variable as independent-groups or within-groups.

## Independent-Groups Factorial Designs

In an independent-groups factorial design (also known as a between-subjects factorial), both independent variables are studied as independent-groups. Therefore, if the design is a 2 × 2, there are four different groups of participants in the experiment. The DeWall team's study on alcohol, aggression, and body weight was an independent-groups factorial: Some lighter-weight men drank a placebo beverage, other light men drank an alcoholic one, some heavier men drank a placebo beverage, and other heavy men drank an alcoholic one. In other words, there were different people in each cell. If the researchers decided to use 50 participants in each cell of the design, they would have needed a full 200 participants: 50 in each of the four groups.

## Within-Groups Factorial Designs

In a within-groups factorial design (also called a repeated-measures factorial), both independent variables are manipulated as within-groups. If the design is 2 × 2, there is only one group of participants but they participate in all four combinations, or cells, of the design. The Bartholow and Heinz study was a within-groups factorial design. All participants saw both alcohol photos and plant photos, counterbalanced over successive trials. In addition, all participants responded to both aggression-related words and neutral words.

A within-groups factorial design requires fewer participants. If Bartholow and Heinz had decided to use 50 people in each cell of their study, they would need a total of only 50 people because every person participates in each of the four cells. Therefore, within-groups designs make efficient use of participants (**Figure 12.20**). Because it was a within-groups design, the researchers counterbalanced the order of presentation of photos and words by having the computer present the photos and their subsequent words in a different random order for each participant.

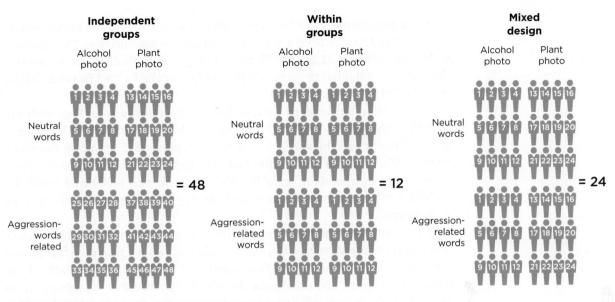

**FIGURE 12.20**
**Within-groups designs are more efficient.**
To achieve a goal of 12 observations per cell, an independent-groups factorial design would need 48 participants. A within-groups factorial design would require 12 participants, and a mixed design would require 24 participants.

## Mixed Factorial Designs

In a mixed factorial design, one independent variable is manipulated as independent-groups and the other is manipulated as within-groups. The Strayer and Drews study on cell phone use while driving for two different age groups is an example of a mixed factorial design. Age was an independent-groups participant variable: Participants in one group were younger and those in the other group were older. But the cell phone condition independent variable was manipulated as within-groups. Each participant drove in both the cell phone and the control conditions of the study. If Strayer and Drews had wanted 50 people in each cell of their 2 × 2 mixed design, they would have needed a total of 100 people: 50 younger drivers and 50 older drivers, each participating at both levels of the cell phone condition.

## Increasing the Number of Levels of an Independent Variable

The discussion so far has focused on the simplest factorial design, the 2 × 2. This design has two independent variables, each with two levels, creating four conditions (2 × 2 = 4). However, researchers can add more levels to each independent variable. For example, Strayer and Drews might have manipulated their cell phone condition using three levels (handheld cell phone, hands-free cell phone, and no cell phone) and then crossed it with age (older and younger drivers). This design is represented in **Figure 12.21**. It still has two independent variables, but one has two levels and the other has three levels. This design is called a 2 × 3 factorial design, and it results in six cells (2 × 3 = 6).

The notation for factorial designs follows a simple pattern. Factorials are notated in the form "— × —." The quantity of numbers indicates the number of independent variables (a 2 × 3 design is represented with two numbers, 2 and 3). The value of each of the numbers indicates how many levels there are for each independent variable (two levels for one and three levels for the other). When you multiply the two numbers, you get the total number of cells in the design.

What would happen if Strayer and Drews also increased the number of levels of the other independent variable, age? For example, what if they used four groups of drivers: drivers in their 20s, 30s, 50s, and 70s? If the cell phone condition had three levels and age had four levels, the new design would be represented as in **Figure 12.22**. There are still two independent variables, but one of them has three levels and the other has four levels. The new design is called a 3 × 4 factorial design, and it results in 12 cells (3 × 4 = 12).

When independent variables have more than two levels, researchers can still investigate main effects and interactions by computing the marginal means and seeing whether they are different. The easiest way to detect interactions is to plot the results on a line graph and see whether the lines run parallel. As in a 2 × 2 factorial design, statistical tests would confirm whether any of the main effects or interactions are statistically significant.

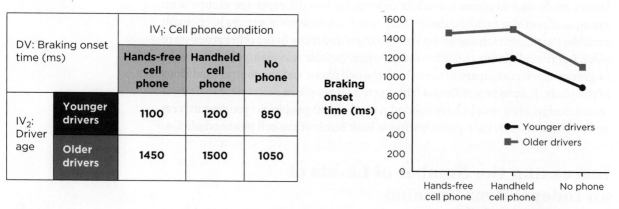

**FIGURE 12.21**

**A 2 × 3 factorial design.**

(Data are fabricated for illustration purposes and error bars are omitted.)

| DV: Braking onset time (ms) | | IV₁: Cell phone condition | | |
|---|---|---|---|---|
| | | **Hands-free cell phone** | **Handheld cell phone** | **No phone** |
| **IV₂: Driver age** | **Age 20–29** | 1100 | 1200 | 850 |
| | **Age 30–49** | 1120 | 1225 | 820 |
| | **Age 50–69** | 1300 | 1400 | 900 |
| | **Age 70+** | 1600 | 1500 | 1050 |

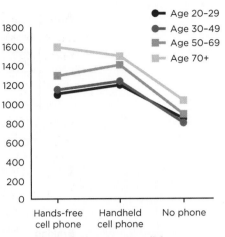

**FIGURE 12.22**

**A 3 × 4 factorial design.**

(Data are fabricated for illustration purposes and error bars are omitted.)

## Increasing the Number of Independent Variables

For some research questions, researchers find it necessary to have more than two independent variables in a crossed factorial design. For instance, suppose Strayer and Drews decided to study not only the cell phone independent variable and the age independent variable, but also two kinds of traffic conditions: dense traffic and light traffic. Would this third independent variable make a difference?

Such a design is called a 2 × 2 × 2 factorial, or a three-way design. There are two levels of the first independent variable, two levels of the second, and two levels of the third. This design would create eight cells, or conditions, in the experiment (2 × 2 × 2 = 8). The best way to depict a three-way design is to construct the original 2 × 2 table twice, once for each level of the third independent variable, as shown in **Figure 12.23A**. To graph a three-way design, you create two side-by-side line graphs, as shown in **Figure 12.23B**.

To make this study a three-way design, Strayer and Drews might manipulate the new variable as independent-groups, having some participants drive in light traffic only and others drive in heavy traffic only. Or they might manipulate the new variable as within-groups, having all participants drive in both light and heavy traffic. Either way, the design is considered a three-way factorial design.

### MAIN EFFECTS AND INTERACTIONS FROM A THREE-WAY DESIGN

When a factorial design has three independent variables, the number of differences to be investigated increases dramatically. In a three-way design, you are concerned with three main effects (one for each independent variable), plus three separate two-way interactions and a three-way interaction.

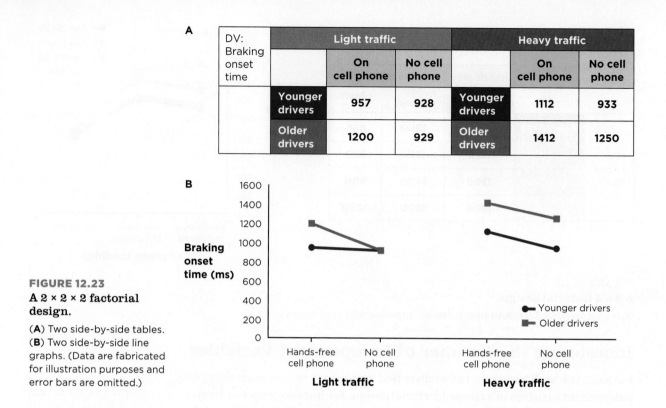

| DV: Braking onset time | Light traffic | | | Heavy traffic | | |
|---|---|---|---|---|---|---|
| | | **On cell phone** | **No cell phone** | | **On cell phone** | **No cell phone** |
| **Younger drivers** | | 957 | 928 | **Younger drivers** | 1112 | 933 |
| **Older drivers** | | 1200 | 929 | **Older drivers** | 1412 | 1250 |

**A**

**B**

**FIGURE 12.23**

**A 2 × 2 × 2 factorial design.**

(**A**) Two side-by-side tables. (**B**) Two side-by-side line graphs. (Data are fabricated for illustration purposes and error bars are omitted.)

## TABLE 12.1

### Main Effects in a Three-Way Factorial Design

**MAIN EFFECT FOR CELL PHONE VS. CONTROL**

| | |
|---|---|
| Cell phone (mean of 957, 1,200, 1,112, 1,412) | 1,170.25 |
| No cell phone (mean of 928, 929, 933, 1,250) | 1,010.00 |

**MAIN EFFECT FOR DRIVER AGE**

| | |
|---|---|
| Younger drivers (mean of 957, 928, 1,112, 933) | 982.50 |
| Older drivers (mean of 1,200, 929, 1,412, 1,250) | 1,197.75 |

**MAIN EFFECT FOR TRAFFIC CONDITIONS**

| | |
|---|---|
| Light traffic (mean of 957, 1,200, 928, 929) | 1,003.50 |
| Heavy traffic (mean of 1,112, 1,412, 933, 1,250) | 1,176.75 |

*Note*: To estimate each main effect in a three-way factorial design, you average the means for braking onset time for each level of each independent variable, ignoring the levels of the other two independent variables. The means come from Figure 12.23. (These estimates assume there are equal numbers of participants in each cell.)

**Main Effects: Is There a Difference?** Because there are three independent variables in a 2 × 2 × 2 design, there will be three main effects to test. Each main effect represents a simple, overall difference: the effect of one independent variable, averaged across the other two independent variables. **Table 12.1** shows how the three main effects were computed. Overall, people brake more slowly in the cell phone condition than in the control condition. Overall, older drivers brake more slowly than younger drivers. And overall, people are slower to brake in heavy traffic than in light traffic. Remember that main effects test only one independent variable at a time. When describing each main effect, you don't mention the other two independent variables because you averaged across them.

**Two-Way Interactions: Is There a Difference in Differences?** In a three-way design, there are three possible two-way interactions. In the driving with cell phone example, these would be:

1. Age × traffic condition (a two-way interaction averaging over the cell phone condition variable).
2. Age × cell phone condition (a two-way interaction averaging over the traffic conditions variable).
3. Cell phone condition × traffic condition (a two-way interaction averaging over the age variable).

To inspect each of these two-way interactions, you construct three 2 × 2 tables, as in **Figure 12.24**. After computing the means, you can investigate the difference

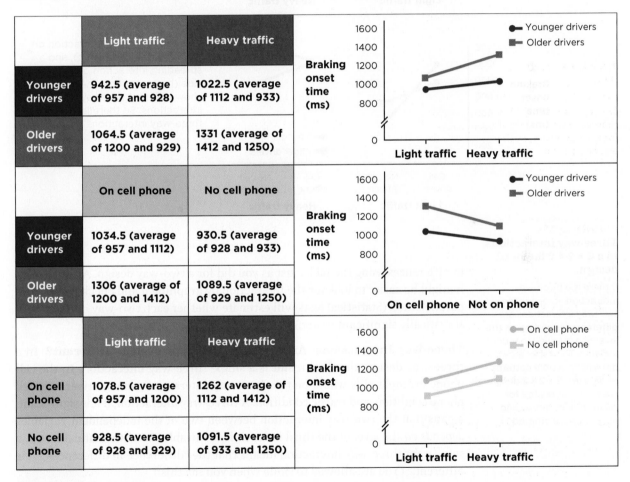

**FIGURE 12.24**

**Two-way interactions in a 2 × 2 × 2 factorial design.**

Data are recombined to estimate the three two-way interactions in this study. The means come from Figure 12.23. (Data are fabricated for illustration purposes and error bars are omitted.)

| Possible outcome | Is there a three-way interaction? |
|---|---|

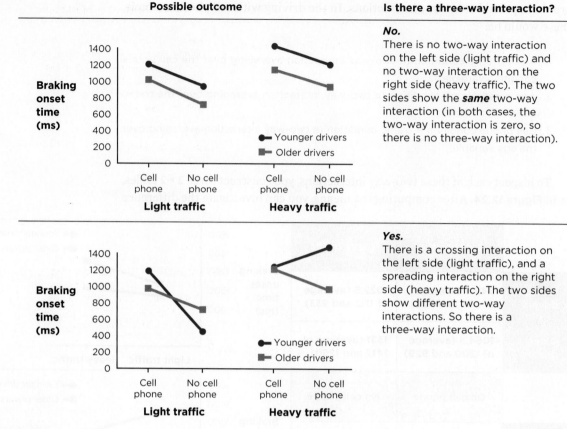

**No.**
There is no two-way interaction on the left side (light traffic) and no two-way interaction on the right side (heavy traffic). The two sides show the *same* two-way interaction (in both cases, the two-way interaction is zero, so there is no three-way interaction).

**Yes.**
There is a crossing interaction on the left side (light traffic), and a spreading interaction on the right side (heavy traffic). The two sides show different two-way interactions. So there is a three-way interaction.

**FIGURE 12.25**
**Three-way interactions in a 2 × 2 × 2 factorial design.**

If there is a three-way interaction, it means the two-way interactions are different, depending on the level of a third independent variable. This table shows different possible patterns of data in a 2 × 2 × 2 design. (Data are fabricated for illustration purposes and error bars are omitted.)

in differences using the table, just as you did for a two-way design. Alternatively, it might be easier to look for the interaction by graphing it and checking for non-parallel lines. (Statistical tests will estimate whether each two-way interaction is statistically significant or not.)

**Three-Way Interactions: Are the Two-Way Interactions Different?** In a three-way design, the final result is a single three-way interaction. In the cell phone example, this would be the three-way interaction among driver age, cell phone condition, and traffic condition. A three-way interaction, if it is significant, means that the two-way interaction between two of the independent variables *depends on* the level of the third independent variable. In mathematical terms, a significant three-way interaction means that the "difference in differences . . . is different." (You are allowed to smile when you say this.)

A three-way interaction is easiest to detect by looking at line graphs of the data. Look again at Figure 12.23B. Notice that in light traffic, there's a two-way

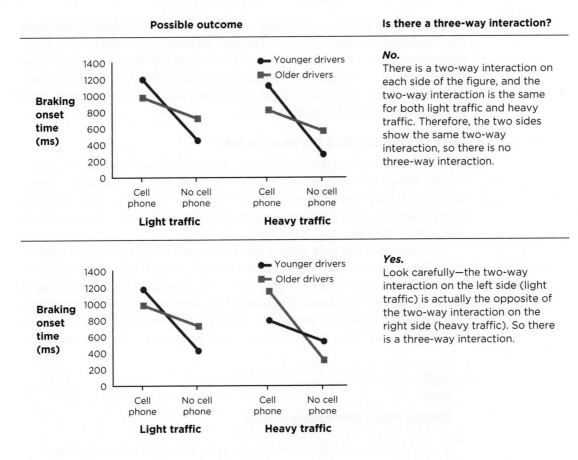

| Possible outcome | Is there a three-way interaction? |
|---|---|

**No.**
There is a two-way interaction on each side of the figure, and the two-way interaction is the same for both light traffic and heavy traffic. Therefore, the two sides show the same two-way interaction, so there is no three-way interaction.

**Yes.**
Look carefully—the two-way interaction on the left side (light traffic) is actually the opposite of the two-way interaction on the right side (heavy traffic). So there is a three-way interaction.

interaction between driver age and cell phone condition, but in heavy traffic, there is no two-way interaction between these two independent variables. The two-way interaction of driver age × cell phone condition therefore depends on the level of traffic conditions. In other words, there is a difference in differences for the light traffic side of the graph, but there is no difference in differences for the heavy traffic side of the graph.

You would find a three-way interaction whenever there is a two-way interaction for one level of a third independent variable but not for the other (because the two-way interactions are different—there is a two-way interaction on one side but not on the other). You will also find a three-way interaction if a graph shows one pattern of two-way interaction on one side but a different pattern of two-way interaction on the other side—in other words, if there are different two-way interactions. However, if you found the same kind of two-way interaction for both levels of the third independent variable, there would not be a three-way interaction. **Figure 12.25** shows some of the possible outcomes of a three-way design.

Factorial designs are a useful way of testing theories and exploring outcomes that depend on multiple factors, and they provide researchers with a way of quantifying the interactions they want to study. Of course, a study can have more than three independent variables, and some may have four or five. With each additional independent variable (or factor), the researchers will be looking at more main effects and even more kinds of interactions.

## WHY TEST ALL THESE INTERACTIONS?

Managing two-way and three-way interactions can be complicated, but in studying psychology and in thinking about daily life, you need to understand interaction effects. Why? Because we don't live in a main effect world. Most outcomes in psychological science studies—and, by extension, in life—are not main effects; they are interactions.

Consider again this main effect question: Is it good to be forgiving in a relationship? The answer would reflect an interaction: It depends on how serious the problems are in the relationship (McNulty, 2010). Here's the other: Does daycare lead to social and emotional problems in children? This has an interaction answer as well: It depends on the quality of the daycare. It might even have a three-way interaction answer: It depends on the quality of the care *and* the nature of the home environment.

✔️

**CHECK YOUR UNDERSTANDING**

1. Describe how the same 2 × 2 design might be conducted as an independent-groups factorial, a within-groups factorial, or a mixed factorial design. Explain how different designs change the number of participants required: Which design requires the most? Which requires the fewest?

2. What does the notation (e.g., 2 × 2, 3 × 4, 2 × 2 × 3) indicate about the number of independent variables in a study? How does it convey the number of cells?

3. In a 2 × 2 × 2 design, what is the number of main effects and interactions?

4. Describe how you can tell whether a study has a three-way interaction.

1. See pp. 382-383; an independent-groups factorial requires the most participants, and a within-in-groups factorial requires the fewest. 2. A 3 x 4 design has two independent variables, one with three levels and one with four levels; see pp. 383-385. 3. See pp. 385-389; three main effects, three two-way interactions, and one three-way interaction. 4. See pp. 388-390 and Figure 12.25.

## IDENTIFYING FACTORIAL DESIGNS IN YOUR READING

Whether you're reading original research published in a journal or secondhand reports of research published in the popular media, certain clues will alert you that the study had a factorial design.

# Identifying Factorial Designs in Empirical Journal Articles

In an empirical journal article, researchers almost always describe the design they used in the Method section. You can tell the researchers used a factorial design if they refer to their study as a 2 × 2 design, a 3 × 2 design, a 2 × 2 × 2 design, or the like. Such descriptions indicate the number of independent variables in the study as well as how many levels there were for each independent variable.

In the study on using a cell phone while driving, for example, the researchers describe their experimental design as follows:

> The design was a 2 (Age: Younger vs. Older adults) × 2 (Task: Single- vs. Dual-task) factorial. Age was a between-subjects factor and the single- vs. dual-task condition was a within-subjects factor. (Strayer & Drews, 2004, p. 643)

In their article, they use "dual-task" for driving while using a cell phone and "single-task" for driving without a cell phone. Notice that Strayer and Drews use the notation 2 × 2, labeling each independent variable in parentheses. They also specify that the design was factorial. You can also infer they used a mixed factorial design because they mention that one independent variable was independent-groups ("between-subjects") and one was within-groups ("within-subjects").

Whereas the Method section outlines the study's design, independent variables, and dependent variables, the Results section of an empirical journal article discusses whether the main effects and interactions are significant. Authors may include the 95% CI, use the term *significant*, the notation $p < 0.05$, or even an asterisk in a table to indicate that a main effect or interaction is statistically significant. Here is how Strayer and Drews described the main effects and interactions in their study:

> The MANOVA indicated significant main effects of age, $F(4, 35) = 8.74$, $p < 0.01$, and single- vs. dual-task, $F(4, 35) = 11.44$, $p < 0.01$. However, the Age × Single-vs. Dual-Task interaction was not significant, $F(4, 35) = 1.46$, $p = 0.23$. This latter finding suggests that older adults do not suffer a significantly greater penalty for talking on a cell phone while driving than do their younger counterparts. (Strayer & Drews, 2004, p. 644)

Your statistics course will teach you what MANOVA and *F* mean in the quoted text above, but you should now be able to recognize the terms *main effect*, *interaction*, and *significant*.

# Identifying Factorial Designs in Popular Media Articles

Whereas empirical journal articles must specify what kind of design was used in a study, popular media articles usually do not. Media outlets probably assume most of their readers would not know what a 2 × 2 factorial design means. Indeed, most journalists gloss over the details of an experimental design to make their articles simpler. However, you can detect a factorial design from a report if you know what to look for.

Here's an example of how a journalist described the DeWall study on alcohol use, aggressive behavior, and body weight in the online news outlet *Pacific Standard*. After explaining the study in some detail, the journalist described the interaction like this: "The researchers found that alcohol, compared to placebo, increased aggression among the heavier men but had little effect on the lighter men" (Best, 2010).

In other cases, you may need to read between the lines in order to know that a study had a factorial design. There are certain clues you can look for to identify factorial designs in the popular media.

## LOOK FOR "IT DEPENDS" OR "ONLY WHEN"

Journalists might gloss over the details of a factorial design, but sometimes they will use a phrase like "it depends" or "only when" to highlight an interaction in a report of a factorial design. This example uses "it depends" to describe which kind of music improves memory:

> The research suggests that it may help, but it depends upon a variety of factors. . . . One study found that musically trained students tended to perform better on learning tests when they listened to neutral music . . . [but] musically naïve students . . . learned better when listening to positive music. (Cherry, 2019)

The example starts with the dependent variable of how much people learn. It mentions one factor (type of music: neutral or positive) as well as a second factor (degree of musical training), using "it depends" to describe the interaction. The relationship between type of music and performance on a learning test depends on a person's musical training.

The passage below describes a 2 × 2 within-groups factorial design in which dogs were trained to willingly lie still in an MRI machine (Andics et al., 2016). The dogs' brains were scanned while the researchers played different words through dog-size headphones (**Figure 12.26**). The researchers were investigating whether dogs' brains process only the intonation of speech, only the lexical content (the words), or both. The CNN reporter uses "only when" to describe the interaction effect:

> Positive or meaningful words such as "well done," "good boy" and "clever" were said in both a praising intonation and a neutral intonation. Neutral or meaningless words, such as "even if," "although" and "however," also were said in both intonations. Only when a praise word was spoken to the dogs in a praising tone of voice did the brain's reward center light up like a Christmas tree in the brain scans. The reward center is the part of the brain that responds to pleasurable stimuli, like food treats or being petted. (Howard, 2016)

**FIGURE 12.26**
**Dogs as subjects in a factorial design.**
According to a study covered in the popular media, researchers learned that, like the human brain, a dog's brain processes both the emotional tone and the lexical content of speech.

This description introduces all four conditions of the factorial first. Then it uses "only when" to explain how one independent variable (type of word: praise words or meaningless words) interacted with the other independent variable (tone of voice: praising tone or neutral tone). The dependent variable was activity in the brain's reward center. Can you sketch a graph of the result described in the dog MRI study?

## LOOK FOR PARTICIPANT VARIABLES

You can sometimes detect factorial designs when journalists discuss a participant variable such as age, personality, gender, or ethnicity. In such stories, the participant variable often moderates another independent variable. And when there is a moderator, there is an interaction (as well as a factorial design to test it).

The following example describes a factorial design with a participant variable (self-esteem). The journalist does not mention the study's factors or design. But you can tell there's an interaction because the author describes different responses to the intervention for participants with high and low self-esteem:

> Joanne Wood of the University of Waterloo in Ontario and two colleagues conducted experiments in which they asked students to repeat statements to themselves such as "I am a lovable person" and then measured how it affected their mood. But in one of their studies involving 32 male and 36 female psychology students, the researchers found that repeating the phrase did not improve the mood of those who had low self-esteem, as measured by a standard test. They actually ended up feeling worse, and the gap between those with high and low self-esteem widened. (Stein, 2009)

The statement "the gap between those with high and low self-esteem widened" is a sign that there was a difference in differences—an interaction (probably a spreading interaction). Because the journalist mentions that mood improved, you can infer the dependent variable was mood. One factor in this design was self-esteem (high or low); the other was whether or not the participants repeated the statement "I am a lovable person." You can work more with this study in the Review Questions and Learning Actively sections at the end of the chapter.

## CHECK YOUR UNDERSTANDING

1. In an empirical journal article, in what section will you find the independent and dependent variables of the study's design? In what section will you find whether the main effects and interactions are statistically significant?

2. Describe at least two cues indicating that a story in the popular media is probably describing a factorial design.

1. The Method section lists the variables and design; the Results section reports the significance of main effects and interactions; see p. 391. 2. You can look for phrases such as "it depends" or for participant variables; see pp. 392–294.

# CHAPTER REVIEW

 It's time to complete your study experience!  Go to INQUIZITIVE to practice actively with this chapter's concepts and get personalized feedback along the way.

## Summary

Simple experiments involve one independent variable and one dependent variable. Many hypotheses in psychological science are more complex; they involve studying two or more independent variables.

### REVIEW: EXPERIMENTS WITH ONE INDEPENDENT VARIABLE

- In a study with one independent variable, researchers look for a simple difference, such as the difference between being drunk or sober or the difference between being on a cell phone or not.

### EXPERIMENTS WITH TWO INDEPENDENT VARIABLES CAN SHOW INTERACTIONS

- When testing more than one variable, researchers are testing for interactions, asking whether the effect of one independent variable depends on the level of the other one. An interaction is a "difference in differences."

- Factorial designs cross two or more independent variables, creating conditions (cells) that represent every possible combination of the levels of each independent variable.

- Factorial designs can describe multiple influences on behavior; they enable researchers to test their theories and determine whether some manipulation affects one type of person more than another.

- Analyzing the data from a factorial design involves looking for main effects for each independent variable by estimating the marginal means, then looking for interaction effects by checking for a difference

in differences (in a line graph, interactions appear as nonparallel lines).

- When there is an interaction effect, it is more important than any main effects found.

### FACTORIAL VARIATIONS

- The factors can be independent-groups or within-groups variables; the factors can be manipulated (independent) variables or measured, participant variables.

- When a factorial design has three or more independent variables, the number of interactions increases to include all possible combinations of the independent variables.

- In a design with three independent variables, the three-way interaction tests whether two-way interactions are the same at the levels of the third independent variable.

### IDENTIFYING FACTORIAL DESIGNS IN YOUR READING

- In empirical journal articles, the type of design is given in the Method section.

- In popular media stories, factorial designs may be indicated by language such as "it depends" and "only when," or descriptions of both participant variables and independent variables.

## Key Terms

interaction effect, p. 365
factorial design, p. 367

cell, p. 367
participant variable, p. 368

main effect, p. 373
marginal means, p. 374

# Review Questions

To investigate the effect of positive self-statements on mood, psychologist Joanne Wood and her colleagues recruited people with different levels of self-esteem (Wood et al., 2009). Participants wrote down their thoughts and feelings for 4 minutes. The researchers randomly assigned half the participants to repeat to themselves a positive self-statement, "I am a lovable person," at 15-second intervals (cued by a bell sound). The other half did not repeat this statement. After the 4-minute session, all participants completed a subtle measure of positive mood. Here are the results:

| DV: POSITIVE MOOD | LOW SELF-ESTEEM PARTICIPANTS | HIGH SELF-ESTEEM PARTICIPANTS |
|---|---|---|
| "I am a lovable person" | 11.18 | 30.47 |
| No statement | 16.94 | 24.59 |

1. Why might the Wood team have conducted their study as a factorial design?

   a. To test how well positive self-statements work, compared to no statements.

   b. To compare the moods of high self-esteem and low self-esteem people.

   c. To test whether the effect of positive self-statements would depend on a person's level of self-esteem.

2. What are the factors in this study?

   a. Self-esteem level: high versus low

   b. Self-statement instructions: positive versus none

   c. Self-esteem level: high versus low; and self-statement instructions: positive versus none

   d. Positive mood

3. There is an interaction in the results. How do you know?

   a. When the cell means are graphed, the lines are not parallel.

   b. The difference between low and high self-esteem is larger for the positive self-statement condition and smaller for the "no statement" condition.

   c. Positive self-statements raised the mood of high self-esteem people and lowered the mood of low self-esteem people.

   d. All of the above.

4. Which of the following sentences describes the *main effect for self-esteem* in the Wood study?

   a. Overall, the moods of high self-esteem people are more positive than the moods of low self-esteem people.

   b. Mood depended on both the participants' level of self-esteem and what self-statement condition they were in.

   c. Overall, the moods of people in the "I am a lovable person" condition are about the same as the moods of people in the "no statement" condition.

   d. Positive self-statements raised the moods of high self-esteem people and lowered the moods of low self-esteem people.

5. This study is an example of a(n):

   a. Independent-groups factorial design

   b. Within-groups factorial design

   c. Mixed factorial design

6. Suppose these researchers ran their study again, but this time they compared how high or low self-esteem people responded to three kinds of statements: Positive self-statements, negative self-statements, and no statements. What kind of design would this be?

   a. 2 × 2

   b. 2 × 3

   c. 2 × 2 × 2

   d. 6 × 1

# Learning Actively

1. Create a line graph from the data in the Review Questions above (the study by Wood et al., 2009). Create the graph both ways: with *self-statement type* on the *x*-axis (representing the two levels of self-statement with two different lines) and with *self-esteem level* on the *x*-axis (with the two self-esteem levels as the two lines). Describe the interaction you see.

2. For practice, compute the marginal means in the two studies shown in the figures below. (Assume each cell has an equal number of participants.) You would need significance tests to be sure, but does it look as if there will be significant main effects for both the cell phone condition and driver age? Why or why not? Does it look as if there are main effects for participant type and the type of item to remember? Why or why not?

| DV: Braking onset time (ms) | IV₁: Cell phone condition | | |
|---|---|---|---|
| | **Cell phone** | **Not on phone** | Main effect for IV₂: Driver age |
| IV₂: Driver age — **Younger drivers** | 912 | 780 | |
| **Older drivers** | 1086 | 912 | |
| Main effect for IV₁: Cell phone condition | | | |

| DV: Items recalled | IV₁: Participant type | | |
|---|---|---|---|
| | **Child chess experts** | **Adult novices** | Main effect for IV₂: Type of item |
| IV₂: Type of item — **Chess pieces** | 9.3 | 5.9 | |
| **Digits** | 6.1 | 7.8 | |
| Main effect for IV₁: Participant type | | | |

3. In one of their studies, Strayer and his students tested whether people would get better at driving while talking on a cell phone if they practiced doing so (Cooper & Strayer, 2008). They had participants drive in a simulator while talking on a hands-free cell phone and while not talking on a phone. The same people participated over several days, so they had a chance to practice this multitasking. On the first day, they were considered to be least experienced; on the last day, the most experienced. On the last day, they were tested in both a familiar environment and a slightly different driving environment, to see if the first days of practice would transfer to a new context. The researchers collected data on how many collisions (accidents) the drivers got into on the simulator at each testing point. Here are their cell means:

| | NUMBER OF COLLISIONS | | |
|---|---|---|---|
| | DAY 1 | DAY 4 (DRIVING IN A FAMILIAR CONTEXT) | DAY 4 (DRIVING IN A NEW CONTEXT) |
| Single-task (not using cell phone) | 15 | 6 | 10 |
| Dual-task (using cell phone) | 20 | 7.5 | 24 |

   a. What kind of design is this? (Put your answer in the form "___ × ___.")

   b. What are the independent and dependent variables?

   c. Indicate whether each independent variable was manipulated as independent-groups or within-groups.

   d. Create a line graph depicting these results.

   e. Estimate and describe any main effects and interactions in this study. (Of course, you would need statistics to determine if the observed effects are statistically significant.)

   f. What might you conclude from the results of this study? Does experience affect cell phone use while driving?

4. Are participant variables independent-groups variables or within-groups variables? Why?

# PART VI

# Balancing Research Priorities

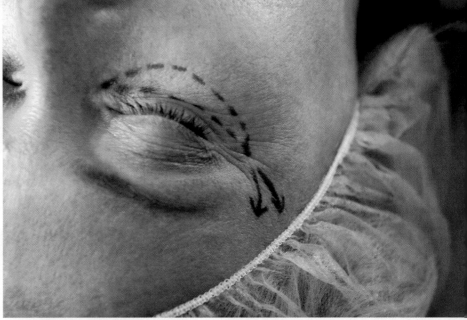

"What if you can't randomly assign participants to the independent variable levels?"

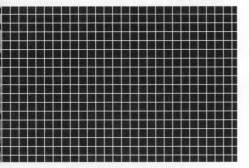

"What is the value of an experiment with just one participant?"

# Quasi-Experiments and Small-*N* Designs

PREVIOUS CHAPTERS HAVE EXPLAINED how to interrogate frequency claims (Chapters 6 and 7), association claims (Chapters 8 and 9), and causal claims (Chapters 10–12). The last two chapters focus on a more general issue: how researchers balance priorities while conducting their studies. Of course, psychological scientists always want to carry out the best studies possible, but they are constrained by logistical issues, and they must perform their work ethically. How do they balance their research goals with practical realities?

This chapter discusses situations in which conducting a true experiment is not feasible. For example, a researcher might not be able to randomly assign participants to different groups or counterbalance conditions in a within-groups experiment. What are the trade-offs? Can they achieve internal validity when full experimental control is impossible? Sometimes researchers may be able to collect data from only one case, such as a single child or a person with an unusual behavioral problem. How can they balance priorities for internal and external validity when they're studying just a single instance?

## QUASI-EXPERIMENTS

**Quasi-experiments** differ from true experiments in that the researchers do not have full experimental control. They start by selecting an independent variable and a dependent variable. Then they

## LEARNING OBJECTIVES

**A year from now, you should still be able to:**

**1.**
Articulate how quasi-experiments differ from true experiments.

**2.**
Use the design and results of quasi-experiments to evaluate the support they provide for causal claims.

**3.**
Explain the major differences between small-*N* designs and large-*N* designs.

**4.**
Use the design and results of small-*N* experiments to evaluate the support they provide for causal claims.

study participants who are exposed to each level of the independent variable. However, in a quasi-experiment, the researchers might not be able to randomly assign participants to one level or the other; they are assigned by teachers, political regulations, acts of nature—or even by their own choice.

## Four Examples of Quasi-Experiments

There are many possible quasi-experimental designs (Shadish et al., 2002). This section introduces four common designs. Each design has an "independent" variable and a dependent variable. Because the researchers do not have full experimental control over the independent variable, we usually call it a **quasi-independent variable**.

### NUDGING PEOPLE TOWARD ORGAN DONATION

Around the world, thousands of people with severe illnesses wait for a suitable donor organ, and many die before one becomes available. Public health researchers have explored ways to increase the number of people who consent to be organ donors.

Organ donation options are framed differently in different countries. Some are framed as opt-in, in which people must take some action (such as checking a box or sending a letter) to express their intent to be an organ donor. Other countries use presumed consent, or opt-out, in which people must take action to *not* to be a donor. These opt-in and opt-out procedures are called *default options*. People are likely to accept default options when making decisions because defaults are effortless (Thaler & Sunstein, 2008). People may also interpret default options as the socially approved course of action.

Researchers Eric Johnson and Daniel Goldstein (2003) tested the effect of default option framing on organ donation rates. They collected data on the numbers of people who consented to organ donation in 11 European countries. As you can see in **Figure 13.1**, the rates of consent for organ donation are almost 100% in most of the countries that use presumed consent as the default. But rates are much lower in the countries that require action to become an organ donor.

In this study, there is a quasi-independent variable (the two default consent options) and a dependent variable (the rate of organ donation). But researchers did not control which countries had which defaults, and people were not randomly assigned to live in the different countries. Therefore, it's a quasi-experiment. The design is called a **nonequivalent control group posttest-only design** because the participants were not randomly assigned to groups and were tested only once, after exposure to one level of the independent variable or the other.

The authors titled their article "Defaults save lives"; in other words, when countries adopt a presumed consent default, it causes much higher rates of organ

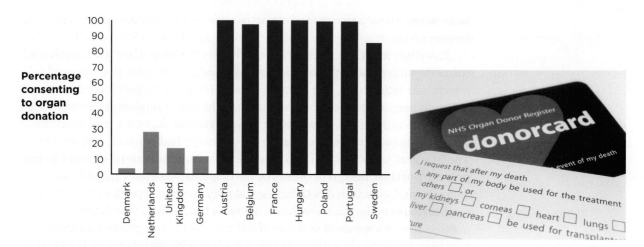

**FIGURE 13.1**

**Defaults save lives.**

Some countries (red bars) require people to take action to become an organ donor; others (blue bars) require people to take action in order to opt out. The rates of organ donation in the population are much higher in countries with opt-out systems. (Source: Johnson & Goldstein, 2003.)

donation. As you read the rest of this chapter, consider what these results mean: Do you think the study supports their causal conclusion?

## THE PSYCHOLOGICAL EFFECTS OF COSMETIC SURGERY

Around the world, plastic surgeons perform about 10.2 million cosmetic surgeries each year (International Society of Aesthetic Plastic Surgery, 2017). Anecdotal evidence indicates that people who undergo such procedures think they'll improve their body image, self-esteem, and overall sense of well-being. But does cosmetic surgery really achieve these results? One approach would be to randomly assign people to have plastic surgery or not. In normal circumstances, though, this would not be ethically or practically feasible because researchers cannot assign people to undergo an unnecessary and possibly risky surgery.

A team of psychological scientists found another way to study the effects of cosmetic surgery (Margraf et al., 2013). They recruited a sample of about 600 patients at a clinic in Germany who had already elected to undergo plastic surgery. The researchers measured this group's self-esteem, life satisfaction, self-rated general attractiveness, and other variables at four time periods: before surgery and then 3 months, 6 months, and 1 year after surgery. As a comparison group, the researchers located a sample of about 250 people who had registered at the same plastic surgery clinic, having indicated their interest in receiving surgery, but who ultimately decided not to have any procedures. This comparison group filled out the self-esteem, life satisfaction, and attractiveness measures at the same times as the surgery group.

This study looks like an experiment. There is an independent variable (having cosmetic surgery or not), and there are dependent variables (measures of self-esteem, life satisfaction, and attractiveness). However, the participants were not randomly assigned to the two conditions, and the lack of random assignment made this a quasi-experiment. People were self-assigned to the two quasi-independent variable groups according to whether they actually had cosmetic surgery or not. The Margraf team's study is an example of a **nonequivalent control group pretest/posttest design** because the participants were not randomly assigned to groups and were tested both before and after some intervention.

The results of the study are shown in **Figure 13.2**. Although both groups started out the same on a standard measure of self-esteem, the two groups had diverged a year later. Similarly, the surgery group started out with slightly higher life satisfaction and general attractiveness than the comparison group, and the surgery group had increased on these measures 1 year later. Does this study allow us to say that the cosmetic surgery *caused* people's self-image and life satisfaction to improve?

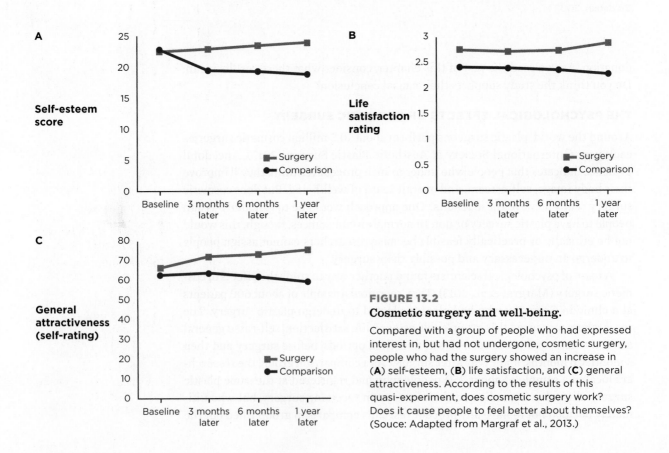

**FIGURE 13.2**

**Cosmetic surgery and well-being.**

Compared with a group of people who had expressed interest in, but had not undergone, cosmetic surgery, people who had the surgery showed an increase in (**A**) self-esteem, (**B**) life satisfaction, and (**C**) general attractiveness. According to the results of this quasi-experiment, does cosmetic surgery work? Does it cause people to feel better about themselves? (Souce: Adapted from Margraf et al., 2013.)

## POPULAR SHOWS AND SUICIDE

Netflix introduced the series *13 Reasons Why* in late March 2017. The show is organized around the suicide of a 17-year-old character named Hannah. In each episode, Hannah describes a reason she decided to kill herself, and one of the early episodes originally depicted Hannah's suicide in graphic detail. Millions of people watched the show and discussed it on social media.

Some mental health advocates cautioned that the show depicted suicide irresponsibly. These critics argued that the series presented suicide as a person's only solution for their suffering. They also worried that the show would lead to copycat suicides or self-harm.

A team of researchers set out to investigate the effect of the show on suicide rates in the United States (Niederkrotenthaler et al., 2019). First, they used social media data to determine the exact months of the year when the show was being discussed. The show debuted on March 21, 2017, and public attention was highest during the four weeks of April 2017, as measured by how many mentions of the show appeared on Twitter and Instagram (**Figure 13.3**).

Next, Niederkrotenthaler and his team investigated whether suicide rates were different during April 2017, when the show was getting the most attention, compared with other months. Using a public database maintained by the Centers for Disease Control (CDC), they recorded the total number of suicides among

≪

The National Suicide Prevention Lifeline is available in the U.S., 24 hours a day, at 1-800-273-8255. In Canada, the number is 1-833-456-4566.

≪

To review reasoning biases, see Chapter 2, pp. 30–35.

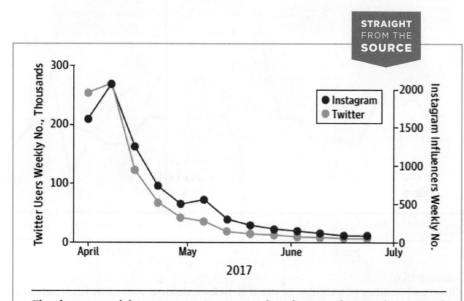

STRAIGHT FROM THE **SOURCE**

The show earned the most attention on social media in April 2017, when 84% of Twitter users and 74% of Instagram influencers posted about the show for the first time within the period analyzed.

**FIGURE 13.3**
**Social Media Attention to *13 Reasons Why*.**

The researchers tracked mentions of the show on Instagram (*y*-axis on the right) and Twitter (*y*-axis on the left) for the weeks before and after the show's release by counting the terms *13RW*, *13 Reasons Why*, *Thirteen reasons why*, *Hannah Baker*, and *Clay Jensen* (Source: Neiderkrotenthaler et al., 2019).

people aged 10 to 19 for each month of the years 2016 and 2017. They plotted the results month by month (**Figure 13.4**), noting a spike in April. (For comparison, they also plotted each month's suicide rate across the previous 18 years.)

The *13 Reasons Why* study is an example of an **interrupted time-series design**. This quasi-experimental design measures a variable repeatedly (in this example, suicide rates in the United States)—before, during, and after the "interruption" caused by some event (in this case, a show's release). Niederkrotenthaler and his team concluded that suicides were 13.3% higher among young people in the 3 months after the series appeared (with a confidence interval of 5.5 to 21.1%) compared with suicide rates for 18 previous Aprils. What do you think: Was the Netflix series responsible for this increase in suicides?

### INVESTIGATING THE EFFECT OF LEGISLATION ON OPIOID ABUSE

Another quasi-experiment took advantage of variability in state laws to investigate whether local policies could slow the opioid crisis in the United States. In 1996, OxyContin (a brand name for extended-release oxycodone) was introduced in the United States. People discovered ways to avoid the time-release nature of the drug and abuse it, and many became addicted. Since that year, more than

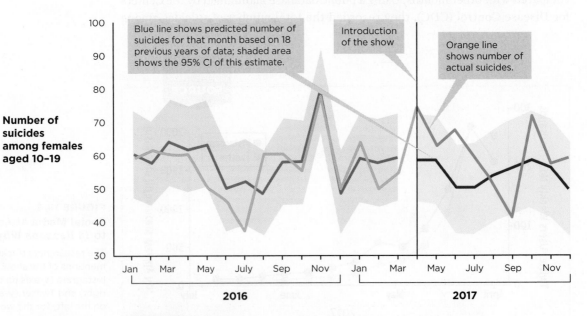

**FIGURE 13.4**

**Observed number of suicides in the U.S. before, during, and after high rates of social media attention to *13 Reasons Why*.**

The vertical line marks April 2017, when the show was first released and social media attention was the highest. The blue line and the shaded area around it represent the average suicide rate and 95% CI in each month for the previous 18 years. The observed suicide rate in April 2017 was outside the 95% CI, which means that the 2017 rate was abnormally high compared with previous Aprils. (Sources: Data from CDC; graphic adapted from Niederkrotenthaler et al., 2019.)

400,000 Americans have died of opioid drug overdoses. The opioid crisis has multiple causes, including changing medical views about pain management, users' despair at poor economic conditions, and aggressive drug marketing practices by Perdue Pharma, the company that produces OxyContin (Alpert, et al., 2019).

Individual states implemented various laws to try to control the crisis. For example, some states began targeting so-called "pill mills," freestanding pain clinics that prescribed and dispensed pain medication, meaning that patients could walk out with large quantities of opioids. In the state of Florida, pain clinics proliferated between 2003 and 2010, and opioid overdose deaths increased alarmingly (Centers for Disease Control and Prevention, 2011).

Starting in 2010, Florida's state government passed laws that prevented pain clinics from dispensing medications on-site and increased criminal penalties for doctors who broke the new laws. Two successful sting operations by federal law enforcement also targeted pill mills in 2011 and 2012.

Did the tough new policies work? A team of public health researchers investigated this question by comparing Florida to a nearby state, North Carolina (Kennedy-Hendricks, et al., 2016). Both states are in the Southeast and have similar poverty levels and median incomes. North Carolina's overdose trajectory was similar to Florida's, but it had passed no new laws during the target time, 2010-12. The researchers tracked opioid overdose deaths from 2003 to 2013. **Figure 13.5**

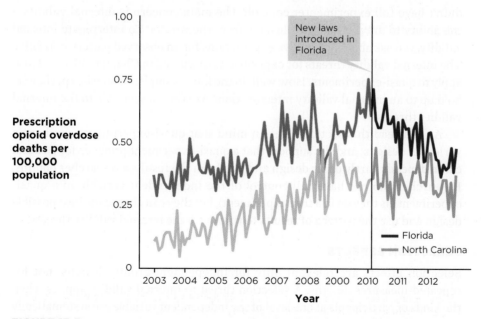

**FIGURE 13.5**

**Prescription opioid and heroin overdose death rates in two U.S. states.**

Prescription opioid overdose rates were increasing between 2003 and 2010 in both Florida and North Carolina. But only Florida showed a decrease in the rate of prescription overdoses after they instituted several anti-pill mill laws between 2010 and 2012; North Carolina's rate leveled off but did not decline. (Source: Kennedy-Hendricks, et al., 2016)

displays the opioid death rates for prescription opioids (i.e., OxyContin) in both Florida and North Carolina. Before 2010, overdoses were rising dramatically in both places. But after 2010, overdose rates, in Florida only, started to decline.

The Kennedy-Hendricks study used a **nonequivalent control group interrupted time-series design**, which combines two of the previous designs (the nonequivalent control group design and the interrupted time-series design). The two states were not randomly assigned to having the pill mill laws or not (that's the nonequivalent control group). And researchers did not have experimental control over the year the laws were passed (that's the interrupted time series). The lack of full experimenter control is what made the study a quasi-experiment. In this study, one quasi-independent variable was pill-mill laws: Florida had passed them but North Carolina did not. Another quasi-independent variable was time period: before and after the new laws. The dependent variable was overdose rates from prescription opioids.

## Internal Validity in Quasi-Experiments

Each of the four previous examples looks like a true experiment: Each one has an independent variable and a dependent variable. What is missing in every case is full experimenter control over the independent variable.

What did the researchers give up when they conducted studies in which they didn't have full experimenter control? The main concern is internal validity—the ability to draw causal conclusions from the results. To interrogate internal validity, you ask about alternative explanations for an observed pattern of results. The internal validity threats for experiments discussed in Chapters 10 and 11 also apply to quasi-experiments. How well do the four examples of quasi-experiments hold up to an internal validity interrogation? Are they susceptible to the internal validity threats?

As you read this section, keep in mind that quasi-experiments can have a variety of designs, and the support that a quasi-experiment provides for a causal claim depends partly on its design and partly on the results a researcher obtains. Researchers do not have full control of the independent variable in a quasi-experiment (as they do in a true experiment), but they can choose the best possible design and use the pattern of results to rule out some internal validity threats.

### SELECTION EFFECTS

Selection effects are relevant only for independent-groups designs, not for repeated-measures designs. A selection threat to internal validity applies when the kinds of participants at one level of the independent variable are systematically different from those at the other level.

Consider the 11-nation study on organ donation in the first example. The results showed that rates of consent for organ donation were much higher in the seven countries with presumed consent policies (Johnson & Goldstein, 2003).

On the basis of these results, can you claim that the presumed consent policies caused the higher rates of consent? We should consider the possibility of a selection effect: Are there systematically different types of people in the presumed consent countries compared with the opt-in countries? Could these seven countries simply have more generous, giving people than the other four countries? Probably not: The four countries with opt-in policies are not systematically different in terms of their economies, religious beliefs, or language from the seven presumed consent countries. Although a selection effect is possible, it is not very plausible.

In the cosmetic surgery study, the people who actually had the surgery may have been different from those who simply expressed interest in it. When the researchers asked, a full 61% of the comparison group reported they had decided against surgery because they couldn't afford it (Margraf et al., 2013). Therefore, there may have been a selection effect in this study; people who had cosmetic surgery might have been more financially well-off than people who did not have the procedure. However, the pretest/posttest nature of the study helps rule out selection effects, too. Financial stability might explain why one group started out higher in life satisfaction, but it does not seem to be a reasonable explanation for why the surgery group increased in self-esteem and general attractiveness over time (see Figure 13.2).

The Margraf team took additional steps to help counteract selection effects in their study. For some of their analyses, they used information on age, gender, body mass index, income, and several other variables to create matched groups, matching 179 people from the surgery group with 179 people from the comparison group. They compared the results from the matched-groups data to the results from the full samples (about 500 people in the surgery group and 264 in the comparison group) and found similar results both times. The matched-groups version of the data gave these researchers confidence that selection effects were not responsible for the differences they observed (**Figure 13.6**).

Some researchers control for selection effects by using a **wait-list design**, in which all the participants plan to receive treatment but are randomly assigned to do so at different times. The Margraf team could have studied a group of people, all of whom were scheduled for cosmetic surgery, instructing half to receive their surgery right away and placing others on a waiting list for surgery at a later time. They could then measure the patterns of self-esteem, life satisfaction, and general

**FIGURE 13.6**
**Selection effect for cosmetic surgery.**
The Margraf team matched people on income to rule out the possibility that people who elected cosmetic surgery were not wealthier than people who decided to wait.

attractiveness in both groups over several months, when only one of the groups would have had surgery. The wait-list design, unlike the original, is a true experiment because it ensures that the same kinds of people are in each group.

## DESIGN CONFOUNDS

In certain quasi-experiments, design confounds can be a problem. Recall that in a design confound, some outside variable accidentally and systematically varies with the levels of the targeted independent variable. In the study on organ donation policies, you might question whether the presumed consent policies co-occur with some other government policy such as greater public awareness of organ donation. Before accusing the Johnson and Goldstein study of this confound, however, we'd have to demonstrate that the alternative explanation was systematic. That is, we'd have to show that *all seven* countries with presumed consent policies also had greater public awareness of organ donation, while the four opt-in countries did not.

## MATURATION THREAT

Maturation threats occur when, in an experimental or quasi-experimental design with a pretest and posttest, an observed change could have emerged more or less spontaneously over time. The cosmetic surgery study had a pretest and posttest, so it was potentially susceptible to a maturation threat. Because the participants who had surgery did improve over time in self-esteem, life satisfaction, and general attractiveness (see Figure 13.2), you might ask whether the surgery was the reason, or whether it was maturation. Perhaps everybody simply improves in these qualities over time. Fortunately, the design of this quasi-experiment included a comparison group, and the results indicated that the comparison group did not improve over time; in fact, they got slightly worse on the same variables. Because of the design and the pattern of results, you can probably rule out maturation as an internal validity threat in this study.

Could maturation be an internal validity threat in the opioid overdose study? Clearly, opioid overdose rates were rising in both states between 2003 and 2010 (indeed, they were rising across the entire country). But the comparison group helps tell the story: The rate of opioid overdose leveled off in North Carolina but started to decline in Florida after 2010. The study's design and results suggest that Florida's pill mill laws helped reduce the rate of opioid deaths above and beyond simple maturation or spontaneous change (**Figure 13.7**).

## HISTORY THREAT

A history threat occurs when an external, historical event happens for everyone in a study at the same time as the treatment. With a history threat, it is unclear whether the outcome is caused by the treatment or by the external event or factor. Perhaps the suicide rates among young people in the United States increased around April 2017 not because of the release of *13 Reasons Why* but because of

**FIGURE 13.7**
**Ruling out internal validity threats.**

The researchers compared two states that were similar in poverty level, median income, and political orientation to help rule out alternative explanations for the pattern of results.

some other well-publicized event in the country at that time, such as the suicide of a celebrity. (Suicide rates can increase after a celebrity suicide, especially if the media coverage suggests that suicide is the only escape for suffering people; Gould et al., 2003.) You could conduct an archival news search to look for events that are potential history threats.

Similarly, in the opioid overdose study, opioid deaths might have shifted in Florida not because of the laws they passed, but because of some change in employment or living conditions at the same time. As you might imagine, history threats can be especially relevant when a quasi-experiment relies on historical events (such as a new law or a media event) to manipulate its key variable. In the opioid study, the comparison group helped the Kennedy-Hendricks team rule out certain history threats. For example, OxyContin was reformulated in 2010 to help prevent abuse; however, this reformulation affected both Florida and North Carolina (indeed, all U.S. states), so we can rule it out as a history threat.

Of course, it's possible that Florida coincidentally experienced some other economic or political event in 2010 that would explain the decrease in opioid death. This would be a selection-history threat: The historical event systematically affects participants only in the treatment group or only in the comparison group, not both. To help minimize selection-history threats, the researchers selected North Carolina and Florida because they are economically and geographically similar. But other studies also help. For example, researchers have compared opioid abuse in a variety of states that have pill mill laws to a variety of states that do not (e.g., Dowell et al., 2016). The states with pill mill laws show a small but meaningful decline in opioid deaths compared with the

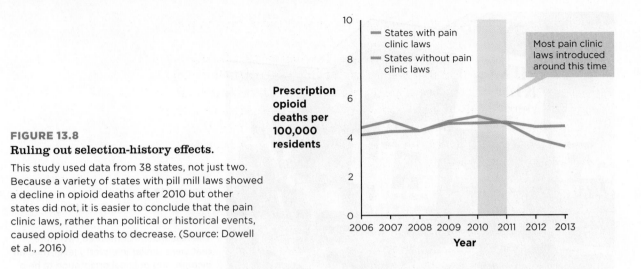

**FIGURE 13.8**

**Ruling out selection-history effects.**

This study used data from 38 states, not just two. Because a variety of states with pill mill laws showed a decline in opioid deaths after 2010 but other states did not, it is easier to conclude that the pain clinic laws, rather than political or historical events, caused opioid deaths to decrease. (Source: Dowell et al., 2016)

others (**Figure 13.8**). Because the states with pill-mill laws are economically and politically diverse, it is plausible to attribute the decline to the laws, rather than to different historical events in each individual state.

## REGRESSION TO THE MEAN

Regression to the mean occurs when an extreme outcome is caused by a combination of random factors that are unlikely to happen in the same combination again, so the extreme outcome gets less extreme over time. Chapter 11 gave the example of Italy's 5–0 win in a World Cup soccer game. That extreme score was a lucky combination of random factors that did not repeat itself in the next game, so the next game's score regressed back toward the average, or mean.

Remember that regression to the mean can threaten internal validity only for pretest/posttest designs, and even then, only when a group is selected because of its initially very high or very low scores. The initial group means are extreme, in part, because of a combination of random factors that will not happen the same way twice.

Could regression to the mean be at play in the cosmetic surgery study? We might suspect that many of the people in the group who elected to have surgery were feeling exceptionally bad about themselves at the time, meaning that their subsequent increase in self-esteem was only a regression effect. Although this explanation is possible, we might rule it out for two reasons. For one, the researchers did not select the surgery group because of unusually low scores at pretest; they simply followed everyone who visited their targeted clinics. Regression is a problem when a group is purposefully selected for its unusually low (or high) mean at pretest. Second, if regression to the mean were the explanation, the surgery group would have started out lower than the comparison group, but they started out the same on self-esteem and started out even a little higher than the comparison group on life satisfaction and general attractiveness (see Figure 13.2).

Regression to the mean has been an alternative explanation for certain other quasi-experiments (Shadish & Luellen, 2006). However, the study designs described in this chapter are generally not susceptible to it. Either the results do not fit the regression pattern or the researchers do not use pretest/posttest designs. Recall, as well, that true experiments use random assignment to place participants into groups, a practice that eliminates regression to the mean as an internal validity threat.

## ATTRITION THREAT

In designs with pretests and posttests, attrition occurs when people drop out of a study over time. Attrition becomes an internal validity threat when *systematic* kinds of people drop out of a study. In the cosmetic surgery study, for example, you might wonder whether people's self-image improved only because individuals who were disappointed with their surgery outcomes stopped responding to the study over time. If only the happiest, most satisfied participants completed the study, that would explain the apparent increase in self-esteem, life satisfaction, and general attractiveness over time. In this case, it would not be the surgery but the attrition of the most dissatisfied participants that caused the increase.

Fortunately, attrition is easy to check for, and the researchers on the Margraf team made sure it was not an explanation for their results. Here is an excerpt from the Method section of the published study:

> *Missing Values Analysis.* Completers were defined as having available data at all four time points, as opposed to dropouts who did not. The comparison group contained more dropouts than the surgery group. . . . Completers did not differ from dropouts with respect to any analyzed outcome variable at baseline, 3- and 6-month follow-up, and neither with respect to the following eight features at baseline: clinic, occupation, treatment type, gender, age, body mass index, income. . . . (Margraf et al., 2013, pp. 7–8)

The statement above indicates that although some people—especially those in the comparison group—dropped out of the study, the dropouts were not systematically different from completers. Because the attrition was unsystematic, the researchers concluded that attrition was not a threat to internal validity.

## TESTING AND INSTRUMENTATION THREATS

Whenever researchers measure participants more than once, they need to be concerned about testing threats to internal validity. A testing threat is a kind of order effect in which participants tend to change as a result of having been tested before. Repeated testing might cause people to improve, regardless of the treatment they received. Repeated testing might also cause performance to decline because of fatigue or boredom.

Instrumentation, too, can be an internal validity threat when participants are tested or observed twice. A measuring instrument could change over repeated uses, and this change would threaten internal validity. If a study uses two versions of a test with different standards (e.g., one test is more difficult) or if a study uses coders who change their standards over time, then participants might appear to change, when in reality there is no change between one observation and the next.

You can use a study's results and design to interrogate testing and instrumentation threats to internal validity. Consider the design and results of the cosmetic surgery study. Participants in both the surgery group and the comparison group were tested multiple times on their self-esteem, life satisfaction, and body image. A simple testing effect or instrumentation effect would have caused both groups to improve or both to worsen, but the surgery group improved over time while the comparison group declined. A comparison group like the one in this study almost always helps rule out a testing threat to internal validity.

## OBSERVER BIAS, DEMAND CHARACTERISTICS, AND PLACEBO EFFECTS

Three final threats to internal validity are related to human subjectivity. Observer bias, in addition to being a threat to construct validity, can also threaten internal validity when the experimenters' expectations influence their interpretation of the results. Other threats include demand characteristics, when participants guess what the study is about and change their behavior in the expected direction, and placebo effects, when participants improve, but only because they believe they are receiving an effective treatment. Fortunately, these three threats are easy to interrogate. For observer bias, you simply ask who measured the behaviors. Was the design blind (masked) or double-blind? For experimental demand, you can think about whether the participants were able to detect the study's goals and respond accordingly. For placebo effects, you can ask whether the design of a study included a comparison group that received an inert, or placebo, treatment.

Consider the study that evaluated the psychological effects of cosmetic surgery (Margraf et al., 2013). Even though this study was not double-blind (participants obviously knew whether or not they had surgery), the chance of observer bias was low because the experimenters asked participants to self-report their own self-esteem and other variables. However, the study might have been susceptible to a placebo effect. People who have cosmetic surgery are usually aware that they chose to undergo such a procedure in order to feel better about themselves. Perhaps it's not surprising, then, that they increased their self-reported self-esteem and life satisfaction! A better way to study the question might be to disguise the fact that the longitudinal study was investigating cosmetic surgery and instead simply present a series of questionnaires. Although this approach might be difficult in terms of practicality, it might reduce the chance for participants in either group to consciously increase or decrease their scores (**Figure 13.9**).

In the study on presumed consent for organ donation, data were analyzed through public records. Because people did not know they were part of a study, demand characteristics were eliminated as an internal validity threat. Thinking about the other examples in this chapter, to what extent can you rule out observer bias, demand characteristics, or placebo effects?

## Balancing Priorities in Quasi-Experiments

What does a researcher gain by conducting a quasi-experiment? If quasi-experimental studies can be vulnerable to internal validity threats, why would a researcher use one?

### REAL-WORLD OPPORTUNITIES

One reason for using quasi-experimental designs, such as those in the opioid study, the cosmetic surgery study, and the *13 Reasons Why* study, is that they present real-world opportunities for studying interesting phenomena and important events. The Kennedy-Hendricks team would never have been able to randomly assign states to change their pill mill laws, but they took advantage of the research opportunity that Florida provided. Similarly, Margraf and his colleagues did not manipulate cosmetic surgery, and the Niederkrotenthaler team did not manipulate the timing of the Netflix show. However, both research teams took advantage of the next-best thing—events that occurred in real-world settings.

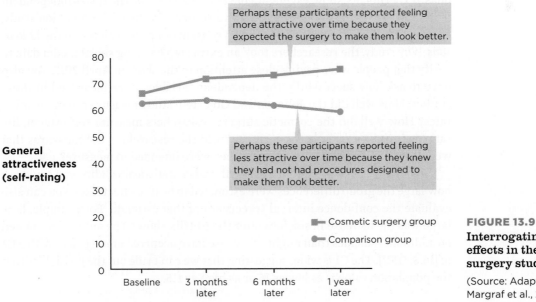

**FIGURE 13.9**

**Interrogating placebo effects in the cosmetic surgery study.**

(Source: Adapted from Margraf et al., 2013.)

## EXTERNAL VALIDITY

The real-world settings of many quasi-experiments can enhance external validity because of the likelihood that the patterns observed will generalize to other circumstances and other individuals. In the organ donation study, one goal was to show that the research on how people make decisions in different default conditions (which had previously been based on true experimental designs conducted on computers) would generalize to the real world. And you don't have to ask whether the *13 Reasons Why* study applies to real-world settings because that's where the study took place. You might still ask whether the study's results would generalize to other countries. In general, quasi-experiments capitalize on real-world situations, even as they give up some control over internal validity. In contrast, as Chapter 14 will discuss, many lab experiments seek to maximize internal validity while giving up some external validity.

## ETHICS

Ethical concerns are another reason researchers might choose a quasi-experimental design. Many questions of interest to researchers would be unethical to study in a true experiment. It would not be ethical to assign a potentially harmful television show to young adults, nor would it be ethical to assign elective cosmetic surgery to people who don't want it. Quasi-experiments can be an ethical option for studying these interesting questions.

## CONSTRUCT VALIDITY AND STATISTICAL VALIDITY IN QUASI-EXPERIMENTS

To interrogate the construct validity of a quasi-experiment, you would interrogate how successfully the study manipulated or measured its variables. Usually, quasi-experiments show excellent construct validity for the quasi-independent variable (as the preceding examples have shown). In the organ donation study, countries really do have either presumed consent or opt-in policies. In the *13 Reasons Why* study, the researchers took an extra step by using social media data to verify that people were paying close attention to the show in April 2017. You also have to ask how successfully the dependent variables were measured in these studies: How well did the Johnson and Goldstein study measure organ donation rates? How well did the cosmetic surgery researchers measure self-esteem, life satisfaction, and general attractiveness? Did the researchers use measures that were reliable and that measured what they were intended to measure?

Finally, to assess a quasi-experimental study's statistical validity, you could ask how large the group differences were estimated to be (the effect size). You can also evaluate the confidence interval (precision) of that estimate. For example, how large was the increase in suicides after the Netflix show? The authors estimated 66 additional suicides than might otherwise have occurred among men, with a CI of [16.3, 115.7]. The CI is wide, suggesting that we can't rule out the possibility that the population value is as low as 16 or as high as 115.

# Quasi-Experiments and Correlational Studies

When a quasi-experiment compares two groups without using random assignment, the groups in the study can look similar to those in other designs. For example, some quasi-experiments seem similar in design to correlational studies (see Chapters 8 and 9).

Consider the Cacioppo et al. (2013) study about meeting one's spouse online and marital satisfaction (from Chapter 8). The categorical variable in that study—whether people met online or in person—looks like a quasi-independent variable. There are two categories (meeting online or not), and couples were not randomly assigned to one or the other category. It seems like a correlational study because there were two measured variables, but it also seems like a quasi-experiment because it studied two groups of people who were not randomly assigned. Quasi-experiments and correlational designs also have similar internal validity concerns: Just as you might ask about third variables or unmeasured "lurking" variables in a correlational study, you might ask about selection effects in a quasi-experimental study.

Although the two are similar, in quasi-experiments the researchers tend to select their samples more intentionally than they do in most correlational designs. In correlational studies, researchers select a sample (such as a large survey sample, as in the Cacioppo study), measure two variables, and test the relationship between them. In quasi-experiments, however, the researchers might target groups with particular qualities (such as those with presumed consent and opt-in policies), target a certain time period (as in the *13 Reasons Why* study), or seek out comparison groups provided by state laws (as in the opioid abuse study).

# Quasi-Independent Variables Compared with Participant Variables

There is also a distinction between a quasi-independent variable and a participant variable. Recall that a participant variable is a categorical variable, such as age, gender, or ethnicity, whose levels are measured rather than manipulated. Many psychologists study people of different ages or social identities. For example, they might compare how many hours of screen time 10-year-olds and 15-year-olds spend daily, or they might compare the aggressive behaviors of men and women. Participant variables look similar to the nonequivalent control groups of quasi-experiments because both involve measured variables that are categorical.

« For more on participant variables, see Chapter 12, p. 368.

Studies with participant variables are intended to document similarities and differences due to social identities (such as gender, social class, ethnicity, religion, or sexuality), development (measured by age), or personality (such as comparing introverts to extroverts). For example, a study might address the question: "Do men and women have different rates of organ donation?" or "Are there differences in organ donation across different age groups?" In a correlational study, all variables are measured, so any study with a participant variable (such as gender) and another measured variable (such as rate of organ donation or aggression) will be a correlational study. In contrast, quasi-independent variables focus less on individual differences and more on potential interventions such as laws, media exposure, or education.

Ultimately, rather than becoming too concerned about categorizing a particular study as either quasi-experimental or correlational, or a variable as a quasi-independent or participant variable, focus on applying what you know about threats to internal validity and evaluating causal claims. These critical thinking tools apply regardless of how you classify the study's design.

✔

**CHECK YOUR UNDERSTANDING**

1. How is a nonequivalent control group design different from a true independent-groups experiment?

2. How are interrupted time-series designs and nonequivalent control group interrupted time-series designs different from true within-groups experiments?

3. Explain why both the design and the results of a study are important for assessing a quasi-experiment's internal validity.

4. What are three reasons a researcher might conduct a quasi-experiment, rather than a true experiment, to study a research question?

1. See p. 402; only a true independent-groups experiment randomly assigns participants to the groups. 2. See pp. 406–409; only a true within-groups experiment can control the order of presentation of the levels of the independent variable. 3. See pp. 408–415. 4. See pp. 415–417.

# SMALL-*N* DESIGNS: STUDYING ONLY A FEW INDIVIDUALS

In previous chapters, you learned that large samples enable researchers to make more precise statistical estimates. Indeed, in the past few years psychology researchers have greatly increased the sample sizes in their studies. These days in psychology, bigger samples are seen as better. But sometimes researchers conduct experiments and studies with just a few participants, and it can still be possible to draw conclusions from a study that uses just one or two participants. What priorities are researchers balancing when they study only a few people or animals at a time?

**TABLE 13.1**

## Differences Between Large-*N* and Small-*N* Designs

| LARGE-*N* DESIGNS | SMALL-*N* DESIGNS |
|---|---|
| 1. *Participants are grouped.* The data from an individual participant are not of interest in themselves; data from all participants in each group are combined and studied together. | 1. *Each participant is treated separately.* Small-*N* designs are almost always repeated-measures designs, in which researchers observe how the person or animal responds to several systematically designed conditions. |
| 2. Data are represented as *group averages*. | 2. Data for *each individual* are presented. |
| 3. Large samples enable group averages to be estimated more precisely. | 3. Careful designs enable us to compare each individual during treatment periods and control periods. |
| 4. These studies are used for both basic and applied research. | 4. These designs are often used in therapeutic settings, to confirm that a treatment works for an individual person. |

When researchers use a **small-*N* design**, instead of gathering a little information from a larger sample, they obtain a lot of information from just a few cases. These studies are still useful and valuable, if done correctly. Large-*N* designs and small-*N* designs differ in four key ways, summarized in **Table 13.1**.

# Research on Human Memory

The famous case of Henry Molaison (1926–2008), known by his initials H.M., is one of the most important in the field of neuroscience and human memory. As a young adult, Henry suffered from repeated, debilitating epileptic seizures. Medication helped, but after several years it no longer controlled the seizures, and the large doses had started to destroy his cerebellum (the brain structure that controls movement and balance). In 1953, at age 27, he had a surgical operation to remove the area of his brain thought to be the origin of his seizures. A surgeon excised the front half of his hippocampus on both the right and left sides (bilaterally), along with other brain areas, including portions of his hippocampal gyrus, amygdala, and medial temporal lobes.

The surgery was successful in that it dramatically reduced Henry's seizures. But as he was recovering, his family and medical staff noticed he didn't recognize the nurses and doctors caring for him. He remembered his parents and could recall memories from before his surgery with varying levels of detail. Yet he'd seemingly lost the ability to learn anything new, including how to find the bathroom in the hospital.

Surgeons at the time did not know that the hippocampus and surrounding brain areas are responsible for memory formation. H.M.'s tragic case filled this gap in their knowledge (Corkin, 2013). After the outcome became clear, surgeon William Scoville expressed deep regret at the memory difficulties he'd inadvertently caused his patient and cautioned other neurosurgeons against removing both sides of the hippocampus in future procedures (Scoville & Milner, 1957).

Henry Molaison's grave memory loss provided neuropsychologists such as Brenda Milner, then a graduate student, an unprecedented opportunity to study the neuroanatomy of human memory. By studying Henry and patients with similar surgeries, Scoville and Milner learned that bilateral hippocampal lesions do not affect intelligence or personality, only the ability to form new memories (Scoville & Milner, 1957).

Milner, and later Suzanne Corkin and her colleagues, studied H.M. extensively over more than 40 years. The tasks they developed, along with the patient's gracious participation, helped document the biological separation between declarative memory, or knowing that something happened, and nondeclarative memory, knowing how to do something. For instance, Corkin's group taught Henry to trace a star pattern with a pencil while seeing his hand only in a mirror (Corkin, 2013). Over repeated trials, his mirror-tracing skill improved just as quickly as that of a control participant with an intact brain (this was his nondeclarative, "knowing how" memory). But each day when he saw the task, he'd claim he'd never tried it before (his declarative, "knowing that" memory); (**Figure 13.10**).

In another task, researchers showed Henry a series of complex pictures from magazines. A few hours later, they showed him two pictures, only one

**FIGURE 13.10**
**Case studies show separate memory systems.**
Henry Molaison (right) got better every day at a mirror-tracing task (nondeclarative memory), even though he claimed each day that he'd never seen the task before (declarative memory).

of which he had seen earlier. Although his declarative memory was impaired (he claimed never to have seen either image), he could almost always guess the correct picture (apparently, he used feelings of familiarity to select one). The same separation was present in his spatial memory. When told there was a secret buzzer hidden under the carpet in a testing room, Henry eagerly walked around looking for it. On the first day, it took him several minutes to find it. On subsequent days, he expressed surprise each time he was told about the secret, but then walked directly to the buzzer, having no trouble locating where it was (Corkin, 2013).

Studies showed that Henry's short-term (working) memory was fairly intact. He could remember a set of numbers (such as "5, 8, 4") for a short period of time, reciting a span he'd heard up to 30 seconds earlier. And if he continually rehearsed a number, he could accurately recite it even an hour later. But if he was distracted for a minute (talking to a nurse, for instance), it was lost. When asked to recall it, he'd say, "What number?"

The contributions this case made to the study of memory and neuroscience were significant. Research on H.M. (and on a few people with similar lesions) helped neuroscientists and psychologists learn the role of hippocampal and medial-temporal brain regions in memory storage. They were able to test hypotheses about the separation of declarative and nondeclarative memory, the difference between feelings of familiarity and feelings of knowing, and even how the brain processes odors. (Interestingly, Henry smelled odors but could not identify them accurately.) From 1957 until a few years before his death, he willingly participated in hundreds of hours of research. Though he didn't always remember hearing he was famous, he enjoyed the attention, and once said, "You just live and learn. I'm living, and you're learning" (Corkin, 2013, p. 113).

## BALANCING PRIORITIES IN CASE STUDY RESEARCH

How convinced should we be by the results of research on special cases such as H.M.? These studies, after all, were conducted with only a small number of participants. (Fortunately, this kind of brain damage is rare.) Can we really conclude anything from research conducted on so few people?

**Experimental Control.** Case studies can effectively advance our knowledge when researchers use careful research designs. Because of the empirical strengths of these studies, we can, in fact, make some conclusions. First, Corkin and her colleagues used the power of experimental control. In some cases, such as testing Henry's ability to remember numbers or recognize magazine photos, researchers compared his performance with that of age-matched control participants who had no brain damage. Second, researchers deliberately designed tasks meant to isolate different elements of memory, such as declarative from nondeclarative memory. And they worked hard to present a range of activities, including visual, spatial, and auditory learning tasks, which helped them distinguish Henry's perceptual processes from memory processes.

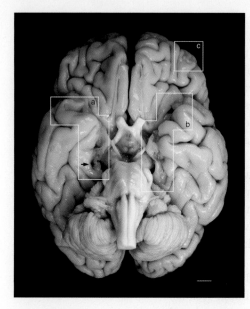

**FIGURE 13.11**
**The brain of Henry Molaison.**

H.M. and his guardians gave written permission for his brain to be studied after his death. After he died in 2008, scientists carried out a plan to study his brain through imaging and surgery. Areas outlined as *a* and *b* show where some of the temporal lobes had been surgically lesioned in 1957. The *c* area shows another lesion in the frontal lobe.

»
For more on pattern and parsimony, see Chapter 9, pp. 260–262.

**Studying Special Cases.** Just as quasi-experiments can take advantage of natural accidents, laws, or historical events, small-*N* studies often take advantage of special medical cases. Studying people like Henry Molaison gave researchers the opportunity to test which kinds of tasks require hippocampal regions and which do not, under controlled conditions.

## Disadvantages of Small-*N* Studies

Brain damage usually affects more than one discrete region, creating an internal validity problem in small-*N* brain damage studies like H.M.'s. The surgeon removed not only the hippocampus but also some areas around it (**Figure 13.11**). Henry's cerebellum was also damaged from antiseizure medications. The multiple types of damage make it more difficult to narrow down the specific region responsible for each behavioral deficit—an internal validity issue.

Another disadvantage involves external validity: Participants in small-*N* studies may not represent the general population very well. It's important that researchers found similar memory deficits in several patients with bilateral hippocampal lesions (Scoville & Milner, 1957). However, any patient who undergoes such surgery usually has health problems not found in the general population. Some, like H.M., had a history of severe epilepsy, and others underwent surgery in the 1950s for the treatment of mental illnesses such as schizophrenia. Still others sustained damage to their hippocampus as a result of encephalitis (Wilson & Wearing, 1995).

Therefore, we cannot be sure whether results from studies on surgery patients would apply to people with no history of epilepsy or schizophrenia. Furthermore, it clearly would be unethical to remove regions of a nonepileptic person's brain to create the necessary comparison. What could a researcher do to explore the generalizability of the findings from such patients? One option would be to triangulate, meaning to compare a case study's results to research using other methods. For example, the Corkin team's results are consistent with contemporary research using functional brain imagery on nonepileptic adults (e.g., Kensinger et al., 2003). The findings from these studies confirm what has been observed behaviorally in individuals with surgical lesions. This is another example of how the weight of a variety of evidence supports a parsimonious theory about how the human brain is organized.

## Behavior-Change Studies in Applied Settings: Three Small-*N* Designs

Research on people with brain damage is only one example of the power of a small-*N* design. In educational, clinical, and work settings, practitioners can use small-*N* designs to learn whether their interventions work. Small-*N* designs are frequently used in behavior analysis, a technique in which practitioners use reinforcement principles to improve a client's behavior. In the examples that follow, an occupational therapist might teach an elderly Alzheimer's patient a new memory strategy and then observe whether the patient's memory has improved. A therapist might try to help a child with autism become less afraid of dogs, or teach a developmentally delayed adult to stop a self-harming behavior. In such applied settings, practitioners, like researchers, need to think empirically: They develop theories about people's behaviors and make predictions about what treatments should help. They then implement changes, observe the results, and modify their theories or treatments in response to these observations.

« For a review of the theory-data cycle, see Chapter 1, pp. 10–15.

When practitioners notice improvement after using some treatment, they might wonder whether the improvement was caused by the intervention or by something else. Would the memory of a person with Alzheimer's have improved anyway, or could the improvement have been caused by, say, a change in medication? Did the therapy decrease a child's fear of dogs, or did her fear subside simply because she got attention from the therapist? Notice that these questions are internal validity questions—questions about alternative explanations for the result. Carefully designed small-*N* or single-*N* studies can help practitioners decide whether changes are caused by their interventions or by some other influence.

## STABLE-BASELINE DESIGNS

A **stable-baseline design** is a study in which a practitioner or researcher observes behavior for an extended baseline period before beginning a treatment or other intervention. If behavior during the baseline is stable, the researcher is more certain of the treatment's effectiveness. One example comes from a study of a memory technique known as expanded rehearsal, which was used with a real Alzheimer's patient, Ms. S (Moffat, 1989). Before teaching her the new strategy, the practitioners spent several weeks recording baseline information, such as how many words Ms. S could recall after hearing them only once. It was important that the baseline data were stable: Ms. S remembered very few words, and there was no upward trend. Then she was taught the new technique, as researchers continued to monitor how many words she could remember. The researchers noticed a sudden improvement in her memory ability (**Figure 13.12**).

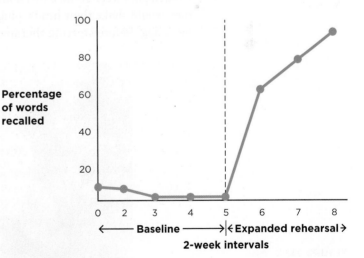

**FIGURE 13.12**

**Using a stable-baseline design.**

In this study, the patient's memory was consistently poor until the new expanded rehearsal technique was introduced; then it dramatically improved. (Source: Adapted from Moffat, 1989.)

Why should these results convince you that the patient's improvement was caused by the new expanded rehearsal technique? One reason is that the baseline was stable. If the researchers had collected only one baseline measure before the new treatment and a single test afterward (a before-and-after comparison), the improvement could be explained by any number of factors, such as maturation (spontaneous change), regression to the mean, or a history effect. (In fact, a single baseline record followed by a single posttreatment measure would have been a small-*N* version of the "really bad experiment"; see Chapter 11.) Instead, the researchers recorded an extended, stable baseline, which made it unlikely that some sudden, spontaneous change just happened to occur right at the time the new therapy began. Furthermore, the stable baseline meant there was not a single, extreme low point from which improvement would almost definitely occur (a regression effect). Performance began low and stayed low until the experimental technique was introduced.

The stable baseline gave this study internal validity, enabling the researcher to rule out some alternative explanations. In addition, the study was later repeated with a few other Alzheimer's clients (**Figure 13.13**). This replication provided further evidence that expanded rehearsal can help people with Alzheimer's.

### MULTIPLE-BASELINE DESIGNS

In a **multiple-baseline design**, researchers stagger their introduction of an intervention across a variety of individuals, times, or situations to rule out alternative explanations. Here's an example. Up to 30% of children with autism express a fear of dogs, and one study attempted to help three such children (Tyner et al., 2016). Participants were John, Sally, and Bob (not their real names), ages 5–10. At first, they would shake their heads, plug their ears, or refuse to enter a room containing a dog. Before starting therapy, the researchers recorded each child's initial

**FIGURE 13.13**

**A speech therapist testing a client at home for Alzheimer's disease.**

Small-*N* designs can help therapists learn which therapies are effective for their clients.

behavior several times. They introduced each child to a gym where a therapy dog sat with a handler about 98 feet away. Children were told to "go as close as you can to the dog," and observers recorded how close, in feet, each child could approach.

After recording baseline behaviors for several days, therapists began a treatment called contact desensitization plus reinforcement. During daily training sessions, each child was accompanied into the gym with a therapy dog at the far end. The child sat with the therapist, playing on a laptop until they appeared calm (that was the contact desensitization). Then the therapist would move 5 feet, saying, "Let's come closer." If the child moved ahead, they got a favorite snack and praise from the therapist (the reinforcement). (Children were allowed to back away 1 foot at a time if they appeared anxious.) Then the cycle was repeated. Each training session lasted 30 minutes or until the child actually touched the dog. Each child received seven to twelve therapy sessions. About 2 weeks after the training ended, children were shown different dogs in different situations (such as a parking lot), and their distance to the dog was recorded.

The results for John, Sally, and Bob are shown in **Figure 13.14**. Notice how each child's baseline distance to the dog was fairly stable, indicating that simply being tested in the gym did not improve their fear. Notice also that each child's treatment began at different times—illustrating the multiple-baseline aspect of this small-$N$ design. And notice that each child's distance to the dog reduced dramatically as treatment sessions began.

Should these results convince you that the children's fear was reduced by the contact desensitization plus reinforcement therapy? Probably. First, each child's baseline distance to the dog showed no improvement until the therapy started. Second, the same pattern was observed in three children, which helps rule out alternative explanations, such as an outside event that could have affected only one child. This multiple-baseline design has the internal validity to support a causal conclusion.

In this example, multiple baselines were represented by three children, starting at different times. In other studies, multiple baselines might be represented by different situations or behaviors. One such study was conducted in the notoriously dangerous mining industry. After collecting baseline data on accident rates, managers used tokens to encourage employees of a strip mine to enact safety rules, prevent accidents, or be a member of an injury-free workgroup (Fox et al., 1987). Managers tested the token system in 1972 at one mining location and in 1974 at another. They found that injury-related absences (the key outcome behavior) decreased only after the system began in each location. The multiple baselines at the two mining locations helped the researchers conclude that the token system, not other factors, was responsible for reducing injuries.

## REVERSAL DESIGNS

In a **reversal design**, as in the other two small-$N$ designs (stable baseline and multiple baseline), researchers observe a problem behavior both with and without

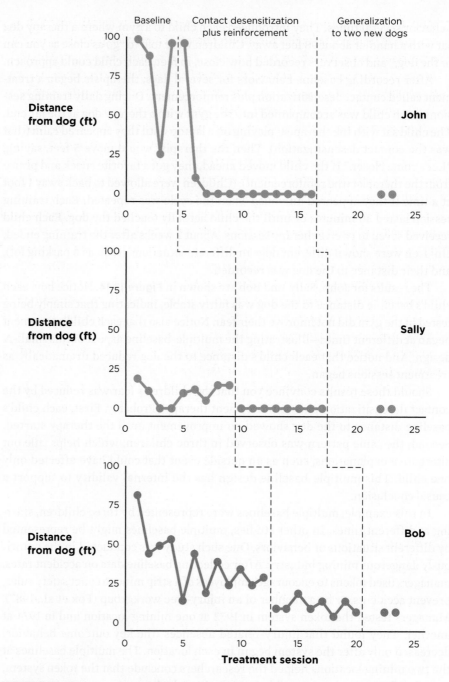

**FIGURE 13.14**

**Using a multiple-baseline design.**

In this study, three children with autism who feared dogs initially stayed a long distance from a dog on the far side of a gym. After several sessions of therapy in which they were praised for moving closer and closer, all three children showed dramatic improvements in their willingness to approach the training dog, and then later, two new dogs. (Source: Adapted from Tyner et al., 2016.)

treatment, but take the treatment away for a while (the reversal period) to see whether the problem behavior returns (reverses). They subsequently reintroduce the treatment to see if the behavior improves again. By observing how the behavior changes as the treatment is removed and reintroduced, the researchers can test for internal validity and make a causal statement: If the treatment is really working, behavior should improve only when the treatment is applied.

An example concerns a man who had autism and severe language deficits. Darnell (not his real name), age 18, lived in a residential treatment center. His therapists wanted to change his behavioral habit of rumination—bringing up food he had previously swallowed. The consequences were serious: Darnell had been hospitalized for weight loss because of this recurring behavior.

Across several treatment sessions, Darnell was first given a healthy snack and a high-calorie shake, and then therapists measured his degree of rumination over the next hour (DeRosa et al., 2016). During baseline sessions, therapists simply stayed in the room with him and observed. In treatment sessions, they placed three of his favorite foods on the table and gave him a little attention (a simple comment or a rub on his head) about every 45 seconds. They were testing the idea that Darnell would not ruminate if he had a favorite food to eat because eating food and ruminating are incompatible behaviors.

**Figure 13.15** shows the results of the series of treatment sessions. At baseline, Darnell's rate of rumination was quite high. During the treatments, his rate of rumination was much less frequent. As the graph shows, over time, the therapists

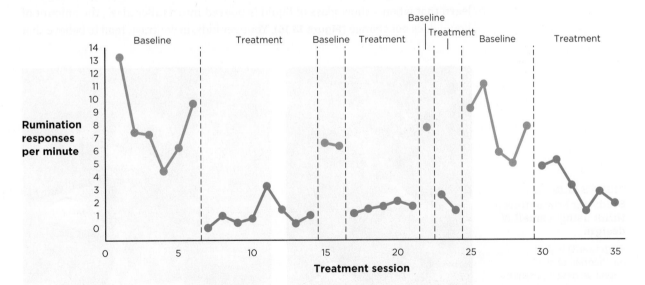

### FIGURE 13.15
**Using a reversal design.**

In this study, the client's rumination behavior was high during baseline sessions and lower during treatment sessions. This pattern supports the idea that the treatment caused his rumination to decrease. (Source: Adapted from DeRosa et al., 2016.)

withheld the treatment and simply observed his rumination: This was the reversal period. Sure enough, during the baseline sessions, Darnell's rates of rumination increased again. The pattern suggests that the treatment of having three favorite foods available was preventing the rumination behavior.

Reversal designs are appropriate mainly for situations in which a treatment may not cause lasting change. Perhaps because of his disabilities, Darnell's rumination seemed to be automatically reinforcing to him, which is probably why the behavior returned during baseline sessions. In contrast, reversal designs would not make sense for an educational intervention. Once a student has learned a new skill (such as Ms. S's expanded rehearsal technique), it's unlikely the skill would simply reverse, or go away.

While a reversal design enables a practitioner to evaluate the effectiveness of a treatment, it may be considered harmful and unethical to withdraw an effective treatment from a patient or client. However, it also may be unethical to use a treatment that is not empirically demonstrated to be effective. (To review a full discussion of ethics in psychology research, see Chapter 4.)

## Other Examples of Small-*N* Studies

Research in psychological science boasts several influential small-*N* and single-*N* studies. The Swiss clinical psychologist Jean Piaget worked out a theory of cognitive development in children through careful, systematic observations of his own three children (Piaget, 1923). He found, for example, that as children get older, they learn that when a short glass of liquid is poured into a taller glass, the amount of liquid does not change (**Figure 13.16**). Younger kids, in contrast, tend to believe that

**FIGURE 13.16**
**Studying how children think using a small-*N* design.**

Piaget (left) tested his theories of child cognitive development by systematically testing his own children (not pictured) on carefully constructed tasks, such as estimating which glass "has more."

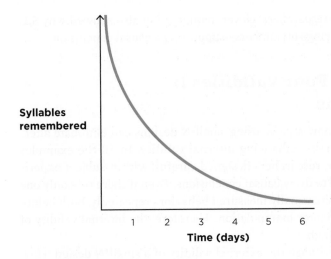

**FIGURE 13.17**

**A single-*N* design: the forgetting curve.**

Ebbinghaus's carefully designed experiments on memory processes contributed to psychology, even though he used only one person—himself—as a subject.

*Syllables remembered* (vertical axis)

*Time (days)* (horizontal axis): 1 2 3 4 5 6

there is more liquid in the taller glass because the level appears higher. Although Piaget observed only a few children, he designed systematic questions, made careful observations, and replicated his extensive interviews with each of them.

The German psychologist Hermann Ebbinghaus was a pioneer in the experimental study of memory. In a series of studies conducted over many years, he made himself memorize long lists of nonsense syllables, such as *pon* and *mip*. He systematically varied the frequency and duration of studying each list, and carefully recorded how many syllables he remembered at different time intervals (Ebbinghaus, 1913). He was the first to document several fundamental memory phenomena, one of which is called the forgetting curve, shown in **Figure 13.17**. It depicts how memory for a newly learned list of nonsense syllables declines most dramatically over the first hour but then declines more slowly after that. Although he studied only himself—a **single-*N* design**—Ebbinghaus created testing situations with experimental precision and, eventually, replicability.

In another example of a single-*N* study, memory researchers recruited an average college student (known as S.F.) and asked him to come to their laboratory three to five times a week for a year and a half (Ericsson et al., 1980). Each day, they read S.F. random numbers—one digit per second. Later, S.F. would try to recall the numbers in the correct order. Ordinarily, the average memory span for retaining numbers is about seven (Miller, 1956). After regularly practicing in the lab, S.F. developed the ability to recite back 79 random numbers at a time (**Figure 13.18**).

S.F.'s remarkable performance resulted, in part, from his strategy of grouping clusters of numbers according to track and field times (e.g., a string of 3392 might become 3:39.2, "a great time for the mile"). In fact, the researchers tested whether the "running time" strategy caused his improved performance by generating some number strings that purposefully did not correspond well to running times. S.F.'s memory span for those special strings dropped down to his beginning level. His incredible memory skill demonstrates what can happen with extensive training

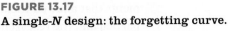

| 2 | 7 | 1 | 2 | 5 | 8 | 2 | 3 |
| 7 | 0 | 8 | 7 | 5 | 0 | 9 | 9 |
| 9 | 2 | 5 | 4 | 1 | 6 | 1 | 8 |
| 7 | 9 | 6 | 1 | 0 | 0 | 5 | 6 |
| 7 | 8 | 0 | 0 | 1 | 1 | 5 | 6 |
| 6 | 2 | 6 | 2 | 5 | 3 | 4 | 8 |
| 2 | 1 | 1 | 9 | 1 | 8 | 4 | 3 |
| 1 | 1 | 3 | 9 | 5 | 4 | 9 | 2 |
| 3 | 9 | 9 | 9 | 5 | 6 | 5 | 8 |
| 7 | 8 | 0 | 5 | 6 | 8 | 5 | 5 |

**FIGURE 13.18**

**Remembering random numbers.**

Do you think you could recall up to 80 random digits like these after hearing them only once? A college student known as S.F. learned to do so by practicing short-term memory skills for a year and a half.

and motivation. And the researchers' clever manipulation also showed why S.F. got so good at learning strings of numbers—supporting a causal conclusion.

## Evaluating the Four Validities in Small-*N* Designs

So far we've focused on how studies using small-*N* designs can eliminate alternative explanations, thereby enhancing internal validity. In all the examples described in this chapter, researchers designed careful, within-subject experiments that allowed them to draw causal conclusions. Even if there was only one participant, the researchers usually measured behaviors repeatedly, both before and after some intervention or manipulation. Therefore, the internal validity of these single-*N* studies is high.

It may seem easy to criticize the external validity of a small-*N* design. How can one person represent a population of interest? Even when researchers can demonstrate that their manipulation, intervention, or procedure replicates in a second or third case, the question of generalizability remains. Remember, though, that researchers can take steps to maximize the external validity of their findings. First, they can triangulate by combining the results of single-*N* studies with other studies on animals or other groups, as the team did when comparing H.M.'s results with subsequent research on people without brain damage. Second, researchers can specify the population to which they want to generalize, and they rarely intend to generalize to everyone. They may not care, for example, if a memory strategy for Alzheimer's clients applies to everybody in the world, but they do care whether it generalizes to other people with Alzheimer's. Understandably, in cases like these, researchers sometimes limit a study's population of interest to a particular subset. Third, sometimes researchers are not concerned about generalizing at all. It may be sufficient to Darnell's caregivers to learn about the one technique that helps him keep down nutritious food. In such cases, even if the causal statement applies only to one person, it is still useful.

When interrogating a small-*N* design, you should also evaluate construct validity. Of course, researchers want to be sure their measurements are reliable and valid. The researchers in the previous examples recorded how well H.M. drew a pattern, how close children got to a dog, and whether Darnell ruminated or not. Construct validity is fairly straightforward when researchers are recording whether a person with a brain lesion reports seeing this picture or that one, and for objective measures such as memory for a string of numbers. But when researchers are recording the distance a child gets to a dog or whether a person is ruminating, they should use multiple observers and check for interrater reliability, in case one observer is biased or the behavior is difficult to identify.

Regarding statistical validity, in single-*N* designs, researchers do not typically use traditional statistics. However, they still draw conclusions from data, and they should treat data appropriately. In many cases, graphs (such as those in

Figures 13.12, 13.14, and 13.15) provide enough quantitative evidence. In addition, you might think about effect sizes more simply in small-*N* cases, by asking: By what margin did the client's behavior improve?

---

✔

## CHECK YOUR UNDERSTANDING

**1.** What are three small-*N* designs used in applied settings?

**2.** Are small-*N* designs within-groups or between-groups designs?

**3.** How is a multiple-baseline design both similar to and different from a nonequivalent control group interrupted time-series design?

**4.** How do small-*N* researchers approach the question of external validity?

1. See pp. 423–428. 2. Within-groups designs, see p. 430. 3. See pp. 425–426; compare Figures 13.5 and 13.14. 4. See pp. 430–431.

# CHAPTER REVIEW

 It's time to complete your study experience! Go to INQUIZITIVE to practice actively with this chapter's concepts and get personalized feedback along the way.

## Summary

Experiments do not always take place in ideal conditions with clean manipulations, large samples of participants, and random assignment. Quasi-experiments and small-N designs use strategies that optimize naturally occurring groups or single individuals.

### QUASI-EXPERIMENTS

- Quasi-experiments can use independent-groups designs such as a nonequivalent control group design and a nonequivalent control group pretest/posttest design. They can also follow within-groups designs, as in an interrupted time-series design or a nonequivalent control group interrupted time-series design.

- When a quasi-experiment includes a comparison group and the right pattern of results, researchers may support a causal claim, even when participants cannot be randomly assigned to conditions and the researchers do not have complete experimental control of the independent variable.

- Examining the results and design of a quasi-experiment reveals its vulnerablity to alternative explanations, such as selection, maturation, history, regression, attrition, testing, and instrumentation effects; observer biases; demand characteristics; and placebo effects—the same kinds of internal validity threats that can occur in true experiments.

- In quasi-experiments, researchers balance confidence in internal validity with other priorities, such as opportunities to study ethically in a real-world situation or to take advantage of a political event.

### SMALL-N DESIGNS: STUDYING ONLY A FEW INDIVIDUALS

- Small-N studies balance an intense, systematic investigation of one or a few people against the usual approach of studying groups of people. The internal validity of small-N studies can be just as high as that of repeated-measures experiments conducted on larger samples.

- Three small-N designs used in applied settings are the stable-baseline design, the multiple-baseline design, and the reversal design.

- Small-N designs can establish excellent construct and internal validity. They can achieve external validity by replicating the results in other settings. In applied settings, researchers might prioritize the ability to establish a treatment's effectiveness for a single individual over broad generalizability.

- Researchers must be aware of the trade-offs of each research decision, making conscious choices about which validities are most important—and most possible—to prioritize as they study a particular issue in psychological science.

# Key Terms

quasi-experiment, p. 401

quasi-independent variable, p. 402

nonequivalent control group posttest-only design, p. 402

nonequivalent control group pretest/posttest design, p. 404

interrupted time-series design, p. 406

nonequivalent control group interrupted time-series design, p. 408

wait-list design, p. 409

small-*N* design, p. 419

stable-baseline design, p. 423

multiple-baseline design, p. 424

reversal design, p. 425

single-*N* design, p. 429

 **To see samples of chapter concepts in the popular media, visit www.everydayresearchmethods.com and click the box for Chapter 13.**

# Review Questions

1. What is the term for a quasi-experimental design with at least one treatment group and one comparison group, in which the participants are measured once and have not been randomly assigned to the groups?

   a. Nonequivalent control group design

   b. Independent-groups design

   c. Factorial design

   d. Reversal design

2. Which of these is not a reason for a researcher to select a quasi-experimental design?

   a. To enhance external validity.

   b. To avoid the ethical issues a true experiment would cause.

   c. To ensure internal validity.

   d. To take advantage of real-world opportunities to study phenomena and events.

3. Researchers studied preteens at an outdoor education camp that prevented kids from using devices with screens, such as cell phones (Uhls et al., 2014). They predicted the camp would improve children's nonverbal communication skills. One group of sixth graders attended the camp in the spring. They were compared with a group of sixth graders from the same school who had not attended the camp. The kids were tested on how well they could read emotions in faces. The camp group took the emotion test on Monday and Friday (the first and last days of their camp week); the control group took the emotion test on Monday and Friday of a regular school week. What type of design was this?

   a. Interrupted time-series design

   b. Nonequivalent control group interrupted time-series design

   c. Nonequivalent control group posttest-only design

   d. Nonequivalent control group pretest/posttest design

4. For the kids' camp study, you could ask: Did the researchers use a reliable and valid test of nonverbal communication skills? You would be asking about which kind of validity?

   a. Construct validity

   b. Statistical validity

   c. Internal validity

   d. External validity

5. The researchers found that the ability to read emotions in faces improved significantly in the kids who had been to the camp, but not in the control kids. Which of the following would be a threat to internal validity in this study?

   a. If the kids who went to camp were selected for their low levels of emotional communication skills, but the control children were not.

   b. If the kids in the two groups were not representative of children from their local school district.

   c. If the sample size of the study was very small.

6. A psychologist is working with four siblings, all of whom exhibit violent behavior toward one another. The children's parents are instructed to record the number of violent behaviors each child exhibits in the hour before dinner for 1 week. The parents then begin using a positive reinforcement technique to shape the behavior of the youngest child, while continuing to record the behavior of all children. The recording continues, and the technique is used on one additional child each week. By the end of 6 weeks, there is a significant decrease in violent behaviors for each of the children. What type of design did the psychologist use?

   a. Stable-baseline design

   b. Multiple-baseline design

   c. Reversal design

   d. Interrupted time-series design

7. Which of these is not a method for addressing the external validity of the conclusions of a small-*N* study?

   a. Triangulate by comparing results with other research.

   b. Specify a limited population to which to generalize.

   c. Randomly assign people to the treatment and control conditions.

   d. Specify that the result applies only to the participant studied.

# Learning Actively

1. Researchers Owens et al. (2010) wanted to investigate the impact of school start time on the sleep patterns of adolescents. They studied teenagers who were enrolled in an American high school, both before (fall semester) and after (spring semester) the entire school had decided to shift its start time from 8:00 a.m. to 8:30 a.m. Students completed a survey asking what time they went to bed the night before, how many hours of sleep they'd gotten, and their daytime sleepiness and level of depressed mood. The researchers found that after the 8:30 start time was implemented, students reported getting 45 minutes more sleep each night, and the percentage of students who reported more than 8 hours per night jumped from 16.4% to 54.7%. In addition, students' level of daytime sleepiness and depressed mood decreased after the 8:30 start time began.

   a. Is this study a nonequivalent control group posttest-only design, a nonequivalent control group pretest/posttest design, an interrupted time-series design, or a nonequivalent control group interrupted time-series design?

   b. Graph the results of the study, according to the results in the description. (There are multiple dependent variables; choose only one to graph.)

   c. What causal statement might the researchers be trying to make, if any? Is it appropriate? Use the results and design to interrogate the study's internal validity.

   d. If you notice any internal validity flaws, can you redesign the study to remove the flaw?

   e. Ask one question to address construct validity and one to address external validity.

2. Suppose you're a dog owner and are working with your 3-year-old Labrador retriever. When the dog goes for walks, he growls fiercely at other dogs. You want to reduce your dog's growling behavior, so you decide to try a technique you learned on television: pressing firmly on the dog's neck and saying a forceful, quick "Shhhhh!" sound when the dog begins to growl at other dogs. You decide to apply a small-*N* design to investigate the effectiveness of your training regimen.

a. Which small-*N* design(s) would be appropriate for this situation?

b. Choose one small-*N* design and describe how you would conduct your study.

c. Sketch a graph of the results you would predict from your design if your treatment worked. Use Figures 13.12, 13.14, and 13.15 as models.

d. Explain whether you could conclude from your study's results that the treatment caused your dog's aggressive behavior to decrease.

"Does This Study Need
a Random Sample of
Participants?"

"Would We Find These Same Results
in Other Cultural Contexts?"

# Replication, Transparency, and Real-World Importance

HOW DO WE IDENTIFY HIGH-QUALITY SCIENCE? Evaluating quality is one of your goals as a consumer of research. You have already learned that the four big validities (construct, statistical, internal, and external) can help you evaluate a study's quality. This chapter revisits these dimensions, taking the broader view of how studies contribute to scientific progress. One aspect of quality science is replication. Another concerns research transparency. Other aspects, such as a study's applicability to real-world contexts, also help us evaluate it. After reading this chapter, you'll be able to draw a nuanced conclusion about a study's quality (how scientifically credible it is) and importance (how valuable it might be in the real world).

## REPLICATION

Responsible researchers always consider whether the results of an investigation could be a fluke or whether they will get the same results if they conduct the same study again—in other words, whether the finding is **replicable** (or *reproducible*). As you have learned, replication is part of interrogating statistical validity: We ask about the size of the estimate (effect size), its precision (95% CI), and what else is known— what do other studies say?

**LEARNING OBJECTIVES**

**A year from now, you should still be able to:**

**1.**
Explain why it is essential for a study to be replicated.

**2.**
Describe why transparent research practices help ensure credible science.

**3.**
Evaluate, in a nuanced way, a study's quality in the context of scientific progress and external validity.

**»**

For more details on
replication, see Chapter 3,
pp. 68–69; Chapter 8,
pp. 214–215; and Chapter 10,
p. 310.

It makes sense that a finding should be replicated in order to be considered high quality. If one research team claimed their therapy cured breast cancer but no other teams could replicate their success, you would not trust the cure. If one study found that playing violent video games increased aggressive behavior but no other studies found the same result, you might consider the first study a fluke. Replication gives a study credibility and is a crucial part of the scientific process.

## Types of Replication

When a researcher performs a study again, it is known as a replication study. Here we discuss three major types: direct replication, conceptual replication, and replication-plus-extension.

### DIRECT REPLICATION

In **direct replication**, researchers repeat an original study as closely as they can to see whether the effect is the same in the newly collected data. For example, in Chapter 10 you learned about a study in which babies watched a model persisting with a toy (Leonard et al., 2017). Babies persisted longer at pushing an inert button when they had watched an adult model effortfully figure out a toy (versus easily succeeding). The researchers published their original study and its successful direct replication side-by-side in the same article (**Figure 14.1**).

Another example of direct replication comes from Chapter 8. You read about Milek et al. (2018), who successfully replicated the effect in which people who engage in more deep talk have higher well-being (see Figure 8.8). This team replicated the basic effect in five separate studies, although there were slight variations in the samples: Some of the samples included older adults and some included college students.

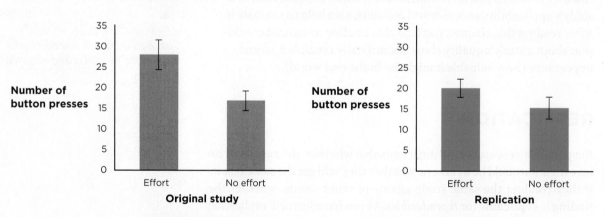

**FIGURE 14.1**

**Direct replication of the baby persistence effect.**

This graph shows the results for the first study (left) and its direct replication study (right) of the baby persistence study. Error bars show the standard error of each mean. (Source: Adapted from open data provided by Leonard et al., 2017.)

Of course, a direct replication cannot replicate the initial study in every detail. In the Leonard experiments, for example, the two samples contained distinct sets of participants. In addition, the two studies were conducted at different times of the year. Despite small variations such as these, in a direct replication researchers try to reproduce the original experiment as closely as possible.

Direct replication makes good sense. However, if there were any threats to internal validity or flaws in construct validity in the original study, such threats would be repeated in the direct replication too. In addition, when successful, a direct replication confirms what we already learned, but it usually does not test the theory in a new context (Crandall & Sherman, 2016). For this reason, researchers value other types of replication as a supplement to direct replication.

## CONCEPTUAL REPLICATION

In a **conceptual replication**, researchers explore the same research question but use different procedures. The conceptual variables in the study are the same, but the procedures for operationalizing the variables are different.

An example of conceptual replication comes from the study described in Chapter 12 that tested whether just thinking about alcohol can make people more aggressive. In that study, the researchers showed people photos of alcohol (versus plants) and then tested their reaction times to aggression-related words versus neutral words (Bartholow & Heinz, 2006). That study found that alcohol cues could prime people to think about aggression (see Figure 12.10).

In a second study, the same researchers conceptually replicated this effect, using the same variables but with different operationalizations. Instead of using photos of alcohol or plants, they exposed people to advertisements for alcohol versus control products. And instead of using reaction time as a measure of aggression, they asked people to read a paragraph about an individual named Donald, who performs a variety of behaviors that could be interpreted as hostile or not (e.g., he refuses to pay his rent until his landlord paints his apartment). If people rate Donald's behavior as more hostile, it's an indication that they are thinking about aggression. In this conceptual replication, Bartholow and Heinz did replicate the core effect: When people had just seen alcohol advertisements (versus control ads), they rated Donald's behavior as more hostile (**Figure 14.2**).

**FIGURE 14.2**

**Conceptual replication: manipulating and measuring the same variables with different operationalizations.**

The abstract (conceptual) level of the variables is the same, but the operational level of the variables changes.

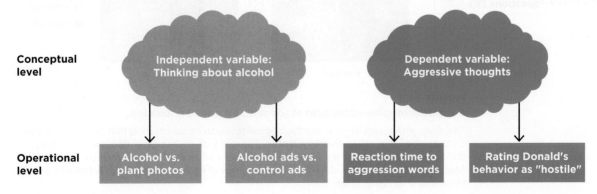

## REPLICATION-PLUS-EXTENSION

In a **replication-plus-extension** study, researchers replicate their original experiment and add variables to test additional questions. One example is the research on notetaking, discussed in Chapter 10 (Mueller & Oppenheimer, 2014). In the original posttest-only design, students taking notes with a laptop performed worse on subsequent exams compared with those taking notes by hand. A team at a different university (Morehead et al., 2019) conducted a replication-plus-extension study of this finding. The new researchers tested the original laptop and longhand conditions in a direct replication attempt. Students took notes on the same TED talk videos as in the original study and were tested on the same factual and conceptual questions. But the Morehead team also extended the study by adding two levels of the independent variable. One group of students took no notes at all, and another group used eWriters, tablets that allow people to make digital notes and drawings.

The results are shown in **Figure 14.3.** The replication portion of the study found, as expected, that longhand notetakers scored a bit higher on factual questions than laptop notetakers ($d$ = 0.27, 95% CI [–0.23, 0.76]). But when it came to the conceptual questions, they found the opposite result: Students in the *laptop* condition scored a bit higher than those in the longhand condition ($d$ = –0.35, 95% CI [–0.84, 0.15]). In other words, the "replication" portion of this replication-plus-extension study did not replicate the original result. In addition, the two "extension" conditions differed only slightly from the rest.

What shall we make of the evidence? Mueller and Oppenheimer's original article presented three studies: the original study (Study 1) plus two conceptual replications (Studies 2 and 3). At time of this writing, a few labs have published attempts to replicate Mueller and Oppenheimer's Study 1. These labs have generally found smaller effects of longhand notetaking and sometimes even the opposite effect (Luo et al., 2018; Urry et al., 2020). Therefore, replication studies do not always replicate the original result. We should consider the original studies along

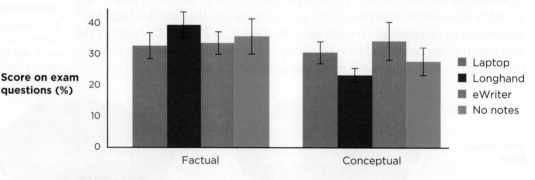

**FIGURE 14.3**

**A replication-plus-extension study with an added condition.**

This study attempted to replicate the original research demonstrating that people do worse on tests when they take notes on a laptop. The researchers also extended the initial study, testing people's performance when they took notes on an eWriter and when they took no notes at all. The error bars show the standard error of each mean. (Source: Adapted from Morehead et al., 2019, Study 2.)

with the replications to evaluate how much different forms of notetaking affect comprehension of TED talks.

## Replication Projects

A generation ago, it was surprisingly difficult to find published examples of direct replication studies, but things have changed in psychological science. Now many prestigious journals encourage replication and reserve pages for publishing direct replication attempts.

### ONE STUDY, MANY LABS

Sometimes multiple groups of scientists work together to conduct replication studies. For example, labs from around the world might agree to conduct a direct replication of one study, all following the same strict research protocol. As a result, a study can be replicated by several labs at one time.

One example involved 17 labs testing the facial feedback hypothesis (**Figure 14.4**). This hypothesis states that our emotional experience can be influenced by our facial expressions: If we are induced to adopt a smile, we will feel happier than if we are induced to adopt a pouting facial expression. In the original study (Strack et al., 1988), the researchers told people they were investigating how we can perform tasks using different parts of their bodies. Participants rated cartoons while holding their pen one of two ways: in their teeth (a smile pose) versus in their lips (a pout). The original study reported that people found the cartoons funnier when they held the smile pose.

In the replication project, each lab collected data from at least 50 participants. The project coordinator consulted with the original author to ensure their

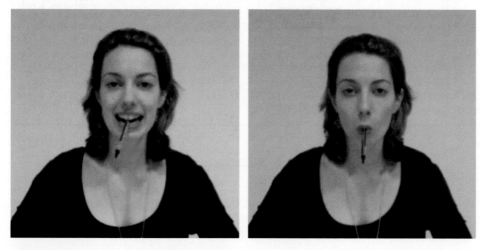

**FIGURE 14.4**
**Testing the facial feedback hypothesis.**
The model shows how participants held the pen in the two conditions, leading to a smile (left) versus a pout (right). (Source: Wagenmakers et al., 2016.)

procedure was as similar as possible to the original. Then the 17 labs collected data and reported their results. The results are depicted in **Figure 14.5**, which shows the funniness ratings estimated by each lab. Here, a positive value means that smilers found the cartoons funnier than pouters. As you can see, the 95% CI for each of the studies included zero. The project's conclusion was that "overall, the results were inconsistent with the original result" (Wagenmakers et al., 2016, p. 924). The original study's author accepted the results but pointed out ways the replication deviated from the original study (Strack, 2016).

### MANY LABS, MANY STUDIES

Other replication projects coordinate many labs around the world to replicate a variety of studies. One of the earliest such projects was called the Open Science Collaboration (OSC, 2015), which selected 100 studies from three major psychology

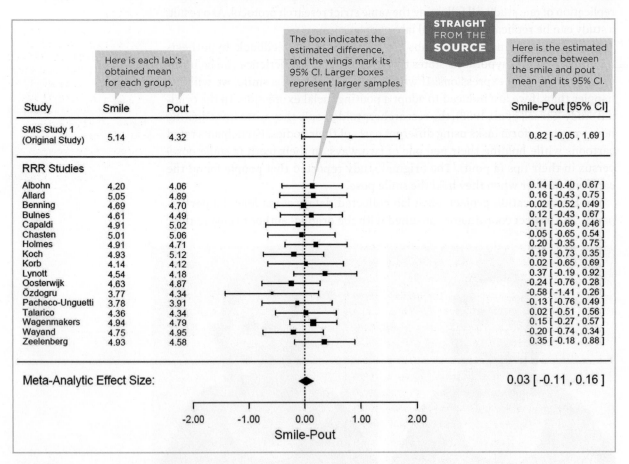

**FIGURE 14.5**

**One study, many labs.**

Results of 17 replications of the facial feedback study. All of the 95% CIs included zero, indicating that the original effect was not replicable. SMS = Strack, Martin, and Stepper (the original authors). RRR = Registered Replication Report. You'll learn about the meta-analytic effect size in the next section.

journals and recruited 100 labs around the world, assigning one lab to each study. This project used different metrics to judge whether a study was a successful replication. By one metric, only 39% of the studies cleanly replicated the original effects—a number that seemed regretfully low to many psychologists (Yong, 2015).

Another example involved 36 labs around the world, each of which replicated 16 simple studies (Klein et al., 2014). One of the effects tested was the anchoring heuristic, in which people are asked to estimate quantities such as how many babies are born every day in the United States. People's estimates are influenced by an arbitrary number. Here are the two conditions for this particular effect:

[Fewer] than 50,000 babies are born per day in the United States. How many babies do you think are born in the U.S. each day?
and
More than 100 babies are born per day in the United States. How many babies do you think are born in the U.S. each day?

In the original study (Jacowitz & Kahneman, 1995), people who saw the anchor of 50,000 tended to give higher estimates than those who saw the anchor of 100, with a *d* of 0.93, 95% CI [0.51, 1.33]. In Klein et al.'s replication project, all 36 labs replicated this finding and the average effect size was actually larger than the original (*d* = 2.60, 95% CI [2.41, 2.79]).

The Klein group successfully replicated 14 of the 16 studies, and even though the participating labs came from all over the world, the location of the lab did not matter very much (**Figure 14.6**).

**FIGURE 14.6**
**Many labs, many studies.**

In this replication project, 36 labs conducted direct replications of 16 studies and their results were combined. Each X represents an original study's effect size. Each small dot represents the effect estimated by one lab. The black square represents the average effect size combined from all 36 labs. (Source: Adapted from Klein et al., 2014.)

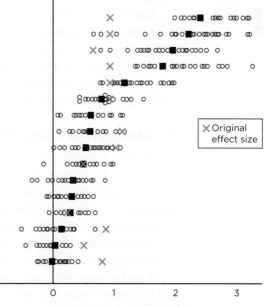

Standardized mean difference (*d*)

## WHY MIGHT A STUDY NOT BE REPLICABLE?

Replication projects have revealed that while many psychological effects are replicable, others are not. When a study fails to replicate, it could be an issue with the replication study itself. Even in direct replications, there are differences in sample, materials, or geography (Van Bavel et al., 2016). Studies may also fail to replicate because of problems with the *original* studies rather than the replications. The original studies might have engaged in research practices that, by today's standards, were likely to lead to fluke results—findings that are not real. During the last 10 years, psychologists have critiqued and improved our ways of doing science, as you will learn later in this chapter.

# Meta-Analysis: What Does the Literature Say?

Progress in psychological science occurs incrementally, as researchers successfully conduct systematic sets of direct replications, conceptual replications, and replication-plus-extension studies. The most credible conclusions are those based on a body of evidence. A **scientific literature** (or simply *literature*) consists of a series of related studies, conducted by various researchers, that have tested similar variables. For example, you might hear your instructors talk about the literature on alcohol and aggression, or the literature on which notetaking form or studying technique is most effective.

Sometimes researchers collect all the studies on a topic and consider them together—generating what is known as a review article, or a literature review (see Chapter 2). One approach is simply to summarize the literature in a narrative way, describing what the studies typically show and explaining how the body of evidence supports a theory.

Researchers can also use the quantitative technique of meta-analysis to create a mathematical summary of a scientific literature. A **meta-analysis**, introduced in Chapter 2, is a way of mathematically averaging the results of all the studies (both published and unpublished) that have tested the same variables to see what conclusion that whole body of evidence supports. The following example will help you understand the basic process involved.

### EXAMPLE: LYING TAKES TIME

A common scene in crime dramas shows a suspect hooked up to lie detection equipment. The theory is that liars experience stress: They display agitated heart rate and sweatier palms when lying than when answering truthfully. However, empirical evidence does not support the accuracy of stress-based lie detection instruments (Saxe, 1991). In fact, they're not permitted in court.

An alternative theory proposes cognitive (rather than emotional) burdens of lying. Liars have to fabricate a story, avoid contradicting themselves, and keep the truth under wraps. As a result, people should take more time to respond to questions when they are lying than when telling the truth. A number of laboratory studies have tested this theory. In one such study, experimenters gave students an envelope containing a jack of spades playing card and a 20-euro bank note, telling them to lie throughout the experiment by saying they'd never seen them (Gamer et al., 2007). Later, during a timed computer task, the students were shown a variety of playing cards and bank notes and were asked if they'd seen them before (**Figure 14.7**). Their reaction times were slower when they denied seeing the jack of spades or 20-euro note than when they denied seeing innocent items ($d = 1.34$, 95% CI [0.62, 2.06]).

A group of researchers conducted a meta-analysis on studies like these (Suchotzki et al., 2017). By searching databases, contacting online groups, and emailing colleagues, they collected 114 experiments. They computed the effect size $d$ of each study, such that the larger the effect size, the greater the reaction time difference between lies and truths. Then they calculated the average of all effect sizes. (Although they used $d$, a meta-analysis can also compute the average of effect sizes as measured by $r$.) The average effect size in the 114 studies was $d = 1.26$, 95% CI [1.14, 1.37]—a very large effect size, supporting the cognitive cost of lying. Notice that the 95% CI is narrow here, reflecting the precision derived from the many studies in a meta-analysis.

**FIGURE 14.7**
**Laboratory studies of lying.**

In some studies, people were shown cards or notes and asked to lie about what they had seen. Why is a meta-analysis more valuable than a single study?

In follow-up analyses, the team separated the studies into different categories. For example, in some studies participants were told to go as fast as possible; in others they were not. The theory predicts that the reaction time difference will be especially noticeable when people are trying to go fast. As expected, the average effect size for the "fast as possible" studies was larger (**Table 14.1**). In other words, speed instructions moderated the relationship between lying and reaction time.

≪
To review moderators,
see Chapter 8, pp. 225–227.

**TABLE 14.1**

**Results for the Reaction Time Difference Between Lying and Truthful Conditions, Categorized by Type of Instructions to Participants**

| TYPE OF STUDY | NUMBER OF STUDIES | TOTAL NUMBER OF PARTICIPANTS | AVERAGE EFFECT SIZE $d$ (LYING CONDITION MINUS TRUTHFUL CONDITION) AND 95% CI |
| --- | --- | --- | --- |
| Participants instructed to go as fast as possible | 100 | 2,866 | 1.29, [1.16, 1.41] |
| Participants not instructed to go fast | 11 | 354 | 0.97, [0.64, 1.30] |

*Note:* Three studies were not able to be categorized.
Source: Adapted from Suchotzki et al., 2017, Table 2.

The researchers also separately analyzed studies in which participants had an incentive to avoid being caught—a situation similar to a criminal interrogation. Motivation to avoid getting caught moderated the influence of lying on reaction time (**Table 14.2**), such that when people were motivated, the reaction time difference was smaller.

## STRENGTHS AND LIMITATIONS OF META-ANALYSIS

The example illustrates several important features of meta-analysis. In a meta-analysis, researchers collect all possible examples of a particular kind of study. Then they average all the effect sizes to find an overall effect size. Using meta-analysis, researchers can also sort the studies into categories (i.e., they can test moderators), computing separate effect size averages for each category. From these follow-up analyses, researchers can detect new patterns in the literature as well as test new questions.

Because meta-analyses usually contain data that have been published in empirical journals, you can be more certain that the data have been peer-reviewed, providing one check on their quality. However, especially in the past, there was a publication bias in psychology: Stronger relationships were more likely to be published than negligible effects. This tendency could lead to the **file drawer problem**, the idea that a meta-analysis might be overestimating the true size of an effect because negligible effects, or even opposite effects, have not been included in the collection process. (The name comes from the notion that instead of being published, these studies sit forgotten in the researchers' filing cabinets.) To combat the problem, researchers who are conducting a meta-analysis should follow the practice of contacting their colleagues (via social media groups and subscription lists), requesting both published and unpublished data for their project.

Here's an illustration of the potential seriousness of the file drawer problem. A group of medical researchers analyzed data from a set of 74 studies in the United States on the effectiveness of antidepressant medications, such as Paxil and Zoloft

TABLE 14.2

### Results for the Reaction Time Difference Between Lying and Truthful Conditions, Categorized by Participants' Motivation to Avoid Detection

| TYPE OF STUDY | NUMBER OF STUDIES | TOTAL NUMBER OF PARTICIPANTS | AVERAGE EFFECT SIZE $d$ (LYING CONDITION MINUS TRUTHFUL CONDITION) AND 95% CI |
|---|---|---|---|
| No motivation | 85 | 2,552 | 1.33, [1.19, 1.47] |
| Instructed to avoid detection | 23 | 626 | 1.00, [0.78, 1.22] |
| Incentive to avoid detection | 6 | 129 | 1.13, [0.84, 1.43] |

Source: Adapted from Suchotzki et al., 2017, Table 2.

(Turner et al., 2008). All the studies had been registered in advance, as required by law, with the U.S. Food and Drug Administration (FDA), which oversees pharmaceutical research. Of the 74 studies, only 38 had shown positive results for these drugs—that is, they alleviated symptoms of depression. Of the rest, 24 studies showed negative and 12 showed "questionable" effects of antidepressants. However, all but one of the positive studies had been published in medical journals, whereas far fewer of the studies with null findings were ever published (**Figure 14.8**). In fact, only 3 of the 36 negative or questionable outcomes were ultimately published. Therefore, if you read only published studies, you would conclude that 94% of them demonstrate that antidepressants are effective, when in fact only 51% of all registered studies have shown that they work.

Literature reviews and meta-analyses are considered valuable by many psychologists because they assess the weight of the evidence in a scientific literature. They tell you whether, across a number of studies, there is a relationship between two variables—and if so, how strong it is. However, a meta-analysis is only as powerful as the data that go into it. If researchers don't work hard to include unpublished results or if studies they do include have followed questionable research practices, the meta-analysis will reach a biased conclusion. New methods try to ensure the studies included in a meta-analysis were well conducted.

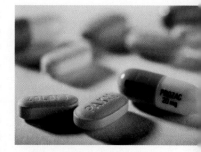

**FIGURE 14.8**
**Selective publication rates.**

About 51% of FDA-registered studies found that antidepressant medications are effective, yet the studies with positive effects are more likely to actually be published in medical journals.

## Replicability and Popular Media

Can you count on the media to tell you which scientific studies are replicable? Not always. For one, journalists do not always consider replicability when they report on science stories. Sometimes journalists will report on a single, hot-off-the-press study because it makes a splashy headline. Responsible journalists, however, not only report on the *latest* studies; they also give readers a sense of what the *entire literature* says on a particular topic. For example, rather than merely announcing the results of a recent study on coffee and depression, a responsible journalist should talk about the context of the entire literature surrounding a study. A study's importance is best judged in the context of the body of evidence.

✔
### CHECK YOUR UNDERSTANDING

1. Describe how the three types of replication studies are similar and different.

2. Explain, in your own words, what a replication project does.

3. Compare the value of a single study to that of a body of evidence, or a scientific literature.

4. In your own words, describe the steps a researcher follows in a meta-analysis. What can a meta-analysis tell you?

1. See pp. 438–441. 2. See pp. 441–443. 3. See p. 444. 4. See pp. 444–447.

# RESEARCH TRANSPARENCY AND CREDIBILITY

You are lucky to be learning research methods now, at a time when psychological research is more transparent and credible than ever. Psychologists have identified questionable research practices and developed strategies to avoid them.

## Questionable Research Practices

In Chapter 1 you learned about Merton's norms of science, which allow science to be self-correcting. For example, scientists should report their own data objectively and make their data public (*communality*), even when the results do not support their hypotheses (*disinterestedness*). Unfortunately, scientists can, even unintentionally, engage in questionable research practices that violate Merton's norms and make scientific progress less likely.

### UNDERREPORTING NULL FINDINGS

One questionable practice is the underreporting of null findings. Researchers normally include multiple dependent variables in an experiment, especially when they are conducting exploratory research. Sometimes only one out of a dozen variables will show a strong effect. However, this practice becomes a problem if, in writing about the research, the researcher reports only the strong effects, not the weak ones. For example, one set of authors failed to report the results of 18 measured variables that did not work out as expected (reported in Rohrer et al., 2015). Underreporting misleads people to think the evidence for a theory is stronger than it really is.

### HARKING

Imagine someone claims they had accurately predicted the outcome of a football game—after it already happened. You would not be that impressed. Similarly, it is questionable to create an after-the-fact hypothesis about a research result, making it appear as if you predicted it all along. This practice is called **HARKing**, for "hypothesizing after the results are known" (Kerr, 1998; **Figure 14.9**). Predictions that happen *before* data are collected are more convincing than those made after the fact, so HARKing misleads readers about the strength of the evidence.

### *p*-HACKING

Researchers can analyze their study's results in a wide variety of ways. They might remove different outliers from the data, compute scores several different ways, or run a few different types of statistics. This exploratory practice has been dubbed **p-hacking**, in part because the goal is to find a *p* value of just under .05, the traditional value for significance testing (corresponding to a 95% CI that does not include zero; Simmons et al., 2011). Researchers do not intentionally *p*-hack, but biases can creep in (Nuzzo, 2015). The practice of *p*-hacking is misleading when others are not told about all the different ways the data were analyzed and only the strongest version is reported.

## Transparent Research Practices

Research transparency helps counter unintentional biases. As physicist Richard Feynman said, "The first principle is that you must not fool yourself, and you are the easiest person to fool" (Feynman, 1974). Transparency helps scientists be more accountable to both themselves and the scientific community. **Table 14.3** summarizes potential biases, the transparent practices meant to reduce them, and the badges a published article might display if researchers followed one of the transparent practices.

**FIGURE 14.9**

**Hypothesizing after the results are known (HARKing).**

One problematic research practice involves creating a hypothesis *after* seeing surprising results (Kerr, 1998). Such findings may be due to chance and cannot be replicated. Careful scientists replicate surprising findings in a new, independent study. The practice of preregistration aims to prevent HARKing, because researchers publish their target (the hypothesis) before they start to collect data.

### OPEN DATA AND OPEN MATERIALS

One transparent practice is **open science**, the practice of sharing one's data and materials freely so others can collaborate, use, and verify the results. With **open data**, psychologists provide their full data set, so other researchers can reproduce the statistical results or even conduct new analyses on it (increasing its usefulness). Open data makes plain the many options available for analysis.

With **open materials**, psychologists provide their study's full set of measures and manipulations so others can conduct replication studies more easily. With open materials, all conditions and measured variables are reported—not just the ones that worked.

### PREREGISTRATION

**Preregistration**, introduced in Chapter 1, occurs when scientists publish their study's method, hypotheses, or statistical analyses in advance of data collection. Preregistrations are time-stamped to help verify that they happened before data were collected. Certain journals treat preregistered studies more favorably; some

## TABLE 14.3

## Questionable Versus Transparent Research Practices

| QUESTIONABLE PRACTICE | EXPLANATION | ALTERNATIVE, TRANSPARENT PRACTICE | EXPLANATION | BADGE USED IN PUBLICATION WHEN THE TRANSPARENT PRACTICE IS USED |
|---|---|---|---|---|
| **Underreporting null effects** | Researchers mislead about the strength of the evidence by not reporting conditions or measures that did not support the hypothesis. | Open materials, in which all study materials are reported publicly | Others can see the full study design and fairly evaluate the strength and consistency of the evidence. | OPEN MATERIALS |
| ***p*-hacking** | Researchers try many ways of analyzing their data, so the result is more likely to be a fluke rather than a true, replicable pattern. | Open data, in which full data sets are provided | Others can re-run and confirm the statistical analyses. They can also use the data to test new questions. | OPEN DATA |
| **HARKing** | The study reveals an unexpected result, but the researcher writes about the study as if the result had been predicted all along. | Preregistration, in which researchers publish the hypothesis and study design before data collection and analysis begin | Others have more confidence in the strength of the evidence. | PREREGISTERED |
| **Using small samples** | In a small sample, a few chance values can influence the data set, so the study's estimate is imprecise and less replicable. | Although it's not part of research transparency, larger samples are now required and encouraged. | Studies with large sample sizes produce estimates that are more precise and replicable. | |

even peer-review the proposal and promise to publish the results regardless of the outcome (these are called *registered reports*). Preregistration gives researchers credit for the importance of the research question and the quality of the study design—not just for the results (Chambers, 2017). Transparent research practices make your job easier as a consumer of information. You probably wouldn't buy a car without checking it out carefully. Similarly, transparent research practices allow anyone to fully check out a study to evaluate its quality before they "buy" it (Vazire, 2018). Transparency helps formalize Merton's norms—it helps science self-correct and progress.

**CHECK YOUR UNDERSTANDING**

1. Describe why underreporting null effects, HARKing, and *p*-hacking are questionable research practices.

2. Explain how open materials, open data, and preregistration help scientists avoid their biases.

1. See pp. 448–449 and Table 14.3. 2. See pp. 449–451.

## MUST A STUDY HAVE EXTERNAL VALIDITY?

Asking about replicability is one way to judge a study's quality. Reproducing a study's results is an essential step that allows researchers to be more confident in the accuracy of their results.

Replicability can also help you interrogate one of the four big validities: external validity—the degree to which a study's results are generalizable to other participants and other settings. Although direct replication studies may not support external validity if they are conducted on the same population as the original, conceptual replications and replication-plus-extension studies can. When researchers test their questions using slightly different methods, different kinds of participants, or different situations, or when they extend their research to study new variables, they are demonstrating how their results generalize to other populations and settings. The more settings and populations in which a study is conducted, the better you can assess the generalizability of the findings.

### Generalizing to Other Participants

Recall that to assess a study's generalizability to other people, you would ask *how* the participants were obtained. If a study is intended to generalize to some population, the researchers must draw a probability sample from that population. If a study uses a convenience sample (such as a haphazard sample of whoever is close by), you can't be sure of the study's generalizability to the population the researcher intends. For example, if a group of researchers wanted to generalize a study's results from a sample of U.S. soldiers to the population of all U.S. soldiers, they would have to use random sampling techniques to draw the sample from the total population of American soldiers.

### IT'S *A* POPULATION, NOT *THE* POPULATION

Bear in mind that the population to which researchers want to generalize usually is not the population of every living person. Instead, when researchers are generalizing from a sample to a population, they will specify what the population of interest is. It might be all the college students in Manitoba. It might be all U.S. soldiers. It might be all the third graders in a Beijing elementary school. It might be a group of lab-reared rhesus monkeys. Researchers are at liberty to specify what their population of interest is based on the theories they are testing.

### EXTERNAL VALIDITY COMES FROM *HOW*, NOT *HOW MANY*

»

For a review of sample size and generalizability, see Chapter 7, pp. 179–192.

Recall that when you are assessing the generalizability of a sample to a population, "how" matters more than "how many." In other words, a randomly selected sample of 200 participants has external validity; a haphazardly selected sample of 2,000 participants does not.

### JUST BECAUSE A SAMPLE COMES FROM A POPULATION DOESN'T MEAN IT GENERALIZES TO THAT POPULATION

Some students assume that if a convenience sample simply includes some members of a population (perhaps dog owners, or Asian men, or Methodist ministers), the sample can therefore generalize to those populations (of all dog owners, Asian men, or Methodist ministers). Instead, the same rules apply: In order to generalize to any population, you would need a probability sample of dog owners, or of Asian men, or Methodist ministers. If you had only a convenience sample, it might primarily contain the dog owners whom the researcher could contact easily and who were willing to participate in the study.

## Generalizing to Other Settings

The other aspect of external validity is a study's generalizability to different settings. Conceptual replications illustrate this aspect of external validity very well. When researchers extended the studies of alcohol and aggression from reaction time to photos to interpretation of Donald's potentially aggressive behavior (p. 439), they showed that the results could generalize from one setting to another setting.

Sometimes you want to know whether a lab situation created for a study generalizes to real-world settings. For example, you might ask whether the studies on lying about playing cards, which took place in the laboratory on a computer, would generalize meaningfully to real-world lies. A study's similarity to real-world contexts is sometimes called its **ecological validity**, or *mundane realism* (explained in detail later in this chapter). Many psychologists consider ecological validity to be one aspect of external validity (Brewer, 2000).

# Does a Study Have to Be Generalizable to Many People?

How is external validity related to a study's quality and importance? Read the following two statements and decide whether you agree with each one:

1. The best research uses random samples from the population.
2. The best research uses people of all genders, ages, and ethnicities, and from all socioeconomic classes, regions, countries, and so on.

Of course, both of these statements address the external validity of a particular study. When the sample for a study has been selected from a population *at random* (using a probability sample), the results from that sample can be generalized to the population it was drawn from. It also makes sense that if a study's sample includes only men, you may not generalize its results to women; if a study's sample includes only college students from Manitoba, you may not generalize its results to elderly residents of Florida. Because most people have a strong intuitive understanding of external validity, they will agree with the two statements above.

However, the two statements are only *sometimes* right. Evaluating the importance of external validity requires a nuanced approach that considers the researcher's priorities. Whether a researcher strives for external validity in a study depends on what research mode he or she is operating in: theory-testing mode or generalization mode.

## THEORY-TESTING MODE

When researchers work in **theory-testing mode**, they are usually designing correlational or experimental research to investigate support for a theory. As discussed in Chapter 1, the theory-data cycle is the process of designing studies to test a theory and using the data from the studies to reject, refine, or support the theory. In theory-testing mode, external validity often matters less than internal validity.

**Example: The Contact Comfort Theory.** Harlow's classic study of attachment in infant monkeys (described in Chapters 1 and 10) is a good example of theory-testing mode (Harlow, 1958). Harlow created two artificial monkey "mothers" in order to test two competing theories of infant attachment: the cupboard theory (babies are attached to their mothers because their mothers feed them) and the contact comfort theory (babies are attached to their mothers because their mothers are soft and cozy). In a real monkey mother, of course, the features of food and coziness are confounded. So Harlow separated the two features by creating one cloth mother that was soft and cozy but did not provide food and one wire mother that was cold and uncomfortable but did provide food. By separating the two confounded variables, Harlow was prioritizing internal validity.

Harlow was clearly in theory-testing mode here, wondering which theory, the cupboard theory or the contact comfort theory, was right. And the results from his study could not have been clearer: The baby monkeys in this study spent almost all of their time cuddling with the soft, cozy mother. The contact comfort theory was overwhelmingly supported.

The monkeys in Harlow's study were hardly representative of monkeys in the wild. He didn't even use a random sample of monkeys from his laboratory. But Harlow didn't care because he was in theory-testing mode: He created the artificial situation to test his *theory*—not to test the truth in some population of monkeys. In fact, according to the cupboard theory, *any* sample of monkeys— no matter how representative—should have been equally or more interested in the wire mother than they were in the cloth mother. The data, however, did not support the cupboard theory of attachment.

**Example: The "Parent-as-Grammar-Coach" Theory.** Another example of a study conducted in theory-testing mode comes from research on how children learn grammar. Some psychologists used to believe that children learn correct grammar through reinforcement, as parents praise a child's grammatically correct sentences and correct the ungrammatical ones. They thought children learned grammar through this constant correction process.

The reinforcement theory predicted that parents would praise their kids for grammatical sentences and correct the ungrammatical sentences. But read the following interaction, audiotaped by Brown and Hanlon in a study that observed parents interacting with their children (1970, cited in Mook, 1989, p. 27):

> **Child:** Mama isn't boy, he girl.
> **Parent:** That's right.
> **Child:** There's the animal farmhouse.
> **Parent:** No, that's a lighthouse.

What Brown and Hanlon noticed—and you probably did, too—is that the parent accepted the child's first sentence, which was ungrammatical but factually true. (*That's right—he girl!*) But the parent corrected the child's second sentence, which was grammatically correct but factually wrong. (*Not a farmhouse—a lighthouse!*) This one incident illustrates the overall trend in the data. After coding hours of conversations between parents and children, Brown and Hanlon found that most of the time, parents corrected their children's sentences for factual accuracy but not for grammar. Furthermore, the reinforcement theory predicted that the children in this study would not learn to speak properly without having their grammar corrected. But even though the parents didn't point out errors, the children did learn to speak grammatically. The reinforcement theory of speech development therefore was not supported.

This study included only upper-middle-class Boston families, so the children and parents were not representative of all children, even of all Boston children (Brown & Hanlon, 1970). Moreover, the parents in the study were willing to let a researcher record their interactions with their children on tape; they might have been especially eager to be involved in research or were more educated than average (**Figure 14.10**). Yet the bias of this sample didn't matter because the researchers were testing a theory: If the reinforcement theory of grammar were true, *any* sample of parents would have corrected ungrammatical sentences, but the parents in this study did not.

Of course, the reinforcement theory of grammar might apply to some other population in the world, and if Brown and Hanlon had studied a wider sample of people, they might have found evidence that some parents, somewhere, do correct their children's grammar. Keep two things in mind. First, the researchers chose a strong test of their theory. If the reinforcement theory of grammar should apply anywhere, it would be among precisely the kinds of parents who volunteered for the study: upper-middle class, well-educated, and interested in research. Such parents presumably use standard grammar themselves and are willing to explain grammar rules to their children. Second, if the researchers had found some other cultural group of parents who did correct their children's grammar, they would have to modify the reinforcement theory to fit these new data. They'd have to change the theory to explain why reinforcement applies only in this population but not in others. In either case, the data from Brown and Hanlon's study mean that the "parent-as-grammar-coach" theory must be rejected or at least modified.

**Other Examples.** The overwhelming majority of studies in psychology are of the theory-testing type (Mook, 1989). Most researchers design studies that enable them to test competing explanations and confirm or disconfirm their hypotheses. For example, research on people's reaction times while lying tested the theory that lying entails a cognitive cost. Strayer's research on cell phone use while driving, which you read about in Chapter 12, tested the theory that cell phones are cognitively distracting to drivers. When researchers are in theory-testing mode, they are not very concerned (at least not yet) with the external validity of their samples or procedures (Berkowitz & Donnerstein, 1982).

## GENERALIZATION MODE

Although psychologists test many of their association and causal claims in theory-testing mode, at certain times theory-testing takes place in **generalization mode**, when researchers want to generalize the findings from the sample in a previous study to a larger population. They are careful, therefore, to use probability samples with appropriate diversity of gender, age, ethnicity, and so on. In other words, researchers in generalization mode are concerned about external validity.

**Frequency Claims: Always in Generalization Mode.** Survey research that is intended to support frequency claims is done in generalization mode. A researcher must have a representative sample in order to answer such questions as: "How many U.S. teenagers text while driving?" "What percentage of voters support the health care law?" "At what age do Dutch children learn to read?" It would not be acceptable to estimate U.S. teenage texting-while-driving rates from a haphazard sample of youths in an upper-middle-class high school in New York

**FIGURE 14.10**
**When is external validity crucial?**

In the "parent-as-grammar-coach" study, the sample included only upper-middle-class Boston families (Brown & Hanlon, 1970). Why was it acceptable to use a nonrandom sample in this research?

City. Estimating the percentage of voters who support a national health care law by interviewing only people living in Dallas, Texas, wouldn't be okay either. And it wouldn't be acceptable to estimate the age at which Dutch children learn to read by asking a self-selected sample on a web page dedicated to gifted children. All these samples would be biased.

As you have learned, representative samples are essential for supporting frequency claims. (For a review, see Chapters 3 and 7.) Therefore, when researchers are testing frequency claims, they are always in generalization mode.

**Association and Causal Claims: Sometimes in Generalization Mode.** Most of the time, association and causal claims are conducted in theory-testing mode. But researchers sometimes conduct them in generalization mode, too.

Suppose a researcher tries out a new therapeutic technique on a limited sample of clients (such as a sample of European-American women) and finds that it works. If the therapy is effective in this sample, the researcher would then want to learn whether it will also be effective more generally, in other samples. Will it work on African-American women? Will it work on men? To learn whether the therapy's effectiveness generalizes to other populations, the researcher has to collect data on samples from those populations. In this case, the researcher cares about generalizability from one sociocultural group to another.

Consider a marketing researcher who learns that a sample of local teenagers prefers an advertising campaign featuring tattoo artists over an ad campaign featuring a professional skateboarder. The researcher would hope to generalize the pattern from this particular sample to the teenagers around the country who will eventually view the ads. Therefore, the marketing researcher would care very much that the sample used in the study represents teenagers nationwide. Are they the same age? Are they of the same social class? Do they show the same distribution of ethnicities? Was the focus group sample unusually interested in tattoos, compared with the rest of the country's teenage population? Only if the external validity were sound would the preferences of this sample be generalizable to the preferences of the nation's teens.

## CULTURAL PSYCHOLOGY: A SPECIAL CASE OF GENERALIZATION MODE

**Cultural psychology** is a subdiscipline of psychology focusing on how cultural contexts shape the way a person thinks, feels, and behaves (Heine, 2020; Markus & Hamedani, 2007; Shweder, 1989). In conducting their studies, cultural psychologists work in generalization mode. They have challenged researchers who work exclusively in theory-testing mode by identifying several theories that were supported by data in one cultural context but not in any other. Here's a strong example.

**The Müller-Lyer Illusion.** You may already be familiar with the Müller-Lyer illusion, illustrated in **Figure 14.11**. Does the vertical line B appear longer than the

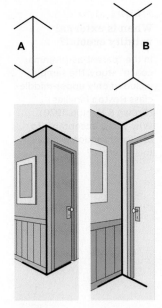

**FIGURE 14.11**
**The Müller-Lyer illusion.**

(Top) The vertical lines labeled A and B are the same length, but North Americans and Europeans usually perceive line B to be longer than line A. That perception is not true for all people worldwide. (Bottom) Researchers propose that only people who grow up in "carpentered worlds" learn how combinations of lines generate depth cues. (Source: Heine, 2020.)

vertical line A? If you take out a ruler and measure the two vertical lines, you'll find they are exactly the same length.

Almost all North Americans and Europeans fall for this illusion, but not all *people* do. Indeed, one team of researchers found that many people around the world, when tested, do not see line B as being longer than line A (Segall et al., 1966). **Figure 14.12** shows the cross-cultural results of this study.

Suppose a group of researchers in theory-testing mode used the Müller-Lyer data from a single North American sample to test a theory about human visual perception. Though they might not think culture would affect such a basic cognitive process—the illusion seems to happen naturally!—they would be wrong. In fact, the Segall team used their global data to conclude that people who grow up in a "carpentered world" have more visual experience with right angles as cues for depth perception than people who grow up in other societies. (Look at the corner of the room you're in right now. Do you see the angles of line B in the Müller-Lyer illusion?) In environments with few square buildings, a child's developing visual system doesn't perceive the end-lines of walls angling in as indicating a corner is near, or end-lines angling out suggesting a corner is farther away. Such culturally learned cues are the proposed explanation for the Müller-Lyer illusion.

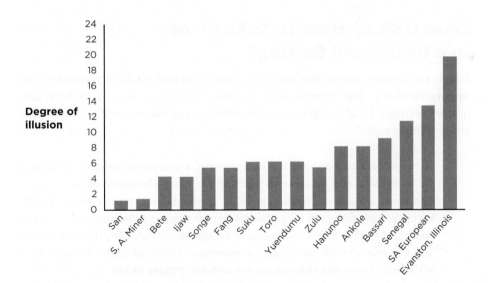

**FIGURE 14.12**

**Cross-cultural results for the Müller-Lyer illusion.**

Segall et al. (1966) tested the Müller-Lyer illusion on adults in 16 societies and found that North Americans are most likely to perceive the illusion. The *y*-axis shows how much longer line B (in Figure 14.11) appears to participants compared with line A. The higher the value, the greater the degree of the illusion. (Source: Adapted from Henrich et al., 2010.)

Cultural studies like these remind other researchers they cannot take generalization for granted. Even psychological processes that seem basic and fundamental can be affected by cultural environments.

### THEORY TESTING USING WEIRD PARTICIPANTS

To understand the importance of cultural psychologists' work, consider that most research in psychological science has been conducted on North American college students. One researcher recorded the samples used in the top six journals in psychology for the year 2007. In these core journals, 68% of the participants were American and 96% of the participants were from North America, Europe, Australia, or Israel (Arnett, 2008). Participants from these countries are from a unique subset of the world's population, which researchers refer to as WEIRD: Western, educated, industrialized, rich, and democratic (Henrich et al., 2010). Obviously, WEIRD samples are not very representative of all the world's people. The Müller-Lyer illusion demonstrates how seemingly basic human processes can work differently in different cultural contexts.

When researchers in psychology operate in theory-testing mode, they do not prioritize external validity and they may even test their theories only on WEIRD participants. However, cultural psychologists raise the alarm, reminding researchers that theories that have been tested only on WEIRD subjects may not apply to everyone (Arnett, 2008; Henrich et al., 2010; Sears, 1986).

## Does a Study Have to Take Place in a Real-World Setting?

People sometimes assume that studies conducted in real-world settings are more important—that is, have more real-world value—than those held in artificial laboratory settings. Read the following descriptions and ask yourself whether each study is important:

1. To investigate recognizing the human form, a researcher dressed a student model in black and taped small lights to her head, shoulders, elbows, wrists, hips, knees, and ankles (Johansson, 1973). The model was videotaped while walking in the dark in the lab. Later, the researcher showed either the video or a still photograph of the model to a group of college students, asking them what they saw. Observers of the photo saw a meaningless jumble of lights, and observers of the movie reported seeing a person walking (**Figure 14.13**).

2. Memory researcher Suzanne Corkin and her colleagues asked the famous patient H.M. to trace a star shape with a pencil while seeing his hand only in a mirror (see Chapter 13). Although his performance improved every day, he had to be reintroduced to the task daily because he claimed he'd never seen it before (Corkin, 2013).

3. Researcher Elizabeth Paluck investigated the positive impact of a radio show in post-genocide Rwanda in Africa. After the mass slaughter of Tutsis by

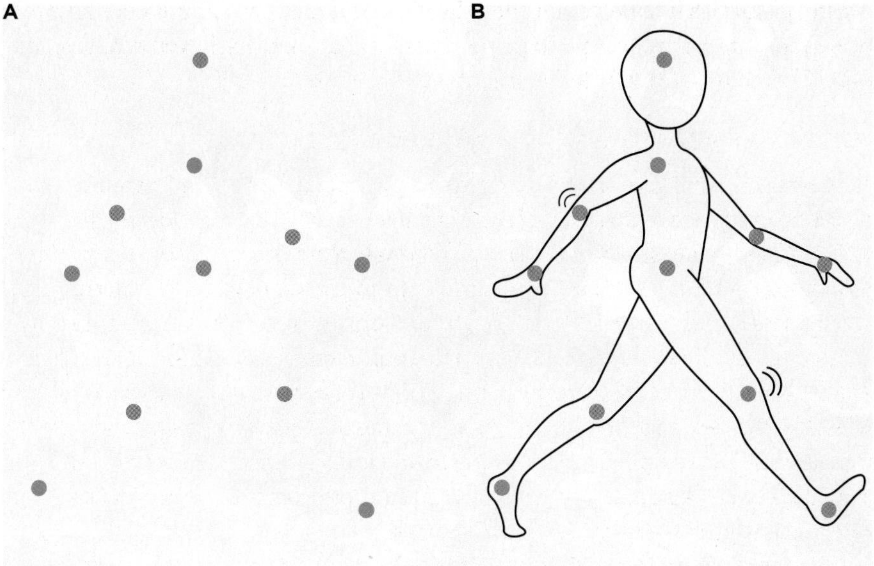

**FIGURE 14.13**
**Recognizing a human form.**

In this study, a model wore lights on several body parts. Participants viewed either (**A**) a still photo of the model or (**B**) a video of the model walking in a dark room. The results demonstrated that people cannot recognize the human form from points of light alone; the figure has to be moving. In the real world, you never observe people walking around in the dark with small lights illuminating their joints. (Source: Adapted from Johansson, 1973.)

Hutus in the 1990s, Rwanda faced a crisis of intergroup trust as returned refugees, victims, and accused perpetrators tried to live together within a single community. One hope for healing came from a radio soap opera called *New Dawn* (*Musekeweya*), about a fictional multiethnic community facing shortages and intergroup violence. The characters later reconcile, and the radio show delivered messages about cooperation and communication. Paluck and her team randomly assigned groups of Rwandan community members to listen to either *New Dawn* or a control program about healthy behavior (Paluck, 2009). Participants listened to the radio in small groups (a common practice in Rwanda) once a month over the course of a year. At the end of the year, the researchers interviewed each participant. The results showed that people who had listened to the *New Dawn* program (compared with controls) endorsed more trusting, cooperative social norms. They were also more likely to express their opinions in a situation that required making a cooperative group decision. The researchers concluded that media programming can improve people's perceptions of cooperation (**Figure 14.14**).

If you were a news producer, which of these three studies would you deem most important to share with your audience? You might argue on the basis of generalizability. For instance, the lights study does not tell you anything about the real world; after all, how often do you see someone walking around in a dark room with lights taped to his or her knees? You might say that most people do not have lesions in their hippocampus, so the mirror-tracing memory study doesn't apply to the majority of people. Finally, you might conclude the radio study is the most important because it took place in a real-world setting and addressed a serious problem. If so, you were probably guided by the assumption that a study

**FIGURE 14.14**
**The power of radio in Rwanda.**

Listening to radio programs in small groups is common in the African country of Rwanda. Divisive radio propaganda played a role in inciting violence in Rwanda in 1994. As the country recovered from genocide, a field experiment tested the power of a healing-oriented radio soap opera to improve social norms of cooperation.

should be similar to real-world contexts and daily life in order to be important. But is this always true?

## EXTERNAL VALIDITY AND THE REAL WORLD

When interrogating a study's external validity, you ask whether the results can generalize not only to other populations but also to other settings. When research takes place in the real world, sometimes referred to as a **field setting**, it has a built-in advantage for external validity because it clearly applies to real-world contexts. As mentioned previously, ecological validity is one aspect of external validity, referring to the extent to which a study's tasks and manipulations are similar to the kinds of situations participants might encounter in their everyday lives. Paluck's study in Rwanda has excellent ecological validity because of its field setting. However, ecological validity is just one factor in generalizability because a study's setting may not represent all possible environments. Would the results of the radio study apply to a different social problem? Would it also apply in a cultural context that doesn't have a tradition of radio dramas?

The situation a researcher creates in a lab can be just as real as one that occurs in a restaurant or workplace. Although it may be easy to dismiss a study that does not seem realistic, remember that in daily life people find themselves in all kinds of settings, all of which are real, including community centers, shops, and theaters, as well as classrooms and research labs. Indeed, the emotions and behaviors generated by a laboratory manipulation (e.g., taking notes during a lecture or having a cell phone conversation during a driving simulator task) can also be quite real, visible, and meaningful. Many lab experiments excel in **experimental realism**: They create situations in which people experience authentic emotions, motivations, and behaviors. People in lab studies have interacted with actual people, drunk real alcoholic beverages, and played games with other participants. Many of these situations are truly engaging and emotionally evocative.

To what extent does the real-world similarity—the ecological validity—of a study affect your ideas about a study's importance? A nuanced answer will consider the mode in which it is conducted: generalization mode or theory-testing mode.

## GENERALIZATION MODE AND THE REAL WORLD

Because external validity is of primary importance when researchers are in generalization mode, they might strive for a representative sample of a population. But they might also try to enhance the ecological validity of a study in order to ensure its generalizability to nonlaboratory settings. By the time Paluck (2009) studied the impact of radio programs in Rwanda, people had already tested the short-term impact of media messages in the lab. For example, one study established that when people feel empathy with others, they feel less prejudice (Batson et al., 1997). Studies had also tested how social norms can affect biased behavior (Crandall & Stangor, 2005). But no one studied the impact of an engaging radio soap opera over the long term with adults in a field setting.

## THEORY-TESTING MODE AND THE REAL WORLD

When a researcher is working in theory-testing mode, external validity and real-world applicability may be lower priorities. Take, for instance, the Johansson (1973) study, in which the model had lights attached to her head and her joints. Of course, no one is going to encounter these circumstances in the real world, but the ecological validity of the situation didn't matter to the researcher. He was testing a research question: How much information do people need before they can conclude they're looking at a human? By keeping the room dark and having lights only on the model's head and joints, the researcher was able to cut out all other visual information. He was concerned with internal validity—eliminating alternative explanations for an interpretation. To narrow down exactly what visual information was necessary to recognize a human form, Johansson had to create an extremely artificial situation.

Was the Johansson study important? In terms of the theory he was testing, it was invaluable because he was able to show that both joint location and movement are necessary and sufficient to recognize a human form. What about generalizability and real-world applicability? On the one hand, both the model and the study's participants were drawn haphazardly, not randomly, from a small group of North American college students. The situation created in the lab would never occur in the real world. On the other hand, the ability to recognize human gestures, postures, and moods is undoubtedly essential for many aspects of social life. The theoretical understanding gained from this seemingly artificial study contributes to our understanding of a perceptual process involved in basic social cognition.

Let's consider the study design that many people (quite correctly) respect as a pinnacle of behavioral research: the randomized, double-blind, placebo-controlled study, introduced in Chapter 11. In such a study, an experimenter goes to extreme artificial lengths to assign people at random to carefully constructed experimental conditions that control for placebo effects, experimenter bias, and experimental demand. Such studies have virtually no equivalent in everyday, real-world settings, yet their results can be among the most valuable in psychological science.

In short, theory-testing mode often demands that experimenters create artificial situations that allow them to minimize distractions, eliminate alternative explanations, and isolate individual features of some situation. Theory-testing mode prioritizes internal validity at the expense of all other considerations, including ecological validity. Nonetheless, such studies make valuable contributions to the field of psychology.

**Table 14.4** summarizes the approach to importance, credibility, and external validity that has been emphasized in this chapter.

**TABLE 14.4**

## Responding Appropriately to the "Latest Scientific Breakthrough"

| SAY THIS | NOT THAT |
| --- | --- |
| "Was that finding replicated?"<br>"That is a single study. How does the study fit in with the entire literature?" | "Look at this single, interesting result!" |
| "How well do the methods of this study get at the theory they were testing?" | "I don't think this study is important because the methods had nothing to do with the real world." |
| "Was the study conducted in generalization mode? If so, were the participants representative of the population of interest?" | "I reject this study because they didn't use a random sample."<br>"This is a bad study because they used only North Americans as participants." |
| "The study had thousands of participants, but were they selected in such a way to allow generalization to the population of interest?" | "They used thousands of participants. It must have great external validity." |
| "Would the result hold up in another cultural context?"<br>"Would that result apply in other settings?" | "That psychological principle seems so basic, I'm sure it's universal." |

## CHECK YOUR UNDERSTANDING

1. Describe the difference between generalization mode and theory-testing mode.

2. Which of the three types of claims (frequency, association, causal) is/are almost always conducted in generalization mode? Which of the three types of claims is/are usually conducted in theory-testing mode?

3. Explain why researchers who are operating in theory-testing mode might not use a random sample in their study. What validity are they prioritizing? What aspects of their research are they emphasizing (for now)?

4. Summarize the goal of cultural psychology. What does this field suggest about working in theory-testing and generalization modes?

5. Even if an experiment tests hypotheses in an artificial laboratory setting, the study's findings may still apply to the real world. Explain why.

1. See pp. 453-458. 2. See pp. 455-456. 3. See pp. 453-455. 4. See pp. 456-458. 5. See pp. 458-462.

# CHAPTER REVIEW

 It's time to complete your study experience! Go to INQUIZITIVE to practice actively with this chapter's concepts and get personalized feedback along the way.

## Summary

A nuanced approach can be used to evaluate a study's credibility and importance. A study must be replicated to be deemed credible, but it might not need to be generalizable or have immediate real-world applicability to be important.

### REPLICATION

- Replication studies determine whether the findings of an original study are reproducible.

- A direct replication repeats the original study exactly. A conceptual replication has the same conceptual variables as the original study but operationalizes the variables differently. A replication-plus-extension study repeats the original study and introduces new participant variables, situations, or independent variable levels.

- Replication projects coordinate labs around the world to conduct direct replication studies of between one and several psychological studies at a time.

- A meta-analysis collects and mathematically averages the effect sizes from all studies that have tested the same variables. It helps quantify whether an effect exists in the literature and, if so, its size and what moderates it.

### RESEARCH TRANSPARENCY AND CREDIBILITY

- Psychologists have identified questionable research practices that include underreporting null results, *p*-hacking, and hypothesizing after the results are known (HARKing). These may produce findings that cannot be replicated.

- Many psychological scientists now promote open data, open materials, and preregistration to strengthen the verifiability and replicability of studies.

### MUST A STUDY HAVE EXTERNAL VALIDITY?

- The importance of external validity depends on whether researchers are operating in generalization mode or theory-testing mode.

- In theory-testing mode, researchers design studies that test a theory, leaving the generalization step for later studies, which will test whether the theory holds in a sample that is representative of another population.

- In generalization mode, researchers focus on whether their samples are representative, whether the data from their sample apply to the population of interest, and even whether the data might apply to a new population of interest.

- In contrast to what many casual observers assume, high-quality research might not always have good external validity. Diverse, representative samples are primarily important when researchers are in generalization mode. In theory-testing mode, researchers do not (yet) consider whether their samples are representative of some population, so external validity is less important than internal validity.

- Researchers who make frequency claims are always in generalization mode. Researchers are also in generalization mode when asking whether an association or causal claim can be generalized to a different group of people.

- Cultural psychologists have documented how psychological discoveries, including basic cognitive or

- visual processes, are not always applicable cross-culturally.
- When researchers collect data only from WEIRD (Western, educated, industrialized, rich, and democratic) samples, they cannot assume the theories they develop in theory-testing mode will apply to all people.
- Research does not necessarily have to be conducted in a field setting to have ecological validity.

- Laboratory studies conducted in theory-testing mode might have strong experimental realism even if they do not resemble real-world situations outside the lab. Yet the data from such artificial settings help researchers test theories in the most internally valid way possible, and the results may still be important and apply to real-world circumstances.

## Key Terms

replicable, p. 437
direct replication, p. 438
conceptual replication, p. 439
replication-plus-extension, p. 440
scientific literature, p. 444
meta-analysis, p. 444
file drawer problem, p. 446

HARKing, p. 448
*p*-hacking, p. 449
open science, p. 449
open data, p. 449
open materials, p. 449
preregistration, p. 449
ecological validity, p. 452

theory-testing mode, p. 453
generalization mode, p. 455
cultural psychology, p. 456
field setting, p. 460
experimental realism, p. 460

 **To see samples of chapter concepts in the popular media, visit www.everydayresearchmethods.com and click the box for Chapter 14.**

## Review Questions

1. If you repeat a study and find the same results as the first time, what can you say about the original study?
   a. It is replicable.
   b. It is statistically significant.
   c. It is valid.
   d. It is consistent.

2. When researchers conduct a replication study in which they have the same variables at an abstract level but use different operationalizations of each variable, what type of study is it?
   a. Direct replication
   b. Meta-analysis
   c. Conceptual replication
   d. Replication-plus-extension

3. Which of these new research practices is most relevant for preventing HARKing?
   a. Open data
   b. Open materials
   c. Preregistration
   d. Using a larger sample

4. Which of the following claims is most likely to have been tested in generalization mode?
   a. Four out of 10 teenagers can't identify fake news when they see it.
   b. Reading stressful news makes adults anxious.
   c. People who walk faster live longer.

5. Which of these is a field setting?

   a. A psychology lab with a hidden camera

   b. A neuropsychology lab with an MRI machine

   c. A preschool playground with video cameras

   d. A biology lab with galvanic skin response detectors

6. Which of these statements is true of external validity?

   a. Psychologists usually strive to generalize to all people.

   b. For generalization to a population, the larger the sample, the better.

   c. External validity comes from how the sample is obtained, rather than sample size.

   d. A sample that contains female college students can generalize to all female college students.

# Learning Actively

1. Consider the study that measured the amount of time people spent sitting and the thickness of their medial-temporal lobes, from Chapter 8 (Siddarth et al., 2018). How would you conduct a direct replication of this study? A conceptual replication? A replication-plus-extension?

2. Search the Internet for the phrase "hack your way to scientific glory" to find an interactive tool that allows you to try *p*-hacking on a real data set. How many different options did you try before you found a statistically significant result?

3. Visit the website for the journal *Psychological Science* and look for articles that have badges for open data, open materials, or preregistration (see examples in Table 14.3). Follow the links provided in the badged article to visit the location of that study's open data, materials, or preregistration. What do you notice?

4. For each short study description below, indicate whether you think it would have been conducted in theory-testing mode or generalization mode or whether it could be done in either mode. Explain your answer. For which of these studies would a random sample of participants be the most important? For which would external validity be the least important?

   a. A study found that most Holocaust survivors struggle with depression, sleep disorders, and emotional distress. The conclusion was based on a government data set that has tracked 220,000 Holocaust survivors ("Most Holocaust Survivors Battle Depression," 2010).

   b. A team of neuropsychologists tested memory in mice, using a pretest/posttest design. The mice's cages were exposed to a typical cell phone's electromagnetic field for 1 hour a day, for 9 months. Later, the researchers tested each mouse's memory and found the mice had better memory after exposure to the electromagnetic fields than before and better memory compared with the no-exposure control group (Hamzelou, 2010).

   c. A group of researchers studied three people in India who were born blind. At ages 7, 12, and 29, each one received surgery and treatment to correct their vision. After the patients regained their sight, the researchers studied how they had developed their newly acquired abilities to decode the visual world. At first, each patient thought that a two-dimensional picture, such as the one labeled B in the figure, depicted three objects instead of two. With several months of experience, however, they all learned to interpret the images correctly. By moving the objects apart from each other on some of the trials, the researchers discovered that all three men could use motion cues to decode what lines belonged to which object (similar to how people in Johansson's study could identify that a lighted model was a walking human only when the model was moving). The researchers concluded that as the brain learns about the visual world, it uses motion cues to decide which lines belong to which objects (Ostrovsky et al., 2009).

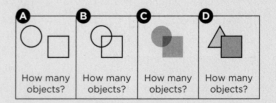

# Statistics Review

## DESCRIPTIVE STATISTICS

In everyday language, the word *statistics* is used to describe quantitative records, such as a baseball player's batting average or the average life span of a country's citizens. In science, the word refers to the set of tools researchers use to make sense of data that they have collected in a study. This supplementary chapter provides a very brief overview of one set of such statistical tools: **descriptive statistics**, used for organizing and summarizing the properties of a set of data. The other set of statistical tools, inferential statistics, is covered in the supplementary chapter that follows this one.

## DESCRIBING DATA

Recall that when a researcher collects data from a group of people or animals, the group is often a sample from a larger population. If we tested 5 rhesus monkeys on their ability to discriminate blue from green, and the 5 came from a larger population of 25 monkeys in the lab, then the 5 monkeys would be the sample. If we tested 50 students on their anagram skills, the 50 students might be a sample from a larger population of students who could have signed up for the research.

However, researchers don't always study a sample from a larger population. If a midterm exam is given to 31 students, the 31 students are a complete set of cases. They are not a sample because they are the whole population of interest. Or we might collect data on the average family income and teen pregnancy rates in all 50 states in the United States. These 50 states are not a sample, either; they are a population. We might simply have a batch of scores—perhaps a set of prices from the local supermarket, or some data on reading speed from a group of third graders. Regardless of whether our data are best described as a sample, a population, or a simple set of scores, we can still apply the descriptive techniques explained here.

Variables are what researchers measure or manipulate in a study. If we study 31 students' grades on a midterm exam, then exam score is the variable. In other studies, variables might be the ability to discriminate blue from green, the average family income, or the pregnancy rate among teenagers. Variables vary: They take on different levels, or values, for the different members of a sample. Thus, the

« For a review of categorical and quantitative variables, see Chapter 5, pp. 122–123.

| Student name | Exam score |
|---|---|
| Henry | 17 |
| Emma | 29 |
| Caitlyn | 19 |
| Lonnie | 27 |
| Lalia | 22 |
| Alek | 27 |
| Rohan | 22 |
| Max | 20 |
| Shane | 29 |
| Yukiko | 29 |
| Alexi | 18 |
| Marianna | 30 |
| Mira | 21 |
| Cristina | 27 |
| Emmanuel | 26 |
| Raul | 30 |
| Ian | 19 |
| Sena | 29 |
| Jordan | 27 |
| Ayase | 32 |
| Luke | 25 |
| Miguel | 32 |
| Jon | 30 |
| Gabriel | 31 |
| Rhianna | 32 |
| Juniper | 24 |
| Malika | 25 |
| Shawn | 30 |
| Adhya | 24 |
| Harriet | 33 |
| Lucio | 25 |

**FIGURE S1.1**

**A data matrix of exam scores.**

A data matrix is the starting point for computing most statistics.

values for an exam score might range from 16 to 33 on a 35-point scale. Ability to discriminate blue from green might have the categorical values of "yes" or "no." Average family income might have quantitative values ranging from $12,000 up to millions of dollars and anything in between.

## Data Matrices

After we collect a set of data, we usually enter the data in a grid format, called a **data matrix**, using a computer program. Programs such as Excel, SPSS, R, or JASP can calculate formulas and facilitate making graphs and organizing data in various ways. **Figure S1.1** shows a data matrix with the scores of 31 students who took a short-answer exam consisting of 35 items. The first column identifies each person by name (this column might contain simple ID numbers instead). The second column shows the person's score on the exam. In a data matrix, each column represents a variable, and each row represents a case (such as a person, an animal, a state, a product, or any other case under study).

## Frequency Distributions and Dot Plots

At first glance, the data matrix shows a disorganized list of scores. However, data visualization techniques such as frequency distributions and dot plots can quickly bring some order to the scores. A **frequency distribution** is a table that gives a visual picture of the observations on a particular variable. It clearly shows how many of the cases scored each possible value on the variable.

To make a frequency distribution, we list possible values for the variable from lowest to highest and tally how many people obtained each score, as in **Figure S1.2A**. Normally, we do not leave the tally marks there; we count them and enter the value in the table, as in **Figure S1.2B**. Based on the data from a frequency distribution, it is a fairly simple step to create a graph called a **frequency histogram** (often called simply a *histogram*), as in **Figure S1.3A**. Note that the possible exam scores are on the *x*-axis, while the frequency of each score is on the *y*-axis. We could also draw the histogram the other way, as in **Figure S1.3B**.

Instead of giving individual numerical scores, we could group the exam score values. For example, if we call any score between 30 and 33 an A, any score between 25 and 29 a B, and so on, the frequency histogram looks simpler, as in **Figure S1.4**.

Another option for data visualization is a **dot plot**. **Figure S1.5** shows the data from the midterm exam in dot plot form. The *y*-axis depicts the possible scores on the exam. Each dot represents a single score. Dot plots can be jittered, like the one in Figure S1.5, meaning that the dots are spread out a little bit horizontally, making it easier to see all of the scores (jittering is especially important when more than one person got the same score). A grouped frequency distribution might tell us that nine students got an A in the class, but we would not know what the students' exact scores were. In contrast, dot plots are increasingly used in the spirit

| A | Possible value | Number of cases |
|---|----------------|-----------------|
| | 17 | I |
| | 18 | I |
| | 19 | II |
| | 20 | I |
| | 21 | I |
| | 22 | II |
| | 23 | |
| | 24 | II |
| | 25 | III |
| | 26 | I |
| | 27 | IIII |
| | 28 | |
| | 29 | IIII |
| | 30 | IIII |
| | 31 | I |
| | 32 | III |
| | 33 | I |

| B | Possible value | Number of cases |
|---|----------------|-----------------|
| | 17 | 1 |
| | 18 | 1 |
| | 19 | 2 |
| | 20 | 1 |
| | 21 | 1 |
| | 22 | 2 |
| | 23 | 0 |
| | 24 | 2 |
| | 25 | 3 |
| | 26 | 1 |
| | 27 | 4 |
| | 28 | 0 |
| | 29 | 4 |
| | 30 | 4 |
| | 31 | 1 |
| | 32 | 3 |
| | 33 | 1 |

**FIGURE S1.2**

**A frequency distribution for the exam scores in Figure S1.1.**

(**A**) List the possible values in one column and tally the number of times each value occurs in the data set in the next column. Then convert the tallies to numerals. (**B**) The final frequency distribution.

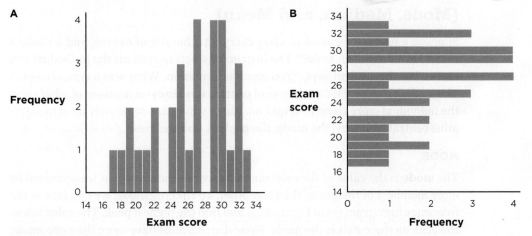

**FIGURE S1.3**

**Frequency histogram of the exam scores in Figure S1.1.**

(**A**) Exam scores are on the *x*-axis. (**B**) Exam scores are on the *y*-axis.

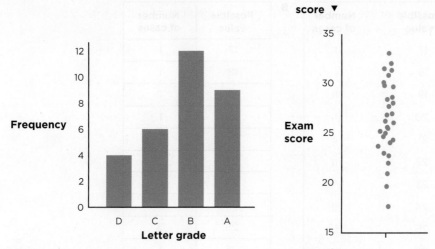

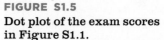

**FIGURE S1.4**
Grouped frequency histogram of
the exam scores in Figure S1.1.

**FIGURE S1.5**
Dot plot of the exam scores
in Figure S1.1.

A dot plot shows each individual's data; each
dot represents one person's score. This dot plot
is jittered, meaning its dots are spread out a bit
horizontally so that it's easy to see where more
than one person earned a particular exam score.

of research transparency: A dot plot reveals every data point and helps us see how spread out the data are.

Compared with a disorganized list of scores, a frequency distribution, frequency histogram, or dot plot makes it easier to visualize the scores collected.

## Describing Central Tendencies (Mode, Median, and Mean)

Suppose a professor comes to class carrying a bundle of exams, and a student asks, "How did the class do?" The instructor starts to read off the individual test scores, but the student says, "Too much information. What was a *typical* score?" The student is asking for a measure of **central tendency**—a measure of what value the individual scores tend to center on. Three values are commonly used to determine central tendency: the mode, the median, and the mean.

### MODE

The **mode** is the value of the most common score—the score that was received by more members of the group than any other. To find the mode, we can look at the frequency histogram (as in Figure S1.3) and find the highest peak. The value below the peak on the *x*-axis is the mode. Some distributions have more than one mode; they are called **bimodal**, having two modes or scores, or **multimodal**, having more than two modes or scores. For an example, see the distribution in Figure S1.3, which has three modes: 27, 29, and 30.

## MEDIAN

The **median** is the value at the middlemost score of a distribution of scores—the score that divides a frequency distribution into halves. The median is a typical score in the sense that if we were to guess that every student in the class received the median score, we would be too high or too low equally often. To find the median of 31 scores, we sort the scores from smallest to largest and find the value of the 16th, or middlemost, score. When we do this, the median is 27.

## MEAN

The **mean**, also called the *average*, is found by adding all the scores in the batch and then dividing by the number of scores. The mean is abbreviated with the symbol $M$. Here is the formula for the mean:

$$M = \frac{\Sigma X}{N}$$

The $X$ in this formula stands for each student's score on the test. The sigma ($\Sigma$) means "the sum of." Therefore, $\Sigma X$ means we must sum all the values of $X$—all the scores. The $N$ stands for the number of scores. In our example, we would find the mean by adding up 33, 32, 32, 32, 31, 30, 30, 30, 30, 29, 29, 29, 29, 27, and so on (down to 17), and then we would divide by 31, the number of people who took the exam. We would find that the mean exam value in this class is 26.16.

## MODE, MEDIAN, MEAN: WHICH TO USE?

The mean is by far the most common measure of central tendency. However, when a set of scores contains a few extreme scores on one end (outliers; see Chapter 8), the median or mode may be a more accurate measure of central tendency. Suppose we want to know the typical family income in a community of only five families: four with modest incomes and a fifth that is very wealthy. Let's say the five incomes are as follows:

$20,000
$30,000
$40,000
$50,000
$1,000,000

The mean (average) would be $228,000—a very misleading idea of the community's income. In such a case, the median income—$40,000—would be a better estimate of what is typical for the community as a whole. In short, the mean is usually the most appropriate measure of central tendency, but when a set of data has outliers, the median (or sometimes the mode) may provide a better description.

When a distribution has a clear mode, the mode can be a good choice for describing central tendency. For example, a class's evaluations of a professor's teaching performance might be distributed as follows:

| Overall, this professor's teaching was: | Number of respondents |
|---|---|
| 1 = poor | 0 |
| 2 = average | 0 |
| 3 = good | 1 |
| 4 = very good | 4 |
| 5 = excellent | 10 |

The professor's mean rating would be 4.60, but she might also wish to report the modal response—that the overwhelming majority of the students rated her "excellent," or 5. (By the way, the median response is also 5. Do you see why?)

## Describing Variability (Variance and Standard Deviation)

Besides describing the central tendency of a set of scores, we can also describe how spread out the scores are. Imagine a teacher has two small classes, A and B. Both classes write an essay that is scored. **Figure S1.6** shows the two classes' essay scores. Notice that both classes have the same number of scores (10), and both

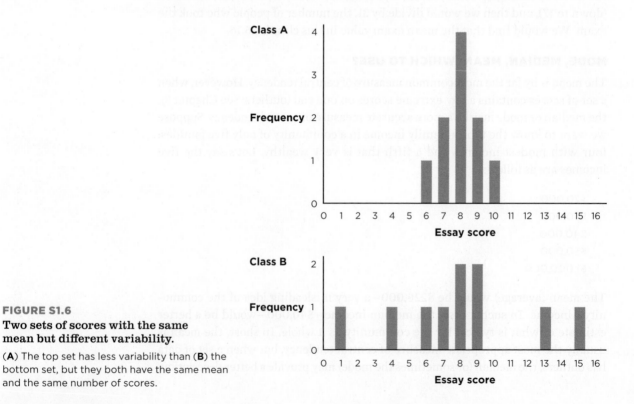

**FIGURE S1.6**

**Two sets of scores with the same mean but different variability.**

(**A**) The top set has less variability than (**B**) the bottom set, but they both have the same mean and the same number of scores.

have the same mean as well. However, Class A (which meets at 11 a.m.) has less variability than Class B (which meets at 7 p.m.). In the top set, scores are, on average, closer to the mean. In the bottom set, scores are, on average, farther from the mean. The teacher suspects that Class B had more variability because its evening time attracted a broader range of students.

The two most common descriptive techniques that capture the relative spread of scores are the variance (sometimes abbreviated as $SD^2$) and the standard deviation (abbreviated $SD$). **Variance** is a computation that quantifies how spread out the scores of a sample are around their mean; it is the square of the standard deviation. **Standard deviation** is a computation that captures how far, on average, each score in a data set is from the mean. It's important to fully understand the logic behind these computations because the logic applies to some other statistics.

When computing the variance of a set of scores, we start by calculating how far each score is from the mean. The first two columns of **Table S1.1** present the set of scores that goes with Class A.

The first step is to calculate the mean of this set of 10 scores. We add up all the scores in the second column, divide by 10, and get the mean: 8.0. Next, we create a

TABLE S1.1

**Variance and Standard Deviation Computations for the Set of Scores in Class A (Figure S1.6A)**

| STUDENT | SCORE | DEVIATION (SCORE – MEAN) | DEVIATION SQUARED |
|---------|-------|--------------------------|-------------------|
| A | 6 | 6 – 8.0 = –2 | 4 |
| B | 7 | 7 – 8.0 = –1 | 1 |
| C | 7 | 7 – 8.0 = –1 | 1 |
| D | 8 | 8 – 8.0 = 0 | 0 |
| E | 8 | 8 – 8.0 = 0 | 0 |
| F | 8 | 8 – 8.0 = 0 | 0 |
| G | 8 | 8 – 8.0 = 0 | 0 |
| H | 9 | 9 – 8.0 = 1 | 1 |
| I | 9 | 9 – 8.0 = 1 | 1 |
| J | 10 | 10 – 8.0 = 2 | 4 |
| | Sum = 80 | | Sum = 12 |
| | Mean = $\frac{80}{10}$ = 8.00 | | Variance = $\frac{12}{10}$ = 1.20 |
| | | | $SD = \sqrt{1.20}$ = 1.10 |

deviation score for each participant. We subtract the mean, 8.0, from each score. The deviation scores are in the third column. One possible way to figure out the "average" deviation score would be simply to add up all the deviation scores in the third column and divide by 10. However, because some of the deviation scores are positive and some are negative, they would cancel each other out when added up. They would add up to zero for any distribution of scores, so merely summing them would not give us any sense of the variability in the scores.

To eliminate this problem, we square each deviation score, since the square of either a positive or a negative number is a positive number. The squared deviations are given in the fourth column of Table S1.1. We now compute the average of the squared deviations by summing them (to get 12) and dividing by the number of scores (10). The result is the variance. Finally, to reverse the step in which we squared the scores, we take the square root of the variance to find the standard deviation, or $SD$ (1.10).

Here is the mathematical formula for the variance when you are interested in describing only your current batch of scores:

$$SD^2 = \frac{\Sigma (X - M)^2}{N}$$

This formula can be explained as follows:

1. From each score $X$, we subtract the mean: $(X - M)$
2. We square each of the resulting deviation scores: $(X - M)^2$
3. We add up all the squared deviation scores: $\Sigma(X - M)^2$ (This quantity is called the "sum of squares" because we *sum* all of the *squared* deviation scores.)
4. We divide the sum of squares by the number of scores to get the mean squared deviation, called the variance:

$$SD^2 = \frac{\Sigma (X - M)^2}{N}$$

Finally, if we take the positive square root of the variance, we get the standard deviation:

$$SD = \sqrt{SD^2}$$

The standard deviation is more commonly reported than the variance because it better captures how far, on average, each score is from the mean. When the standard deviation is large, there is a great deal of variability in the set; the scores are spread out far from the mean, either above or below. When the standard deviation is small, there is less variability in the set; most of the scores are closer to the mean, above or below. Indeed, the standard deviation for Class A is 1.10 but the standard deviation for Class B is 3.82. The standard deviation computations for Class B are shown in **Table S1.2**. The standard deviation for Class B is higher than the one we computed for Class A because the scores in Class B are more spread out.

When you are computing the standard deviation from a batch of scores and your goal is to estimate the population's standard deviation, you should know

**Variance and Standard Deviation Computations for the Set of Scores in Class B (Figure S1.6B)**

| STUDENT | SCORE | DEVIATION (SCORE − MEAN) | DEVIATION SQUARED |
|---|---|---|---|
| K | 1 | 1 − 8.0 = −7 | 49 |
| L | 4 | 4 − 8.0 = −4 | 16 |
| M | 6 | 6 − 8.0 = −2 | 4 |
| N | 7 | 7 − 8.0 = −1 | 1 |
| O | 8 | 8 − 8.0 = 0 | 0 |
| P | 8 | 8 − 8.0 = 0 | 0 |
| Q | 9 | 9 − 8.0 = 1 | 1 |
| R | 9 | 9 − 8.0 = 1 | 1 |
| S | 13 | 13 − 8.0 = 5 | 25 |
| T | 15 | 15 − 8.0 = 7 | 49 |
| | Sum = 80 | | Sum = 146 |
| | Mean = $\frac{80}{10}$ = 8.00 | | Variance = $\frac{146}{10}$ = 14.60 |
| | | | SD = $\sqrt{14.60}$ = 3.82 |

that the formula for $SD$ changes a bit. Instead of using $N$ in the denominator, you use $N - 1$. This small adjustment makes the $SD$ from your sample a more accurate estimate of the true $SD$ in the population from which your sample was drawn. Here are the formulas to use in that case:

$$SD^2 = \frac{\Sigma (X - M)^2}{N - 1}$$

$$SD = \sqrt{SD^2}$$

## HOW MEAN AND STANDARD DEVIATION ARE REPRESENTED IN JOURNAL ARTICLES

In an empirical journal article, the mean and standard deviation information is usually presented either within the text of the Results section or as part of a table. Following are two examples of mean and standard deviation data that appeared in actual journal articles.

The first is an example of how mean and standard deviation information can be presented in a text. Read the following excerpt from an article (discussed in Chapter 2) on using a punching bag to express anger (Bushman, 2002, p. 728):

> How hard the punching bag was hit. . . . Overall, men hit the punching bag harder than did women, $M = 6.69$, $SD = 2.05$, and $M = 4.73$, $SD = 1.88$, $F(1, 396) = 99.14$, $p < .0001$, $d = 1.00$. No other effects were significant ($ps > .05$).
>
> *Number of times punching bag was hit.* Participants who thought about becoming physically fit hit the punching bag more times than did participants who thought about the person who insulted them, $M = 127.5$, $SD = 63.5$, and $M = 112.2$, $SD = 57.5$, $F(1, 396) = 6.31$, $p < .05$, $d = 0.25$. In other words, participants in the rumination group vented less than did participants in the distraction group. No other effects were significant ($ps > .05$).

Even if other statistical symbols are not familiar to you, look for the mean (*M*) and standard deviation (*SD*).

## TEST YOURSELF 1

In the excerpt above, can you find the average force with which men hit the punching bag? Can you find the average force with which women hit the punching bag? Which group, men or women, has the higher variability? How can you tell?

· The second example comes from a series of studies described in Chapter 10, in which people took notes while watching a video and then answered factual and conceptual questions about its content (Mueller & Oppenheimer, 2014). In Mueller and Oppenheimer's third study, people were randomly assigned to take notes on a laptop or longhand and were tested on the material a week later. Some people were given the chance to study their notes before the test and others were not. **Figure S1.7** shows how mean and standard deviation information were presented

STRAIGHT FROM THE SOURCE

**Table 2.** Raw Means for Overall, Factual, and Conceptual Performance in the Four Conditions of Study 3

| Question type | Longhand-study | Longhand–no study | Laptop-study | Laptop–no study |
|---|---|---|---|---|
| Factual only | 7.1 (4.0) | 3.8 (2.8) | 4.5 (3.2) | 3.7 (3.1) |
| Conceptual only | 18.5 (7.8) | 15.6 (7.8) | 13.8 (6.3) | 16.9 (8.1) |
| Overall | 25.6 (10.8) | 19.4 (9.9) | 18.3 (9.0) | 20.6 (10.7) |

Note: Standard deviations are given in parentheses.

**FIGURE S1.7**

**Mean and standard deviation information might be presented as a table in an empirical journal article.**

(Source: Mueller & Oppenheimer, 2014, Study 3.)

in the article. Depending on the article and the journal, tables will differ, but you can use the column labels or table captions to locate the means and standard deviations of particular cells.

## TEST YOURSELF 2

According to Figure S1.7, what were the mean and *SD* for the factual score of people who took notes longhand and were allowed to study them? What were the mean and *SD* for the factual score of people who took notes on a laptop and were allowed to study them?

## VISUALIZING CENTRAL TENDENCY AND VARIABILITY

We can use a **box plot** (sometimes called a *box and whisker diagram*) to visualize central tendency and variability. **Figure S1.8A** shows side-by-side box plots of the essay scores for Class A and Class B. The bold horizontal line in the middle of each box shows the median of each class. The boxed area shows where the middle 50% of the scores lie (called the *interquartile range*, or the 25th and 75th percentiles). The wider the boxed area is, the more variability there is in the data. The whiskers show the "minimum" and "maximum" values. The minimum and maximum on a box plot are not the actual smallest and largest values. Instead, the minimum and maximum are computed by multiplying 1.5 times the interquartile range

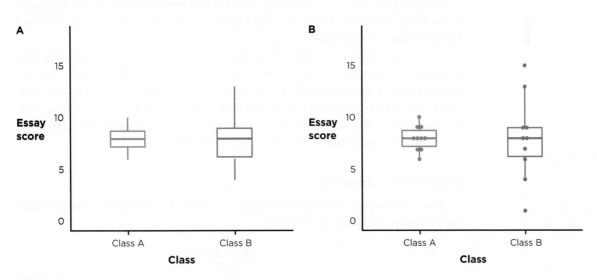

**FIGURE S1.8**

**Box plot of essay scores for two classes.**

(**A**) The box plot makes it clear that although the two classes have the same median, Class B's data are more spread out. (**B**) This combination box plot and dot plot adds full transparency about a study's data.

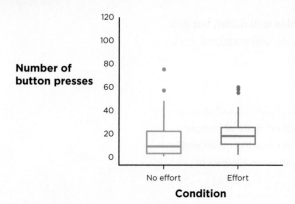

**Number of button presses**

Condition: No effort / Effort

**FIGURE S1.9**

**Box plot from the baby effort study (replication study).**

Babies were shown a model who either succeeded with some toys right away (No effort) or succeeded only after trying (Effort). Babies were subsequently measured on how many times they pressed an inert button on a toy. (Source: Leonard et al., 2017.)

and plotting that value. Individual scores sometimes lie outside the whiskers, and these are often called **outliers**. **Figure S1.8B** shows the same box plot overlaid with dot plot data, an increasingly common format. **Figure S1.9** shows a box plot that was presented in the Leonard et al. (2017) article described in Chapter 10.

## Describing Relative Standing (z Scores)

We can also describe where an individual score stands in relation to the whole batch of scores. A **z score** describes whether an individual's score is above or below the mean and how far it is from the mean in standard deviation units.

### DESCRIBING RELATIVE STANDING IN STANDARD DEVIATION UNITS

Let's start with the exam scores we used to illustrate frequency distributions, in Figure S1.1. Suppose Max, who has a score of 20, wants to know how good his exam score was in relation to the scores of the rest of the class. Because we already know that the mean score was 26.16, we can tell Max that his score, 20, was 6.16 points below the mean.

Perhaps Max also wants to know whether 6.16 points was far below the mean or just a little below the mean. We might answer Max's question by using standard deviation units of distance.

The standard deviation for this group of test scores was 4.52—meaning that on average, scores were 4.52 points away from the mean. We can tell Max his score was 6.16 points below the mean, and that the standard deviation was 4.52. Therefore, Max's score was 1.36 standard deviation units below the mean. Now Max has learned that he did worse than average, by a fairly large margin. His score was more than one standard deviation below the mean.

### COMPUTING z SCORES

To describe people's relative standing in standard deviation units, we compute z scores using the following formula:

$$z = \frac{(X - M)}{SD}$$

We start with the individual score, $X$, and subtract the mean from that score. Then we divide the difference by the standard deviation. When we follow the z score formula, any score below the mean (like Max's) will have a negative z score. Any score above the mean will have a positive *z* score. Any score that is directly at the mean will have a *z* score of zero.

**TEST YOURSELF 3**

Can you compute the *z* score for Sena, who got a 29 on the same exam Max took?

## USING *z* SCORES

One of the useful qualities of a *z* score is that it lets us compare cases that might have been measured in different units. (For this reason, the *z* score is sometimes referred to as a *standardized score*.) Suppose, for example, the first exam was a midterm exam with only 35 questions on it, and Max's score was 20. Now imagine the final exam has 100 questions, and Max's score was 65. Was Max's score on the final, relative to those of his classmates, better than his relative score on the midterm? We could use *z* scores to find out.

If the mean score on the final was 80, with a standard deviation of 14 points, we can use this information to compute Max's *z* score on the final exam:

$$z = \frac{(65 - 80)}{14} = -1.07$$

Max's *z* score for the first exam was –1.34, and for the final it was –1.07. Both scores are below average, but his final exam score was closer to the mean than his midterm score. Therefore, Max's performance on the final was a little better, relatively, than his performance on the midterm.

**TEST YOURSELF 4**

Sena's score on the final exam was 94. Which test did she perform better on (the first exam or the final), relative to her classmates?

In this way, to describe the relative standing of the scores in a set, we can convert each score to a *z* score. The *z* score lets us describe how far any individual's score on a variable is from the mean, in standard deviation units. In addition, if we convert each person's scores on two or more variables to *z* scores, we can meaningfully compare the relative standings of each person on those variables, even when the variables are measured in different units.

One variable, for instance, might be height, measured in centimeters, and the other variable might be weight, measured in kilograms. If a person's *z* score for height is $z = 0.58$ and their *z* score for weight is $z = 0.00$, for example, we could conclude they are above average in height but at the mean in weight (and thus probably a rather thin person). Or perhaps one variable, such as a state's average family income, is measured in dollars, and the other variable, teen pregnancy rate, is measured as the number of pregnancies per 100,000 teens. The $z$ scores can tell us whether a state is relatively wealthy or not and whether its teen pregnancy rate is higher or lower than average.

## Describing Associations Using Scatterplots or the Correlation Coefficient $r$

Three chapters in the main text introduced the logic of scatterplots and the correlation coefficient $r$ (see Chapters 3, 5, and 8). We use scatterplots and $r$ to describe the association between two variables that are measured in the same set of cases. For example, we might want to describe the association between 2-year-old height and adult height. Or we might want to describe the association between how much time people spend sitting and the thickness of certain brain regions.

### SCATTERPLOTS

As discussed previously, one way to describe associations between two variables is to draw a scatterplot. With one variable on the $x$-axis and another variable on the $y$-axis, we plot each case as a dot on the graph so that it represents the person's score on both variables.

**Figure S1.10** shows a hypothetical scatterplot for the association between 2-year-old height and adult height. The marked dot represents Eliana, one member of the group. The scatterplot shows that Eliana was fairly short at age 2 and is also fairly short as an adult. Other dots on the scatterplot represent other members of the group, showing their height at the two different ages.

Similarly, **Figure S1.11** shows a scatterplot of the association between how many hours people report sitting per day and the thickness of their medial-temporal lobes (MTLs). The black dot represents a person who reported sitting about

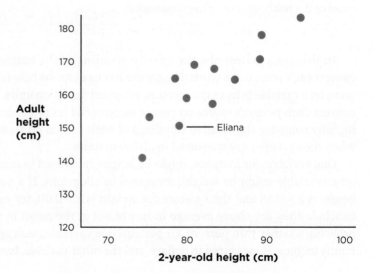

**FIGURE S1.10**

Scatterplot of adult height and 2-year-old height.

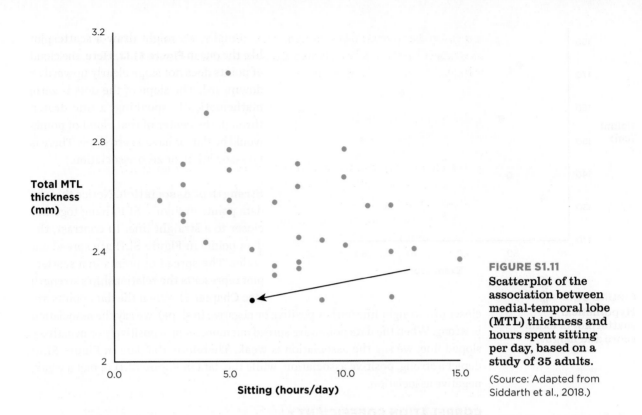

**FIGURE S1.11**
**Scatterplot of the association between medial-temporal lobe (MTL) thickness and hours spent sitting per day, based on a study of 35 adults.**

(Source: Adapted from Siddarth et al., 2018.)

6 hours per day and had a smaller-than-average MTL thickness. The other dots on that scatterplot represent other members of the sample.

By inspecting a scatterplot, we can describe two important aspects of an association: the *direction* of the relationship between two variables (positive, negative, or zero) and the *strength* of the positive or negative relationship (strong or weak).

**Direction of Association: Positive, Negative, or Zero.** In Figure S1.10, notice that the cloud of points on the scatterplot slopes upward from left to right. The slope of the dots is positive; mathematically speaking, a line drawn through the center of that cloud of points would have a positive slope. Because the slope is positive, we call the association between the two variables positive. High scores on one variable go with high scores on the other variable, and low scores on one variable go with low scores on the other variable. In a positive association, "high goes with high and low goes with low."

In contrast, in Figure S1.11 notice that the cloud of points on the scatterplot slopes downward from left to right. Because the slope of the dots is negative—mathematically speaking, a line drawn through the center of that cloud of points would have a negative slope—the association between the two variables is referred to as negative (or an inverse association). High scores on one variable go with low scores on the other variable. In a negative association, "high goes with low and low goes with high."

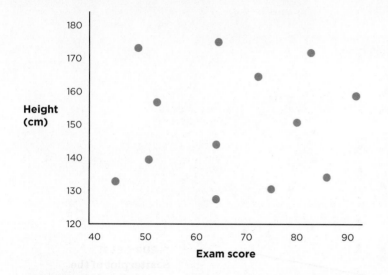

Height (cm)

Exam score

**FIGURE S1.12**

Hypothetical scatterplot of exam score and height.

Finally, we might draw a scatterplot like the one in **Figure S1.12.** Here, the cloud of points does not slope clearly upward or downward. The slope of the dots is zero; mathematically speaking, a line drawn through the center of that cloud of points would be flat, or have a zero slope. There is no association, or zero association.

**Strength of Association.** Notice that the data points in Figure S1.10 hang together closer to a straight line. In contrast, the data points in Figure S1.11 are spread out wider. The spread of points in a scatter-plot represents the relationship's strength (see Chapter 5). When the data points are closer to a straight line (either positive or negative in slope), we say the association is strong. When the data points are spread out more along a positively or negatively sloped line, we say the association is weak. Therefore, the data in Figure S1.10 depict a strong, positive association, while the data in Figure S1.11 depict a weak, negative association.

### CORRELATION COEFFICIENT $r$

Researchers use the correlation coefficient $r$ to capture the direction and strength of an association (see Chapters 3, 5, and 8). The value of $r$ can range from –1.0, which represents the strongest possible negative correlation, to 1.0, which represents the strongest possible positive correlation. For example, the relationship depicted in Figure S1.10 is $r = .75$; the relationship depicted in Figure S1.11 is $r = -.37$.

The sign of $r$ indicates the direction of the relationship. If $r$ is positive (such as $r = .75$), the relationship between the two variables is positive. If $r$ is negative (such as $r = -.37$), the relationship between the two variables is negative. If $r$ is zero, or very close to zero (such as $r = .02$), then the relationship between the two variables is essentially zero, or negligible.

The magnitude of the absolute value of $r$ indicates the strength of the relation-ship. If $r$ is large (such as .75), the relationship between two variables is strong (the dots on the scatterplot would be closer together). If $r$ is smaller, the relationship between two variables is weaker (the dots on the scatterplot would be more spread out). The strength of a correlation is independent of its sign, so an $r$ of –.45 would represent a stronger correlation than an $r$ of .11.

**Computing $r$.** The formula for computing the correlation coefficient $r$ can be represented in many ways. Here is the formula used by most statistical software packages:

$$r = \frac{\sum z_x z_y}{N - 1}$$

**TABLE S1.3**

## Computing the Correlation Coefficient $r$

| (1) PERSON | (2) SCORE ON X (2-YEAR-OLD HEIGHT, IN CM) | (3) SCORE ON Y (ADULT HEIGHT, IN CM) | (4) $z_x$ (Z SCORE FOR 2-YEAR-OLD HEIGHT) | (5) $z_Y$ (Z SCORE FOR ADULT HEIGHT) | (6) $z_x z_Y$ |
|---|---|---|---|---|---|
| Eliana | 78 | 150 | −1.00, or $\frac{(78 - 83.28)}{5.28}$ | −1.88, or $\frac{(150 - 165.29)}{8.16}$ | 1.88, or (−1.00 × −1.88) |
| Ella | 80 | 160 | −0.62 | −0.65 | 0.40 |
| Eshaan | 91 | 170 | 1.45 | 0.58 | 0.84 |
| Ava | 84 | 168 | 0.13 | 0.33 | 0.04 |
| Annamaria | 79 | 165 | −0.81 | −0.04 | 0.03 |
| Oscar | 90 | 175 | 1.26 | 1.19 | 1.50 |
| Oliver | 81 | 169 | −0.43 | 0.45 | −0.19 |
| | $M = 83.28$ | $M = 165.29$ | | | $\Sigma z_x z_Y = 4.50$ |
| | $SD = 5.28$ | $SD = 8.16$ | | | $\frac{\Sigma z_x z_Y}{N - 1} = 0.75$ |
| | | | | | $r = .75$ |

Let's break it down step by step. First, we have two variables per case (often that means two variables per person). **Table S1.3** shows how to carry out the steps in calculating $r$ for a set of seven people. Notice that the first three columns of the table represent a data matrix for this data set, including one column for each variable ($X$ and $Y$) and one row for each person. The three right-hand columns show the computations for $r$. In the formula, the variables are labeled $X$ and $Y$. If we are computing the correlation between 2-year-old height and adult height, for example, 2-year-old height would be variable $X$ (column 2), and adult height would be variable $Y$ (column 3).

The second step is converting each person's scores on $X$ and $Y$ to $z$ scores, $z_X$ and $z_Y$, using the formula for computing $z$ given earlier. If someone's 2-year-old height was above the mean, his or her $z$ score ($z_X$) would be positive; if someone's 2-year-old height was below the mean, his or her $z$ score ($z_X$) would be negative (columns 4 and 5 of Table S1.3). The third step is to multiply these two $z$ scores, $z_X$ and $z_Y$, for each person (column 6). Finally, we sum the products of the $z$ scores and divide by the number of cases—in this example, seven people—to get $r$.

**The Logic of the r Formula.** It is worth reflecting on two aspects of the formula for $r$. First, notice that $r$ can easily capture the association between adult height and 2-year-old height, even though the two variables have very different ranges of scores. The height for 2-year-olds ranges from 78 to 91 cm; adult height ranges from 150 to 175 cm. However, the formula for $r$ converts each height value to its $z$ score first. That way, it does not matter that the two heights fall within very different ranges.

Second, think about what it means that $r$ multiplies the two $z$ scores for each person. Take Eliana, for example. Her height is below average at age 2 and below average at adulthood, so both of her $z$ scores are negative. When we multiply them together, we get a positive number. Now consider Oscar, whose height is above average at age 2 and above average at adulthood. Both of his $z$ scores are positive, so when we multiply them, we also get a positive number. In Table S1.3, most of the products are positive, though some are negative. After summing all these products and dividing by $N - 1$, we get an $r$ value of .75—a positive $r$, meaning that "high goes with high and low goes with low." This makes sense; people with high 2-year-old height tend to have high adult height, and people with low 2-year-old height tend to have low adult height.

In contrast, if the relationship between two variables is negative, high goes with low and low goes with high. In this situation, when we compute the $r$, positive $z$ scores for one variable will tend to be multiplied with negative $z$ scores for the other variable, so the products will be mostly negative. When we sum these negative products and divide by $N - 1$, the result will be a negative number, or a negative $r$, meaning that "high goes with low and low goes with high." Normally researchers use computers to calculate $r$ values. However, knowing the mathematics behind the formula for $r$ can help you understand what $r$ values represent.

## Describing Effect Size

Because the value of $r$ indicates the strength of the relationship between two variables, many researchers use $r$ as a measure of effect size, a computation that describes the magnitude of a study's result (see Chapters 8, 10, and 14). There are several measures of effect size and all of them are used for the same purpose: to describe the strength of the relationship between two variables. For example, when a study's outcome demonstrates a difference between two groups, the effect size describes how large or small that difference is.

### DESCRIBING EFFECT SIZE WITH COHEN'S *d*

When a study involves group or condition means (such as when we compare the mean score when taking notes on a laptop versus taking notes longhand), we can describe the effect size in terms of how far apart the two means are, in standard deviation units. This will also tell us how much overlap there is between the two sets of scores. This commonly used effect size measure is called $d$, also known as **Cohen's *d***.

Let's revisit the notetaking study (Mueller & Oppenheimer, 2014; see Figure S1.7). If we were to ask about this study's effect size, we would ask *how much better* people did on the test after taking longhand versus laptop notes. Was it just a little better or a lot better? We are asking: Is the effect size large or small?

For simplicity, let's focus only on the factual scores for people who were allowed to study their notes in Mueller and Oppenheimer's study (see Figure S1.7):

- When people took notes longhand and were allowed to study them, they got a mean of 7.1 factual questions right, with a standard deviation of 4.0 questions. (A perfect score would have been 8.0.)
- When people took notes on laptops and were allowed to study them, they got a mean of 4.5 factual questions right, with a standard deviation of 3.2 questions.

To determine how far apart these two means are in standard deviation units, we use the following formula for $d$:

$$d = \frac{M_1 - M_2}{SD_{(pooled)}}$$

The numerator is the mean of one group minus the mean of the other group. The denominator is the $SD$ of these two groups, "pooled." To get the pooled $SD$, you average the variances for the two groups and take the square root of that average. If the two groups are the same size, we can take a simple mean of the two variances, but when the two groups are different sizes, we need to compute a weighted mean of the two variances; that is, we weight the $SD^2$ of the larger group more.[1]

If we apply this formula to Mueller and Oppenheimer's data, the numerator is simply the mean difference between the two groups (the longhand group and the laptop group), or 7.1 – 4.5. The denominator is the pooled $SD$, which is 3.62. So we would compute the effect size as follows:

$$d = \frac{7.10 - 4.50}{3.62} = \frac{2.60}{3.62} = 0.72$$

In other words, the effect size of taking notes on a laptop versus longhand when people are allowed to study their notes is $d = 0.72$. (We omit any negative sign when it is clear which group is higher than the other.)

What does a $d$ of 0.72 mean? It means that the factual test score average of the longhand group is 0.72 standard deviations higher than the average of the laptop group. But is that large or small? As you learned in Chapter 10, the interpretation depends on the context. Some psychologists use a rule of thumb that calls a $d$ of 0.2 small, a $d$ of 0.5 moderate, and a $d$ of 0.8 strong. According to this convention, the effect size in Mueller and Oppenheimer's study was fairly large. However, as described in Chapters 8 and 10, you need context. Many effect sizes smaller than $d = 0.2$ might still be considered very important. And sometimes a small sample can lead to large effect sizes just by chance.

Or suppose we conduct an experiment in which we praise the appearance of one group of people and say something neutral to members of another group. Later

---

[1]The general formula for a pooled $SD$ is as follows, where $n_1$ and $n_2$ are the number of observations in the two groups, and $SD_1^2$ and $SD_2^2$ are the variances of each group.

$$SD_{(pooled)} = \sqrt{\frac{(n_1 - 1)SD_1^2 + (n_2 - 1)SD_2^2}{n_1 + n_2 - 2}}$$

we ask each group to take a self-esteem test that uses a 5-point scale. We compute the two group means and find a mean of 4.13 ($SD$ = 1.46) for the people whose appearance was praised and a mean of 3.98 ($SD$ = 1.50) for those who were not praised. When we compute the effect size, $d$, we come up with $d$ = 0.10. Therefore, the groups are about 0.10 of a standard deviation unit apart on self-esteem. If we rely only on conventions, this could be described as a small effect of appearance praise on self-esteem.

**Effect Size $d$ and Group Overlap.** Another way of looking at group-difference effect sizes such as $d$ is to know that $d$ represents the amount of overlap between two groups or conditions. Parts A and B of **Figure S1.13** show how two groups might overlap at different effect sizes in our examples. The larger the effect size, the less overlap between the two experimental groups; the smaller the effect size, the more overlap. If the effect size is zero, there is full overlap between the two groups (Figure S1.13C).

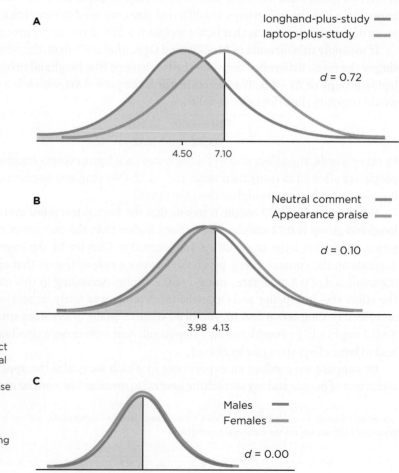

**FIGURE S1.13**

**The larger the effect size, the less overlap between the two experimental groups.**

(**A**) At an effect size of 0.72, 76.4% of the laptop-plus-study group members scored lower than the average member of the longhand-plus-study group. (**B**) At an effect size of 0.10, 54% of people hearing a neutral phrase had lower self-esteem than the average member of the group hearing praise for their appearance. (**C**) An effect size of 0.00 represents full overlap between the two groups, the greatest possible overlap, with 50% of Group 1 members (males) falling below the average member of Group 2 (females).

## WHICH EFFECT SIZE MEASURE TO USE?

Researchers often use the effect size $r$ to determine the strength of the relationship between two quantitative variables. The effect size $d$ is more often used when one variable is categorical. These two measures of effect size are based on different scales: $r$ can only range between 1 and –1, but $d$ can be higher than 1 or lower than –1. When judging effect size, context matters, as discussed fully in Chapters 8 and 10.

## OTHER EFFECT SIZE MEASURES

As you read empirical journal articles, you may notice other indicators of effect size, such as Hedge's $g$. Hedge's $g$ is very similar to $d$. Like $d$, it gives the distance between two means in standard deviation units, but it is computed with a different formula.

Another effect size measure you might encounter is $\eta^2$, or eta squared. This effect size may be used when researchers describe differences among several groups (i.e., more than two means), or when they describe the effect sizes of interaction effects.

## EFFECT SIZE AND IMPORTANCE

Chapters 8 and 10 explain the relationship between effect size and importance. Generally speaking, the larger an effect size is, the more important a result seems to be. However, the converse is not always true: A small effect size is not always an unimportant one. Chapter 8 introduced the example of a very small effect size ($r = .05$) for the relationship between agreeableness and the friendliness of a single social encounter. This seemingly very small effect size could translate into a real gain in popularity for agreeable people when aggregated over many social encounters. Therefore, small effect sizes are generally less important than large ones—but sometimes even small effect sizes are important and valuable. It depends on scale and the theoretical and real-world context of the research.

## EFFECT SIZES AND ORIGINAL UNITS

Effect sizes can certainly help indicate whether a study's result is strong, moderate, or weak. In some cases, however, we may not need to compute an effect size to assess the magnitude of some intervention. For example, in the notetaking study, instead of calculating the effect size $d$, we could have looked at the means and found that people studying their longhand notes got 2.6 more factual questions right, on average, than those studying their laptop notes, out of 8 factual questions. Or recall the Mrazek team's (2013) mindfulness intervention for GRE scores (see Chapter 10). They reported that the mindfulness training group improved their GRE scores by about 16 percentile points.

In these examples, it is relatively easy to evaluate the strength of the manipulation's impact: The longhand group got an additional 2.6 questions right out of 8 possible questions. Mindfulness training improves scores by 16 percentile points. These results may seem substantial and important even without effect size values.

Other times we must rely only on effect size values to evaluate a result's strength. Effect sizes are especially useful when we're not familiar with the scale on which a variable is measured. Consider the hypothetical experiment in which people in one group were praised for their appearance and people in another group heard a neutral remark. Because self-esteem was measured on an arbitrary 5-point scale, it would be hard to put the difference between the two means into practical terms. Praising people's appearance made their scores on self-esteem increase about 0.15 points on the 5-point scale, so we might say the two group means were about 15% of a "self-esteem unit" apart. Is that a large difference or a small one? Indeed, it is difficult to translate this into a practical outcome; it's not the same as GRE percentile points or questions on a test.

However, knowing that the effect size in the self-esteem study was $d = 0.10$ provides a somewhat better understanding of its magnitude, especially if we compare the effect size to something else we know. For example, we might say the effect size of praising someone's *appearance* on self-esteem is $d = 0.10$, but the effect size of praising someone's *personal qualities* on self-esteem is larger, say $d = 0.18$.

In addition, the effect size from one study can be compared to the effect size from another study—even a study using different variables. Consult **Table S1.4** to see examples of different benchmarks we might use to evaluate the effect size of a study.

## TABLE S1.4

### Comparing and Evaluating Effect Sizes

| ASSUMING IT WAS BASED ON A LARGE SAMPLE (1,500 OR MORE), AN $r$ OF: | IS APPROXIMATELY EQUIVALENT TO A $d$ OF: | BEFORE CONSIDERING CONTEXT, THIS EFFECT SIZE MIGHT INITIALLY BE DESCRIBED AS: | A NONPSYCHOLOGICAL EXAMPLE OF THIS EFFECT SIZE |
|---|---|---|---|
| .05 | 0.10 | Very small or very weak | Correlation between a baseball player's overall batting average and success at any one batting turn ($r = .05$, $d = 0.10$) |
| .10 | 0.20 | Small or weak | Correlation between taking antihistamine medication and runny nose symptoms ($r = .11$, $d = 0.22$) |
| .20 | 0.40 | Moderate | Difference between men and women in average weight (males higher, $r = .26$, $d = 0.54$) |
| .30 | 0.63 | Having a fairly powerful effect | Correlation between a town's elevation above sea level and its annual temperature ($r = -.34$, $d = 0.72$) |
| .40 | 0.87 | Unusually large in psychology— either very powerful or possibly too good to be true (if based on a small sample) | Correlation between height and weight in adults ($r = .44$, $d = 0.98$) |

Sources: Funder & Ozer, 2019; also Abelson, 1985; Meyer et al., 2001; Ozer & Benet-Martínez, 2006.

**TEST YOURSELF 1** The average force for men was 6.69. The average force for women was 4.73. Men had a slightly higher *SD* on this variable (2.05) than women (1.88).

**TEST YOURSELF 2** The mean and *SD* for the factual score of people who took notes longhand and were allowed to study them were *M* = 7.1, *SD* = 4.0. The mean and *SD* for the factual score of people who took notes on a laptop and were allowed to study them were *M* = 4.5, *SD* = 3.2.

**TEST YOURSELF 3** Sena's *z* score on the midterm exam was 0.63. Her score is less than one standard deviation above the mean.

**TEST YOURSELF 4** Sena's *z* score on the final was 1.0, so she did better on the final than she did on the midterm—relative to the rest of the class, at least.

# Key Terms

descriptive statistics, p. 467

data matrix, p. 468

frequency distribution, p. 468

frequency histogram, p. 468

dot plot, p. 468

central tendency, p. 470

mode, p. 470

bimodal, p. 470

multimodal, p. 470

median, p. 471

mean, p. 471

variance, p. 473

standard deviation, p. 473

box plot, p. 477

outlier, p. 478

*z* score, p. 478

Cohen's *d*, p. 484

# Statistics Review

## INFERENTIAL STATISTICS

The preceding section reviewed descriptive statistics, a set of tools for organizing and summarizing certain characteristics of a sample. Here we cover **inferential statistics**, a set of techniques that use data from a sample to estimate what is happening in the population. When we use inferential statistics, we estimate some value in the population and compute a range of precision for that estimate to indicate how much uncertainty we have about it.

## ESTIMATION AND PRECISION

Estimation is something we do every day. Suppose you're going to have a party next weekend. You invited about 60 people, telling each person they could bring a friend. How many people will show up? You might estimate about 75. But you're not certain, so you might tell your roommate, "I predict we'll have between 60 and 90 people" (**Figure S2.1**).

Or suppose you're headed to the urgent care center with a sore throat. How long will you have to wait? You might estimate that you'll be seen by a doctor in about 25 minutes. But you're uncertain, so you might plan to wait anywhere

**FIGURE S2.1**

**Everyday estimation.**

A fisherman might use his hands to estimate the size of a fish he caught. When we use inferential statistics, we do something similar—we estimate the size of some percentage, correlation, or difference. Our fisherman might spread his arms wide not to exaggerate the size of the fish but to be sure that his estimate actually includes its true size.

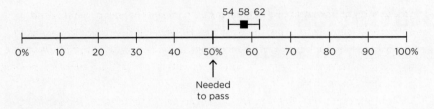

**FIGURE S2.2**

**Straw-ban support.**

The poll estimated 58% support for the straw ban. This point estimate is marked with the dark black box. The margin of error in the poll was +/- 4% and is depicted by the wings to each side of the box.

between 15 minutes and an hour. Of course, it could be that you'll have to wait much less or much more than that.

In both of these cases, you estimated a value you did not know (how many people would come to the party or how long you'd have to wait), and you gave a range of precision around your estimate.

## A Formal Example of Estimation

When we do estimation in a research study, we get more formal than these everyday examples, but the same idea applies. Imagine that the community of Springfield is proposing a ban on plastic straws to reduce landfill waste. The "straw proposition" will be put to a vote at the next election, and if more than 50% of voters vote in favor of it, it will pass. A news channel wanted to estimate the support for the straw proposition, so they conducted an opinion poll (you might call it a straw poll!) by selecting a random sample of 500 likely voters from the community. The poll revealed that support for the straw ban was 58%, with a margin of error of 4%. Based on this information, do you think the straw ban will pass?

The result of the poll is presented in **Figure S2.2**. The square represents the estimate of 58%, and the line extends from 4% below the dot to 4% above, to represent the margin of error. Based on this result, we might predict the straw ban will pass because the estimate of support from the poll goes from 54% to 62%, and this range is well above the 50% needed to pass.

The straw ban story activates several intuitions that are relevant for understanding inferential statistics:

- **Our research question is about the whole population.** The news channel pollsters conducted the poll on a sample, but they are ultimately interested in making a prediction about what all of the people who are going to vote on the plastic straw ban will do.

- **The quality of the sample data matters.** The news channel pollsters used data from a sample to make the estimate. However, if they had used a biased sample (such as including only younger voters), the estimate would probably be incorrect. A random sample of community voters is necessary to make the best predictions (see Chapter 7).
- **The population value is unknown.** After the poll is conducted, we don't know what the true support for the straw ban is in the population. We only know what the *sample*'s level of support is.
- **Larger samples give more certain estimates.** If the sample had only 10 people in it, we would feel especially uncertain about the estimate, even if these 10 people were drawn randomly. In contrast, if the sample had 1,000 randomly selected people in it, we would feel more certain (our estimate would be more precise).
- **To get a better estimate, we should do more than one poll.** One well-conducted poll is good, but if other polls had been conducted, we could combine the results of them all and get a more precise estimate.

## Point Estimates and Confidence Intervals

In statistical language, the name for the initial estimate is the **point estimate**. The point estimate is a single estimate (for example, 58%), based on our sample data, of the true value in the population. The point estimate might be a percentage (as in a poll). It might be a difference between means (an effect size, $d$) or a relationship between two variables (an $r$; see Statistics Review: Descriptive Statistics).

The name for the range of precision—for example, the range of 54% to 62%—is the **confidence interval**, or **CI**. The confidence interval is a range that fairly often contains the true level (the population level) of some variable—in this case, the level of support for the straw ban. Of course, the true level of population support might be lower than 54 or higher than 62. However, we expect that the true value will be between between 54 and 62. We report the CI in square brackets, like this: [54, 62].

To compute a confidence interval, we need to decide how often we want our intervals to contain the true value. The usual approach in statistics is to compute an interval that will contain the population value 95% of the time. Of course, we might wish to include it 99% of the time—in that case, our interval needs to be wider, say [51, 65] instead of the original [54, 62]. A 99% CI needs to be wider to be more certain to contain the population value. For example, when you estimate how many guests will be at your party, you might increase your uncertainty range to be more confident: "I'm 99% confident there will be between 10 to 1,000 guests!" (And you'd be *extremely* surprised if you got fewer than 10 or more than 1,000.) In other cases, we might feel comfortable being 80% confident, in which case our interval would be smaller, for example [55, 61]. Our 80% confidence intervals usually contain the population value (80% of the time) but will miss it 20% of the time.

(For example, when you predict the size of your party, if you were 80% confident you'll have 50 to 80 guests, then you wouldn't be all that surprised if you had many more or fewer of them.) In this chapter, CIs represent 95% confidence, which is the typical level in psychology.

In sum, the inference process used in statistics takes data from a sample, whose characteristics are known, to make a point estimate about some population, whose characteristics are often unknown. The point estimate is accompanied by a range of uncertainty called the confidence interval.

Election polls are an interesting example of inferential statistics. Before election day, we use poll samples to estimate the population levels of support. After the election, we have the true population value—the result of the election. But in many other kinds of research, we may never know the population value, so we are always only estimating.

## The Steps of Estimation and Precision

Several of the steps described in the straw ban poll example illustrate what researchers do when they practice statistical inference. These steps are adapted from a longer list by Cumming and Calin-Jageman (2016). Please see their book for a full treatment.

### STEP 1: STATE A RESEARCH QUESTION USING TERMS SUCH AS "HOW MUCH" OR "TO WHAT EXTENT"

"How much support is there for the straw ban?"

### STEP 2: DESIGN A STUDY: OPERATIONALIZE THE QUESTION IN TERMS OF VARIABLES THAT ARE EITHER MANIPULATED OR MEASURED

Select a random sample of voters and ask them whether or not they plan to support the straw ban.

### STEP 3: COLLECT THE DATA AND COMPUTE THE POINT ESTIMATE AND CONFIDENCE INTERVAL

On average, 58% of the sample supports the ban, with a margin of error of 4%, leading to a confidence interval of [54, 62].

### STEP 4: INTERPRET THE RESULTS IN THE CONTEXT OF YOUR RESEARCH QUESTION

We expect that the straw ban proposition will pass on election day because the predicted range of support [54, 62] is well above 50%. (Of course, we might have missed the true range of support.)

## STEP 5: IF POSSIBLE, CONDUCT THE STUDY AGAIN AND META-ANALYZE THE RESULTS

It's important to replicate the results of any research study. We can combine the estimates of multiple studies into one overall estimate using meta-analysis, introduced in Chapters 2 and 14.

## Types of Point Estimates (Overview)

The straw ban example we started with—predicting a single percentage—is one of the simplest. Other types of studies require different computations, but they all lead to a point estimate and confidence interval. In this chapter, you'll learn how to compute point estimates and confidence intervals for:

- A single percentage estimate, such as from a poll (Chapters 6 and 7)
- The difference between the same set of people, measured twice (a repeated-measures experiment; Chapter 10)
- The difference between two independent groups (an independent-groups experiment; Chapter 10)
- Differences among several independent groups (Chapter 12)
- The correlation, or $r$, between two variables (Chapter 8)
- The beta from a regression analysis (Chapter 9)

## Determining the Confidence Interval for a Percentage Estimate

The example about community support for the plastic straw ban involved a frequency claim—a single, measured variable. We followed the first two steps of the inference process as follows: **Step 1:** The research question concerned the degree of support for the straw ban. **Step 2:** The research design involved asking a random sample of 500 voters in the community whether or not they supported the straw ban. **Step 3:** We collected the data and computed a point estimate of 58% and a CI of [54, 62]. But where did these numbers come from?

### STEP 3: COLLECT THE DATA AND COMPUTE THE POINT ESTIMATE AND CONFIDENCE INTERVAL

In a poll, the point estimate is a simple percentage—you merely count the number of people who support the straw ban and divide by the total size of the sample:

Percent support = number supporting the ban / total sample size

$$\text{or } \frac{290}{500} = 58\%$$

What about the confidence interval? The CI takes the form of the point estimate plus and minus the margin of error. In our example, the margin of error was 4%. The margin of error is the product of three components: a *variability component* (such as a standard deviation), a *sample size component*, and the *constant associated with the 95% level of confidence*—a *z* score (**Figure S2.3**). As an overview, here is the full formula for the margin of error of a percentage estimate:

$$SD * \sqrt{\left(\frac{1}{N}\right)} * 1.96$$

**The Variability Component.** To estimate the variability of a percentage estimate, we use the standard deviation of the percentage. There are several ways to do this, but one is to assign a 0 to every "no" vote and 1 to every "yes" vote. The mean of this column of numbers is the point estimate (for example, if there are 290 yes votes out of 500, the mean of this set of numbers is 0.58, or 58%). Then we can compute the standard deviation of this set of numbers using the formula you learned in Statistics Review: Descriptive Statistics. In our example, the standard deviation (that is, the *SD*) is 0.494, or 4.94%.

**The Sample Size Component.** The second element of a margin of error is a sample size component. Here we use the square root of 1 over the sample size, or

$$\sqrt{\left(\frac{1}{N}\right)}$$

The product of these first two components, the *SD* times $\sqrt{\left(\frac{1}{N}\right)}$, is known as the **standard error**. Notice that because the sample size component is in the denominator, it means that as the sample size gets bigger, the margin of error will get smaller.

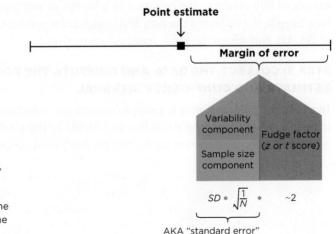

**FIGURE S2.3**
**Building a CI.**

The 95% CI of a statistic consists of a point estimate and the margin of error. The margin of error contains three parts: a variability component, a sample size component, and a constant (the fudge factor, usually something around 2.0 for the 95% confidence level). The first two components (variability and sample size) are known as the standard error. Therefore, if you approximately double the standard error, you get one wing of a 95% CI.

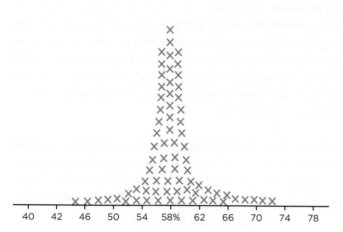

The sampling distribution here was created based on polling results about the straw ban. If we conducted our 500-person poll an infinite number of times, computed the percentage support in each sample, and put an X on this graph representing each poling result, we'd get a distribution of approximately this shape. Each X represents the estimated percentage from one poll of 500 people. The mean of this distribution is equal to that of our original sample estimate, 58%. The standard error is the standard deviation of the distribution and is equal to 2.2%. If we conduct multiple polls, about half of them will be closer to the truth than 2.2%, and about half will be farther away. Later, we multiply the standard error by 1.96 to get the margin of error.

What is the standard error and what does it represent? In a full-length statistics class, you will learn it is the typical, or average, error we make when we are estimating a population value. The standard error concerns the sampling distribution of the mean, the characteristics of which are derived from the central limit theorem. Briefly, the sampling distribution of the mean is a hypothetical (i.e., theoretically derived) distribution you would get if you conducted the same poll an infinite number of times and plotted the estimates you got. In the plastic straw example, most of the polling results would be near 58%, but some would be a bit larger and others would be a bit smaller. The standard deviation (the width) of this sampling distribution is the standard error (**Figure S2.4**).

**The Constant Associated with 95% Confidence.** The third component of the margin of error is a constant that is associated with 95% confidence—you might call it a "fudge factor." In the case of a polling result (a percentage), the constant will be 1.96. The margin of error, then, is the product of these values: the variability component (the *SD* of 4.94%), the sample size component $\left(\sqrt{\left(\frac{1}{500}\right)}\right)$, and 1.96. This gives 4.3%. (We rounded this number to 4 in our opening story, as media outlets often do.) Because the constant is 1.96—around 2—we approximately double the standard error to get the margin of error. (In other words, we take the standard error and enlarge it, creating a margin of error that covers most magnitudes of errors we could make.)

The 1.96 value is a *z* score (see Statistics Review: Descriptive Statistics) from a normal distribution. When we compute the margin of error for a polling result (a percentage), we base our fudge factor on the normal curve (see Appendix B and **Figure S2.5**).

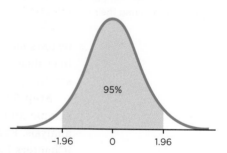

**FIGURE S2.5**
**The normal distribution, showing the constant associated with 95% confidence.**

When we want 95% of our confidence intervals to contain the population value, we multiply our standard error by 1.96. This constant comes from the *z* scores associated with the normal distribution, where 95% of the scores fall between these two values.

The values of 1.96 (and –1.96) are the $z$ scores that capture the middle 95% of any normal curve, leaving out 2.5% on each tail. This middle range is 95% because we are computing a 95% confidence interval. The $z$ score of 1.96 that is used for a 95% confidence interval is well known in statistics, and many people use it as a benchmark, even for a footrace (**Figure S2.6**).

**Computing the Confidence Interval from the Margin of Error.** Now that we have the margin of error, we can compute the 95% confidence interval. We add and subtract the margin of error from the point estimate of 58%:

lower limit: 58% – 4.3% = 53.7
upper limit: 58% + 4.3% = 62.3

And then we present the CI in square brackets: [53.7, 62.3].

To continue the five inferential statistics steps, **Step 4** involves interpreting the results in the context of the research question. Our CI of [53.7, 62.3] means we are a bit uncertain about support for the straw ban. The low end of the CI is 53.7, which would mean that a slim majority supports the ban. The upper end is 62.3, which is fairly dramatic support. From this poll alone, we would estimate that support is somewhere between a slim to a very solid majority. We would probably guess that the ban will pass, because the entire CI lies above the 50% needed for approval. On the other hand, we should keep in mind that 5% of 95% CIs miss the population value—so we shouldn't be too shocked if the election results are not within our CI range. We would want to evaluate this estimate in light of what else we know, such as what other polls say, the quality of the sample, the political trends in this town, and so on.

**Step 5** in the research process involves doing the poll again with a new sample and combining the results of multiple studies or polls using meta-analysis. Earlier in this book, you learned about the importance of replication (Chapters 1 and 14) and meta-analysis (Chapters 2 and 14). During an election season, it's common for polls to be replicated many times, often by different polling organizations, and then combined to make the most accurate election forecasts possible.[1]

**FIGURE S2.6**
**The value 1.96 is a benchmark.**
When computing a confidence interval for a percent estimate, we multiply the standard error by the constant of 1.96. This constant is so well known among statisticians that they sometimes run 1.96-mile races during their conferences!

---

[1]The margin of error formulae presented here do not work as well for small frequencies. Therefore, most statistical software uses the approach from Newcombe and Altman (2000). If students notice a small difference between hand calculations based on this chapter's approach and statistical software, they should prefer the CI from the statistical software.

# Determining the Point Estimate and Confidence Interval for a Dependent, or Paired Design

How does the process for calculating the point estimate and CI differ for a repeated-measures experiment, in which each participant experiences two conditions—both levels of the independent variable (Chapter 10)? Another name for this type of data is a **dependent sample**, or a *paired design*. These terms refer to data in which each person has two scores (perhaps they were tested under two conditions, or perhaps they took a pretest and a posttest), and we are interested in the difference between them. To compute the point estimate and confidence interval in this case, we'll use a difference score.

In Chapter 10 you read about a study by Boothby et al. (2014) in which people tasted chocolate under two conditions—alone and with a partner. Each participant rated some sweet chocolate two times: as an unshared experience and as a shared experience. Let's work through the steps, using Boothby et al.'s Study 1 and the steps from Cumming and Calin-Jageman (2016).

## STEP 1: STATE A RESEARCH QUESTION USING TERMS SUCH AS "HOW MUCH" OR "TO WHAT EXTENT"

"How much more do people like the chocolate when they taste it under the shared condition compared with the unshared condition?"

## STEP 2: DESIGN A STUDY: OPERATIONALIZE THE QUESTION IN TERMS OF VARIABLES THAT ARE EITHER MANIPULATED OR MEASURED

Chapter 10 presents the details on this study, including how its independent variable was manipulated. You might recall that people rated each piece of chocolate using a scale from 1 to 10.

## STEP 3: COLLECT THE DATA AND COMPUTE THE POINT ESTIMATE AND CONFIDENCE INTERVAL

In this study, the dependent variable was measured once during each condition. How will we compute the point estimate and confidence interval for these data?

In this repeated-measures design, each person has two scores—one for the shared condition and one for the unshared condition. To compute the point estimate—the difference between the two conditions—we first compute a difference score for each person. For example, if Aliyah rated her chocolate as an 8 under the shared condition and as a 6 under the unshared condition, her difference score would be 2 (see **Table S2.1**).

After we find the difference score for each person in the study (see the last column of Table S2.1), we can find the mean of this column of differences, as well as its standard deviation. When Boothby et al. conducted their study, they found the mean of the difference scores to be 1.54. That's the point estimate: a difference of 1.54 rating points (on a scale of 1 to 10).

To create the confidence interval, we again start with the point estimate and add and subtract the margin of error from it. As before, the margin of error is the product of three components—a variability component and a sample size component (which together make up the standard error), as well as a constant associated with our 95% confidence level.

**The Variability Component.** In a paired design (i.e., a dependent-groups design), we use the standard deviation (*SD*) of the column of difference scores. In this example, it's 2.77.

**The Sample Size Component.** For this, we use the number of participants. In this study there were 23, so we use the formula:

$$\sqrt{\left(\frac{1}{N}\right)}$$

where *N* is the number of participants.

**TABLE S2.1**

**Computing Difference Scores for a Repeated-Measures Design**

| PARTICIPANT | RATING IN SHARED CONDITION | RATING IN UNSHARED CONDITION | DIFFERENCE (SHARED MINUS UNSHARED) |
|---|---|---|---|
| Aliyah | 8 | 6 | 2 |
| Benjamin | 7 | 7 | 0 |
| Carolyn | 5 | 4 | 1 |
| Danae | 5 | 7 | -2 |
| ... | | | |
| Mean difference score | | | 1.54 |
| Standard deviation of difference scores | | | 2.77 |
| Standard error of difference scores (*N* = 23) | | | 0.58 |

We then multiply these first two components to get the standard error:

$$\text{standard error} = SD_{\text{differences}} * \sqrt{\left(\frac{1}{N}\right)}$$

Here is the computation for this example:

$$\text{standard error} = 2.77 * \sqrt{\left(\frac{1}{23}\right)}$$

$$\text{standard error} = 0.58$$

**The Constant for the Difference Between Two Means.** To get the margin of error, we multiply the standard error by the 95% CI constant. In the example with polling data, we used the constant of 1.96, which was a $z$ score. We can use this same constant as long as our $N$ is large (say, 500 or greater) or if we happen to know the $SD$ of the population (we usually do not).

When the sample size is small (and the $N$ of 23 qualifies as very small here), we use a $t$ value as our constant instead of a $z$ score. The $t$ distribution is a family of distributions (see **Figure S2.7**) that takes different shapes depending on the size of the sample. To find the $t$ value we need for our particular sample, we need to know the *degrees of freedom*, or *df*. In a paired design, the *df* is equal to the number of participants (or pairs of scores) minus 1:

$$df = (N - 1)$$
$$df = (23 - 1)$$
$$df = 22$$

Using the *df* value, we can look up the $t$ value we need for our constant, using a computer or a table such as the one in Appendix B, p. 577. In this example, the *df* is 22, so the $t$ value we'll use for our constant is 2.074. (Notice that this $t$ value constant is still close to 2.0.)

**Putting It All Together.** Now we're ready to compute the margin of error and the CI. We already combined the first two elements into the standard error (0.58),

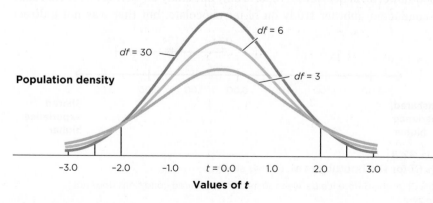

**Population density**

Values of *t*

*df* = 6

*df* = 30

*df* = 3

−3.0    −2.0    −1.0    *t* = 0.0    1.0    2.0    3.0

**FIGURE S2.7**
**Sampling distributions of t for small samples (degrees of freedom = 3 and 6) and large samples (degrees of freedom = 30 or larger).**

As the sample size increases, the *t* distribution gets thinner and approximates a normal distribution.

so we'll multiply this by the constant (2.074) to get the margin of error for this difference score, which is 1.20. Then we add and subtract this from the mean of the differences to get each piece:

$$\text{upper bound} = 1.54 + 1.20$$
$$= 2.74$$
$$\text{lower bound} = 1.54 - 1.20$$
$$= 0.34$$
$$\text{95\% CI for the difference} = [0.34, 2.74]$$

## STEP 4: INTERPRET THE RESULTS IN THE CONTEXT OF YOUR RESEARCH QUESTION

We estimate that when people taste sweet chocolate under shared conditions, they like it more than when they taste it under unshared conditions. How much more? Our 95% CI is 0.34 to 2.74. This means the sample is consistent with differences near 0.34, which would be negligible given the 1–10 rating scale used. On the other hand, our sample data is also consistent with differences near 2.74, which would be a notable difference. So our estimate leaves considerable uncertainty—tasting chocolate in the shared condition could change the experience a lot, could just barely change it, or anything in between. If we want more certainty we would need to collect more data to narrow the CI (**Figure S2.8**).

In this example, we have a CI that does not include 0 difference. If a value of 0 is not inside the 95% CI, we don't have to strongly consider zero as a true population parameter. Still, we need to remember that 5% of 95% CIs will miss the true population value, and our lower end, 0.34, is not far from 0. In sum, in this sample, it seems that the shared experience has at least some effect on the enjoyment of chocolate, but this is a tentative conclusion. We would also want to think about how this result fits in with what else we know. (Have shared experience effects been found with other foods? Is a change of this magnitude reasonable given other research into taste-testing?)

## STEP 5: IF POSSIBLE, CONDUCT THE STUDY AGAIN AND META-ANALYZE THE RESULTS

The Boothby et al. article (2016) reports only one study on tasting sweet chocolate (they conducted another study on bitter chocolate, but that was not a direct

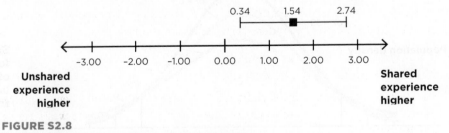

**FIGURE S2.8**
**A 95% CI for the Boothby et al. (2014) study.**

The 95% CI for the difference between shared and unshared conditions does not contain zero.

replication). Ideally, the researchers should conduct a direct replication of Study 1, report its results, and then combine all similar studies using meta-analysis. This is especially important when the estimate is uncertain. Because our first CI was broad, it will be difficult for the original lab to tell others what they should expect if they conduct a similar study: Should they expect a very small difference or a large one?

## Determining the Confidence Interval for a Difference Between Two Groups (an Independent-Groups Experiment)

How does the process for calculating the point estimate and CI differ when we have scores from two different groups, rather than two scores from the same set of people? Once again, we will turn the two means into a single difference score.

Let's work with an example from Chapter 10, the independent-groups experiment that compared two groups of babies (Leonard et al., 2017). All the babies watched a model open a tricky box and take a toy off a carabiner clip. In the "effort" condition, the model tried three times to solve each problem and finally succeeded. In the "no-effort" condition, the model simply succeeded three times in a row. Then the model handed the baby a block-shaped musical toy with a large, misleading button. The dependent variable was how long the babies would persist at trying to turn on the music—how many times did they press the inert button?

This was an independent-groups experiment—specifically, a posttest-only design. Babies were randomly assigned to one condition or the other (effort or no-effort), and they were measured on the dependent variable only once.

What is the appropriate way to analyze the data from this design? Let's work through the steps, using Leonard et al.'s Study 1 and the steps from Cumming and Calin-Jageman (2016).

### STEP 1: STATE A RESEARCH QUESTION USING TERMS SUCH AS "HOW MUCH" OR "TO WHAT EXTENT"

"How many more times will babies press the button in the effort condition compared with the no-effort condition?"

### STEP 2: DESIGN A STUDY: OPERATIONALIZE THE QUESTION IN TERMS OF VARIABLES THAT ARE EITHER MANIPULATED OR MEASURED

Chapter 10 presents the full details on this study and how its independent variable was manipulated and its dependent variable was measured.

### STEP 3: COLLECT THE DATA AND COMPUTE THE POINT ESTIMATE AND CONFIDENCE INTERVAL

In this study, the dependent variable can be stated as "the number of button presses babies were observed to use on the musical toy." How will we compute the point estimate and confidence interval for these data?

There were two groups (effort and no-effort), but we want to calculate a single point estimate, so we'll use the difference between the two groups. The babies in the effort group pressed the button an average of 28.06 times, and the babies in the no-effort group pressed it an average of 16.94 times. The difference between these two groups is 11.12. That's the point estimate: a difference of 11.12 button presses.

To compute the confidence interval around this difference, we start with the point estimate and add and subtract the margin of error from it. As before, the margin of error is the product of three components—a variability component, a sample size component, and a constant (in this case, a $t$) associated with our 95% confidence level. Here is the overview of the formula:

$$\text{margin of error} = SD_{pooled} * \sqrt{\left(\frac{1}{N_1} + \frac{1}{N_2}\right)} * t(df)$$

**The Variability Component.** We estimate the variability in the sample using the standard deviation of the two groups. We start by finding the $SD$ of each group separately. Then we pool these two $SD$s because two estimates are better than one. Pooling the two $SD$s involves averaging the two variances ($SD^2$s) from the two groups if the $N$s are equal and taking the square root. If the $N$s are not equal, we weight the two variances according to their sample size. In the Leonard et al. study, the effort group's $SD$ was 21.09 and the no-effort group's $SD$ was 13.86. Both were based on the same sample size of 34, so we get the $SD_{pooled}$ of 17.84.

**The Sample Size Component.** When we are testing two independent groups, the sample size component reflects the sizes of each group, so in our margin of error calculations, we use the following sample size component:

$$\sqrt{\left(\frac{1}{N_1} + \frac{1}{N_2}\right)}$$

In this example, our sample size is 34:

$$\sqrt{\left(\frac{1}{34} + \frac{1}{34}\right)}$$

As before, the product of the $SD$ and the sample size component above is known as the standard error.

$$\text{standard error} = 17.84 * \sqrt{\left(\frac{1}{34} + \frac{1}{34}\right)}$$
$$\text{standard error} = 4.33$$

**The Constant.** As before, we might be able to use the $z$ score constant of 1.96 if our $N$ is large or if we happen to know the $SD$ of the population.

In the Leonard study, $N$ is relatively small (68), and we don't know the $SD$ of the population of difference scores, so we need to use a $t$ value as our constant. To find the $t$ value we need for our particular sample, we need to know the degrees of freedom, or $df$.

The $df$ is equal to:

$$df = (N_1 - 1) + (N_2 - 1)$$
$$df = (34 - 1) + (34 - 1)$$
$$df = 66$$

Using this *df* value, we look up the *t* value we need for our constant, using a computer or a table such as the one in Appendix B, p. 577. In this example, the *df* is 66, and we want the .95 confidence value (which corresponds to the .05 *t* value in the table). That *t* value is 1.997 (very close to 2). This is our constant—the fudge factor that we will multiply by the standard error.

**Putting It All Together.** Now we're ready to compute the margin of error and the CI. We multiply the standard error (4.33) by the constant (1.997) to get the margin of error for this difference score, which is 8.64. We add and subtract this from the difference to get the upper and lower bounds:

$$\text{upper bound} = 11.12 + 8.64$$
$$= 19.76$$
$$\text{lower bound} = 11.12 - 8.64$$
$$= 2.48$$
$$95\% \text{ CI for difference} = [2.48, 19.76]$$

### STEP 4: INTERPRET THE RESULTS IN THE CONTEXT OF YOUR RESEARCH QUESTION

From our sample, we estimate a difference of 11.12 button presses 95% CI [2.48, 19.76]. In other words, when babies see an adult modeling effort, they press an inert button more often than babies who see an adult modeling no effort. How many more presses? Our estimate is not very certain. Values around 2.48 are plausible, which would be a rather small amount of additional button pressing. Values around 19.76 are also plausible, which indicate much more button pressing. So the adult model could have a fairly small influence on infant behavior, a very large influence, or anywhere in between (and we also need to keep in mind that some estimates don't capture the true population value).

In this example, you might have noticed that the CI does not include the value of 0.00. This information supports the inference that in the population, the difference between effort and no-effort is probably something larger than zero (**Figure S2.9**).

We might be wrong about our estimate. After all, when we use 95% CIs, 5% of them will miss the population difference, meaning the true population difference

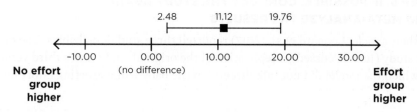

**FIGURE S2.9**

**A 95% CI for the Leonard study.**

The 95% CI for the difference in the number of button presses between the effort group and the no-effort group does not include zero.

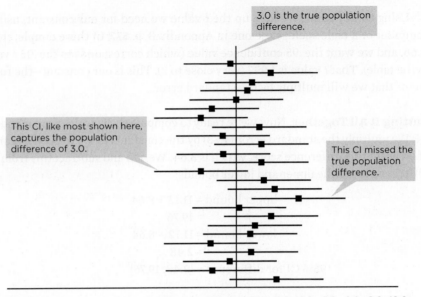

3.0 is the true population difference.

This CI, like most shown here, captures the population difference of 3.0.

This CI missed the true population difference.

-7.0 -6.0 -5.0 -4.0 -3.0 -2.0 -1.0 0.0 1.0 2.0 3.0 4.0 5.0 6.0 7.0 8.0 9.0 10.0

**FIGURE S2.10**

**CIs capture the population value 95% of the time.**

Every study will give us only one confidence interval (CI), which either includes the true population difference or does not. Over the long run, if we run the study many times, 95% of our CIs will include the true population difference, but 5% of the time, our CI will miss it. Note that some CIs are wider than others. This happens because every time we run the study, we may have a slightly different estimate of variability (and we may even have a slightly different N), so each CI will change to reflect the realities of the particular sample. In this example, we know that the true population difference is 3.0 points, but we usually do not know the population difference.

might be smaller than 2.48 or larger than 19.76. Is our CI one that captures the truth or one of the ones that misses? There's no way to know for sure without conducting more research. If we run this study multiple times, we'll get slightly different CIs each time. But over the long run, 95% of our CIs will include the true population difference.[2] **Figure S2.10** illustrates how a CI works.

## STEP 5: IF POSSIBLE, CONDUCT THE STUDY AGAIN AND META-ANALYZE THE RESULTS

In their article, Leonard et al. (2017) reported three studies on babies. The original study (just discussed), a replication of the original study, and a third version, in which the model did not talk directly to the baby while exerting effort (or no

---

[2]If we conduct another study, about 83% of the time it will have a point estimate inside the original study's 95% CI. Why not 95%? Because both the first study and the subsequent study are prone to sampling error—so with two sources of error, the rate of agreement falls.

effort). The researchers reported the results for all three studies, including the 95% CIs for all three. They could meta-analyze the results of these three studies by combining them into an average point estimate and an average CI.

## Effect Size *d* or Original Units?

We just worked through two examples of how to conduct inferential statistics on difference scores. One found an average difference on a rating for chocolate, which we calculated to be around 1.54 points on a scale from 1 to 10. Another study found an average difference in button presses, which we calculated to be 11.12 button presses on a musical toy. It made sense to present the difference scores in these original units because it was easy to picture what 1.54 points on a 10-point scale might mean and what 11.12 button presses look like, in practical terms. But we could also express these differences using effect size, *d*. Recall from Statistics Review: Descriptive Statistics that *d* tells us the difference between two means in SD units.

In the Leonard et al. study, the effect size associated with the 11.12 difference in button presses can be converted to a *d* of 0.62. (Recall that when calculating *d*, we divide the mean difference by the pooled *SD*, in this case $\frac{11.12}{17.84}$). We can also calculate a CI around *d*. The CI for this study's *d* was [0.13, 1.11]. In the Boothby et al. study, the effect size associated with the 1.54 difference on the rating scale was reported by the authors as *d* = 0.56, 95% CI for *d* [0.09, 1.03][3].

The importance of an effect size depends on context, as explained in Chapters 8, 10, and Statistics Review: Descriptive Statistics. Some psychologists start out assuming a *d* of 0.2 to be small, 0.5 to be medium, and 0.8 to be large. Using these benchmarks, the two *d*s above are considered medium in size.

Which measure of difference should we use—original units or *d*? In many cases it makes good sense to use the original units (such as button presses) because this gives your reader a practical sense of how large the difference is. The reader might say, "Oh! The babies pressed the button around 11 extra times in the effort condition—that seems like a pretty big difference—but not a huge one."

Other times, such as when you want to compare results, it might make sense to use *d*. For example, Leonard and her colleagues not only measured button presses with the musical toy; they also measured how long (in seconds) each baby spent playing with the toy. They found that babies in the effort condition played about 3.26 seconds longer, 95% CI [−12.33, 18.86]. As you can see, seconds of play and number of button presses are on different scales, so it is hard to compare 11.1 button presses with 3.26 seconds. However, the 3.26 seconds corresponds to a *d* of 0.10. When we compare the *d* of 0.62 to the *d* of 0.10, we can see that the difference for button presses appears to be stronger (because 0.62 is larger than 0.10). You might also have noticed that the CI for the difference in time spent playing

---

[3]When calculating *d* for a paired *t* test, we use the pooled *SD* of the two conditions, not the *SD* of the difference scores.

included both negative and positive values [–12.33, 18.86]. This wide range of values includes the possibility that there is no difference between the groups (0.00) or that the difference even goes the opposite way. The CI range is also compatible with the conclusion that the effect of the effort (versus no-effort) condition on time spent playing is not very large.

## A Study with More Than Two Means

So far you have read how to compute the point estimate and confidence interval for two independent groups and for two dependent (paired) groups. In each case, we estimated how large the difference was and computed its CI.

But what if you have three or more means to compare with each other? When a study compares three or more groups with each other (let's call the groups A, B, and C), we might be tempted to estimate everything we can: How big is the A to B difference? How big is the B to C difference? How big is the C to A difference? The more groups you have, the more differences you can estimate, right? But that's the problem: You might be tempted to look at everything and report only the largest differences. That's cherry-picking, which is a questionable research practice.

Instead, when you have multiple comparisons, the appropriate thing to do is preregister a small number of differences you intend to estimate. Then you can compute point estimates and CIs for those differences in ways very similar to what we did before.

Here's an example of an experiment with three independent groups, from an example in Chapter 2. As you may recall, Bushman (2002) was testing the hypothesis that venting one's anger (by punching a punching bag) would reduce a person's subsequent anger and aggression more than sitting quietly or exercising would. This study had three stages. In the first stage, a student wrote an essay that was subsequently criticized by another student, who called it "one of the worst essays I have ever read!" In the second stage, Bushman divided the insulted (and angry) participants into three groups. The first group sat quietly in the lab room. The second group had the chance to punch a punching bag and was told to imagine the insulting student's face on it (this was the venting group). The third group had the chance to punch a punching bag, but they were told they were doing so for exercise. In the final stage, all three groups of participants rated their anger and had a chance to punish the insulting student by playing a very loud noise blast.

Let's work through the analysis steps for this example.

### STEP 1: STATE A RESEARCH QUESTION USING TERMS SUCH AS "HOW MUCH" OR "TO WHAT EXTENT"

To avoid cherry-picking, we will decide in advance to estimate only two theory-relevant differences, both focused on the venting group. One is "How large is the difference in anger between the venting group and the group sitting quietly?" Two is "How large is the difference in anger between the venting group and the exercise group?"

## STEP 2: DESIGN A STUDY: OPERATIONALIZE THE QUESTION IN TERMS OF VARIABLES THAT ARE EITHER MANIPULATED OR MEASURED

The introduction to this section laid out the key details of this study, and you can read the full design in Bushman (2002).

## STEP 3: COLLECT THE DATA AND COMPUTE THE POINT ESTIMATE AND CONFIDENCE INTERVAL

The researchers obtained a mean rating of angry mood for each of the three groups. Here are the means representing how angry each group reported feeling after they either sat or punched the bag (the anger rating scale had a low of 15 and a high of 75). Each group had 200 people.

Mean of group who sat quietly: 26.25 ($SD$ = 10.98)
Mean of venting group: 29.78 ($SD$ = 11.56)
Mean of exercise group: 27.32 ($SD$ = 10.88)

We will estimate two point estimates (difference scores)—one for each of the research questions in Step 1. The first compares the anger of the venting group with that of the group sitting quietly:

$$= 29.78 - 26.25$$
$$= 3.53$$

The second compares the anger of the venting group with that of the exercise group:

$$= 29.78 - 27.32$$
$$= 2.46$$

To create the confidence intervals, as usual we start with the point estimate and add and subtract the margin of error from it. And as before, the margin of error is the product of three components—variability, sample size, and a constant associated with the 95% confidence level.

**The Variability Component.** You might recall that when we estimated the difference between two means, we found the $SD$ of each group and then pooled these two $SD$s because two estimates are better than one. When our study involves three or more means, we pool the $SD$s from *all* groups to get an even better estimate of the $SD$.

If the $N$s of the groups are equal, pooling the $SD$s involves simply averaging the variances ($SD^2$s) and taking the square root. If the $N$s are not equal, we weight the two $SD$s according to their sample size, using this formula:

$$SD_{\text{pooled}} = \sqrt{\frac{(N_1 - 1)SD_1^2 + (N_2 - 1)SD_2^2 + (N_3 - 1)SD_3^2}{N_1 + N_2 + N_3 - 3}}$$

In Bushman's study, the groups were all the same size ($N = 200$), so we can average the three *SD* estimates to get $SD_{pooled} = 11.14$.

**The Sample Size Component.** Once we find the pooled *SD*, the sample size component is the same as it was for comparing two independent groups—it reflects both of the groups' *N*s.

$$\sqrt{\left( \frac{1}{N_1} + \frac{1}{N_2} \right)}$$

We multiply the variability component by the sample size component to get the standard error for this comparison. Here's the standard error for the first comparison, between the venting and the sitting quietly groups:

standard error for difference between venting and sitting quietly:

$$11.14 * \sqrt{\left( \frac{1}{200} + \frac{1}{200} \right)} = 1.11$$

The standard error for the second comparison, between the venting and the exercising groups, happens to be exactly the same because these groups also have *N*s of 200:

standard error for difference between venting and exercising:

$$11.14 * \sqrt{\left( \frac{1}{200} + \frac{1}{200} \right)} = 1.11$$

**The Constant.** The constant is a *t* value, as in the last two examples. When the sample size is small or we don't know the *SD* of the population, we use a *t* value as our constant instead of a *z* score. To find the *t* value, we need to know the degrees of freedom. In the multiple-group case, the *df* is based on all groups, to reflect the fact that the $SD_{pooled}$ estimate was based on all three groups. Therefore, the *df* is equal to:

$$df = (N_1 - 1) + (N_2 - 1) + (N_3 - 1)$$
$$df = (200 - 1) + (200 - 1) + (200 - 1)$$
$$df = 597$$

Using this *df* value, we look up the *t* value we need for our constant, using a computer or a table such as the one in Appendix B, p. 577. In this example, the *df* is 597, so the *t* value is 1.97. (Because our sample is fairly large, our *t* value is almost the same as the benchmark *z* score constant, 1.96.)

**Putting It All Together.** Now we're ready to compute the margins of error and the CIs. The standard error happens to be the same for both of the comparisons because they are based on the same sample size. We multiply our pooled *SD* (11.14) by our sample size component $\sqrt{\frac{1}{200} + \frac{1}{200}}$ to get the standard error (1.11). Then we multiply this by our $t$ constant (1.97) to get the margin of error for this difference score, which is 2.19. We add and subtract the margin of error from our differences to get our two CIs.

CI for the comparison between venting and sitting quietly:

$$\text{upper bound} = 3.53 + 2.19$$
$$= 5.72$$
$$\text{lower bound} = 3.53 - 2.19$$
$$= 1.34$$
$$95\% \text{ CI for difference} = [1.34, 5.72]$$

CI for the comparison between venting and exercising:

$$\text{upper bound} = 2.46 + 2.19$$
$$= 4.65$$
$$\text{lower bound} = 2.46 - 2.19$$
$$= 0.27$$
$$95\% \text{ CI for difference} = [0.27, 4.65]$$

## STEP 4: INTERPRET THE RESULTS IN THE CONTEXT OF YOUR RESEARCH QUESTION

Our first estimate concerns the difference in anger between venting and sitting quietly: We estimate that venting actually increased feelings of anger by 3 points, but we're a bit uncertain about how much, 95% CI [1.34, 5.72]. Bushman's data is compatible with venting increasing anger by just 1.34 points. Given the scale is from 15 to 75, that level of increase might be considered fairly small. But the data is also compatible with increases around 5.72 points, which might be considered a notable increase. However, it is clear that venting didn't *help*, because the CI does not include any values reflecting a decrease in anger. So this evidence does not support the idea that venting is a good strategy for dealing with anger. Of course, our 95% CI might be one of the 5% that misses the population value, but it's plausible that the conventional wisdom about venting is wrong.

From this same study, Bushman could also estimate the difference in anger between venting and exercise [0.27, 4.65]. This comparison also suggests that venting increases anger, and again we are uncertain by how much. The lower end of the CI is only 0.27, which would be a tiny increase. The top end is 4.65, which might be meaningful. As before, this estimate also goes against the hypothesis that venting helps, because the CI is not compatible with any values reflecting a *decrease* in anger. Neither of the differences we estimated from this study provides compelling evidence that venting helps manage anger.

## The Analysis of Variance Approach

The previous approach, in which we preregistered a small number of comparisons, is arguably the most reasonable approach to analyzing a data set that has multiple groups (Cumming & Calin-Jageman, 2016). However, when you read empirical articles about studies that compare three or more groups, you will often see another approach used: the analysis of variance, or ANOVA, which computes an *F* ratio.

The top of the *F* ratio is an estimate of the variability between the groups (for example, how much variability there is among the three group means). The bottom of the *F* ratio is an estimate of the pooled variability within the groups (for example, how much variability there is among the individuals in each group). If the *F* ratio is a large number (usually much greater than 2.0 or 3.0), it means that the group means are fairly different from each other—far apart—compared with the variability within each group. If the *F* ratio is small (i.e., 1.0 or less), it means that the group means are not very different from each other.

When you read empirical journal articles that include ANOVAs and *F* ratios, these values are usually followed up with planned comparisons. These planned comparisons are similar to the preregistered difference estimates we just walked through.

## Determining the Point Estimate and Confidence Interval for a Correlation Coefficient

So far we have described how to calculate point estimates and confidence intervals for three types of differences: a difference between two independent groups, a difference between two conditions within the same group (a paired design, or repeated-measures design), and a difference among three or more independent groups. We might also estimate the strength and direction of an association between two variables. To estimate such a relationship, we use *r* as our point estimate. Here's how we would work through the research steps in this situation, using an example from Statistics Review: Descriptive Statistics (the correlation between 2-year-old height and adult height).

### STEP 1: STATE A RESEARCH QUESTION USING TERMS SUCH AS "HOW MUCH" OR "TO WHAT EXTENT"

Here our question is phrased in terms of the strength of the correlation: "To what extent does 2-year-old height correlate with adult height?" Or "How strong is the relationship between 2-year-old height and adult height?"

### STEP 2: DESIGN A STUDY: OPERATIONALIZE THE QUESTION IN TERMS OF VARIABLES THAT ARE EITHER MANIPULATED OR MEASURED

We measured a set of seven people as adults and looked up their height on their medical records at age 2. We recorded both values for each person, in cm (see Table S1.3).

## STEP 3: COLLECT THE DATA AND COMPUTE THE POINT ESTIMATE AND CONFIDENCE INTERVAL

You learned in detail about the correlation coefficient $r$ in Chapter 8 and Statistics Review: Descriptive Statistics, including how to compute it. In Table S1.3, you can see the point estimate for our data: $r = .75$.

Next, we need to estimate a confidence interval around $r$. As with all other examples here, we need to estimate the margin of error for the correlation and then add and subtract the margin of error from our point estimate $r$.

You would not compute the margin of error of a correlation coefficient by hand. You can estimate it using software such as JASP or R. When you run the correlation in these programs, you ask the program for the correlation as well as its 95% CI. After we analyze the data for this correlation using JASP (and check the box to get the confidence interval), the output reports that the CI for this $r$ was [–.003, .961].

## STEP 4: INTERPRET THE RESULTS IN THE CONTEXT OF YOUR RESEARCH QUESTION

The point estimate of .75 is a fairly strong positive correlation (especially compared with the effect sizes listed in Table S1.4). But our estimate is very uncertain: The 95% CI is very wide [–.003, .961] and even includes zero (see **Figure S2.11**). The wide interval may surprise you, especially given our strong intuition that these two variables (child height and adult height) should be highly correlated. The reason is that the estimate is based on only seven individuals. When we have such a small sample, any estimate will be much less precise, and the wide interval reflects that lack of precision. Over the long run, 95% of such intervals will contain the true population correlation between 2-year-old height and adult height. If we ran our study again with more people, the CI would be narrower, meaning the estimate would be more precise, but we don't know where the new CI will be, and the new CI based on more data may even fall outside our first CI.

## STEP 5: IF POSSIBLE, CONDUCT THE STUDY AGAIN AND META-ANALYZE THE RESULTS

Especially since this was an example with a very small $N$, we would want to conduct a study with a larger sample size to get a more precise estimate of the correlation. If we meta-analyzed the two resulting correlations (one based on a small

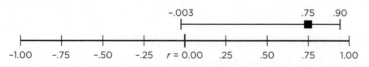

**FIGURE S2.11**

**The 95% CI for the relationship between 2-year-old height and adult height.**

This 95% CI is extremely wide, representing the small sample it was estimated from ($N = 7$). In addition, the 95% CIs for $r$ are often asymmetrical like this, in part because $r$ can only be as high as 1.0.

*N* and one based on a larger *N*), the one based on the larger *N* would be weighted more in the meta-analytic estimate.

## Determining the Point Estimate and Confidence Interval for Beta (Multiple Regression)

Chapter 9 introduced beta, a value obtained from the multiple-regression process. Beta is similar to *r* in that both are used to estimate the association between two variables. However, beta goes further than *r*, because it usually represents the relationship between a predictor (independent) variable and a dependent variable, *controlling for* other ("third") variables. For example, Chapter 9 presented a study that estimated the relationship between viewing sexual content on TV and teen pregnancy rates, controlling for other variables such as age, grades in school, parent education, ethnicity, and peer characteristics.

The betas in this study are the point estimates. For example, in the TV study, the beta for exposure to sex on TV predicting pregnancy was beta = 0.44, controlling for other variables such as age, grades, parent education, ethnicity, and so on.

Next, we would compute the 95% CI around each beta to indicate how precise these estimates are. When you encounter regression analyses in empirical journal articles, you may not actually see these CIs for beta. In fact, the Chandra study (2008) on sexual TV content did not report them, perhaps because reporting of CIs was not as common when the paper was published more than a decade ago. You will see more CIs in recent articles, because most journals now require them.

If Chandra et al. (2008) had reported a 95% CI for their beta of 0.44, it might have been reported as a range such as [0.23, 0.63]. The interpretation would be as follows: We see that 0 is relatively far outside the CI, so these data support at least some level of relationship. Still, we are somewhat uncertain how strong the relationship is, because the CI is compatible with both weaker relationships (0.23) and stronger relationships (0.63). Interpretation of strength depends on research context. Teen pregnancy is a serious issue, so even a weak relationship may be worth documenting. We would also compare this relationship to other predictors of teen pregnancy (such as sex education) to help us judge the importance of TV. Finally, we should remember that our estimate is a 95% CI—we expect that 95% of estimates like this will capture the true population parameter, but our CI could be one of the 5% that does not.

## THE CONFIDENCE INTERVAL APPROACH VERSUS NHST

So far, we have focused on the estimation and precision (point estimates and confidence intervals) approach to inferential statistics, an approach known as the new statistics (Cumming, 2012, 2014). The name reflects modern statistical practices in psychology. In addition to point estimates and confidence intervals, this approach emphasizes replication, meta-analysis, open science, and preregistration. New statistics represents the direction psychology is heading in the future, and many people find the approach intuitive.

However, the statistical reporting in some empirical journal articles is based on another inferential statistics approach known as **null hypothesis significance testing (NHST)**. You might learn NHST in full-length statistics classes. It's helpful for you to know about this approach too—especially what a **_p_ value** is and what "statistical significance" means.

The fundamental distinction between the two approaches is that they are based on different research questions. The research questions in the new statistics are _estimation based_, so they are phrased in terms of "how much" or "to what extent" (for example, "How large is the difference between groups?"). In contrast, the NHST research questions are phrased in _binary_, yes/no terms ("Is there a significant difference between groups, or not?").

## The NHST Procedure

NHST begins with an assumption called the null hypothesis. If we are testing the difference between two conditions—for example, the difference between unshared and shared experiences (Boothby et al., 2014)—we would take the following steps.

### STEP 1: ASSUME THAT THERE IS NO EFFECT (THE NULL HYPOTHESIS)

The null hypothesis states that there is no effect in the population: "There is no difference between chocolate ratings in the shared and unshared conditions." In other words, the assumed population difference between the two conditions should be around 0.00.

### STEP 2: COLLECT DATA AND CALCULATE YOUR RESULT

In Study 1, Boothby et al. found that ratings of the sweet chocolate were higher in the shared condition than the unshared condition (1.54 points higher).

### STEP 3: CALCULATE THE PROBABILITY OF GETTING A RESULT OF THAT MAGNITUDE, OR ONE EVEN MORE EXTREME, IF THE NULL HYPOTHESIS IS TRUE

In this step of NHST, we calculate a probability, or _p_ value. Using knowledge of the _t_ distribution (including the standard error of our difference), we compute the probability that we would obtain a difference of 1.54 or larger if the null hypothesis was true. For example, assuming there is no difference in the population and our sample comes from that null hypothesis population, we would not be surprised to find differences near 0.00 most of the time. We might find a difference of −0.12 or a difference of 0.89. These would not surprise us if there's no difference in the population. But how likely would it be to find a difference of 1.54? Is this difference a rare result or a common one? Using NSHT, that probability turns out to be $p = .01$.

## STEP 4: DECIDE WHETHER TO REJECT OR RETAIN THE NULL HYPOTHESIS

Here we make a decision based on the probability we computed in Step 3. The $p$ of .01 means that the probability of obtaining a difference of 1.54 or even more extreme is very rare if the null hypothesis is true. In fact, the $p$ value of .01 tells us that we would get a difference this large or larger only 1% of the time if the null hypothesis were true. This result is so rare under the assumption of the null hypothesis that we decide to reject the null hypothesis. When we reject the null, we call that result **statistically significant**.

When making the Step 4 decision in NHST, we decide in advance how "rare" a result has to be in order to reject the null. Conventionally, we use a $p = .05$ decision rule (this decision rule of .05 is also known as **alpha**). That is, we plan in advance that if the result we obtain in our study (or a result more extreme) would happen less than 5% of the time (or $p < .05$) under the null hypothesis, we will reject the null.

You might have noticed that this cutoff of $p = .05$ corresponds to the 95% CI we have been using. That's no coincidence: The 95% CI is the complement to a conventional $p$ of .05 (5%). In fact, when we compute a 95% CI and the CI does not include zero, it's the same thing as saying our result is statistically significant.

Sometimes we find out that our result would *not* be so rare under the null hypothesis assumption. For example, say we conducted our study and found a small difference (say, a difference of only 0.89 in Boothby's study). We might calculate that such a result (or one more extreme) would occur $p = .25$ (25%) of the time if the null hypothesis is true. In this case, we decide not to reject the null, because the $p$ we obtained is *larger* than our decision point of $p = .05$. Instead, we say that we *retain the null hypothesis*, or that our result is **not statistically significant** (often abbreviated **n.s.**). **Table S2.2** summarizes these decision possibilities of NHST and compares them with the confidence interval method.

As you can see, NHST has its own logic focused on rejecting or retaining a null hypothesis about the population. In contrast, the new statistics focuses on estimating the size of some effect and calculating the precision of that estimate. What NHST and the new statistics have in common is that they make inferences about a population (which is unknown) based on the characteristics of a sample (which is known). In addition, the assumptions, computations, and tests are often the same: Both approaches require variability components, sample size components, $t$ and $z$ distributions, and standard errors. Both approaches involve uncertainty. **Table S2.3** summarizes some of the key similarities and differences between these two approaches to inferential statistics. **Table S2.4** summarizes the inferential statistics to be used for analyzing different types of data.

## Summary of NHST Possible Outcomes

| THIS TERM | MEANS THE SAME AS: | IN OTHER WORDS: | YOU MAY SEE, IN PUBLISHED WORK: | IN A RESEARCH CONTEXT, MAY MEAN: | IN TERMS OF THE CONFIDENCE INTERVAL: |
|---|---|---|---|---|---|
| Rejecting the null hypothesis | The result is statistically significant. | The probability of getting a result this extreme or more extreme, by chance, if the null hypothesis is true, is less than 5%. | $p < .05$ <br> * (asterisk) | The difference or association is not compatible with zero. | The confidence interval does not contain 0. |
| Retaining the null hypothesis | The result is not statistically significant. | The probability of getting a result this extreme or more extreme, by chance, if the null hypothesis is true, is greater than or equal to 5%. | $p \geq .05$ <br> n.s. | We cannot conclude that the difference is larger than zero. We cannot conclude that the relationship is stronger than zero. | The confidence interval includes 0. |

## The Major Differences and Commonalities Between the New Statistics and Null Hypothesis Significance Testing (NHST)

| | NEW STATISTICS | NHST |
|---|---|---|
| **Focus** | Estimation and precision (point estimate and confidence interval) | Decision to reject or retain the null hypothesis, based on a $p$ value |
| **Types of questions** | Questions of magnitude: How large is the difference? <br> How strong is the relationship? | Yes/no questions: Is the difference significantly different from zero or not? <br> Is the relationship significantly different from zero or not? |
| **Inference goals** | Uses results from a sample (which is known) to make estimates about a population value (which is unknown). | Uses results from a sample (which is known) to make a yes/no inference about the characteristics of a population (which is unknown). |
| **Typical output** | Computes a point estimate (such as a difference score, a $d$, or an $r$) and a confidence interval around that estimate. | Computes a test statistic (such as a $t$, $r$, or $F$) and compares it to the null hypothesis distribution, resulting in a $p$ value. |

*(continued)*

## The Major Differences and Commonalities Between the New Statistics and Null Hypothesis Significance Testing (NHST) *(Continued)*

| | NEW STATISTICS | NHST |
|---|---|---|
| **Translating between the two (part 1)** | When a 95% CI does not include zero, it is the same as rejecting the null hypothesis under NHST ($p < .05$). The CI also provides information about the magnitude of the effect and the precision with which it is estimated. | When the *p* value is less than .05, you reject the null. Rejecting the null hypothesis does not provide, in itself, any information about the magnitude of the significant effect. |
| **Translating between the two (part 2)** | When a 95% CI includes zero, it is the same as retaining the null hypothesis (n.s.).<br><br>A 95% CI that includes zero indicates that the population value may be so small that it might even be zero. | When the *p* value is *greater than* .05, we retain the null and the result is called not significant (n.s.). Retaining the null hypothesis means only that we cannot reject the idea that the null hypothesis is true. |
| **Role of sample size** | When a study uses a large sample, it usually leads to more precise estimates, represented as narrower 95% CIs. | When a study uses a large sample, it is usually easier to reject the null hypothesis (i.e., obtain statistical significance). |
| **Role of values like *t*** | The *t* associated with a certain *df* is part of the margin of error calculation, which is used to create the 95% CI. | We compute a *t* value for our sample and compare it to the kinds of *t*s we would get if the null hypothesis is true. If the *t* from the sample is very large (usually larger than 2.00, depending on sample size), we can usually reject the null. |
| **Role of standard errors** | Standard errors play a role in calculating the CI. When standard error is small, the precision of the estimate is better, and the CI is narrower. | Standard errors play a role in calculating the test statistic for the sample. When standard error is small, the test statistic (such as *t*) becomes larger, making it easier to reject the null hypothesis. |
| **Possible inference errors** | When we set the CI at 95%, we expect 95% of our intervals to contain the true population value, but 5% will miss it. For each result, we won't know whether the CI we obtained is a hit or a miss. Over the long run, if we do the study multiple times, the CI will miss the true population value 5% of the time. | When we reject the null hypothesis, we have a 5% chance of making a mistake by saying a result did not come from the null hypothesis distribution when it really did (this is called a Type I error).<br><br>When we retain the null, we might fail to reject the null hypothesis when it actually should be rejected (this is called a Type II error). |
| **Common misconceptions to avoid** | Remember that the population value we are estimating does not change—it is some unknown, but stable, value. In contrast, the CIs from each study we run will be slightly different from each other, and over the long run, 95% of these CIs will capture the true population value. | First, finding a "statistically significant" result may sound impressive, but we should still check the effect size. Sometimes a result will be statistically significant but very small in practical terms.<br><br>Second, finding a nonsignificant result does not mean that "the null hypothesis is true." It simply means we cannot reject the null hypothesis. |

**TABLE S2.4**

## Inferential Statistics You Can Use to Analyze Different Kinds of Data

| SITUATION | ONE VARIABLE IS: | THE OTHER VARIABLE IS: | NEW STATISTICS RESEARCH QUESTION | POINT ESTIMATE | CI INTERPRETATION | NHST RESEARCH QUESTION | NHST TEST TYPICALLY USED AND ITS INTERPRETATION |
|---|---|---|---|---|---|---|---|
| Estimating a single percentage | Quantitative (e.g., a count of yes votes) | (There is only one variable in this scenario.) | How much support is there for Proposition Q? | Percentage of support (e.g., 57%) | Our approach captures the true percentage of support in the population 95% of the time. | Is the degree of support significantly different from zero? | Same: point estimate and CI |
| Two independent groups (comparing two group means) | Categorical/ nominal (e.g., treatment vs. control group) | Quantitative (e.g., severity of symptoms) | How much of a reduction in symptom severity was experienced by the treatment group? | Difference between two means in original units, or difference between two means in effect size, $d$ | Our approach captures the true difference between groups in the population 95% of the time. | Does the treatment group score significantly higher than the control group? | Independent-groups $t$ test and associated $p$ value Is the difference in conditions significantly different from zero? |
| Testing a difference between two scores measured in the same sample (paired design) | Categorical (e.g., kind of cola: regular or diet; people taste both kinds of cola) | Quantitative (e.g., rating of cola flavor on a scale of 1 to 10) | How much higher do people rate regular cola compared with diet cola? | Paired difference between the two conditions in original units, or difference between two means in effect size, $d$ | Our approach captures the true difference between colas 95% of the time. | Do people rate regular cola significantly higher than diet cola? | Dependent groups $t$ test and associated $p$ value Is the difference in conditions significantly different from zero? |

*(continued)*

## Inferential Statistics You Can Use to Analyze Different Kinds of Data *(Continued)*

| SITUATION | ONE VARIABLE IS: | THE OTHER VARIABLE IS: | NEW STATISTICS RESEARCH QUESTION | POINT ESTIMATE | CI INTERPRETATION | NHST RESEARCH QUESTION | NHST TEST TYPICALLY USED AND ITS INTERPRETATION |
|---|---|---|---|---|---|---|---|
| Testing the significance of a difference between two or more groups (comparing group means) | Categorical (e.g., major: chemistry, psychology, or biology) | Quantitative (e.g., exam scores) | How much higher do chemistry majors score than biology majors? How much higher do psychology majors score than biology majors? | We preregister a limited number of comparisons among the three groups (e.g., chemistry to biology, and psychology to biology). | We have one CI for each planned comparison. Our approach means that 95% of the CIs will capture the true difference between groups. | Are these three means significantly different from each other? | Analysis of variance (between-groups ANOVA), returning an $F$ and associated $p$ value. Is there some significant difference among these means? |
| Testing an association between two variables | Quantitative (e.g., hours of study for exam) | Quantitative (e.g., grade on exam) | How strong is the association between hours of studying and exam grades? | Correlation coefficient (returns an $r$ value) | Our approach means that 95% of the CIs will capture the true association between hours of study and grades. | Is the association (measured in $r$) between hours of study and exam grades statistically significant? | Correlation, or $r$, with an associated $p$ value. Is the difference in conditions significantly different from zero? |
| Testing an association between two variables, controlling for a third variable | Quantitative (e.g., hours of study for exam) | Quantitative (e.g., grade on exam; other quantitative variables also controlled for) | How strong is the association between hours of studying and exam grades when people's preference for the material is controlled for? | Multiple regression (returns beta values or $b$ values) | Our approach means that 95% of the CIs will capture the true association between hours of study and grades when preference is controlled for. | Is the association (measured in beta or $b$) between hours of study and exam grades statistically significant when preference for the material is controlled for? | Beta, or $b$, whose significance is evaluated by an associated $t$ statistic and $p$ value. Is the relationship significantly different from zero? |

| SITUATION | ONE VARIABLE IS: | THE OTHER VARIABLE IS: | NEW STATISTICS RESEARCH QUESTION | POINT ESTIMATE | CI INTERPRETATION | NHST RESEARCH QUESTION | NHST TEST TYPICALLY USED AND ITS INTERPRETATION |
|---|---|---|---|---|---|---|---|
| Testing an association between two or more categories (comparing group percentages) | Categorical (e.g., major: psychology, English, chemistry) | Percentage on some variable (e.g., pass/fail rate) | How different are the passing rates in these three groups? | Percent passing rates plus margins of error | By comparing the CIs of the three percent estimates (and how much the CIs overlap), we can make inferences about how different they are. | Is there a difference in passing rates among the three groups, or not? | Chi-square test of goodness of fit (returns an $X^2$ value and p value) Are the two passing rates significantly different from each other? |
| Testing an association between two variables | Categorical (e.g., class year: freshman, sophomore, junior, senior) | Categorical (e.g., form of transportation to campus: bike, bus, car) | How different are these proportions from each other? Are these two categorical variables related? | Differences in proportions Relatedness of two ordinal categories | It is possible to compute CIs for differences in proportion or a CI for the degree of relatedness between two ordinal categories. | Do people in different class years differ systematically in what form of transportation they use? | Chi-square test of independence (returns an $X^2$ value and p value) Are the forms of transportation significantly different across class year? |
| Testing two or more independent variables at a time and their interaction (see Chapter 11) | First independent variable is categorical (e.g., being on cell phone or not) | Dependent variable is quantitative (e.g., time to brake when presented with a hazard in a driving simulator) | Focus is the difference in differences: How much faster do people brake when on a cell phone (compared to control) in light traffic? How much faster do people brake when on a cell phone (compared to control) in heavy traffic? | Two point estimates: 1. the difference in brake time between cell phone and control; 2. the difference in brake time between cell phone and control in the heavy traffic condition. | Our approach means that 95% of CIs will contain the true cell phone/control difference in the light condition, and 95% of CIs will contain the true cell phone/ no distraction difference in the heavy condition. Overlap between the CIs shows how different the differences are. | Do people brake faster in the cell phone or control condition? (main effect) Do people brake faster in light or heavy traffic? (main effect) Does the effect of cell phone depend on traffic conditions? (interaction) | Factorial analysis of variance (returns F values for each main effect and each interaction) |

*Note:* Not all of the statistical tests in this table are included in this supplementary chapter.

# Key Terms

inferential statistics, p. 491

point estimate, p. 493

confidence interval (CI), p. 493

standard error, p. 496

dependent sample, p. 499

null hypothesis significance testing
(NHST), p. 515

$p$ value, p. 515

statistically significant, p. 516

alpha, p. 516

not statistically significant (n.s.), p. 516

# Presenting Results

## APA-STYLE REPORTS AND CONFERENCE POSTERS

Communication is essential to the scientific method. Scientists make the results of their research public in order to tell others about the advances they have made or the phenomena they have documented. Publication is part of the theory-data cycle (Chapter 1) because researchers may publish their hypotheses in advance (via preregistration) and also because researchers write about the results in terms of how well they support a theory. Published data become the basis for replication and theory development. Through the peer-review process, methods and results are scrutinized by peers who evaluate the quality of the research and the importance of the findings.

This supplementary chapter covers two forms in which psychological scientists present their data: the written research report and the conference poster.

## WRITING RESEARCH REPORTS IN APA STYLE

As part of your psychology courses, you will probably be required to prepare a research report. The most common format for report writing is APA style, outlined in the *Publication Manual of the American Psychological Association* (7th edition, 2020). In the classroom, your research reports will be read only by your professors and fellow students. However, psychological scientists use the same APA style to write research reports that may become empirical journal articles.

# APA Style Overview

A scientific research report is different from other kinds of nonfiction writing you may have tried. All APA-style research reports contain the same sections, which present particular kinds of information (see Chapter 2). An APA-style report includes the following elements:

Title

Abstract

Introduction

Method

Results

Discussion

References

APA style prescribes not only the content that belongs in each section, but also the format, including margin specifications, heading styles, and the presentation of statistical tests.

## TITLE

By reading the title alone, readers should understand the main idea of the article. The *APA Manual* recommends that the title be no more than 12 words long.

**Table S3.1** presents examples of titles of research papers cited in this textbook. You can see that, overall, they are informative and concise. In some cases, they even communicate their message with style. Most of the titles in the table contain a colon and a subtitle. The main title (the words before the colon) is intended to attract readers' interest; the subtitle (the words after the colon) specifies the article's content.

---

**TABLE S3.1**

### Titles of Empirical Journal Articles

| ARTICLE TITLE | AUTHORS |
|---|---|
| Well-being from the knife? Psychological effects of aesthetic surgery | Margraf et al., 2013 |
| Profiles in driver distraction: Effects of cell phone conversations on younger and older drivers | Strayer & Drews, 2004 |
| Eavesdropping on happiness: Well-being is related to having less small talk and more substantive conversations | Mehl et al., 2010 |

## TITLE CHECKLIST

- A title should communicate the purpose of the research in about 12 words or less.
- A title does not typically contain abbreviations.
- A title does not use the words "method," "results," "a study of," or "an experimental investigation of."
- In an APA-style manuscript, the title is centered and presented in uppercase and lowercase letters; it is boldfaced. It appears in two places in the typed manuscript: on the cover page, which is page 1, and on the first page of the introduction (see the sample paper, pp. 545 and 547).

## ABSTRACT

The abstract is a summary of the article's content. It does not present the nuances and details of the research—for that, readers will consult the full report. However, the abstract should clearly communicate the report's main research question, the methods used to test it, the major results, and an indication of why the results are important—for example, how the results support or shape a theory.

The abstract is the first section of your paper that most readers will encounter, but it is often the last thing you will write. After you complete the other sections of the paper, you can easily create an abstract by writing one or two sentences each to capture the introduction and the Method, Results, and Discussion sections. Above all, the abstract should be concise, accurate, and clear. Readers should be able to get a good sense of your research question and the results you obtained by reading the abstract alone.

## ABSTRACT CHECKLIST

- An abstract clearly and accurately summarizes the research question, methods used, primary results, and interpretation of the results in terms of some theory or application.
- An abstract should be about 150 words long. (Different journals have different word limits for abstracts, and the *APA Manual* does not specify abstract length; ask your professor how long your abstract should be.)
- In an APA-style manuscript, the abstract is presented on its own page, page 2. The page is labeled with the word "Abstract" in boldface text at the top center. The abstract itself should be typed as a single paragraph with no indentation (see the sample paper, p. 546).

## INTRODUCTION

The first major section of your paper is the introduction. This is where the main narrative of the research report begins.

**Components of an Introduction.** The main body of the introduction introduces the problem you studied and explains why it is important—usually because it tests some element of a theory. Your study may also be important because your particular approach or method has not been used in past research. Therefore, the bulk of your introduction describes the theory your study is testing and explains past research on the problem you studied. You describe what other researchers have found and explain why their research is relevant to yours.

The last paragraph of the introduction briefly introduces the method you used. (Was it a correlational study? A single-*N* design? An experiment? Did you use a factorial design?) The introduction is not the place to explain all the methodological details, such as how many participants you used or what questionnaires or tasks they completed; that information belongs in the Method section. However, you tell your readers whether your method was correlational or experimental and what your primary variables were. Then, usually in the same paragraph, you state your hypothesis or research question. If you had a clear prediction about what would happen in the study, that's your hypothesis. If you conducted a study to see which of several interesting outcomes might happen (Will A happen? Or will B?), that's your research question. The hypothesis or research question is stated in terms of the variables you mentioned when you briefly described the method. If you preregistered your hypothesis, you'll say so in the introduction.

Here's a paragraph from a study featured in Chapter 10 (Boothby et al., 2014) illustrating how to describe the method and hypotheses (predictions) in the introduction:

> In two laboratory studies, we investigated the difference between experiencing a stimulus simultaneously with someone else (i.e., shared experience) and experiencing a stimulus while that other person is present but not sharing the experience of the stimulus (i.e., unshared experience). We predicted that sharing an experience, even in the absence of communication with the coexperiencer, would render the experienced stimulus more intense. Thus, we expected that generally pleasant stimuli would be perceived more positively and generally unpleasant stimuli would be perceived more negatively when they were part of a shared experience. (p. 2)

Here's another example, from Chapter 12's study on cell phones while driving (Strayer & Drews, 2004). In this excerpt, "dual task" means talking on the phone while driving:

> In this article, we explore the extent to which older adults are penalized by this real-world dual-task activity. Based on the aging and dual-task literature, we predict that as the dual-task demands increase, the driving performance of older adults will deteriorate more rapidly than that of younger drivers. (p. 641)

**Writing the Introduction.** For many students, the introduction is the hardest section to write. Although you'll probably have read review articles or empirical journal articles that inspired your study, writing about these sources to create a coherent introduction is a challenge.

If you are writing an introduction for the first time, try writing the last paragraph first. Write about the method you used and the variables you studied. State your research question or hypothesis. (If you preregistered your hypotheses, you already started on this part.)

Next, try writing the first paragraph. Introduce the main area of research (perhaps it is stereotyping, eating preferences, cultural differences, or brain activity during reading). You may introduce your topic in a creative way to describe why this area of research is potentially interesting. However, the balance can be tricky. It might be appropriate to link your topic to contemporary events, but it is not appropriate to explain why you personally became interested in the research topic. For the sake of your readers, you should avoid being too broad in this opening paragraph, lest you sound trite or say things you cannot back up (such as "From the dawn of time, stereotypes have plagued humankind" or "Cultural differences are a common source of tension in our society today"). You also want to avoid jumping into technical waters too early. A good balance is to link your topic to a concrete story—but to do so briefly. Here's how Brad Bushman (2002) introduced his report of an experimental study on venting anger, described in Chapter 2:

> The belief in the value of venting anger has become widespread in our culture. In movies, magazine articles, and even on billboards, people are encouraged to vent their anger and "blow off steam." For example, in the movie *Analyze This*, a psychiatrist (played by Billy Crystal) tells his New York gangster client (played by Robert De Niro), "You know what I do when I'm angry? I hit a pillow. Try that." The client promptly pulls out his gun, points it at the couch, and fires several bullets into the pillow. "Feel better?" asks the psychiatrist. "Yeah, I do," says the gunman. (p. 724)

It can be particularly challenging to organize the middle portion of the introduction—the paragraphs after the opening paragraph and before those containing the statement of your hypothesis or research question. In general, it's not effective simply to summarize each empirical journal article in isolation, one after another. Instead, try using past studies to build an argument that leads to your hypothesis. This requires planning. Reread the background articles you have. Write each article's results and arguments on separate cards, summarizing the main point, and move the cards around as you explore the most logical way to arrange them. What order of presentation will let you explain the past research so it leads to your hypothesis? Then you can turn your card arrangement into an outline and start writing.

When summarizing past research, keep in mind that psychologists do not generally use direct quotes when describing work by other researchers. They almost always paraphrase it, putting it into their own words.

As you write your introduction, alternate between summaries of past research, including brief paraphrased descriptions (e.g., "In one study, Strayer and Drews (2004) asked younger and older drivers to complete a driving simulator task either undistracted or while talking on a hands-free cell phone") and statements that reflect your own interpretations and arguments (e.g., "This study demonstrated that people drive much worse when they are talking on a cell phone; it does not test whether people will also drive worse if they are talking to the navigation app in their car"). It might help to think of the past research descriptions as the "bricks" of your introduction, and the interpretations, arguments, and transitions you provide as the "mortar." As you build your introduction, you arrange the bricks in a logical order and then provide the mortar that connects them. By the end, it should be very clear to the reader why you conducted your study the way you did and why you formed your hypothesis.

## INTRODUCTION CHECKLIST

- Follow the typical introduction format:
  - The first paragraph of the introduction describes the general area of research.
  - The middle paragraphs summarize past research studies (the "bricks") and give your interpretation of their meaning and importance (the "mortar"), arranged in a way that logically leads to your hypothesis.
  - The last paragraphs briefly describe the method used and the primary variables studied, and they state the hypothesis or research question.
- Document the sources you are summarizing by listing the authors' last names and year of publication, using parentheses or a signal phrase, as described below (in Citing Sources in APA Style, pp. 541–544). You should not type the full titles of the articles you describe.
- Describe past research by paraphrasing or summarizing, not quoting. Be careful to avoid plagiarizing (see pp. 539–541), and be sure to cite each article you describe.
- In general, it is appropriate to write the entire introduction in the past tense.
- If needed for organizing a long introduction, use subheadings.
- Avoid phrases that are vague and undocumentable, such as "in our society today" and "since the beginning of time."
- In an APA-style manuscript, the introduction begins at the top of page 3. Retype the paper's title at the top of the introduction and begin the text on the next line. (The heading "Introduction" is not used.) Do not insert any extra line breaks or extra spacing throughout the introduction. If you use subheadings to organize a long introduction, they should be boldfaced, capitalized, and flush left.

## METHOD

The Method section explains, in concise and accurate detail, the procedures you followed in conducting your study. When you write the Method section, your goal is to communicate the details of your study so completely that a reader who had only your report to go on could conduct a direct replication study. Aim to be completely transparent in your Method section and don't leave any measures or manipulations out. If you are able, provide your complete set of materials on an open science website such as the Open Science Framework, osf.io.

A conventional Method section contains about four subsections. They will vary according to the study. Possible subsections include Design, Participants, Measures, Materials (or, alternatively, Apparatus), and Procedure.

**Design.** It can be helpful to open the Method section with a statement of the study's design, naming its independent and dependent variables. You state whether the independent variables were manipulated as between-subjects or within-subjects. For example, you might write, "We conducted a 3 (distraction condition: none, cell phone, or navigation app) × 2 (type of driver: younger or older) between-subjects factorial experiment. The dependent variable was the delay in braking time in the driving simulator."

A complex study may require a section headed Overview, in which you describe the variables you measured and the procedure you followed.

**Participants (or for Animals: Subjects).** Here you describe the number, type, and characteristics of the people or animals you studied. Human participants are referred to as "participants" and animals are usually called "subjects" in psychological science writing. For human participants, you say how many people participated and give relevant demographic information, such as gender identity, ethnicity, socioeconomic status, age range, immigrant status, and native language. In addition, other characteristics may be relevant to report. Participants' intellectual abilities or disabilities may be relevant for a study on educational techniques; participants' sexual orientation may be relevant for a study on dating behaviors. In describing human participants, you also indicate how the participants were selected (randomly? by convenience?), recruited (by e-mail? in a shopping mall? in psychology classes?), and compensated (Were they paid? Did they get course credit? Did they volunteer?).

When describing animal subjects, it is conventional to give the species' common name and taxonomic name (e.g., "We observed 10 piping plovers [*Charadrius melodus*] in their natural environment") and indicate for laboratory animals the strain and provider used.

**Materials (or Apparatus).** Here you describe in detail the instruments you used to measure or manipulate the variables in your study. If you presented information on a computer screen, indicate how large the screen was and how far participants sat from it. If you used a commercially available computer program, specify the program you used. If animals were exposed to a particular piece of equipment, give its dimensions, manufacturer, and model.

If you used questionnaires or published scales to measure well-being or self-esteem, devote one paragraph to each measurement scale. Indicate who wrote the items by citing the authors who first published the scale. Give one or two sample items from the questionnaire and indicate what the response scale was (e.g., "a 5-point scale ranging from 1 [*strongly disagree*] to 5 [*strongly agree*]"). Explain how you combined items for the scales—for example, if you computed a mean or a sum. Indicate what higher and lower scores signify (e.g., "high scores indicated higher self-esteem"). Also indicate the scale's reliability and validity. For example, you might give the Cronbach's alpha value you obtained in your own study and the extent to which past researchers have validated the measure.

» For types of reliability and validity that might be relevant, see Chapter 5, pp. 125–143.

Although the Materials section should be complete and detailed, you don't have to describe obvious features, such as what kind of paper a questionnaire was printed on (unless there was something special about it) or whether the participants used pens or pencils to record their answers.

**Procedure.** This is where you describe what happened in your study, in what order. Did participants come to a laboratory or classroom or did they participate online? What did participants do first, next, and last? If there was a series of trials, what happened in each trial? If there were counterbalanced orders of presentation, what were they, and how were participants assigned to each order? How were participants assigned to independent variable groups (randomly or not)? Were participants or experimenters blind to conditions in the study? If so, how was this achieved? If there was a confederate in the study, what did the confederate say (exactly), and when? How were participants debriefed?

In writing the Procedure subsection, be careful not to repeat information you already described in other sections. In the Method section, each element is presented only once, in the most appropriate place and the most appropriate order. Often it makes sense to put Procedure last, but in some cases it may need to go earlier in the Method section for more clarity.

### METHOD CHECKLIST

- The reader should be able to use the Method section to conduct a direct replication study, without asking any further questions.
- In APA style, the heading is "Method," not "Methods."
- Use subsections such as Design, Participants, Materials, and Procedure, presented in the order that is most appropriate and clear.
- Do not put the same information in more than one section. If you describe a measure in the Materials subsection, don't describe it again or give more detail about it in the Procedure subsection.

- If you used published questionnaires, describe each one in its own short paragraph, citing its source, sample items, relevant computations, and response options. Indicate relevant reliability and validity results for each questionnaire.
- If you can, publish your complete set of materials on an open science website such as the Open Science Framework (osf.io).
- In an APA-style manuscript, the Method section is labeled "Method" in boldface, centered. The Method section does not start on a new page; it begins directly after the introduction with no extra line spacing. Subheadings for Participants, Materials, or Procedure should be typed flush left, boldfaced, and capitalized. Do not insert extra line spacing between subsections.

## RESULTS

The Results section of a research report presents the study's numerical results, including any statistical tests and their significance, sometimes in the form of a table or figure. Don't report the values for individual participants; present group means or overall associations. In the Results section, you type numerals for means, standard deviations, correlation coefficients, effect sizes, or other descriptive statistics. You also enter the results and symbols for any statistical tests you calculated. The *APA Manual* provides precise guidelines for presenting these values. Generally, the symbols for statistical computations and means (such as $M$ for mean, $SD$ for standard deviation, $t$ for $t$ test, and $F$ for ANOVA) are presented in italics, but the numerals themselves are not (e.g., $M = 3.25$).

A well-organized Results section is systematic, and its sentence structure may even be a little repetitive. The priority is to be crystal clear. It is often best to begin with simple results and then move to more complicated ones. For example, if you included a manipulation check in an experiment, begin with its results. Then move to group means, followed by tests of significance. If your study was correlational, begin by presenting the simple bivariate correlations and then present multiple-regression results. If your study was a factorial design, present main effects first and then interactions. If your study included multiple dependent variables, present the results for each one in turn, but try to keep the sentence structure the same for each dependent variable, so the reader can follow a predictable pattern.

It might also be appropriate to refer to your study's hypothesis and expectations as you write your Results section. For example, you might write, "As predicted, driving performance was worse in the driving app condition than the no-distraction condition."

**Tables and Figures.** It is good practice to present certain results in a table or figure. While a sentence is appropriate for presenting one to three numerical values, a table can summarize a larger set of descriptive statistics, such as four or more means and standard deviations, much more clearly and easily than you could do in a sentence. Tables are also appropriate for presenting multiple-regression results.

Tables must follow APA style guidelines. They may be single- or double-spaced, but they must include only horizontal lines as spacers, not vertical lines. You should not simply copy and paste tables of output from a statistical program into your manuscript. Instead, you must reformat them in APA style, usually retyping the numbers and formatting them appropriately. Tables may be included within the main body of the text or at the end, after the References. If you have more than one table, number each one consecutively (Table 1, Table 2, and so on). The label (e.g., **Table 1**) is in boldface text, and the title itself appears on the next line, italicized, in upper- and lowercase letters. In the text of the Results section, call out each table you created (e.g., "Means and standard deviations for the main dependent variables are presented in Table 1"). An example of an APA-style table is provided in the sample paper (see p. 557).

A figure can often highlight your data's strongest result. For example, if your factorial design found a predicted interaction, you might want to present the result as a line graph or bar graph. Figures should be created using a computer program. Each figure should have clearly labeled axes and should be presented in black and white rather than color, whenever feasible. Figures may be placed within the body of the text or at the end, after the References. If you have more than one figure, number each one consecutively (Figure 1, Figure 2, and so on). As with tables, you must call out each figure that you are including in the text of the Results section (e.g., "Figure 1 depicts the effect of distraction type on braking response time"). Provide a descriptive caption for each figure, typed below it. The label (e.g., **Figure 1**) appears in boldface followed by a period. The caption appears on the next line, italicized, in upper- and lowercase letters.

If you present results in a table or figure, do not repeat the same numerical values (such as the same group means) in the text of the Results section. Mention the general pattern in the text, and refer readers to the table or figure for the full story (e.g., "As Figure 2 depicts, people braked the fastest when they were distracted, regardless if they were older or younger").

The key guideline for the Results section is to state the numerical findings clearly, concisely, and accurately, and then stop writing. The Results section is likely to be the shortest section of a student research report.

Ideally, provide your data openly for others to access and confirm (for example, on a website such as the Open Science Framework, osf.io). Before you make your data open, remove all columns that contain participant identifiers (such as IP addresses or emails) and make sure each variable name is labeled in way that is clear to others. You can also upload your syntax or data analysis scripts.

## RESULTS CHECKLIST

- A good Results section is well organized and crystal clear. Present simple results first, and use repetitive sentence structures when presenting multiple, related results.
- Use a table to present multiple values such as means, correlations, or multiple inferential tests.

- Figures are always called figures, not graphs. Use figures to present the strongest results in your study. Don't overdo it; most papers contain only one to three figures.
- Call out all tables and figures in the text of the Results section, and place them approximately after the paragraph in which they are called out or at the end, after the References.
- Do not present the same results twice. If you present a result in the text, do not repeat it in a table or figure, and don't present the same data in both table and figure form.
- In an APA-style manuscript, the Results section begins right after the Method section, with no page break or extra line spacing. It is labeled with the word "Results" in boldface. You may insert additional subheadings to organize a long Results section; such subheads should be boldfaced, capitalized, and flush left.
- Check the *APA Manual* or the sample paper on pp. 545–559 for examples of how to present statistical results.

## DISCUSSION

A well-written Discussion section achieves three goals. First, you summarize the results of your study and describe the extent to which the results support your hypothesis or answer your research question. You tell the reader how well the results fit with the theory or background literature that you described in the introduction. Second, you evaluate your study, advocating for its strengths and defending its weaknesses. Third, you suggest what the next step might be for the theory-data cycle.

**Summarizing and Linking to the Theory-Data Cycle.** The first paragraphs of the Discussion section summarize the hypotheses and major results of your study. Clearly indicate which results supported your hypothesis and which did not. Tie the results back to the literature and theories you mentioned in the introduction. In this sense, the Discussion section and introduction are like bookends to your paper—they both address the theory-data cycle. Describe how your results support the broader theory and why (or why not). If the results support the theory you were testing, you should explain how.

If the results do not support your theory, it will mean one of two things: Either the theory is incorrect (and therefore must be modified in some way), or your study was flawed (and therefore a better study should be conducted). The Discussion is the place to explore these options and explain what you think is going on. For example, if you conducted an experiment that found a null result, what factors might be responsible?

« For a review of the theory-data cycle, see Figure 1.5, p. 13. For some common reasons for a null result, see Table 11.3, pp. 352–353.

**Evaluating Your Study.** In the next paragraphs of the Discussion section, you evaluate the choices you made in conducting your study. Generally speaking, authors advocate for the strengths of their own studies and anticipate criticisms others might make so they can deflect them in advance. An excellent strategy is to write about the four big validities one by one.

Start by addressing the construct validity of your study, explaining how well your variables were manipulated or measured, and how you know (review the evidence). Then, if you conducted an experiment, assess how well your study addressed potential internal validity threats. If your study was correlational, you might remind your readers that your data do not allow you to make a causal statement, and explain why. Address the statistical validity of your study by discussing the statistical choices you made. Finally, you might address the study's external validity. Because many student papers are not based on random samples of participants, you may need to consider how much this matters. Maybe it does not—if you were in theory-testing mode, for example. Reviewing your study in terms of the four big validities is an excellent way to make sure you have thoroughly evaluated and defended your study. The average student paper can probably include about one paragraph for each of the four big validities.

» To review balancing research priorities, see Chapters 13 and 14.

**Specifying the Next Step.** In the last paragraph or two, you write about some directions for further research. It's not sufficient to use a vague statement such as "Future research is needed." Suggest a specific, theory-driven direction for the next study to take. If your study was flawed in some way, could specific steps be taken to correct the flaws, and what results would you expect? If your study was conducted well, what part of the theory should be tested next? How could you test it, what results would you expect, and what would such results mean? If your study was correlational, could you conduct an experiment next? If so, how would you do so, what results would you expect, and what would those results mean? Could the next study be a conceptual replication? If so, what new contexts might you test, what results would you expect, and what would those results mean?

Push yourself to answer these questions so you can write thoughtful suggestions about the next step. Who knows—you might even inspire yourself to conduct another study.

## DISCUSSION CHECKLIST

- The Discussion section has three components.
- The first couple of paragraphs summarize the results and interpret how the results fit with the theory and literature discussed in the introduction.
- The middle paragraphs evaluate your study. Work through each of the four big validities in turn, explaining the extent to which your study has fulfilled each one.
- The last couple of paragraphs give suggestions for future research. For each suggestion, explain four things: why you would study that question, how you would study it, what your results might be, and what those results would mean.
- Do not report new statistical findings in the Discussion section; numerals and statistics belong in the Results section.
- The Discussion section and introduction are bookends; they both describe how your particular study fits in with the larger body of literature on a topic. If you

opened your paper with a real-world example or story, you might consider closing it by reflecting on how your findings can help interpret that same example.

- In an APA-style manuscript, the Discussion section starts directly after the Results section with no page break or extra line spacing. Head the section with the word Discussion, boldfaced and centered. You may insert additional subheadings to organize a long Discussion section; such subheads should be boldfaced, capitalized, and flush left.

## REFERENCES

In the course of writing the introduction and the Discussion section, you consulted and summarized articles written by other authors. You cited these papers within the text using the authors' last names and the year of publication. Near the end of your paper, in a section titled References, you provide the full bibliographic information for each of the sources you cited, in an alphabetized list. The format is shown on pp. 542–543 and pp. 555–556.

## Formatting an APA-Style Manuscript

When you prepare a research report in APA style, you'll follow a number of specific guidelines. It can be hard to assimilate all the rules the first time. A good strategy is to use the sample paper on pp. 545–559. Pay attention to every detail, such as line spacing, font size and style, and the use of boldface and italic terms. Here's an overview of APA format rules that apply to all sections of the research report:

- In an APA-style paper, everything is double-spaced with the exception of tables and figures, which may contain single-spaced text.
- All text is in the same-sized font (usually 12-point) and printed in black. Section headings are the same font size and color as the main text.
- Margins on all sides should be 1 inch (2.54 centimeters). Do not right-justify the text. This means to leave the right side ragged.
- The paper's title is boldfaced but is centered and capitalized, both on the first page and at the top of page 3.
- Headings are boldfaced. The first-level heading—used for section headings such as Method, Results, and Discussion—is centered and capitalized. The second-level heading is boldfaced and flush left, and the first letters of major words are capitalized; the text following the heading begins on the next line. The third-level heading, if any, is boldfaced, italicized, and flush left, and the first letters of major words are capitalized; the text following the heading begins on the next line.

- The title page of the paper contains the title, the authors' names, the authors' institutional affiliations, an author note with contact information. Journals and some instructors also require a running head, which is a shortened version of the title that appears at the top of each page.
- The following sections start on a new page: abstract, introduction, and References. (The Method, Results, and Discussion sections do not start on new pages.)
- The order of pages is as follows: title page, abstract, main body of paper (including introduction and Method, Results, and Discussion sections), References, footnotes (if any), appendices (if any). Tables and figures may be placed directly in the text if desired; otherwise, they should be presented one per page after the References.
- Page number should be flush right at the top of each page. If a running head is required, use a three- to four-word shortened title, printed in all capitals and flush left. Use "insert header" or "view header" to add this information.

## Writing Style: Five Suggestions

In general, research writing is straightforward, not fancy. An APA-style research report should be written in clear, concise language. This is not the place to use long, complex sentences or show off a large vocabulary.

Such writing is easier said than done: It takes practice, feedback, and attention. Here are five suggestions that can go a long way toward making your research report writing more sophisticated and clear. Your course instructor may have further suggestions to help you improve your writing.

### WRITE IN THE FIRST PERSON

In APA style, the first person ("I" or "we") is permitted because it can make a sentence more readable. First-person writing sounds especially natural and clear when there are two or more authors on a paper. Compare the following sentences:

The authors presented participants with three distraction conditions: none, cell phone conversation, and navigation app. It was expected that participants would brake slower in the two distraction conditions.

We presented participants with three distraction conditions: none, cell phone conversation, and navigation app. We expected that participants would brake more slowly in the two distraction conditions.

Whereas the first-person singular pronoun "I" is acceptable in report writing, it can sound awkward, so use it sparingly. In addition, the second person ("you") is considered too casual for report writing; in a research report, do not refer to the reader directly.

## CHOOSE THE MOST APPROPRIATE SUBJECT FOR EACH SENTENCE

Sometimes when you are comparing competing theories or briefly describing past research, it makes sense to use the author names as the subject of the sentence, as in the following example:

> Darley and Latané's (1968) laboratory studies supported a theory of bystander intervention known as diffusion of responsibility, but Shaffer and colleagues (1975) wanted to test the theory in a real-world context.

Often, however, when you are primarily describing the behavior of people, children, students, or animals, it is better to start a sentence with them, not with the researchers who studied them. Compare the following two sentences:

> Latané and Darley (1970) have found that in an emergency, people are less likely to help others when there are other people around who might also offer help.

> In an emergency, people are less likely to help others when there are other people around who might also offer help (Latané & Darley, 1970).

The first sentence emphasizes the *names* of the researchers, whereas the second sentence more appropriately emphasizes the *findings*: what people do in an emergency. Emphasizing the findings will make your descriptions of past research more vivid and interesting. Notice that in the second sentence above, the citation in parentheses makes it clear that the preceding statement is a research finding by Latané and Darley.

## PREFER THE ACTIVE VOICE

The subject you use for a sentence can also determine whether the sentence is written in the active voice or the passive voice. Sentences in the active voice are more direct and usually easier to read, so you should strive to write in the active voice as much as possible. Compare the following examples:

> **Passive:** The toys were never seen by the children.

> **Active:** The children never saw the toys.

> **Passive:** Some of the action sequences were verbally commented upon by the adults.

> **Active:** The adults verbally commented on some of the action sequences.

In these examples, both options are grammatically correct, but the active sentences are clearer, shorter, and easier to read.

Sometimes, however, the passive voice makes the most sense. For example:

The rats were injected with ethanol 2 hours before each trial.

This sentence is written in the passive voice, but it appropriately places the focus of the sentence on the rats, not the people who injected them.

## USE STRONG VERBS

A precise verb can improve a sentence's clarity and style. Search your paragraphs for linking verbs such as *is, are,* and *be.* Try to replace them with stronger verbs, as in the following examples:

Our results are consistent with past research on eating behavior.
Our results replicate past research on eating behavior.

Cell phones are an important influence on how people drive.
Cell phones distract people when they drive.

The manual was the guide for how to conduct the study.
The manual explained how to conduct the study.

## CUT CLUTTER

Concise writing is more readable. You can often write clearer sentences simply by cutting needless words. For example, the following sentence originally appeared in an early draft of this material:

A precise verb can improve a sentence's clarity and make your writing easier to read. (15 words)

This shorter sentence conveys the same meaning without being repetitive:

A precise verb can improve a sentence's clarity. (8 words)

In the next example, the writer streamlined a long sentence by trimming unnecessary words:

When challenged to do so by their professors, most students find that they can cut out 20% of their manuscript's length simply by taking out a few extra words from each sentence. (32 words)

> Most students can shorten their manuscript by 20% by removing unnecessary words from each sentence. (15 words)

Your writing becomes more readable when you cut redundant phrases and replace strings of short words with a single, effective one.

## Avoiding Plagiarism[1]

When you use the words or ideas of others, you must acknowledge that by crediting the original published source. If you don't credit your sources, you are guilty of plagiarism. Plagiarism is often unintentional, such as when a writer paraphrases someone else's ideas in language that is close to the original. It is essential, therefore, to know what constitutes plagiarism: (1) using another writer's words or ideas without in-text citation and documentation, (2) using another writer's exact words without quotation marks, and (3) paraphrasing or summarizing someone else's ideas using language or sentence structures that are too close to the original, even if you cited the source in parentheses. The following practices will help you avoid plagiarizing:

- **Take careful notes,** clearly labeling quotations and using your own phrasing and sentence structure in paraphrases and summaries.
- **Know what sources you must document,** and credit them both in the text and in the reference list.
- **Be especially careful with online material;** copying material from a website directly into a document you are writing is all too easy. Like other sources, information from the web must be acknowledged.
- **Check all paraphrases and summaries** to be sure they are in your words and your style of sentence structure, and that you put quotation marks around any of the source's original phrasing.
- **Check to see that all quotations are documented;** it is not enough just to include quotation marks or indent a block quotation. (Remember, however, that in APA style it is not conventional to quote; you should paraphrase instead.)

» For more on avoiding plagiarism, see Figure 4.11, p. 106.

Whether deliberate or accidental, plagiarism has consequences. Students who plagiarize may automatically fail a course or even be expelled from school. If you are having trouble completing an assignment, ask your instructor for help, or seek assistance at your school's writing center.

---

[1] This section is adapted from "Avoiding Plagiarism" in *The Norton Field Guide to Writing, 3rd Edition* by Richard Bullock. Copyright © 2013, 2009, 2006 by W. W. Norton & Company, Inc. Used by permission of W. W. Norton & Company, Inc. This selection may not be reproduced, stored in a retrieval system, or transmitted in any form or by any means without the prior written permission of the publisher.

# Using Appropriate Paraphrasing[2]

When you paraphrase, you restate information from a source in your own words, using your own sentence structures. (APA style requires paraphrasing and restricts direct quotes to very special circumstances.) Paraphrase when the source material is important but the original wording is not. Because it includes all the main points of the source, a paraphrase is usually about the same length as the original.

Here is an excerpt from a source, followed by three paraphrased versions. The first two demonstrate some of the challenges of paraphrasing:

**Original Source**

In 1938, in a series of now-classic experiments, exposure to synthetic dyes derived from coal and belonging to a class of chemicals called aromatic amines was shown to cause bladder cancer in dogs. These results helped explain why bladder cancers had become so prevalent among dyestuffs workers. With the invention of mauve in 1854, synthetic dyes began replacing natural plant-based dyes in the coloring of cloth and leather. By the beginning of the twentieth century, bladder cancer rates among this group of workers had skyrocketed, and the dog experiments helped unravel this mystery.

—Sandra Steingraber, 2008, p. 976

**Unacceptable Paraphrase: Wording Too Close to Original**

Now-classic experiments in 1938 showed that when dogs were exposed to aromatic amines, chemicals used in synthetic dyes derived from coal, they developed bladder cancer. Similar cancers were prevalent among dyestuffs workers, and these experiments helped to explain why. Mauve, a synthetic dye, was invented in 1854, after which cloth and leather manufacturers replaced most of the natural plant-based dyes with synthetic dyes. By the early twentieth century, this group of workers had skyrocketing rates of bladder cancer, a mystery the dog experiments helped to unravel (Steingraber, 2008).

This paraphrase borrows too much of the language of the original or changes it only slightly, as the underlined words and phrases show.

**Unacceptable Paraphrase: Sentence Structure Too Close to Original**

In 1938, several path-breaking experiments showed that being exposed to synthetic dyes that are made from coal and belong to a type of chemicals called

---

[2]This section is from "Using Appropriate Paraphrasing" in *The Norton Field Guide to Writing, 3rd Edition* by Richard Bullock.

aromatic amines caused dogs to get bladder cancer. These results helped researchers identify why cancers of the bladder had become so common among textile workers who worked with dyes. With the development of mauve in 1854, synthetic dyes began to be used instead of dyes based on plants in the dyeing of leather and cloth. By the end of the nineteenth century, rates of bladder cancer among these workers had increased dramatically, and the experiments using dogs helped clear up this oddity (Steingraber, 2008).

This paraphrase uses different language but follows the sentence structure of Steingraber's text too closely.

### Acceptable Paraphrase

Biologist Sandra Steingraber (2008) explains that path-breaking experiments in 1938 demonstrated that dogs exposed to aromatic amines (chemicals used in coal-derived synthetic dyes) developed cancers of the bladder that were similar to cancers common among dyers in the textile industry. After mauve, the first synthetic dye, was invented in 1854, leather and cloth manufacturers replaced most natural dyes made from plants with synthetic dyes, and by the early 1900s textile workers had very high rates of bladder cancer. The experiments with dogs proved the connection.

Use your own words and sentence structure. If you use a few words from the original, put them in quotation marks.

## Citing Sources in APA Style

As you write, you must briefly document the sources you use within the text. You must also include the full documentation of every cited source in the References.

### BRIEF DOCUMENTATION IN TEXT

When you are describing another researcher's ideas, words, methods, instruments, or research findings in your research report, you cite the source by indicating the author's last name and the year of publication. There are two ways to provide in-text documentation: by using a signal phrase or by placing the entire citation in parentheses.

When using a signal phrase, you present the last names as part of the sentence and place only the year of publication in parentheses:

Results by Strayer and Drews (2004) indicate . . .

According to Brummelman and his colleagues (2015), . . .

Alternatively, you can provide in-text documentation by putting both the author name(s) and the date in parentheses:

One study showed that both older and younger drivers brake more slowly when talking on the phone (Strayer & Drews, 2004).

With the second method, remember to use an ampersand (&) and to place the sentence's period outside the closing parenthesis.

As mentioned earlier, in APA-style papers, you will not usually quote directly; instead, you paraphrase the research descriptions in your own words. However, if you do quote directly from another author, use quotation marks and indicate the page number:

> "It is also important to note that performance decrements for cell phone drivers were obtained even when there was no possible contribution from the manual manipulation of the cell phone" (Strayer & Drews, 2004, p. 648).

When a source is written by either one or two authors, cite their names and the date every time you refer to that source, as in the previous example. When a source is written by three or more authors, cite the first author's name followed by "et al." and the date:

> Parental overvaluation predicted higher levels of child narcissism over time (Brummelman et al., 2015).

These are the rules for sources with obvious authors—the most common types of sources used by psychology students. You might need to cite other sources, such as websites with no author or government agency reports. In those cases, consult the *APA Manual* for the correct documentation style.

## FULL DOCUMENTATION IN THE REFERENCES

The References section contains an alphabetized list of all the sources you cited in your paper—and only those sources. If you did not cite an article, chapter, or book in the main body of your text, it does not belong in the References. Do not list the sources in the order in which you cited them in the text; alphabetize them by the first author's last name.

In the following examples, notice the capitalization patterns for the titles of different types of publications—articles, journals, books, and book chapters—and whether they are italicized or formatted as plain text. Notice that while the journal's name is capitalized, only the first word of the article title is capitalized. Pay attention to the placement of periods and commas. Finally, note that if the journal article includes a digital object identifier (DOI), it is included at the end.

**Journal Articles with One Author.** Here and in the next set of examples, notice that both the volume and issue number of a journal are included (if available), and that the volume number is italicized along with the journal title. Only the second example had an issue number and DOI available to report.

> McNulty, J. K. (2010). When positive processes hurt relationships. *Current Directions in Psychological Science, 19*(3), 167–171. https://doi.org/10.1177/0963721410370298

**Journal Articles with Two or More Authors.** These examples follow the same pattern as a single-authored article. Notice how a list of authors is separated with commas in APA style.

Brummelman, E., Thomaes, S., Nelemans, S. A., Orobio de Castro, B., Overbeek, G., & Bushman, B. J. (2015). Origins of narcissism in children. *Proceedings of the National Academy of Sciences of the United States of America, 112*(12), 3659–3662. https://doi.org/10.1073/pnas.1420870112

Mueller, C. M., & Dweck, C. S. (1998). Intelligence praise can undermine motivation and performance. *Journal of Personality and Social Psychology, 75*(1), 33–52. https://doi.org/10.1037/0022-3514.75.1.33

**Books.** In the next two sets of examples, pay attention to how the publisher is listed.

Eberhardt, J. L. (2019). *Biased: Uncovering the hidden prejudice that shapes what we see, think, and do.* Viking.

Heine, S. J. (2017). *DNA is not destiny: The remarkable, completely misunderstood relationship between you and your genes.* W. W. Norton.

**Chapters in Edited Books.** Here, compare the way the chapter authors' names and those of the book editors are given, and notice how and where the page numbers appear.

Geen, R. G., & Bushman, B. J. (1989). The arousing effects of social presence. In H. Wagner & A. Manstead (Eds.), *Handbook of psychophysiology* (pp. 261–281). John Wiley.

Kitayama, S., & Bowman, N. A. (2010). Cultural consequences of voluntary settlement in the frontier: Evidence and implications. In M. Schaller, A. Norenzayan, S. J. Heine, T. Yamagishi, & T. Kameda (Eds.), *Evolution, culture, and the human mind* (pp. 205–227). Psychology Press.

## CHECKLIST FOR DOCUMENTING SOURCES

- In the References, entries are listed in alphabetical order by the author's last name. They are not listed in the order in which you mentioned them in the paper.
- Within a source entry, the order of the authors matters; often the first author contributed the most to the paper. Therefore, if an article or book chapter has multiple authors, list them all in the same order that they appeared in the publication.

- The entry for each source starts on a new line, using a hanging indent format (see the examples and the sample paper). Do not insert extra line spacing between entries.
- The list is double-spaced and starts on a new page, after the Discussion section. The heading References appears at the top of the page, boldfaced and centered. (Do not label this section "Bibliography" or "Works Cited.")

A running head—the short version of the title—appears on the top of every page, in all caps. Use the "Insert" menu to edit the header in MS Word. For student papers, the running head may not be required, so ask your instructor.

Page numbers start with 1 on the title page and appear on the right corner of each page.

**Teaching as an Underdog: The Benefits of Being a Struggling Professor**

Jane Mafale[1]

[1]Department of Psychology, Muhlenberg College

If there are multiple authors, list all their names. On the next line, list the institutions. Use superscript numbers to link names to institutions.

Author Note

This research was conducted as part of an independent research project with support from a faculty mentor, Kenneth Michniewicz.

Data and materials are openly available on osf.io/xnb53

Correspondence concerning this article should be addressed to Jane Mafale, Muhlenberg College, Allentown, PA, 18104; janemafale@muhlenberg.edu

If your study has open data or open materials, you would include the link here.

The word "Abstract" is centered and bold. The abstract begins on Page 2. For student papers, the Abstract may not be required, so ask your instructor.

The abstract text is not indented.

It is appropriate to use the first person (I, we) in a research report. If you are presenting the results of a group project, "we" is appropriate.

Avoid sexist language by using plural or the singular pronoun "they."

The abstract should be about 150 words long; some journals allow an abstract to be as long as 250 words. Ask your instructor how long your abstract should be.

Provide three to five keywords for your paper, indented under the abstract. Use the Thesaurus of Psychological Index Terms, available in PsycINFO, for appropriate keywords.

**Abstract**

Professor identities and relatability in the classroom play an important role in the quality of education students receive. In the present study, I examine the extent to which an *underdog* identity, in which the professor struggles against difficult odds, affects student perceptions of their teaching skill and ability to relate and connect to their students. Students ($N = 70$) read a hypothetical scenario about a professor who was either an underdog (had struggled) or a "topdog" (had not struggled). Students rated the target's level of caring and competence as well as overall quality. They evaluated the underdog professor as more caring, but not more competent, than the topdog professor. These results suggest that an underdog identity can confer some benefits, notably increased relatability that can lead to other potential benefits. I discuss this work in light of teacher identity presentation in the classroom.

*Keywords:* underdog identity, caring, professional competence, relatability, teacher quality

The introduction begins on Page 3 (or on Page 2 if there is no abstract).

**Teaching as an Underdog: The Benefits of Being a Struggling Professor**

Repeat the title of the manuscript at the top of the introduction.

Underdogs can be defined as individuals or groups who are at a disadvantage based on factors outside of their control (Vandello et al., 2007). People still tend to root for the underdog, perhaps because they, too, have experienced a situation in which they struggled against difficult odds (Kim et al., 2008). Additionally, people often make more favorable character judgments about those who are at a disadvantage (Vandello et al., 2007). These ideas may help to explain and justify the underdog effect, defined as people's tendency to root for an individual or group who is seen as trying to accomplish a difficult task with a clear disadvantage or obstacle to overcome and is not expected to succeed (Kim et al., 2008).

There is no extra space or heading between the title and the introduction text.

Citation format for a paper with three or more authors.

While there has been research on the effects of having an underdog identity in many contexts, there is a gap in the research surrounding the outcomes of the underdog effect in the classroom, specifically when a teacher reveals their underdog background to students. There are many important qualities associated with successful and effective teachers (Stronge et al., 2004), one of which is a caring nature. Caring teachers create student-teacher relationships where respect and learning are fostered. A study done by Peart and Campbell (1999) found that when adults were asked to reflect on their most influential teachers, the majority indicated the caring nature of these teachers as an important key in their success. The notion that an effective teacher is actively caring and supportive bolsters the idea that underdogs would make effective teachers, seeing as they are perceived as having higher levels of

When possible, do not simply discuss past research articles one at a time; integrate them into an argument, as the student has done here.

Signal phrase citation format for a paper with two authors. Notice that "and" is spelled out because the authors are mentioned as part of the sentence.

these qualities. Wolk (2002) claimed that "teachers need to allow students to see them as complete people with emotions, opinions, and lives outside of school" (p. 18), thus suggesting that teachers who share their background with students may be more relatable. Therefore, this study predicts there is some benefit to teachers who identify as an underdog when revealing this background to students.

In the present experiment, I exposed college students to one of two professor profiles—an underdog or a topdog. I measured students' ratings of the professor's level of caring, competence, and overall quality. I hypothesized that underdogs would be seen as somewhat more caring and supportive, and this would be associated with students rating them as better-quality teachers overall. (Hypotheses were not preregistered.)

## Method

We report how we determined our sample size, all data exclusions, all manipulations, and all measures in the study.

### Design

This was a posttest-only experiment with teacher status (topdog/underdog) as the independent variable and students' impressions of the teacher as dependent variables.

### Participants

Seventy undergraduate psychology students from Muhlenberg College participated in this study. Sample size was not determined in advance; it reflects the number of people who completed the study within the time allowed. The participants' ages ranged from 18 to 22 ($M = 19.72$, $SD = 1.11$),

Citation format for a direct quotation; includes quotation marks and the page number.

The final paragraph of the introduction describes the method briefly and explains the hypotheses of the study in terms of this method.

If you preregistered your study, you would state that here and provide a link to the preregistration.

There is no extra space between the introduction and the Method heading.

Format for a first-level heading: centered and boldfaced.

This statement is recommended by Simmons et al. (2012) to improve the transparency of research reporting. You may include it if you have actually reported the things it mentions.

It's helpful to start your Method section with a design paragraph detailing the primary independent and dependent variables. If your design is factorial, you'll mention that here.

At the start of a sentence, any number should be written as a word.

Numbers equal to or greater than 10 are presented as numerals. Numbers less than 10 are presented as words. Any statistical results are presented as numerals.

and 79.5% identified as women, 7.7% identified as men, and 2.2% identified as neither. The racial identity of the participants consisted of 79.5% identifying as White, 5.1% identifying as Asian, 2.6% identifying as biracial, and 1.3% identifying as other or not listed.

## Materials

### *Teacher Ratings of Competence and Caring*

The Teacher Behavior Checklist (TBC; Keeley et al., 2006) was adapted to measure participants' beliefs about the fictitious professor. This scale was originally designed by Buskist et al. (2002), who surveyed students and award-winning teachers to come up with the traits and behaviors associated with excellent teachers (these traits included *passionate*, *respectful*, *approachable*, *creative*, *fair*, *understanding*, and *well prepared*).

The TBC separates items into two categories, some of which capture professional competence and some of which capture caring and supportive nature.

**Professional Competence.** We used the 14 TBC items that measure professional competence, including *establishes daily and academic term goals*, *is professional*, and *is prepared* ($\alpha = .92$). Participants were prompted to rate the extent to which they would expect the target professor to be someone who engaged in each behavior. Responses were given on a Likert scale that ranged from 1 = *not at all* to 7 = *very much*. Higher scores indicated that participants believed the professor would exhibit the behavior to a greater extent.

**Caring and Supportive Nature.** We also used the TBC items that measure caring and supportive nature (Keeley et al., 2006). The original subscale contained 14 teacher qualities, such as *good listener*, *is approachable/personable*,

---

Format for a second-level heading: flush left, boldfaced, title case. The text begins on the next indented line.

Format for a third-level heading: flush left, boldfaced, italicized, title case. The text begins on the next indented line.

Format for a fourth-level heading: indented, boldfaced, title case, followed by a period. The text begins on the same line.

It is appropriate to present construct validity results, such as these Cronbach's alpha results, in the Method section.

Indicate rating scales and anchors when describing self-report scales. Use numerals for the point numbers and anchors of scales. Italicize scale anchors.

*is humble.* Due to a coding error on the survey, one original item, *has a happy/positive attitude/humorous,* was split into two items, *has a happy/positive attitude* and *is humorous.* This yielded 15 items ($\alpha = .93$). Responses were given on a Likert scale that ranged from 1 = *not at all* to 7 = *very much.* Higher scores indicated that participants believed the professor would exhibit the behavior to a greater extent.

### Overall Teacher Quality

Teacher quality was assessed using a single item: "Overall, I think this is a good professor." Responses were given on a Likert scale that ranged from 1 = *not at all* to 7 = *very much.* Higher scores indicated that participants believed the professor would exhibit the behavior to a greater extent. (The overall teacher quality item was the last of seven teacher-quality items participants rated; the other six items were not analyzed here.)

### Teacher Descriptions

The two teacher descriptions, adapted from Michniewicz and Edelman (2019), are contained in Appendix A.

### Belief in a Just World

Participants also completed the 7-item measure of Global Beliefs in a Just World Scale (Lipkus, 1991); however, these data were not analyzed.

### Procedure

This study received Institutional Review Board approval through Muhlenberg College. Participants completed an online survey that ostensibly measured their perceptions of a professor based only on a short vignette about the professor's background. Participants were randomly assigned to receive either the biography of an underdog professor or the biography of a topdog

*Give example items when describing self-report scales.*

*Refer to appendices in the main text. Place appendices after any figures or tables.*

*When a number is used in a hyphenated phrase, it is written as a numeral.*

*For full research transparency, you should mention everything your participants did. If you did not include these tasks in your statistical analyses, simply say so.*

professor. After reading these fictitious biographies, participants then answered questions about their perceptions of this professor's caring and supportive nature, professional competence, and overall teaching quality. The survey concluded with demographic questions. Participants were thanked and debriefed.

## Results

Descriptive statistics for the three dependent variables are presented in Table 1.

I hypothesized that underdogs, relative to topdogs, would receive heightened evaluations of professional competence, caring and supportive nature, and teacher quality. I examined the extent to which teacher status (underdog, topdog) influenced these three measures.

For professional competence, students rated underdogs as a little bit less competent ($M = 5.18$, $SD = 0.79$) than topdogs ($M = 5.29$, $SD = 0.91$). The difference in ratings on a 7-point scale was 0.11, 95% CI [−0.30, 0.52], and the effect size was rather small $d = 0.13$, 95% CI [−0.35, 0.60]. The confidence interval for the difference contains both positive and negative values and includes zero. The results suggest that the manipulation only negligibly influenced perceptions of professional competence, if at all.

For caring and supportive nature, students rated underdogs as more caring and supportive ($M = 5.30$, $SD = 0.84$) than topdogs ($M = 4.84$, $SD = 0.85$). The difference in ratings on a 7-point scale was 0.45, 95% CI [0.05, 0.86], and the effect size was moderate, $d = 0.54$, 95% CI [0.05, 1.01]. The confidence interval for the difference suggests that the manipulation influenced ratings of caring and supportive, somewhere from a very small amount to a large amount.

There is no extra space between the end of the Method section and the Results heading.

Call out all tables in the text. Do not repeat values presented in a table in the text. Tables may be inserted in the body of the text itself (for example, at the end of the paragraph in which they are called out) or may be placed at the end, after the References.

Format for reporting a mean difference and its 95% CI.

Format for reporting an effect size and its 95% CI.

Use a repetitive sentence structure when describing related results.

Use a zero before a decimal fraction when the statistic can be greater than 1 (e.g., $d$ values). Do not use a zero before a decimal fraction when the statistic cannot be greater than 1 (e.g., correlations, proportions, and $p$ values).

For perceptions of overall quality, students rated underdog teachers as higher in overall quality ($M = 5.91$, $SD = 1.08$) compared to topdogs ($M = 5.37$, $SD = 1.03$). The difference in ratings on a 7-point scale was 0.54, 95% CI [0.03, 1.05], and the effect size was moderate, $d = 0.51$, 95% CI [0.03, 0.99]. The result suggests that the manipulation influenced ratings of overall quality, from a very small amount to a large amount. Figure 1 summarizes the results for the two conditions.

Finally, I explored caring and supportive nature as a mediator in the relationship between underdog status and teacher quality. I used an analysis of covariance (ANCOVA) with underdog status as the independent variable, teacher quality as the dependent variable, and caring and supportive nature as the covariate. Supporting a mediation model, caring and supportive nature significantly predicted overall teaching quality, $F(1,66) = 72.17$, $p < .001$, $\eta_p^2 = 0.52$, and underdog status no longer significantly predicted overall teacher quality when caring and supportive nature was in the model, $F(1,66) < 1$, $p = .48$.

## Discussion

In the present study, I predicted that underdogs would be seen as more caring and supportive, and that these ratings would be associated with students seeing them as better quality teachers overall. The results supported this hypothesis, because participants rated underdog professors as somewhat more caring and supportive as well as better overall quality professors. A basic mediational test was consistent with the interpretation that caring and supportive nature mediates the relationship between underdog status and ratings of overall

---

**Call out all figures in the text. Figures may be placed in the main body of the text (for example, at the end of the paragraph in which they are called out) or at the end, after the References and Tables.**

**Format for presenting an *F* statistic, degrees of freedom, and a *p* value.**

**Report exact *p* values between .001 and .99. If *p* is less than .001, report *p* < .001.**

**There is no extra space between the end of the Results section and the Discussion heading.**

**The first paragraph of the Discussion section summarizes the hypotheses and major results.**

quality. These findings suggest that students' perceptions of teacher identity are an important element of the classroom environment.

    The study is consistent with previous research on student-teacher relationships. A supportive foundation is provided by high-quality student-teacher relationships (Hamre & Pianta, 2001). Students may do better when teachers like them (Wang & Eccles, 2013) and when teachers show social emotional support toward their students (Prewett et al., 2019). Since underdogs are seen as more caring, supportive, and relatable, having an underdog identity should make a teacher appear to be even more caring and supportive and thus be able to maintain a stronger relationship with students and be an effective teacher. Ultimately, the present study proposes that there are benefits to students knowing the struggling stories and background of their teachers who identify as underdogs, and thus teachers should not worry if students find out details about their lives, and should instead actively share them.

    The study was designed with good internal validity. I used a between-subjects design so that participants would not be aware of the comparison we were making. The two professor profiles were identical except for the underdog/topdog status manipulation. As for construct validity, I used a validated measure of teacher quality, the TBC, which helps ensure that our measures of caring and supportive nature, professional competence, and overall quality were more valid. The study's external validity is unknown; I used a convenience sample of students at my own college, so I do not know if it generalizes to other campus populations.

The middle paragraphs of the Discussion section evaluate the study's strengths and weaknesses.

Citation format for a two-author source. In an in-text citation for two authors, use an ampersand (&).

In a student paper, address how well the study meets the four big validities.

**Limitations and Future Research**

A limitation of the present study was that the background of each professor was simply handed to students as part of a study. Further research would be necessary to see the best way to reveal this background in a real-life setting. A future study on the different ways to share an underdog background to students, whether this be verbally on the first day, over time in small increments, or even in a letter to students, would be beneficial to see how this experimental data would translate to a real classroom setting.

Another direction of future research could examine whether students' own identity moderates their perception—for example, to see if students who identify as underdogs are especially likely to prefer a teacher who identifies as an underdog. Similarly, academic discipline could be manipulated to see if the subject area makes a difference in student responses to underdog teachers, as the present study explicitly stated that the professor was teaching psychology.

At the end of the Discussion, point to future research questions, explain what you would expect, and explain why they would be important.

## References

Buskist, W., Sikorski, J., Buckley, T., & Saville, B. K. (2002). Elements of master teaching. In S. F. Davis & W. Buskist (Eds.), *The teaching of psychology: Essays in honor of Wilbert J. McKeachie and Charles L. Brewer* (pp. 27–39). Lawrence Erlbaum Associates, Inc.

Hamre, B. K., & Pianta, R. C. (2001). Early teacher-child relationships and the trajectory of children's school outcomes through eighth grade. *Child Development, 72*(2), 625–638. https://doi.org/10.1111/1467-8624.00301

Keeley, J., Smith, D., & Buskist, W. (2006). The teacher behaviors checklist: Factor analysis of its utility for evaluating teaching. *Teaching of Psychology, 33*(2), 84–91. https://doi.org/10.1207/s15328023top3302_1

Kim, J., Allison, S. T., Eylon, D., Goethals, G. R., Markus, M. J., Hindle, S. M., & Mcguire, H. A. (2008). Rooting for (and then abandoning) the underdog. *Journal of Applied Social Psychology, 38*(10), 2550–2573. https://doi.org/10.1111/j.1559-1816.2008.00403.x

Lipkus, I. (1991). The construction and preliminary validation of a global belief in a just world scale and the exploratory analysis of the multidimensional belief in a just world scale. *Personality and Individual Differences, 12*(11), 1171–1178. https://doi.org/10.1016/0191-8869(91)90081-L

Peart, N. A., & Campbell, F. A. (1999). At-risk students' perceptions of teacher effectiveness. *Journal for a Just and Caring Education, 5*(3), 269–284.

The reference list begins on a new page. The heading is boldfaced and centered. Sources are listed in alphabetical order by first author.

Reference format for a chapter in an edited book.

Reference format for an empirical journal article with more than one author. The title of the article is in sentence case. Notice that the journal name is capitalized and italicized. The journal volume is italicized and the issue number and page numbers are not.

When a DOI is available for a source, provide it at the end of the citation.

Within a single source, preserve the order of authorship; do not list authors alphabetically unless they originally appeared that way.

Reference format for a single-author empirical article.

Prewett, S. L., Bergin, D. A., & Huang, F. L. (2018). Student and teacher perceptions on student-teacher relationship quality: A middle school perspective. *School Psychology International, 40*(1), 66–87. https://doi .org/10.1177/0143034318807743

Stronge, J. H., Tucker, P. D., & Hindman, J. L. (2004). *Handbook for qualities of effective teachers*. Association for Supervision and Curriculum Development.

Vandello, J. A., Goldschmied, N. P., & Richards, D. A. R. (2007). The appeal of the underdog. *Personality and Social Psychology Bulletin, 33*(12), 1603–1616. https://doi.org/10.1177/0146167207307488

Wang, M.-T., & Eccles, J. S. (2013). School context, achievement motivation, and academic engagement: A longitudinal study of school engagement using a multidimensional perspective. *Learning and Instruction, 28*, 12–23. https://doi.org/10.1016/j.learninstruc.2013.04.002

Wolk, S. (2002). *Being good: Rethinking classroom management and student discipline*. Heinemann.

Reference format for a book.

**Table 1**

*Descriptive Statistics for Attributes of an Effective Professor (Total Sample)*

| Variable | Cronbach's alpha | $M$ | $SD$ |
|---|---|---|---|
| Caring and supportive nature | .93 | 5.07 | 0.87 |
| Professional competence | .92 | 5.23 | 0.85 |
| Overall quality (single item) | -- | 5.64 | 1.08 |

*Note.* $N$ = 69 for all values. All values ranged from 1 (*not at all*) to 7 (*very much*).

Tables are numbered consecutively and placed one per page if they are placed at the end of the manuscript.

Table titles are presented in italics and are printed in title case.

Do not simply copy output from a statistical program into a table. Retype the data and its labels in the APA format.

Tables may be double- or single-spaced.

Table format can include horizontal separation lines, but no vertical lines.

Use the table note to describe any abbreviations or explain the nature of measures used in the table. The note should be double-spaced.

**Figure 1**

*Participants' Mean Ratings of Underdog and Topdog Professors*

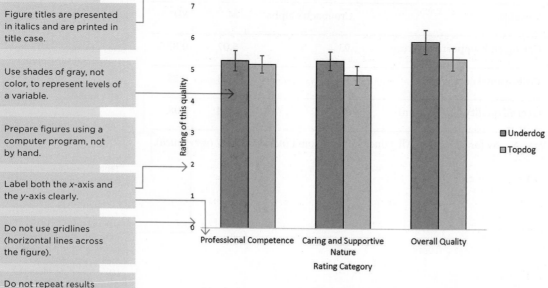

*Note.* Error bars represent the 95% CI of each condition mean.

Each figure goes on its own page if figures are placed at the end of the manuscript. Figures are numbered consecutively. Figure labels are boldfaced.

Figure titles are presented in italics and are printed in title case.

Use shades of gray, not color, to represent levels of a variable.

Prepare figures using a computer program, not by hand.

Label both the *x*-axis and the *y*-axis clearly.

Do not use gridlines (horizontal lines across the figure).

Do not repeat results in a figure if they are also in the text.

There should be no outline around the figure.

Most figures should include error bars. Error bars can indicate either standard error or confidence intervals, so indicate which one applies to your figure.

## Appendix: Teacher Descriptions

An appendix is appropriate for presenting the full text of research materials when such information is too long to present in the Method section.

If there is more than one appendix, they are called Appendix A, Appendix B, and so on.

**Underdog:**

Dr. J is a college professor recently hired to teach at a small liberal arts college. They received their doctoral degree with a training in psychology and plan to teach courses such as Introductory Psychology, Research Methods in Psychology, and senior-level applied psychology courses. The road for Dr. J to become a college professor has not been an easy one. Dr. J is a first-generation college student, meaning that their parents did not go to college. As a result, Dr. J received less guidance from family about the process of going to undergraduate and graduate school; moreover, Dr. J received no financial assistance from family members throughout the process. Despite these struggles, Dr. J looks forward to being a psychology professor for years to come.

**Topdog:**

Dr. J is a college professor recently hired to teach at a small liberal arts college. They received their doctoral degree with a training in psychology and plan to teach courses such as Introductory Psychology, Research Methods in Psychology, and senior-level applied psychology courses. The road for Dr. J to become a college professor has been a relatively easy one. Dr. J is a third-generation college student, meaning that their parents and grandparents went to college. As a result, Dr. J received ample guidance from family about the process of going to undergraduate and graduate school; moreover, Dr. J received financial assistance from family members throughout the process. As a result of this, Dr. J looks forward to being a psychology professor for years to come.

# PREPARING POSTERS FOR CONFERENCES

If you become involved in conducting original research—whether as part of a class project, for a student thesis, or as a research assistant for a professor—you may have the opportunity to present your research in a poster session. A poster is a brief summary of a research study, typed in a large, easy-to-read font and printed on a page as large as 4 to 5 feet wide. Poster sessions, in which several researchers present their posters simultaneously, are a common part of psychology conferences, both at undergraduate psychology conferences (where undergraduate research is the sole focus) and at regional and national psychology conferences (where faculty and graduate student research is the primary focus).

## The Purpose of a Poster Session

A poster session is an informal way to share research results with the scientific community. At a typical poster session, dozens of researchers stand next to their posters in a large conference room (as in **Figure S3.1**). Other researchers mingle, stopping to read posters that attract their interest, and perhaps talking one-on-one with the poster authors about the research.

Besides sharing results with the scientific community, the other goal of a poster session is to enable researchers to talk informally. The one-on-one conversations and the nonthreatening context let people talk to potential collaborators, meet people they admire, or simply learn more about research conducted at other colleges and universities.

**FIGURE S3.1**
**A poster session at a psychology conference.**

## Preparing the Poster

An APA-style research report will be the starting point for your poster, which should contain sections labeled "Introduction," "Method," "Results," "Discussion," and "References." The poster format lends itself to less text and more images, as shown in the sample poster on pp. 562–563.

### KEEP THE TEXT SHORT

A poster should give only a *brief* summary of the study you conducted. Many posters contain more text than most people are willing to read as they walk by, and it's best to keep the text short. In fact, a recent trend is to put a one-line message in the center in large font (as the sample poster illustrates) and move other details to the sides. On the rest of the poster, limit yourself to one or two paragraphs (perhaps even bulleted statements) for the Introduction and Discussion sections. Keep the Method section focused on the bare minimum of information (such as the number of participants and the operationalizations of the primary variables). Let your tables and figures tell the story of your results.

### SHOW, DON'T TELL

Present as much information as you can in tables, images, and figures. Visual art attracts an audience: People are more likely to stop by a poster that contains a large, interesting photo or a colorful figure. Tables and figures can also help you talk about your results in an interactive way. (For example, while pointing to your poster, you could explain, "Here are the two distraction groups we used. And you can see in this figure that the two distraction groups braked much more slowly than the undistracted group").

### MAKE THE POSTER READABLE AND ATTRACTIVE

The typeface and formatting rules for a poster are flexible. Any text should be in a font that is large enough to read from a distance—at least 20-point. The title of your poster (printed across the top edge) should be even larger—at least 40-point. You can combine a variety of font sizes, colors, and backgrounds if you wish, as long as the poster is readable. (Be careful not to go overboard with visual effects.)

## Attending a Poster Session

When you participate in a poster session, you will find your assigned space, hang up your poster with the pushpins provided, and stand next to it wearing your best outfit and a friendly expression. As people approach your poster, give them a moment to look it over, and then offer to explain your work. Some people prefer to read silently, but most of your audience will appreciate the chance to talk one-on-one.

It is a good idea to practice delivering a "poster talk," in which you describe your research in 1 minute or less. Using your poster's images as props, practice delivering the key points—the purpose of the study, the method, and the results—in this very short time period. After your brief description, a visitor can ask follow-up questions, and you can begin a conversation about the research. Congratulations—you are now participating in the scientific community!

In addition to your poster, prepare a handout—a regular-sized page with the text of your poster. You can make copies or post the handout online and put a QR code on the poster. Include your name and e-mail address so people can contact you with questions.

Finally, during a poster session, it is perfectly appropriate to leave your poster for a few minutes to mingle and look at the other posters. This is especially important if your conference contains only one poster session. Don't miss this chance to learn about others' research as well as show off your own.

# Teaching as an Underdog: The Benefits of Being a

JANE MAFALE AND KENNETH MICHNIEWICZ, MUHLENBERG COLLEGE, ALLENTOWN, PA

## INTRODUCTION

Students' impressions of professors are determined by many factors, including teaching style and emotional relatedness (Pianta et al., 2012).

Generally, underdogs are simultaneously described as *heroic* and *losers*. While there may therefore be costs to an underdog identity, people like and support underdogs more (Vandello et al., 2007), and people identify with underdogs (Kim et al., 2008). We hypothesized that underdogs, relative to "topdogs," would receive heightened evaluations of professional competence, caring, and teacher quality.

## METHOD

Participants: undergraduate psychology students ($N = 70$) randomly assigned to underdog professor description or topdog professor description.

- Racial identity: 79.5% White, 5.1% Asian, 2.6% Biracial, 1.3% Other or not listed
- Gender: 79.5% Women, 7.7% Men, 2.6% Neither
- Age $M = 19.72$

We measured participants' perceptions of this professor on:

- Overall quality: "Overall, I think this is a good professor."
- Professional competence scale: (Ex: "I would expect quality mentorship from this professor.")
- Caring and supportive nature scale: (Ex: "I could see this professor as someone who puts effort and energy into the lessons in the classroom.")

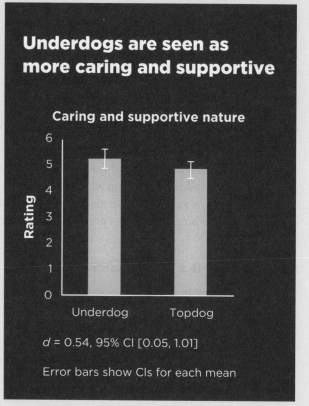

**Underdogs are seen as more caring and supportive**

Caring and supportive nature

$d = 0.54$, 95% CI [0.05, 1.01]

Error bars show CIs for each mean

## RESULTS

- No difference in professional competence rating of underdog and topdog professors. Underdogs received greater liking and support generally and were viewed as more caring and supportive.
- Underdog teachers were expected to be of higher quality; when controlling for caring nature, this effect became n.s.

# Struggling Professor

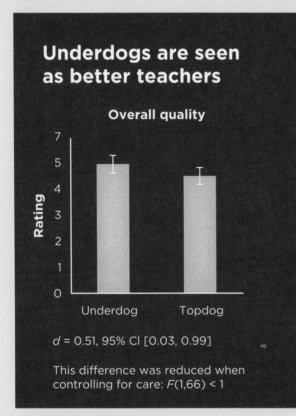

**Underdogs are seen as better teachers**

Overall quality

$d$ = 0.51, 95% CI [0.03, 0.99]

This difference was reduced when controlling for care: $F(1,66) < 1$

- Underdog professors may benefit as a result of being seen as more caring, though future research is needed to experimentally test this as a mediating factor.
- Follow-up study to test additional factors, such as instructor gender or discipline, which may be differently associated with struggling

## REFERENCES

Kim, J., Allison, S. T., Eylon, D., Goethals, G. R., Markus, M. J., Hindle, S. M., & McGuire, H. A. (2008). Rooting for (and then abandoning) the underdog. *Journal of Applied Social Psychology, 38*(10), 2550–2573. https://doi.org/10.1111/j.1559-1816.2008.00403.x

Pianta, R. C., Hamre, B. K., & Allen, J. P. (2012). Teacher-student relationships and engagement: Conceptualizing, measuring, and improving the capacity of classroom interactions. In S. L. Christenson, A. L. Reschly, & C. Wylie (Eds.), *Handbook of research on student engagement* (pp. 365–386). Springer.

Vandello, J. A., Goldschmied, N. P., & Richards, D. A. R. (2007). The appeal of the underdog. *Personality and Social Psychology Bulletin, 33*(12), 1603–1616. https://doi.org/10.1177/0146167207307488

## DISCUSSION

- Overall, our results thus far suggest that sharing an underprivileged background with students only benefits teachers. This is important given the potential stigma the underprivileged may experience upon sharing their life stories. Students' perception of underdog professors as more caring, supportive, and likable suggests a benefit to underdog status.

# Appendix A
## RANDOM NUMBERS AND
## HOW TO USE THEM

There are two uses of the term *randomization* in psychology, and it is important not to confuse them. Sometimes it refers to *probability sampling* (often called *random sampling*) from a population, and sometimes it refers to *random assignment* of participants to groups in a between-subjects experiment. Whereas random sampling (probability sampling) is a method for selecting participants from some population in an unbiased way, random assignment is a method for assigning participants to two or more experimental conditions in an unbiased way. Random sampling enhances a study's external validity, and random assignment enhances a study's internal validity. (For more on probability sampling, see Chapter 7; for more on random assignment, see Chapter 10.)

**Table A.1** contains a random series of two-digit numbers, from 00 to 99. This kind of random number table is useful for both probability sampling and random assignment, but they are used differently in each case.

## RANDOM SAMPLING (PROBABILITY SAMPLING)

Suppose we have a classroom with no more than 100 people in it; that's our population. We want to sample 20 cases from this population using *simple random sampling*. The first step is to assign a number to each member of the population, from 00 to 99. Using the random numbers table, we select a starting value haphazardly—by dropping a pen onto the page, perhaps. Starting with this value, we then read across the rows. For example, if the pen drops on the third entry in the first row, 78, person number 78 will be sampled in our study. Then we continue moving along the row from there—persons 71, 21, 28, and so on—until we sample 20 cases. If a number is duplicated, we simply ignore the duplicate and go to the next number. If the population has fewer than 100 people in it—say, only 60 people—we ignore any random numbers that are greater than 60.

The example assumes we have a population of no more than 100 cases. If the population is larger than 100, we take the numbers in pairs, making the first entry on the table 7,917. By using two columns at a time, we can handle populations up to 10,000 members.

We can also use the random number table for *systematic sampling,* another variation of random sampling. We drop a pen on Table A.1 and choose a value—say, 98. We split this into two digits, 9 and 8. Then we count off. Starting with the ninth person in a group, we select every eighth person after that until we have a full sample.

## RANDOM ASSIGNMENT

Now let's assume we have already selected some sample of people who are going to be subjects in an experiment, and we're ready to assign participants to each experimental condition.

We plan to have 90 participants in our study, which includes three groups (say, laptop, notebook, and no notes). Ninety participants have agreed to be in our study, and we decide that laptop will be Group 1, notebook will be Group 2, and no notes will be Group 3. We can start anywhere on the random number table (perhaps by dropping a pen on it) and read along the row, considering only the digits 1, 2, and 3; we ignore any other numbers.

We assign our participants in sets of three. If we had a prearranged list of participant names, we would start with the first three on the list. If we did not have names in advance, we could set up a schedule based on the order in which participants show up for the experiment and start with the first three participants who arrive. Suppose we drop the pen on a part of the table that starts with the following row of random numbers:

93    94    17    15    28    07    16    87    22    06

Starting with the 9 in 93 and reading across, the first value of 1, 2, or 3 we encounter is a 3. That means the first person in the first set of three people will be in Group 3—no notes. The next value we encounter is 1, so the second person will be in Group 1—laptop. Therefore, by elimination, the final person in this group of three will be in Group 2—notebook.

Now we start again with the next set of three people. The next appropriate value we encounter is a 1, so the fourth person is in Group 1. Next is a 2, so the fifth person will be in Group 2, and, by elimination, the sixth person will be in Group 3, and so on.

Of course, if we had four experimental groups, we would consider the numbers 1, 2, 3, and 4. If we had two experimental groups, we might consider numbers 1 and 2. Or we could consider odd and even numbers—any odd number would mean an assignment to Group 1, and any even number would mean an assignment to Group 2. (In the case of two groups, we can also flip a coin to assign people to conditions.)

# Random Numbers

| | | | | | | | | | |
|---|---|---|---|---|---|---|---|---|---|
| 79 | 17 | 78 | 71 | 21 | 28 | 49 | 08 | 47 | 79 |
| 17 | 33 | 72 | 97 | 86 | 45 | 44 | 65 | 97 | 29 |
| 27 | 65 | 06 | 82 | 98 | 28 | 36 | 03 | 72 | 93 |
| 33 | 57 | 70 | 34 | 39 | 91 | 78 | 99 | 64 | 53 |
| 76 | 81 | 31 | 42 | 31 | 04 | 00 | 10 | 82 | 13 |
| 27 | 72 | 54 | 77 | 94 | 97 | 92 | 56 | 20 | 98 |
| 97 | 95 | 39 | 36 | 02 | 43 | 10 | 08 | 19 | 00 |
| 87 | 84 | 51 | 57 | 65 | 03 | 46 | 70 | 94 | 69 |
| 40 | 80 | 05 | 81 | 12 | 90 | 02 | 90 | 44 | 38 |
| 21 | 90 | 78 | 37 | 47 | 61 | 92 | 69 | 35 | 30 |
| 40 | 61 | 04 | 23 | 42 | 76 | 72 | 13 | 08 | 83 |
| 59 | 02 | 28 | 10 | 82 | 77 | 75 | 89 | 13 | 34 |
| 91 | 37 | 80 | 64 | 61 | 39 | 19 | 38 | 91 | 28 |
| 24 | 42 | 44 | 77 | 45 | 44 | 03 | 46 | 25 | 94 |
| 66 | 49 | 81 | 89 | 88 | 40 | 81 | 60 | 25 | 26 |
| 57 | 55 | 52 | 54 | 53 | 31 | 49 | 38 | 14 | 72 |
| 83 | 26 | 59 | 05 | 42 | 05 | 89 | 74 | 68 | 10 |
| 16 | 97 | 26 | 84 | 41 | 14 | 94 | 94 | 94 | 03 |
| 53 | 16 | 08 | 29 | 29 | 28 | 19 | 28 | 01 | 83 |
| 87 | 73 | 84 | 55 | 94 | 57 | 52 | 68 | 56 | 90 |
| 56 | 55 | 60 | 96 | 53 | 21 | 18 | 59 | 55 | 86 |
| 83 | 59 | 56 | 38 | 86 | 84 | 07 | 40 | 77 | 20 |
| 37 | 39 | 88 | 49 | 43 | 00 | 49 | 13 | 02 | 51 |
| 14 | 20 | 68 | 04 | 90 | 94 | 70 | 05 | 83 | 10 |
| 11 | 16 | 82 | 54 | 39 | 36 | 56 | 00 | 52 | 07 |
| 46 | 97 | 32 | 82 | 63 | 13 | 42 | 30 | 20 | 64 |
| 25 | 04 | 76 | 44 | 88 | 19 | 61 | 20 | 56 | 97 |
| 05 | 54 | 35 | 78 | 93 | 94 | 17 | 15 | 28 | 07 |
| 16 | 87 | 66 | 77 | 22 | 06 | 50 | 76 | 95 | 09 |
| 67 | 78 | 65 | 43 | 99 | 96 | 82 | 04 | 48 | 30 |
| 50 | 70 | 46 | 81 | 33 | 52 | 89 | 59 | 09 | 49 |
| 57 | 90 | 31 | 77 | 96 | 04 | 97 | 17 | 87 | 54 |
| 51 | 85 | 26 | 99 | 70 | 46 | 88 | 58 | 00 | 99 |
| 45 | 07 | 47 | 13 | 64 | 79 | 44 | 06 | 15 | 07 |
| 46 | 72 | 46 | 81 | 14 | 12 | 17 | 48 | 07 | 33 |
| 04 | 62 | 90 | 98 | 01 | 48 | 00 | 54 | 91 | 65 |

*(continued)*

# Random Numbers (*continued*)

| | | | | | | | | | |
|---|---|---|---|---|---|---|---|---|---|
| 75 | 83 | 67 | 58 | 01 | 28 | 14 | 42 | 41 | 00 |
| 84 | 72 | 63 | 83 | 39 | 67 | 62 | 67 | 28 | 05 |
| 61 | 91 | 27 | 17 | 24 | 76 | 64 | 22 | 20 | 75 |
| 01 | 05 | 20 | 78 | 51 | 19 | 23 | 31 | 44 | 61 |
| 71 | 71 | 55 | 10 | 29 | 62 | 30 | 90 | 52 | 04 |
| 08 | 98 | 57 | 51 | 73 | 55 | 96 | 67 | 02 | 36 |
| 57 | 83 | 20 | 73 | 45 | 93 | 21 | 48 | 23 | 95 |
| 33 | 51 | 57 | 26 | 11 | 16 | 82 | 56 | 63 | 55 |
| 10 | 35 | 48 | 50 | 12 | 09 | 09 | 83 | 81 | 46 |
| 26 | 07 | 34 | 35 | 97 | 89 | 11 | 71 | 88 | 75 |
| 94 | 08 | 05 | 65 | 43 | 55 | 83 | 00 | 20 | 64 |
| 03 | 80 | 52 | 12 | 55 | 86 | 62 | 79 | 39 | 72 |
| 50 | 86 | 61 | 36 | 18 | 43 | 48 | 01 | 71 | 04 |
| 24 | 58 | 31 | 51 | 91 | 55 | 43 | 43 | 17 | 27 |
| 76 | 96 | 32 | 12 | 33 | 99 | 74 | 96 | 26 | 65 |
| 41 | 63 | 83 | 68 | 38 | 74 | 97 | 45 | 30 | 82 |
| 22 | 25 | 34 | 52 | 80 | 38 | 18 | 62 | 53 | 15 |
| 79 | 88 | 43 | 73 | 32 | 02 | 38 | 51 | 22 | 47 |
| 28 | 37 | 38 | 51 | 44 | 13 | 10 | 03 | 18 | 97 |
| 95 | 09 | 89 | 59 | 94 | 87 | 96 | 44 | 55 | 82 |
| 53 | 37 | 57 | 01 | 72 | 33 | 79 | 00 | 85 | 10 |
| 84 | 83 | 02 | 29 | 98 | 81 | 77 | 79 | 49 | 28 |
| 86 | 67 | 93 | 57 | 32 | 17 | 50 | 69 | 42 | 12 |
| 18 | 61 | 05 | 12 | 59 | 12 | 71 | 25 | 42 | 60 |
| 26 | 09 | 16 | 23 | 90 | 39 | 33 | 49 | 11 | 64 |
| 48 | 83 | 61 | 38 | 67 | 06 | 46 | 03 | 18 | 83 |
| 88 | 46 | 69 | 96 | 53 | 83 | 10 | 91 | 06 | 15 |
| 89 | 34 | 46 | 69 | 45 | 65 | 42 | 29 | 04 | 04 |
| 58 | 06 | 18 | 26 | 65 | 07 | 55 | 36 | 54 | 05 |
| 85 | 87 | 13 | 15 | 14 | 37 | 25 | 31 | 61 | 36 |
| 01 | 81 | 81 | 80 | 61 | 99 | 67 | 81 | 14 | 25 |
| 14 | 46 | 11 | 80 | 94 | 45 | 75 | 84 | 92 | 28 |
| 17 | 04 | 08 | 18 | 02 | 51 | 04 | 84 | 31 | 76 |
| 79 | 72 | 38 | 16 | 74 | 54 | 22 | 00 | 51 | 22 |
| 71 | 17 | 12 | 26 | 47 | 03 | 30 | 51 | 27 | 95 |
| 08 | 64 | 24 | 69 | 14 | 90 | 49 | 53 | 37 | 89 |
| 65 | 79 | 53 | 49 | 56 | 27 | 20 | 15 | 10 | 59 |

| | | | | | | | | | |
|----|----|----|----|----|----|----|----|----|----|
| 33 | 13 | 86 | 60 | 94 | 48 | 27 | 27 | 98 | 84 |
| 14 | 78 | 26 | 31 | 01 | 57 | 02 | 92 | 55 | 81 |
| 56 | 57 | 03 | 39 | 92 | 45 | 53 | 36 | 69 | 25 |
| 42 | 54 | 21 | 57 | 40 | 71 | 99 | 66 | 91 | 48 |
| 93 | 10 | 88 | 86 | 67 | 14 | 03 | 16 | 38 | 89 |
| 32 | 61 | 47 | 42 | 04 | 94 | 25 | 65 | 84 | 76 |
| 60 | 44 | 66 | 51 | 94 | 34 | 21 | 32 | 12 | 86 |
| 06 | 70 | 13 | 90 | 90 | 05 | 68 | 01 | 98 | 87 |
| 76 | 38 | 70 | 73 | 55 | 62 | 94 | 24 | 47 | 06 |
| 66 | 22 | 83 | 26 | 59 | 77 | 97 | 79 | 04 | 97 |
| 80 | 38 | 89 | 80 | 14 | 96 | 13 | 64 | 16 | 12 |
| 51 | 16 | 75 | 12 | 20 | 77 | 85 | 30 | 59 | 76 |
| 87 | 74 | 55 | 86 | 74 | 38 | 76 | 81 | 30 | 94 |
| 00 | 16 | 08 | 49 | 50 | 55 | 59 | 33 | 65 | 93 |
| 75 | 61 | 81 | 62 | 03 | 92 | 94 | 27 | 41 | 67 |
| 23 | 87 | 37 | 06 | 08 | 56 | 34 | 86 | 06 | 86 |
| 41 | 48 | 68 | 45 | 23 | 89 | 04 | 83 | 37 | 38 |
| 84 | 34 | 63 | 36 | 22 | 31 | 02 | 53 | 42 | 53 |
| 35 | 20 | 23 | 20 | 76 | 56 | 73 | 88 | 60 | 17 |
| 80 | 49 | 38 | 13 | 41 | 00 | 93 | 37 | 62 | 53 |
| 70 | 35 | 78 | 06 | 05 | 91 | 52 | 81 | 98 | 14 |
| 33 | 14 | 40 | 54 | 94 | 39 | 20 | 69 | 69 | 15 |
| 54 | 42 | 74 | 80 | 12 | 98 | 76 | 28 | 42 | 91 |
| 30 | 55 | 14 | 38 | 26 | 06 | 33 | 44 | 94 | 24 |
| 96 | 28 | 58 | 93 | 82 | 45 | 63 | 13 | 15 | 79 |
| 85 | 46 | 30 | 34 | 09 | 39 | 37 | 55 | 46 | 01 |
| 53 | 57 | 10 | 83 | 57 | 51 | 79 | 05 | 90 | 76 |
| 17 | 19 | 89 | 90 | 27 | 01 | 50 | 84 | 55 | 09 |
| 40 | 09 | 81 | 67 | 07 | 32 | 52 | 40 | 68 | 71 |
| 49 | 17 | 66 | 61 | 97 | 30 | 20 | 66 | 54 | 53 |
| 22 | 32 | 35 | 81 | 47 | 32 | 70 | 73 | 87 | 77 |
| 89 | 97 | 08 | 70 | 87 | 39 | 11 | 40 | 15 | 46 |
| 46 | 74 | 00 | 02 | 80 | 39 | 85 | 92 | 57 | 65 |
| 42 | 75 | 86 | 23 | 09 | 75 | 28 | 28 | 40 | 73 |
| 94 | 43 | 80 | 48 | 64 | 63 | 01 | 02 | 80 | 22 |
| 54 | 72 | 93 | 31 | 34 | 07 | 50 | 42 | 60 | 66 |
| 55 | 16 | 04 | 74 | 47 | 21 | 43 | 16 | 70 | 89 |
| 07 | 92 | 33 | 15 | 38 | 36 | 86 | 79 | 95 | 71 |
| 54 | 11 | 73 | 86 | 13 | 49 | 10 | 10 | 89 | 36 |

# Appendix B
## STATISTICAL TABLES

## AREAS UNDER THE NORMAL CURVE (DISTRIBUTION OF $z$)

After computing a $z$ score, use this table to look up the percentage of the scores between that $z$ score and the mean in a normal distribution or the percentage of scores that lie beyond that $z$ score in a normal distribution.

The percentage of scores in the entire normal distribution is 100%, or an area of 1.00. A score that is directly at the mean would have a $z$ score of 0.00, in the exact center of the distribution. Therefore, 0% of the scores fall between a $z$ score of 0.00 and the mean, and 50% (i.e., half) of them fall beyond that $z$ score. For a $z$ score of 1.11, using the table we can see that 36.65% of the scores fall between that $z$ score and the mean, and 13.35% fall beyond that $z$ score.

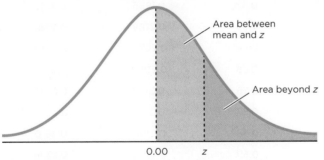

The normal distribution is symmetrical, so if the $z$ score is negative, use the absolute value of $z$ to look up the relevant areas.

| z SCORE | AREA BETWEEN MEAN AND z | AREA BEYOND z | z SCORE | AREA BETWEEN MEAN AND z | AREA BEYOND z |
|---|---|---|---|---|---|
| 0.00 | 0.0000 | 0.5000 | 0.34 | 0.1331 | 0.3669 |
| 0.01 | 0.0040 | 0.4960 | 0.35 | 0.1368 | 0.3632 |
| 0.02 | 0.0080 | 0.4920 | 0.36 | 0.1406 | 0.3594 |
| 0.03 | 0.0120 | 0.4880 | 0.37 | 0.1443 | 0.3557 |
| 0.04 | 0.0160 | 0.4840 | 0.38 | 0.1480 | 0.3520 |
| 0.05 | 0.0199 | 0.4801 | 0.39 | 0.1517 | 0.3483 |
| 0.06 | 0.0239 | 0.4761 | 0.40 | 0.1554 | 0.3446 |
| 0.07 | 0.0279 | 0.4721 | 0.41 | 0.1591 | 0.3409 |
| 0.08 | 0.0319 | 0.4681 | 0.42 | 0.1628 | 0.3372 |
| 0.09 | 0.0359 | 0.4641 | 0.43 | 0.1664 | 0.3336 |
| 0.10 | 0.0398 | 0.4602 | 0.44 | 0.1700 | 0.3300 |
| 0.11 | 0.0438 | 0.4562 | 0.45 | 0.1736 | 0.3264 |
| 0.12 | 0.0478 | 0.4522 | 0.46 | 0.1772 | 0.3228 |
| 0.13 | 0.0517 | 0.4483 | 0.47 | 0.1808 | 0.3192 |
| 0.14 | 0.0557 | 0.4443 | 0.48 | 0.1844 | 0.3156 |
| 0.15 | 0.0596 | 0.4404 | 0.49 | 0.1879 | 0.3121 |
| 0.16 | 0.0636 | 0.4364 | 0.50 | 0.1915 | 0.3085 |
| 0.17 | 0.0675 | 0.4325 | 0.51 | 0.1950 | 0.3050 |
| 0.18 | 0.0714 | 0.4286 | 0.52 | 0.1985 | 0.3015 |
| 0.19 | 0.0753 | 0.4247 | 0.53 | 0.2019 | 0.2981 |
| 0.20 | 0.0793 | 0.4207 | 0.54 | 0.2054 | 0.2946 |
| 0.21 | 0.0832 | 0.4168 | 0.55 | 0.2088 | 0.2912 |
| 0.22 | 0.0871 | 0.4129 | 0.56 | 0.2123 | 0.2877 |
| 0.23 | 0.0910 | 0.4090 | 0.57 | 0.2157 | 0.2843 |
| 0.24 | 0.0948 | 0.4052 | 0.58 | 0.2190 | 0.2810 |
| 0.25 | 0.0987 | 0.4013 | 0.59 | 0.2224 | 0.2776 |
| 0.26 | 0.1026 | 0.3974 | 0.60 | 0.2257 | 0.2743 |
| 0.27 | 0.1064 | 0.3936 | 0.61 | 0.2291 | 0.2709 |
| 0.28 | 0.1103 | 0.3897 | 0.62 | 0.2324 | 0.2676 |
| 0.29 | 0.1141 | 0.3859 | 0.63 | 0.2357 | 0.2643 |
| 0.30 | 0.1179 | 0.3821 | 0.64 | 0.2389 | 0.2611 |
| 0.31 | 0.1217 | 0.3783 | 0.65 | 0.2422 | 0.2578 |
| 0.32 | 0.1255 | 0.3745 | 0.66 | 0.2454 | 0.2546 |
| 0.33 | 0.1293 | 0.3707 | 0.67 | 0.2486 | 0.2514 |

| z SCORE | AREA BETWEEN MEAN AND z | AREA BEYOND z | z SCORE | AREA BETWEEN MEAN AND z | AREA BEYOND z |
|---|---|---|---|---|---|
| 0.68 | 0.2517 | 0.2483 | 1.01 | 0.3438 | 0.1562 |
| 0.69 | 0.2549 | 0.2451 | 1.02 | 0.3461 | 0.1539 |
| 0.70 | 0.2580 | 0.2420 | 1.03 | 0.3485 | 0.1515 |
| 0.71 | 0.2611 | 0.2389 | 1.04 | 0.3508 | 0.1492 |
| 0.72 | 0.2642 | 0.2358 | 1.05 | 0.3531 | 0.1469 |
| 0.73 | 0.2673 | 0.2327 | 1.06 | 0.3554 | 0.1446 |
| 0.74 | 0.2704 | 0.2296 | 1.07 | 0.3577 | 0.1423 |
| 0.75 | 0.2734 | 0.2266 | 1.08 | 0.3599 | 0.1401 |
| 0.76 | 0.2764 | 0.2236 | 1.09 | 0.3621 | 0.1379 |
| 0.77 | 0.2794 | 0.2206 | 1.10 | 0.3643 | 0.1357 |
| 0.78 | 0.2823 | 0.2177 | 1.11 | 0.3665 | 0.1335 |
| 0.79 | 0.2852 | 0.2148 | 1.12 | 0.3686 | 0.1314 |
| 0.80 | 0.2881 | 0.2119 | 1.13 | 0.3708 | 0.1292 |
| 0.81 | 0.2910 | 0.2090 | 1.14 | 0.3729 | 0.1271 |
| 0.82 | 0.2939 | 0.2061 | 1.15 | 0.3749 | 0.1251 |
| 0.83 | 0.2967 | 0.2033 | 1.16 | 0.3770 | 0.1230 |
| 0.84 | 0.2995 | 0.2005 | 1.17 | 0.3790 | 0.1210 |
| 0.85 | 0.3023 | 0.1977 | 1.18 | 0.3810 | 0.1190 |
| 0.86 | 0.3051 | 0.1949 | 1.19 | 0.3830 | 0.1170 |
| 0.87 | 0.3078 | 0.1922 | 1.20 | 0.3849 | 0.1151 |
| 0.88 | 0.3106 | 0.1894 | 1.21 | 0.3869 | 0.1131 |
| 0.89 | 0.3133 | 0.1867 | 1.22 | 0.3888 | 0.1112 |
| 0.90 | 0.3159 | 0.1841 | 1.23 | 0.3907 | 0.1093 |
| 0.91 | 0.3186 | 0.1814 | 1.24 | 0.3925 | 0.1075 |
| 0.92 | 0.3212 | 0.1788 | 1.25 | 0.3944 | 0.1056 |
| 0.93 | 0.3238 | 0.1762 | 1.26 | 0.3962 | 0.1038 |
| 0.94 | 0.3264 | 0.1736 | 1.27 | 0.3980 | 0.1020 |
| 0.95 | 0.3289 | 0.1711 | 1.28 | 0.3997 | 0.1003 |
| 0.96 | 0.3315 | 0.1685 | 1.29 | 0.4015 | 0.0985 |
| 0.97 | 0.3340 | 0.1660 | 1.30 | 0.4032 | 0.0968 |
| 0.98 | 0.3365 | 0.1635 | 1.31 | 0.4049 | 0.0951 |
| 0.99 | 0.3389 | 0.1611 | 1.32 | 0.4066 | 0.0934 |
| 1.00 | 0.3413 | 0.1587 | 1.33 | 0.4082 | 0.0918 |

*(continued)*

| z SCORE | AREA BETWEEN MEAN AND z | AREA BEYOND z | z SCORE | AREA BETWEEN MEAN AND z | AREA BEYOND z |
|---|---|---|---|---|---|
| 1.34 | 0.4099 | 0.0901 | 1.68 | 0.4535 | 0.0465 |
| 1.35 | 0.4115 | 0.0885 | 1.69 | 0.4545 | 0.0455 |
| 1.36 | 0.4131 | 0.0869 | 1.70 | 0.4554 | 0.0446 |
| 1.37 | 0.4147 | 0.0853 | 1.71 | 0.4564 | 0.0436 |
| 1.38 | 0.4162 | 0.0838 | 1.72 | 0.4573 | 0.0427 |
| 1.39 | 0.4177 | 0.0823 | 1.73 | 0.4582 | 0.0418 |
| 1.40 | 0.4192 | 0.0808 | 1.74 | 0.4591 | 0.0409 |
| 1.41 | 0.4207 | 0.0793 | 1.75 | 0.4599 | 0.0401 |
| 1.42 | 0.4222 | 0.0778 | 1.76 | 0.4608 | 0.0392 |
| 1.43 | 0.4236 | 0.0764 | 1.77 | 0.4616 | 0.0384 |
| 1.44 | 0.4251 | 0.0749 | 1.78 | 0.4625 | 0.0375 |
| 1.45 | 0.4265 | 0.0735 | 1.79 | 0.4633 | 0.0367 |
| 1.46 | 0.4279 | 0.0721 | 1.80 | 0.4641 | 0.0359 |
| 1.47 | 0.4292 | 0.0708 | 1.81 | 0.4649 | 0.0351 |
| 1.48 | 0.4306 | 0.0694 | 1.82 | 0.4656 | 0.0344 |
| 1.49 | 0.4319 | 0.0681 | 1.83 | 0.4664 | 0.0336 |
| 1.50 | 0.4332 | 0.0668 | 1.84 | 0.4671 | 0.0329 |
| 1.51 | 0.4345 | 0.0655 | 1.85 | 0.4678 | 0.0322 |
| 1.52 | 0.4357 | 0.0643 | 1.86 | 0.4686 | 0.0314 |
| 1.53 | 0.4370 | 0.0630 | 1.87 | 0.4693 | 0.0307 |
| 1.54 | 0.4382 | 0.0618 | 1.88 | 0.4699 | 0.0301 |
| 1.55 | 0.4394 | 0.0606 | 1.89 | 0.4706 | 0.0294 |
| 1.56 | 0.4406 | 0.0594 | 1.90 | 0.4713 | 0.0287 |
| 1.57 | 0.4418 | 0.0582 | 1.91 | 0.4719 | 0.0281 |
| 1.58 | 0.4429 | 0.0571 | 1.92 | 0.4726 | 0.0274 |
| 1.59 | 0.4441 | 0.0559 | 1.93 | 0.4732 | 0.0268 |
| 1.60 | 0.4452 | 0.0548 | 1.94 | 0.4738 | 0.0262 |
| 1.61 | 0.4463 | 0.0537 | 1.95 | 0.4744 | 0.0256 |
| 1.62 | 0.4474 | 0.0526 | 1.96 | 0.4750 | 0.0250 |
| 1.63 | 0.4484 | 0.0516 | 1.97 | 0.4756 | 0.0244 |
| 1.64 | 0.4495 | 0.0505 | 1.98 | 0.4761 | 0.0239 |
| 1.65 | 0.4505 | 0.0495 | 1.99 | 0.4767 | 0.0233 |
| 1.66 | 0.4515 | 0.0485 | 2.00 | 0.4772 | 0.0228 |
| 1.67 | 0.4525 | 0.0475 | 2.01 | 0.4778 | 0.0222 |

| z SCORE | AREA BETWEEN MEAN AND z | AREA BEYOND z | z SCORE | AREA BETWEEN MEAN AND z | AREA BEYOND z |
|---------|------------------------|---------------|---------|------------------------|---------------|
| 2.02 | 0.4783 | 0.0217 | 2.35 | 0.4906 | 0.0094 |
| 2.03 | 0.4788 | 0.0212 | 2.36 | 0.4909 | 0.0091 |
| 2.04 | 0.4793 | 0.0207 | 2.37 | 0.4911 | 0.0089 |
| 2.05 | 0.4798 | 0.0202 | 2.38 | 0.4913 | 0.0087 |
| 2.06 | 0.4803 | 0.0197 | 2.39 | 0.4916 | 0.0084 |
| 2.07 | 0.4808 | 0.0192 | 2.40 | 0.4918 | 0.0082 |
| 2.08 | 0.4812 | 0.0188 | 2.41 | 0.4920 | 0.0080 |
| 2.09 | 0.4817 | 0.0183 | 2.42 | 0.4922 | 0.0078 |
| 2.10 | 0.4821 | 0.0179 | 2.43 | 0.4925 | 0.0075 |
| 2.11 | 0.4826 | 0.0174 | 2.44 | 0.4927 | 0.0073 |
| 2.12 | 0.4830 | 0.0170 | 2.45 | 0.4929 | 0.0071 |
| 2.13 | 0.4834 | 0.0166 | 2.46 | 0.4931 | 0.0069 |
| 2.14 | 0.4838 | 0.0162 | 2.47 | 0.4932 | 0.0068 |
| 2.15 | 0.4842 | 0.0158 | 2.48 | 0.4934 | 0.0066 |
| 2.16 | 0.4846 | 0.0154 | 2.49 | 0.4936 | 0.0064 |
| 2.17 | 0.4850 | 0.0150 | 2.50 | 0.4938 | 0.0062 |
| 2.18 | 0.4854 | 0.0146 | 2.51 | 0.4940 | 0.0060 |
| 2.19 | 0.4857 | 0.0143 | 2.52 | 0.4941 | 0.0059 |
| 2.20 | 0.4861 | 0.0139 | 2.53 | 0.4943 | 0.0057 |
| 2.21 | 0.4864 | 0.0136 | 2.54 | 0.4945 | 0.0055 |
| 2.22 | 0.4868 | 0.0132 | 2.55 | 0.4946 | 0.0054 |
| 2.23 | 0.4871 | 0.0129 | 2.56 | 0.4948 | 0.0052 |
| 2.24 | 0.4875 | 0.0125 | 2.57 | 0.4949 | 0.0051 |
| 2.25 | 0.4878 | 0.0122 | 2.58 | 0.4950 | 0.0050 |
| 2.26 | 0.4881 | 0.0119 | 2.59 | 0.4952 | 0.0048 |
| 2.27 | 0.4884 | 0.0116 | 2.60 | 0.4953 | 0.0047 |
| 2.28 | 0.4887 | 0.0113 | 2.61 | 0.4955 | 0.0045 |
| 2.29 | 0.4890 | 0.0110 | 2.62 | 0.4956 | 0.0044 |
| 2.30 | 0.4893 | 0.0107 | 2.63 | 0.4957 | 0.0043 |
| 2.31 | 0.4896 | 0.0104 | 2.64 | 0.4959 | 0.0041 |
| 2.32 | 0.4898 | 0.0102 | 2.65 | 0.4960 | 0.0040 |
| 2.33 | 0.4901 | 0.0099 | 2.66 | 0.4961 | 0.0039 |
| 2.34 | 0.4904 | 0.0096 | 2.67 | 0.4962 | 0.0038 |

*(continued)*

| z SCORE | AREA BETWEEN MEAN AND z | AREA BEYOND z | z SCORE | AREA BETWEEN MEAN AND z | AREA BEYOND z |
|---|---|---|---|---|---|
| 2.68 | 0.4963 | 0.0037 | 3.02 | 0.4987 | 0.0013 |
| 2.69 | 0.4964 | 0.0036 | 3.03 | 0.4988 | 0.0012 |
| 2.70 | 0.4965 | 0.0035 | 3.04 | 0.4988 | 0.0012 |
| 2.71 | 0.4966 | 0.0034 | 3.05 | 0.4989 | 0.0011 |
| 2.72 | 0.4967 | 0.0033 | 3.06 | 0.4989 | 0.0011 |
| 2.73 | 0.4968 | 0.0032 | 3.07 | 0.4989 | 0.0011 |
| 2.74 | 0.4969 | 0.0031 | 3.08 | 0.4990 | 0.0010 |
| 2.75 | 0.4970 | 0.0030 | 3.09 | 0.4990 | 0.0010 |
| 2.76 | 0.4971 | 0.0029 | 3.10 | 0.4990 | 0.0010 |
| 2.77 | 0.4972 | 0.0028 | 3.11 | 0.4991 | 0.0009 |
| 2.78 | 0.4973 | 0.0027 | 3.12 | 0.4991 | 0.0009 |
| 2.79 | 0.4974 | 0.0026 | 3.13 | 0.4991 | 0.0009 |
| 2.80 | 0.4974 | 0.0026 | 3.14 | 0.4992 | 0.0008 |
| 2.81 | 0.4975 | 0.0025 | 3.15 | 0.4992 | 0.0008 |
| 2.82 | 0.4976 | 0.0024 | 3.16 | 0.4992 | 0.0008 |
| 2.83 | 0.4977 | 0.0023 | 3.17 | 0.4992 | 0.0008 |
| 2.84 | 0.4977 | 0.0023 | 3.18 | 0.4993 | 0.0007 |
| 2.85 | 0.4978 | 0.0022 | 3.19 | 0.4993 | 0.0007 |
| 2.86 | 0.4979 | 0.0021 | 3.20 | 0.4993 | 0.0007 |
| 2.87 | 0.4979 | 0.0021 | 3.21 | 0.4993 | 0.0007 |
| 2.88 | 0.4980 | 0.0020 | 3.22 | 0.4994 | 0.0006 |
| 2.89 | 0.4981 | 0.0019 | 3.23 | 0.4994 | 0.0006 |
| 2.90 | 0.4981 | 0.0019 | 3.24 | 0.4994 | 0.0006 |
| 2.91 | 0.4982 | 0.0018 | 3.25 | 0.4994 | 0.0006 |
| 2.92 | 0.4982 | 0.0018 | 3.26 | 0.4994 | 0.0006 |
| 2.93 | 0.4983 | 0.0017 | 3.27 | 0.4995 | 0.0005 |
| 2.94 | 0.4984 | 0.0016 | 3.28 | 0.4995 | 0.0005 |
| 2.95 | 0.4984 | 0.0016 | 3.29 | 0.4995 | 0.0005 |
| 2.96 | 0.4985 | 0.0015 | 3.30 | 0.4995 | 0.0005 |
| 2.97 | 0.4985 | 0.0015 | 3.31 | 0.4995 | 0.0005 |
| 2.98 | 0.4986 | 0.0014 | 3.32 | 0.4995 | 0.0005 |
| 2.99 | 0.4986 | 0.0014 | 3.33 | 0.4996 | 0.0004 |
| 3.00 | 0.4987 | 0.0013 | 3.34 | 0.4996 | 0.0004 |
| 3.01 | 0.4987 | 0.0013 | 3.35 | 0.4996 | 0.0004 |

| z SCORE | AREA BETWEEN MEAN AND z | AREA BEYOND z | z SCORE | AREA BETWEEN MEAN AND z | AREA BEYOND z |
|---|---|---|---|---|---|
| 3.36 | 0.4996 | 0.0004 | 3.51 | 0.4998 | 0.0002 |
| 3.37 | 0.4996 | 0.0004 | 3.52 | 0.4998 | 0.0002 |
| 3.38 | 0.4996 | 0.0004 | 3.53 | 0.4998 | 0.0002 |
| 3.39 | 0.4997 | 0.0003 | 3.54 | 0.4998 | 0.0002 |
| 3.40 | 0.4997 | 0.0003 | 3.55 | 0.4998 | 0.0002 |
| 3.41 | 0.4997 | 0.0003 | 3.56 | 0.4998 | 0.0002 |
| 3.42 | 0.4997 | 0.0003 | 3.57 | 0.4998 | 0.0002 |
| 3.43 | 0.4997 | 0.0003 | 3.58 | 0.4998 | 0.0002 |
| 3.44 | 0.4997 | 0.0003 | 3.59 | 0.4998 | 0.0002 |
| 3.45 | 0.4997 | 0.0003 | 3.60 | 0.4998 | 0.0002 |
| 3.46 | 0.4997 | 0.0003 | 3.70 | 0.4999 | 0.0001 |
| 3.47 | 0.4997 | 0.0003 | 3.80 | 0.4999 | 0.0001 |
| 3.48 | 0.4997 | 0.0003 | 3.90 | 0.49995 | 0.00005 |
| 3.49 | 0.4998 | 0.0002 | 4.00 | 0.49997 | 0.00003 |
| 3.50 | 0.4998 | 0.0002 | | | |

*Note:* This table is included for basic statistical reference. It is not discussed in detail in this book.

## CRITICAL VALUES OF *t*

To compute a 95% confidence interval (CI), read down the column labeled ".05" under "Two-tailed tests" to find the *t* value that corresponds to the degrees of freedom (this column is shaded in the table). For example, for a 95% CI with 20 degrees of freedom, use a *t* of 2.086. Then multiply this *t* value by the standard error to get the margin of error (one side of the CI).

To conduct null hypothesis significance testing, use this table to find the critical value of *t*. First decide whether a one- or a two-tailed test is appropriate. Then decide the level of significance and read down the corresponding column to the number of degrees of freedom. The table entry gives the value of *t* that must be *exceeded* in order to be significant. For example, if we do a two-tailed test with 20 degrees of freedom, *t* must be greater than 2.086 to be significant at the 0.05 level.

| | ONE-TAILED TESTS | | | TWO-TAILED TESTS | | |
|---|---|---|---|---|---|---|
| df | .10 | .05 | .01 | .10 | .05 | .01 |
| 1 | 3.078 | 6.314 | 31.821 | 6.314 | 12.706 | 63.657 |
| 2 | 1.886 | 2.920 | 6.965 | 2.920 | 4.303 | 9.925 |
| 3 | 1.638 | 2.353 | 4.541 | 2.353 | 3.182 | 5.841 |
| 4 | 1.533 | 2.132 | 3.747 | 2.132 | 2.776 | 4.604 |
| 5 | 1.476 | 2.015 | 3.365 | 2.015 | 2.571 | 4.032 |
| 6 | 1.440 | 1.943 | 3.143 | 1.943 | 2.447 | 3.708 |
| 7 | 1.415 | 1.895 | 2.998 | 1.895 | 2.365 | 3.500 |
| 8 | 1.397 | 1.860 | 2.897 | 1.860 | 2.306 | 3.356 |
| 9 | 1.383 | 1.833 | 2.822 | 1.833 | 2.262 | 3.250 |
| 10 | 1.372 | 1.813 | 2.764 | 1.813 | 2.228 | 3.170 |
| 11 | 1.364 | 1.796 | 2.718 | 1.796 | 2.201 | 3.106 |
| 12 | 1.356 | 1.783 | 2.681 | 1.783 | 2.179 | 3.055 |
| 13 | 1.350 | 1.771 | 2.651 | 1.771 | 2.161 | 3.013 |
| 14 | 1.345 | 1.762 | 2.625 | 1.762 | 2.145 | 2.977 |
| 15 | 1.341 | 1.753 | 2.603 | 1.753 | 2.132 | 2.947 |
| 16 | 1.337 | 1.746 | 2.584 | 1.746 | 2.120 | 2.921 |
| 17 | 1.334 | 1.740 | 2.567 | 1.740 | 2.110 | 2.898 |
| 18 | 1.331 | 1.734 | 2.553 | 1.734 | 2.101 | 2.897 |
| 19 | 1.328 | 1.729 | 2.540 | 1.729 | 2.093 | 2.861 |
| 20 | 1.326 | 1.725 | 2.528 | 1.725 | 2.086 | 2.846 |
| 21 | 1.323 | 1.721 | 2.518 | 1.721 | 2.080 | 2.832 |
| 22 | 1.321 | 1.717 | 2.509 | 1.717 | 2.074 | 2.819 |
| 23 | 1.320 | 1.714 | 2.500 | 1.714 | 2.069 | 2.808 |
| 24 | 1.318 | 1.711 | 2.492 | 1.711 | 2.064 | 2.797 |
| 25 | 1.317 | 1.708 | 2.485 | 1.708 | 2.060 | 2.788 |
| 26 | 1.315 | 1.706 | 2.479 | 1.706 | 2.056 | 2.779 |
| 27 | 1.314 | 1.704 | 2.473 | 1.704 | 2.052 | 2.771 |
| 28 | 1.313 | 1.701 | 2.467 | 1.701 | 2.049 | 2.764 |
| 29 | 1.312 | 1.699 | 2.462 | 1.699 | 2.045 | 2.757 |

| | ONE-TAILED TESTS | | | TWO-TAILED TESTS | | |
|---|---|---|---|---|---|---|
| df | .10 | .05 | .01 | .10 | .05 | .01 |
| 30 | 1.311 | 1.697 | 2.458 | 1.698 | 2.042 | 2.750 |
| 35 | 1.306 | 1.690 | 2.438 | 1.690 | 2.030 | 2.724 |
| 40 | 1.303 | 1.684 | 2.424 | 1.684 | 2.021 | 2.705 |
| 45 | 1.301 | 1.680 | 2.412 | 1.680 | 2.014 | 2.690 |
| 50 | 1.299 | 1.676 | 2.404 | 1.676 | 2.009 | 2.678 |
| 55 | 1.297 | 1.673 | 2.396 | 1.673 | 2.004 | 2.668 |
| 60 | 1.296 | 1.671 | 2.390 | 1.671 | 2.001 | 2.661 |
| 65 | 1.295 | 1.669 | 2.385 | 1.669 | 1.997 | 2.654 |
| 70 | 1.294 | 1.667 | 2.381 | 1.667 | 1.995 | 2.648 |
| 75 | 1.293 | 1.666 | 2.377 | 1.666 | 1.992 | 2.643 |
| 80 | 1.292 | 1.664 | 2.374 | 1.664 | 1.990 | 2.639 |
| 85 | 1.292 | 1.663 | 2.371 | 1.663 | 1.989 | 2.635 |
| 90 | 1.291 | 1.662 | 2.369 | 1.662 | 1.987 | 2.632 |
| 95 | 1.291 | 1.661 | 2.366 | 1.661 | 1.986 | 2.629 |
| 100 | 1.290 | 1.660 | 2.364 | 1.660 | 1.984 | 2.626 |
| $\infty$ | 1.282 | 1.645 | 2.327 | 1.645 | 1.960 | 2.576 |

# CRITICAL VALUES OF *F*

This table can handle up to seven independent treatment groups. To use it, decide the level of significance (.01, .05, or .10). Then determine the degrees of freedom for the numerator (number of conditions minus 1) and degrees of freedom for the denominator (sum of the number of subjects, minus 1 in each group). The table entry gives the value of *F* that must be *exceeded* to be significant at the specified level.

Thus, if we have three treatment groups with 10 subjects each, we have 2 *df* for the numerator and 9 + 9 + 9 = 27 *df* for the denominator. If we set our significance criterion at .05, we need an *F* larger than 3.36 to reject the null hypothesis.

| DENOMINATOR df | SIGNIFICANCE LEVEL | NUMERATOR DEGREES OF FREEDOM | | | | | |
|---|---|---|---|---|---|---|---|
| | | 1 | 2 | 3 | 4 | 5 | 6 |
| 1 | .01 | 4,052 | 5,000 | 5,404 | 5,625 | 5,764 | 5,859 |
| | .05 | 162 | 200 | 216 | 225 | 230 | 234 |
| | .10 | 39.9 | 49.5 | 53.6 | 55.8 | 57.2 | 58.2 |

*(continued)*

| DENOMINATOR df | SIGNIFICANCE LEVEL | NUMERATOR DEGREES OF FREEDOM | | | | | |
|---|---|---|---|---|---|---|---|
| | | 1 | 2 | 3 | 4 | 5 | 6 |
| 2 | .01 | 98.50 | 99.00 | 99.17 | 99.25 | 99.30 | 99.33 |
| | .05 | 18.51 | 19.00 | 19.17 | 19.25 | 19.30 | 19.33 |
| | .10 | 8.53 | 9.00 | 9.16 | 9.24 | 9.29 | 9.33 |
| 3 | .01 | 34.12 | 30.82 | 29.46 | 28.71 | 28.24 | 27.91 |
| | .05 | 10.13 | 9.55 | 9.28 | 9.12 | 9.01 | 8.94 |
| | .10 | 5.54 | 5.46 | 5.39 | 5.34 | 5.31 | 5.28 |
| 4 | .01 | 21.20 | 18.00 | 16.70 | 15.98 | 15.52 | 15.21 |
| | .05 | 7.71 | 6.95 | 6.59 | 6.39 | 6.26 | 6.16 |
| | .10 | 4.55 | 4.33 | 4.19 | 4.11 | 4.05 | 4.01 |
| 5 | .01 | 16.26 | 13.27 | 12.06 | 11.39 | 10.97 | 10.67 |
| | .05 | 6.61 | 5.79 | 5.41 | 5.19 | 5.05 | 4.95 |
| | .10 | 4.06 | 3.78 | 3.62 | 3.52 | 3.45 | 3.41 |
| 6 | .01 | 13.75 | 10.93 | 9.78 | 9.15 | 8.75 | 8.47 |
| | .05 | 5.99 | 5.14 | 4.76 | 4.53 | 4.39 | 4.28 |
| | .10 | 3.78 | 3.46 | 3.29 | 3.18 | 3.11 | 3.06 |
| 7 | .01 | 12.25 | 9.55 | 8.45 | 7.85 | 7.46 | 7.19 |
| | .05 | 5.59 | 4.74 | 4.35 | 4.12 | 3.97 | 3.87 |
| | .10 | 3.59 | 3.26 | 3.08 | 2.96 | 2.88 | 2.83 |
| 8 | .01 | 11.26 | 8.65 | 7.59 | 7.01 | 6.63 | 6.37 |
| | .05 | 5.32 | 4.46 | 4.07 | 3.84 | 3.69 | 3.58 |
| | .10 | 3.46 | 3.11 | 2.92 | 2.81 | 2.73 | 2.67 |
| 9 | .01 | 10.56 | 8.02 | 6.99 | 6.42 | 6.06 | 5.80 |
| | .05 | 5.12 | 4.26 | 3.86 | 3.63 | 3.48 | 3.37 |
| | .10 | 3.36 | 3.01 | 2.81 | 2.69 | 2.61 | 2.55 |
| 10 | .01 | 10.05 | 7.56 | 6.55 | 6.00 | 5.64 | 5.39 |
| | .05 | 4.97 | 4.10 | 3.71 | 3.48 | 3.33 | 3.22 |
| | .10 | 3.29 | 2.93 | 2.73 | 2.61 | 2.52 | 2.46 |

| DENOMINATOR df | SIGNIFICANCE LEVEL | NUMERATOR DEGREES OF FREEDOM | | | | | |
|---|---|---|---|---|---|---|---|
| | | 1 | 2 | 3 | 4 | 5 | 6 |
| 11 | .01 | 9.65 | 7.21 | 6.22 | 5.67 | 5.32 | 5.07 |
| | .05 | 4.85 | 3.98 | 3.59 | 3.36 | 3.20 | 3.10 |
| | .10 | 3.23 | 2.86 | 2.66 | 2.55 | 2.45 | 2.39 |
| 12 | .01 | 9.33 | 6.93 | 5.95 | 5.41 | 5.07 | 4.82 |
| | .05 | 4.75 | 3.89 | 3.49 | 3.26 | 3.11 | 3.00 |
| | .10 | 3.18 | 2.81 | 2.61 | 2.48 | 2.40 | 2.33 |
| 13 | .01 | 9.07 | 6.70 | 5.74 | 5.21 | 4.86 | 4.62 |
| | .05 | 4.67 | 3.81 | 3.41 | 3.18 | 3.03 | 2.92 |
| | .10 | 3.14 | 2.76 | 2.56 | 2.43 | 2.35 | 2.28 |
| 14 | .01 | 8.86 | 6.52 | 5.56 | 5.04 | 4.70 | 4.46 |
| | .05 | 4.60 | 3.74 | 3.34 | 3.11 | 2.96 | 2.85 |
| | .10 | 3.10 | 2.73 | 2.52 | 2.40 | 2.31 | 2.24 |
| 15 | .01 | 8.68 | 6.36 | 5.42 | 4.89 | 4.56 | 4.32 |
| | .05 | 4.54 | 3.68 | 3.29 | 3.06 | 2.90 | 2.79 |
| | .10 | 3.07 | 2.70 | 2.49 | 2.36 | 2.27 | 2.21 |
| 16 | .01 | 8.53 | 6.23 | 5.29 | 4.77 | 4.44 | 4.30 |
| | .05 | 4.49 | 3.63 | 3.24 | 3.01 | 2.85 | 2.74 |
| | .10 | 3.05 | 2.67 | 2.46 | 2.33 | 2.24 | 2.18 |
| 17 | .01 | 8.40 | 6.11 | 5.19 | 4.67 | 4.34 | 4.10 |
| | .05 | 4.45 | 3.59 | 3.20 | 2.97 | 2.81 | 2.70 |
| | .10 | 3.03 | 2.65 | 2.44 | 2.31 | 2.22 | 2.15 |
| 18 | .01 | 8.29 | 6.01 | 5.09 | 4.58 | 4.25 | 4.02 |
| | .05 | 4.41 | 3.56 | 3.16 | 2.93 | 2.77 | 2.66 |
| | .10 | 3.01 | 2.62 | 2.42 | 2.29 | 2.20 | 2.13 |
| 19 | .01 | 8.19 | 5.93 | 5.01 | 4.50 | 4.17 | 3.94 |
| | .05 | 4.38 | 3.52 | 3.13 | 2.90 | 2.74 | 2.63 |
| | .10 | 2.91 | 2.61 | 2.40 | 2.27 | 2.18 | 2.11 |

*(continued)*

| DENOMINATOR df | SIGNIFICANCE LEVEL | NUMERATOR DEGREES OF FREEDOM | | | | | |
|---|---|---|---|---|---|---|---|
| | | 1 | 2 | 3 | 4 | 5 | 6 |
| 20 | .01 | 8.10 | 5.85 | 4.94 | 4.43 | 4.10 | 3.87 |
| | .05 | 4.35 | 3.49 | 3.10 | 2.87 | 2.71 | 2.60 |
| | .10 | 2.98 | 2.59 | 2.38 | 2.25 | 2.16 | 2.09 |
| 21 | .01 | 8.02 | 5.78 | 4.88 | 4.37 | 4.04 | 3.81 |
| | .05 | 4.33 | 3.47 | 3.07 | 2.84 | 2.69 | 2.57 |
| | .10 | 2.96 | 2.58 | 2.37 | 2.23 | 2.14 | 2.08 |
| 22 | .01 | 7.95 | 5.72 | 4.82 | 4.31 | 3.99 | 3.76 |
| | .05 | 4.30 | 3.44 | 3.05 | 2.82 | 2.66 | 2.55 |
| | .10 | 2.95 | 2.56 | 2.35 | 2.22 | 2.13 | 2.06 |
| 23 | .01 | 7.88 | 5.66 | 4.77 | 4.26 | 3.94 | 3.71 |
| | .05 | 4.28 | 3.42 | 3.03 | 2.80 | 2.64 | 2.53 |
| | .10 | 2.94 | 2.55 | 2.34 | 2.21 | 2.12 | 2.05 |
| 24 | .01 | 7.82 | 5.61 | 4.72 | 4.22 | 3.90 | 3.67 |
| | .05 | 4.26 | 3.40 | 3.01 | 2.78 | 2.62 | 2.51 |
| | .10 | 2.93 | 2.54 | 2.33 | 2.20 | 2.10 | 2.04 |
| 25 | .01 | 7.77 | 5.57 | 4.68 | 4.18 | 3.86 | 3.63 |
| | .05 | 4.24 | 3.39 | 2.99 | 2.76 | 2.60 | 2.49 |
| | .10 | 2.92 | 2.53 | 2.32 | 2.19 | 2.09 | 2.03 |
| 26 | .01 | 7.72 | 5.53 | 4.64 | 4.14 | 3.82 | 3.59 |
| | .05 | 4.23 | 3.37 | 2.98 | 2.74 | 2.59 | 2.48 |
| | .10 | 2.91 | 2.52 | 2.31 | 2.18 | 2.08 | 2.01 |
| 27 | .01 | 7.68 | 5.49 | 4.60 | 4.11 | 3.79 | 3.56 |
| | .05 | 4.21 | 3.36 | 2.96 | 2.73 | 2.57 | 2.46 |
| | .10 | 2.90 | 2.51 | 2.30 | 2.17 | 2.07 | 2.01 |
| 28 | .01 | 7.64 | 5.45 | 4.57 | 4.08 | 3.75 | 3.53 |
| | .05 | 4.20 | 3.34 | 2.95 | 2.72 | 2.56 | 2.45 |
| | .10 | 2.89 | 2.50 | 2.29 | 2.16 | 2.07 | 2.00 |

| DENOMINATOR df | SIGNIFICANCE LEVEL | NUMERATOR DEGREES OF FREEDOM | | | | | |
|---|---|---|---|---|---|---|---|
| | | 1 | 2 | 3 | 4 | 5 | 6 |
| 29 | .01 | 7.60 | 5.42 | 4.54 | 4.05 | 3.73 | 3.50 |
| | .05 | 4.18 | 3.33 | 2.94 | 2.70 | 2.55 | 2.43 |
| | .10 | 2.89 | 2.50 | 2.28 | 2.15 | 2.06 | 1.99 |
| 30 | .01 | 7.56 | 5.39 | 4.51 | 4.02 | 3.70 | 3.47 |
| | .05 | 4.17 | 3.32 | 2.92 | 2.69 | 2.53 | 2.42 |
| | .10 | 2.88 | 2.49 | 2.28 | 2.14 | 2.05 | 1.98 |
| 35 | .01 | 7.42 | 5.27 | 4.40 | 3.91 | 3.59 | 3.37 |
| | .05 | 4.12 | 3.27 | 2.88 | 2.64 | 2.49 | 2.37 |
| | .10 | 2.86 | 2.46 | 2.25 | 2.11 | 2.02 | 1.95 |
| 40 | .01 | 7.32 | 5.18 | 4.31 | 3.83 | 3.51 | 3.29 |
| | .05 | 4.09 | 3.23 | 2.84 | 2.61 | 2.45 | 2.34 |
| | .10 | 2.84 | 2.44 | 2.23 | 2.09 | 2.00 | 1.93 |
| 45 | .01 | 7.23 | 5.11 | 4.25 | 3.77 | 3.46 | 3.23 |
| | .05 | 4.06 | 3.21 | 2.81 | 2.58 | 2.42 | 2.31 |
| | .10 | 2.82 | 2.43 | 2.21 | 2.08 | 1.98 | 1.91 |
| 50 | .01 | 7.17 | 5.06 | 4.20 | 3.72 | 3.41 | 3.19 |
| | .05 | 4.04 | 3.18 | 2.79 | 2.56 | 2.40 | 2.29 |
| | .10 | 2.81 | 2.41 | 2.20 | 2.06 | 1.97 | 1.90 |
| 55 | .01 | 7.12 | 5.01 | 4.16 | 3.68 | 3.37 | 3.15 |
| | .05 | 4.02 | 3.17 | 2.77 | 2.54 | 2.38 | 2.27 |
| | .10 | 2.80 | 2.40 | 2.19 | 2.05 | 1.96 | 1.89 |
| 60 | .01 | 7.08 | 4.98 | 4.13 | 3.65 | 3.34 | 3.12 |
| | .05 | 4.00 | 3.15 | 2.76 | 2.53 | 2.37 | 2.26 |
| | .10 | 2.79 | 2.39 | 2.18 | 2.04 | 1.95 | 1.88 |
| 65 | .01 | 7.04 | 4.95 | 4.10 | 3.62 | 3.31 | 3.09 |
| | .05 | 3.99 | 3.14 | 2.75 | 2.51 | 2.36 | 2.24 |
| | .10 | 2.79 | 2.39 | 2.17 | 2.03 | 1.94 | 1.87 |

*(continued)*

| DENOMINATOR df | SIGNIFICANCE LEVEL | NUMERATOR DEGREES OF FREEDOM | | | | | |
|---|---|---|---|---|---|---|---|
| | | 1 | 2 | 3 | 4 | 5 | 6 |
| 70 | .01 | 7.01 | 4.92 | 4.08 | 3.60 | 3.29 | 3.07 |
| | .05 | 3.98 | 3.13 | 2.74 | 2.50 | 2.35 | 2.23 |
| | .10 | 2.78 | 2.38 | 2.16 | 2.03 | 1.93 | 1.86 |
| 75 | .01 | 6.99 | 4.90 | 4.06 | 3.58 | 3.27 | 3.05 |
| | .05 | 3.97 | 3.12 | 2.73 | 2.49 | 2.34 | 2.22 |
| | .10 | 2.77 | 2.38 | 2.16 | 2.02 | 1.93 | 1.86 |
| 80 | .01 | 6.96 | 4.88 | 4.04 | 3.56 | 3.26 | 3.04 |
| | .05 | 3.96 | 3.11 | 2.72 | 2.49 | 2.33 | 2.22 |
| | .10 | 2.77 | 2.37 | 2.15 | 2.02 | 1.92 | 1.85 |
| 85 | .01 | 6.94 | 4.86 | 4.02 | 3.55 | 3.24 | 3.02 |
| | .05 | 3.95 | 3.10 | 2.71 | 2.48 | 2.32 | 2.21 |
| | .10 | 2.77 | 2.37 | 2.15 | 2.01 | 1.92 | 1.85 |
| 90 | .01 | 6.93 | 4.85 | 4.01 | 3.54 | 3.23 | 3.01 |
| | .05 | 3.95 | 3.10 | 2.71 | 2.47 | 2.32 | 2.20 |
| | .10 | 2.76 | 2.36 | 2.15 | 2.01 | 1.91 | 1.84 |

## r TO z' CONVERSION

| r | z' | r | z' | r | z' |
|---|---|---|---|---|---|
| 0.00 | 0.0000 | 0.10 | 0.1003 | 0.20 | 0.2027 |
| 0.01 | 0.0100 | 0.11 | 0.1104 | 0.21 | 0.2132 |
| 0.02 | 0.0200 | 0.12 | 0.1206 | 0.22 | 0.2237 |
| 0.03 | 0.0300 | 0.13 | 0.1307 | 0.23 | 0.2342 |
| 0.04 | 0.0400 | 0.14 | 0.1409 | 0.24 | 0.2448 |
| 0.05 | 0.0500 | 0.15 | 0.1511 | 0.25 | 0.2554 |
| 0.06 | 0.0601 | 0.16 | 0.1614 | 0.26 | 0.2661 |
| 0.07 | 0.0701 | 0.17 | 0.1717 | 0.27 | 0.2769 |
| 0.08 | 0.0802 | 0.18 | 0.1820 | 0.28 | 0.2877 |
| 0.09 | 0.0902 | 0.19 | 0.1923 | 0.29 | 0.2986 |

| r | z' | r | z' | r | z' |
|---|-----|---|-----|---|-----|
| 0.30 | 0.3095 | 0.54 | 0.6042 | 0.77 | 1.0203 |
| 0.31 | 0.3205 | 0.55 | 0.6184 | 0.78 | 1.0454 |
| 0.32 | 0.3316 | 0.56 | 0.6328 | 0.79 | 1.0714 |
| 0.33 | 0.3428 | 0.57 | 0.6475 | 0.80 | 1.0986 |
| 0.34 | 0.3541 | 0.58 | 0.6625 | 0.81 | 1.1270 |
| 0.35 | 0.3654 | 0.59 | 0.6777 | 0.82 | 1.1568 |
| 0.36 | 0.3769 | 0.60 | 0.6931 | 0.83 | 1.1881 |
| 0.37 | 0.3884 | 0.61 | 0.7089 | 0.84 | 1.2212 |
| 0.38 | 0.4001 | 0.62 | 0.7250 | 0.85 | 1.2562 |
| 0.39 | 0.4118 | 0.63 | 0.7414 | 0.86 | 1.2933 |
| 0.40 | 0.4236 | 0.64 | 0.7582 | 0.87 | 1.3331 |
| 0.41 | 0.4356 | 0.65 | 0.7753 | 0.88 | 1.3758 |
| 0.42 | 0.4477 | 0.66 | 0.7928 | 0.89 | 1.4219 |
| 0.43 | 0.4599 | 0.67 | 0.8107 | 0.90 | 1.4722 |
| 0.44 | 0.4722 | 0.68 | 0.8291 | 0.91 | 1.5275 |
| 0.45 | 0.4847 | 0.69 | 0.8480 | 0.92 | 1.5890 |
| 0.46 | 0.4973 | 0.70 | 0.8673 | 0.93 | 1.6584 |
| 0.47 | 0.5101 | 0.71 | 0.8872 | 0.94 | 1.7380 |
| 0.48 | 0.5230 | 0.72 | 0.9076 | 0.95 | 1.8318 |
| 0.49 | 0.5361 | 0.73 | 0.9287 | 0.96 | 1.9459 |
| 0.50 | 0.5493 | 0.74 | 0.9505 | 0.97 | 2.0923 |
| 0.51 | 0.5627 | 0.75 | 0.9730 | 0.98 | 2.2976 |
| 0.52 | 0.5763 | 0.76 | 0.9962 | 0.99 | 2.6467 |
| 0.53 | 0.5901 | | | | |

*Note:* This table is included for basic statistical reference. Its use is not discussed in detail in this book.

## CRITICAL VALUES OF r

This table assists null hypothesis significance testing for $r$. (To estimate the confidence interval around $r$, use the online tool at http://vassarstats.net/rho.html.) To use the table, first decide whether a one- or a two-tailed test is appropriate. Then decide the level of significance. Read down the corresponding column to the row associated with the number of degrees of freedom in the correlation (the number of pairs of scores minus 2). The table entry gives the value of $r$ that must be exceeded in order to be statistically significant. If the obtained $r$ is negative, use the absolute value of it. For example, if we do a two-tailed test with 40 degrees of freedom, our $r$ must be more extreme than .304 (or −.304) to be significant at the .05 level.

| | LEVEL OF SIGNIFICANCE FOR A ONE-TAILED TEST | | | | |
|---|---|---|---|---|---|
| | .10 | .05 | .025 | .01 | .0005 |
| | LEVEL OF SIGFINICANCE FOR A TWO-TAILED TEST | | | | |
| df | .20 | .10 | .05 | .02 | .001 |
| 1 | .951 | .988 | .997 | .9995 | .99999 |
| 2 | .800 | .900 | .950 | .980 | .999 |
| 3 | .687 | .805 | .878 | .934 | .991 |
| 4 | .608 | .729 | .811 | .882 | .974 |
| 5 | .551 | .669 | .755 | .833 | .951 |
| 6 | .507 | .621 | .707 | .789 | .925 |
| 7 | .472 | .582 | .666 | .750 | .898 |
| 8 | .443 | .549 | .632 | .715 | .872 |
| 9 | .419 | .521 | .602 | .685 | .847 |
| 10 | .398 | .497 | .576 | .658 | .823 |
| 11 | .380 | .476 | .553 | .634 | .801 |
| 12 | .365 | .457 | .532 | .612 | .780 |
| 13 | .351 | .441 | .514 | .592 | .760 |
| 14 | .338 | .426 | .497 | .574 | .742 |
| 15 | .327 | .412 | .482 | .558 | .725 |
| 16 | .317 | .400 | .468 | .542 | .708 |
| 17 | .308 | .389 | .456 | .529 | .693 |
| 18 | .299 | .378 | .444 | .515 | .679 |
| 19 | .291 | .369 | .433 | .503 | .665 |
| 20 | .284 | .360 | .423 | .492 | .652 |

| | LEVEL OF SIGNIFICANCE FOR A ONE-TAILED TEST | | | | |
|---|---|---|---|---|---|
| | .10 | .05 | .025 | .01 | .0005 |
| | LEVEL OF SIGFINICANCE FOR A TWO-TAILED TEST | | | | |
| df | .20 | .10 | .05 | .02 | .001 |
| 21 | .277 | .352 | .413 | .482 | .640 |
| 22 | .271 | .344 | .404 | .472 | .629 |
| 23 | .265 | .337 | .396 | .462 | .618 |
| 24 | .260 | .330 | .388 | .453 | .607 |
| 25 | .255 | .323 | .381 | .445 | .597 |
| 26 | .250 | .317 | .374 | .437 | .588 |
| 27 | .245 | .311 | .367 | .430 | .579 |
| 28 | .241 | .306 | .361 | .423 | .570 |
| 29 | .237 | .301 | .355 | .416 | .562 |
| 30 | .233 | .296 | .349 | .409 | .554 |
| 40 | .202 | .257 | .304 | .358 | .490 |
| 60 | .165 | .211 | .250 | .295 | .408 |
| 120 | .117 | .150 | .178 | .210 | .294 |
| 500 | .057 | .073 | .087 | .103 | .146 |

*Note:* This table is included for basic statistical reference. Its use is not discussed in detail in this book.

# Glossary

## A

**acquiescence** Answering "yes" or "strongly agree" to every item in a survey or interview. Also called *yea-saying*.

**alpha level** The value, determined in advance, at which researchers decide whether the *p* value obtained from a sample statistic is low enough to reject the null hypothesis or too high, and thus retain the null hypothesis.

**anonymous study** A research study in which identifying information is not collected, thereby completely protecting the identity of participants. *See also* confidential study.

**applied research** Research whose goal is to find a solution to a particular real-world problem. *See also* basic research, translational research.

**association claim** A claim about two variables, in which the value (level) of one variable is said to vary systematically with the value of another variable.

**attrition threat** In a pretest/posttest, repeated-measures, or quasi-experimental study, a threat to internal validity that occurs when a systematic type of participant drops out of the study before it ends.

**autocorrelation** In a longitudinal design, the correlation of one variable with itself, measured at two different times.

**availability heuristic** A bias in intuition, in which people incorrectly estimate the frequency of something, relying predominantly on instances that easily come to mind rather than using all possible evidence in evaluating a conclusion.

**average inter-item correlation** A measure of internal reliability for a set of items; it is the mean of all possible correlations computed between each item and the others.

## B

**basic research** Research whose goal is to enhance the general body of knowledge, without regard for direct application to practical problems. *See also* applied research, translational research.

**beneficence** *See* principle of beneficence.

**bias blind spot** The tendency for people to think that compared to others, they themselves are less likely to engage in biased reasoning.

**biased sample** A sample in which some members of the population of interest are systematically left out, and therefore the results cannot generalize to the population of interest. Also called *unrepresentative sample*. *See also* unbiased sample.

**bimodal** Having two modes, or most common scores.

**bivariate correlation** An association that involves exactly two variables. Also called *bivariate association*.

**box plot** A data visualization technique that depicts a sample's median, interquartile range (25th and 75th percentiles), and outliers.

## C

**carryover effect** A type of order effect, in which some form of contamination carries over from one condition to the next.

**categorical variable** A variable whose levels are categories (e.g., male and female). Also called *nominal variable*.

**causal claim** A claim arguing that a specific change in one variable is responsible for influencing the value of another variable.

**ceiling effect** An experimental design problem in which independent variable groups score almost the same on a dependent variable, such that all scores fall at the high end of their possible distribution. *See also* floor effect.

**cell** A condition in an experiment; in a simple experiment, a cell can represent the level of one independent variable; in a factorial design, a cell represents one of the possible combinations of two independent variables.

**census** A set of observations that contains all members of the population of interest.

**central tendency** A value that the individual scores in a data set tend to center on. *See also* mean, median, mode.

**claim** The argument a journalist, researcher, or scientist is trying to make.

**cluster sampling** A probability sampling technique in which clusters of participants within the population of interest are selected at random, followed by data collection from all individuals in each cluster.

**Cohen's *d*** A measure of effect size indicating how far apart two group means are, in standard deviation units.

**communality** One of Merton's four scientific norms, stating that scientific knowledge is created by a community, and its findings belong to the community. *See also* universalism, disinterestedness, organized skepticism.

**comparison group** A group in an experiment whose levels on the independent variable differ from those of the treatment group in some intended and meaningful way. Also called *comparison condition*.

**conceptual definition** A researcher's definition of a variable at the theoretical level. Also called *construct*. *See also* conceptual variable.

**conceptual replication** A replication study in which researchers examine the same research question (the same conceptual variables) but use different procedures for operationalizing the variables. *See also* direct replication, replication-plus-extension.

**conceptual variable** A variable of interest, stated at an abstract, or conversational, level. Also called *construct*. *See also* conceptual definition.

**concurrent-measures design** An experiment using a within-groups design in which participants are exposed to all the levels of an independent variable at roughly the same time, and a single attitudinal or behavioral preference is the dependent variable.

**condition** One of the levels of the independent variable in an experiment.

**confederate** An actor who is directed by the researcher to play a specific role in a research study.

**confidence interval (CI)** A given range indicated by a lower and upper value that is designed to capture the population value for some point estimate (e.g., percentage, difference, or correlation); a high proportion of CIs will capture the true population value.

**confidential study** A research study in which identifying information is collected, but protected from disclosure to people other than the researchers. *See also* anonymous study.

**confirmation bias** The tendency to consider only the evidence that supports a hypothesis, including asking only the questions that will lead to the expected answer.

**confound** A general term for a potential alternative explanation for a research finding; a threat to internal validity.

**constant** An attribute that could potentially vary but that has only one level in the study in question.

**construct** A variable of interest, stated at an abstract level, usually defined as part of a formal statement of a psychological theory. *See also* conceptual variable.

**construct validity** An indication of how well a variable was measured or manipulated in a study.

**content validity** The extent to which a measure captures all parts of a defined construct.

**control for** Holding a potential third variable at a constant level (statistically or experimentally) while investigating the association between two other variables. *See also* control variable, multiple regression.

**control group** A level of an independent variable that is intended to represent "no treatment" or a neutral condition. Also called *control condition*.

**control variable** In an experiment, a variable that a researcher holds constant on purpose.

**convenience sampling** Choosing a sample based on those who are easiest to access and readily available; a biased sampling technique.

**convergent validity** An empirical test of the extent to which a self-report measure correlates with other measures of a theoretically similar construct. *See also* discriminant validity.

**correlate** To occur or vary together (covary) systematically, as in the case of two variables. *See also* correlational study, covariance.

**correlation coefficient *r*** A single number, ranging from –1.0 to 1.0, that indicates the strength and direction of an association between two variables.

**correlational study** A study that includes two or more variables, in which all of the variables are measured; can support an association claim.

**counterbalancing** In a repeated-measures experiment, presenting the levels of the independent variable to participants in different sequences to control for order effects. *See also* full counterbalancing, partial counterbalancing.

**covariance** The degree to which two variables go together. Also one of three criteria for establishing a causal claim, which states that, in a study's results, the proposed causal variable must vary systematically with changes in the proposed outcome variable. *See also* internal validity, temporal precedence.

**criterion validity** An empirical form of measurement validity that establishes the extent to which a measure is associated with a behavioral outcome with which it should be associated.

**criterion variable** The variable in a multiple-regression analysis that the researchers are most interested in understanding or predicting. Also called *dependent variable*.

**critical value** A value of a statistic that is associated with a desired alpha level.

**Cronbach's alpha** A correlation-based statistic that measures a scale's internal reliability. Also called *coefficient alpha*.

**cross-lag correlation** In a longitudinal design, a correlation between an earlier measure of one variable and a later measure of another variable.

**cross-sectional correlation** In a longitudinal design, a correlation between two variables that are measured at the same time.

**cultural psychology** A subdiscipline of psychology concerned with how cultural settings shape a person's thoughts, feelings, and behavior, and how these in turn shape cultural settings.

**curvilinear association** An association between two variables which is not a straight line; instead, as one variable increases, the level of the other variable increases and then decreases (or vice versa). *See also* positive association, negative association, zero association.

## D

**data** (plural; singular **datum**) A set of observations representing the values of some variable, collected from one or more research studies.

**data fabrication** A form of research misconduct in which a researcher invents data that fit the hypothesis.

**data falsification** A form of research misconduct in which a researcher influences a study's results, perhaps by deleting observations from a data set or by influencing participants to act in the hypothesized way.

**data matrix** A grid presenting collected data.

**debrief** To inform participants afterward about a study's true nature, details, and hypotheses.

**deception** The withholding of some details of a study from participants (deception through omission) or the act of actively lying to them (deception through commission).

**demand characteristic** A cue that leads participants to guess a study's hypotheses or goals; a threat to internal validity. Also called *experimental demand*.

**dependent samples design** A design in which each person has two scores because they were tested under two conditions, and we are interested in the difference between them. Also called a *paired design*.

**dependent variable** In an experiment, the variable that is measured. In a multiple-regression analysis, the single outcome, or criterion variable the researchers are most interested in understanding or predicting. Also called *outcome variable*. *See also* independent variable.

**descriptive statistics** A set of statistics used to organize and summarize the properties of a set of data.

**design confound** A threat to internal validity in an experiment in which a second variable happens to vary systematically along with the independent variable and therefore is an alternative explanation for the results.

**direct replication** A replication study in which researchers repeat the original study as closely as possible to see whether the original effect shows up in the newly collected data. *See also* conceptual replication, replication-plus-extension.

**directionality problem** In a correlational study, the occurrence of both variables being measured around the same time, making it unclear which variable in the association came first. *See also* temporal precedence.

**discriminant validity** An empirical test of the extent to which a self-report measure does not correlate strongly with measures of theoretically dissimilar constructs. Also called *divergent validity*. *See also* convergent validity.

**disinformation** A news story, photo, or video deliberately created to be false or misleading.

**disinterestedness** One of Merton's four scientific norms, stating that scientists strive to discover the truth whatever it is; they are not swayed by conviction, idealism, politics, or profit. *See also* universalism, communality, organized skepticism.

**dot plot** A data visualization technique in which every data point for a given variable is represented.

**double-barreled question** A type of question in a survey or poll that is problematic because it asks two questions in one, thereby weakening its construct validity.

**double-blind placebo control study** A study that uses a treatment group and a placebo group and in which neither the researchers nor the participants know who is in which group.

**double-blind study** A study in which neither the participants nor the researchers who evaluate them know who is in the treatment group and who is in the comparison group.

## E

**ecological validity** The extent to which the tasks and manipulations of a study are similar to real-world contexts; an aspect of external validity. Also called *mundane realism*.

**effect size** The magnitude, or strength, of a relationship between two or more variables.

**empirical journal article** A scholarly article that reports for the first time the results of a research study.

**empiricism** The use of verifiable evidence as the basis for conclusions; collecting data systematically and using it to develop, support, or challenge a theory. Also called *empirical method, empirical research*.

**evidence-based treatment** A psychotherapy technique whose effectiveness has been supported by empirical research.

**experiment**  A study in which at least one variable is manipulated and another is measured.

**experimental realism**  The extent to which a laboratory experiment is designed so that participants experience authentic emotions, motivations, and behaviors.

**external validity**  An indication of how well the results of a study generalize to, or represent, individuals or contexts besides those in the study itself. *See also* generalizability.

## F

**face validity**  The extent to which a measure is subjectively considered a plausible operationalization of the conceptual variable in question.

**factorial design**  A study in which there are two or more independent variables, or factors.

**faking bad**  Giving answers on a survey (or other self-report measure) that make one look worse than one really is.

**faking good**  *See* socially desirable responding.

**falsifiable**  A feature of a scientific theory, in which it is possible to collect data that will indicate that the theory is wrong.

**fence sitting**  Playing it safe by answering in the middle of the scale for every question in a survey or interview.

**field setting**  A real-world setting for a research study.

**file drawer problem**  A problem relating to literature reviews and meta-analyses based only on published literature, which might overestimate the support for a theory because studies finding null effects are less likely to be published than studies finding significant results, and are thus less likely to be included in such reviews.

**floor effect**  An experimental design problem in which independent variable groups score almost the same on a dependent variable, such that all scores fall at the low end of their possible distribution. *See also* ceiling effect.

**forced-choice question**  A survey question format in which respondents give their opinion by picking the best of two or more options.

**frequency claim**  A claim that describes a particular rate or degree of a single variable.

**frequency distribution**  A table showing how many of the cases in a batch of data scored each possible value, or range of values, on the variable.

**frequency histogram**  A data visualization technique showing how many of the cases in a batch of data scored each possible value, or range of values, on the variable.

***F* test**  A statistical test based on analysis of variance that determines the degree of difference among two or more group means.

**full counterbalancing**  A method of counterbalancing in which all possible condition orders are represented. *See also* counterbalancing, partial counterbalancing.

## G

**generalizability**  The extent to which the subjects in a study represent the populations they are intended to represent; how well the settings in a study represent other settings or contexts.

**generalization mode**  The intent of researchers to generalize the findings from the samples and procedures in their study to other populations or contexts. *See also* theory-testing mode.

## H

**HARKing (hypothesizing after the results are known)**  A questionable research practice in which researchers create an after-the-fact hypothesis about an unexpected research result, making it appear as if they predicted it all along.

**history threat**  A threat to internal validity that occurs when it is unclear whether a change in the treatment group is caused by the treatment itself or by an external or historical factor that affects most members of the group.

**hypothesis**  A statement of the specific result the researcher expects to observe from a particular study, if the theory is accurate. Also called *prediction*.

## I

**independent-groups design**  An experimental design in which different groups of participants are exposed to different levels of the independent variable, such that each participant experiences only one level of the independent variable. Also called *between-subjects design*, *between-groups design*.

**independent variable**  In an experiment, a variable that is manipulated. In a multiple-regression analysis, a predictor variable used to explain variance in the criterion variable. *See also* dependent variable.

**inferential statistics**  A set of techniques that uses the laws of chance and probability to help researchers make decisions about what their data mean and what inferences they can make from them.

**informed consent**  The right of research participants to learn about a research project, know its risks and benefits, and decide whether to participate.

**institutional review board (IRB)**  A committee responsible for ensuring that research using human participants is conducted ethically.

**instrumentation threat**  A threat to internal validity that occurs when a measuring instrument changes over time.

**interaction effect**  A result from a factorial design, in which the difference in the levels of one independent variable changes, depending on the level of the other independent variable; a difference in differences. Also called *interaction*.

**internal reliability** In a measure that contains several items, the consistency in a pattern of answers, no matter how a question is phrased. Also called *internal consistency*.

**internal validity** One of three criteria for establishing a causal claim; a study's ability to rule out alternative explanations for a causal relationship between two variables. Also called *third-variable criterion*. *See also* covariance, temporal precedence.

**interrater reliability** The degree to which two or more coders or observers give consistent ratings of a set of targets.

**interrupted time-series design** A quasi-experiment in which participants are measured repeatedly on a dependent variable before, during, and after the "interruption" caused by some event.

**interval scale** A quantitative measurement scale that has no "true zero," and in which the numerals represent equal intervals (distances) between levels (e.g., temperature in degrees). *See also* ordinal scale, ratio scale.

**J**

**journal** A monthly or quarterly periodical containing peer-reviewed articles on a specific academic discipline or subdiscipline, written for a scholarly audience. Also called *scientific journal*.

**journalism** News and commentary published or broadcast in the popular media and produced for a general audience.

**justice** *See* principle of justice.

**K**

**known-groups paradigm** A method for establishing criterion validity, in which a researcher tests two or more groups who are known to differ on the variable of interest, to ensure that they score differently on a measure of that variable.

**L**

**Latin square** A formal system of partial counterbalancing to ensure that every condition in a within-groups design appears in each position at least once.

**leading question** A type of question in a survey or poll that is problematic because its wording encourages one response more than others, thereby weakening its construct validity.

**level** One of the possible variations, or values, of a variable. Also called *condition*.

**Likert scale** A survey question format using a rating scale containing multiple response options anchored by the specific terms *strongly agree, agree, neither agree nor disagree, disagree,* and *strongly disagree*. A scale that does not follow this format exactly is called a *Likert-type scale*.

**longitudinal design** A study in which the same variables are measured in the same people at different points in time.

**M**

**main effect** In a factorial design, the overall effect of one independent variable on the dependent variable, averaging over the levels of the other independent variable.

**manipulated variable** A variable in an experiment that a researcher controls, such as by assigning participants to its different levels (values). *See also* measured variable.

**manipulation check** In an experiment, an extra dependent variable researchers can include to determine how well a manipulation worked.

**margin of error of the estimate** In the context of a percentage estimate, an inferential statistic providing a range of values that has a high probability of containing the true population value. *See also* confidence interval.

**marginal means** In a factorial design, the arithmetic means for each level of an independent variable, averaging over the levels of another independent variable.

**masked design** A study design in which the observers are unaware of the experimental conditions to which participants have been assigned. Also called *blind design*.

**matched groups** An experimental design technique in which participants who are similar on some measured variable are grouped into sets; the members of each matched set are then randomly assigned to different experimental conditions. Also called *matching*.

**maturation threat** A threat to internal validity that occurs when an observed change in an experimental group could have emerged more or less spontaneously over time.

**mean** An arithmethic average; a measure of central tendency computed from the sum of all the scores in a set of data, divided by the total number of scores.

**measured variable** A variable in a study whose levels (values) are observed and recorded. *See also* manipulated variable.

**measurement error** The degree to which the recorded measure for a participant on some variable differs from the true value of the variable for that participant. Measurement errors may be random, such that scores that are too high and too low cancel each other out; or they may be systematic, such that most scores are biased too high or too low.

**median** A measure of central tendency that is the value at the middlemost score of a distribution of scores, dividing the frequency distribution into halves.

**mediator** A variable that helps explain the relationship between two other variables. Also called *mediating variable*.

**meta-analysis** A way of mathematically averaging the effect sizes of all the studies that have tested the same variables to see what conclusion that whole body of evidence supports.

**mode** A measure of central tendency that is the most common score in a set of data.

**moderator** A variable that, depending on its level, changes the relationship between two other variables.

**multimodal** Having two or more modes, or most common scores.

**multiple-baseline design** A small-*N* design in which researchers stagger their introduction of an intervention across a variety of contexts, times, or situations.

**multiple regression** A statistical technique that computes the relationship between a predictor variable and a criterion variable, controlling for other predictor variables. Also called *multivariate regression*.

**multistage sampling** A probability sampling technique involving at least two stages: a random sample of clusters followed by a random sample of people within the selected clusters.

**multivariate design** A study designed to test an association involving more than two measured variables.

## N

**negative association** An association in which high levels of one variable go with low levels of the other variable, and vice versa. Also called *inverse association, negative correlation. See also* curvilinear association, positive association, zero association.

**negatively worded question** A question in a survey or poll that contains negatively phrased statements, making its wording complicated or confusing and potentially weakening its construct validity.

**noise** Unsystematic variability among the members of a group in an experiment, which might be caused by situation noise, individual differences, or measurement error. Also called *error variance, unsystematic variance*.

**nonequivalent control group design** A quasi-experiment that has at least one treatment group and one comparison group, but participants have not been randomly assigned to the two groups.

**nonequivalent control group interrupted time-series design** A quasi-experiment with two or more groups in which participants have not been randomly assigned to groups; participants are measured repeatedly on a dependent variable before, during, and after the "interruption" caused by some event, and the presence or timing of the interrupting event differs among the groups.

**nonequivalent control group pretest/posttest design** A quasi-experiment that has at least one treatment group and one comparison group, in which participants have not been randomly assigned to the two groups, and in which at least one pretest and one posttest are administered.

**nonprobability sampling** A category name for nonrandom sampling techniques, such as convenience, purposive, and quota sampling, that result in a biased sample. *See also* biased sample, probability sampling.

**not statistically significant** In NHST, the conclusion assigned when $p > .05$; that is, when it is likely the result came from the null-hypothesis population.

**null effect** A finding that an independent variable did not make a difference in the dependent variable; there is no significant covariance between the two. Also called *null result*.

**null hypothesis** In a common form of statistical hypothesis testing, the assumption that there is no difference, no relationship, or no effect in a population.

**null hypothesis significance testing (NHST)** An inferential statistical technique in which a result is compared to a hypothetical population in which there is no relationship or no difference.

## O

**observational measure** A method of measuring a variable by recording observable behaviors or physical traces of behaviors. Also called *behavioral measure*.

**observational research** The process of watching people or animals and systematically recording how they behave or what they are doing.

**observer bias** A bias that occurs when observer expectations influence the interpretation of participant behaviors or the outcome of the study.

**observer effect** A change in behavior of study participants in the direction of observer expectations. Also called *expectancy effect*.

**one-group, pretest/posttest design** An experiment in which a researcher recruits one group of participants; measures them on a pretest; exposes them to a treatment, intervention, or change; and then measures them on a posttest.

**open access** Term referring to a peer-reviewed academic journal that anyone, even the general public, can read without paying for access.

**open data** When psychologists provide their full data set on the Internet so other researchers can reproduce the statistical results or even conduct new analyses on it.

**open-ended question** A survey question format that allows respondents to answer any way they like.

**open materials** When psychologists provide their study's full set of measures and manipulations on the Internet so others can see the full design or conduct replication studies.

**open science** The practice of sharing one's data, hypotheses, and materials freely so others can collaborate, use, and verify the results.

**operational definition** The specific way in which a concept of interest is measured or manipulated as a variable in a study. Also called *operationalization, operational variable.*

**operational variable** *See* operational definition.

**operationalize** To turn a conceptual definition of a variable into a specific measured variable or manipulated variable in order to conduct a research study.

**order effect** In a within-groups design, a threat to internal validity in which exposure to one condition changes participant responses to a later condition. *See also* carryover effect, practice effect, testing threat.

**ordinal scale** A quantitative measurement scale whose levels represent a ranked order, and in which distances between levels are not equal (e.g., order of finishers in a race). *See also* interval scale, ratio scale.

**organized skepticism** One of Merton's four scientific norms, stating that scientists question everything, including their own theories, widely accepted ideas, and "ancient wisdom." *See also* universalism, communality, disinterestedness.

**outlier** A score that stands out as either much higher or much lower than most of the other scores in a sample.

**oversampling** A form of probability sampling; a variation of stratified random sampling in which the researcher intentionally overrepresents one or more groups.

**P**

**parsimony** The degree to which a theory provides the simplest explanation of some phenomenon. In the context of investigating a claim, the simplest explanation of a pattern of data; the best explanation that requires making the fewest exceptions or qualifications.

**partial counterbalancing** A method of counterbalancing in which some, but not all, of the possible condition orders are represented. *See also* counterbalancing, full counterbalancing.

**participant variable** A variable such as age, gender, or ethnicity whose levels are selected (i.e., measured), not manipulated.

**paywalled** Term referring to a peer-reviewed academic journal that the general public must pay to access; only people who are members of subscribing institutions can access the content.

***p*-hacking** A family of questionable data analysis techniques, such as adding participants after the results are initially analyzed, looking for outliers, or trying new analyses in order to obtain a *p* value of just under .05, which can lead to nonreplicable results.

**physiological measure** A method of measuring a variable by recording biological data.

**pilot study** A study completed before (or sometimes after) the study of primary interest, usually to test the effectiveness or characteristics of the manipulations.

**placebo effect** A response or effect that occurs when people receiving an experimental treatment experience a change only because they believe they are receiving a valid treatment.

**placebo group** A control group in an experiment that is exposed to an inert treatment, such as a sugar pill. Also called *placebo control group.*

**plagiarism** Representing the ideas or words of others as one's own; a form of research misconduct.

**point estimate** A single estimate of some population value (such as a percentage, a correlation, or a difference) based on data from a sample.

**poll** A method of posing questions to people on the telephone, in personal interviews, on written questionnaires, or via the Internet. Also called *survey.*

**population** A larger group from which a sample is drawn; the group to which a study's conclusions are intended to be applied. Also called *population of interest.*

**positive association** An association in which high levels of one variable go with high levels of the other variable, and low levels of one variable go with low levels of the other variable. Also called *positive correlation. See also* curvilinear association, negative association, zero association.

**posttest-only design** An experiment using an independent-groups design in which participants are tested on the dependent variable only once. Also called *equivalent groups, posttest-only design.*

**power** The likelihood that a study will show a statistically significant result when an independent variable truly has an effect in the population; the probability of not making a Type II error.

**practice effect** A type of order effect in which participants' performance improves over time because they become practiced at the dependent measure (not because of the manipulation or treatment). Also called *fatigue effect. See also* order effect, testing threat.

**predictor variable** A variable in multiple-regression analysis that is used to explain variance in the criterion variable. Also called *independent variable.*

**preregistered** A term referring to a study in which, before collecting any data, the researcher has stated publicly what the study's outcome is expected to be.

**present/present bias** A bias in intuition, in which people incorrectly estimate the relationship between an event and its outcome, focusing on times the event and outcome are present, while failing to consider evidence that is absent and harder to notice.

**pretest/posttest design** An experiment using an independent-groups design in which participants are tested on the key dependent variable twice: once before and once after exposure to the independent variable.

**principle of beneficence** An ethical principle from the Belmont Report stating that researchers must take precautions to protect participants from harm and to promote their well-being. *See also* principle of justice, principle of respect for persons.

**principle of justice** An ethical principle from the Belmont Report calling for a fair balance between the kinds of people who participate in research and the kinds of people who benefit from it. *See also* principle of beneficence, principle of respect for persons.

**principle of respect for persons** An ethical principle from the Belmont Report stating that research participants should be treated as autonomous agents and that certain groups deserve special protection. *See also* principle of beneficence, principle of justice.

**probabilistic** Describing the empirical method, stating that science is intended to explain a certain proportion (but not necessarily all) of the possible cases.

**probability sampling** A category name for random sampling techniques, such as simple random sampling, stratified random sampling, and cluster sampling, in which a sample is drawn from a population of interest so each member has an equal and known chance of being included in the sample. Also called *random sampling*. *See also* nonprobability sampling, unbiased sample.

**purposive sampling** A biased sampling technique in which only certain kinds of people are included in a sample.

***p* value** In NHST, the probability of getting the result in a sample or one more extreme, by chance, if there is no relationship or difference in the population.

## Q

**quantitative variable** A variable whose values can be recorded as meaningful numbers.

**quasi-experiment** A study similar to an experiment except that the researchers do not have full experimental control (e.g., they may not be able to randomly assign participants to the independent variable conditions).

**quasi-independent variable** A variable that resembles an independent variable, but the researcher does not have true control over it (e.g., cannot randomly assign participants to its levels or cannot control its timing). *See also* independent variable.

**quota sampling** A biased sampling technique in which a researcher identifies subsets of the population of interest, sets a target number for each category in the sample, and nonrandomly selects individuals within each category until the quotas are filled.

## R

***r*** *See* correlation coefficient.

**random assignment** The use of a random method (e.g., flipping a coin) to assign participants into different experimental groups.

**ratio scale** A quantitative measurement scale in which the numerals have equal intervals and the value of zero truly means "none" of the variable being measured. *See also* interval scale, ordinal scale.

**reactivity** A change in behavior of study participants (such as acting less spontaneously) because they are aware they are being watched.

**regression threat** A threat to internal validity related to regression to the mean, a phenomenon in which any extreme finding is likely to be closer to its own typical, or mean, level the next time it is measured (with or without the experimental treatment or intervention). *See also* regression to the mean.

**regression to the mean** A phenomenon in which an extreme finding is likely to be closer to its own typical, or mean, level the next time it is measured, because the same combination of chance factors that made the finding extreme are not present the second time. *See also* regression threat.

**reliability** The consistency of the results of a measure.

**repeated-measures design** An experiment using a within-groups design in which participants respond to a dependent variable more than once, after exposure to each level of the independent variable.

**replicable** Describing a study whose results have been reproduced when the study was repeated, or replicated. Also called *reproducible*. *See also* conceptual replication, direct replication, replication-plus-extension.

**replication** The process of conducting a study again to test whether the result is consistent.

**replication-plus-extension** A replication study in which researchers replicate their original study but add variables or conditions that test additional questions. *See also* conceptual replication, direct replication.

**representative sample** A sample in which all members of the population of interest are equally likely to be included (usually through some random method), and therefore the results can generalize to the population of interest. Also called *unbiased sample*.

**respect for persons** *See* principle of respect for persons.

**response set** A shortcut respondents may use to answer items in a long survey, rather than responding to the content of each item. Also called *nondifferentiation*.

**restriction of range** In a bivariate correlation, the absence of a full range of possible scores on one of the variables, so the relationship from the sample underestimates the true correlation.

**reversal design** A small-*N* design in which a researcher observes a problem behavior both before and during treatment, and then discontinues the treatment for a while to see if the problem behavior returns.

**review journal article** An article summarizing all the studies that have been published in one research area.

# S

**sample** The group of people, animals, or cases used in a study; a subset of the population of interest.

**sampling distribution** A theoretical prediction about the kinds of statistical outcomes likely to be obtained if a study is run many times and the null hypothesis is true.

**scatterplot** A graphical representation of an association, in which each dot represents one participant in the study measured on two variables.

**scientific literature** A series of related studies, conducted by various researchers, that have tested similar variables. Also called *literature*.

**selection-attrition threat** A threat to internal validity in which participants are likely to drop out of either the treatment group or the comparison group, not both.

**selection effect** A threat to internal validity that occurs in an independent-groups design when the kinds of participants at one level of the independent variable are systematically different from those at the other level.

**selection-history threat** A threat to internal validity in which a historical or seasonal event systematically affects only the participants in the treatment group or only those in the comparison group, not both.

**self-correcting** A process in which scientists make their research available for peer review, replication, and critique, with the goal of identifying and correcting errors in the research.

**self-plagiarism** A potentially unethical practice in which researchers recycle their own previously published text, verbatim and without attribution, in a subsequent article.

**self-report measure** A method of measuring a variable in which people answer questions about themselves in a questionnaire or interview.

**self-selection** A form of sampling bias that occurs when a sample contains only people who volunteer to participate.

**semantic differential format** A survey question format using a response scale whose numbers are anchored with contrasting adjectives.

**simple random sampling** The most basic form of probability sampling, in which the sample is chosen completely at random from the population of interest (e.g., drawing names out of a hat).

**single-*N* design** A study in which researchers gather information from only one animal or one person.

**situation noise** Unrelated events or distractions in the external environment that create unsystematic variability within groups in an experiment.

**slope direction** The upward, downward, or neutral slope of the cluster of data points in a scatterplot.

**small-*N* design** A study in which researchers gather information from just a few cases.

**snowball sampling** A variation on purposive sampling, a biased sampling technique in which participants are asked to recommend acquaintances for the study.

**socially desirable responding** Giving answers on a survey (or other self-report measure) that make one look better than one really is. Also called *faking good*.

**spurious association** A bivariate association that is attributable only to systematic mean differences on subgroups within the sample; the original association is not present within the subgroups.

**stable-baseline design** A small-*N* design in which a researcher observes behavior for an extended baseline period before beginning a treatment or other intervention, and continues observing behavior after the intervention.

**standard deviation** A computation that captures how far, on average, each score in a data set is from the mean.

**standard error** The typical, or average, error researchers make when estimating a population value.

**statistically significant** In NHST, the conclusion assigned when when $p < .05$; that is, when it is unlikely the result came from the null-hypothesis population.

**statistical validity** The extent to which statistical conclusions derived from a study are accurate and reasonable. Also called *statistical conclusion validity*.

**stemplot** A graphical representation of the values obtained on some variable in a sample of data. Also called *stem-and-leaf plot*.

**stratified random sampling** A form of probability sampling; a random sampling technique in which the researcher identifies particular demographic categories, or strata, and then randomly selects individuals within each category.

**strength** A description of an association indicating how closely the data points in a scatterplot cluster along a line of best fit drawn through them.

**survey** A method of posing questions to people on the telephone, in personal interviews, on written questionnaires, or via the Internet. Also called *poll*.

**systematic sampling** A probability sampling technique in which the researcher uses a randomly chosen number *N*, and counts off every $N$th member of a population to achieve a sample.

**systematic variability** In an experiment, a description of when the levels of a variable coincide in some predictable way with experimental group membership, creating a potential confound. *See also* unsystematic variability.

## T

**temporal precedence** One of three criteria for establishing a causal claim, stating that the proposed causal variable comes first in time, before the proposed outcome variable. *See also* covariance, internal validity.

**testing threat** In a repeated-measures experiment or quasi-experiment, a kind of order effect in which scores change over time just because participants have taken the test more than once; includes practice effects.

**test-retest reliability** The consistency in results every time a measure is used.

**theory** A statement or set of statements that describes general principles about how variables relate to one another.

**theory-testing mode** A researcher's intent for a study, testing association claims or causal claims to investigate support for a theory. *See also* generalization mode.

**third-variable problem** In a correlational study, the existence of a plausible alternative explanation for the association between two variables. *See also* internal validity.

**translational research** Research that uses knowledge derived from basic research to develop and test solutions to real-world problems. *See also* applied research, basic research.

**treatment group** The participants in an experiment who are exposed to the level of the independent variable that involves a medication, therapy, or intervention.

**$t$ test** A statistical test used to evaluate the size and significance of the difference between two means.

**Type I error** A "false positive" result in the statistical inference process, in which researchers conclude that there is an effect in a population, when there really is none.

**Type II error** A "miss" in the statistical inference process, in which researchers conclude that their study has not detected an effect in a population, when there really is one.

## U

**unbiased sample** A sample in which all members of the population of interest are equally likely to be included (usually through some random method), and therefore the results can generalize to the population of interest. Also called *representative sample*. *See also* biased sample.

**universalism** One of Merton's four scientific norms, stating that scientific claims are evaluated according to their merit, independent of the researcher's credentials or reputation. The same preestablished criteria apply to all scientists and all research. *See also* communality, disinterestedness, organized skepticism.

**unobtrusive observation** An observation in a study made indirectly, through physical traces of behavior, or made by someone who is hidden or is posing as a bystander.

**unsystematic variability** In an experiment, a description of when the levels of a variable fluctuate independently of experimental group membership, contributing to variability within groups. *See also* systematic variability.

## V

**validity** The appropriateness of a conclusion or decision. *See also* construct validity, external validity, internal validity, statistical validity.

**variable** An attribute that varies, having at least two levels, or values. *See also* dependent variable, independent variable, manipulated variable, measured variable.

**variance** A computation that quantifies how spread out the scores of a sample are around their mean; it is the square of the standard deviation.

## W

**wait-list design** An experimental design for studying a therapeutic treatment, in which researchers randomly assign some participants to receive the therapy under investigation immediately, and others to receive it after a time delay.

**weight of the evidence** A conclusion drawn from reviewing scientific literature and considering the proportion of studies that is consistent with a theory.

**within-groups design** An experimental design in which each participant is presented with all levels of the independent variable. Also called *within-subjects design*.

## Z

**zero association** A lack of systematic association between two variables. Also called *zero correlation*. *See also* curvilinear association, positive association, negative association.

**$z$ score** A computation that describes how far an individual score is above or below the mean, in standard deviation units. Also called *standardized score*.

# Answers to End-of-Chapter Questions

## Review Questions

### Chapter 1
1. b
2. a
3. d
4. b
5. d

### Chapter 2
1. a
2. c
3. b
4. b
5. a
6. a

### Chapter 3
1. c, e
2. c
3. b
4. a
5. a
6. c
7. a

### Chapter 4
1. d
2. c
3. d
4. b
5. a
6. c

### Chapter 5
1. a. Quantitative, ratio
   b. Quantitative, ratio
   c. Quantitative, ordinal
   d. Categorical
   e. Categorical
   f. Quantitative, interval
2. b
3. a. Test-retest reliability
   b. Interrater reliability
   c. Internal reliability
4. a. Criterion validity
   b. Convergent and discriminant validity
   c. Face validity
   d. Content validity

### Chapter 6
1. c
2. d
3. b, c
4. b
5. c
6. a

### Chapter 7
1. d
2. c
3. c
4. a

### Chapter 8
1. b
2. c
3. d
4. d
5. a

### Chapter 9
1. a
2. a
3. b
4. c
5. c
6. b
7. b
8. a

### Chapter 10
1. b
2. d
3. a
4. b
5. b

### Chapter 11
1. a
2. d
3. b
4. a
5. a
6. d

### Chapter 12
1. c
2. c
3. d
4. a
5. a
6. b

### Chapter 13
1. a
2. c
3. d
4. a
5. a
6. b
7. c

### Chapter 14
1. a
2. c
3. c
4. a
5. c
6. c

# Guidelines for Selected Learning Actively Exercises

## Chapter 1

Answers will vary.

## Chapter 2

1. Example A.

   a. How upset does the dog get when we don't use the thunder blanket?

   b.

   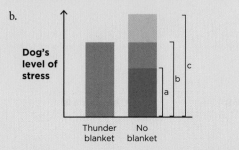

   c. Perhaps the dog is doing better with the thunder blanket because when she's using it, the fireworks happen to be less severe. The lower severity of the sound, not the thunder blanket, is responsible for the dog's reaction. Or perhaps the dog is doing better with the thunder blanket because the owners are also paying extra attention to her when they use it. The attention, not the thunder blanket, is responsible for the dog's increased calmness.

   Example C.

   a. Would your GRE score have improved without the course? (No course is the comparison group.)

   b.

   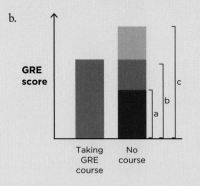

   c. What might be confounded with taking a GRE course? Perhaps the math and science courses you were enrolled in at the same time were helping to improve your scores. Or perhaps you were simply more motivated to do well on the test the second time.

2. a. This statement reflects the availability heuristic. The speaker bases the conclusion on evidence that comes easily to mind (what they see the cousin eating).

   b. The conclusion the speaker is talking about seems to be supported by empirical evidence, so this is a good source of evidence. You might also want to ask whether the newspaper source reported the research findings accurately.

   c. This statement reflects confirmation bias: While watching the debate, the speaker was more motivated to notice the preferred candidate's successes and to ignore the candidate's lapses.

   d. This speaker is relying on authority; in this case, information from marketing and advertising. She should ask: How good is the science on which this advertisement's conclusions are based, and is the ad reporting the science accurately?

   e. This statement reflects intuitive reasoning, namely the availability heuristic (students who are drinking are more visible than those who are in their rooms, at work, or at the movies) or the present-present bias (it's easier to notice the students who are drinking and more difficult to factor in the many students on campus who are not drinking).

   f. This speaker is basing her conclusions on her own experience. Experience lacks a comparison group. (What would have happened if the speaker didn't declutter the closet?) Experience may have confounds. (Maybe decluttering the closet coincided with other positive changes, such as eating better or getting more sleep.)

   g. This is likely confirmation bias. The speaker may notice examples that fit his theory (cars that drive around him when he's wearing a brewery jersey and cars that buzz him when he's wearing a different jersey) and ignore or discount exceptions (cars that buzz him when wearing a brewery jersey and cars that drive around him when he's wearing a different one).

3. Answers will vary.
4. Answers will vary.
5. Answers will vary.
6. Answers will vary.

# Chapter 3

1.

| VARIABLE IN CONTEXT | CONCEPTUAL VARIABLE NAME | OPERATIONALIZATION OF THIS VARIABLE | LEVELS OF THIS VARIABLE | MEASURED OR MANIPULATED |
|---|---|---|---|---|
| A questionnaire study asks for various demographic information, including participants' **level of education**. | Level of education | Asking participants to circle their highest level of education from this list:<br><br>High school diploma<br>Some college<br>College degree<br>Graduate degree | High school diploma<br>Some college<br>College degree<br>Graduate degree | Measured |
| A questionnaire study asks about **anxiety**, measured on a 20-item Spielberger Trait Anxiety Inventory. | Anxiety | Score on 20-item Spielberger Trait Anxiety Inventory | Anxiety from low to high, represented by a numerical score | Measured |
| A study of readability has people read a passage of text printed in one of two **fonts: sans-serif or serif.** | Font of text | Sans-serif font or serif font | Sans-serif, serif | Manipulated |
| A study of **school achievement** asks participants to report their SAT scores, as a measure of college readiness. | School achieve-ment | SAT score | SAT score, from 600 to 2400 | Measured |
| A researcher studying self-control and **blood sugar levels** gives participants one of two glasses of sweet-tasting lemonade: one has sugar, one is sugar-free. | Blood sugar (glucose) levels | Drinking sugared lemonade or sugar-free lemonade | High glucose and low glucose | Manipulated |

2. a.  This is a causal claim.

Variables: chewing gum (or not), level of focus.

- You might ask: How well did they measure level of focus? (Construct validity)
- How well did they manipulate chewing gum or not? (Construct validity)
- Did they conduct an experiment, randomly assigning people to chew gum or not? (Internal validity)
- How did they get their sample? Did they use random sampling? (External validity)
- How strong is the relationship between chewing gum and focus? What is the confidence interval of the estimate? What do other studies say? (Statistical validity)

b.  This is an association claim.

Variables: workaholism (workaholic or not), presence of psychiatric disorder.

- How well did they measure workaholism? How carefully did they diagnose psychiatric disorders? (Construct validity)

- How strong is the relationship between workaholism and psychiatric disorders? How precise is the estimate?

What do other studies say? (Statistical validity)
- How did they get their sample? Is the sample representative? (External validity)

c.  This is a frequency claim.

Variable: feeling dissatisfied with one's body or not.

- How well did they measure people's body satisfaction? (Construct validity)
- How did they get their sample? Is the sample representative of women? (External validity)

- What is the margin of error of this estimate? Can we compare it to other estimates of the same thing? (Statistical validity)

3.  You would randomly assign a sample of people to either chew gum or not, then have everyone participate in a task that requires careful focus (or to study the other variable, you could also measure mood). The two variables would be gum chewing (or not) and degree of focus.

The results may be graphed as follows:

Degree of focus

Gum    No gum

The experiment would fulfill covariance if the results turned out as depicted in the graph, because the causal variable (gum chewing) is covarying with the outcome (degree of focus). The method ensured temporal precedence: Because gum chewing was manipulated, it came before task focus was measured. There would be internal validity as long as participants were randomly assigned and all other aspects were kept the same (the two groups performed the same task under the same conditions).

## Chapter 4

1. The IRB members might consider that publicly observable behavior is usually exempt from informed consent requirements, but children are considered a "vulnerable population." Children may not be able to give informed consent, and they may not monitor their public behavior to the same extent as adults do. Depending on the case, the IRB may require the researcher to request informed consent from parents in the play area before proceeding. In addition, the researcher has not yet explained what the purpose of the study will be. The IRB, in its evaluation of the research proposal, should consider the benefits of the knowledge to be gained from the study.

2. Normally, researchers using anonymous, low-risk questionnaires may be exempted from informed consent procedures, but a review board might be concerned about the risk of coercion in this situation. The IRB might wonder if students in the professor's class will feel coerced into completing the questionnaire, even if they do not wish to. (However, if there is truly no way to link responses back to the participants, then a student who does not wish to participate might be instructed to turn in a blank questionnaire.) In a small class, the students' handwriting might be recognized by the professor, so the surveys may not be truly anonymous unless they are online. The IRB would probably evaluate this proposal more negatively if the questions on the survey were about personal values or private behaviors rather than study habits.

3. You might have listed some of the following costs and benefits: Deception might harm participants by making them feel tricked or embarrassed. Such negative feelings may make participants less likely to participate in future research and may make them less willing to accept or read research findings in the future. On the one hand, people might become aware of negative information about themselves, such as what kinds of actions they will perform—knowledge that may not be welcome or comfortable (e.g., in the Milgram studies, delivering shocks to the "learner"). On the other hand, deceived research participants may gain some valuable self-knowledge from their participation, thereby feeling they are contributing to the enterprise of science.

Deception studies can be valuable to society because, as noted in the chapter, the results of such studies may provide important lessons about obedience, helping behavior, persuasion, or other research topics. In addition, human welfare might be improved when scientists or practitioners apply the knowledge from a deception study. However, when members of society read or hear about deceptive research studies, they may begin to mistrust scientists. They may also become more suspicious of others around them. (Text from this question and answer is based on an analysis by Dunn, 2009.)

4. Answers will vary.

5. Answers will vary.

## Chapter 5

1. a. Coders will need to be tested on their interrater reliability. A scatterplot should have "Coder 1" on the x-axis and "Coder 2" on the y-axis; there would be a tight, upward-sloping cloud of points to show strong interrater reliability. Test-retest reliability may also be relevant. You would have to measure cell phone use in the same students at two different points in time. If you assume people's cell phone habits are stable over time, you should observe a positive relationship on a scatterplot, or a strong, positive correlation coefficient. The labels on the scatterplot should be "Rate of cell phone use at first recording" on one axis and "Rate of cell phone use at second recording" on the other axis.

   b. Because this scale has seven items that are likely to be averaged together, it will be important to establish internal reliability (through a high value on Cronbach's alpha), to make sure all seven items are answered consistently by most people. In addition, since risk for panic disorder is something that should be fairly stable over time, you should assess test-retest reliability. For test-retest reliability, a scatterplot should have "Time 1 test" on the x-axis and "Time 2 test" on the y-axis. There would be a tight, upward-sloping cloud of points to show strong interrater reliability.

c. Since observers are coding the eyeblink response, coders will need to be tested on their interrater reliability. A scatterplot should have "Coder 1" on the x-axis and "Coder 2" on the y-axis; there would be a tight, upward-sloping cloud of points to show strong interrater reliability.

d. Interrater (interteacher) reliability may be relevant here. Test-retest reliability is also relevant because you can assume that shyness is stable over time. If you ask teachers to rate the same children once at the beginning of the year and once at the middle, you should see a positive correlation between these two ratings.

2. To measure criterion validity, you would see whether the teacher ratings correlated with some behavioral measure of classroom shyness. For example, you might see if the shyness ratings correlated (negatively) with the number of times the student was seen to raise their hand in a classroom setting during the day.

   For convergent validity, you would want to show that the classroom shyness rating is correlated with other ratings of shyness, perhaps parent ratings of shyness in the children or therapist ratings of shyness. To show convergent and discriminant validity, the ratings of shyness should be more strongly correlated with a measure of shyness than they are with a measure of autism or a measure of anxiety, for example.

3. Answers will vary.

## Chapter 6

1. Answers will vary.

2. This is a forced-choice item (people must choose among options from 0 to 7). This question does not seem to be leading, negatively worded, or double-barreled. However, it seems possible that people would overrepresent their frequency of exercising because they believe they should exercise.

3. Your decisions will depend on where you are planning to code, but the one thing to attend carefully to is interrater reliability. To establish interrater reliability, you will need to have two coders each rate each driver, yielding two ratings per observation. The association between the two coders' ratings is the interrater reliability.

4. You could ask about the interrater reliability of the coders' rating of each face's gender and race, as well as the reliability of their coding of how long faces were in the babies' visual field. To ask about possible observer bias, you could find out if the coders knew the race of the babies from which each recording came. (If the coders knew the race of the babies, that might affect their judgment of the race of the faces in the video.)

## Chapter 7

1. Many people are frustrated that opinion pollsters never call them, and they may even volunteer to contribute polling data for opinion polls during an election. Of course, the polling organizations cannot accept volunteer respondents. If they did, their polls would have poor external validity—or at least, they would be able to generalize only to other people who voluntarily call pollsters to share their opinions.

   One reason this woman has not been called by pollsters is that each poll needs to sample only about 1,000 to 2,000 voters. With millions of voters in the population, the chance of being selected by a poll is extremely small.

2. a. The sample is the 200 titles you select and the population is the entire set of 13,000 titles.

   b. To collect a simple random sample, use the database of all 13,000 titles. In that list, assign each book a random number, use the computer to sort the books into a list with the smallest numbers on top, and select the first 200 books on the sorted list. For each of the 200 books in the sample, you would record the price and take the average. That sample average would be a good estimate of the average price of the full book population in the store.

   c. To collect a stratified random sample, you would first choose some categories, or strata, that are meaningful. For example, you might stratify the sample into textbooks and trade books. If the population includes 60% textbooks and 40% trade books, you could select a random sample of 120 textbooks and 80 trade books (in stratified random sampling, the sample size in each stratum is proportional to that in the population). Alternatively, you could categorize according to whether the books are paperback or hardback, fiction or nonfiction, or you might even stratify by topic (literature, foreign language, self-help, etc.). After identifying the categories, you would select at random the number of books you need in each stratum, according to the proportion they represent in the full list of titles.

   d. A convenience sample would involve recording the price of the first 200 books you can pick up in the store, simply by walking around and choosing books. (This would bias your sample toward books on the most reachable shelves.) Or you could stand by the cash register and record the price of the next 200 books sold at that store. (This convenience sample might bias your sample to include mainly the cheaper books, or mainly the sale books, or mainly the popular books.)

   e. To conduct a systematic random sample, you would select two random numbers (say, 15 and 33). You would list the 13,000 books in the store, start with the 15th book, and then count off, selecting every 33rd book in the list until you get 200 books. Record the prices and take the average of the 200 books in the sample.

f. To conduct a cluster sample, you would first decide on some arbitrary clusters you could use; for example, you might use the last initial of the author as the cluster, creating 26 possible clusters. Of the 26 possible last initials, you could randomly select six letters, and then record the price of all the books in those six clusters. Alternatively, you could randomly sample 50 books from each of the six selected letters (this would be multistage sampling).

g. To conduct a quota sample, you would first choose some categories that might be important to you. For example, you might decide to study textbooks and trade books. If the population includes 60% textbooks and 40% trade books, you would decide to study 120 textbooks and 80 trade books. However, you would choose these books nonrandomly—perhaps by choosing the first 120 textbooks and the first 80 trade books you encounter.

## Chapter 8

1. a. Measured variables: degree of stomach pain in childhood (present or absent) and level of anxiety disorders as adults. This should be plotted with a bar graph, since stomach pain was a categorical, yes or no variable. The $x$-axis should have "Stomach pain in childhood" or "No stomach pain" and the $y$-axis should have "Level of anxiety disorders in adulthood." The bar for "Stomach pain in childhood" should be higher.

   Construct validity: How accurately can they measure the degree of stomach pain in childhood? (The measures are probably good because they were medically diagnosed.) How well did they measure anxiety disorders as adults? Are self-reports appropriate here?

   Statistical validity: As for effect size, the rate of 51% is 31 points higher than the rate of 20%, so the effect size seems large. You could ask about the confidence interval on this difference. You would also ask what else is known—what do other estimates of the same relationship suggest?

   External validity: This was probably a purposive sample; they started by identifying kids who had stomach pain. Because purposive sampling is not a representative sampling technique, you do not know if the results will generalize to a population.

   If you chose to ask about internal validity, you might wonder whether you can support the claim that "Stomach pain in childhood causes anxiety disorders later on." Clearly there is covariance: Stomach pain goes with anxiety. There is also temporal precedence: The stomach pain is measured before the anxiety disorder. However, there may be third variables that provide alternative explanations. For example, perhaps family stress is associated with both stomach pain and anxiety disorders.

b. Measured variables: diagnosis of ADHD and likelihood of bullying. If ADHD is considered categorical (ADHD diagnosis or not), it could be plotted as a bar graph, but if it is considered quantitative (severity of ADHD), then a scatterplot is appropriate.

   To interrogate construct validity, you could ask how well the researchers measured each of the two variables in this association: level of ADHD and level of bullying. You could first ask how the ADHD diagnosis was made. If a professional psychologist diagnosed each child, you could feel more confident in the construct validity of this measure. You would then ask about the measure of bullying. How well was this variable measured? The article mentions only that the researchers asked the children about bullying. You might wonder how valid a child's report of his or her own bullying behavior would be. Would a child's self-ratings correlate with teachers' ratings?

   For statistical validity, you could ask about effect size first. The article reports that children with ADHD are "four times more likely to bully" than non-ADHD children, which seems like a strong effect size. You would also ask about the confidence interval of this estimate and ask about other studies of the same relationship—what do other results say? Finally, when the variables are categorical, as they seem to be in this study (children either have ADHD or they don't, and they are either bullies or not), outliers are typically not a problem, because a person cannot have an extreme score on a categorical variable.

   For external validity, the article reports that all the children in one grade level were studied. This study used a census, not a sample, so the findings clearly generalize to children in this Swedish town.

2. a. This strong negative correlation means that scientists who drank more beer published fewer articles.

b. This means we have some uncertainty about the true relationship between beer and publications—we wouldn't be surprised to learn that it is as weak as −.24 or a strong as −.74. We can probably rule out that the relationship is zero. However, CIs are created to capture the population value 95% of the time, so there is also a chance this CI has missed the population value.

c. The correlation would become stronger with this outlier.

d. No, the result establishes covariance, but it does not establish temporal precedence. (It could also be the case that the scientists drank beer to cope with a lower publication rate.) It does not establish internal validity, either: A third variable might be institution type; scientists working at universities might publish more and socialize less with beer, while scientists working at companies might publish less and socialize more with beer.

e. One possible table:

| | Correlation between beer consumption and publication rate |
| --- | --- |
| Science faculty | −.63 |
| Humanities faculty | −.14 |

## Chapter 9

1. a. The autocorrelations are those in the top row: .489, .430, .446, as well as those in the bottom row: .466, .486, .471.

b. There are no cross-sectional correlations in this figure. The authors chose to omit them, perhaps because they were not the focus of the article.

c. The cross-lag correlations are similar in strength. The correlations between parental warmth at one time period and child self-esteem at the next time period are about as strong as the correlations between child self-esteem at one time period and parental warmth at a later time period. The pattern of results is consistent with the conclusion that parental warmth and child self-esteem are mutually reinforcing over time.

2. a. Number of health problems is a third-variable problem.

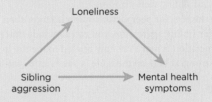

b. Household status (living alone or living with others) is a moderator (data below are fabricated).

| Household status | Relationship between having a dog and lifespan |
| --- | --- |
| Living alone | .21 |
| Living with others | .09 |

c. Exercise is a mediator.

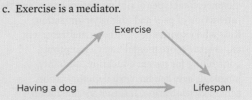

d. Birth order is a moderator (data below are fabricated).

| Birth order | Relationship between sibling aggression and mental health symptoms |
| --- | --- |
| Firstborn | .10 |
| Later-born | .18 |

e. Loneliness is a mediator.

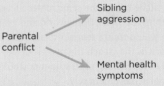

f. Parental conflict is a third-variable problem.

3. a. The criterion variable is mental health, measured by the Trauma Symptom Checklist. It is at the top of the table and in the table title.

b. There are 17 predictors in this table (you don't count $R^2$ as a predictor).

c. Kids who experience more total types of sibling victimization experience more mental health symptoms, controlling for parent education, ethnicity, language, age, gender, child maltreatment, sexual victimization, school victimization, Internet victimization, witnessing family or community violence, total types of peer victimization, and the interaction of peer and sibling victimization.

d. Kids who experience more total types of peer victimization experience more mental health symptoms, controlling for parent education, ethnicity, language, age, gender, child maltreatment, sexual victimization, school victimization, Internet victimization, witnessing family or community violence, total types of sibling victimization, and the interaction of peer and sibling victimization.

e. Kids who experience childhood maltreatment experience more mental health symptoms, controlling for parent education, ethnicity, language, age, gender, sexual victimization, school victimization, Internet victimization, witnessing family or community violence, total peer victimization, total types of sibling victimization, and the interaction of peer and sibling victimization.

f. Kids who experience Internet victimization do not experience significantly more mental health symptoms, at least when controlling for parent education, ethnicity, language, age, gender, sexual victimization, school victimization, witnessing family or community violence, total peer victimization, total types of sibling victimization, and the interaction of peer and sibling victimization.

g. Since the beta for peer victimization is larger than the beta for sibling aggression, you can conclude that peer victimization is more strongly related to mental health. The strongest beta on the table is peer victimization.

## Chapter 10

1. (*Sample answer*)
   a. You could randomly assign students to two groups. Both groups will be taught the same material, using the same teaching methods, homework, and examples. However, you would train a teacher to act either friendly or stern as they teach the two groups of students. After the teaching unit, students would take the same school achievement test.

   The bar graph should look something like this:

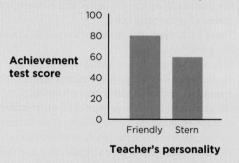

**Teacher's personality**

The independent (manipulated) variable is the teacher's personality, with two levels (friendly and stern). The dependent (measured) variable is the achievement test score. The control variables might include the teacher's appearance, the content of the material taught, the teaching method, the examples used, and the homework used.

Your assessment of covariance will depend on how your graph is prepared; however, this study would show covariance if the results came out as depicted in the graph shown earlier, in which the achievement test scores covary with the teacher's personality. This study also shows temporal precedence: The teacher's personality was manipulated, so it came first in time, followed by the achievement test. This study would also have internal validity if the researchers controlled for potential alternative explanations—for example, by keeping the teaching methods and homework the same. If the study has met all three causal rules, you can make a causal statement that a friendlier teacher causes students to score higher on school achievement tests.

2. (*Sample answer*)
   b. If you manipulated the piano practice independent variable as independent-groups, you would have some participants practice the piano for 10 minutes per day and other participants practice for 30 minutes per day. You would randomly assign people to the two groups.

   If you manipulated the piano practice variable as within-groups, you could have participants alternate blocks of practice months—some months practicing 10 minutes per day, and other months practicing 30 minutes per day. You would measure piano performance at the end of each monthly block. To control for order effects, you would counterbalance the months, so that some participants practice 10 minutes a day first, and others practice 30 minutes a day first.

   For this independent variable, the advantage to using the independent-groups design is that most participants probably believe that 30 minutes of practice will work better than 10, so this design may be more susceptible to demand characteristics or placebo effects. In an independent groups design, participants would be less aware of what the experiment is testing. The within-groups design has the advantage that each participant will be serving as his or her own control for the two experimental conditions; their original piano playing ability will be constant for all conditions. In addition, the within-groups design has the advantage of needing fewer participants.

3. a. The independent variable is whether participants were doing their questionnaires alone or with a passive confederate. The dependent variable was whether people stopped filling out their questionnaires to investigate the "accident" or help the "victim." The control variables were the tape recording of the accident (always the same), the room in which the study was held, the appearance and behavior of the female experimenter, and the questionnaires participants completed.

b.

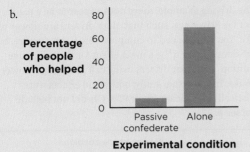

c. This was an independent-groups manipulation. People were in either the alone group or the passive confederate group, not both.

d. For construct validity, you would ask whether getting up to help is a good measure of helping behavior (it seems to be). You would also ask whether participating alone or with a passive confederate is a reasonable manipulation of the presence of bystanders. For internal validity, you would make sure that the experimenters used random assignment (they did) and appropriate control variables to avoid confounds. Are any other control variables unaccounted for? For external validity, you would ask how the experimenters gathered their sample: Was it a random sample of some population of interest? You can also ask if this situation—helping a woman falling from a chair in another room—would generalize to other emergencies, such as helping a man bleeding on the street, helping somebody who fainted, or helping in other kinds of situations.

For statistical validity, you could ask how large the effect size was. Indeed, the difference was 7% versus 70%, and this is an extremely large effect size—a 63% difference. You would estimate the 95% CI of this difference. And ideally, you'd compare the estimate to other estimates from similar studies.

## Chapter 11

1. a. IV: exposure to alcohol advertising or not. DV: reported level of drinking.
   b. Design: one-group, pretest/posttest design (a within-groups design).
   c.

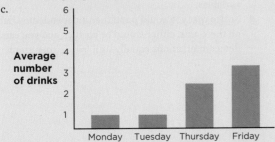

d. IV threats: Because this is a one-group, pretest/posttest design, it is subject to multiple internal validity threats. Perhaps the most obvious is history: It is plausible that students drank more after exposure to the advertising simply because the posttest was on a weekend.

e. To redesign the study, Jack could add a comparison group that is also tested on the same days but does not see the alcohol advertising.

2. a. IV: the use of the categorization strategy. DV: the memory rate.
   b. Design: one-group, pretest/posttest (a within-groups design).
   c.

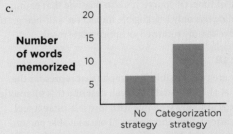

d. Because this is a one-group, pretest/posttest design, it is subject to multiple internal validity threats. Perhaps the most obvious here is testing: The students probably recalled more words the second time because they had a second chance to learn the same list of words.

e. To fix this problem, the student presenters should use a new word list the second time—when categorization is used as a mnemonic. To control for the possibility that one word list might be more difficult than the other (which would be a design confound), the presenters should also counterbalance the use of the two word lists.

3. a. IV: the meditation training. DV: symptoms of anxiety and depression.
   b. Design: one-group, pretest/posttest design.
   c. The x-axis should have "Before training" and "After training," and the y-axis should read "Anxiety and depression symptoms." The line or bar graph should show a decline in symptoms.
   d. Because this is a one-group, pretest/posttest design, it is subject to multiple internal validity threats. Regression to the mean could be at play (if the workers' symptoms were especially keen at pretest), as well as maturation (in many cases, people's ability to cope with a stressful event simply improves on its own over time).
   e. As always, a comparison group receiving no meditation training would improve the internal validity of this design.

4. *Increasing between-groups variability*: Was 1 ounce of chocolate enough to cause a difference in well-being? Was the well-being questionnaire sensitive enough to detect differences in this variable?

*Reducing within-group differences:* With such a small sample, Dr. Dove might need to use a within-groups design, because there are likely to be individual differences in well-being. Otherwise, she might try using a larger number of participants (at least 50 in each group might be better), thus reducing the impact of measurement errors or irrelevant individual differences. The participants in this study also seemed to be going about their normal routines in real-world settings. There may have been innumerable sources of situation noise in their lives over this 4-week period. In a future study, Dr. Dove might consider quarantining participants for some period of time. Of course, it's also possible that eating chocolate has only a negligible impact on well-being, so Dr. Dove's study returned an appropriate result.

## Chapter 12

1. Below are two possible line graphs that represent the Wood et al. (2009) data. You can describe this interaction in words as follows: People with low self-esteem feel worse after telling themselves "I am a lovable person," but people with high self-esteem feel better after telling themselves "I am a lovable person."

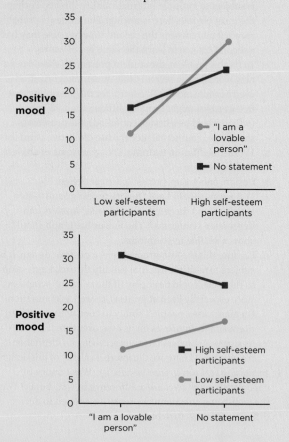

2. In the driving example, there does appear to be a main effect for driver age, such that older drivers are slower to brake. You would need to compute 95% CIs to be sure, but there does appear to be a main effect for the cell phone condition, such that drivers using cell phones are slower to brake. In the actual study, both main effects were statistically significant (their 95% CIs did not include zero; see p. 374).

| DV: Braking onset time (ms) | | IV₁: Cell phone condition | | |
|---|---|---|---|---|
| | | **On cell phone** | **Not on phone** | Main effect for IV₂: Driver age |
| IV₂: Driver age | **Younger drivers** | 912 | 780 | 846 |
| | **Older drivers** | 1086 | 912 | 989 |
| Main effect for IV₁: Cell phone condition | | 989 | 846 | |

In the chess pieces example, there does not appear to be a main effect for type of item, since the two marginal means are fairly close to each other. There also does not appear to be a large main effect for participant type, since the two marginal means are almost the same here, too. You would need to compute 95% CIs to determine whether the differences between the marginal means are statistically significant.

| DV: Items recalled | | IV₁: Participant type | | |
|---|---|---|---|---|
| | | **Child chess experts** | **Adult novices** | Main effect for IV₂: Type of item |
| IV₂: Type of item | **Chess pieces** | 9.3 | 5.9 | 7.6 |
| | **Digits** | 6.1 | 7.8 | 7.0 |
| Main effect for IV₁: Participant type | | 7.7 | 6.9 | |

3. a. This is a 3 × 2 within-groups factorial design.
   b. The independent variables are cell phone condition (two levels) and testing condition (three levels). The dependent variable is the number of collisions.
   c. Both independent variables are within-groups variables.
   d. Notice that you could put either independent variable on the *x*-axis; either would be correct, and you can detect interactions equally well from either graph.

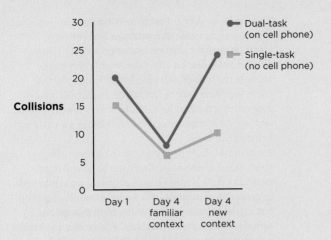

Dual-task (on cell phone)

Single-task (no cell phone)

Collisions

30
25
20
15
10
5
0

Day 1    Day 4 familiar context    Day 4 new context

e. There is a main effect for cell phone condition, such that talking on a cell phone causes more collisions. (You can say "cause" here because this was an experimental design with no confounds.) There is also a main effect for testing day: People had the fewest collisions on Day 4, familiar context, and the most collisions on Day 4, new context. There appears to be an interaction: The difference between single- and dual-task is about the same on Day 1 and Day 4, familiar context, but the difference is greater on Day 4, new context.

f. The results of this study seem to show that regardless of experience level, using cell phones impairs people's driving skill.

4. Participant variables are usually independent-groups variables. In the case of gender, participants usually identify as one or the other or neither. Ethnicity, too, is an independent-groups variable. Sometimes personality traits (such as high self-esteem versus low self-esteem or introversion versus extroversion) are used as participant variables; these, too, are independent-groups variables. Age, however, could go either way. Strayer and his colleagues recruited some people in their 20s and other people in their 70s, so age was an independent-groups variable in this design. However, if a researcher recruits one sample of people and tests them in their 20s, 30s, 40s, and 50s, age becomes a participant variable that is studied as a repeated-measures variable. (This kind of study is called a longitudinal design; see Chapter 9.)

## Chapter 13

1. a. This is an interrupted time-series design.
   b. Your graph could have "Hours of sleep per night" on the y-axis and "Before change" and "After change" on the x-axis. The line should be increasing from left to right.

c. The causal claim would be that starting school later caused students to get more sleep. This result shows covariance (students got more sleep when the school time started later) and temporal precedence (the school's change in start time preceded the measurement of how much sleep they were getting). However, in this quasi-experimental design, it is possible there are threats to internal validity. Increases in sleep could have been caused by seasonal changes from fall to spring, or by systematic changes in the school's activities or curriculum (if school events in the fall are more numerous or intense compared to spring).

d. One alternative design would be a nonequivalent control group interrupted time-series design, where you could study sleep patterns in two high schools, only one of which changed its school start time at mid-year. Another option would be to measure the students on the dependent variable, sleep, more frequently and for a longer time. The study could measure sleep patterns for multiple semesters first, then implement the start time change, and then continue to measure sleep patterns. By inspecting the results, you could tease apart seasonal changes in sleep from start time changes.

e. Construct validity of the dependent variable: How well does a survey operationalize the amount of sleep students are getting? External validity: To what extent does the result from this one school generalize to other schools? Does it generalize to younger children?

2. a. Either the stable-baseline design or the reversal design is appropriate here. Since there is only one context for the growling behavior, the multiple-baseline design would not be appropriate.

b. Using a stable-baseline design, you would observe and record your dog's growling behavior daily in the presence of other dogs for a long period of time (2–3 weeks). Then you would continue to observe and record your dog's growling behavior daily as you began to implement the behavioral technique.

c. The graph would look similar to Figure 13.12, except the growling behavior would be consistently high (rather than low) during the baseline period and would then decrease after the intervention starts.

d. If the results were as depicted in the graph you drew, you could rule out maturation and regression explanations for the dog's behavior, because the stable-baseline period shows that the dog's behavior has not changed on its own. A history threat might still apply to your data if some other change (such as a change in diet) happened to occur in the dog's life at the same time you started using the behavioral technique.

However, in the absence of some other explanation, you could infer the causal success of the therapy if the dog's growling behavior began to decrease at the time you started the therapy.

## Chapter 14

1. Answers will vary.
2. Answers will vary.
3. Answers will vary.
4. a. This study could be conducted in theory-testing mode, because it may test a theory that exposure to a very stressful event is a potential cause of mental suffering and emotional problems. However, this study is also being conducted in generalization mode, since it appears to be testing a frequency claim about the population of Holocaust survivors: What percentage of survivors experience mood or sleep disorders? Frequency claims are always in generalization mode.

   b. This study appears at first to be conducted in theory-testing mode. It is testing a link between electromagnetic radiation and brain activity. (Does this kind of radiation affect the brain?) However, because the type of radiation is tied to cell phones, the researchers may be interested, eventually, in generalizing the results to humans who use cell phones and may be worried about the technology's long-term benefits and risks.

   c. Because this study used a restricted sample of a special kind of person—being born blind and later regaining sight is rare—it probably was not conducted in generalization mode. It is a good example of theory-testing mode because the results from this special sample allowed the researchers to learn that the brain uses motion (more than color or lines) to decode the visual world.

# References

Abelson, R. P. (1995). *Statistics as principled argument.* Erlbaum.

Alpert, A., Evans, W., Lieber, E. M. J., & Powell, D. (2019). *Origins of the opioid crisis and its enduring impacts.* NBER Working Paper No. 26500. National Bureau of Economic Research. https://doi.org/10.3386/w26500

American Psychological Association. (2002, with 2010 and 2016 amendments). *Ethical principles of psychologists and code of conduct.* http://www.apa.org/ethics/code/index.aspx

American Psychological Association. (2020). *Publication manual of the American Psychological Association* (7th ed). American Psychological Association.

Anderson, C. A., Berkowitz, L., Donnerstein, E., Huesmann, L. R., Johnson, J., Linz, D., Malamuth, N. M., & Wartella, E. (2003). The influence of media violence on youth. *Psychological Science in the Public Interest, 4*(3), 81–110. https://doi.org/10.1111/j.1529-1006.2003.pspi_1433.x

Anderson, C. A., Shibuya, A., Ihori, N., Swing, E. L., Bushman, B. J., Sakamoto, A., Rothstein, H. R., & Saleem, M. (2010). Violent video game effects on aggression, empathy, and prosocial behavior in Eastern and Western countries: A meta-analytic review. *Psychological Bulletin, 136*(2), 151–173. https://doi.org/10.1037/a0018251

Andics, A., Gábor, A., Gácsi, M., Faragó, T., Szabó, D., & Miklósi, A. (2016, September 2). Neural mechanisms for lexical processing in dogs. *Science, 353*(6303), 1–4. https://doi.org/10.1126/science.aaf3777

Animal Welfare Act. (1966). Title 9 Code of Federal Regulations (CF), Chapter 1, Subchapter A: Animal Welfare. http://www.gpo.gov/fdsys/pkg/CFR-2009-title9-vol1/xml/CFR-2009-title9-vol1-chapI-subchapA.xml

Arnett, J. (2008). The neglected 95%: Why American psychology needs to become less American. *American Psychologist, 63*(7), 602–614. https://doi.org/10.1037/0003-066x.63.7.602

Aron, A. (2009). *Instructor's manual with tests for statistics for psychology* (5th ed.). Pearson.

Aschwanden, C. (2018, December 6). *Psychology's replication crisis has made the field better.* FiveThirtyEight. https://fivethirtyeight.com/features/psychologys-replication-crisis-has-made-the-field-better/

Association for Psychological Science. (n.d.). APS Wikipedia initiative. http://www.psychologicalscience.org/index.php/members/aps-wikipedia-initiative

Baird, B., Mrazek, M. D., Phillips, D. T., & Schooler, J. W. (2014). Domain-specific enhancement of metacognitive ability following meditation training. *Journal of Experimental Psychology, 143*(5), 1972–1979. https://doi.org/10.1037/a0036882

Baird, B., Smallwood, J., Mrazek, M. D., Kam, J. W. Y., Franklin, M. S., & Schooler, J. W. (2012). Inspired by distraction mind wandering facilitates creative incubation. *Psychological Science, 23*(10), 1117–1122. https://doi.org/10.1177/0956797612446024

Barnett, W. S. (1998). Long-term effects on cognitive development and school success. In W. S. Barnett & S. S. Boocock (Eds.), *Early care and education for children in poverty: Promises, programs, and long-term outcomes* (pp. 11–44). SUNY Press.

Baron, R. M., & Kenny, D. A. (1986). The moderator-mediator variable distinction in social psychological research: Conceptual, strategic and statistical considerations. *Journal of Personality and Social Psychology, 51*(6), 1173–1182. https://doi.org/10.1037//0022-3514.51.6.1173

Bartholow, B. D., & Heinz, A. (2006). Alcohol and aggression without consumption: Alcohol cues, aggressive thoughts, and hostile perception bias. *Psychological Science, 17*(1), 30–37. https://doi.org/10.1111/j.1467-9280.2005.01661.x

Batson, C. D., Polycarpou, M. P., Harmon-Jones, E., Imhoff, H. J., Mitchener, E. C., Bednar, L. L., Klein, T. R., & Highberger, L. (1997). Empathy and attitudes: Can feeling for a member of a stigmatized group improve feelings toward the group? *Journal of Personality and Social Psychology, 72*(1), 105–118. https://doi.org/10.1037//0022-3514.72.1.105

Baumrind, D. (1964). Some thoughts on the ethics of research: After reading Milgram's "Behavioral Study of Obedience." *American Psychologist, 19*(6), 421–423. https://doi.org/10.1037/h0040128

Beck, A. T., Ward, C., Mendelson, M., Mock, J., & Erbaugh, J. (1961). An inventory for measuring depression. *Archives of General Psychiatry, 4*, 561–571. https://doi.org/10.1001/archpsyc.1961.01710120031004

Becker-Blease, K. A., Freyd, J. J. (2006). Research participants telling the truth about their lives: The ethics of asking and not asking about abuse. *American Psychologist, 61*(3), 218–226. https://doi.org/10.1037/0003-066X.61.3.218

Beecher, H. K. (1955). The powerful placebo. *Journal of the American Medical Association, 159*(17), 1601–1606. https://doi.org/10.1001/jama.1955.02960340022006

Benedetti, F., Amanzio, M., Vighetti, S., & Asteggiano, G. (2006). The biochemical and neuroendocrine bases of the hyperalgesic nocebo effect. *Journal of Neuroscience, 26*(46), 12014–12022. https://doi.org/10.1523/jneurosci.2947-06.2006

Berkowitz, L. (1973, July). The case for bottling up rage. *Psychology Today, 7,* 24–31.

Berkowitz, L., & Donnerstein, E. (1982). External validity is more than skin deep: Some answers to criticisms of laboratory experiments. *American Psychologist, 37*(3), 245–257. https://doi.org/10.1037//0003-066X.37.3.245

Best, E. (2010, May 18). Alcohol makes bigger guys more aggressive. *Pacific Standard.* http://www.psmag.com/culture-society/alcohol-makes-bigger-guys-more-aggressive-15485/

Bianchi, E. C., & Vohs, K. D. (2016). Social class and social worlds: Income predicts the frequency and nature of social contact. *Social Psychological and Personality Science, 7*(5), 479–486. https://doi.org/10.1177/1948550616641472

BioMed Central & COPE. (n.d.). Text recycling guidelines for editors. https://publicationethics.org/text-recycling-guidelines

Blackman, A. (2014, November 10). Can money buy you happiness? *The Wall Street Journal.* http://www.wsj.com/articles/can-money-buy-happiness-heres-what-science-has-to-say-1415569538

Bland, C. S. (1981). The Halsted mastectomy: Present illness and past history. *Western Journal of Medicine, 134*(6), 549–555.

Blass, T. (2002, March). The man who shocked the world. *Psychology Today, 35,* 68–74.

Blumberg, S. F., & Luke J. V. (2015). Wireless substitution: Early release estimates from the National Health Interview Survey, July–December 2015. http://www.cdc.gov/nchs/data/nhis/earlyrelease/wireless201605.pdf

Bogg, T., & Roberts, B. W. (2004). Conscientiousness and health-related behaviors: A meta-analysis of the leading behavioral contributors to mortality. *Psychological Bulletin, 130*(6), 887–919. https://doi.org/10.1037/0033-2909.130.6.887

Bohannon, J. (2013). Who's afraid of peer review? *Science, 342,* 60–65.

Bohannon, J. (2015, May 27). *I fooled millions into thinking chocolate helps weight loss: Here's how.* Io9.gizmodo. http://io9.gizmodo.com/i-fooled-millions-into-thinking-chocolate-helps-weight-1707251800

Boothby, E. J., Clark, M. S., & Bargh, J. A. (2014). Shared experiences are amplified. *Psychological Science, 25*(12), 2209–2217. https://doi.org/10.1177/0956797614551162

Borsboom, D., & Wagenmakers, E. J. (2013, January). Derailed: The rise and fall of Diederik Stapel [Review of the book *Onstporing,* by Diederik Stapel]. *APS Observer.* http://www.psychologicalscience.org/index.php/publications/observer/2013/january-13/derailed-the-rise-and-fall-of-diederik-stapel.html

Bothwell, R. K., Deffenbacher, K. A., & Brigham, J. C. (1987). Correlations of eyewitness accuracy and confidence: Optimality hypothesis revisited. *Journal of Applied Psychology, 72*(4), 691–695. https://doi.org/10.1037/0021-9010.72.4.691

Bowker, A., Boekhoven, B., Nolan, A., Bauhaus, S., Glover, P., Powell, T., & Taylor, S. (2009). Naturalistic observations of spectator behavior at youth hockey games. *Sport Psychologist, 23*(3), 301–316. https://doi.org/10.1123/tsp.23.3.301

Brewer, M. (2000). Research design and issues of validity. In H. Reis & C. Judd (Eds.), *Handbook of research methods in social and personality psychology.* Cambridge University Press.

Brewer, N., & Wells, G. L. (2006). The confidence-accuracy relationship in eyewitness identification: Effects of lineup instructions, foil similarity, and target-absent base rates. *Journal of Experimental Psychology: Applied, 12*(1), 11–30. https://doi.org/10.1037/1076-898x.12.1.11

Bröder, A. (1998). Deception can be acceptable. *American Psychologist, 53*(7), 805–806. https://doi.org/10.1037/h0092168

Brown, R., & Hanlon, C. (1970). Derivational complexity and order of acquisition in child speech. In J. R. Hayes (Ed.), *Cognition and the development of language* (pp. 11–54). Wiley.

Brummelman, E., Crocker, J., & Bushman, B. J. (2016). The praise paradox: When and why praise backfires in children with low self-esteem. *Child Development Perspectives, 10*(2), 111–115. https://doi.org/10.1111/cdep.12171

Brummelman, E., Thomaes, S., Nelemans, S. A., Orobio de Castro, B., Overbeek, G., & Bushman, B. J. (2015). Origins of narcissism in children. *Proceedings of the National Academy of Sciences, 112*(12), 3659–3662. https://doi.org/10.1073/pnas.1420870112

Buddy, T. (2019, October 23). *The link between alcohol and aggression.* Verywellmind. https://www.verywellmind.com/alcohol-facilitates-aggression-62647

Bushman, B. J., & Anderson, C. A. (2001). Media violence and the American public: Scientific facts versus media misinformation. *American Psychologist, 56*(6–7), 477–489. https://doi.org/10.1037/0003-066x.56.6-7.477

Bushman, B. J., Baumeister, R. F., & Phillips, C. M. (2001). Do people aggress to improve their mood? Catharsis beliefs, affect regulation opportunity, and aggressive responding. *Journal of Personality and Social Psychology, 81*(1), 17–32. https://doi.org/10.1037//0022-3514.81.1.17

Cacioppo, J. T., Cacioppo, S., Gonzaga, G. C., Ogburn, E. L., & VanderWeele, T. J. (2013). Marital satisfaction and break-ups differ across on-line and off-line meeting venues. *Proceedings of the National Academy of Sciences, 110*(25), 10135–10140. https://doi.org/10.1073/pnas.1222447110

Camara, W. J., & Echternacht, G. (2000). The SAT I and high school grades: Utility in predicting success in college. College Entrance Examination Board. https://eric.ed.gov/?q=camara&ff1=autCamara%2c+Wayne+J.&pg=3&id=ED446592

Campos, B., Wang, S., Plaksina, T., Repetti, R. L., Schoebi, D., Ochs, E., & Beck, M. E. (2013). Positive and negative emotion in the daily life of dual-earner couples with children. *Journal of Family Psychology, 27*(1), 76–85. https://doi.org/10.1037/a0031413

Cantril, H. (1965). *The pattern of human concerns.* Rutgers University Press.

Carlson, N. (2009). *Physiology of behavior* (10th ed.). Allyn & Bacon.

Carroll, L. (2008, January 29). *Kids with ADHD may be more likely to bully.* NBC News. http://www.nbcnews.com/id/22813400/ns/health-childrens_health/t/kids-adhd-may-be-more-likely-bully/#.U1bKavldV8E

Carroll, L. (2013, August 12). *Chronic stomach pain in kids linked to later anxiety.* NBC News. http://www.nbcnews.com/health/chronic-stomach-pain-kids-linked-later-anxiety-6C10887554

Carter, S. P., Greenberg, K., & Walker, M. (2016). The impact of computer usage on academic performance: Evidence from a randomized trial at the United States Military Academy. Working paper for the MIT School Effectiveness and Inequality Initiative. https://seii.mit .edu/wp-content/uploads/2016/05/SEII-Discussion-Paper-2016.02-Payne-Carter-Greenberg-and-Walker-2.pdf

Caruso, E. M., Vohs, K. D., Baxter, B., & Waytz, A. (2013). Mere exposure to money increases endorsement of free-market systems and social inequality. *Journal of Experimental Psychology: General, 142*(2), 301–306. https://doi.org/10.1037/a0029288

CBS Local. (2016, July 14). *AAA: 8 out of 10 drivers experience aggression behind the wheel.* http://newyork.cbslocal.com/2016/07/14/aaa-road-rage-survey/

CBS News. (2008, November 3). *Study links sex on TV to teen pregnancy.* http://www.cbsnews.com/news/study-links -sex-on-tv-to-teen-pregnancy/

Centers for Disease Control and Prevention. (2000). Clinical growth charts. http://www.cdc.gov/growthcharts/clinical_ charts.htm

Centers for Disease Control and Prevention (2001). Drug overdose deaths—Florida, 2003–2009. *Morbidity and Mortality Weekly Report, 60*(26), 869–872.

Centers for Disease Control and Prevention. (2008). Youth risk behavior surveillance—United States 2007. http://www.cdc .gov/mmwr/preview/mmwrhtml/ss5704a1.htm

Centers for Disease Control and Prevention. (2010). *Morbidity and Mortality Weekly Report, 59*(49), 1609–1613. https://www .cdc.gov/mmwr/preview/mmwrhtml/mm5949a1.htm

Centers for Disease Control and Prevention. (2016). The Tuskegee timeline. http://www.cdc.gov/tuskegee/timeline.htm

Centers for Disease Control and Prevention. (2017). Youth risk behavior surveillance, United States, 2017. *Morbidity and Mortality Weekly Report, 67*(8). https://www.cdc.gov/healthyyouth/data/yrbs/results.htm

Centers for Disease Control and Prevention. (n.d). Distracted driving. http://www.cdc.gov/motorvehiclesafety/Distracted_ Driving/index.html

Chambers, C. D. (2017). *The seven deadly sins of psychology: A manifesto for reforming the culture of scientific practice.* Princeton University Press.

Chandra, A., Martino, S. C., Collins, R. L., Elliott , M. N., Berry, S. H., Kanouse, D. E., & Miu, A. (2008). Does watching sex on television predict teen pregnancy? Findings from a National Longitudinal Survey of Youth. *Pediatrics, 122*(5), 1047–1054. https://doi.org/10.1542/peds.2007-3066

Chen, A. (2019, October 26). *Dog people live longer. But why?* NPR. www.npr.org/sections/health-shots/2019/10/26/773531999/dog-people-live-longer-but-why

Cherry, K. (2019, December 10). *How listening to music can have psychological benefits.* Verywellmind. https://www.verywellmind .com/surprising-psychological-benefits-of-music-4126866

Chi, M. T. H. (1978). Knowledge structures and memory development. In R. Siegler (Ed.), *Children's thinking: What develops?* (pp. 73–96). Erlbaum.

Childress, J. F., Meslin, E. M., & Shapiro, H. T. (2005). *Belmont revisited: Ethical principles for research with human subjects.* Georgetown University Press.

Christian, L., Keeter, S., Purcell, K., & Smith, A. (2010). Assessing the cell phone challenge. Pew Research Center. http://pewresearch.org/pubs/1601/assessing-cell-phone-challenge-in-public-opinion-surveys

Clark, L. A., & Watson, D. (1995). Constructing validity: Basic issues in objective scale development. *Psychological Assessment, 7*(3), 309–319. https://doi.org/10.1037/1040-3590.7.3.309

Clark, L. A., & Watson, D. (2019). Constructing validity: New developments in creating objective measuring instruments. *Psychological Assessment, 31*(12), 1412–1427. https://doi.org/10.1037/pas0000626

Clifford, S., Jewell, R. M., & Waggoner, P. D. (2015). Are samples drawn from Mechanical Turk valid for research on political ideology? *Research and Politics, 2*(4), 1–9. https://doi.org/10.1177/2053168015622072

Clifton, J. (2016, March 16). The happiest people in the world? Gallup. http://www.gallup.com/opinion/gallup/189989/happiest-people-world.aspx

Cohen, J. (1992). A power primer. *Psychological Bulletin, 112*(1), 155–159. https://doi.org/10.1037/0033-2909.112.1.155

Cohen, S., Kamarck, T., & Mermelstein, R. (1983). A global measure of perceived stress. *Journal of Health and Social Behavior, 24*(4), 385–396. https://doi.org/10.2307/2136404

Coile, D. C., & Miller, N. E. (1984). How radical animal activists try to mislead humane people. *American Psychologist, 39*(6), 700–701. https://doi.org/10.1037//0003-066x.39.6.700

Collins, R. L., Martino, S. C., Elliott, M. N., & Miu, A. (2011). Relationships between adolescent sexual outcomes and exposure to sex in media: Robustness to propensity-based analysis. *Developmental Psychology, 47*(2), 585–591. https://doi.org/10.1037/a0022563

Cook, T. D. (1979). *Quasi-experimentation: Design & analysis issues for field settings* (First Edition). Houghton Mifflin.

Cooper, C. (2015, September 14). Serving food on a larger plate "makes people eat more." *Independent.* http://www.independent .co.uk/life-style/health-and-families/health-news/serving-food-on-a-larger-plate-makes-people-eat-more-10500767.html

Copeland, J., & Snyder, M. (1995). When counselors confirm: A functional analysis. *Personality and Social Psychology Bulletin, 21*(11), 1210–1220. https://doi.org/10.1177/01461672952111009

Coren, S. (2016, April 13). The data says, "Don't hug the dog!" *Psychology Today.* https://www.psychologytoday.com/blog/canine-corner/201604/the-data-says-dont-hug-the-dog

Corkin, S. (2013). *Permanent present tense: The unforgettable life of the amnesic patient, H.M.* Basic Books.

Cozby, P. C. (2007). *Methods in behavioral research* (9th ed.). McGraw-Hill.

Crabtree, Steve. (2019, Sept. 16). Inside Afghanistan: Nearly nine in 10 Afghans are suffering. Gallup. https://news.gallup.com/poll/266825/inside-afghanistan-nearly-nine-afghans-suffering .aspx

Craik, F. I., & Lockhart, R. S. (1972). Levels of processing: A framework for memory research. *Journal of Verbal Learning & Verbal Behavior, 11*(6), 671–684. http://dx.doi.org/10.1016/S0022-5371(72)80001-X

Crandall, C. S., & Sherman, J. W. (2016). On the scientific superiority of conceptual replications for scientific progress.

*Journal of Experimental Social Psychology, 66*, 93–99. https://doi.org/10.1016/j.jesp.2015.10.002

Crandall, C. S., & Stangor, C. (2005). Conformity and prejudice. In J. F. Dovidio, P. Glick, & L. A. Rudman (Eds.), *On the nature of prejudice: Fifty years after Allport* (pp. 295–309). Wiley-Blackwell.

Cronbach, L. J., & Meehl, P. E. (1955). Construct validity in psychological tests. *Psychological Bulletin, 52*(4), 281–302. https://doi.org/10.1037/h0040957

Crowne, D. P., & Marlowe, D. (1960). A new scale of social desirability independent of psychopathology. *Journal of Consulting Psychology, 24*(4), 349–354. https://doi.org/10.1037/h0047358

Crume, D. M. (n.d.). *Six great ways to vent your frustrations.* Lifehack. http://www.lifehack.org/articles/featured/six-great-ways-to-vent-your-frustrations.html

Cumming, G., & Calin-Jageman, R. J. (2016). *Introduction to the new statistics* (1st ed.). Routledge.

Cumming, G., & Finch, S. (2005). Inference by eye: Confidence intervals and how to read pictures of data. *American Psychologist, 60*(2), 170–180. https://doi.org/10.1037/0003-066x.60.2.170

Dahl, M. (2016, April 25). Your dog hates hugs. *New York Magazine.* http://nymag.com/scienceofus/2016/04/your-dog-hates-hugs.html

Daniels, J. (2009). Cloaked websites: Propaganda, cyber-racism and epistemology in the digital era. *New Media and Society, 11*(5), 659–683.

Dart, T. (2016, May 24). "They're here for therapy": Houston's "rage room" a smash as economy struggles. *The Guardian.* https://www.theguardian.com/us-news/2016/may/24/rage-room-anger-management-unemployment-houston-texas

Deary, I. J., Penke, J., & Johnson, W. (2010). The neuroscience of human intelligence differences. *Nature Reviews: Neuroscience, 11*(3), 201–211. https://doi.org/10.1038/nrn2793

De Langhe, B., Fernbach, P. M., & Lichtenstein, D. R. (2016). Navigating by the stars: Investigating the actual and perceived validity of online user ratings. *Journal of Consumer Research, 42*(6), 817–833. https://doi.org/10.1093/jcr/ucv047

DeNoon, D. J. (2008, May 7). *Perk of a good job: Aging mind is sharp.* WebMD. http://www.webmd.com/brain/news/20080507/perk-of-good-job-aging-mind-is-sharp

DeRosa, N. M., Roane, H. S., Bishop, J. R., & Silkowski, E. L. (2016). The combined effects of noncontingent reinforcement and punishment on the reduction of rumination. *Journal of Applied Behavior Analysis, 49*(3), 680–685. https://doi.org/10.1002/jaba.304

DeWall, C. N., Bushman, B. J., Giancola, P. R., & Webster, G. D. (2010). The big, the bad, and the boozed-up: Weight moderates the effect of alcohol on aggression. *Journal of Experimental Social Psychology, 46*(4), 619–623. https://doi.org/10.1016/j.jesp.2010.02.008

Diener, E., & Diener, C. (1996). Most people are happy. *Psychological Science, 7*(3), 181–185. https://doi.org/10.1111/j.1467-9280.1996.tb00354.x

Diener, E., Emmons, R. A., Larsen, R. J., & Griffin, S. (1985). The satisfaction with life scale. *Journal of Personality Assessment, 49*(1), 71–75. https://doi.org/10.1207/s15327752jpa4901_13

Diener, E., Horwitz, J., & Emmons, R. A. (1985). Happiness of the very wealthy. *Social Indicators, 16*, 263–274. https://doi.org/10.1007/BF00415126

DiResta, R., et al. (2018). The tactics and tropes of the Internet Research Agency. New Knowledge Report. https://int.nyt.com/data/documenthelper/533-read-report-internet-research-agency/7871ea6d5b7bedafbf19/optimized/full.pdf#page=1

Dowell, D., Zhang, K., Noonan, R. K., & Hockenberry, J. M. (2016). Mandatory provider review and pain clinic laws reduce the amounts of opioids prescribed and overdose death rates. *Health Affairs, 35*(10), 1876–1883. https://doi.org/10.1377/hlthaff.2016.0448

Doyen, S., Klein, O., Pichon, C., & Cleeremans, A. (2012). Behavioral priming: It's all in the mind, but whose mind? *PLOS ONE, 7*(1), 7. https://doi.org/10.1371/journal.pone.0029081

Doyle, A. C. (1892/2002). Silver Blaze. In *The complete Sherlock Holmes.* Gramercy.

Duke, A. A., Giancola, P. R., Morris, D. H., Holt, J. C. D., & Gunn, R. L. (2011). Alcohol dose and aggression: Another reason why drinking more is a bad idea. *Journal of Studies on Alcohol and Drugs, 72*(1), 34–43. https://doi.org/10.15288/jsad.2011.72.34

Dunn, D. (2009). *Research methods for social psychology.* Wiley-Blackwell.

Dunn, L. M., & Dunn, L. M. (1981). *PPVT: Revised manual.* American Guidance Service.

Ebbinghaus, H. (1913). *Memory: A contribution to experimental psychology.* Columbia University Press. (Originally published 1885)

Ericsson, K. A., Chase, W. G., & Faloon, S. (1980, June 6). Acquisition of a memory skill. *Science, 208*(4448), 1181–1182. https://doi.org/10.1126/science.7375930

Family dinner benefits: Do meals together really make a difference for children? (POLL) (2012, September 26). *HuffPost.* http://www.huffingtonpost.com/2012/09/26/family-dinner-benefits-make-a-difference-poll_n_1916602.html

*Federal Register.* (2000, December 6). 65 F.R. 76260–76264. Doc 06de00-72. Federal Research Misconduct Policy. Department of Health and Human Services.

*Federal Register.* (2001, December 11). 66 F.R. 64266. Doc 01-30627. Findings of Scientific Misconduct. Department of Health and Human Services.

Feshbach, S. (1956). The catharsis hypothesis and some consequences of interaction with aggression and neutral play objects. *Journal of Personality, 24*(4), 449–462. https://doi.org/10.1111/j.1467-6494.1956.tb01281.x

Feynman, R. (1974, June). Cargo cult science. Commencement address delivered at California Institute of Technology. http://calteches.library.caltech.edu/3043/1/CargoCult.pdf

Fisher, B., Jeong, H. H., Anderson, S., Bryant, J., Fisher, E. R., & Wolmark, N. (2002). Twenty-five year follow-up of a randomized trial comparing radical mastectomy, total mastectomy, and total mastectomy followed by irradiation. *New England Journal of Medicine, 347*, 567–575.

Fisher, B., Redmond, C., Fisher, E. R., Bauer, M., Wolmark, N., Wickerham, D. L., Deutsch, M., Montague, E., Margolese, R., & Foster, R. (1985). Ten-year follow-up of a randomized clinical trial comparing radical mastectomy and total mastectomy with or without radiation. *New England Journal of Medicine, 312*, 674–681.

Flake, J. K., Pek, J., & Hehman, E. (2017). Construct validation in social and personality research: Current practice and recommendations. *Social Psychological and Personality Science, 8*, 370–378.

Flick, C. (2016). Informed consent and the Facebook emotional manipulation study. *Research Ethics, 12*(1), 14–28.

Foa, E. B., Gillihan, S. J., & Bryant, R. A. (2013). Challenges and successes in dissemination of evidence-based treatments for posttraumatic stress: Lessons learned from prolonged exposure therapy for PTSD. *Psychological Science in the Public Interest, 14*(2), 65–111. https://doi.org/10.1177/1529100612468841

Fox, D. K., Hopkins, B. L., & Anger, W. K. (1987). The long-term effects of a token economy on safety performance in open-pit mining. *Journal of Applied Behavior Analysis, 20*(3), 215–224. https://doi.org/10.1901/jaba.1987.20-215

Fraley, R. C., & Vazire, S. (2014). The N-pact factor: Evaluating the quality of empirical journals with respect to sample size and statistical power. *PLOS ONE, 9*(10), 12. https://doi.org/10.1371/journal.pone.0109019

Franchak, J. M., Kretch, K. S., & Adolph, K. E. (2016). See and be seen: Infant-caregiver social looking during locomoter free play. *Developmental Science, 21*(4), e12626. https://doi.org/10.1111/desc.12626

Freakonomics. (2013, June 21). *Couples who meet online have better marriages*. http://freakonomics.com/2013/06/21/couples-who-meet-online-have-better-marriages/

Frey, D., & Stahlberg, D. (1986). Selection of information after receiving more or less reliable self-threatening information. *Personality and Social Psychology Bulletin, 12*(4), 434–441. https://doi.org/10.1177/0146167286124006

Friedman, R. (2018, April 19). Standing up at your desk could make you smarter. *The New York Times*. https://www.nytimes.com/2018/04/19/opinion/standing-up-at-your-desk-could-make-you-smarter.html

Funder, D. C., & Ozer, D. J. (2019). Evaluating effect size in psychological research: Sense and nonsense. *Advances in Methods and Practices in Psychological Science, 2*(2), 156–168. https://doi.org/10.1177/2515245919847202

Gallup. (2019). Global Emotions Report. https://www.gallup.com/analytics/248906/gallup-global-emotions-report-2019.aspx

Gallup. (n.d.). Gallup Daily: Frequent exercise. http://www.gallup.com/poll/182252/gallup-daily-frequent-exercise.aspx

Gallup. (n.d.). The Well-Being 5: Development and validation of a diagnostic instrument to improve population well-being (trends). http://www.gallup.com/services/178469/development-validation-diagnostic-instrument-improve-population-trends.aspx

Gamer, M., Bauermann, T., Stoeter, P., & Vessel, G. (2007). Covariations among fMRI, skin conductance, and behavioral data during processing of concealed information. *Human Brain Mapping, 28*(12), 1287–1301. https://doi.org/10.1002/hbm.20343

Gay, P. (Ed.). (1989). *A Freud reader*. Norton.

Geen, R. G., & Quanty, M. B. (1977). The catharsis of aggression: An evaluation of a hypothesis. *Advances in Experimental Social Psychology, 10*, 1–37. https://doi.org/10.1016/s0065-2601(08)60353-6

Gernsbacher, M. A. (2003). Is one style of autism early intervention "scientifically proven"? *Journal of Developmental and Learning Disorders, 7*, 19–25.

Giancola, P. R. (2000). Executive functioning: A conceptual framework for alcohol-related aggression. *Experimental and Clinical Psychopharmacology, 8*(4), 576–597. https://doi.org/10.1037//1064-1297.8.4.576

Gignac, G. E., & Szodorai, E. T. (2016). Effect size guidelines for individual differences researchers. *Personality and Individual Differences, 102*, 74–78. https://doi.org/10.1016/j.paid.2016.06.069

Gilbert, D. (2005). *Stumbling on happiness*. Vintage.

Gilbert, D. T., King, G., Pettigrew, S., & Wilson, T. D. (2016, March 4). Comment on "Estimating the reproducibility of psychological science." *Science, 351*(6277), 1037. https://doi.org/10.1126/science.aad7243

Goodman, J. K., Cryder, C. E., & Cheema, A. (2013). Data collection in a flat world: The strengths and weaknesses of Mechanical Turk samples. *Journal of Behavioral Decision Making, 26*(3), 213–224. https://doi.org/10.1002/bdm.1753

Gordon, A. M. (2013, February 5). Gratitude is for lovers. Greater Good. http://greatergood.berkeley.edu/article/item/gratitude_is_for_lovers

Gordon, A. M., Impett, E. A., Kogan, A., Oveis, C., & Keltner, D. (2012). To have and to hold: Gratitude promotes relationship maintenance in intimate bonds. *Journal of Personality and Social Psychology, 103*(2), 257–274. https://doi.org/10.1037/a0028723

Gottfredson, L. S. (Ed.). (1997). Foreword to special issue: Intelligence and social policy. *Intelligence, 24*(1), https://doi.org/10.1016/S0160-2896(97)90010-6

Gould, M., Jamieson, P., & Romer, D. (2003). Media contagion and suicide among the young. *American Behavioral Scientist, 46*(9), 1269–1284.

Gould, S. J. (1996). *The mismeasure of man* (revised and expanded). Norton.

Gray, F. D. (1998). *The Tuskegee syphilis study: The real story and beyond*. River City Publishers.

Greenwald, A. G., Nosek, B. A., & Banaji, M. R. (2003). Understanding and using the Implicit Association Test: I. An improved scoring algorithm. *Journal of Personality and Social Psychology, 85*(2), 197–216. https://doi.org/10.1037/0022-3514.85.2.197

Grim, T. (2008). A possible role of social activity to explain differences in publication output among ecologists. *Oikos, 117*(4), 484–487. https://doi.org/10.1111/j.0030-1299.2008.16551.x

Gross, J. J. (2014). *The handbook of emotion regulation* (2nd ed.). Guilford Press.

Gross, J. J., & John, O. P. (2002). Wise emotion regulation. In L. F. Barrett & P. Salovey (Eds.), *The wisdom in feeling: Psychological processes in emotional intelligence* (pp. 297–319). Guilford Press.

Haller, M. (2012, January). The reason why you're an angry drunk. *Men's Health*. http://menshealth.com/health/a19528649/the-reason-why-you-re-an-angry-drunk/

Hamzelou, J. (2010, January). Cell phone radiation is good for Alzheimer's mice. *New Scientist Health*. http://www.newscientist.com/article/dn18351-cellphone-radiation-is-good-for-alzheimers-mice.html

Hardt, J., & Rutter, M. (2004). Validity of adult retrospective reports of adverse childhood experiences: Review of the evidence. *Journal of Child Psychology and Psychiatry, 45*(2), 260–273.

Harlow, H. (1958). The nature of love. *American Psychologist, 13*(12), 673–685. https://doi.org/10.1037/h0047884

Harms, W. (2013, June 3). Meeting online leads to happier, more enduring marriages. University of Chicago News. https://news.uchicago.edu/article/2013/06/03/meeting-online-leads-happier-more-enduring-marriages

Hastorf, A., & Cantril, H. (1954). They saw a game: A case study. *Journal of Abnormal and Social Psychology, 49*(1), 129–134. https://doi.org/10.1037/h0057880

Hattie, J. (2008). *Visible learning: A synthesis of meta-analyses relating to achievement.* Taylor Francis.

Hayes, A. F. (2017). *Introduction to mediation, moderation, and conditional process analysis* (2nd ed.). Guilford Press.

Heine, S. J. (2020). *Cultural psychology* (4th ed.). Norton.

Heinzen, T., Lilienfeld, S., & Nolan, S. A. (2015). *The horse that won't go away: Clever Hans, facilitated communication, and the need for clear thinking.* Worth.

Heller, J. (1972, July 26). Syphilis victims in U.S. study went untreated for 40 years. *The New York Times.* https://www.nytimes.com/1972/07/26/archives/syphilis-victims-in-us-study-went-untreated-for-40-years-syphilis.html

Henrich, J., Heine, S. J., & Norenzayan, A. (2010). The weirdest people in the world? (Target article, commentaries, and response.). *Behavioral and Brain Sciences, 33*(2–3), 61–83. https://doi.org/10.1017/S0140525X0999152X

Herzog, H. A., Jr. (1993). "The movement is my life": The psychology of animal rights activism. *Journal of Social Issues, 49*(1), 103–119. https://doi.org/10.1111/j.1540-4560.1993.tb00911.x

Hill, C. J., Bloom, H. S., Black, A. R., & Lipsey, M. W. (2008). Empirical benchmarks for interpreting effect sizes in research. *Child Development Perspectives, 2*(3), 172–177. https://doi.org/10.1111/j.1750-8606.2008.00061.x

Hill, P. L., & Roberts, B. W. (2011). The role of adherence in the relationship between conscientiousness and perceived health. *Health Psychology, 30*(6), 797–804. https://doi.org/10.1037/a0023860

Holmes, T. H., & Rahe, R. H. (1967). The social readjustment rating scale. *Journal of Psychosomatic Research, 11*(2), 213–218. https://doi.org/10.1016/0022-3999(67)90010-4

Horrey, W. J., & Wickens, D. C. (2006). Examining the impact of cell phone conversations on driving using meta-analytic techniques. *Human Factors: The Journal of the Human Factors and Ergonomics Society, 48*(1), 196–205.

Howard, J. (2016, August 31). *Your dog understands what you are saying, sort of.* CNN. http://www.cnn.com/2016/08/31/health/dogs-words-mri-study/

Hsu, J. (2009, April 12). *Facebook users get worse grades in college.* Live Science. https://www.livescience.com/3495-facebook-users-worse-grades-college.html

Hubbard, F. O. A., & Van Ijzendoorn, M. H. (1991). Maternal unresponsiveness and infant crying across the first 9 months: A naturalistic longitudinal study. *Infant Behavior and Development, 14*(3), 299–312. https://doi.org/10.1016/0163-6383(91)90024-M

Hume, David (1888). *Hume's treatise of human nature* (L. A. Selby Bigge, Ed.). Clarendon Press. (Originally published 1739–40)

Inbar, Y. (2016). Association between contextual dependence and replicability in psychology may be spurious. *Proceedings of the National Academy of Sciences, 113*(34), E4933–E4934. https://doi.org/10.1073/pnas.1608676113

International Society of Aesthetic Plastic Surgery. (2017). *ISAPS International Survey on Aesthetic/Cosmetic Procedures Performed in 2010.* http://www.isaps.org/isaps-global-statistics-2011.html

Jacowitz, K. E., & Kahneman, D. (1995). Measures of anchoring in estimation tasks. *Personality and Social Psychology Bulletin, 21*(11), 1161–1166. https://doi.org/10.1177/01461672952111004

Johansson, G. (1973). Visual perception of biological motion and a model for its analysis. *Perception and Psychophysics, 14*(2), 201–211. https://doi.org/10.3758/BF03212378

Johnson, J. G., Cohen, P., Smailes, E. M., Kasen, S., & Brook, J. S. (2002, March 29). Television viewing and aggressive behavior during adolescence and adulthood. *Science, 295*(5564), 2468–2471. https://doi.org/10.1126/science.1062929

Jones, J. H. (1993). *Bad blood: The Tuskegee syphilis experiment* (Rev. ed.). Free Press.

Jones, J. T., Pelham, B. W., Carvallo, M., & Mirenberg, M. C. (2004). How do I love thee? Let me count the J's: Implicit egotism and interpersonal attraction. *Journal of Personality and Social Psychology, 87*(5), 665–683. https://doi.org/10.1037/0022-3514.87.5.665

Jonsen, A. R. (2005). On the origins and future of the Belmont Report. In J. F. Childress, E. M. Meslin, & H. T. Shapiro (Eds.), *Belmont revisited: Ethical principles for research with human subjects* (pp. 3–11). Georgetown University Press.

Jost, J. (2018). The IAT is dead. Long live the IAT. *Current Directions in Psychological Science, 28*(1). https://doi.org/10.1177/0963721418797309

Kabat-Zinn, J. (2013). *Full catastrophe living: Using the wisdom of your body and mind to face stress, pain, and illness* (2nd ed.). Bantam/Random House.

Kagay, M. (1994, July 8). Poll on doubt of Holocaust is corrected. *The New York Times.* https://www.nytimes.com/1994/07/08/us/poll-on-doubt-of-holocaust-is-corrected.html.

Kaplan, R. M., & Pascoe, G. C. (1977). Humorous lectures and humorous examples: Some effects upon comprehension and retention. *Journal of Educational Psychology, 69*(1), 61–66. https://doi.org/10.1037/0022-0663.69.1.61

Kay, A. C., & Jost, J. T. (2003). Complementary justice: Effects of "poor but happy" and "poor but honest" stereotype exemplars on system justification and implicit activation of the justice motive. *Journal of Personality and Social Psychology, 85*(5), 823–837. https://doi.org/10.1037/0022-3514.85.5.823

Keeter, S., (2019, February 27). Growing and improving Pew Research Center's American Trends Panel. Pew Research Center. https://www.pewresearch.org/methods/2019/02/27/growing-and-improving-pew-research-centers-american-trends-panel/

Keeter, S., Christian, L., & Dimock, M. (2010). The growing gap between landline and dual-frame election polls. Pew Research Center. http://www.pewresearch.org/2010/11/22/the-growing-gap-between-landline-and-dual-frame-election-polls

Kennedy, C., & Hartig, H. (2019, February 27). Response rates in telephone surveys have resumed their decline. Pew Research Facttank: News in the Numbers. https://www.pewresearch.org/fact-tank/2019/02/27/response-rates-in-telephone-surveys-have-resumed-their-decline/

Kennedy-Hendricks, A., Richey, M., McGinty, E. E., Stuart, E. A., Barry, C. L., & Webster, D. W. (2016). Opioid overdose deaths and Florida's crackdown on pill mills. *American Journal of Public Health, 106*(2), 291–297. https://doi.org/10.2105/AJPH.2015.302953

Kenny, D. A. (2008). Mediation. http://davidakenny.net/cm/mediate.htm

Kenny, D. A. (2009). Moderator variables. http://davidakenny.net/cm/moderation.htm

Kenny, D. A., & West, T. V. (2008). Zero acquaintance: Definitions, statistical model, findings, and process. In J. Skowronski & N. Ambady (Eds.), *First impressions* (pp. 129–146). Guilford Press.

Kensinger, E. A., Clarke, R. J., & Corkin, S. (2003). What neural correlates underlie successful encoding and retrieval? A functional magnetic resonance imaging study using a divided attention paradigm. *Journal of Neuroscience, 23*(6), 2407–2415. https://doi.org/10.1523/JNEUROSCI.23-06-02407.2003

Kerr, N. L. (1998). HARKing: Hypothesizing after the results are known. *Personality and Social Psychology Review, 2*(3), 196–217. https://doi.org/10.1207/s15327957pspr0203_4

Kienle, G. S., & Kiene, H. (1997). The powerful placebo effect: Fact or fiction? *Journal of Clinical Epidemiology, 50*(12), 1311–1318. https://doi.org/10.1016/S0895-4356(97)00203-5

Kimmel, A. J. (2007). *Ethical issues in behavioral research* (2nd ed.). Blackwell.

Kimmel, A. J. (2012). Deception in research. In S. J. Knapp, M. C. Gottlieb, M. M. Handelsman, & L. D. VandeCreek (Eds.), *APA handbook of ethics in psychology* (Vol. 2, pp. 401–421). American Psychological Association. https://doi.org/10.1037/13272-019

Kirsch, I., & Sapirstein, G. (1998). Listening to Prozac and hearing placebo: A meta-analysis of antidepressant medication. *Prevention & Treatment, 1*(2), Article 2a. https://doi.org/10.1037/1522-3736.1.1.12a

Klayman, J., & Ha, Y. W. (1987). Confirmation, disconfirmation, and information in hypothesis testing. *Psychological Review, 94*(2), 211–228. https://doi.org/10.1037/0033-295x.94.2.211

Klein, R. A., Ratliff, K. A., Vianello, M., Adams, R. B., Jr., Bahník, Š., Bernstein, M. J., Bocian, K., Brandt, M. J., Brooks, B., Brumbaugh, C. C., Cemalcilar, Z., Chandler, J., Cheong, W., Davis, W. E., Devos, T., Eisner, M., Frankowska, N., Furrow, D., Galliani, E. M., . . . Nosek, B. A. (2014). Investigating variation in replicability: A "many labs" replication project. *Social Psychology, 45*(3), 142–152. https://doi.org/10.1027/1864-9335/a000178

Kosteas, V. D. (2012). The effect of exercise on earnings: Evidence from the NLSY. *Journal of Labor Research, 33*(2), 225–250.

Kraft, M. A. (in press). Interpreting effect sizes of education interventions. *Educational Researcher.*

Kramer, A. D. I., Guillory, J. E., & Hancock, J. T. (2014). Experimental evidence of massive-scale emotional contagion through social networks. *Proceedings of the National Academy of Sciences, 111*(24), 8788–8790. https://doi.org/10.1073/pnas.1320040111

Kringelbach, M. L., & Berridge, K. C. (2009). Towards a functional neuroanatomy of pleasure and happiness. *Trends in Cognitive Sciences, 13*(11), 479–487. https://doi.org/10.1016/j.tics.2009.08.006

Krosnick, J. (1999). Survey research. *Annual Review of Psychology, 50*, 537–567. https://doi.org/10.1146/annurev.psych.50.1.537

Kubicek, L. F., & Emde, R. N. (2012). Emotional expression and language: A longitudinal study of typically developing earlier and later talkers from 15 to 30 months. *Infant Mental Health Journal, 33*(6), 553–584. https://doi.org/10.1002/imhj.21364

LaBouff, J. P., Rowatt, W. C., Johnson, M. K., & Finkle, C. (2012). Differences in attitudes toward outgroups in religious and nonreligious contexts in a multinational sample: A situational context priming study. *International Journal for the Psychology of Religion, 22*(1), 1–9. https://doi.org/10.1080/10508619.2012.634778

Langer, E. J., & Abelson, R. P. (1974). A patient by any other name . . . : Clinician group differences in labeling bias. *Journal of Consulting and Clinical Psychology, 42*(1), 4–9. https://doi.org/10.1037/h0036054

Latané, B., & Darley, J. M. (1969). Bystander "apathy." *American Scientist, 57*(2), 244–268.

Lee, J. (1993). *Facing the fire: Experiencing and expressing anger appropriately.* Bantam.

Lelkes, Y., Krosnick, J. A., Marx, D. M., Judd, C. M., & Park, B. (2012). Complete anonymity compromises the accuracy of self-reports. *Journal of Experimental Social Psychology, 48*(6), 1291–1299. https://doi.org/10.1016/j.jesp.2012.07.002

Leonard, J. A., Lee, Y., & Schulz, L. E. (2017). Infants make more attempts to achieve a goal when they see adults persist. *Science, 357*(6357), 1290–1294. https://doi.org/10.1126/science.aan2317

Likert, R. (1932). A technique for the measurement of attitudes. *Archives of Psychology, 22*, 1–55.

Lin-Siegler, X., Ahn, J. N., Chen, J., Fang, F. A., & Luna-Lucero, M. (2016). Even Einstein struggled: Effects of learning about great scientists' struggles on high school students' motivation to learn science. *Journal of Educational Psychology, 108*(3), 314–328. https://doi.org/10.1037/edu0000092

Lister-Landman, K., Domoff, S. E., & Dubow, E. F. (2017). The role of compulsive texting in adolescents' academic functioning. *Psychology of Popular Media Culture, 6*(4), 311–325. https://doi.org/10.1037/ppm0000100

Loevinger, J. (1957). Objective tests as instruments of psychological theory. *Psychological Reports, 3*(3), 635–694. https://doi.org/10.2466/PR0.3.7.635-694

Lohr, J. M., Olatunji, B. O., Baumeister, R. F., & Bushman, B. J. (2007). The psychology of anger venting and empirically supported alternatives that do no harm. *Scientific Review of Mental Health Practice, 5*(1), 53–64.

Lovaas, O. I. (1987). Behavioral treatment and normal educational and intellectual functioning in young autistic children. *Journal of Consulting and Clinical Psychology, 55*(1), 3–9. https://doi.org/10.1037/0022-006x.55.1.3

Lucas, R. E., & Lawless, N. M. (2013). Does life seem better on a sunny day? Examining the association between daily weather conditions and life satisfaction judgments. *Journal of Personality and Social Psychology, 104*(5), 872–884. https://doi.org/10.1037/a0032124

Lucas, R. E., & Schimmack, U. (2009). Income and well-being: How big is the gap between the rich and the poor? *Journal of Research in Personality, 43*(1), 75–78. https://doi.org/10.1016/j.jrp.2008.09.004

Luo, L., Kiewra, K. A., Flanigan, A. E., & Peteranetz, M. S. (2018). Laptop versus longhand note taking: Effects on lecture notes and achievement. *Instructional Science, 46*(6), 947–971. https://doi.org/10.1007/s11251-018-9458-0

Lutsky, N. (2008). Arguing with numbers: A rationale and suggestions for teaching quantitative reasoning through argument and writing. In B. L. Madison & L. A. Steen (Eds.), *Calculation vs. context: Quantitative literacy and its implications for teacher education* (pp. 59–74). Mathematical Association of America.

Lyubomirsky, S., King, L., & Diener, E. (2005). The benefits of frequent positive affect: Does happiness lead to success? *Psychological Bulletin, 131*(6), 803–855. https://doi.org/10.1037/0033-2909.131.6.803

Margraf, J., Meyer, A. H., & Lavallee, K. L. (2013). Well-being from the knife? Psychological effects of aesthetic surgery. *Clinical Psychological Science, 1*(3), 239–252. https://doi.org/10.1177/2167702612471660

Markus, H. R., & Hamedani, M. G. (2007). Sociocultural psychology: The dynamic interdependence among self systems and social systems. In S. Kitayama & D. Cohen (Eds.), *Handbook of cultural psychology* (pp. 3–39). Guilford Press.

Markus, H. R., & Kitayama, S. (1991). Culture and the self: Implications for cognition, emotion, and motivation. *Psychological Review, 98*(2), 224–253. https://doi.org/10.1037//0033-295x.98.2.224

Maxwell, S. E., & Cole, D. A. (2007). Bias in cross-sectional analyses of longitudinal mediation. *Psychological Methods, 12*(1), 23–44. https://doi.org/10.1037/1082-989X.12.1.23

May, D. (2014, June 3). A learning secret: Don't take notes with a laptop. *Scientific American.* http://www.scientificamerican.com/article/a-learning-secret-don-t-take-notes-with-a-laptop

McCallum, J. M., Arekere, D. M., Green, B. L., Katz, R. V., & Rivers, B. M. (2006). Awareness and knowledge of the U.S. Public Health Service syphilis study at Tuskegee: Implications for biomedical research. *Journal of Health Care for the Poor and Underserved, 17*(4), 716–733. https://doi.org/10.1353/hpu.2006.0130

McCartney, K., & Rosenthal, R. (2000). Effect size, practical importance, and social policy for children. *Child Development, 71*(1), 173–180. https://doi.org/10.1111/1467-8624.00131

McKey, R., Condelli, L., Ganson, H., Barrett, B., McConkey, C., & Plantz, M. (1985). *The impact of Head Start on children, families, and communities* (Final report of the Head Start Evaluation, Synthesis, and Utilization Project). U.S. Department of Health and Human Services.

McNulty, J. K. (2010). When positive processes hurt relationships. *Current Directions in Psychological Science, 19*(3), 167–171. https://doi.org/10.1177/0963721410370298

Mehl, M. R., Gosling, S. D., & Pennebaker, J. W. (2006). Personality in its natural habitat: Manifestations and implicit folk theories of personality in daily life. *Journal of Personality and Social Psychology, 90*(5), 862–877. https://doi.org/10.1037/0022-3514.90.5.862

Mehl, M. R., & Pennebaker, J. W. (2003). The sounds of social life: A psychometric analysis of students' daily social environments and natural conversations. *Journal of Personality and Social Psychology, 84*(4), 857–870. https://doi.org/10.1037/0022-3514.84.4.857

Mehl, M. R., Vazire, S., Holleran, S. E., & Clark, C. S. (2010). Eavesdropping on happiness: Well-being is related to

having less small talk and more substantive conversations. *Psychological Science, 21*(4), 539–541. https://doi.org/10.1177/0956797610362675

Mehl, M. R., Vazire, S., Ramirez-Esparza, N., Slatcher, R. B., & Pennebaker, J. W. (2007, July 6). Are women really more talkative than men? *Science, 317*(5834), 82. https://doi.org/10.1126/science.1139940

Merrick, M. T., Ford, D. C., Ports, K. A., & Guinn, A. S. (2018). Prevalence of adverse childhood experiences from the 2011–2014 Behavioral Risk Factor Surveillance System in 23 States. *JAMA Pediatrics, 172*(11), 1038–1044.

Metzger, M. M. (2015). Knowledge of the Animal Welfare Act and animal welfare regulations influences attitudes toward animal research. *Journal of the American Association for Laboratory Animal Science, 54*(1), 70–75.

Meyer, G. J., Finn, S. E., Eyde, L. D., Kay, G. G., Moreland, K. L., Dies, R. R., Eisman, E. J., Kubiszyn, T., & Reed, G. M. (2001). Psychological testing and psychological assessment. *American Psychologist, 56*(2). https://doi: 10.1037//0003-066X.56.2.128

Milek, A., Butler, E. A., Tackman, A. M., Kaplan, D. M., Raison, C. L., Sbarra, D. A., Vazire, S., & Mehl, M. R. (2018). "Eavesdropping on happiness" revisited: A pooled, multisample replication of the association between life satisfaction and observed daily conversation quantity and quality. *Psychological Science, 29*(9), 1451–1462. https://doi.org/10.1177/0956797618774252

Milgram, S. (1963). Behavioral study of obedience. *Journal of Abnormal and Social Psychology, 67*(4), 371–378. https://doi.org/10.1037/h0040525

Milgram, S. (1974). *Obedience to authority.* Harper & Row.

Miller, D. P., Waldfogel, J., & Han, W. J. (2012). Family meals and child academic and behavioral outcomes. *Child Development, 83*(6), 2104–2120. https://doi.org/10.1111/j.1467-8624.2012.01825.x

Miller, G. A. (1956). The magic number seven plus or minus two: Some limits on our capacity for processing information. *Psychological Review, 63*(2), 81–97. https://doi.org/10.1037/h0043158

Miller, J. M., & Krosnick, J. A. (1998). The impact of candidate name order on election outcomes. *Public Opinion Quarterly, 62*(3), 291–330.

Mitchell, L. (2015, March 30). Has the world gone coco? Eating chocolate can help you LOSE weight. *Daily Star.* http://www.dailystar.co.uk/diet-fitness/433688/Chocolate-diet-how-to-lose-weight

Moffat, N. J. (1989). Home-based cognitive rehabilitation with the elderly. In L. W. Poon, D. C. Rubin, & B. A. Wilson (Eds.), *Everyday cognition in adulthood and late life* (pp. 659–680). Cambridge University Press.

Mook, D. (1989). The myth of external validity. In L. W. Poon, D. C. Rubin, & B. A. Wilson (Eds.), *Everyday cognition in adulthood and late life* (pp. 25–43). Cambridge University Press.

Mook, D. (2001). *Psychological research.* Norton.

Morehead, K., Dunlosky, J., & Rawson, K. A. (2019). How much mightier is the pen than the keyboard for note-taking? A replication and extension of Mueller and Oppenheimer (2014). *Educational Psychology Review, 31*(3), 753–780. https://doi.org/10.1007/s10648-019-09468-2

*Most Holocaust survivors battle depression.* (2010, January 26). NBC News. http://www.nbcnews.com/id/35082451/ns/health-mental_health/t/most-holocaust-survivors-battle-depression/#.U1bHs_ldV8E

Moyer, M. W. (2010, July 1). Skip the small talk: Meaningful conversations linked to happier people. *Scientific American.* http://www.scientificamerican.com/article/skip-the-small-talk/

Mrazek, M. D., Franklin, M. S., Phillips, D. T., Baird, B., & Schooler, J. W. (2013). Mindfulness training improves working memory capacity and GRE performance while reducing mind wandering. *Psychological Science, 24*(5), 776–781. https://doi.org/10.1177/0956797612459659

Mueller, C. M., & Dweck, C. S. (1998). Praise for intelligence can undermine children's motivation and performance. *Journal of Personality and Social Psychology, 75*(1), 33–52. https://doi.org/10.1037//0022-3514.75.1.33

Mueller, P. A., & Oppenheimer, D. M. (2014). The pen is mightier than the keyboard: Advantages of longhand over laptop note taking. *Psychological Science, 25*(6), 1–10. https://doi.org/10.1177/0956797614524581

Mukherjee, S. (2010). *The emperor of all maladies: A biography of cancer.* Scribner.

Myers, D. G. (2000). The funds, friends, and faith of happy people. *American Psychologist, 55*(1), 56–67. https://doi.org/10.1037//0003-066x.55.1.56

National Institutes of Health, Office of Human Subjects Research. (1979). *Belmont Report.* http://ohsr.od.nih.gov/guidelines/belmont.html

National Research Council. (2011). *Guide for the care and use of laboratory animals* (8th ed.). National Academies Press.

Nazareth, A., Huang, X., Voyer, D., & Newcombe, N. (2019). A meta-analysis of sex differences in human navigation skills. *Psychonomic Bulletin & Review, 26*(5), 1503–1528. https://doi.org/10.3758/s13423-019-01633-6

Neisser, U., & Harsch, N. (1992). Phantom flashbulbs: False recollections of hearing the news about Challenger. In E. Winograd and U. Neisser (Eds.), *Affect and accuracy in recall.* Cambridge University Press.

Nelson, S. K., Kushlev, K., English, T., Dunn, E. W., & Lyubomirsky, S. (2013). In defense of parenthood: Children are associated with more joy than misery. *Psychological Science, 24*(1), 3–10. https://doi.org/10.1177/0956797612447798

Newcombe, R. G., & Altman, D. G. (2000). Proportions and their differences. In D. Altman, D. Machin, T. Bryant, & M. Gardner (Eds.), *Statistics with confidence: Confidence intervals and statistical guidelines* (2nd ed., pp. 45–56). BMJ Books.

*New York Times* (2009, July 18). Should cell phone use by drivers be illegal? http://roomfordebate.blogs.nytimes.com/2009/07/18/should-cellphone-use-by-drivers-be-illegal/

Nicholson, C. (2006, March 28). Mindfulness may improve test scores. *Scientific American.* http://www.scientificamerican.com/podcast/episode/mindfulness-may-improve-test-scores-13-03-28/

Niederkrotenthaler, T., Stack, S., Till, B., Sinyor, M., Pirkis, J., Garcia, D., Rockett, I. R. H., & Tran, U. S. (2019). Association of increased youth suicides in the United States with the release of *13 Reasons Why. JAMA Psychiatry.* https://doi.org/10.1001/jamapsychiatry.2019.0922

Nisbett, R. E., & Wilson, T. D. (1977). Telling more than we can know: Verbal reports on mental processes. *Psychological Review, 84*(3), 231–259. https://doi.org/10.1037//0033-295X.84.3.231

Nuzzo, R. (2015). How scientists fool themselves—and how they can stop. *Nature, 526*(7572), 182–185. https://doi.org/10.1038/526182a

O'Connor, A. (2012). The chocolate diet? *The New York Times Well Blog.* http://well.blogs.nytimes.com/2012/03/26/the-chocolate-diet/?src=me&ref=general

Oettingen, G. (2014). *Rethinking positive thinking: Inside the new science of motivation.* Penguin/Current.

Oishi, S., Rothman, A. J., Snyder, M., Su, J., Zehm, K., Hertel, A. W., Gonzales, M. H., & Sherman, G. D. (2007). The socioecological model of procommunity action: The benefits of residential stability. *Journal of Personality and Social Psychology, 93*(5), 831–844. https://doi.org/10.1037/0022-3514.93.5.831

Open Science Collaboration. (2015, August 28). Estimating the reproducibility of psychological science. *Science, 349*(6251), 1–8. https://doi.org/10.1126/science.aac4716

Ortmann, A., & Hertwig, R. (1997). Is deception acceptable? *American Psychologist, 52*(7), 746–747. https://doi.org/10.1037//0003-066x.52.7.746

Ostrovsky, Y., Meyers, E., Ganesh, S., Mathur, U., & Sinha, P. (2009). Visual parsing after recovery from blindness. *Psychological Science, 20*(12), 1484–1491. https://doi.org/10.1111/j.1467-9280.2009.02471.x

Otway, L. J., & Vignoles, V. L. (2006). Narcissism and childhood recollections: A quantitative test of psychoanalytic predictions. *Personality and Social Psychology Bulletin, 32*(1), 104–116. https://doi.org/10.1177/0146167205279907

Owens, J. A., Belon, K., & Moss, P. (2010). Impact of delaying school start time on adolescent sleep, mood, and behavior. *Archives of Pediatric Adolescent Medicine, 164*(7), 608–614. https://doi.org/10.1001/archpediatrics.2010.96

Ozer, D. J., & Benet-Martínez, V. (2006). Personality and the prediction of consequential outcomes. *Annual Review of Psychology, 57*(1), 401–421. https://doi.org/10.1146/annurev.psych.57.102904.190127

Paluck, E. L. (2009). Reducing intergroup prejudice and conflict using the media: A field experiment in Rwanda. *Journal of Personality and Social Psychology, 96*(3), 574–587. https://doi.org/10.1037/a0011989

Pande, A. H., Ross-Degnan, D., Zaslavsky, A. M., & Salomon, J. A. (2011). Effects of healthcare reforms on coverage, access, and disparities: Quasi-experimental analysis of evidence from Massachusetts. *American Journal of Preventive Medicine, 41*(1), 1–8. https://doi.org/10.1016/j.amepre.2011.03.010

Paulhus, D. L., & Vazire, S. (2007). The self-report method. In R. W. Robins, R. C. Fraley, & R. Krueger (Eds.), *Handbook of research methods in personality psychology* (pp. 224–239). Guilford Press.

Pavot, W., & Diener, E. (1993). Review of the Satisfaction with Life Scale. *Psychological Assessment, 5*(2), 164–172. https://doi.org/10.1037/1040-3590.5.2.164

Pearson, C. (2015, August 6). *Science proves reading to kids really does change their brains. HuffPost.* http://www.huffingtonpost.com/entry/science-proves-reading-to-kids-changes-their-brains_us_55c26bf4e4b0f1cbf1e38740

Pelham, B. W., Carvallo, M., & Jones, J. T. (2005). Implicit egotism. *Current Directions in Psychological Science, 14*(2), 106–110. https://doi.org/10.1111/j.0963-7214.2005.00344.x

Pelham, B. W., Mirenberg, M. C., & Jones, J. T. (2002). Why Susie sells seashells by the seashore: Implicit egotism and major life decisions. *Journal of Personality and Social Psychology, 82*(4), 469–487. https://doi.org/10.1037/0022-3514.82.4.469

Perry, G. (2013). *Behind the shock machine: The untold story of the notorious Milgram psychology experiments.* New Press.

Petrosino, A., Turpin-Petrosino, C., & Finckenauer, J.O. (2000). Well-meaning programs can have harmful effects! Lessons from experiments of programs such as Scared Straight. *Crime and Delinquency, 46*(3), 354–379. https://doi.org/10.1177/0011128700046003006

Pew Research Center. (2015, May 12). *America's Changing Religious Landscape.* RLS-08-26-full-report.pdf

Pew Research Center (2015). *Americans, Politics, and Science Issues.* http://www.pewinternet.org/2015/07/01/chapter-7-opinion-about-the-use-of-animals-in-research/

Pew Research Center. (n.d.). Cell phone surveys. http://www.people-press.org/methodology/collecting-survey-data/cell-phone-surveys/

Pew Research Center. (n.d.). Random digit dialing—Our standard method. http://people-press.org/methodology/sampling/#1

Pezdek, K. (2003). Event memory and autobiographical memory for the events of September 11, 2001. *Applied Cognitive Psychology, 17*(9), 1033–1045. https://doi.org/10.1002/acp.984

Pfungst, O. (1911). *Clever Hans (The horse of Mr. Von Osten): A contribution to experimental animal and human psychology.* Henry Holt.

Piaget, J. (1923). *The language and thought of the child* (M. Worden, trans.). Harcourt, Brace, & World.

Piff, P. K., Stancato, D. M., Côté, S., Mendoza-Denton, R., & Keltner, D. (2012). Higher social class predicts increased unethical behavior. *Proceedings of the National Academy of Sciences, 109*(11), 4086–4091. https://doi.org/10.1073/pnas.1118373109

Pittenger, D. J. (2008). Deception in research: Distinctions and solutions from the perspective of utilitarianism. In D. N. Bersoff (Ed.), *Ethical conflicts in psychology* (4th ed., pp. 417–422). American Psychological Association.

Plous, S. (1996a). Attitudes toward the use of animals in psychological research and education: Results from a national survey of psychologists. *American Psychologist, 51*(11), 1167–1180. https://doi.org/10.1037/0003-066x.51.11.1167

Plous, S. (1996b). Attitudes toward the use of animals in psychological research and education: Results from a national survey of psychology majors. *Psychological Science, 7*(6), 352–358. https://doi.org/10.1111/j.1467-9280.1996.tb00388.x

Plous, S. (1998). Signs of change within the animal rights movement: Results from a follow-up survey of activists. *Journal of Comparative Psychology, 112*(1), 48–54. https://doi.org/10.1037/0735-7036.112.1.48

Plous, S., & Herzog, H. A., Jr. (2000, October 27). Poll shows researchers favor lab animal protection. *Science, 290*(5492), 711. https://doi.org/10.1126/science.290.5492.711b

Pronin, E., Gilovich, T., & Ross, L. (2004). Objectivity in the eye of the beholder: Divergent perceptions of bias in self versus others. *Psychological Review, 111*(3), 781–799. https://doi.org/10.1037/0033-295x.111.3.781

Pronin, E., Lin, D. Y., & Ross, L. (2002). The bias blind spot: Perceptions of bias in self versus others. *Personality and Social Psychology Bulletin, 28*(3), 369–381. https://doi.org/10.1177/0146167202286008

Quinn, P. C., Yahr, J., Kuhn, A., Slater, A. M., & Pascalis, O. (2002). Representation of the gender of human faces by infants: A preference for female. *Perception, 31*(9), 1109–1121. https://doi.org/10.1068/p3331

Rampell, C. (2010, April 19). Want a higher GPA? Go to a private college. *The New York Times.* https://economix.blogs.nytimes.com/2010/04/19/want-a-higher-g-p-a-go-to-a-private-college/

Raskin, R., & Terry, H. (1988). A principal components analysis of the Narcissistic Personality Inventory and further evidence of its construct validity. *Journal of Personality and Social Psychology, 54*(5), 890–902. https://doi.org/10.1037/0022-3514.54.5.890

Rauscher, F. H., Shaw, G. L., & Ky, K. N. (1993). Music and spatial task performance. *Nature, 365*(6447), 611.

Raven, J. C. (1976). *Standard progressive matrices.* Oxford Psychologists Press.

Rayner, K., Schotter, E. R., Masson, M. E. J., Potter, M.C., & Treiman, R. (2016). So much to read, so little time: How do we read, and can speed reading help? *Psychological Science in the Public Interest, 17*(1), 4–34. https://doi.org/10.1177/1529100615623267

Reiss, J. E., & Hoffman, J. E. (2006). Object substitution masking interferes with semantic processing: Evidence from event-related potentials. *Psychological Science, 17*(12), 1015–1020. https://doi.org/10.1111/j.1467-9280.2006.01820.x

Remen, T., Pintos, J., Abrahamowicz, M., & Siemiatycki, J. (2018). Risk of lung cancer in relation to various metrics of smoking history: A case-control study in Montreal. *BMC Cancer, 18*(1), 1275. https://doi.org/10.1186/s12885-018-5144-5

Rentfrow, P. J., & Gosling, S. D. (2003). The do-re-mi's of everyday life: The structure and personality correlates of music preferences. *Journal of Personality and Social Psychology, 84*(6), 1236–1256. https://doi.org/10.1037/0022-3514.84.6.1236

Reproducibility Project: Psychology. https://osf.io/EZcUj/wiki/home/

Reverby, S. (2009). *Examining Tuskegee: The infamous syphilis study and its legacy.* University of North Carolina Press.

Riedeger, M., & Klipker, K. (2014). Emotional regulation in adolescence. In J. J. Gross (Ed.), *The handbook of emotion regulation* (2nd ed., pp. 187–202). Guilford Press.

Roberts, B. W., & Robins, R. W. (2000). Broad dispositions, broad aspirations: The intersection of personality traits and major life goals. *Personality and Social Psychology Bulletin, 26*(10), 1284–1296. https://doi.org/10.1177/0146167200262009

Rohrer, D., Pashler, H., & Harris, C. R. (2015). Do subtle reminders of money change people's political views? *Journal of Experimental Psychology: General, 144*(4), e73–e85. https://doi.org/10.1037/xge0000058

Rohrer, J. M. (2018). Thinking clearly about correlations and causation: Graphical causal models for observational data. *Advances in Methods and Practices in Psychological Science, 1*(1), 27–42. https://doi.org/10.1177/2515245917745629

Ropeik, D. (2010). *How risky is it, really?: Why our fears don't always match the facts*. McGraw-Hill Education.

Ropeik, D., & Gray, G. (2002). *Risk: A practical guide for deciding what's really safe and what's really dangerous in the world around you*. Houghton Mifflin.

Rosenberg, M. (1965). *Society and the adolescent self-image*. Princeton University Press.

Rosenthal, R., & Fode, K. L. (1963). The effect of experimenter bias on the performance of the albino rat. *Behavioral Science, 8*(3), 183–189. https://doi.org/10.1002/bs.3830080302

Rubio-Aparicio, M., Marín-Martínez, F., Sánchez-Meca, J., & López-López, J. A. (2018). A methodological review of meta-analyses of the effectiveness of clinical psychology treatments. *Behavior Research Methods, 50*(5), 2057–2073. https://doi.org/10.3758/s13428-017-0973-8

Sabin, L. (2015, March 10). The origins of narcissism: Children more likely to be self-centered if they are praised too much. *Independent*. http://ind.pn/2d10Zk7

Sasaki, J. Y., & Kim, H. S. (2011). At the intersection of culture and religion: A cultural analysis of religion's implications for secondary control and social affiliation. *Journal of Personality and Social Psychology, 101*(2), 401–414. https://doi.org/10.1037/a0021849

Sathyanarayana Rao, T. S., & Andrade, C. (2011). The MMR vaccine and autism: Sensation, refutation, retraction, and fraud. *Indian Journal of Psychiatry, 53*(2), 95–96. https://doi.org/10.4103/0019-5545.82529

Sawilowsky, S. S. (2004). Teaching random assignment: Do you believe it works? Theoretical and behavioral foundations of education. *Journal of Modern Applied Statistical Methods, 3*(1), 221–226. https://doi.org/10.22237/jmasm/1083370980

Saxe, L. (1991). Lying: Thoughts of an applied social psychologist. *American Psychologist, 46*(4), 409–415. https://doi.org/10.1037//0003-066X.46.4.409

Schäfer, T., & Schwarz, M. A. (2019). The meaningfulness of effect sizes in psychological research: Differences between sub-disciplines and the impact of potential biases. *Frontiers in Psychology, 10*, https://doi.org/10.3389/fpsyg.2019.00813

Schwarz, N., & Clore, G. L. (1983). Mood, misattribution, and judgments of well-being: Informative and directive functions of affective states. *Journal of Personality and Social Psychology, 45*(3), 513–523. https://doi.org/10.1037/0022-3514.45.3.513

Schwarz, N., & Oyserman, D. (2001). Asking questions about behavior: Cognition, communication, and questionnaire construction. *American Journal of Evaluation, 22*(2), 127–160. https://doi.org/10.1016/s1098-2140(01)00133-3

ScienceDaily. (2015, September 11). *Pressure to be available 24/7 on social media causes teen anxiety, depression*. https://www.sciencedaily.com/releases/2015/09/150911094917.htm

Scoville, W. B., & Milner, B. (1957). Loss of recent memory after bilateral hippocampal lesions. *Journal of Neurology, Neurosurgery, and Psychiatry, 20*, 11–21. https://doi.org/10.1136/jnnp.20.1.11

Sears, D. O. (1986). College sophomores in the laboratory: Influences of a narrow data base on social psychology's view of human nature. *Journal of Personality and Social Psychology, 51*(3), 515–530. https://doi.org/10.1037//0022-3514.51.3.515

Segal, D. L., Coolidge, F. L., Cahill, B. S., & O'Riley, A. A. (2008). Psychometric properties of the Beck Depression Inventory-II (BDI-II) among community-dwelling older adults. *Behavior Modification, 32*(1), 3–20. https://doi.org/10.1177/0145445507303833

Segall, M. H., Campbell, D. T., & Herskovits, M. J. (1966). *The influence of culture on visual perception*. Bobbs-Merrill.

Shadish, W. R., Cook, T. D., & Campbell, D. T. (2002). *Experimental and quasi-experimental designs for generalized causal inference*. Houghton Mifflin.

Shadish, W. R., & Luellen, J. K. (2006). Quasi-experimental design. In J. L. Green, G. Camilli, & P. B. Elmore (Eds.), *Handbook of complementary methods in education research* (pp. 539–550). Erlbaum.

Shane, S., & Frenkel, S. (2018, December 17). Russian 2016 influence operation targeted African-Americans on social media. *The New York Times*. https://www.nytimes.com/2018/12/17/us/politics/russia-2016-influence-campaign.html

Sharpe, D., Adair, J. G., & Roese, N. J. (1992). Twenty years of deception research: A decline in subjects' trust? *Personality and Social Psychology Bulletin, 18*(5), 585–590. https://doi.org/10.1177/0146167292185009

Shuster, E. (1997). Fifty years later: The significance of the Nuremberg Code. *New England Journal of Medicine, 337*(20), 1436–1440. https://doi.org/10.1056/nejm199711133372006

Shweder, R. (1989). Cultural psychology: What is it? In J. Stigler, R. Shweder, & G. Herdt (Eds.), *Cultural psychology: The Chicago symposia on culture and development* (pp. 1–46). Cambridge University Press.

Siddarth, P., Burggren, A. C., Eyre, H. A., Small, G. W., & Merrill, D. A. (2018). Sedentary behavior associated with reduced medial temporal lobe thickness in middle-aged and older adults. *PLOS ONE, 13*(4), e0195549. https://doi.org/10.1371/journal.pone.0195549

Silver, N. (2012). Fivethirtyeight: Nate Silver's political calculus. *The New York Times*. http://fivethirtyeight.blogs.nytimes.com

Silverman, C., & Singer-Vine, J. (2016). Most Americans who see fake news believe it, new survey says. Buzzfeed News. https://www.buzzfeednews.com/article/craigsilverman/fake-news-survey

Simmons, J. P., Nelson, L. D., & Simonsohn, U. (2011). False-positive psychology: Undisclosed flexibility in data collection and analysis allows presenting anything as significant. *Psychological Science, 22*(11), 1359–1366. https://doi.org/10.1177/0956797611417632

Simmons, J. P., Nelson, L. D., & Simonsohn, U. (2012). A 21-word solution. SSRN. https://doi.org/10.2139/ssrn.2160588

Simonsohn, U. (2011). Spurious? Name similarity effects (implicit egotism) in marriage, job, and moving decisions. *Journal of Personality and Social Psychology, 101*(1), 1–24. https://doi.org/10.1037/a0021990

Simonsohn, U. (2015). Small telescopes: Detectability and the evaluation of replication results. *Psychological Science, 26*(5), 559–569. https://doi.org/10.1177/0956797614567341

Simon-Thomas, E. R. (2016, June 4). Are the rich more lonely? *Huff-Post*. http://www.huffingtonpost.com/greater-good-science-center/are-the-rich-more-lonely_b_10296990.html

Smith, G. T. (2005a). On construct validity: Issues of method and measurement. *Psychological Assessment, 17*(4), 396–408. https://doi.org/10.1037/1040-3590.17.4.396

Smith, G. T. (2005b). On the complexity of quantifying construct validity. *Psychological Assessment, 17*(4), 413–414. https://doi.org/10.1037/1040-3590.17.4.413

Smith, S. S., & Richardson, D. (1983). Amelioration of deception and harm in psychological research: The important role of debriefing. *Journal of Personality and Social Psychology, 44*(5), 1075–1082. https://doi.org/10.1037//0022-3514.44.5.1075

Snibbe, A. C., & Markus, H. R. (2005). You can't always get what you want: Educational attainment, agency, and choice. *Journal of Personality and Social Psychology, 88*(4), 703–720. https://doi.org/10.1037/0022-3514.88.4.703

Snyder, M., & Campbell, B. (1980). Testing hypotheses about other people: The role of the hypothesis. *Personality and Social Psychology Bulletin, 6*(3), 421–426. https://doi.org/10.1177/014616728063015

Snyder, M., & Swann, W. B. (1978). Hypothesis-testing processes in social interaction. *Journal of Personality and Social Psychology, 36*(11), 1202–1212. https://doi.org/10.1037/0022-3514.36.11.1202

Snyder, M., & White, P. (1981). Testing hypotheses about other people: Strategies of verification and falsification. *Personality and Social Psychology Bulletin, 7*(1), 39–43. https://doi.org/10.1177/014616728171007

Spiegel, A. (2010, June 28). "Mozart effect" was just what we wanted to hear. National Public Radio transcript. http://www.npr.org/templates/story/story.php?storyId=128104580

Stapel Investigation. (2012). Flawed science: The fraudulent research practices of social psychologist Diederik Stapel. https://www.commissielevelt.nl

Steenhuysen, J. (2010, April 26). Depressed? You must like chocolate. MSNBC. http://www.msnbc.msn.com/id/36786824/ns/health-mental_health

Stein, R. (2009, June 22). Positive thinking may be a negative. *The Canton Repository*. https://www.cantonrep.com/article/20090622/NEWS/306229815?template=ampart

Steinberg, L., & Monahan, K. (2011). Adolescents' exposure to sexy media does not hasten the initiation of sexual intercourse.*Developmental Psychology, 47*(2), 562–576. https://doi.org/10.1037/a0020613

Steingraber, S. (2008). Pesticides, animals, and humans. In L. H. Peterson & J. C. Brereton (Eds.), *The Norton Reader* (11th ed., pp. 971–982). Norton. (Reprinted from *Living downstream: An ecologist looks at cancer and the environment*, by S. Steingraber, 1997, New York: Perseus Books.)

Strack, F. (2016). Reflection on the smiling registered replication report. *Perspectives on Psychological Science, 11*(6), 929–930. https://doi.org/10.1177/1745691616674460

Strack, F., Martin, L. L., & Stepper, S. (1988). Inhibiting and facilitating conditions of the human smile: A nonobtrusive test of the facial feedback hypothesis. *Journal of Personality and Social Psychology, 54*(5), 768–777. https://doi.org/10.1037/0022-3514.54.5.768

Strauss, M. (2018). Americans divided over the use of animals in scientific research. Pew Research Center. https://www.pewresearch.org/fact-tank/2018/08/16/americans-are-divided-over-the-use-of-animals-in-scientific-research/

Strayer, D. L., & Drews, F. A. (2004). Profiles in distraction: Effects of cell phone conversations on younger and older drivers. *Human Factors, 46*(4), 640–650. https://doi.org/10.1518/hfes.46.4.640.56806

Strayer, D. L., Drews, F. A., & Johnston, W. A. (2003). Cell phone-induced failures in visual attention during simulated driving. *Journal of Experimental Psychology: Applied, 9*(1), 23–32. https://doi.org/10.1037/1076-898X.9.1.23

Stroebe, W., Postmes, T., & Spears, R. (2012). Scientific misconduct and the myth of self-correction in science. *Psychological Science, 7*(6), 670–688. https://doi.org/10.1177/1745691612460687

Strube, M. J. (1991). Small sample failure of random assignment: A further examination. *Journal of Consulting and Clinical Psychology, 59*(2), 346–350. https://doi.org/10.1037//0022-006x.59.2.346

Suchotzki, K., Verschuere, B., Van Bockstaele, B., Ben-Shakhar, G., & Crombez, G. (2017). Lying takes time: A meta-analysis on reaction time measures of deception. *Psychological Bulletin, 143*(4), 428–453. https://doi.org/10.1037/bul0000087

Suds seem to skew scientific success. (2008, March 18). *The San Diego Union Tribune*. http://www.utsandiego.com/uniontrib/20080318/news_1n18science.html

Sugden, N. A., Mohamed-Ali, M. I., & Moulson, M. C. (2013). I spy with my little eye: Typical, daily exposure to faces documented from a first-person infant perspective. *Developmental Psychobiology, 56*(2), 249–261. https://doi.org/10.1002/dev.21183

Talarico, J. M., & Rubin, D. C. (2003). Confidence, not consistency, characterizes flashbulb memories. *Psychological Science, 14*(5), 455–461. https://10.1111/1467-9280.02453

Tavris, C. (1989). *Anger: The misunderstood emotion*. Simon & Schuster.

Taylor, L. E., Swerdfeger, A. L., & Eslick, G. D. (2014). Vaccines are not associated with autism: An evidence-based meta-analysis of case-control and cohort studies. *Vaccine, 32*(29), 3623–3629. https://doi.org/10.1016/j.vaccine.2014.04.085

Thaler, R., & Sunstein, C. (2008). *Nudge: Improving decisions about health, wealth, and happiness*. Penguin Books.

Tighe, M. (2008, November 3). Study Links Teen Pregnancy to Sex on TV Shows. Newsmax. http://www.newsmax.com/Newsfront/sex-tv-abstinence-teen/2008/11/03/id/326321/

Tucker, C. J., Finkelhor, D., Turner, H., & Shattuck, A. (2013). Association of sibling aggression with child and adolescent mental health. *Pediatrics, 132*(1), 79–84. https://doi.org/10.1542/peds.2012-3801

Turner, E. H., Matthews, A. M., Linardatos, E., Tell, R. A., & Rosenthal, R. (2008). Selective publication of antidepressant trials and its influence on apparent efficacy. *New England Journal of Medicine, 358*(3), 252–260. https://doi.org/10.1056/NEJMsa065779

Tversky, A., & Kahneman, D. (1974). Judgments under uncertainty: Heuristics and biases. *Science, 185*(4157), 1124–1131. https://doi.org/10.1126/science.185.4157.1124

Twachtman-Cullen, D. (1997). *A passion to believe: Autism and the facilitated communication phenomenon*. Westview Press.

Tyner, S., Brewer, A., Helman, M., Leon, Y., Pritchard, J., & Schlund, M. (2016) Nice doggie! Contact desensitization plus reinforcement decreases dog phobias for children with autism. *Behavior Analysis and Practice, 9*(1), 54–57. https://doi.org/10.1007/s40617-016-0113-4

Uhls, Y. T., Michikyan, M., Morris, J., Garcia, D., Small, G. W., Zgourou, E., & Greenfield, P. M. (2014). Five days at outdoor education camp without screens improves preteen skills with nonverbal cues. *Computers in Human Behavior, 39,* 387–392. https://doi.org/10.1016/j.chb.2014.05.036

Urry, H. L. (2019, February 9). Don't ditch the laptop just yet: A direct replication of Mueller and Oppenheimer's (2014) Study 1 Plus Mini-Meta-Analyses Across Similar Studies. https://doi.org/10.31234/osf.io/vqyw6

U.S. Department of Health and Human Services. (2012). Summary health statistics for U.S. adults: National Health Interview Survey, 2011. http://www.cdc.gov/nchs/data/series/sr_10/sr10_256.pdf

U.S. Department of Health and Human Services, National Institutes of Health. (2009). Public welfare, protection of human subjects. Code of Federal Regulations: HHS Regulation 45 CFR, Part 46. http://www.hhs.gov/ohrp/humansubjects/guidance/45cfr46.html

U.S. Public Health Service (1973). Final Report of the Tuskegee Syphilis Study Ad Hoc Advisory Panel. U.S. Department of Health, Education, and Welfare.

Van Bavel, J. J., Mende-Siedlecki, P., Brady, W. J., & Reinero, D. A. (2016). Contextual sensitivity in scientific reproducibility. *Proceedings of the National Academy of Sciences, 113*(23), 6454–6459. https://doi.org/10.1073/pnas.1521897113

Vandell, D., Henderson, L. V., & Wilson, K. S. (1988). A longitudinal study of children with day-care experiences of varying quality. *Child Development, 59*(5), 1286–1292. https://doi.org/10.1111/j.1467-8624.1988.tb01497.x

Van Orden, K. A., Witte, T. K., Cukrowicz, K. C., Braithwaite, S. R., Selby, E. A., & Joiner, T. E. (2010). The interpersonal theory of suicide. *Psychological Review, 117*(2), 575–600. https://doi.org/10.1037/a0018697

Vazire, S. (2018). Implications of the credibility revolution for productivity, creativity, and progress. *Perspectives on Psychological Science, 13*(4), 411–417. https://doi.org/10.1177/1745691617751884

Vazire., S., & Carlson, E. N. (2011). Others sometimes know us better than we know ourselves. *Current Directions in Psychological Science, 20*(2), 104–108. https://doi.org/10.1177/0963721411402478

Vedantam, S. (2016, June 7). How stories told of brilliant scientists affect kids' interest in the field. *Morning Edition, National Public Radio.* http://www.npr.org/2016/06/07/481058613/how-the-stories-told-of-brilliant-scientists-affect-kids-interest-in-the-field

Vickery, T. J., Chun, M. M., & Lee, D. (2011). Ubiquity and specificity of reinforcement signals throughout the human brain. *Neuron, 72*(1), 166–177. https://doi.org/10.1016/j.neuron.2011.08.011

Vohs, K. D. (2015). Money priming can change people's thoughts, feelings, motivations, and behaviors: An update on 10 years of experiments. *Journal of Experimental Psychology: General, 144*(4), e86–e93. https://doi.org/10.1037/xge0000091

Waelde, L. C., Uddo, M., Marquett, R., Ropelato, M., Freightman, S., Pardo, A., & Salazar, J. (2008). A pilot study of meditation for mental health workers following Hurricane Katrina. *Journal of Traumatic Stress, 21*(5), 497–500. https://doi.org/10.1002/jts.20365

Wagenmakers, E.-J., Beek, T., Dijkhoff, L., Gronau, Q. F., Acosta, A., Adams, R. B., Albohn, D. N., Allard, E. S., Benning, S. D., Blouin-Hudon, E.-M., Bulnes, L. C., Caldwell, T. L., Calin-Jageman, R. J., Capaldi, C. A., Carfagno, N. S., Chasten, K. T., Cleeremans, A., Connell, L., DeCicco, J. M., . . . Zwaan, R. A. (2016). Registered Replication Report: Strack, Martin, & Stepper (1988). *Perspectives on Psychological Science, 11*(6), 917–928. https://doi.org/10.1177/1745691616674458

Wakefield, A., Murch, S., Anthony, A., Linnell, J., Casson, D., Malik, M., Berelowitz, M., Dhillon, A., Thomson, M., Harvey, P., Valentine, A., Davies, S., & Walker-Smith, J. (1998). RETRACTED: Ileal-lymphoid-nodular hyperplasia, nonspecific colitis, and pervasive developmental disorder in children. *The Lancet, 351*(9103), 637–641. https://doi.org/10.1016/S0140-6736(97)11096-0

Wardle, C. (2017, February 16). Fake news. It's complicated. First Draft News. https://firstdraftnews.org/fake-news-complicated/

Warner, J. (2008, January 7). Family meals curb eating disorders. WebMD. http://www.webmd.com/parenting/news/20080107/family-meals-curb-teen-eating-disorders

Webb, E., Campbell, D., Schwartz, R., & Sechrest, L. (1966). *Unobtrusive measures: Nonreactive research in the social sciences.* Rand McNally.

Wechsler, D. (2004). *The Wechsler Intelligence Scale for Children* (4th ed.). Pearson Assessment.

Welsh, J. (2012, May 17). Parents are happier than non-parents. Live Science. http://www.livescience.com/20391-parents-happier-parents.html

Westfall, J., & Yarkoni, T. (2016). Statistically controlling for confounding constructs is harder than you think. *PLOS ONE, 11*(3), e0152719. https://doi.org/10.1371/journal.pone.0152719

Williams, L. M. (1994). Recall of childhood trauma: A prospective study of women's memories of child sexual abuse. *Journal of Consulting and Clinical Psychology, 62*(6), 1167–1176. https://doi.org/10.1037/0022-006X.62.6.1167

Wilson, B. A., & Wearing, D. (1995). Prisoner of consciousness: A state of just awakening following herpes simplex encephalitis. In R. Campbell, & M. A. Conway (Eds.), *Broken memories: Case studies in memory impairment* (pp. 14–30). Blackwell.

Wilson, D. C. (2006, December). Framing the future of race relations. *Public Opinion Pros.* http://www.publicopinionpros.norc.org

Wilson, D. C., & Brewer, P. R. (2016). Do frames emphasizing harm to age and racial-ethnic groups reduce support for voter ID laws? *Social Science Quarterly, 97*(2), 391–406. https://doi.org/10.1111/ssqu.12234

Wilson, D. C., Moore, D. W., McKay, P. F., & Avery, D. R. (2008). Affirmative action programs for women and minorities: Expressed support affected by question order. *Public Opinion Quarterly, 72*(3), 514–522. https://doi.org/10.1093/poq/nfn031

Wilson, T. D. (2011). *Redirect: The surprising new science of psychological change.* Little Brown/Hachette Book Group.

Wineburg, S., & McGrew, S. (2017). Lateral reading: Reading less and learning more when evaluating digital information. Stanford history education group working paper no. 2017-A1.

Witkower, Z., & Tracy, J. L. (2019). A facial-action imposter: How head tilt influences perceptions of dominance from a neutral face. *Psychological Science, 30*(6), 893–906. https://doi.org/10.1177/0956797619838762

Witters, D., H., D. (2020, April 14). *In U.S., Life Ratings Plummet to 12-Year Low.* Gallup.com. https://news.gallup.com/poll/308276/life-ratings-plummet-year-low.aspx

Wolfers, J. (2014, October 31). How confirmation bias can lead to a spinning of wheels. *The New York Times.* https://www.nytimes.com/2014/11/01/upshot/how-confirmation-bias-can-lead-to-a-spinning-of-wheels.html

Wolraich, M. L., Lindgren, S. D., Stumbo, P. J., Stegink, L. D., Appelbaum, M. I., & Kiritsy, M. C. (1994). Effects of Diets High in Sucrose or Aspartame on The Behavior and Cognitive Performance of Children. *New England Journal of Medicine, 330*(5), 301–307. https://doi.org/10.1056/NEJM199402033300501

Wood, J. V., Perunovic, E. W. Q., & Lee, J. W. (2009). Positive self-statements: Power for some, peril for others. *Psychological Science, 20*(7), 860–866. https://doi.org/10.1111/j.1467-9280.2009.02370.x

Yeager, D. S., Hanselman, P., Walton, G. M., Murray, J. S., Crosnoe, R., Muller, C., Tipton, E., Schneider, B., Hulleman, C. S., Hinojosa, C. P., Paunesku, D., Romero, C., Flint, K., Roberts, A., Trott, J., Iachan, R., Buontempo, J., Yang, S. M., Carvalho, C. M., . . . Dweck, C. S. (2019). A national experiment reveals where a growth mindset improves achievement. *Nature, 573*(7774), 364–369. https://doi.org/10.1038/s41586-019-1466-y

Yong, E. (2015, August 27). How reliable are psychology studies? *The Atlantic.* https://www.theatlantic.com/science/archive/2015/08/psychology-studies-reliability-reproducability-nosek/402466/

Yong, E. (2017, September 21). Infants can learn the value of perseverance by watching adults. *The Atlantic.* https://www.theatlantic.com/science/archive/2017/09/infants-can-learn-the-value-of-perseverance-by-watching-adults/540471/

Yorio, N. (2010). Seven secrets of low-stress families. WebMD. http://www.webmd.com/parenting/features/seven-secrets-of-low-stress-families#1

# Credits

## Frontmatter

**Page ii**: Hero Images/Getty Images; **Page viii**: Courtesy of Sarah Franczyk; **Page xx**: weestock Images/Alamy Stock Photo; **Page xxii**: littleny/Shutterstock; **Page xxiii**: Trio Images/Getty Images; **Page xxiv**: Muslim Girl/Getty Images; **Page xxv**: Courtesy of the author; **Page xxvii**: cbpix/Getty Images

## Part Opener I

**Pages 2–3**: weestock Images/Alamy Stock Photo

## Chapter 1

**Page 4 (left)**: A&E/Everett Collection; **(right)**: Tribune Content Agency LLC/Alamy Stock Photo; **Page 7**: AP Photo/Nati Harnik; **Page 8**: A&E/Everett Collection; **Page 11**: fizkes/Shutterstock; **Page 12**: Harlow Primate Laboratory; **Page 14**: Los Angeles Times; **Page 15**: © Walt Disney/Everett Collection; **Page 16 (left)**: Courtesy of Jeff Miller/University of Wisconsin-Madison; **(right)**: Steve Liss/The LIFE Images Collection/Getty Images; **Page 18**: PHD Comics.com; **Page 19**: Jim Wilson/The New York Times/Redux

## Chapter 2

**Page 22 (top)**: eclipse_images/Getty Images; **(bottom)**: frederic REGLAIN/Alamy Stock Photo; **Page 24 (top)**: opturadesign/Alamy Stock Photo; **(bottom)**: Rossana V. Morales/Shutterstock; **Page 32**: Our World in Data; **Page 34**: Wavebreak Media ltd/Alamy; **Page 35**: BURGER/PHANIE/Alamy Stock Photo; **Page 37 (left)**: Darren Gerrish/WireImage/Getty Images; **(right)**: Kevin Mazur/Getty Images for TB12; **Page 40**: Bushman Brad J.: Does Venting Anger Feed or Extinguish the Flame? Personality and Social Psychology Bulletin. Sage Publications 06/01/2002. ©2002 Society for Personality and Social Psychology Inc. Reprinted by Permission of SAGE Publications; **Page 41**: Courtesy of the author; **Page 45**: © Signe Wilkinson, 2016/The Washington Post; **Page 47**: Good Morning America

## Chapter 3

**Page 54 (top)**: Imperia Staffieri/agefotostock; **(left)**: YouTube; **(right)**: weestock Images/Alamy Stock Photo; **Page 56**: Courtesy of the author; **Page 59 (left)**: Christina K. Betz; **(right)**: Sean Gallup/Getty Images; **Page 73 (Figure 3.4)**: Republished with permission of The Society for Research in Child Development, Blackwell Publishing, Inc., John Wiley & Sons, from "The 'Batman Effect': Improving Perseverance in Young Children," in *Child Development*, Rachel E. White, Emily O. Prager, Catherine Schaefer, Ethan Kross, Angela L. Duckworth, Stephanie M., Vol 88, Issue 5, pp 1563–1571, © 2016; permission conveyed through Copyright Clearance Center, Inc.; **Page 77**: Joshua Resnick/Shutterstock; **Page 80**: Zachary Witkower and Jessica L. Tracy, Psychological Science Volume 30 issue 6, pp 893–906

## Part Opener II

**Pages 86–87**: littleny/Shutterstock

## Chapter 4

**Page 88 (left)**: Oli Scarff/Getty Images; **(right)**: Ryan Smith/Getty Images; **(bottom)**: littleny/Shutterstock; **Page 90**: National Archives and Records Administration Southeast Region (Atlanta); **Page 91**: Paul J. Richards/AFP/Getty Images; **Pages 92–93**: From the film Obedience © 1965 by Stanley Milgram. © Renewed 1993 by Alexandra Milgram. Distributed by Alexander Street Press; **Page 95**: Voisin/Phanie/Science Source; **Page 97**: Courtesy of the author; **Page 98**: Copyright 2017 by the American Psychological Association. Reproduced [or Adapted] with permission. The official citation that should be used in referencing this material is the APA ethics code here: https://www.apa.org/ethics/code/index.aspx. No further reproduction or distribution is permitted without written permission from the American Psychological Association; **Page 101**: Diego Cervo/Fotolia; **Page 102**: Thierry Berrod, Mona Lisa Production/Science Source; **Page 104 (left)**: Diomedia/BSIP; **(right)**: Sathyanarayana Rao T.S. & Andrade C. (2011). The MMR vaccine and autism: Sensation refutation and fraud. Indian Journal of Psychiatry 53 95–96; **Page 106**: Witkower, Tracy, et al. 2019; **Page 108**: Stephen Bell/Alamy Stock Photo; **Page 109**: Edmond Terakopian - PA Images/Getty Images; **Page 111**: Brendan O'Sullivan/Getty Images

## Chapter 5

**Page 116 (top)**: Donatas Dabravolskas/Shutterstock; **(left)**: James Doberman/Shutterstock; **(right)**: Ingus Kruklitis/Shutterstock; **Page 121**: Vickery et al. (2011). Ubiquity and specificity of reinforcement signals throughout the human brain. Neuron *72*(1): 166–177 supplemental Figure S1 panel B. © 2011 Elsevier; **Page 132**: Table 2 p. 167 from Pavot W. & Diener E. (1993). Review of the Satisfaction With Life Scale. Psychological Assessment *5*(2) 164–172. doi:10.1037/1040-3590.5.2.164; **Page 133**: GagliardiImages/Shutterstock; **Page 134**: Courtesy of the author; **Page 144**: Folio Images/Shutterstock; **Page 145**: James Doberman/Shutterstock

## Part Opener III

**Pages 150–151**: Trio Images/Getty Images

## Chapter 6

**Page 152 (top)**: Trio Images/Getty Images; **(left)**: Vox.com; **(right)**: Jill Freedman/Getty Images; **Page 156**: Yelp; **Page 160**: Broward County Board of Elections; **Page 161**: Courtesy of the author; **Page 164**: FG Trade/Getty Images; **Page 165**: Christina K. Betz; **Page 167 (right)**: Science 317/5834/82 Title: Are Women Really More Talkative Than Men? Matthias R. Mehl, Simine Vazire, Nairán Ramírez-Esparza; **(left)**: Matthias Mehl; **Page 168 (all)**: John M. Franchak, Kari S. Kretch, Karen E. Adolph/Developmental Science V21 Issue 4/John Wiley & Sons Ltd.; **Page 169**: Copyright 2013 by the American Psychological Association. Reproduced with permission. Campos et al. (2013). Positive and negative emotion in the daily life of dual-earner couples with children. Journal of Family Psychology *27*(1) 76–85. doi:10.1037/a0031413 No further reproduction or distribution is permitted without written permission from the American Psychological Association; **Page 171**: Mary Evans Picture Library/Alamy Stock Photo; **Page 172**: Copyright 2013 by the American Psychological Association. Reproduced with permission. Campos et al. (2013). Positive and negative emotion in the daily life of dual-earner couples with children. Journal of Family Psychology *27*(1) 76–85. doi:10.1037/a0031413 No further reproduction or distribution is permitted without written permission from the American Psychological Association; **Page 173**: Spencer Grant/Science Source; **Page 177**: Courtesy of Nicole Sugden and Margaret Moulson/Ryerson University

## Chapter 7

**Page 178 (top)**: Fedor Eremin/Shutterstock; **(middle)**: Heathcliff O'Malley/Camera Press/Redux; **(bottom)**: Zappos.com; **Page 183**: Sipa USA/Alamy Stock Photo; **Page 184**: Travis Carr; **Page 185**: Buzzfeed.com; **Page 186**: © AAA 2016. Reprinted with permission; **Page 187**: Urbaniak G. C.& Plous S. (2015). Research Randomizer (Version 4.0) [Computer software]. Retrieved on January 20, 2017 from http://www.randomizer.org; **Page 194**: Courtesy of the author

## Part Opener IV

**Pages 200–201**: Muslim Girl/Getty Images

## Chapter 8

**Page 202 (left)**: ZenShui/Sigrid Olson/Getty Images; **(right)**: Nick Sinclair/Alamy Stock Photo; **(bottom)**: Matthew Staver/The New York Times/ Redux; **Page 206 (Figure 8.2)**: Siddarth et al. "Sedentary behavior associated with reduced medial temporal lobe thickness in middle-aged and older adults," PLoS ONE *13*(4): e0195549; **Page 211**: ZUMA Press Inc/Alamy Stock Photo; **Page 214 (Figure 8.8)**: Milek, Anne, et al. "'Eavesdropping on Happiness' Revisited: A Pooled, Multisample Replication of the Association Between Life Satisfaction and Observed Daily Conversation Quantity and Quality," in *Psychological Science 29*(9) © 2018, SAGE Publications; **Page 226 (Figure 8.18)**: Shigehiro Oishi et al., "The socioecological model of procommunity action: The benefits of residential stability," *Journal of Personality and Social Psychology*, Vol. *93*(5), Nov. 2007, 831–844. Copyright 2007 by the American Psychological Association; **Page 228**: Sofi photo/Shutterstock; **Pages 235–237**: Courtesy of the author

## Chapter 9

**Page 241 (top)**: InspiredFootage/Getty Images; **(bottom)**: Richard Cartwright/ABC via Getty Images; **Page 247**: asisee-it/Getty Images; **Page 258**: Dimitrios Pappas/Dreamstime.com; **Page 259**: Phovoir/Shutterstock; **Page 261**: pixelrain/Shutterstock

## Part Opener V

**Pages 274–275**: Courtesy of the author

## Chapter 10

**Page 276 (top)**: Courtesy of the author; **(bottom)**: Myrleen Pearson/Alamy Stock Photo; **Page 278**: Hongqi Zhang/Alamy Stock Photo; **Page 279 (Figure 10.2)**: Mueller, P. A. & D. M. Oppenheimer. "Corrigendum: The Pen Is Mightier Than the Keyboard: Advantages of Longhand Over Laptop

Note Taking," Psychological Science 25:1159–1168 © 2018, SAGE Publications; **Page 280**: Julia A. Leonard, Yuna Lee, Laura E. Schulz. Science 22 Sep 2017: Vol. 357, Issue 6357, pp. 1290–1294 DOI: 10.1126/science.aan2317; **Page 294**: Michael D. Mrazek et al. Psychological Science. Vol *24*(5) pp 776–781 © 2013. Reprinted by Permission of SAGE Publications Inc.; **Page 307**: Luka Lajst/Getty Images; **Pages 317–319**: Courtesy of the author

## Chapter 11

**Page 322 (top)**: Camille Tokerud/Getty Images; **(bottom)**: Mike Cullen; **Page 336**: The Photo Works/Alamy Stock Photo; **Page 337**: Michael D. Mrazek et al. Psychological Science, Vol *24*(5) pp 776–781 © 2013. Reprinted by Permission of SAGE Publications Inc.; **Page 340**: Susan Chiang/Getty Images; **Page 356**: Figure 2, p. e76 , from Rohrer, D., Pashler, H., & Harris, C. R. (2015). Do subtle reminders of money change people's political views? Journal of Experimental Psychology: General, *144*(4), e73–e85. https://doi.org/10.1037/xge0000058

## Chapter 12

**Page 362 (top)**: Edward Frazer/Corbis; **(bottom)**: Adrian Hancu/iStock Editorial; **Page 366 (Figure 12.4)**: Graph: "Rated deliciousness of sandwich." Reprinted by permission of Vanessa Loaiza; **Page 368**: Strayer D. L. & Drews F. A. (2004). Profiles in driver distraction: Effects of cell phone conversations on younger and older drivers. Human Factors 46 640–649. Photo courtesy David Strayer; **Page 393**: Courtesy of Eniko Kubinyi

## Part Opener VI

**Pages 398–399**: cbpix/Getty Images

## Chapter 13

**Page 400 (top)**: PHOTOINKE/Alamy Stock Photo; **(bottom)**: Jose L. Stephens/Shutterstock; **Page 403**: Cordelia Molloy/Science Source; **Page 405**: Reports of Adolescent Psychiatric Outpatients on the Impact of the TV Series "13 Reasons Why": A Qualitative Study, by Benedikt Till, Christine Vesely, Dunja Mairhofer, Marlies Braun, Thomas Niederkrotenthaler, Journal of Adolescent Health; **Page 406 (Figure 13.4)**: Republished with permission of the Society for Adolescent Medicine and Elsevier Science & Technology Journals, from "Reports of Adolescent Psychiatric Outpatients on the Impact of the TV Series '13 Reasons Why': A Qualitative Study" in *Journal of Adolescent Health: Official publication of the Society for Adolescent Medicine,* Till B, Vesely C, Mairhofer D, Braun M, Niederkrotenthaler T, Vol 64, Issue 3, pp 414–415, © 1991; permission conveyed

through Copyright Clearance Center, Inc.; **Page 407 (Figure 13.5)**: Republished with permission of the American Public Health Association, from "Opioid Overdose Deaths and Florida's Crackdown on Pill Mills" by Alene Kennedy-Hendricks, PhD, Matthew Richey, PhD, Emma E. McGinty, PhD, MS, Elizabeth A. Stuart, Phd in *American Journal of Public Health: JPH, 106*(2), pp 291–297, © 2016; permission conveyed through Copyright Clearance Center, Inc.; **Page 409**: Blend Images /JGI/Jamie Grill/Media Bakery; **Page 411**: David Crigger/Bristol Herald Courier/Associated Press; **Page 412 (Figure 13.8)**: Republished with permission of Project Hope, from "Mandatory Provider Review And Pain Clinic Laws Reduce The Amounts Of Opioids Prescribed And Overdose Death Rates" by Deborah Dowell, Kun Zhang, Rita K. Noonan, and Jason M. Hockenberry in *Health Affairs Journal, 35*(10), pp 1876–1883, © 1981; permission conveyed through Copyright Clearance Center, Inc.; **Page 420 (left)**: From NOVA ScienceNow, How Memory Works (https://www.pbs.org/wgbh/nova/article/corkin-hm-memory/) ©1997–2020 WGBH Educational Foundation; **(right)**: Henry Molaison, aged 60, at MIT in 1986. Photograph by Jenni Ogden, author of book *Trouble in Mind: Stories from a Neuropsychologist's Casebook*; **Page 422**: Annese J. et al. Postmortem examination of patient H.M.'s brain based on histological sectioning and digital 3D reconstruction. Nat. Commun. 5:3122 doi: 10.1038/ncomms4122 (2014); **Page 424**: BSIP SA/Alamy Stock Photo; **Page 428 (left)**: Patrick Grehan/Getty Images; **(right)**: Maya Barnes Johansen/TopFoto

## Chapter 14

**Page 436 (top)**: Juice Images/age fotostock; **(left)**: robertharding/Alamy Stock Photo; **(right)**: Benoit Decout/REA/Redux; **Pages 441–442**: Wagenmakers, E. J., Beek, T., Dijkhoff, L., Gronau, Q. F., Acosta, A., Adams, R. B., Jr., . . . Zwaan, R. A. (2016). Registered Replication Report: Strack, Martin, & Stepper (1988). Perspectives on Psychological Science, 11, 917–928; **Page 443 (Figure 14.6)**: From "Investigating Variation in Replicability: A 'Many Labs' Replication Project," by Richard A. Klein et al. in *Social Psychology* 45:142–152, © 2014. Reprinted by permission of Richard A. Klein; **Page 445 (top)**: carlos cardetas/Alamy Stock Photo; **(Table 14.1)**: From "Lying takes time: A meta-analysis on reaction time measures of deception," by Kristina Suchotzki et al. in *Psychological Bulletin 143*(4):428–453, © 2017 The American Psychiatric Association; **Page 447**: Jonathan Nourok/Getty Images; **Page 450 (all)**: Courtesy of OSF | Center for Open Science; **Page 455**: Natalia Rapoport/Shutterstock; **Page 460**: Lifeline Energy Foundation

## Statistics Review: Descriptive Statistics

**Page 476**: Mueller, P. A., & Oppenheimer, D. M. (2014); **Page 481 (Figure S1.11)**: Siddarth, et. al. "Sedentary behavior associated with reduced medial temporal lobe thickness in middle-aged and older adults," PLoS ONE 13(4): e0195549

## Statistics Review: Inferential Statistics

**Page 491**: MichaelSvoboda/Getty Images; **Page 498**: Courtesy of Luke Wilcox and Erica Chauvet; **Page 506 (Figure S2.10)**: Republished with permission of Taylor and Francis, from *Introduction to the New Statistics: Estimation, Open Science, and Beyond*, by Cumming, Geoff; Calin-Jageman, Robert. © 2016. Permission conveyed through Copyright Clearance Center, Inc.

## Presenting Results: APA-Style Reports and Conference Posters

**Pages 539–540**: From *The Norton Field Guide to Writing, Third Edition* by Richard Bullock. Copyright © 2013, 2009, 2006 by W. W. Norton & Company, Inc. Used by permission of W. W. Norton & Company, Inc.; **Pages 545–559**: "Teaching as an Underdog: The Benefits of Being a Struggling Professor." Reprinted by permission of Jane Mafale; **Page 558 (Figure 1)**: Courtesy of Jane Mafale; **Page 560**: Courtesy of Wesleyan University; **Pages 562–563**: Courtesy of Jane Mafale

# Names Index

# Subject Index

basic research, 16
Beck Depression Inventory (BDI)
    convergent validity of, 140–41
    discriminant validity of, 141, 142
    known-group evidence for, 138–39
behavioral measures. *see* observational
    measures
behavior-change studies, 422–28
Belmont Report, 94–97, 98, 108, 109
benchmarks, 212, 498
beneficence. *see* principle of beneficence
beta
    inferential statistics for, 514
    to test for third variables, 252–55,
        256–57, 514
    between-groups/between subjects
        designs. *see* independent-groups
        designs
    between-groups differences, 356
    insufficient, 344–47
    within-groups variability obscuring,
        347–53
bias
    confirmation, 34–35
    of intuition, 30–36
    observer (*see* observer bias)
    present/present, 33–34
    publication, 446–47
bias blind spot, 35
biased samples (unrepresentative
        samples), 181–86, 191–92
    characteristics of, 182–86
    defined, 181
    in different populations of interest, 182*t*
bimodal distributions, 470
bivariate correlational research, 203–39
    construct validity of, 209–10
    defined, 204
    example, 228–30
    external validity of, 223–27
    internal validity of, 219–23
    statistical validity of, 210–19
bivariate correlations (bivariate
        associations), 204–8
blind design. *see* masked design
books
    chapters in edited, 39–41, 45, 543
    citing sources from, 543
    full-length, 39–41
box plots (box and whisker diagrams),
        477–78
brain scans, 121–22
breast cancer, radical mastectomy for. *see*
        mastectomy, radical
butter consumption and happiness, 56, 57
Buxtun, Peter, 90–91
BuzzFeed.com, 185, 196

## C

Cabell's blacklist of predatory journals, 42
carpentered world, 457
carryover effects, 299
categorical variables (nominal variables)
    associations described with, 207–8
    characteristics and examples, 124*t*
    defined, 122
    quantitative variables *vs.*, 122–23
catharsis. *see* anger, venting
causal claims
construct validity of, 77, 303–6
    defined, 64
    examples, 60, 61*t*
    external validity of, 77, 306–8
    in generalization mode, 456
    interrogating, 70–78, 303–11
    mistaken, 74–77
    observational research as basis of, 166
    statistical validity of, 77–78, 308–10
    verbs distinguishing association claims
        from, 64–65, 70–71, 203
    *see also* experiments; multivariate
        correlational research
causation
    association insufficient to establish,
        219–23
    criteria for, 65, 71–72 (*see also*
        covariance; internal validity;
        temporal precedence)
CDC. *see* Centers for Disease Control
        and Prevention
ceiling effects, 345–46, 352*t*, 353*t*
celebrities
    suicide in, 411
    trusting, 37*f*
cell phone use
    driving and (*see under* driving)
    "horns on head" story, 46–47
cells, 367–68
census, 180
Center for Epidemiological Studies
        Depression scale (CES-D), 140, 141
Centers for Disease Control and
        Prevention (CDC), 90, 405
central tendencies, 470–72
    defined, 470
    visualizing, 477–78
    *see also* mean; median; mode
CES-D. *see* Center for Epidemiological
        Studies Depression scale
Chabot, Steve, 154
Cham, Jorge, 18*f*
cherry-picking, 508
children
    adverse experiences and (*see* adverse
        childhood experiences)

cognitive development in, 428–29
daycare and development of,
    64, 367, 390
ethical research guidelines, 95, 100
food insecurity in, 61
happiness and, 228–30
memory capacity development in, 372,
    373*f*, 378
narcissism in (*see* narcissism and
    parental overpraise)
superhero play and staying on task, 60,
    64, 72–74, 77–78, 101
chocolate
    body mass and, 258
    shared experience of tasting (*see*
        shared experience effects)
CIs. *see* confidence intervals
CITI program, 97
claims, 60–79
    defined, 60
    interrogating using validities, 66–79
    non-research based, 65–66
    *see also* association claims; causal
        claims; frequency claims
Clever Hans, 171, 173
Clinton, Bill, 91
cluster sampling, 188, 189*f*
CNN, 392
codebooks, 171–72
coefficient alpha. *see* Cronbach's alpha
coercion, 95
coffee consumption and depression rate,
    61, 62, 64, 69, 447
Cohen's *d*, 308–9, 445, 484–86, 487,
    507–8
Common Rule, 97
communality, 15*t*, 17, 43, 105, 448
comparison groups, 284–85
    defined, 24, 284
    experience lacking, 24–26
    internal validity threats and, 327–28,
        332, 334, 336, 337
    present/present bias and, 33
concept maps, 38*f*, 135*f*
conceptual definitions, 118,
    135–36, 145
conceptual knowledge, 303
conceptual replication, 439, 451, 452
conceptual variables (constructs)
    defined, 57
    examples, 59*t*
    operationalization of, 57–58, 118–20
    concurrent-measures design,
        296–97, 303*t*
conditions, 281
confederates, 27
conference posters, 560–63

ceilings, floors, and, 345–46, 353*t*
construct validity and, 303
defined, 72, 281
mnemonic for remembering, 282
*see also* criterion variables
depression. *see* Beck Depression
  Inventory; Center for Epidemiological
  Studies Depression scale; coffee
  consumption and depression rate
descriptive statistics, 467–89
  for associations, 481–82
  for central tendencies, 470–72
  data matrices, 468
  defined, 467
  dot plots, 468–70
  for effect size, 484–88
  frequency distributions, 468–70
  for relative standing (*see z* scores)
  for variability, 472–78
design confounds, 286–89, 324
defined, 286, 338*t*
  examples, 338*t*, 340
  null effects and, 346–47
  quasi-experiments and, 410
  within-groups designs and, 299
Design subsection, 529
difference scores, 499–500
digital object identifier (DOI), 542
directionality problem, 219
direct replication, 438–39, 451
discriminant validity (divergent validity),
  141–42
  defined, 140
  example, 146
Discussion section
  in empirical journal articles, 44
  in research reports, 533–35
  self-plagiarism in, 105
disinformation (fake news), 47–48, 59*t*
  defined, 47
  inability to identify, 56, 61, 64
disinterestedness, 15*t*, 104, 448
divergent validity. *see* discriminant
  validity
dogs
  hugging and, 284
  lifespan and ownership of, 257–58
  in MRI machines, 392–93
dot plots, 468–70
double-barreled questions, 157–58
double-blind placebo control studies,
  336–37, 462
double-blind studies, 335
driving
  cell phone use and, 45, 364, 365,
    367–69, 370, 376–77, 379, 380–81*f*,
    383–89, 391, 455, 526, 528, 541, 542

road rage and, 180, 186, 193
  texting and, 60, 67, 68
drug abuse. *see* opioid abuse and drug
  legislation

# E

eating disorders and family meals.
  *see under* family meals
ecological validity (mundane realism),
  452, 460, 461
EEG (electroencephalography), 122
effect size
  defined, 39, 210
  descriptive statistics for, 484–88
  group overlap and, 486
  importance and, 487
  inferential statistics for, 507–8
  meta-analysis and, 445–46
  original units and, 487–88
  statistical validity and, 210–12, 308–9
election polls, 153, 154, 180, 183–84, 193,
  195, 196*f*
electroencephalography (EEG), 122
empirical journal articles
  accuracy of, 55
  components of, 43–44
  defined, 39
  example, 40*f*
  factorial designs in, 391
  mean and standard deviation in, 475–77
  reading with a purpose, 44–45
  on reliability and validity, 143–44
empiricism/empirical method/empirical
  research, 5, 6, 10, 35–36
equivalent groups, posttest-only design.
  *see* posttest-only design
equivalent groups, pretest/posttest
  design. *see* pretest/posttest design
error variance. *see* noise
"especially," 366
"especially for," 378
estimation, 491–93
  determining CI for a percentage,
    495–98
  explained, 491–92
  formal example of, 492–93
  steps of, 494–95
  *see also* point estimates
et al., 542
eta squared ($\eta^2$), 487
Ethical Principles of Psychologists and
  Code of Conduct (APA), 98
ethics, 89–115
  animal research, 107–9, 110
  APA principles, 98–109
  Belmont Report, 94–97, 98, 99*t*, 108, 109
  core principles, 94–97

debriefing, 93, 102–3, 112
deception, 101–2, 112
historical examples, 89–94
informed consent, 95, 97, 100–101,
  110, 112
IRBs and (*see* institutional review
  boards)
in observational research, 174
openness and, 105
plagiarism avoidance (*see* plagiarism)
quasi-experiments and, 416
research misconduct, 103–5
in reversal design, 428
thoughtful balance in, 110
transparency and (*see* transparency)
evidence-based treatments, 7
exercise and income, 60, 61, 62, 64, 69, 70
exit polls, 183–84
expanded rehearsal technique,
  423–24, 428
expectancy effects. *see* observer effects
experience, 24–29
  comparison group lacking, 24–26
  confounds in, 26–27
  research superiority to, 27–29
experimental control, 421
experimental demands. *see* demand
  characteristics
experimental realism, 460–61
experimental variables, 280–82
experiments, 323–61
  defined, 72, 281
  how causal claims are supported
    by, 72–73
  longitudinal studies in lieu of, 247–48
  with more than one independent
    variable, 365–97 (*see also* factorial
    designs)
  null effects in (*see* null effects)
  with one independent variable, 363–64
  quasi- (*see* quasi-experiments)
  really bad, 324–25, 326*f*
  simple (*see* simple experiments)
  small-*N* (*see* small-*N* designs)
  threats to internal validity in, 324–41
exposure therapy for PTSD, 45
external validity
  of association claims, 69, 223–27
  of causal claims, 77, 306–8
  defined, 67
  description, 69*t*
examples, 81, 230
  of frequency claims, 67–68, 179–80, 193
  good *vs.* unknown, 180–81
  importance of, 224–25, 451–58
  interrogating, 193–97
  limit testing and, 369–70

Juvenile Justice and Delinquency
   Prevention Act of 1974, 9

**K**

Kaiser Permanente, 195
kappa, 130
Kashdan, Todd, 29
known-groups paradigm, 137–39

**L**

Ladder of Life, 119, 120, 137, 139
Lancet, The, 104
large-*N* designs, 419
Latin square, 301
leading questions, 156
levels (values) of variables, 56, 59*t*
lie detectors, 138, 444
Likert scales, 155, 156
Likert-type scales, 155
limit testing, 368–70
line graphs, 376, 377*f*
longitudinal designs, 234–48
causation criteria and, 246–47
defined, 243
interpreting results from, 243–44
lying and reaction times, 444–46,
   452, 455

**M**

Mafale, Jane, 545, 562
main effects, 373–75
   defined, 373
   estimating size of, 374–75
   interactions compared with, 379,
      380–81*f*
   as overall effect, 375
   from a three-way design, 385, 386
manipulated variables, 56–57, 72–73
   defined, 56, 281
   examples, 59*t*
   factorial designs for studying, 368
manipulation checks, 304, 346, 347*f*
marginal means, 373*f*, 374
margin of error of the estimate, 68, 196–97,
   496–98, 500–503, 504–5, 509–11
   computing the CI from, 498
   constant associated with 95%
      confidence, 497–98, 501, 504, 510
   sample size component, 496, 500–501,
      504, 510
   variability component, 496, 500, 504,
      509–10
marital satisfaction and meeting online,
   203, 204–5, 207–8, 209–10, 211, 212,
   213–14, 219, 221, 417
masked design (blind design), 173, 335

mastectomy, radical, 24–26, 29, 30–31, 32,
   33, 37, 355
matched groups (matching), 291, 297
Materials subsection, 44, 529–30
maturation threats
   defined, 326, 338*t*
   examples, 338*t*, 341
   preventing, 326–27
   in quasi-experiments, 410
mean (average)
   defined, 208, 471
   in journal articles, 475–77
   marginal, 373*f*, 374
   regression to (*see* regression to the mean)
   studies with more than two, 508–11
   when to use, 471–72
measured variables, 56–57, 72–73
   defined, 56, 281
   examples, 59*t*
measurement, 117–49
   common types of, 120–22
   process of, 118–24
   reliability of, 125–32
   scales of, 122–24
   validity of, 133–44
measurement error, 348–50, 351*t*, 353*t*
medial-temporal lobe (MTL) thickness
      and sitting. *see* sitting and MTL
      thickness
median, 471–72
mediators (mediating variables), 263–66
memory
   capacity development, 372, 373*f*, 378
   declarative, 420–21
   expanded rehearsal technique,
      423–24, 428
   flashbulb, 165
   humor effect on, 304
   Molaison case (*see* Molaison, Henry)
   music and, 392
   nondeclarative, 420, 421
   processing deeply and, 316–21
   for random numbers, 429–30
   self-reporting on, 164–65
   spatial, 421
Merton's scientific norms, 15–16, 448, 450
*see also* communality; disinterestedness;
      organized skepticism; universalism
meta-analysis
   defined, 39, 444
   inferential statistics step, 495, 502–3,
      506, 513–14
   replication and, 444–47
   strengths and limitations of, 446–47
Method section
   in empirical journal articles, 44,
      143, 391

in research reports, 529–31
   self-plagiarism in, 105
Michniewicz, Kenneth, 545, 562
Milgram obedience studies, 92–94, 96, 101
mindfulness and test scores, 9, 14, 16,
   293–95, 301–2, 337, 340–41, 487
mining industry, safety improvement
   in, 425
mirror-tracing task, 420, 458, 459
mixed factorial designs, 383
mode, 470–72
moderators (moderating variables),
      225–27
   defined, 225
   interactions showing, 370
   mediators *vs.*, 265, 266*f*
Molaison, Henry (H.M.), 419–22, 430, 458
money
   exercise-income association, 60, 61, 62,
      64, 69, 70
   happiness and, 119, 355
   political views and, 356–57
   *see also* wealth
monkeys, attachment in. *see* attachment
      theory
mortality, 331
Mozart effect, 18–19
MTL (medial-temporal lobe) thickness
      and sitting. *see* sitting and MTL
      thickness
Müller-Lyer illusion, 456–58
multimodal distributions, 470–71
multiple-baseline designs, 424–25, 426*f*
multiple-regression analyses, 248–59
   adding more predictors in, 256–57
   causation not established by, 259
   inferential statistics and, 514
   measuring variables in, 249–51
   in popular media articles, 257–58
multistage sampling, 188
multivariate correlational research,
      241–73
   defined, 242
   longitudinal designs (*see* longitudinal
      designs)
   mediation in, 263–66
   multiple-regression analyses (*see*
      multiple-regression analyses)
   pattern and parsimony approach,
      260–62
   validities and, 267–69
multivariate regression. *see* multiple-
      regression analyses
mundane realism. *see* ecological validity
music
   intelligence and (*see under* intelligence)
   memory and, 392